Lecture Notes in Computer Science 4281

Commenced Publication in 1973
Founding and Former Series Editors:
Gerhard Goos, Juris Hartmanis, and Jan van Leeuwen

Kamel Barkaoui   Ana Cavalcanti
Antonio Cerone (Eds.)

Theoretical Aspects of Computing - ICTAC 2006

Third International Colloquium
Tunis, Tunisia, November 20-24, 2006
Proceedings

 Springer

Volume Editors

Kamel Barkaoui
Conservatoire National des Arts et Métiers Départment STIC
292 Rue Saint-Martin
75141 Paris Cedex 03, France
E-mail: barkaoui@cnam.fr

Ana Cavalcanti
University of York
Department of Computer Science
York YO10 5DD, England
E-mail: Ana.Cavalcanti@cs.york.ac.uk

Antonio Cerone
The United Nations University
International Institute for Software Technology
P.O. Box 3058, Macau
E-mail: antonio@itee.uq.edu.au

Library of Congress Control Number: 2006935418

CR Subject Classification (1998): F.1, F.3, F.4, D.3, D.2, C.2.4

LNCS Sublibrary: SL 1 – Theoretical Computer Science and General Issues

ISSN   0302-9743
ISBN-10   3-540-48815-4 Springer Berlin Heidelberg New York
ISBN-13   978-3-540-48815-6 Springer Berlin Heidelberg New York

Springer is a part of Springer Science+Business Media

springer.com

© Springer-Verlag Berlin Heidelberg 2006
Printed in Germany

Typesetting: Camera-ready by author, data conversion by Scientific Publishing Services, Chennai, India
Printed on acid-free paper   SPIN: 11921240   06/3142   5 4 3 2 1 0

Preface

The International Colloquium on Theoretical Aspects of Computing (ICTAC) held in 2006 in Tunis, Tunisia, was the third of a series of events created by the International Institute for Software Technology of the United Nations University. The aim of the colloquium is to bring together researchers from academia, industry, and government to present their results, and exchange experience, ideas, and solutions for their problems in theoretical aspects of computing.

The previous events were held in Guiyang, China (2004), and Hanoi, Vietnam (2005). Beyond its scholarly goals, another main purpose of ICTAC is to promote cooperation in research and education between participants and their institutions, from developing and industrial countries, as in the mandate of the United Nations University.

These proceedings record the contributions from the invited speakers and from the technical sessions. We present four invited papers, 21 technical papers, selected out of 78 submissions from 24 countries, and two extended abstracts of tutorials.

The Programme Committee includes researchers from 27 countries. Each of the 78 papers was evaluated by at least three reviewers. After the evaluation, reports were returned to the Programme Committee for discussion and resolution of conflicts. Based on their recommendations, we concluded the consensus process, and selected the 21 papers that we present here. For the evaluation of the submitted tutorials, this year we had the help of a separate Programme Committee especially invited for that purpose.

We are grateful to all members of the Programme and Organizing Committees, and to all referees for their hard work. The support and encouragement of the Advisory Committee were invaluable assets. Without the support of our sponsoring institutions, ICTAC 2006 could not have been a reality. Their recognition of the importance of this event is greatly appreciated.

Finally, we would like to thank all the authors of the invited and submitted papers and tutorials, and all the participants of the colloquium. They are the main focus of the whole event.

November 2006   Kamel Barkaoui, Ana Cavalcanti, and Antonio Cerone
Programme Chairs
ICTAC 2006

Organization

ICTAC 2006 was organized by the International Institute for Software Technology of the United Nations University, the University of Tunis El Manar, the Ecole Nationale d'Ingènieurs de Tunis, the University of York, and the Conservatoire National des Arts et Métiers.

Conference Chairs

Programme Chairs	Kamel Barkaoui (CNAM Paris, France)
	Ana Cavalcanti (University of York, UK)
	Antonio Cerone (UNU-IIST, Macau, SAR China)
Conference Chairs	Mohamed Bettaz (Philadelphia University, Jordan)
	Ali Mili (NJIT and SEI/CMU, USA)
Finance Chairs	Rahma Ben Ayed (Ecole Nationale d'Ingénieurs de Tunis, Tunisia)
	Dang Van Hung (UNU-IIST, Macau, SAR China)
Publicity Chairs	Chris George (UNU-IIST, Macau, SAR China)
	Karim Djouani (Université Paris 12, France)

Advisory Committee

Dines Bjørner	Technical University of Denmark and Japan Advanced Institute of Science and Technology
Manfred Broy	Technische Universität München, Germany
José Luiz Fiadeiro	University of Leicester, UK
Jifeng He	East China Normal University, China
Mathai Joseph	TATA Consultancy Services Limited, India
Shaoying Liu	Hosei University, Japan
Zhiming Liu	UNU-IIST, Macau, SAR China
Zohar Manna	Stanford University, USA
Tobias Nipkow	Technische Universität München, Germany

Mike Reed   UNU-IIST, Macau, SAR China

Jim Woodcock   University of York, UK

Programme Committee

Marc Aiguier	University of Evry, France
Eric Badouel	INRIA, France
Kamel Barkaoui (Co-chair)	CNAM Paris, France
José Barros	Universidade do Minho, Portugal
Hubert Baumeister	Technical University of Denmark, Denmark
Rahma Ben Ayed	Ecole Nationale d'Ingénieurs de Tunis, Tunisia
Mohamed Bettaz	Philadelphia University, Jordan
Jonathan Bowen	Museophile Limited, UK
Khaled Bsaies	Faculté des Sciences de Tunis, Tunisia
Christian Calude	University of Auckland, New Zealand
Ana Cavalcanti (Co-chair)	University of York, UK
Antonio Cerone (Co-chair)	UNU-IIST, Macau, SAR China
Jessica Chen	University of Windsor, Canada
Yifeng Chen	Durham University, UK
Jim Davies	University of Oxford, UK
Mourad Debbabi	Concordia University, Canada
David Deharbe	Federal University of Rio Grande do Norte, Brazil
Jin Song Dong	National University of Singapore, Singapore
Wan Fokkink	Vrije Universiteit, Netherlands
Marcelo Frias	University of Buenos Aires, Argentina
Maurizio Gabbrielli	Università di Bologna, Italy
Valentin Goranko	University of the Witwatersrand, South Africa
Susanne Graf	VERIMAG, France
Lindsay Groves	Victoria University of Wellington, New Zealand
Michael Hansen	Technical University of Denmark, Denmark
Thomas Henzinger	EPFL, Switzerland
Dang Van Hung	UNU-IIST, Macau, SAR China
Purush Iyer	North Carolina State University, USA
Petr Jančar	Technical University of Ostrava, Czech Republic
Takuya Katayama	JAIST, Japan
Maciej Koutny	Newcastle University, UK
Xuandong Li	Nanjing University, China
Xinxin Liu	Chinese Academy of Sciences, China
Antonia Lopes	University of Lisbon, Portugal
Andrea Maggiolo-Schettini	University of Pisa, Italy
Antoni Mazurkiewicz	Polish Academy of Sciences, Poland

Mohamed Mezguiche	Université de Boumerdes, Algeria
Ali Mili	NJIT and SEI/CMU, USA
Roland Mittermeir	Klagenfurt University, Austria
Carroll Morgan	University of New South Wales, Australia
Alberto Pardo	Universidad de la República, Uruguay
Jean-Eric Pin	LIAFA and CNRS, France
R. Ramanujam	Institute of Mathematical Sciences, India
Anders Ravn	Aalborg University, Denmark
Wolfgang Reif	University of Augsburg, Germany
Ingrid Rewitzky	University of Stellenbosch, South Africa
Mark Ryan	University of Birmingham, UK
Augusto Sampaio	Federal University of Pernambuco, Brazil
Bernhard Schätz	Technische Universität München, Germany
Emil Sekerinski	McMaster University, Canada
Carolyn Talcott	SRI International, USA
Tayssir Touili	LIAFA and CNRS, France
Do Long Van	Institute of Mathematics, Vietnam
Martin Wirsing	Ludwig-Maximilians-Universität Munich, Germany
Hongjun Zheng	The MathWorks, USA

Tutorial Programmme Committee

Kamel Barkaoui (Co-chair)	CNAM Paris, France
Faiza Belala	University Mentouri of Constantine, Algeria
Rahma Ben Ayed	Ecole Nationale d'Ingénieurs de Tunis, Tunisia
Ana Cavalcanti (Co-chair)	University of York, UK
Antonio Cerone (Co-chair)	UNU-IIST, Macau, SAR China
Karim Djouani	Université Paris 12, France
Serge Haddad	Université Paris-Dauphine, France
Ryszard Janicki	McMaster University, Canada
Ali Jaoua	University of Quatar, Quatar
Tiziana Margaria	University of Potsdam, Germany
Mourad Maouche	Philadelphia University, Jordan
Salma Mouline	Faculté des Sciences de Rabat, Morocco
Ahmed Nacer	USTHB Algiers, Algeria
Hung Ngo	State University of New York at Buffalo, USA
Gianna Reggio	Università di Genova, Italy
Yahya Slimani	Faculté des Sciences de Tunis, Tunisia
Helen Treharne	University of Surrey, UK

Additional Referees

| Stanisław Ambroszkiewicz | Eugene Asarin |
| Agnès Arnould | Jeremy Avigad |

Marek Bednarczyk
Francine Blanchet-Sadri
Iovka Boneva
Roberto Bruni
Carlos Camarão
Choe Changil
Krishnendu Chatterjee
Jean-paul Comet
Stephanie Delaune
Raymond Devillers
Clelia De Felice
Cinzia Di Giusto
Alessandra Di Pierro
Moreno Falaschi
Adalberto Farias
Wit Foryś
Mickael Foursov
Goran Frehse
Rudolf Freund
Blaise Genest
Patrice Godefroid
Massimiliano Goldwurm
Roberta Gori
Kunihiro Hiraishi
Phan Trung Huy
Ying Jiang
Zhi Jin
Victor Khomenko
Leonid Kof
Martin Kot
Hanna Kozankiewicz
S. N. Krishna
Martin Leucker
Francesca Levi
Kamal Lodaya
Etienne Lozes
Linyun Luo

Assia Mahboubi
Florence Maraninchi
Nicolas Markey
Maria Chiara Meo
Alexandre Miquel
Ben Moszkowski
Regina Motz
Madhavan Mukund
Paritosh Pandya
Dave Parker
Pascal Poizat
Agata Półrola
Daniel Ratiu
Zdeněk Sawa
Guido Sciavicco
Laura Semini
Paula Severi
Natarajan Shankar
Luis Sierra
Mihaela Sighireanu
Ana Sokolova
Jason Steggles
S. P. Suresh
Nguyen Truong Thang
Marcel Tonga
Laurent Van Begin
Vincent van Oostrom
Tran Van Dung
Marcos Viera
Cesar Viho
Phan Cong Vinh
Józef Winkowski
Bożena Woźna
Naijun Zhan
Liming Zhu
Rosalba Zizza

Sponsoring Institutions

International Institute for Software Technology of the United Nations University

Tunisian Ministry of Higher Education

Tunisian Ministry of Scientific Research, Technology and Competency
Development

Tunisian Ministry of Communication Technologies

Tunis Science City

The University of Tunis El Manar and l' Ecole Nationale d'Ingénieurs
de Tunis

University of York

Table of Contents

Invited Papers

Semantics

Concurrency

Model Checking

Formal Languages

Logic and Type Theory

Real-Time and Mobility

Tutorials: Extended Abstracts

Verifying a Hotel Key Card System

Tobias Nipkow

Institut für Informatik, TU München

Abstract. Two models of an electronic hotel key card system are contrasted: a state based and a trace based one. Both are defined, verified, and proved equivalent in the theorem prover Isabelle/HOL. It is shown that if a guest follows a certain safety policy regarding her key cards, she can be sure that nobody but her can enter her room.

1 Introduction

This paper presents two models for a hotel key card system and the verification of their safety (in Isabelle/HOL [5]). The models are based on Section 6.2, *Hotel Room Locking*, and Appendix E in the book by Daniel Jackson [2]. Jackson employs his Alloy system to check that there are no small counterexamples to safety. We confirm his conjecture of safety by a formal proof.

Most hotels operate a digital key card system. Upon check-in, you receive a card with your own key on it (typically a pseudorandom number). The lock for each room reads your card and opens the door if the key is correct. The system is decentralized, i.e. each lock is a stand-alone, battery-powered device without connection to the computer at reception or to any other device. So how does the lock know that your key is correct? There are a number of similar systems and we discuss the one described in Appendix E of [2]. Here each card carries two keys: the old key of the previous occupant of the room (key_1), and your own new key (key_2). The lock always holds one key, its "current" key. When you enter your room for the first time, the lock notices that its current key is key_1 on your card and recodes itself, i.e. it replaces its own current key with key_2 on your card. When you enter the next time, the lock finds that its current key is equal to your key_2 and opens the door without recoding itself. Your card is never modified by the lock. Eventually, a new guest with a new key enters the room, recodes the lock, and you cannot enter anymore.

After a short introduction of the notation we discuss two very different specifications, a state based and a trace based one, and prove their safety and their equivalence. The complete formalization is available online in the *Archive of Formal Proofs* at afp.sf.net.

1.1 Notation

HOL conforms largely to everyday mathematical notation. This section introduces further non-standard notation and in particular a few basic data types with their primitive operations.

K. Barkaoui, A. Cavalcanti, and A. Cerone (Eds.): ICTAC 2006, LNCS 4281, pp. 1–14, 2006.
© Springer-Verlag Berlin Heidelberg 2006

Types The type of truth values is called *bool*. The space of total functions is denoted by $\Rightarrow$. Type variables start with a quote, as in $'a$, $'b$ etc. The notation $t::\tau$ means that term t has type τ.

Functions can be updated at x with new value y, written $f(x := y)$. The range of a function is *range f*, *inj f* means f is injective.

Pairs come with the two projection functions $fst :: 'a \times 'b \Rightarrow 'a$ and $snd :: 'a \times 'b \Rightarrow 'b$.

Sets have type $'a\ set$.

Lists (type $'a\ list$) come with the empty list $[]$, the infix constructor $\cdot$, the infix @ that appends two lists, and the conversion function *set* from lists to sets. Variable names ending in "s" usually stand for lists.

Records are constructed like this $(\!|f_1 = v_1, \ldots|\!)$ and updated like this $r(\!|f_i := v_i, \ldots|\!)$, where the f_i are the field names, the v_i the values and r is a record.

Datatype *option* is defined like this

$$\textbf{datatype}\ 'a\ option = None \mid Some\ 'a$$

and adjoins a new element *None* to a type $'a$. For succinctness we write $\lfloor a \rfloor$ instead of *Some a*.

Note that $[\![A_1; \ldots; A_n]\!] \Longrightarrow A$ abbreviates $A_1 \Longrightarrow \ldots \Longrightarrow A_n \Longrightarrow A$, which is the same as "If A_1 and ... and A_n then A".

2   A State Based Model

The model is based on three opaque types *guest*, *key* and *room*. Type *card* is just an abbreviation for $key \times key$.

The state of the system is modelled as a record which combines the information about the front desk, the rooms and the guests.

record *state* =
owns :: *room* $\Rightarrow$ *guest option*
currk :: *room* $\Rightarrow$ *key*
issued :: *key set*
cards :: *guest* $\Rightarrow$ *card set*
roomk :: *room* $\Rightarrow$ *key*
isin :: *room* $\Rightarrow$ *guest set*
safe :: *room* $\Rightarrow$ *bool*

Reception records who *owns* a room (if anybody, hence *guest option*), the current key *currk* that has been issued for a room, and which keys have been *issued* so far. Each guest has a set of *cards*. Each room has a key *roomk* recorded in the lock and a set *isin* of occupants. The auxiliary variable *safe* is explained further below; we ignore it for now.

In specification languages like Z, VDM and B we would now define a number of operations on this state space. Since they are the only permissible operations on the state, this defines a set of *reachable* states. In a purely logical environment like Isabelle/HOL this set can be defined directly by an inductive definition. Each clause of the definition corresponds to a transition/operation/event. This is the standard approach to modelling state machines in theorem provers.

The set of reachable states of the system (called *reach*) is defined by four transitions: initialization, checking in, entering a room, and leaving a room:

init:
$inj\ initk \Longrightarrow$
$(\!|\ owns = (\lambda r.\ None),\ currk = initk,\ issued = range\ initk,$
$\quad cards = (\lambda g.\ \{\}),\ roomk = initk,\ isin = (\lambda r.\ \{\}),$
$\quad safe = (\lambda r.\ True)\ |\!) \in reach$

check-in:
$[\![\ s \in reach;\ k \notin issued\ s\ ]\!] \Longrightarrow$
$s(\!|\ currk := (currk\ s)(r := k),\ issued := issued\ s \cup \{k\},$
$\quad cards := (cards\ s)(g := cards\ s\ g \cup \{(currk\ s\ r,\ k)\}),$
$\quad owns := (owns\ s)(r := Some\ g),$
$\quad safe := (safe\ s)(r := False)\ |\!) \in reach$

enter-room:
$[\![\ s \in reach;\ (k,k') \in cards\ s\ g;\ roomk\ s\ r \in \{k,k'\}\ ]\!] \Longrightarrow$
$s(\!|\ isin := (isin\ s)(r := isin\ s\ r \cup \{g\}),$
$\quad roomk := (roomk\ s)(r := k'),$
$\quad safe := (safe\ s)(r := owns\ s\ r = \lfloor g \rfloor \wedge isin\ s\ r = \{\} \wedge k' = currk\ s\ r$
$\qquad\qquad\qquad\qquad \vee safe\ s\ r)$
$|\!) \in reach$

exit-room:
$[\![\ s \in reach;\ g \in isin\ s\ r\ ]\!] \Longrightarrow$
$s(\!|\ isin := (isin\ s)(r := isin\ s\ r - \{g\})\ |\!) \in reach$

There is no check-out event because it is implicit in the next check-in for that room: this covers the cases where a guest leaves without checking out (in which case the room should not be blocked forever) or where the hotel decides to rent out a room prematurely, probably by accident. Neither do guests have to return their cards at any point because they may loose cards or may pretended to have lost them. We will now explain the events.

init Initialization requires that every room has a different key, i.e. that *currk* is injective. Nobody owns a room, the keys of all rooms are recorded as issued, nobody has a card, and all rooms are empty.

enter-room A guest may enter if either of the two keys on his card equal the room key. Then g is added to the occupants of r and the room key is set to the second key on the card. Normally this has no effect because the second key is already the room key. But when entering for the first time, the first key on the card equals the room key and then the lock is actually recoded.

exit-room removes an occupant from the occupants of a room.

check-in for room r and guest g issues the card $(currk\ s\ r,\ k)$ to g, where k is new, makes g the owner of the room, and sets $currk\ s\ r$ to the new key k.

The reader can easily check that our specification allows the intended distributed implementation: entering only reads and writes the key in that lock, and check-in only reads and writes the information at reception.

In contrast to Jackson we require that initially distinct rooms have distinct keys. This protects the hotel from its guests: otherwise a guest may be able to enter rooms he does not own, potentially stealing objects from those rooms. Of course he can also steal objects from his own room, but in that case it is easier to hold him responsible. In general, the hotel may just want to minimize the opportunity for theft.

The main difference to Jackson's model is that his can talk about transitions between states rather than merely about reachable states. This means that he can specify that unauthorized entry into a room should not occur. Because our specification does not formalize the transition relation itself, we need to include the *isin* component in order to express the same requirement. In the end, we would like to establish that the system is *safe*: only the owner of a room can be in a room:

$$[\![s \in reach;\ g \in isin\ s\ r]\!] \implies owns\ s\ r = \lfloor g \rfloor$$

Unfortunately, this is just not true. It does not take a PhD in computer science to come up with the following scenario: because guests can retain their cards, there is nothing to stop a guest from reentering his old room after he has checked out (in our model: after the next guest has checked in), but before the next guest has entered his room. Hence the best we can do is to prove a conditional safety property: under certain conditions, the above safety property holds. The question is: which conditions? It is clear that the room must be empty when its owner enters it, or all bets are off. But is that sufficient? Unfortunately not. Jackson's Alloy tool took 2 seconds [2, p. 303] to find the following "guest-in-the-middle" attack:

1. Guest 1 checks in and obtains a card (k_1, k_2) for room 1 (whose key in the lock is k_1). Guest 1 does not enter room 1.
2. Guest 2 checks in, obtains a card (k_2, k_3) for room 1, but does not enter room 1 either.
3. Guest 1 checks in again, obtains a card (k_3, k_4), goes to room 1, opens it with his old card (k_1, k_2), finds the room empty, and feels safe ...

After Guest 1 has left his room, Guest 2 enters and makes off with the luggage.

Jackson now assumes that guests return their cards upon check-out, which can be modelled as follows: upon check-in, the new card is not added to the guest's set of cards but it replaces his previous set of cards, i.e. guests return old cards the next time they check in. Under this assumption, Alloy finds no more counterexamples to safety — at least not up to 6 cards and keys and 3 guests and rooms. This is not a proof but a strong indication that the given assumptions suffice for safety. We prove that this is indeed the case.

It should be noted that the system also suffers from a liveness problem: if a guest never enters the room he checked in to, that room is forever blocked. In practice this is dealt with by a master key. We ignore liveness.

2.1 Formalizing Safety

It should be clear that one cannot force guests to always return their cards (or, equivalently, never to use an old card). We can only prove that if they do, their room is safe. However, we do not follow Jackson's approach of globally assuming everybody returns their old cards upon check-in. Instead we would like to take a local approach where it is up to each guest whether he follows this safety policy. We allow guests to keep their cards but make safety dependent on how they use them. This generality requires a finer grained model: we need to record if a guest has entered his room in a safe manner, i.e. if it was empty and if he used the latest key for the room, the one stored at reception. The auxiliary variable *safe* records for each room if this was the case at some point between his last check-in and now. The main theorem will be that if a room is safe in this manner, then only the owner can be in the room. Now we explain how *safe* is modified with each event:

init sets *safe* to *True* for every room.
check-in for room r resets *safe* s r because it is not safe for the new owner yet.
enter-room for room r sets *safe* s r if the owner entered an empty room using
   the latest card issued for that room by reception, or if the room was already
   safe.
exit-room does not modify *safe*.

The reader should convince his or herself that *safe* corresponds to the informal safety policy set out above. Note that a guest may find his room non-empty the first time he enters, and *safe* will not be set, but he may come back later, find the room empty, and then *safe* will be set. Furthermore, it is important that *enter-room* cannot reset *safe* due to the disjunct $\lor$ *safe* s r. Hence *check-in* is the only event that can reset *safe*. That is, a room stays safe until the next *check-in*. Additionally *safe* is initially *True*, which is fine because initially injectivity of *initk* prohibits illegal entries by non-owners.

Note that because none of the other state components depend on *safe*, it is truly auxiliary: it can be deleted from the system and the same set of reachable states is obtained, modulo the absence of *safe*.

We have formalized a very general safety policy of always using the latest card. A special case of this policy is the one called *NoIntervening* by Jackson [2, p. 200]: every *check-in* must immediately be followed by the corresponding *enter-room*.

2.2 Verifying Safety

All of our lemmas are invariants of *reach*. The complete list, culminating in the main theorem, is this:

Lemma 1.   *1. $s \in reach \implies currk\ s\ r \in issued\ s$*
   2. $[\![s \in reach;\ (k,\ k') \in cards\ s\ g]\!] \implies k \in issued\ s$
   3. $[\![s \in reach;\ (k,\ k') \in cards\ s\ g]\!] \implies k' \in issued\ s$

4. $s \in reach \implies roomk\ s\ k \in issued\ s$
5. $s \in reach \implies \forall r\ r'.\ (currk\ s\ r = currk\ s\ r') = (r = r')$
6. $s \in reach \implies (currk\ s\ r, k') \notin cards\ s\ g$
7. $[\![s \in reach;\ (k_1, k) \in cards\ s\ g_1;\ (k_2, k) \in cards\ s\ g_2]\!] \implies g_1 = g_2$
8. $[\![s \in reach;\ safe\ s\ r]\!] \implies roomk\ s\ r = currk\ s\ r$
9. $[\![s \in reach;\ safe\ s\ r;\ (k', roomk\ s\ r) \in cards\ s\ g]\!] \implies owns\ s\ r = \lfloor g \rfloor$

Theorem 1. If $s \in reach$ and $safe\ s\ r$ and $g \in isin\ s\ r$ then $owns\ s\ r = \lfloor g \rfloor$.

The lemmas and the theorem are proved in this order, each one is marked as a simplification rule, and each proof is a one-liner: induction on $s \in reach$ followed by *auto*.

Although, or maybe even because these proofs work so smoothly one may like to understand why. Hence we examine the proof of Theorem 1 in more detail. The only interesting case is *enter-room*. We assume that guest g_1 enters room r_1 with card (k_1, k_2) and call the new state t. We assume $safe\ t\ r$ and $g \in isin\ t\ r$ and prove $owns\ t\ r = \lfloor g \rfloor$ by case distinction. If $r_1 \neq r$, the claim follows directly from the induction hypothesis using $safe\ s\ r$ and $g \in isin\ t\ r$ because $owns\ t\ r = owns\ s\ r$ and $safe\ t\ r = safe\ s\ r$. If $r_1 = r$ then $g \in isin\ t\ r$ is equivalent with $g \in isin\ s\ r \vee g = g_1$. If $g \in isin\ s\ r$ then $safe\ s\ r$ follows from $safe\ t\ r$ by definition of *enter-room* because $g \in isin\ s\ r$ implies $isin\ s\ r \neq \emptyset$. Hence the induction hypothesis implies the claim. If $g = g_1$ we make another case distinction. If $k_2 = roomk\ s\ r$, the claim follows immediately from Lemma 1.9 above: only the owner of a room can possess a card where the second key is the room key. If $k_1 = roomk\ s\ r$ then, by definition of *enter-room*, $safe\ t\ r$ implies $owns\ s\ r = \lfloor g \rfloor \vee safe\ s\ r$. In the first case the claim is immediate. If $safe\ s\ r$ then $roomk\ s\ r = currk\ s\ r$ (by Lemma 1.8) and thus $(currk\ s\ r, k_2) \in cards\ s\ g$ by assumption $(k_1, k_2) \in cards\ s\ g_1$, thus contradicting Lemma 1.6.

This detailed proof shows that a number of case distinctions are required. Luckily, they all suggest themselves to Isabelle via the definition of function update ($:=$) or via disjunctions that arise automatically.

2.3   An Extension

To test the flexibility of our model we extended it with the possibility for obtaining a new card, e.g. when one has lost one's card. Now reception needs to remember not just the current but also the previous key for each room, i.e. a new field $prevk :: room \Rightarrow key$ is added to *state*. It is initialized with the same value as *currk*: though strictly speaking it could be arbitrary, this permits the convenient invariant $prevk\ s\ r \in issued\ s$. Upon check-in we set *prevk* to $(prevk\ s)(r := currk\ s\ r)$. Event *new-card* is simple enough:

$[\![s \in reach;\ owns\ s\ r = \lfloor g \rfloor]\!]$
$\implies s(\!| cards := (cards\ s)(g := cards\ s\ g \cup \{(prevk\ s\ r, currk\ s\ r)\}) |\!) \in reach$

The verification is not seriously affected. Some additional invariants are required

$s \in reach \implies prevk\ s\ r \in issued\ s$

$[\![s \in reach;\ owns\ s\ r' = \lfloor g \rfloor]\!] \implies currk\ s\ r \neq prevk\ s\ r'$

$[\![s \in reach;\ owns\ s\ r = \lfloor g \rfloor;\ g \neq g']\!] \implies (k,\ currk\ s\ r) \notin cards\ s\ g'$

but the proofs are still of the same trivial induct-auto format.

Adding a further event for loosing a card has no impact at all on the proofs.

3   A Trace Based Model

The only clumsy aspect of the state based model is *safe*: we use a state component to record if the sequence of events that lead to a state satisfies some property. That is, we simulate a condition on traces via the state. Unsurprisingly, it is not trivial to convince oneself that *safe* really has the informal meaning set out at the beginning of subsection 2.1. Hence we now describe an alternative, purely trace based model, similar to Paulson's inductive protocol model [6]. The events are:

datatype *event* =
   Check-in guest room card | *Enter guest room card* | *Exit guest room*

Instead of a state, we have a trace, i.e. list of events, and extract the state from the trace:

$initk\ ::\ room \Rightarrow key$
$owns\ ::\ event\ list \Rightarrow room \Rightarrow guest\ option$
$currk\ ::\ event\ list \Rightarrow room \Rightarrow key$
$issued\ ::\ event\ list \Rightarrow key\ set$
$cards\ ::\ event\ list \Rightarrow guest \Rightarrow card\ set$
$roomk\ ::\ event\ list \Rightarrow room \Rightarrow key$
$isin\ ::\ event\ list \Rightarrow room \Rightarrow guest\ set$
$hotel\ ::\ event\ list \Rightarrow bool$

Except for *initk*, which is completely unspecified, all these functions are defined by primitive recursion over traces:

$owns\ [] \ r = None$
$owns\ (e \cdot s)\ r =$
(**case** e **of** *Check-in* $g\ r'\ c \Rightarrow$ **if** $r' = r$ **then** $\lfloor g \rfloor$ **else** $owns\ s\ r$
 | - $\Rightarrow owns\ s\ r)$

$currk\ [] \ r = initk\ r$
$currk\ (e \cdot s)\ r =$
(**let** $k = currk\ s\ r$
 in case e **of** *Check-in* $g\ r'\ c \Rightarrow$ **if** $r' = r$ **then** $snd\ c$ **else** k | - $\Rightarrow k)$

$issued\ [] = range\ initk$
$issued\ (e \cdot s) = issued\ s \cup ($**case** e **of** *Check-in* $g\ r\ c \Rightarrow \{snd\ c\}$ | - $\Rightarrow \emptyset)$

$cards\ [] \ g = \emptyset$
$cards\ (e \cdot s)\ g =$
(**let** $C = cards\ s\ g$
 in case e **of** *Check-in* $g'\ r\ c \Rightarrow$ **if** $g' = g$ **then** $\{c\} \cup C$ **else** C | - $\Rightarrow C)$

roomk [] *r* = *initk r*
roomk (*e* · *s*) *r* =
(**let** *k* = *roomk s r*
 in case *e* **of** *Enter g r'* (*x*, *y*) ⇒ **if** *r'* = *r* **then** *y* **else** *k* | - ⇒ *k*)

isin [] *r* = ∅
isin (*e* · *s*) *r* =
(**let** *G* = *isin s r*
 in case *e* **of** *Check-in g r c* ⇒ *G*
    | *Enter g r' c* ⇒ **if** *r'* = *r* **then** {*g*} ∪ *G* **else** *G*
    | *Exit g r'* ⇒ **if** *r'* = *r* **then** *G* − {*g*} **else** *G*)

However, not every trace is possible. Function *hotel* tells us which traces correspond to real hotels:

hotel [] = *True*
hotel (*e* · *s*) =
(*hotel s* ∧
 (**case** *e* **of** *Check-in g r* (*k*, *k'*) ⇒ *k* = *currk s r* ∧ *k'* ∉ *issued s*
  | *Enter g r* (*k*, *k'*) ⇒ (*k*, *k'*) ∈ *cards s g* ∧ *roomk s r* ∈ {*k*, *k'*}
  | *Exit g r* ⇒ *g* ∈ *isin s r*))

Alternatively we could have followed Paulson [6] in defining *hotel* as an inductive set of traces. The difference is only slight.

3.1   Formalizing Safety

The principal advantage of the trace model is the intuitive specification of safety. Using the auxiliary predicate *no-Check-in*

no-Check-in s r ≡ ¬(∃ *g c*. *Check-in g r c* ∈ *set s*)

we define a trace to be *safe$_0$* for a room if the card obtained at the last *Check-in* was later actually used to *Enter* the room:

safe$_0$ s r ≡ ∃ *s$_1$ s$_2$ s$_3$ g c*.
   s = *s$_3$* @ [*Enter g r c*] @ *s$_2$* @ [*Check-in g r c*] @ *s$_1$* ∧ *no-Check-in* (*s$_3$* @ *s$_2$*) *r*

A trace is *safe* if additionally the room was empty when it was entered:

safe s r ≡ ∃ *s$_1$ s$_2$ s$_3$ g c*.
   s = *s$_3$* @ [*Enter g r c*] @ *s$_2$* @ [*Check-in g r c*] @ *s$_1$* ∧
   no-Check-in (*s$_3$* @ *s$_2$*) *r* ∧ *isin* (*s$_2$* @ [*Check-in g r c*] @ *s$_1$*) *r* = {}

The two notions of safety are distinguished because, except for the main theorem, *safe$_0$* suffices.

The alert reader may already have wondered why, in contrast to the state based model, we do not require *initk* to be injective. If *initk* is not injective, e.g. *initk r$_1$* = *initk r$_2$* and *r$_1$* ≠ *r$_2$*, then [*Enter g r$_2$* (*initk r$_1$*, *k*), *Check-in g r$_1$* (*initk r$_1$*, *k*)] is a legal trace and guest *g* ends up in a room he is not the owner of. However, this is not a safe trace for room *r$_2$* according to our definition. This reflects that hotel rooms are not safe until the first time their owner has entered them. We no longer protect the hotel from its guests.

3.2   Verifying Safety

Lemma 1 largely carries over after replacing $s \in reach$ by $hotel\ s$ and $safe$ by $safe_0$. Only properties 5 and 6 no longer hold because we no longer assume that $roomk$ is initially injective. They are replaced by two somewhat similar properties:

Lemma 2.

1. $[\![hotel\ (s_2\ @\ Check\text{-}in\ g\ r\ (k,\ k') \cdot s_1);$
   $k' = currk\ (s_2\ @\ Check\text{-}in\ g\ r\ (k,\ k') \cdot s_1)\ r]\!]$
   $\implies r' = r$
2. $[\![hotel\ (s_2\ @\ [Check\text{-}in\ g\ r\ (k,\ k')]\ @\ s_1);\ no\text{-}Check\text{-}in\ s_2\ r]\!]$
   $\implies (k',\ k'') \notin cards\ (s_2\ @\ Check\text{-}in\ g\ r\ (k,\ k') \cdot s_1)\ g'$

Both are proved by induction on s_2. In addition we need some easy structural properties:

Lemma 3.   1. $issued\ (s\ @\ s') = issued\ s\ \cup\ issued\ s'$
2. $no\text{-}Check\text{-}in\ s_2\ r \implies owns\ (s_2\ @\ s_1)\ r = owns\ s_1\ r$
3. $no\text{-}Check\text{-}in\ s_2\ r \implies currk\ (s_2\ @\ s_1)\ r = currk\ s_1\ r$

The main theorem again correspond closely to its state based counterpart:

Theorem 2. If $hotel\ s$ and $safe\ s\ r$ and $g \in isin\ s\ r$ then $owns\ s\ r = \lfloor g \rfloor$.

Let us examine the proof of this theorem to show how it differs from the state based version. For the core of the proof let $s = s_3\ @\ [Enter\ g'\ r\ (k,\ k')]\ @\ s_2$ $@\ [Check\text{-}in\ g'\ r\ (k,\ k')]\ @\ s_1$ and assume $isin\ (s_2\ @\ [Check\text{-}in\ g'\ r\ (k,\ k')]\ @$ $s_1)\ r = \emptyset$ (0). By induction on s_3 we prove

$[\![hotel\ s;\ no\text{-}Check\text{-}in\ (s_3\ @\ s_2)\ r;\ g \in isin\ s\ r]\!] \implies g' = g$

The actual theorem follows by definition of $safe$. The base case of the induction follows from (0). For the induction step let $t = (e \cdot s_3)\ @\ [Enter\ g'\ r\ (k,\ k')]$ $@\ s_2\ @\ [Check\text{-}in\ g'\ r\ (k,\ k')]\ @\ s_1$. We assume $hotel\ t$, $no\text{-}Check\text{-}in\ ((e \cdot s_3)$ $@\ s_2)\ r$, and $g \in isin\ s\ r$, and show $g' = g$. The proof is by case distinction on the event e. The cases $Check\text{-}in$ and $Exit$ follow directly from the induction hypothesis because the set of occupants of r can only decrease. Now we focus on the case $e = Enter\ g''\ r'\ c$. If $r' \neq r$ the set of occupants of r remains unchanged and the claim follow directly from the induction hypothesis. If $g'' \neq g$ then g must already have been in r before the $Enter$ event and the claim again follows directly from the induction hypothesis. Now assume $r' = r$ and $g'' = g$. From $hotel\ t$ we obtain $hotel\ s$ (1) and $c \in cards\ s\ g$ (2), and from $no\text{-}Check\text{-}in\ (s_3$ $@\ s_2)\ r$ and (0) we obtain $safe\ s\ r$ (3). Let $c = (k_1, k_2)$. From Lemma 1.8 and Lemma 3.3 we obtain $roomk\ s\ r = currk\ s\ r = k'$. Hence $k_1 \neq roomk\ s\ r$ by Lemma 2.2 using (1), (2) and $no\text{-}Check\text{-}in\ (s_3\ @\ s_2)\ r$. Hence $k_2 = roomk\ s\ r$ by $hotel\ t$. With Lemma 1.9 and (1–3) we obtain $owns\ t\ r = \lfloor g \rfloor$. At the same time we have $owns\ t\ r = \lfloor g' \rfloor$ because $hotel\ t$ and $no\text{-}Check\text{-}in\ ((e \cdot s_3)\ @\ s_2)\ r$: nobody has checked in to room r after g'. Thus the claim $g' = g$ follows.

   The details of this proof differ from those of Theorem 1 but the structure is very similar.

theorem *safe*: **assumes** *hotel s* **and** *safe s r* **and** $g \in isin\ s\ r$
$\qquad\qquad$ **shows** *owns s r* $= \lfloor g \rfloor$
proof −
$\quad$ { **fix** $s_1\ s_2\ s_3\ g'\ k\ k'$
$\quad$ **let** $?s = s_3$ @ $[Enter\ g'\ r\ (k,k')]$ @ s_2 @ $[Check\text{-}in\ g'\ r\ (k,k')]$ @ s_1
$\quad$ **assume** *0*: *isin* (s_2 @ $[Check\text{-}in\ g'\ r\ (k,k')]$ @ s_1) $r = \{\}$
$\quad$ **have** $\llbracket$ *hotel ?s; no-Check-in* (s_3 @ s_2) r; $g \in isin\ ?s\ r$ $\rrbracket \Longrightarrow g' = g$
$\quad$ **proof**(*induct* s_3)
$\quad\quad$ **case** *Nil* **thus** *?case* **using** *0* **by** *simp*
$\quad\quad$ **next**
$\quad\quad$ **case** (*Cons e* s_3')
$\quad\quad$ **let** $?b = [Enter\ g'\ r\ (k,k')]$ @ s_2 @ $[Check\text{-}in\ g'\ r\ (k,k')]$ @ s_1
$\quad\quad$ **let** $?s = s_3'$ @ $?b$ **and** $?t = (e \cdot s_3')$ @ $?b$
$\quad\quad$ **show** *?case*
$\quad\quad$ **proof**(*cases e*)
$\quad\quad\quad$ **case** (*Enter* $g''\ r'\ c$)[*simp*]
$\quad\quad\quad$ **show** $g' = g$
$\quad\quad\quad$ **proof** *cases*
$\quad\quad\quad\quad$ **assume** [*simp*]: $r' = r$
$\quad\quad\quad\quad$ **show** $g' = g$
$\quad\quad\quad\quad$ **proof** *cases*
$\quad\quad\quad\quad\quad$ **assume** [*simp*]: $g'' = g$
$\quad\quad\quad\quad\quad$ **have** *1*: *hotel ?s* **and** *2*: $c \in cards\ ?s\ g$ **using** ⟨*hotel ?t*⟩ **by** *auto*
$\quad\quad\quad\quad\quad$ **have** *3*: *safe ?s r* **using** ⟨*no-Check-in* $((e \cdot s_3')$ @ $s_2)\ r$⟩ *0*
$\quad\quad\quad\quad\quad\quad$ **by**(*simp add:safe-def*) *blast*
$\quad\quad\quad\quad\quad$ **obtain** $k_1\ k_2$ **where** [*simp*]: $c = (k_1,k_2)$ **by** *force*
$\quad\quad\quad\quad\quad$ **have** *roomk ?s r* $= k'$
$\quad\quad\quad\quad\quad\quad$ **using** *safe-roomk-currk*[*OF 1 safe-safe*[*OF 3*]]
$\quad\quad\quad\quad\quad\quad$ ⟨*no-Check-in* $((e \cdot s_3')$ @ $s_2)\ r$⟩ **by** *auto*
$\quad\quad\quad\quad\quad$ **hence** $k_1 \neq roomk\ ?s\ r$
$\quad\quad\quad\quad\quad\quad$ **using** *no-checkin-no-newkey*[**where** $s_2 = s_3'$ @ $[Enter\ g'\ r\ (k,k')]$ @ s_2]
$\quad\quad\quad\quad\quad\quad$ *1 2* ⟨*no-Check-in* $((e \cdot s_3')$ @ $s_2)\ r$⟩ **by** *auto*
$\quad\quad\quad\quad\quad$ **hence** $k_2 = roomk\ ?s\ r$ **using** ⟨*hotel ?t*⟩ **by** *auto*
$\quad\quad\quad\quad\quad$ **with** *only-owner-enter-normal*[*OF 1 safe-safe*[*OF 3*]] *2*
$\quad\quad\quad\quad\quad$ **have** *owns ?t r* $= \lfloor g \rfloor$ **by** *auto*
$\quad\quad\quad\quad\quad$ **moreover have** *owns ?t r* $= \lfloor g' \rfloor$
$\quad\quad\quad\quad\quad\quad$ **using** ⟨*hotel ?t*⟩ ⟨*no-Check-in* $((e \cdot s_3')$ @ $s_2)\ r$⟩ **by** *simp*
$\quad\quad\quad\quad\quad$ **ultimately show** $g' = g$ **by** *simp*
$\quad\quad\quad\quad$ **next**
$\quad\quad\quad\quad\quad$ **assume** $g'' \neq g$ **thus** $g' = g$ **using** *Cons* **by** *auto*
$\quad\quad\quad\quad$ **qed**
$\quad\quad\quad$ **next**
$\quad\quad\quad\quad$ **assume** $r' \neq r$ **thus** $g' = g$ **using** *Cons* **by** *auto*
$\quad\quad\quad$ **qed**
$\quad\quad$ **qed** (*insert Cons, auto*)
$\quad$ **qed**
$\quad$ } **with** *prems* **show** *owns s r* $= \lfloor g \rfloor$ **by**(*auto simp:safe-def*)
qed

Fig. 1. Isar proof of Theorem 2

3.3 Eliminating *isin*

In the state based approach we needed *isin* to express our safety guarantees. In the presence of traces, we can do away with it and talk about *Enter* events instead. We show that if somebody enters a safe room, he is the owner:

Theorem 3. If *hotel* (*Enter g r c · s*) and *safe₀ s r* then *owns s r* = $\lfloor g \rfloor$.

From *safe₀ s r* it follows that *s* must be of the form s_2 @ [*Check-in g₀ r c*] @ s_1 such that *no-Check-in s_2 r*. Let $c = (x, y)$ and $c' = (k, k')$. By Lemma 1.8 we have *roomk s r* = *currk s r* = k'. From *hotel* (*Enter g r c · s*) it follows that $(x, y) \in$ *cards s g* and $k' \in \{x, y\}$. By Lemma 2.2 $x = k'$ would contradict $(x, y) \in$ *cards s g*. Hence $y = k'$. With Lemma 1.9 we obtain *owns s r* = $\lfloor g \rfloor$.

Having dispensed with *isin* we could also eliminate *Exit* to arrive at a model closer to the ones in [2].

Finally one may quibble that all the safety theorems proved so far assume safety of the room at that point in time when somebody enters it. That is, the owner of the room must be sure that once a room is safe, it stays safe, in order to profit from those safety theorems. Of course, this is the case as long as nobody else checks in to that room:

Lemma 4. If *safe₀ s r* and *no-Check-in s' r* then *safe₀* (*s' @ s*) *r*.

It follows easily that Theorem 3 also extends until check-in:

Corollary 1. If *hotel* (*Enter g r c · s' @ s*) and *safe₀ s r* and *no-Check-in s' r* then *owns s r* = $\lfloor g \rfloor$.

3.4 Completeness of *safe*

Having proved correctness of *safe*, i.e. that safe behaviour protects against intruders, one may wonder if *safe* is complete, i.e. if it covers all safe behaviour, or if it is too restrictive. It turns out that *safe* is incomplete for two different reasons. The trivial one is that in case *initk* is injective, every room is protected against intruders right from the start. That is, [*Check-in g r c*] will only allow *g* to enter *r* until somebody else checks in to *r*. The second, more subtle incompleteness is that even if there are previous owners of a room, it may be safe to enter a room with an old card *c*: one merely needs to make sure that no other guest checked in after the check-in where one obtained *c*. However, formalizing this is not only messy, it is also somewhat pointless: this liberalization is not something a guest can take advantage of because there is no (direct) way he can find out which of his cards meets this criterion. But without this knowledge, the only safe thing to do is to make sure he has used his latest card. This incompleteness applies to the state based model as well.

4 Equivalence

Although the state based and the trace based model look similar enough, the nagging feeling remains that they could be subtly different. Hence I wanted to show the equivalence formally. This was very fortunate, because it revealed some unintended discrepancies (no longer present). Although I had proved both systems safe, it turned out that the state based version of safety was more restrictive than the trace based one. In the state based version of *safe* the room had to be empty the first time the owner enters with the latest card, whereas in the trace based version any time the owner enters with the latest card can make a room safe. Such errors in an automaton checking a trace property are very common and show the superiority of the trace based formalism.

When comparing the two models we have to take two slight differences into account:

– The initial setting of the room keys *initk* in the trace based model is an arbitrary but fixed value. In the state based model any injective initial value is fine.
– As a consequence (see the end of Section 3.1) *state.safe* is initially true whereas *Trace.safe* is initially false.

Since many names occur in both models they are disambiguated by the prefixes *state* and *Trace*.

In the one direction I have shown that any hotel trace starting with an injective *initk* gives rise to a reachable state when the components of that state are computed by the trace functions:

$[\![inj\ initk;\ hotel\ t]\!]$
$\Longrightarrow (\![state.owns = Trace.owns\ t,\ currk = Trace.currk\ t,$
$\quad\quad issued = Trace.issued\ t,\ cards = Trace.cards\ t,\ roomk = Trace.roomk\ t,$
$\quad\quad isin = Trace.isin\ t,$
$\quad\quad safe = \lambda r.\ Trace.safe\ t\ r \vee Trace.owns\ t\ r = None)\!)$
$\quad \in reach$

Conversely, for any reachable state there is a hotel trace leading to it:

$s \in reach \Longrightarrow$
$\exists t\ ik.$
$\quad initk = ik \longrightarrow$
$\quad hotel\ t \wedge$
$\quad state.cards\ s = Trace.cards\ t \wedge$
$\quad state.isin\ s = Trace.isin\ t \wedge$
$\quad state.roomk\ s = Trace.roomk\ t \wedge$
$\quad state.owns\ s = Trace.owns\ t \wedge$
$\quad state.currk\ s = Trace.currk\ t \wedge$
$\quad state.issued\ s = Trace.issued\ t \wedge$
$\quad state.safe\ s = (\lambda r.\ Trace.safe\ t\ r \vee Trace.owns\ t\ r = None)$

The precondition *initk* = *ik* just says that we can find some interpretation for *initk* that works, namely the one that was chosen as the initial setting for the keys in *s*.

The proofs are almost automatic, except for the *safe* component. In essence, we have to show that the procedural *state.safe* implements the declarative *Trace.safe*. The proof was complicated by the fact that initially it was not true and I had to debug *Trace.safe* by proof. Unfortunately Isabelle's current counterexample finders [1,7] did not seem to work here due to search space reasons. Once the bugs were ironed out, the following key lemma, together with some smaller lemmas, automated the correspondence proof for *safe*:

hotel (*Enter g r* (*k, k'*) · *t*) ⟹
Trace.safe (*Enter g r* (*k, k'*) · *t*) *r* =
(*Trace.owns t r* = ⌊*g*⌋ ∧ *Trace.isin t r* = ∅ ∧ *k'* = *Trace.currk t r* ∨
  Trace.safe t r)

In addition we used many lemmas from the trace model, including Theorem 2.

5   Conclusion

We have seen two different specification styles in this case study. The state based one is conceptually simpler, but may require auxiliary state components which express properties of the trace that lead to that state. And it may not be obvious if the definition of the state component correctly captures the desired property of the trace. A trace based specification expresses those properties directly. The proofs in the state based version are all automatic whereas in the trace based setting 4 proofs (out of 15) require special care, thus more than doubling the overall proof size. It would be interesting to test Isabelle's emerging link with automatic first-order provers [3] on the trace based proofs.

There are two different proof styles in Isabelle: unstructured apply-scripts [5] and structured Isar proofs [8,4]. Figure 1 shows an example of the latter. Even if the reader is unfamiliar with Isar, it is easy to see that this proof is very close to the version given in the text. Although apply-scripts are notoriously obscure, and even the author may not have an intuitive grasp of the structure of the proof, in our kind of application they also have advantages. In the apply-style, Isabelle's proof methods prove as much as possible automatically and leave the remaining cases to the user. This leads to much shorter (but more brittle) proofs: The (admittedly detailed) proof in Figure 1 was obtained from an apply-script of less than half the size.

The models given in this paper are very natural but by no means the only possible ones. Jackson himself uses an alternative trace based one which replaces the list data structure by an explicit notion of time. It would be interesting to see further treatments of this problem in other formalisms, for example temporal logics.

Acknowledgments. Daniel Jackson got me started on this case study, Stefano Berardi streamlined my proofs, and Larry Paulson commented on the paper at short notice.

References

1. Stefan Berghofer and Tobias Nipkow. Random testing in Isabelle/HOL. In J. Cuellar and Z. Liu, editors, *Software Engineering and Formal Methods (SEFM 2004)*, pages 230–239. IEEE Computer Society, 2004.
2. Daniel Jackson. *Software Abstractions. Logic, Language, and Analysis.* MIT Press, 2006.

3. Jia Meng, Claire Quigley, and Lawrence C. Paulson. Automation for interactive proof: First prototype. *Information and Computation*. In press.
4. Tobias Nipkow. Structured Proofs in Isar/HOL. In H. Geuvers and F. Wiedijk, editors, *Types for Proofs and Programs (TYPES 2002)*, volume 2646, pages 259–278, 2003.
5. Tobias Nipkow, Lawrence Paulson, and Markus Wenzel. *Isabelle/HOL — A Proof Assistant for Higher-Order Logic*, volume 2283. 2002. http://www.in.tum.de/~nipkow/ LNCS2283/.
6. Lawrence C. Paulson. The inductive approach to verifying cryptographic protocols. *J. Computer Security*, 6:85–128, 1998.
7. Tjark Weber. Bounded model generation for Isabelle/HOL. In W. Ahrendt, P. Baumgartner, H. de Nivelle, S. Ranise, and C. Tinelli, editors, *Selected Papers from the Workshops on Disproving and the Second International Workshop on Pragmatics of Decision Procedures (PDPAR 2004)*, volume 125(3) of *Electronic Notes in Theoretical Computer Science*, pages 103–116, 2005.
8. Markus Wenzel. *Isabelle/Isar — A Versatile Environment for Human-Readable Formal Proof Documents*. PhD thesis, Institut für Informatik, Technische Universität München, 2002. http://tumb1.biblio.tu-muenchen.de/publ/diss/in/2002/ wenzel.html.

Z/Eves and the Mondex Electronic Purse

Jim Woodcock and Leo Freitas

Department of Computer Science
University of York, UK
{jim, leo}@cs.york.ac.uk
www.cs.york.ac.uk/~jim

Abstract. We describe our experiences in mechanising the specification, refinement, and proof of the *Mondex Electronic Purse* using the Z/Eves theorem prover. We took a conservative approach and mechanised the original LaTeX sources, without changing their technical content, except to correct errors: we found problems in the original texts and missing invariants in the refinements. Based on these experiences, we present novel and detailed guidance on how to drive Z/Eves successfully. The work contributes to the research objectives of building the Repository for the Verified Software Grand Challenge.

Keywords: electronic finance, Grand Challenge, Mondex, refinement, security, smart cards, software archaeology, theorem proving, Verified Software Repository, the Z notation, Z/Eves.

1 Introduction

The Mondex case study is a year-long pilot project launched in January 2006 as part of the International Grand Challenge in Verified Software [8, 12]. The case study demonstrates how research groups can collaborate and compete in scientific experiments to generate artefacts to populate the Grand Challenge's Verified Software Repository [1]. The objective is to verify a key property of the Mondex smart card in order to assess the current state of proof mechanisation.

Mondex [11] is an electronic purse hosted on a smart card and developed about ten years ago to the high-assurance standard ITSEC Level E6 [5] by a consortium led by NatWest, a UK high-street bank. Purses interact using a communications device, and strong guarantees are needed that transactions are secure in spite of power failures and mischievous attacks. These guarantees ensure that electronic cash cannot be counterfeited, although transactions are completely distributed. There is no centralised control: all security measures are locally implemented, with no real-time external audit logging or monitoring.

Mondex is a seriously security-critical system that required careful justification. Logica, a commercial software house, with assistance from the University of Oxford, used the Z notation [17, 21] for the development process [20, 18, 2]. We built formal models of the system and its abstract security policy, and conducted hand-written proofs that the system design possesses the required security properties. The abstract security policy specification is about 20 pages of Z; the

K. Barkaoui, A. Cavalcanti, and A. Cerone (Eds.): ICTAC 2006, LNCS 4281, pp. 15–34, 2006.

concrete specification (an n-step protocol) is about 60 pages of Z; the verification, suitable for external evaluation, is about 200 pages of proofs; and the derivation of new refinement rules is about 100 pages [20, 2].

The original proof was carefully structured for understanding, something much appreciated by Mondex case study groups. The original proof was vital in successfully getting the required certification. It was also useful in finding and evaluating different models. The original team made a key modelling discovery, which led to an abstraction that gave the precise security property and invariants that explain why the protocol is secure. The resulting proof revealed a bug in the implementation of a secondary protocol, explained what had gone wrong, and produced a convincing counterexample that the protocol was flawed. This led to an insight to change the design to correct the problem. Third-party evaluators also found a bug: an undischarged assumption in the hand-written proofs.

A commercially sanitised version of the documentation of the Mondex development is publicly available [20]. It contains the Z specifications of security properties; the abstract specification; the intermediate-level design; the concrete design; and rigorous correctness proofs of security and conformance. Originally, there was absolutely no question of mechanising proofs: it was believed that the extra cost would far outweigh the benefit of greater assurance in this case [19]. The feeling that mechanising such a large proof *cost-effectively* was beyond the state of the art ten years ago gives us two sharply focused questions. (a) Was that really true then? (b) Is it true now?

Six groups came together to collaborate and compete. The teams were:

Alloy [6, 7]	Daniel Jackson/Tahina Ramananandro	*MIT*
Event-B [9]	Michael Butler	*Southampton*
OCL [10]	Martin Gogolla	*Bremen*
PerfectDeveloper [3]	David Crocker	*Escher Ltd*
Raise [4]	Chris George/Anne Haxthausen	*Macao/DTU*
Z [17, 21]	Leo Freitas/Jim Woodcock	*York*

We all agreed to work for one year, without funding. Meanwhile, separately and silently, a group led by Gerhard Schellhorn at the University of Augsburg began work using KIV and ASMs [15, 16].

Two distinct approaches emerged amongst the six. The *Archaeologists* made as few changes as possible to the original documentation. They reasoned that models should not be changed just to make verification easier, because how else would we know that our results had anything to do with the original specification? The *Technologists* wanted to use the best proof technology now available. Since these new tools do not work for Z, they had two choices: translate existing models into new languages; or create new models better suited to new tools.

We spend the rest of this paper describing our archaeological experiment in mechanising the proof of Mondex in Z/Eves. As a side effect of our work, we discovered undocumented techniques for driving Z/Eves, and we present these in section 2. We discuss our formalisation in section 3, including the fidelity of our mechanisation, suggestions for improvement of the existing models, and completeness of our work. Section 4 contains a list of the problems, omissions, and errors that we found. Benchmarks might be useful in calibrating tools and comparing experiments, and we have collected some of these in section 5. In section 6, we briefly describe only one of the other experiments currently being conducted on Mondex. Finally, in section 7, we present a few conclusions, suggestions for further work, and call on interested colleagues to join in similar experiments on Mondex and other challenges in the future.

2 Driving Z/Eves

In this section we provide general information about proving theorems in Z/Eves. It is useful to understand how the theorem prover works, in order to explain how to handle a specification as big and complex as Mondex.

2.1 Ability and Usage Directives

The level of automation in Z/Eves can be fine tuned by selecting abilities (boolean enabling conditions) and usages (scope control) [13]. Usages may be assumption (**grule**), forward (**frule**), and rewriting (**rule**), and they define the scope of definitions and theorems with respect to available transformation tactics. These directives must be chosen carefully in a theory to prevent the prover taking wrong turns while transforming goals. Although some guidelines exist for the proper selection of usages, it is difficult to predict the appropriate ability values without experience with the theory being proved and the prover itself.

2.2 Housekeeping Rules

Rewriting rules can be used for fine-grained automation, since they are used by the specialised tactics that rewrite the goal: rewrite, reduce, prove, prove by reduce, and their corresponding trivial and normalised forms. Assumption rules can be used for coarse-grained automation, commonly needed for non-maximal type consistency checks that often appear in proofs, since they are used by every tactic that rewrites the goal. Forward rules are normally used to expose implicit facts about schema components and invariants, without expanding schema definitions. This is particularly valuable when there are complex schema expressions, because we can surgically guide specific aspects of the goal without cluttering the proof with a mass of unrelated assumptions from included schemas. The resulting proofs are easier to conduct, understand, and amend. For instance, for

$$S \;==\; [\, x : \mathbb{N};\; s : \operatorname{seq} \mathbb{N} \mid x = \#s \,]$$

the following forward rules could be added

theorem frule *fSSMaxType*   **theorem** frule *fSSInv*
$$\forall S \bullet s \in \mathbb{P}\,(\mathbb{Z} \times \mathbb{Z})$$ $$\forall S \bullet x = \#s$$

giving access to simple properties of S required by almost all subsequent proofs.

2.3   Automation for Schemas and Bindings

Z/Eves adds theorems for each schema: for S, we get an assumption rule defining the maximal type of the set of bindings for S and a forward rule to infer the types of each schema component.

theorem grule $S\$declaration$
$$S \in \mathbb{P}\,\langle\!\langle x : \mathbb{Z} \rangle\!\rangle$$

theorem frule $S\$declarationPart$
$$S \Rightarrow x \in \mathbb{N} \land s \in s \in \operatorname{seq}\mathbb{N}$$

Rules to reason about θ expressions are also added into context, and we describe them in order of relevance for automation.

– θ and binding expressions

>   **theorem** rule S\$thetaInSet
> $$\theta S \in \langle\!\langle x : x';\ s : s' \rangle\!\rangle \Leftrightarrow x \in x' \land s \in s'$$

– θ expression as schema inclusion

>   **theorem** rule S\$thetaMember
> $$\theta S \in S \Leftrightarrow S$$

– θ expression equality, which is useful for Ξ inclusions

>   **theorem** rule S\$thetasEqual
> $$\theta S = \theta S' \Leftrightarrow x = x' \land s = s'$$

– θ binding selection expression (for each schema component)

>   **theorem** rule S\$select\$x
> $$\theta S.x = x$$

– θ expression as variables of type S

>   **theorem** disabled rule S\$member
> $$x\$ \in S \Leftrightarrow (\exists\, S \bullet x\$ = \theta S)$$

– θ expression as variables of the binding type of S

>   **theorem** disabled rule S\$inSet
> $$x\$ \in \langle\!\langle x : x';\ s : s' \rangle\!\rangle \Leftrightarrow (\exists\, x : x';\ s : s' \bullet x\$ = \theta S)$$

– the meaning of the set of bindings of S

>   **theorem** disabled rule S\$setInPowerSet
> $$\langle\!\langle x : x;\ s : s \rangle\!\rangle \in \mathbb{P}\,\langle\!\langle x : x';\ s : s' \rangle\!\rangle \Leftrightarrow$$
> $$x \in \mathbb{P}\,x' \land s \in \mathbb{P}\,s' \lor x = \{\} \lor s = \{\}$$

Although this gives a powerful automation toolkit for schema mechanisation, when schema components are quite complex, such as layered inclusions or components with binding type, one still might need to expose implicit facts about schemas. For instance, the following frule is needed in Mondex for discharging goals involving $StartFromPurseEafromOkay$ [20, p.30], where some of its components refer to bindings of the $CounterPartyDetails$ schema.

> **theorem** frule fCounterPartyDetailsValueType
> $x \in CounterPartyDetails \Rightarrow x.value \in \mathbb{N}$

Luckily, with the above toolkit, such theorems are often proved quite trivially.

2.4   Free-Type Rules

We usually need the implicit fact that the constructors are injective when we reason about a free type. For example, for the free type $List$, $cons$ is injective:

$$List ::= nil \mid cons\langle\!\langle \mathbb{Z} \times List \rangle\!\rangle \qquad\qquad \textbf{theorem grule } gConsPInjType$$
$$cons \in (\mathbb{N} \times List) \rightarrowtail List$$

To prove this rule, we often need to provide intermediate theorems for expressions that appear as side conditions on goals. These are similar theorems stating that $cons$ is a partial function, a relation, or even a set of pairs.

In the $Mondex$ case study, free-type constructors appear frequently in the specification of the protocol messages, with schema bindings as parameters to give an extra complexity. For instance, the schema $ValidStartFrom$ refers to the expression $startFrom^\sim\ m?$, where the result is a $CounterPartyDetails$ schema. Thus, we need not only the injectivity theorems, but also forward rules about the binding type of the $CounterPartyDetails$ schema as

> **theorem** frule fCounterPartyDetailsMember
> $x \in CounterPartyDetails$
> $\qquad \Rightarrow x \in \langle\!\langle name : NAME;\ nextSeqNo : \mathbb{N};\ value : \mathbb{N} \rangle\!\rangle$

> **theorem** frule fCounterPartyDetailsInSetMember
> $x \in \langle\!\langle name : NAME;\ nextSeqNo : \mathbb{N};\ value : \mathbb{N} \rangle\!\rangle$
> $\qquad \Rightarrow x \in CounterPartyDetails$

Thanks to the automation for θ and binding expressions provided by Z/Eves, these forward rules are relatively easy to prove.

2.5   Rules for Axiomatically Declared Functions

The successful automation of proofs involving functions requires additional rules about the function's (maximal) type, the type of its result, and about its totality. Depending on the structure of the function type and which toolkit theorems are used, we often need more than one type theorem, and we must predict these in advance for the best automation. Fortunately, there is a pattern to these rules. For instance, in a function f declared as

$$f : \text{seq}\,(\mathbb{F}\,\mathbb{N}) \to \text{seq}\,\mathbb{N}$$
$$\cdots$$

we might need to add type information as assumptions (*grules*), such as

$$f \in \mathbb{P}\,(\mathbb{P}\,(\mathbb{Z} \times \mathbb{P}\,\mathbb{Z}) \times \mathbb{P}\,(\mathbb{Z} \times \mathbb{P}\,(\mathbb{Z} \times \mathbb{Z})))$$

which is often required in applying rules, or

$$f \in \text{seq}\,(\mathbb{P}\,\mathbb{Z}) \leftrightarrow \text{seq}\,\mathbb{Z}$$

which might appear when relational definitions from the toolkit are used.

When using a free type we usually need to prove a theorem about the injectivity of its constructors. It gets more complicated when the free type refers to a schema binding, as is the case with *MESSAGE*s in Mondex [20, p.26].

$$MESSAGE \quad ::= \quad startFrom \langle\!\langle CounterPartyDetails \rangle\!\rangle \mid \cdots$$

In Mondex, we have expressions such as

$$cpd \in CounterPartyDetails \land m? \in MESSAGE \land cpd = startFrom^{\sim} m?$$

To discharge the consistency checks about this expression, the injectivity theorem is given with the maximal type of *CounterParyDetails* as

theorem grule gStartFromInjType
$$startFrom \in \langle\!\langle name : NAME;\ value : \mathbb{N};\ nextSeqNo : \mathbb{N} \rangle\!\rangle \rightarrowtail MESSAGE$$

It establishes that the *startFrom* is an injection between *CounterPartyDetails* and *MESSAGE*. Furthermore, to prove this injectivity theorem, we need auxiliary lemmas about functional and relational types of *startFrom*, as well as extra (maximal) type rules for *CounterPartyDetails*, presented above.

2.6   Schema Invariants and Preconditions

While proving theorems involving schema inclusion, it is often necessary to expose particular elements and predicates of the state invariant. Nevertheless, it is not productive to expand the inclusion, as this leads to lengthy and complex predicates. Thus, in order to surgically expose schema components, we need to introduce forward (*frule*) rules. For instance, let us define a state schema S as

$$S \;\; \widehat{=} \;\; [\,x : \mathbb{N};\ s : \text{seq}\,\mathbb{N} \mid x \geq \# s \land s \neq \langle\rangle\,]$$

and an operation over this state as

$$Op \;\; \widehat{=} \;\; [\,\Delta S;\ i? : \mathbb{N} \mid x' = x + 1 \land s' = s \frown \langle i? \rangle\,]$$

Due to the nature of the predicates involved in the operations, as well as the theorems we might be proving about them (such as precondition calculation or refinement simulation), we might want to expose parts of the state invariant in the middle of a proof without expanding S. This careful control is necessary to avoid the hypothesis and goal explosion problem, but it should also be as automatic as possible to avoid the need for micro-management of the proof. In order to achieve all this, we introduce forward rules, such as

theorem frule *fSSInv1*
$$\forall S \bullet s \neq \langle \rangle$$

theorem frule *fSSInv2*
$$\forall S \bullet x \geq \# s$$

They are trivially proved by expanding S; nevertheless, they allow us to conclude the invariants of S without expansion, provided that S appears as part of our original goal.

As occurred before for functions and free types, we might also need to expose the (maximal) type of the schema components, hence theorems like

theorem frule fSSMaxType
$$\forall S \bullet s \in \mathbb{P}\,(\mathbb{Z} \times \mathbb{Z})$$

could be defined. The rationale of when such theorems should be introduced depends on the kind of goals that appear in proofs about the schema in question.

During the refinement proofs in Mondex, it is often mentioned that particular elements of *BetweenWorld* should be used/exposed. To do that without expanding the schema, one just needs to add a forward rule such as

theorem frule fBetweenWorldMaybeLostExpansion
$$\forall \, BetweenWorld \bullet maybeLost = (fromInEpa \cup fromLogged) \cap toInEpv$$

which is again trivially true from the definition of *BetweenWorld* [20, p.42].

A strategy is need for the proof of the preconditions of complex promoted operations in Mondex. Additional lemmas are needed for the precondition of the promoted operation, and although these lemmas cannot be used directly in the promoted precondition proofs, they define how to instantiate the quantifiers in the promoted precondition. This strategy turned out to be very effective.

2.7   Z Idioms

One-point-mu. It is notoriously hard to reason about definite descriptions in Z, mainly because the notion is primitive to the language: it is not easy to eliminate an arbitrary μ-term. There are three very specific automation rules in Z/Eves: two symmetric rules concerning equality with a μ-term; and a third rule concerning a definite description drawn from a singleton set. In each rule there is a candidate value for the expression, and we can call them one-point rules, by analogy with predicate calculus. Definite description is used in Mondex to build bindings with components defined pointwise, and we devised another one-point rule to eliminate a μ-term in favour of an explicit binding: a θ-term with substitutions for each component. That is, to replace $(\mu\,S \mid x = e \wedge \cdots \wedge z = g)$ by $\theta S[x := e, \cdots, z := g]$. The special Z/Eves assignments are a shorthand for schema substitution with expressions rather than names:

$$\theta S[x := e] \Leftrightarrow (\exists\, e : type(x) \mid e = x \bullet S[e/x])$$

For example, here is such a theorem involving the schema *PayDetails*:

> **theorem** rule rStartFromMuPayDetailsValue
> $\forall\, name : NAME;\ nextSeqNo : \mathbb{N};\ cpd : CounterPartyDetails \mid$
> $\quad name \neq cpd.name \bullet$
> $\quad\quad (\mu\,PayDetails \mid from = name \wedge to = cpd.name \wedge$
> $\quad\quad\quad\quad value = cpd.value \wedge fromSeqNo = nextSeqNo \wedge$
> $\quad\quad\quad\quad toSeqNo = cpd.nextSeqNo)$
> $\quad\quad = \theta PayDetails[from := name, to := cpd.name,$
> $\quad\quad\quad\quad value := cpd.value, fromSeqNo := nextSeqNo,$
> $\quad\quad\quad\quad toSeqNo := cpd.nextSeqNo]$

This is useful because Z/Eves has better automation support for bindings, and because it is an automatic rewriting rule, equality substitution takes place fully automatically. This is also useful in proving the next three rules, which are necessary for every proof involving definite descriptions of this sort. First, $\mu\,PayDetails$ maximal type in *StartFromPurseEafromOkay*:

> **theorem** rule rStartFromMuPayDetailsMaxType
> $\forall\, name : NAME;\ nextSeqNo : \mathbb{N};\ cpd : CounterPartyDetails \mid$
> $\quad name \neq cpd.name \bullet$
> $\quad\quad (\mu\,m : \{PayDetails \mid from = name \wedge to = cpd.name \wedge$
> $\quad\quad\quad\quad value = cpd.value \wedge fromSeqNo = nextSeqNo \wedge$
> $\quad\quad\quad\quad toSeqNo = cpd.nextSeqNo\})$
> $\quad\quad \in \langle\!\langle from : NAME;\ fromSeqNo : \mathbb{Z};$
> $\quad\quad\quad\quad to : NAME;\ toSeqNo : \mathbb{Z};\ value : \mathbb{Z}\rangle\!\rangle$

Second, $\mu\,PayDetails$ non-maximal type in *StartFromPurseEafromOkay*:

> **theorem** rule rStartFromMuPayDetailsType
> $\forall\, name : NAME;\ nextSeqNo : \mathbb{N};\ cpd : CounterPartyDetails \mid$
> $\quad name \neq cpd.name \bullet$
> $\quad\quad (\mu\,m : \{PayDetails \mid from = name \wedge to = cpd.name \wedge$
> $\quad\quad\quad\quad value = cpd.value \wedge fromSeqNo = nextSeqNo \wedge$
> $\quad\quad\quad\quad toSeqNo = cpd.nextSeqNo\}) \in PayDetails$

Third, $\mu\,PayDetails$ *from* purse type in *StartFromPurseEafromOkay*:

> **theorem** rule rStartFromMuPayDetailsFromType
> $\forall\, name : NAME;\ nextSeqNo : \mathbb{N};\ cpd : CounterPartyDetails \mid$
> $\quad name \neq cpd.name \bullet$
> $\quad\quad (\mu\,m : \{PayDetails \mid from = name \wedge to = cpd.name \wedge$
> $\quad\quad\quad\quad value = cpd.value \wedge fromSeqNo = nextSeqNo \wedge$
> $\quad\quad\quad\quad toSeqNo = cpd.nextSeqNo\}).from \in NAME$

Finally, four more rules are added to establish the θ-μ *PayDetails* expressions equivalence for *to* purses, with the same shape but *name* = *to*.

Keep declarations non-finite. There is very limited automation for reasoning about finite sets in Z/Eves, and so the best advice is to avoid doing so unnecessarily. A useful tip is not to declare a set as finite, but rather to give its finiteness as a property. This is important because the side conditions and rules available in the automation toolkit are always with respect to the *maximal type*. For example, instead of declaring *abAuthPurse* as a finite function

$$AbWorld \;\widehat{=}\; [\,abAuthPurse : NAME \nrightarrow AbPurse\,]$$

declare it as a function and constrain it to be finite:

$$[\,abAuthPurse : NAME \rightarrow AbPurse \mid abAuthPurse \in NAME \nrightarrow AbPurse\,]$$

Avoid binding selection on free-type constructor results. In schema *BetwInitIn* [20, p.52], the use of $(req^{\sim} m?).from$ directly is a bad idea for Z/Eves automation, as it incurs rather complex lemmas involving the functionality of the inverse function. Instead, one could simply declare a variable to hold such value: Z/Eves would then know the type of this expression, the main problem appearing in the domain check. Nevertheless, for the sake of keeping to the original as much as possible, we left it unchanged. The alternative would be to have something like the following:

$$BetwInitIn == [\,\cdots; \; x : PayDetails \mid x = req^{\sim} m? \wedge \cdots \wedge x.from\,]$$

2.8   Extending the Z Toolkit

Functional overriding. Although there are useful rules for relational overriding, there are no rules specifically for functional overriding. This operator plays a central role in updating the state in the abstract specification and security model. We added three simple rules in the proofs from [20, Chap.8].

> **theorem** rule rPFunElement $[X, Y]$
> $\forall f : X \rightarrow Y; \; x : X; \; y : Y \mid x \in \operatorname{dom} f \wedge y = f\,x \bullet (x, y) \in f$

> **theorem** rule rPFunSubsetOplusRel $[X, Y]$
> $\forall f, g : X \rightarrow Y \mid g \subseteq f \bullet f \oplus g = f \oplus (\operatorname{dom} g \vartriangleleft f)$

> **theorem** lPFunSubsetOplusUnitRel $[X, Y]$
> $\forall f : X \rightarrow Y; \; x : X; \; y : Y \mid x \in \operatorname{dom} f \wedge y = f\,x \bullet$
> $\qquad f = f \oplus \{(x \mapsto y)\}$

Finiteness. As mentioned above, reasoning about finiteness is difficult; there are four reasons for this. (a) Proofs about finiteness often require reasoning about total functions, injections, bijections, and set cardinality. (b) Pointwise instantiation is needed. (c) There is a lack of automation rules and toolkit theorems about finiteness. (d) Low-level rewriting for set membership is not restricted to finite sets. The definition for the finite powerset constructor is

$$\mathbb{F}\, X == \{\, S : \mathbb{P}\, X \mid \exists\, n : \mathbb{N} \bullet \exists\, f : 1 \mathinner{\ldotp\ldotp} n \to S \bullet \operatorname{ran} f = S \,\}$$

and for cardinality

$$
\begin{array}{l}
\underline{\hspace{0.5em}[X]\hspace{0.5em}} \\
\#\, : \mathbb{F} \to \mathbb{N} \\
\hline
\forall\, S : \mathbb{F}\, X \bullet \exists\, f : 1 \mathinner{\ldotp\ldotp} (\#S) \rightarrowtail\!\!\!\to S \bullet \mathit{true}
\end{array}
$$

An alternative, inductive definition is given in the ISO Z Standard.

$$\mathbb{F}_{new}\, X == \bigcap \{\, A : \mathbb{P}\,(\mathbb{P}\, X) \mid \{\} \in A \wedge (\forall\, a : A;\ x : X \bullet a \cup \{x\} \in A) \}$$

This is useful because there is no need to deal with instantiations, and it gives a better pattern for proofs involving the bijection present in cardinality.

The need to prove that a set is finite arises most often from proving properties involving the cardinality operator. Here are some extra theorems to help reason about set sizes. First, smaller sets have smaller sizes.

theorem disabled sizeOfPSubset $[X]$
$$\forall\, T : \mathbb{F}\ X \mid S \subset T \bullet 0 \leq \#S < \#T$$

Next we have the maximal type of cardinality, which is useful for discharging side conditions/type checks on proofs involving $\#$.

theorem disabled grule cardType $[X]$
$$\forall\, x : \mathbb{F}\ X \bullet \#\, x \in \mathbb{Z}$$

The next two theorems reason about the relationship between set membership and the cardinality operator on sets.

theorem disabled rule cardDiffIsSmaller $[X]$
$$\forall\, S : \mathbb{F}\ X;\ x : X \mid x \in S \bullet (\#(S \setminus \{x\}) < \#S)$$

theorem disabled rule cardDiffLower $[X]$
$$\forall\, S : \mathbb{F}\ X;\ x : X \mid x \in S \bullet (0 \leq \#(S \setminus \{x\}))$$

Finite relations have finite domains and ranges.

theorem disabled finRelHasFinDom $[X, Y]$
$$\forall\, R : X \leftrightarrow Y \mid R \in \mathbb{F}\,(X \times Y) \bullet \operatorname{dom} R \in \mathbb{F}\ X$$

theorem disabled finRelHasFinRan $[X, Y]$
$$\forall\, R : X \leftrightarrow Y \mid R \in \mathbb{F}\,(X \times Y) \bullet \operatorname{ran} R \in \mathbb{F}\ Y$$

We also use a variation on the last rule that abstracts the sets involved.

Similar rules apply to sequences.

theorem grule seqIsFinite $[X]$
$\quad \forall\, s : \text{seq } X \bullet s \in \mathbb{F}\,(\mathbb{Z} \times X)$

theorem disabled seqHasFinRan $[X]$
$\quad \forall\, s : \text{seq } X \bullet \text{ran } s \in \mathbb{F}\ X$

theorem disabled seqHasFinRan2 $[X]$
$\quad \forall\, A : \mathbb{P}\ X \bullet \forall\, s : \text{seq } A \bullet \text{ran } s \in \mathbb{F}\ A$

theorem disabled iseqHasFinRan $[X]$
$\quad \forall\, s : \text{iseq } X \bullet \text{ran } s \in \mathbb{F}\ X$

theorem disabled iseqHasFinRan2 $[X]$
$\quad \forall\, A : \mathbb{P}\ X \bullet \forall\, s : \text{iseq } A \bullet \text{ran } s \in \mathbb{F}\ A$

There are other mathematical datatypes in the toolkit that are not used in Mondex (for example, bags), but they could be handled in the same way.

3 Formalisation

3.1 Fidelity

Our formalisation is a carbon copy of *Oxford Monograph PRG-126*, except in two respects. The definition of *PayDetails* [20, p.24] required modification in order to make it finite. In the original *PRG* this is a bug, which leads many claims about finiteness unprovable (see 4.2 below).

The auxiliary toolkit definitions from [20, App.D] are inappropriate for mechanisation because they require reasoning about finiteness and cardinality; they also require witnesses in their instantiation. For instance,

$$\begin{array}{l}
\mid\ totalAbBalance : (NAME \nrightarrow AbPurse) \rightarrow \mathbb{N} \\
\hline
\mid\ totalAbBalance\ \emptyset = 0 \\
\mid\ \forall\, w : (NAME \nrightarrow AbPurse);\ n : NAME;\ AbPurse \mid n \notin \text{dom } w \bullet \\
\mid\qquad totalAbBalance(\{n \mapsto \theta AbPurse\} \cup w) = balance + totalAbBalance\ w
\end{array}$$

In order to use the inductive case of *totalAbBalance*, we need to partition the argument into two parts, the first being a singleton. Without a witness for this element, this rule is useless for automation.

We kept this definition in our formalisation, but did not prove the theorems from [20, Sect.2.4], which is related to *totalAbBalance* and the other auxiliary function from [20, App.D]. Moreover, the proofs given in [20, Sect.2.4] are informal, as the suggested instantiations are not possible as mentioned in the text.

3.2   Suggestion of Improvement

Alternative definition for totalAbBalance. Although there is little automation for finite functions in general, there is good automation for sequences. An alternative definition for *totalAbBalance* using sequences and induction avoids both finiteness and instantiation problems by relying on the rich toolkit theorems for sequences. Summation over sequences is very simple:

$$
\begin{array}{|l}
sum : \text{seq}\,\mathbb{Z} \to \mathbb{Z} \\
\hline
sum \langle\rangle = 0 \\
\forall\, n : \mathbb{Z} \bullet sum\,\langle n \rangle = n \\
\forall\, s, t : \text{seq}\,\mathbb{Z} \bullet sum\,(s \,^\frown t) = sum\,s + sum\,t
\end{array}
$$

An inductive update over sequences is given by

$$
\begin{array}{|l}
update : \text{seq}\,\mathbb{Z} \times \mathbb{Z} \times \mathbb{Z} \to \text{seq}\,\mathbb{Z} \\
\hline
\forall\, i, n : \mathbb{Z} \bullet update(\langle\rangle, i, n) = \langle\rangle \\
\forall\, i, x, n : \mathbb{Z} \bullet update(\langle x \rangle, i, n) = \textbf{if } i = 1 \textbf{ then } \langle n \rangle \textbf{ else } \langle x \rangle \\
\forall\, s, t : \text{seq}\,\mathbb{Z};\ i, n : \mathbb{Z} \bullet update((s \,^\frown t), i, n) = \\
\quad \textbf{if } i \in \text{dom}\,s \textbf{ then } update(s, i, n) \,^\frown t \\
\quad \textbf{else if } i - \#s \in \text{dom}\,t \textbf{ then } s \,^\frown update(t, (i - \#s), n) \\
\quad \textbf{else } s \,^\frown t
\end{array}
$$

The effect an update is given in terms of the changing sum:

theorem tSumUpdate
$$
\forall\, s : \text{seq}\,\mathbb{Z};\ i, n : \mathbb{Z} \mid i \in \text{dom}\,s \bullet \\
sum(update(s, i, n)) = sum\,s - s\,i + n
$$

theorem rule rSumPos
$$
\forall\, s : \text{seq}\,\mathbb{N} \bullet sum\,s \in \mathbb{N}
$$

These definitions are much simpler than the ones using finite functions.

Better structuring of precondition proofs. The precondition proofs in Chapter 8 are understated: they mention that various operations have trivial preconditions because they are disjoined with *Ignore*, a schema with a very easy proof of totality. Nevertheless, if one tries to calculate the preconditions in Z/Eves without relying on *Ignore*, they turn out to be quite challenging, and the informal proof is of little help. The reasons for this are as follows.

- Z/Eves does not support compositional precondition calculation (as described in [21]), so there is no way to mimic the informal proof without doing a lot of calculation.

- There are many variables to instantiate, and so a lot of ingenuity is required to find appropriate values. This cannot be automated.
- The proof needs to be structured with auxiliary lemmas, one for each conjunct of the formulas; mainly the one on page 47, *StartFromEafromOkay*.
- The precondition proof of *StartFromEafromOkay* is missing; it requires the precondition proof of various other parts of the specification.
- Several lemmas are needed for precondition proofs to deal with promoted operations and appropriate instantiations.
- The hand-written proofs avoid analysis of promoted operations.
- Other lemmas are stated but not used (yet).
- No informal explanation is given for harder proofs.

Clearer proof explanation. As the promoted proofs for *Eafrom* operations cannot rely on disjunction with *Ignore*, the whole proof is much more complex, as we need to tackle the entire operation itself. Because of the various quantifiers and schema inclusions, it is quite hard to figure out what the appropriate instantiations would be, hence we have pretty hard precondition proofs to discharge. We decided to break then down into the various schema inclusion parts, so that the appropriate instantiations are clearly understood.

The definition of *StartFromEafromOkay* is given in [20, Sect.5.6.1] as

$$StartFromEafromOkay$$
$$\mathrel{\widehat=} \exists \Delta ConPurse \bullet PhiBOp \land StartFromPurseEafromOkay$$

Thus, at first, we want to prove the precondition of *StartFromPurseEafromOkay* alone. Because of the way these promoted operations are defined, we need to include additional automation lemmas even before this first precondition. More precisely, the use of pointwise definite descriptions in the definition of *StartFromPurseEaFromOkay* makes automation hard.

The hand-written proofs in [20] are nicely written, and we have found this informal help very useful (so far): the proofs are thoroughly explained, especially in later chapters; the mechanised proofs are mostly the same as the explanation.

Minor suggestions. There are some minor mistakes in the text. First, there is a mistaken LaTeX markup involving a subscript and a stroke (Chapters 7 and 10), which in fact turned out to be a bug in the Z standard. Consider the following quantified predicate: $\exists x_1', x_1' : \mathbb{N} \bullet x_1' \neq x_1'$. It parses; it is type correct; and it evaluates to *true*. The two variables in the predicate are actually different, even though they are typeset identically, as can be seen from the LaTeX source used:

```
\exists x_1', x'_1: \nat @ x_1' \neq x'_1
```

This confusion is present in the Mondex source text: a variable is marked up in both ways, introducing an undeclared variable and a failed type-check.

An operation and a theorem are both called *AbOp* (p.63, Chapter 8), causing the type checker to fail, and the proofs in Chapter 10 refer to lemmas in [20, App.C] without proper referencing.

3.3   How Complete Is It?

At the time of writing, the following parts of Mondex have been mechanically verified using Z/Eves:

- Models
  - $\mathcal{A}$ model [20, Chap.3]
  - $\mathcal{B}$ model: purse, world, init., final [20, Chap.4,5,6]
  - $\mathcal{C}$ model [20, Chap.7]
  - applicability proofs [20, Chap.8]
- Refinement: $\mathcal{A}$ to $\mathcal{B}$
  - retrieve definitions [20, Chap.10]
  - $\mathcal{A}$ to $\mathcal{B}$ initialisation [20, Chap.11]
  - $\mathcal{A}$ to $\mathcal{B}$ finalisation [20, Chap.12]
  - $\mathcal{A}$ to $\mathcal{B}$ applicability [20, Chap.13]
  - *Abs* to *Betw* lemmas for backward simulation [20, Chap.14,App.C]
- Security properties [20, Chap.2]
  - all definitions (but [20, Sect.2.4])
  - proofs in [20, Sect.2.4] contain informal arguments
  - *totalAbBalance* [20, App.D] is inadequate for mechanisation
  - mechanisable using suggested model of sequences

It is expected that the remaining chapters will be mechanised shortly.

4   Problems Found

4.1   Are After Purses Authentic?

There is a state invariant that requires all abstract purses involved in a transaction to be authentic: *abAuthPurse*. This invariant is not required in the after-state of the operations *AbTransferOkayTD* and *AbTransferLostTD* (p.20, 21), although it should be. We demonstrated the necessity of the after-invariant by showing that the original definitions can lead to a state with inauthentic purses.

4.2   Four Missing Properties of *BetweenWorld*

BetweenWorld is inconsistent when *val* or *ack* messages are handled. For property *B*3 (p.42), the original purse is missing additional information about the authenticity of *val* messages in the *ether* for *to* and *from* purses. This does not apply to *rel* messages, as property *B*1 shows. We include the new properties in the predicate part to have a uniform signature across *BetweenWorld* properties.

$$\forall\, pd : PayDetails \mid val\ pd \in ether \bullet pd \in authenticTo$$
$$\forall\, pd : PayDetails \mid val\ pd \in ether \bullet pd \in authenticFrom$$

Similarly, for property *B*4, we need to include the authenticity of *ack* messages in the *ether* for *to* and *from* purses.

$$\forall\, pd : PayDetails \mid ack\ pd \in ether \bullet pd \in authenticTo$$
$$\forall\, pd : PayDetails \mid ack\ pd \in ether \bullet pd \in authenticFrom$$

For *B5* nothing else is needed because the *from* purses in *fromLogged* are already authentic, from the definition in *AuxWorld*. Similarly, for *B6*, *B7*, and *B8*, the *to* purses in *toLogged* and *from* purses in *fromLogged* are already authentic.

4.3   Retrieve Relations

The proof of the first refinement [20, Chap.10] reaches the following goal:

$$RabCl \Rightarrow (\exists \, pdThis : PayDetails \bullet true)$$

which requires that at least one *PayDetails* schema exists. For this to be true, we must have at least two different names for *from* and *to* components. Of course this is a reasonable assumption, but it has not been made explicitly in the original specification. This problem also appears in lemmas from [20, Chap.14,App.C].

5   Benchmarks

In August 2006, more than half of Mondex has been verified: this discharges the verification conditions of 160 definitions. Tables 1 and 2 present some statistics from the proof work so far, which we explain in detail.

There are four kinds of conjectures that we needed to prove about Mondex: additional rules for language constructs and mathematical toolkit definitions; theorems stating consistency properties and verification conditions for the correctness of refinements: lemmas used to structure theorems; and domain checks. Most of the additional rules arise from automating the type-checking of free-types and schemas, as described above.

We have proved 160 verification conditions to do with consistency and correctness properties. There are two parts to proving the consistency of a Z specification of a system as an abstract datatype: first, the existence of a model for the specification; and second, the non-triviality of that datatype.

Is there a model for the definitions? This question asks whether the specification is satisfiable, or are the definitions in contradiction? Notice from the table that most paragraphs analysed so far are used to define schemas. Any contradictions in the declarations and constraints of a schema result in the definition of an empty set of bindings, so there is always a model for a schema, albeit perhaps a trivial one. So the problem becomes one of finding carriers for the two given sets that can lead to existence proofs for the free-typ and axiomatic definitions. A total of nine proofs will be needed. Z/Eves has a further requirement for consistency: it generates *domain checks* to guarantee the definedness of expressions involving partial functions; it generates these checks for every definition involving such functions, even the definition is never subsequently used.

Does the specification define a non-trivial abstract datatype? This question is addressed by proving state initialisation and operation precondition theorems.

An interesting metric for a proof is the number of interactions required for its successful completion by a mechanical theorem prover, but this metric can be misleading. A proof with few interactions is rather like a successful attempt

Table 1. Mondex Z/Eves statistics I

Paragraph type	
Original given sets	2
Original free types	4
Oroginal axiomatic definitions	3
Original schemas	105
Original number of paragraphs	**114**
New axiomatic definitions	12
New schemas	34
Total number of paragraphs	**160**

Verification conditions	
Original lemmas	4
Original theorems	15
Number of original proofs	**19**
New Z/Eves rules	59
New lemmas	44
New theorems	43
New domain checks	63
Number of new proofs	**209**
Total number of proofs	**228**

Automation	**grule**	**frule**	**rule**	**lemmas**	
Free types	14	0	4	0	18
Schemas/bindings	0	14	3	4	21
μ-θ expressions	0	0	4	3	7
Extended toolkit	0	0	4	3	7
Finiteness	3	5	6	12	26
Structured names	2	0	0	6	8
Precondition proofs	0	0	0	20	20
Total	**19**	**19**	**21**	**48**	**107**

at push-button model-checking: it does not reveal what has gone on behind the scenes to get to this stage. Our archaeological approach to Mondex meant that we have not restructured the specification to make mechanisation easier: like Peter Lely's portrait of Oliver Cromwell, we have taken Mondex, warts and all.

About 43% of our proof steps are *trivial*, relying on the automation we included for Z/Eves to discharge verification conditions. Another 43% rely on an *intermediate* level of skill: this involves understanding how the proof is going, often using repetitive steps from previous proofs or on knowledge of how Z/Eves works internally. The final 14% rely on *creative* steps requiring domain knowledge, such as instantiating existential variables.

The specification takes Z/Eves (GUI 1.5, Python 2.4) 2sec to parse and typecheck and the proofs scripts take 11min 20sec to run to completion. This is on a Tablet PC with a dual Pentium T2400 CPU, running at 1.83GHz with 2GB RAM 2005 under Windows XP SP2 with 48% CPU load.

Table 2. Mondex Z/Eves statistics II

Trivial		Creative	
invoke	135	use	41
rearrange	121	invoke	3
cases	49	equalitysubstitute	40
next	99	rearrange	5
simplify	78	instantiate	130
rewrite	234	simplify	10
prove/proveby reduce	147	rewrite	20
instantiate	16	split	30
Total	**879**	**Total**	**279**

Intermediate		Proof steps	
prenex	64	Chapter 3	198
invoke	340	Chapter 4	98
rearrange	5	Chapter 5	364
split	13	Chapter 6	76
apply	139	Chapter 7	4
use	102	Chapter 8	1065
simplify	20	Chapter 10	231
rewrite	50	**Total**	**2036**
reduce	1		
trivialrewrite	11	Trivial	43.2%
withenabled/disabled	46	Intermediate	43.1%
with normalization	2	Creative	13.7%
instantiate	80		
equality substitute	5	Chapter 3	9.7%
Total	**878**	Chapter 4	4.8%
		Chapter 5	17.9%
		Chapter 6	3.7%
		Chapter 7	0.2%
		Chapter 8	52.3%
		Chapter 10	11.4%

The work so far has involved around eight or nine days working with Z/Eves, as well as additional effort studying the problem and planning the mechanisation. In particular, the finiteness strategy took quite a lot of effort, which we hope to amortise over future work.

6   Augsburg (KIV)

The team from Augsburg can claim the prize of being first to mechanise the entire Mondex proof [15, 16]. They used the KIV specification and verification system and ASMs, discovering the same small errors as we did in the original rigorous hand-made proofs. They produced alternative, operational formalisation of the communication protocol in ASM, working as technologists, but with some archaeology, since the models and proofs are clearly inspired by original work. They produced a mechanical verification of the full Mondex case study, except for transcription of failure logs to the central archive, a matter orthogonal to the money-transfer protocol.

The Augburg team mimicked the Mondex data refinement proofs faithfully, completing the work in four weeks: one week to get familiar with the case study and specify the ASMs; one week to verify the proof obligations of correctness and invariance; one week to specify the Mondex refinement theory; and one week to prove data refinement and polish the work for publication. The existence of a (nearly) correct refinement relation helped considerably. The main data refinement proofs require 1,839 proof steps, with 372 interactions. The work is interesting, both technically and organisationally: the group took up the challenge and worked independently.

7   Conclusions

We have conducted an experiment to find out how the proof of the Mondex electronic purse can be automated. Perhaps the most surprising result from this experiment is that half of it can be accomplished in an order of magnitude less effort than it took to conduct the original Mondex work. This has been possible due to the existence of good models with their precise invariants. In other words, we should not see this experiment as saying that the original work could be slashed to one-tenth of its effort, but rather that a mechanical proof could be added for an extra 10% of the overall effort. Since the theorem prover that we used was available in the same release ten years ago, this contradicts the popular opinion that it would not be cost-effective.

Our work discovered some unknown bugs as the payback for our efforts: the missing properties of *BetweenWorld* reported in this paper affect six operations, allowing operations involving inauthentic purses. Schema *PayDetails* not being finite affects mostly everywhere in *Betw* and *Conc*.

Our future work involves comparing our results and methods in detail with those of our colleagues working with different tools and notations. Our work can act as a reference model for those not using Z. If they find suspect bug in Mondex, then we can check to see if this behaviour is genuine, or simply an artifact of translation or remodelling. Similarly, we can check to see if the bugs we found are also found by our colleagues.

The Mondex case study shows that the verification community is willing to undertake competitive and collaborative projects—and that there is some value in doing this. A challenge now is to find the most effective way of curating all our results in the Verified Software Repository. We urge all those interested in this work to join the next project!

Acknowledgements. First, we warmly acknowledge our collaboration with Mark Saaltink: he helped our work in many ways, both directly and indirectly.

We would like to thank the other members of the Mondex club, especially those who have been working directly on the verification effort. This includes Michael Butler, David Crocker, Chris George, Martin Gogolla, Anne Haxthausen, and Tahina Ramananandro. Cliff Jones and Ken Pierce have been working on a model in the π-calculus. Juan Bicarregui, Jonathan Bowen, and Jim Davies have all attended our workshops and given valuable criticism and feedback. Tony Hoare inspired the work as part of the Grand Challenge, and Cliff Jones and Peter O'Hearn guided our efforts as members of the steering committee for Grand Challenge 6 on *Dependable Systems Evolution*. The work on Z/Eves and Mondex was presented at Dagstuhl Seminar 06281 on *The Challenge of Software Verification* in July 2006. The authors are grateful for the financial support of QinetiQ Malvern (the *Circus-based Development* project) and the EPSRC (*VSR-net: A network for the Verified Software Repository*). The work of the Mondex club started from a smaller collaboration with Daniel Jackson and others, now recorded in the Alloy book [6].

References

1. Juan Bicarregui, Tony Hoare, and Jim Woodcock. The verified software repository: a step towards the verifying compiler. *FACJ* **18**(2): 143–151 (2006).
2. David Cooper, Susan Stepney, Jim Woodcock. *Derivation of Z Refinement Proof Rules*. Technical Report YCS-2002-347, University of York. December 2002.
3. David Crocker, Safe object-oriented software: the verified design-by-contract paradigm. In F. Redmill and T. Anderson (eds). *Practical Elements of Safety: Proceedings of the 12th Safety-Critical Systems Symposium*. Springer-Verlag.
4. Hung Dang Van, Chris George, Tomasz Janowski, and Richard Moore (eds). *Specification Case Studies in RAISE*. FACIT (Formal Approaches to Computing and Information Technology) series. Springer. 2002.
5. ITSEC. Information Technology Security Evaluation Criteria (ITSEC): Preliminary Harmonised Criteria. Document COM(90) 314, Version 1.2. Commission of the European Communities (1991).
6. Daniel Jackson. *Software Abstractions: Logic, Language, and Analysis*. The MIT Press 2006. pp.350.
7. Daniel Jackson. Dependable Software by Design. *Scientific American*. June 2006.
8. Cliff Jones, Peter O'Hearn, Jim Woodcock. Verified Software: A Grand Challenge. *IEEE Computer* **39**(4): 93–95 (2006).
9. C. Métayer, J.-R. Abrial, and L. Voisin. *Event-B Language*. Project IST-511599 RODIN Rigorous Open Development Environment for Complex Systems. RODIN Deliverable 3.2 Public Document. 31st May 2005. `rodin.cs.ncl.ac.uk`.
10. *UML 2.0 OCL Specification*. OMG Adopted Specification ptc/03-10-14. 2004.
11. Mondex smart cards. `www.mondex.com`.
12. The QPQ Deductive Software Repository. `qpq.csl.sri.com`.
13. Mark Saaltink. *The Z/EVES User's Guide*. ORA Canada (1997).
14. Mark Saaltink. The Z/EVES System. Jonathan Bowen, Michael Hinchey, and David Till (eds). *ZUM '97: The Z Formal Specification Notation, 10th International Conference of Z Users*. Reading April 3–4 1997. *Lecture Notes in Computer Science* **1212** Springer. 1997.

15. G. Schellhorn, H. Grandy, D. Haneberg, W. Reif. The Mondex Challenge: Machine Checked Proofs for an Electronic Purse. *Technical Report.* Institute of Computer Science, University of Augsburg. 2006.
16. Gerhard Schellhorn, Holger Grandy, Dominik Haneberg, Wolfgang Reif. The Mondex Challenge: Machine Checked Proofs for an Electronic Purse. Jayadev Misra *et al.* (eds). *FM 2006: Formal Methods, 14th International Symposium on Formal Methods*, Hamilton, Canada, August 21–27, 2006. Springer. pp.16–31.
17. J. M. Spivey. *The Z Notation: A Reference Manual.* Prentice Hall International Series in Computer Science. 2nd edition. 1992. pp.150.
18. Susan Stepney, David Cooper, Jim Woodcock. More powerful Z data refinement: Pushing the State of the Art in industrial refinement. *ZUM '98.* Berlin, Germany. *LNCS* **1493**:284–307, Springer, 1998.
19. Susan Stepney. A Tale of Two Proofs. *BCS-FACS Third Northern Formal Methods Workshop.* Ilkley, September 1998. EWICS Springer 1998.
20. Susan Stepney, David Cooper, Jim Woodcock. *An Electronic Purse: Specification, Refinement, and Proof.* Technical Monograph PRG-126, Oxford University Computing Laboratory. July 2000.
21. Jim Woodcock and Jim Davies. *Using Z: Specification, Refinement, and Proof.* Prentice Hall International Series in Computer Science 1996. pp.391. The complete text is available from: `www.usingz.com`

Verification Constraint Problems with Strengthening

Aaron R. Bradley and Zohar Manna*

Computer Science Department
Stanford University
Stanford, CA 94305-9045
{arbrad, manna}@cs.stanford.edu

Abstract. The deductive method reduces verification of safety properties of programs to, first, proposing inductive assertions and, second, proving the validity of the resulting set of first-order verification conditions. We discuss the transition from *verification conditions* to *verification constraints* that occurs when the deductive method is applied to parameterized assertions instead of fixed expressions (*e.g.*, $p_0 + p_1 j + p_2 k \geq 0$, for parameters p_0, p_1, and p_2, instead of $3 + j - k \geq 0$) in order to discover inductive assertions. We then introduce two new verification constraint forms that enable the incremental and property-directed construction of inductive assertions. We describe an iterative method for solving the resulting constraint problems. The main advantage of this approach is that it uses off-the-shelf constraint solvers and thus directly benefits from progress in constraint solving.

1 Introduction

The deductive method of program verification reduces the verification of *safety* and *progress* properties to proving the validity of a set of first-order *verification conditions* [13]. In the safety case, the verification conditions assert that the given property is *inductive*: it holds initially (initiation), and it is preserved by taking any transition (consecution). Such an assertion is an *invariant* of the program. In the progress case, the verification conditions assert that a given function is bounded from below (bounded), yet decreases when any transition is taken (ranking). The existence of such a function, called a *ranking function*, guarantees that the program terminates. In this paper, we focus on the generation of inductive assertions. Section 5 briefly discusses the application of similar techniques to the synthesis of ranking functions.

We discuss a natural shift in perspective from verification conditions to *verification constraints*. This shift is achieved by replacing the given assertion with a *parameterized* assertion. The task is then to find some instantiation of the parameters that validates the verification conditions. This task is a constraint

---

* This research was supported in part by NSF grants CCR-01-21403, CCR-02-20134, CCR-02-09237, CNS-0411363, and CCF-0430102, by ARO grant DAAD19-01-1-0723, and by NAVY/ONR contract N00014-03-1-0939. The first author was additionally supported by a Sang Samuel Wang Stanford Graduate Fellowship.

K. Barkaoui, A. Cavalcanti, and A. Cerone (Eds.): ICTAC 2006, LNCS 4281, pp. 35–49, 2006.

satisfaction problem. Now, each verification condition is a constraint on the parameters. Instantiating the parameters of the parameterized assertion with a solution produces an inductive assertion. This method of generating inductive invariants is known as the *constraint-based* method [7].

In general, these verification constraint problems (VCPs) have many solutions, only some of which are interesting. In particular, a solution is only interesting if it provides more information than what is already known. If χ_i is the currently known inductive invariant and φ is a new solution to a safety VCP, then $\chi_{i+1} \overset{\text{def}}{=} \chi_i \wedge \varphi$ should be stronger: χ_{i+1} implies χ_i, but χ_i should not imply χ_{i+1}. We introduce the new verification constraint form called strengthening to ensure this property.

Additionally, we could have a safety property Π in mind when analyzing a program. A safety property is an assertion that holds on all reachable states of the program. In this context, solutions that strengthen Π are sometimes more interesting than solutions that simply strengthen the currently known invariant χ_i. We introduce the new verification constraint form called Π-strengthening to facilitate property-directed invariant generation.

We present basic concepts in Section 2. In Section 3, we introduce verification constraints as a natural generalization of verification conditions through a set of examples. We also introduce the two new forms of verification constraints that enable an incremental construction of invariants. Section 4 then turns to the task of solving the verification constraint problems. To address the existential constraints arising from the new forms of verification constraints, we describe an iterative method of constructing incrementally stronger inductive assertions using general constraint solvers. Section 5 then reviews past work on posing and solving verification constraint problems in areas ranging from program analysis to continuous and hybrid systems. Section 6 concludes.

2   Preliminaries

It is standard practice to formalize programs as mathematical objects called transition systems. For our purposes in this paper, we define a simple form of transition system.

Definition 1 (Transition System). A *transition system* $\mathcal{S}: \langle \overline{x}, \theta, \mathcal{T} \rangle$ contains three components:

- a set of *variables* $\overline{x} = \{x_1, \dots, x_n\}$ that range over the integers $\mathbb{Z}$ or reals $\mathbb{R}$;
- an assertion $\theta[\overline{x}]$ over $\overline{x}$ specifying the *initial condition*;
- and a set of transitions $\mathcal{T} = \{\tau_1, \dots, \tau_k\}$, where each transition τ is specified by its *transition relation* $\rho_\tau[\overline{x}, \overline{x}']$, an assertion over $\overline{x}$ and $\overline{x}'$.

Primed variables $\overline{x}'$ represent the next-state values of their corresponding variables $\overline{x}$.

Thus, in this paper, a transition system consists simply of a set of transitions that loop around a single program point. Variables have integer or real type. Finally, the computation model is sequential, as formalized next.

Definition 2 (State & Computation). A *state* s of a transition system $\mathcal{S}$ is an assignment of values to its variables. A *computation* $\sigma\colon s_0, s_1, s_2, \ldots$ is an infinite sequence of states such that

- s_0 is an initial state: $s_0 \models \theta$;
- for each $i \geq 0$, each adjacent pair of states is related by some transition: $\exists \tau \in \mathcal{T}.\ (s_i, s_{i+1}) \models \rho_\tau$.

Definition 3 (Invariant). An assertion φ is an *invariant* of $\mathcal{S}$, or is $\mathcal{S}$-*invariant*, if for all computations $\sigma\colon s_0, s_1, s_2, \ldots$, for all $i \geq 0$, $s_i \models \varphi$. An assertion φ is $\mathcal{S}$-*inductive* if

- it holds initially: $\forall \overline{x}.\ \theta[\overline{x}] \ \rightarrow\ \varphi[\overline{x}]$; (initiation)
- it is preserved by every $\tau \in \mathcal{T}$: $\forall \overline{x}, \overline{x}'.\ \varphi[\overline{x}] \wedge \rho_\tau[\overline{x}, \overline{x}'] \ \rightarrow\ \varphi[\overline{x}']$. (consecution)

If φ is $\mathcal{S}$-inductive, then it is $\mathcal{S}$-invariant.

For convenience, we employ the following abbreviation: $\varphi \ \Rightarrow\ \psi$ abbreviates $\forall \overline{x}.\ \varphi \ \rightarrow\ \psi$; $\Rightarrow$ is the logical entailment operator. Then, for example, initiation and consecution are expressed as $\theta \ \Rightarrow\ \varphi$ and $\varphi \wedge \rho_\tau \ \Rightarrow\ \varphi'$, respectively.

A *safety property* $\square\Pi$ asserts that a transition system $\mathcal{S}$ does not do anything bad: it never reaches a $\neg\Pi$-state. In other words, Π is $\mathcal{S}$-invariant. Proving safety properties in practice typically consists of finding a *strengthening* inductive assertion. That is, to prove that Π is $\mathcal{S}$-invariant, find an $\mathcal{S}$-inductive assertion φ that entails $\Pi\colon \varphi \ \Rightarrow\ \Pi$.

Recall that a computation was defined to be an *infinite* sequence of states. Thus, if $\mathcal{S}$ terminates, it does not have any computations according to the current definition of transition systems. Let us agree that every transition system $\mathcal{S}$ has an extra *idling* transition τ_{idle} that does not modify any of $\overline{x}$. Then if $\mathcal{S}$ terminates, only this transition is taken. Thus, the computations of a terminating $\mathcal{S}$ all have infinite τ_{idle}-suffixes.

The first-order formulae that arise according to the initiation and consecution conditions of an assertion and program are called *verification conditions*.

3 Verification Constraint Problems with Strengthening

Having formalized our computation model, we now turn to the main topic: *verification constraints* and *verification constraint problems* (VCPs). In the last section, we saw that *verification conditions* are imposed on a given assertion φ. Suppose instead that φ is a *parameterized assertion*.

Definition 4 (Parameterized Assertion). A *parameterized assertion* over variables $\overline{x}$ has the form

$$p_0 + p_1 t_1 + \cdots + p_m t_m \geq 0 \ ,$$

where t_i are monomials over $\overline{x}$ (*e.g.*, x_1, x_1^2, $x_1 x_4^3$), and $\overline{p}$ are parameters.

```
int j, k;
@ j = 2 ∧ k = 0
while (···) do
    if (···)
    then  j := j + 4;
    else  j := j + 2;
          k := k + 1;
done
```

(a) SIMPLE

```
int x₁, x₂, y₁, y₂, y₃, y₄;
@ ( y₁ = x₁  ∧  y₂ = x₂  ∧
    y₃ = x₂  ∧  y₄ = 0     )
while (y₁ ≠ y₂) do
    if (y₁ > y₂)
    then  y₁ := y₁ − y₂;
          y₄ := y₄ + y₃;
    else  y₂ := y₂ − y₁;
          y₃ := y₃ + y₄;
done
```

(b) GCD-LCM

```
int u, w, x, z;
@ x ≥ 1 ∧ u = 1 ∧ w = 1 ∧ z = 0
while (w ≤ x) do
    (z, u, w) := (z + 1, u + 2, w + u + 2);
done
```

(c) SQRT

Fig. 1. Example functions

For a given set of parameters that range over some domain, a parameterized assertion represents a set of assertions — one assertion for each instantiation of the parameters. Then the verification conditions become constraints over the parameters. The constraint problem is to find an instantiation of the parameters such that the verification conditions are valid. Usually, the parameters are considered to range over the rationals, although considering only the integers is sufficient since only the ratio between parameters matters, not their absolute values.

In this section, we examine a set of examples illustrating VCPs and their solutions. The first two examples perform invariant generation to discover information about the loops. The **strengthening** condition guides the solver to discover new information on each iteration of constraint solving. The final example illustrates property-directed invariant generation, in which the Π-**strengthening** condition guides the solver to discover inductive assertions that eliminate error states.

Example 1 (Simple). Consider the loop SIMPLE in Figure 1(a), which first appeared in [11]. The corresponding transition system $\mathcal{S}$ is the following:

$$\begin{aligned}
\overline{x}: & \ \{j, k\} \\
\theta: & \ j = 2 \ \wedge \ k = 0 \\
\rho_{\tau_1}: & \ j' = j + 4 \ \wedge \ k' = k \\
\rho_{\tau_2}: & \ j' = j + 2 \ \wedge \ k' = k + 1
\end{aligned}$$

Because the guards are replaced by nondeterministic choice (··· in Figure 1(a)), the transitions τ_1 and τ_2 are always enabled.

To prove that the assertion $k \geq 0$ is $\mathcal{S}$-inductive requires checking the validity of the following verification conditions:

$$- \; j = 2 \;\wedge\; k = 0 \;\Rightarrow\; k \geq 0 \hspace{3cm} \text{(initiation)}$$
$$- \; k \geq 0 \;\wedge\; j' = j + 4 \;\wedge\; k' = k \;\Rightarrow\; k' \geq 0 \hspace{1.5cm} \text{(consecution 1)}$$
$$- \; k \geq 0 \;\wedge\; j' = j + 2 \;\wedge\; k' = k + 1 \;\Rightarrow\; k' \geq 0 \hspace{1cm} \text{(consecution 2)}$$

Simplifying according to equations yields:

$$- \; 0 \geq 0 \hspace{5cm} \text{(initiation)}$$
$$- \; k \geq 0 \;\Rightarrow\; k \geq 0 \hspace{3cm} \text{(consecution 1)}$$
$$- \; k \geq 0 \;\Rightarrow\; k + 1 \geq 0 \hspace{2.4cm} \text{(consecution 2)}$$

These verification conditions are clearly valid.

Now suppose that we want to discover facts about the loop in the form of a conjunction of affine assertions that is $\mathcal{S}$-invariant. An affine expression is a linear combination of variables with an additional constant; an affine assertion asserts that an affine expression is nonnegative. Our strategy is to construct incrementally an $\mathcal{S}$-inductive assertion χ by solving a sequence of VCPs.

Suppose that χ_{i-1} has been discovered so far, where $\chi_0 \stackrel{\text{def}}{=}$ true. On the ith iteration, construct the parameterized assertion

$$\underbrace{p_0 + p_1 j + p_2 k \geq 0}_{I[j,k]} \;,$$

and solve the following VCP:

$$\begin{aligned}
& I[2, 0] \geq 0 && \text{(initiation)} \\
\wedge \;\; & \chi_{i-1} \;\wedge\; I \geq 0 \;\Rightarrow\; I[j + 4, k] \geq 0 && \text{(consecution 1)} \\
\wedge \;\; & \chi_{i-1} \;\wedge\; I \geq 0 \;\Rightarrow\; I[j + 2, k + 1] \geq 0 && \text{(consecution 2)} \\
\wedge \;\; & \exists j, k. \; \chi_{i-1} \;\wedge\; I < 0 && \text{(strengthening)}
\end{aligned}$$

The notation $I[j + 4, k] \geq 0$ simplifies $j' = j + 4 \;\wedge\; k' = k \;\Rightarrow\; I[j', k'] \geq 0$. The first conjunct imposes initiation; the next two conjuncts impose consecution for each of the two paths of the loop. Together, these three conjuncts constrain $I \geq 0$ to be inductive relative to χ_{i-1}. The final conjunct asserts that there is some χ_{i-1}-state s that is excluded by the new invariant. We call this constraint the strengthening condition.

Any solution for (p_0, p_1, p_2) of this VCP represents an inductive assertion φ_i that strengthens χ_{i-1}. Set $\chi_i \stackrel{\text{def}}{=} \chi_{i-1} \;\wedge\; \varphi_i$, and generate the next VCP with χ_i instead of χ_{i-1}. If a solution does not exist, then halt the incremental construction.

Section 4 discusses how to solve the sequence of VCPs. For now, one possible sequence of discovered inductive assertions is the following:

$$\varphi_1 : \; k \geq 0 \hspace{1cm} \varphi_2 : \; j \geq 0 \hspace{1cm} \varphi_3 : \; j \geq 2k + 2 \;,$$

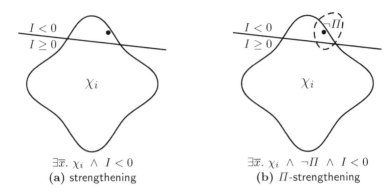

$$\exists \overline{x}.\ \chi_i \wedge I < 0$$

(a) strengthening

$$\exists \overline{x}.\ \chi_i \wedge \neg \Pi \wedge I < 0$$

(b) Π-strengthening

Fig. 2. Illustration of the two strengthening conditions

corresponding to the following sequence of χ_i's:

$$
\begin{aligned}
\chi_0 &\stackrel{\text{def}}{=} \text{true} &&\Rightarrow& \chi_0 &: \text{true} \\
\chi_1 &\stackrel{\text{def}}{=} \chi_0 \wedge \varphi_1 &&\Rightarrow& \chi_1 &: k \geq 0 \\
\chi_2 &\stackrel{\text{def}}{=} \chi_1 \wedge \varphi_2 &&\Rightarrow& \chi_2 &: k \geq 0 \wedge j \geq 0 \\
\chi_3 &\stackrel{\text{def}}{=} \chi_2 \wedge \varphi_3 &&\Rightarrow& \chi_3 &: k \geq 0 \wedge j \geq 0 \wedge j \geq 2k + 2
\end{aligned}
$$

Conjuncts $k \geq 0$ and $j \geq 2k + 2$ entail $j \geq 2$. Therefore, χ_3 as well as $j \geq 2$ are $\mathcal{S}$-invariant. Moreover, every χ_i and $j \geq 2$ are $\mathcal{S}$-inductive.

The strengthening condition is essential for making progress. For example, the sequence of inductive assertions

$$\varphi_1: k \geq 0 \qquad \varphi_2: k \geq 0 \qquad \varphi_3: k \geq 0 \qquad \dots$$

is a solution to the sequence of VCPs constructed without the strengthening condition, but not to the sequence of VCPs constructed with the strengthening condition.

Figure 2(a) illustrates the strengthening condition. The new invariant consists of all states at and below the line. This invariant satisfies the strengthening condition: there exists some χ_i-state (the dot) that the invariant excludes.

In the next example, we look at nonlinear properties.

Example 2 (GCD-LCM). The loop GCD-LCM in Figure 1(b) computes the greatest common divisor (y_1 and y_2) and the least common multiple ($y_3 + y_4$) of (x_1, x_2). As in Example 1, our goal is to discover information about the loop. In this case, our strategy is to construct an $\mathcal{S}$-inductive conjunction of quadratic polynomial inequalities. Therefore, in each iteration, we use the parameterized assertion

$$\underbrace{\mathsf{Quadratic}(x_1, x_2, y_1, y_2, y_3, y_4)}_{I[\overline{x}, \overline{y}]} \geq 0\ .$$

Quadratic forms the most general parameterized quadratic expression over the given variables; *e.g.,*

$$\mathsf{Quadratic}(x, y) = p_0 + p_1 x + p_2 y + p_3 xy + p_4 x^2 + p_5 y^2 \ .$$

In this case, $I[\overline{x}, \overline{y}]$ contains 28 parameterized monomials.

Suppose that χ_{i-1} has been constructed so far. On the ith iteration, solve the following VCP:

$$
\begin{array}{ll}
\forall \overline{x}. \ I[x_1, x_2, x_1, x_2, x_2, 0] \geq 0 & \text{(initiation)} \\
\wedge \ \chi_{i-1} \wedge I \geq 0 \wedge y_1 > y_2 \Rightarrow I[x_1, x_2, y_1 - y_2, y_2, y_3, y_4 + y_3] \geq 0 & \\
\wedge \ \chi_{i-1} \wedge I \geq 0 \wedge y_1 < y_2 \Rightarrow I[x_1, x_2, y_1, y_2 - y_1, y_3 + y_4, y_4] \geq 0 & \\
& \text{(consecution)} \\
\wedge \ \exists \overline{x}, \overline{y}. \ \chi_{i-1} \wedge I < 0 & \text{(strengthening)}
\end{array}
$$

The first conjunct imposes initiation; the next two impose consecution; and the final conjunct imposes the strengthening condition, expressing that the new assertion strengthens χ_{i-1}.

One possible sequence of inductive assertion discovery is the following:

$$
\begin{array}{ll}
\chi_0 \ \overset{\text{def}}{=} \ \mathsf{true} \\
\chi_1 \ \overset{\text{def}}{=} \ \chi_0 \wedge \varphi_1 : \ x_1 x_2 - y_1 y_3 - y_2 y_4 \geq 0 \\
\chi_2 \ \overset{\text{def}}{=} \ \chi_1 \wedge \varphi_2 : \ x_1 x_2 - y_1 y_3 - y_2 y_4 \geq 0 \wedge -x_1 x_2 + y_1 y_3 + y_2 y_4 \geq 0
\end{array}
$$

Thus, χ_2 implies that

$$x_1 x_2 = y_1 y_3 + y_2 y_4$$

is $\mathcal{S}$-invariant.

In many cases, we have a safety property in mind that we would like to prove. The next example describes such a case. We introduce a variant of the **strengthening** condition to direct the invariant generation toward proving the property.

Example 3 (Integer Square-Root). The loop SQRT in Figure 1(**c**) computes the integer square-root z of a positive integer x. On exit, the following relation should hold between z and x:

$$z^2 \leq x < (z + 1)^2 \ .$$

Taking preconditions reveals that the following should be invariant at the top of the loop:

$$\Pi : \ (w \leq x \ \rightarrow \ (z + 1)^2 \leq x) \wedge (w > x \ \rightarrow \ x < (z + 1)^2) \ .$$

Π is not $\mathcal{S}$-inductive. The goal is to prove that Π is $\mathcal{S}$-invariant by generating a strengthening inductive assertion χ such that $\chi \Rightarrow \Pi$. As in Example 2, our strategy is to construct a conjunction of at most quadratic polynomial inequalities. Unlike in previous examples, however, our goal is not to discover properties of the loop; rather, it is to prove $\Box \Pi$.

On each iteration, we use the parameterized assertion

$$\underbrace{\mathsf{Quadratic}(u, w, x, z)}_{I[u,w,x,z]} \geq 0 \ .$$

Suppose that χ_{i-1} has been generated so far; on the ith iteration, solve the following VCP:

$$x \geq 0 \;\Rightarrow\; I[1,1,x,0] \geq 0 \qquad \text{(initiation)}$$
$$\wedge\; \chi_{i-1} \;\wedge\; I \geq 0 \;\wedge\; w \leq x \;\Rightarrow\; I[u+2, w+u+2, x, z+1] \geq 0$$
$$\text{(consecution)}$$
$$\wedge\; \exists u, w, x, z.\; \chi_{i-1} \;\wedge\; \neg\Pi \;\wedge\; I < 0 \qquad (\Pi\text{-strengthening})$$

The first two conjuncts express initiation and consecution, respectively. The final conjunct is a variant of strengthening called Π-strengthening: the new inductive assertion should exclude some state that is both a χ_{i-1}-state (so that χ_{i-1} is strengthened) and a $\neg\Pi$-state (so that an error state is excluded, and thus Π is strengthened).

It is not always possible to exclude a $\neg\Pi$-state with an inductive assertion of a fixed form, so some iterations should use the weaker strengthening condition instead.

One run of this incremental construction produces the following assertions, listed in order from the discovered inductive assertion of the first iteration (top-left) to that of the final iteration (bottom-right).

$$\varphi_1 : \quad -x + ux - 2xz \geq 0 \qquad\qquad \varphi_7 : \qquad\qquad\qquad -1 + u \geq 0$$
$$\varphi_2 : \qquad\qquad\qquad u \geq 0 \qquad\qquad \varphi_8 : \qquad -2u - u^2 + 4w \geq 0$$
$$\varphi_3 : u - u^2 + 4uz - 4z^2 \geq 0 \qquad\qquad \varphi_9 : \qquad -3 - u^2 + 4w \geq 0$$
$$\varphi_4 : \qquad\quad 3u + u^2 - 4w \geq 0 \qquad\qquad \varphi_{10} : \qquad -5u - u^2 + 6w \geq 0$$
$$\varphi_5 : \qquad\quad x - ux + 2xz \geq 0 \qquad\qquad \varphi_{11} : -15 + 22u - 11u^2 + 4uw \geq 0$$
$$\varphi_6 : \quad 1 + 2u + u^2 - 4w \geq 0 \qquad\qquad \varphi_{12} : \qquad -1 - 2u - u^2 + 4w \geq 0$$

Thus, $\chi_{12} \stackrel{\text{def}}{=} \varphi_1 \wedge \cdots \wedge \varphi_{12}$. Each assertion is inductive relative to the previous assertions.

On the thirteenth iteration, it is discovered that no $(\chi_{12} \wedge \neg\Pi)$-state exists, proving $\Box\Pi$. Specifically, φ_1 and φ_5 entail $u = 1 + 2z$, while φ_6 and φ_{12} entail $4w = (u+1)^2$. Thus, $w = (z+1)^2$, entailing Π.

In the next section, we discuss how the new assertion of each iteration is actually found.

Figure 2(b) illustrates the Π-strengthening condition. The new invariant consists of all states at and below the line. This invariant satisfies the Π-strengthening condition: there exists some $(\chi_i \wedge \neg\Pi)$-state (the dot) that the invariant excludes. Therefore, this new invariant strengthens both χ_i and Π, making progress toward proving $\Box\Pi$.

4   Solving VCPs with Strengthening

Section 5 discusses previous work on solving specific forms of VCPs. In this section, we discuss a refinement of the techniques introduced in [7] and [10]. The method of [7] is complete for linear VCPs, while the method of [10] is sound and efficient but incomplete for polynomial VCPs [10]. In particular, we show how to solve VCPs with a **strengthening** or Π-**strengthening** condition, which have not been studied before. Solving constraints with such conditions enables a simple incremental construction of invariants, as illustrated in the examples of the previous section.

4.1   Farkas's Lemma

To begin, we review the constraint-solving method based on *Farkas's Lemma* [7] or *Lagrangian relaxation* [10]. Farkas's Lemma relates a constraint system over the *primal* variables (the variables of the transition system $\mathcal{S}$) to a *dual* constraint system over the parameters [23]. It is restricted to affine constraints, as in Example 1.

Theorem 1 (Farkas's Lemma). *Consider the following universal constraint system of affine inequalities over real variables* $\overline{x} = \{x_1, \ldots, x_m\}$:

$$
S : \begin{bmatrix} a_{1,0} + a_{1,1}x_1 + \cdots + a_{1,m}x_m \geq 0 \\ \vdots \qquad\qquad \vdots \qquad\qquad \vdots \\ a_{n,0} + a_{n,1}x_1 + \cdots + a_{n,m}x_m \geq 0 \end{bmatrix}
$$

If S is satisfiable, it entails affine inequality $c_0 + c_1x_1 + \cdots + c_mx_m \geq 0$ iff there exist real numbers $\lambda_1, \ldots, \lambda_n \geq 0$ such that

$$
c_1 = \sum_{i=1}^{n} \lambda_i a_{i,1} \quad \cdots \quad c_m = \sum_{i=1}^{n} \lambda_i a_{i,m} \quad c_0 \geq \left(\sum_{i=1}^{n} \lambda_i a_{i,0} \right).
$$

Example 4 (Simple). Consider the VCP developed in Example 1 for SIMPLE of Figure 1(a). Using the tabular notation, the first three conjuncts have this form:

(initiation)

$$
\overline{}
$$
$$
p_0 + 2p_1 + 0p_2 \geq 0
$$

(consecution 1)	(consecution 2)
χ_i	χ_i
$p_0 \qquad\quad +p_1j +p_2k \geq 0$	$p_0 \qquad\quad +p_1j +p_2k \geq 0$
$(p_0 + 4p_1) +p_1j +p_2k \geq 0$	$(p_0 + 2p_1 + p_2) +p_1j +p_2k \geq 0$

Suppose that this is the first iteration so that $\chi_0 \overset{\text{def}}{=} \text{true}$. Then dualizing according to the lemma produces the following set of existential constraints over the parameters and λ-multipliers $\{p_0, p_1, p_2, \lambda_1, \lambda_2\}$:

$p_0 + 2p_1 \geq 0 \ \wedge$	(initiation)
$p_0 + 4p_1 \geq \lambda_1 p_0 \ \wedge \ p_1 = \lambda_1 p_1 \ \wedge \ p_2 = \lambda_1 p_2 \ \wedge$	(consecution 1)
$p_0 + 2p_1 + p_2 \geq \lambda_2 p_0 \ \wedge \ p_1 = \lambda_2 p_1 \ \wedge \ p_2 = \lambda_2 p_2$	(consecution 2)

Clearly, $\lambda_1 = \lambda_2 = 1$, so the constraints are equivalent to

$$p_0 + 2p_1 \geq 0 \ \wedge \ p_1 \geq 0 \ \wedge \ 2p_1 + p_2 \geq 0 \ ,$$

for which solutions for (p_0, p_1, p_2) include $(0, 0, 1)$, $(0, 1, 0)$, and $(-2, 1, -2)$. These solutions correspond to the three assertions computed in Example 1:

$$k \geq 0 \ , \quad j \geq 0 \ , \quad \text{and} \quad j \geq 2k + 2 \ .$$

Any one of these solutions could be returned by the constraint solver.

On later iterations, χ_i consists of a conjunction of affine assertions. These assertions are added as additional rows in the tables, resulting in more λ-variables and more complicated dual constraints.

Farkas's Lemma states that the relationship between the primal and dual constraint systems is strict: the universal constraints of the primal system are valid if and only if the dual (existential) constraint system has a solution. Generalizing to polynomials preserves soundness but drops completeness.

Corollary 1 (Polynomial Lemma). *Consider the universal constraint system S of polynomial inequalities over real variables $\bar{x} = \{x_1, \ldots, x_m\}$:*

$$
A: \begin{cases} a_{1,0} + \displaystyle\sum_{i=1}^{m} a_{1,i} t_i \geq 0 \\[2mm] \vdots \\[2mm] a_{n,0} + \displaystyle\sum_{i=1}^{m} a_{n,i} t_i \geq 0 \end{cases}
$$

$$
C: \quad c_0 + \sum_{i=1}^{m} c_i t_i \ \geq 0
$$

where the t_i are monomials over $\bar{x}$. That is, $S: \forall \bar{x}. \ A \ \rightarrow \ C$. Construct the dual constraint system as follows. For monomials t_i of even power (e.g., 1, x^2, $x^2 y^4$, etc.), impose the constraint

$$c_i \geq \lambda_j a_{1,i} + \cdots + \lambda_n a_{n,i} \ ;$$

for all other terms, impose the constraint

$$c_i = \mu_j a_{1,i} + \cdots + \lambda_n a_{n,i} \ .$$

If the dual constraint system is satisfiable (for all $\lambda_j \geq 0$), then the primal constraint system is valid.

In particular, if the constraint system S is parameterized, then a solution to the dual constraint system provides an instantiation of the parameters that validates the primal constraints.

4.2   Solving Iterative VCPs

Farkas's Lemma and its polynomial generalization provide a method for solving the universal constraints of a VCP. However, the strengthening and Π-strengthening conditions impose existential constraints. One possibility is to ignore these existential constraints and apply the methods of [7] and [10]. The authors of [7] solve the constraints using a specialized solver described in [18]. The method of [10] is essentially restricted to verification constraints in which a single solution solves the problem (*e.g.*, to prove termination by finding a ranking function; see Section 5).

Unfortunately, dropping the existential constraints prevents us from performing iterative strengthening easily. Even with a strong χ_i, the constraint solver can always return the same solution that it has returned previously. For example, in Example 4, ignoring the strengthening constraint would allow the solution $k \geq 0$ to be returned again and again, even after setting $\chi_1 \stackrel{\text{def}}{=} k \geq 0$.

Instead, we describe a *sampling-based iterative method* in this section. Unlike the specialized solver of [18], this method is applicable to many types of constraint systems and allows applying off-the-shelf constraint solvers.

As in the examples of Section 3, suppose we have a parameterized assertion $I[\bar{p}, \bar{x}] \geq 0$, where $\bar{p}$ are the parameters and $\bar{x}$ are the system variables. On iteration i, we have already computed inductive assertion χ_{i-1} and would like to compute a stronger inductive assertion χ_i. Let $\psi_i[\bar{p}]$ be the universal constraints (arising from initiation and consecution) of the ith VCP; that is, ψ_i does not include a strengthening or Π-strengthening constraint. Perform the following steps:

1. Solve the existential constraint system χ_{i-1} if the strengthening condition is imposed, or the constraint system $\chi_{i-1} \wedge \neg \Pi$ if the Π-strengthening condition is imposed. In the latter case, if the system does not have a solution, then declare that $\Box \Pi$ is invariant. Otherwise, the solution is a state s.
2. Solve the existential constraint system

   $$I[\bar{p}, s] < 0 \wedge \mathsf{dual}(\psi_i[\bar{p}])$$

   for $\bar{p}$, where dual constructs the dual constraint system (recall that ψ_i contains only universal constraints). If a solution is not found, return to Step 1; if a Π-strengthening condition is imposed, possibly weaken it to a strengthening condition. Otherwise, the solution $\bar{q}$ is an assignment to $\bar{p}$.
3. Optimize the discovered solution $\bar{q}$ of $\bar{p}$. Let $J[\bar{p}, \bar{x}]$ be the non-constant part of I (*e.g.*, $p_1 j + p_2 k$ in $p_0 + p_1 j + p_2 k$). Then solve the following optimization problem for the parameter p_0 of I:

   $$\begin{aligned}&\textbf{minimize } p_0\\&\textbf{subject to}\\&\quad p_0 + J[\bar{q}, \bar{x}] \geq 0 \wedge \mathsf{dual}(\psi_i[p_0, q_1, \ldots, q_k])\end{aligned}$$

   At most the value of q_0 from Step 2 is returned as the minimum of p_0. Set q_0 to the new solution.
4. Let $\chi_i \stackrel{\text{def}}{=} \chi_{i-1} \wedge I[\bar{q}, \bar{x}] \geq 0$.

Thus, Step 1 addresses the strengthening or Π-strengthening constraint, while Steps 2 and 3 address the other (universal) constraints.

The constraint problem of Step 1 can be solved in numerous ways, including using decision procedures or numerical constraint solvers for solving linear and semi-algebraic constraint problems. It is best if these solvers can be randomized so that a wide selection of sample points is possible. The constraint problem of Step 2 can be solved using linear or convex programming. If the Polynomial Lemma is used, then linear programming is sufficient. Many implementations of such constraint solvers are available.

Note that the strict inequality of Step 2 is easily handled by transforming the feasibility problem into an optimization problem:

$$\textbf{maximize } \epsilon$$
$$\textbf{subject to}$$
$$I[\bar{p}, s] \leq -\epsilon \ \wedge \ \mathsf{dual}(\psi_i[\bar{p}])$$

The original system is feasible if and only if the maximum is positive. The optimization of Step 3 is inspired by the optimization that is performed in [21].

The inductive invariants constructed incrementally in Examples 1, 2, and 3 were obtained using this approach.

Example 5 (Simple). Consider the first iteration of solving the VCP of Examples 1 and 4. According to the steps of the procedure, we have the following:

1. Solve the constraint problem χ_0 (recall $\chi_0 \stackrel{\text{def}}{=}$ true), producing, for example, state $(j : -1, \ k : -3)$.
2. Solve

$$\underbrace{p_0 - p_1 - 3p_2 < 0}_{I[-1,-3] \,<\, 0} \ \wedge \ \underbrace{p_0 + 2p_1 \geq 0 \ \wedge \ p_1 \geq 0 \ \wedge \ 2p_1 + p_2 \geq 0}_{\text{dual system, simplified from Example 4}} \ .$$

   One solution is $(p_0 : 1, \ p_1 : 0, \ p_2 : 1)$, corresponding to $1 + k \geq 0$.
3. Optimize

$$\textbf{minimize } p_0$$
$$\textbf{subject to}$$
$$p_0 + k \geq 0 \ \wedge \ p_0 \geq 0$$

   The optimal value of p_0 is 0, corresponding to assertion $k \geq 0$.
4. Let $\chi_1 \stackrel{\text{def}}{=} \chi_0 \wedge k \geq 0$.

The assertion $\chi_1 : \ k \geq 0$ excludes the sample state $(j : -1, \ k : -3)$, as well as any other state in which $k < 0$. Thus, no future iteration can again discover $k \geq 0$ (or any weaker assertion).

On the next iteration, Step 1 could find, for example, sample point $(j : -1, \ k : 5)$, satisfying $\chi_1 : \ k \geq 0$. Then discovering inductive assertion $j \geq 0$ in Steps 2 and 3 eliminates this point.

5   Related Work

Set-Constraint Based Analysis. Set constraint-based program analyses (see, *e.g.*, [2, 1]) pose classical program analysis problems — *e.g.*, standard dataflow equations, simple type inference, and monomorphic closure analysis — as set constraint problems and then solve them. Domains are discrete.

Ranking Function Synthesis. Synthesis of affine expressions for verification purposes was first studied extensively in the context of ranking function synthesis. A function $\delta \colon \overline{x} \to \mathbb{Z}$ is a *ranking function* if

- if $\tau \in \mathcal{T}$ is enabled, then δ is nonnegative: $\varphi \wedge \rho_\tau \Rightarrow \delta \geq 0$;   (bounded)
- δ decreases when any $\tau \in \mathcal{T}$ is taken: $\varphi \wedge \rho_\tau \Rightarrow \delta > \delta'$.   (ranking)

Unlike in the consecution condition of inductive assertions, the parameterized expression appears only in the consequent of the bounded and ranking conditions. Examining Farkas's Lemma shows that synthesis of linear ranking functions over linear loops with real variables is therefore polynomial-time computable: the dual constraint system is linear and thus polynomial-time solvable.

[12] shows how to generate constraint systems over loops with linear assertional guards and linear assignments for which solutions are linear ranking functions. In [8, 9], it is observed that duality of linear constraints achieves efficient synthesis. [15] proves that this duality-based method is complete for single-path loops. [3] presents a complete method for the general case and shows how lexicographic linear ranking functions can also be computed efficiently in practice. In [10], the approach is generalized by using semidefinite programming to approximate the polynomial case.

Several extensions of the constraint-based approach have been explored. [4] extends the method to generate *polyranking* functions [6], which generalize ranking functions. A polyranking function need not always decrease. Finally, [5] addresses loops with integer variables.

Invariant Generation. Invariant generation is harder than pure ranking function synthesis. [7] proposes using Farkas's Lemma and nonlinear constraint solving to generate affine invariants. A specialized solver for this method is described in [18]. [17] specializes the technique to Petri nets, for which the problem is efficiently solvable. In [20], polynomial equation invariants are generated using tools from algebra. [5] addresses loops with integer variables.

Analysis of Continuous and Hybrid Systems. Lyapunov functions of continuous systems have been generated using convex optimization for over a decade (see, *e.g.*, [14]). In [19], the methods of [20] are adapted to generating polynomial equation invariants of hybrid systems. [16] introduces *barrier certificates*, which is a continuous analogue of program invariants. They describe a semidefinite relaxation that approximates consecution. [22] introduces a general method for constructing a *time elapse operator* for overapproximating the reachable space during a continuous mode of a hybrid system.

6   Conclusion

It is natural to view verification conditions as constraints on parameterized expressions. In the constraint context, we show that the two new conditions strengthening and Π-strengthening guide the incremental construction of inductive assertions. Unlike previous approaches to incremental strengthening, our proposed sampling-based incremental method applies standard constraint solvers. Thus, it directly benefits from progress in constraint solving. Additionally, the Π-strengthening condition facilitates property-directed invariant generation without imposing a fixed limit on the size of the discovered inductive assertion.

We have a simple implementation of the iterative technique. To avoid numerical issues involved in floating-point computations, we always use the Polynomial Lemma to produce a parametric-linear constraint problem in which only terms with parameters are nonlinear (they are bilinear: the product of a parameter and a dual λ-multiplier). We then solve this constraint problem by lazily instantiating λ-multipliers over a fixed set of values (typically, $\{0, 1\}$) and passing the linear part of the problem to a rational linear program solver. We thus obtain rational instantiations of the parameters. As solvers for convex programs improve, we can use stronger versions [10] of the Polynomial Lemma to obtain more invariants and to analyze nonlinear transition systems. The iterative method extends to applications of these solvers without modification.

References

1. AIKEN, A. Introduction to set constraint-based program analysis. *Science of Computer Programming 35* (1999), 79–111.
2. AIKEN, A., AND WIMMERS, E. Solving systems of set constraints. In *LICS* (1992), pp. 329–340.
3. BRADLEY, A. R., MANNA, Z., AND SIPMA, H. B. Linear ranking with reachability. In *Proc. 17th Intl. Conference on Computer Aided Verification (CAV)* (July 2005), K. Etessami and S. K. Rajamani, Eds., vol. 3576 of *LNCS*, Springer Verlag, pp. 491–504.
4. BRADLEY, A. R., MANNA, Z., AND SIPMA, H. B. The polyranking principle. In *ICALP* (2005).
5. BRADLEY, A. R., MANNA, Z., AND SIPMA, H. B. Termination analysis of integer linear loops. In *CONCUR* (2005).
6. BRADLEY, A. R., MANNA, Z., AND SIPMA, H. B. Termination of polynomial programs. In *Proc. of Verification, Model Checking and Abstract Interpretation (VM-CAI)* (Paris, France, January 2005), R. Cousot, Ed., vol. 3385 of *LNCS*, Springer Verlag.
7. COLÓN, M., SANKARANARAYANAN, S., AND SIPMA, H. Linear invariant generation using non-linear constraint solving. In *Computer Aided Verification* (July 2003), vol. 2725 of *LNCS*, Springer-Verlag, pp. 420–433.
8. COLÓN, M., AND SIPMA, H. Synthesis of linear ranking functions. In *7th International Conference on Tools and Algorithms for the Construction and Analysis of Systems (TACAS)* (April 2001), T. Margaria and W. Yi, Eds., vol. 2031 of *LNCS*, Springer Verlag, pp. 67–81.

9. COLÓN, M., AND SIPMA, H. Practical methods for proving program termination. In *Proc. 14th Intl. Conference on Computer Aided Verification* (2002), vol. 2404 of *LNCS*, Springer Verlag, pp. 442–454.

10. COUSOT, P. Proving program invariance and termination by parametric abstraction, lagrangian relaxation and semidefinite programming. In *Proc. Verification, Model Checking, and Abstract Interpretation: 5th International Conference (VMCAI)* (2005), pp. 1–24.

11. COUSOT, P., AND HALBWACHS, N. Automatic discovery of linear restraints among the variables of a program. In *5th ACM Symp. Princ. of Prog. Lang.* (Jan. 1978), pp. 84–97.

12. KATZ, S. M., AND MANNA, Z. A closer look at termination. *Acta Informatica 5*, 4 (1975), 333–352.

13. MANNA, Z., AND PNUELI, A. *Temporal Verification of Reactive Systems: Safety.* Springer-Verlag, New York, 1995.

14. PAPACHRISTODOULOU, A., AND PRAJNA, S. On the construction of lyapunov functions using the sum of squares decomposition. In *CDC* (2002).

15. PODELSKI, A., AND RYBALCHENKO, A. A complete method for the synthesis of linear ranking functions. In *VMCAI* (2004), pp. 239–251.

16. PRAJNA, S., AND JADBABAIE, A. Safety verification of hybrid systems using barrier certificates. In *HSCC* (2004), vol. 2993 of *LNCS*, Springer.

17. SANKARANARAYANAN, S., SIPMA, H. B., AND MANNA, Z. Petri net analysis using invariant generation. In *Verification: Theory and Practice* (Taurmina, Italy, 2003), N. Derschowitz, Ed., vol. 2772 of *LNCS*, Springer Verlag, pp. 682–701.

18. SANKARANARAYANAN, S., SIPMA, H. B., AND MANNA, Z. Constraint-based linear relations analysis. In *11th Static Analysis Symposium (SAS'2004)* (2004), vol. 3148 of *LNCS*, Springer-Verlag, pp. 53–68.

19. SANKARANARAYANAN, S., SIPMA, H. B., AND MANNA, Z. Constructing invariants for hybrid systems. In *Hybrid Systems: Computation and Control, 7th International Workshop, HSCC 2004, Philadelphia, PA, USA, March 25-27, 2004, Proceedings* (2004), vol. 2993 of *LNCS*, Springer-Verlag, pp. 539–554.

20. SANKARANARAYANAN, S., SIPMA, H. B., AND MANNA, Z. Non-linear loop invariant generation using Gröbner bases,. In *31th ACM Symp. Princ. of Prog. Lang.* (Venice, Italy, January 2004), pp. 318–329.

21. SANKARANARAYANAN, S., SIPMA, H. B., AND MANNA, Z. Scalable analysis of linear systems using mathematical programming. In *Proc. of Verification, Model Checking and Abstract Interpretation (VMCAI)* (Paris, France, January 2005), R. Cousot, Ed., vol. 3385 of *LNCS*, Springer Verlag.

22. SANKARANARAYANAN, S., SIPMA, H. B., AND MANNA, Z. Fixed point iteration for computing the time elapse operator. In *HSCC* (2006).

23. SCHRIJVER, A. *Theory of Linear and Integer Programming.* Wiley, 1986.

Quantitative μ-Calculus Analysis of Power Management in Wireless Networks

AK McIver

Dept. Computer Science, Macquarie University, NSW 2109 Australia,
and National ICT Australia*
anabel@ics.mq.edu.au

Abstract. An important concern in wireless network technology is battery conservation. A promising approach to saving energy is to allow nodes periodically to enter a "low power mode", however this strategy contributes to message delay, and careful management is required so that the system-wide performance is not severely compromised.

In this paper we show how to manage power schedules using the quantitative modal μ-calculus which allows the specification of a quantitative performance property as a game in which a maximising player's optimal strategy corresponds to optimising overall performance relative to the specified property.

We extend the standard results on discounted games to a class of infinite state systems, and illustrate our results on a small case study.

Keywords: Probabilistic abstraction and refinement, structured specification and analysis of performance, probabilistic model checking.

1 Introduction

The theme of this paper is the specification and analysis of performance-style properties for wireless networks. The problem is particularly challenging in this domain because of the many sources of underlying uncertainty, including collision avoidance, clock-drift and degrading battery life [29]. We model such uncertainties with *probability* or standard *nondeterminism*, using the former when the uncertainty may be quantified and appealing to the latter when it cannot [19].

The formal investigation of probabilistic distributed systems (*i.e.* those combining both probability and nondeterminism) is normally limited to the consideration of *probabilistic temporal properties* [1], such as "the system eventually satisfies predicate *Pred* with probability at least 1/3". There are however many other performance-style quantities which cannot be specified in this way, as they are examples of the more general *stochastic parity games* [6, 15] in which two players try to optimise a quantitative cost function according to their opposing goals.

---

* National ICT Australia is funded through the Australian Government's *Backing Australia's Ability* initiative, in part through the Australian Research Council.

K. Barkaoui, A. Cavalcanti, and A. Cerone (Eds.): ICTAC 2006, LNCS 4281, pp. 50–64, 2006.

Our principal aim in this paper is to illustrate how the quantitative modal μ-calculus [15], a generalisation of the standard μ-calculus of Kozen [12] to probabilistic systems, may be used as a convenient language for specifying and analysing such a stochastic parity game relevant to power-management schemes in wireless networks [29] — indeed careful power management is a pressing concern, where the integrity of the communication relies on preserving battery lives of the individual nodes that make up the network.

Our specific topic is how to optimise a scheme in which nodes periodically enter a low power mode during which communication via so-called "sleeping" nodes is impossible — the obvious drawback here is that messages may be severely delayed, as they are forced to wait for nodes to wake up. Thus the scheduling problem is to decide how to choose the length of a sleep time so that an interval of low power lasts as long as possible without significantly compromising throughput.

Our approach is to specify a game, via the quantitative μ-calculus, in which one player seeks to maximise power savings; we show that computing the optimal strategies of the maximising player is equivalent to optimising the power management scheme so that the low power modes may be applied most advantageously. Our particular contributions are as follows:

1. *The extension* of stochastic parity games to a class of infinite state systems normally lying outside the scope of standard game frameworks [15, 7] (Sec. 2.5);
2. *A formal model* of a wireless communication protocol incorporating power management (Sec. 3) using labelled *probabilistic action systems* (Sec. 2.1);
3. *A novel stochastic-parity-game specification* using quantitative μ-calculus, $qM\mu$ for analysing the optimal expected time in the low power mode constrained by the relative cost of message delay (Sec. 3.1). Using this we are able to compute the optimal sleep schedules.

The advantage of using the framework presented here is that they come equipped with a full theory of abstraction and refinement, and thus we anticipate that a formal proof will establish that this paper's results apply even to large-scale networks [14]. Moreover action systems also give access to detailed numerical experiments using state-of-the-art probabilistic model checkers whose results may be used to determine the optimal schedule, as well as computing detailed expected delays and power savings.We illustrate our formal models in Sec. 3.2 using the PRISM probabilistic model checker [24].

The notational conventions used are as follows. Function application is represented by a dot, as in $f.x$. We use an abstract state space S, and denote the set of discrete probability distributions over S by $\overline{S}$ (that is the sub-normalised functions from S into the real interval $[0, 1]$, where function f is sub-normalised if $\sum_{s:\,S} f.s \leq 1$). Given predicate $Pred$ we write $[Pred]$ for the *characteristic* function mapping states satisfying $Pred$ to 1 and to 0 otherwise, so that 1 and 0 correspond respectively with "True" and "False". The $(p, 1-p)$-weighted average of distributions d and d' is denoted $d\,_p\oplus d'$.

2 Probabilistic Guarded Commands

When programs incorporate probability, their properties can no longer be guaranteed "with certainty", but only "up to some probability". For example the program

$$coin \quad \hat{=} \quad b\colon = 1 \ {}_{2/3}\oplus \ b\colon = 0 \ , \tag{1}$$

sets the variable b to 1 only with probability $2/3$ — in practice this means that if the statement were executed a large number of times, and the final values of b tabulated, roughly $2/3$ of them would record b having been set to 1 (up to well-known statistical confidence).

The language pGCL and its associated *quantitative logic* [19] were developed to express such programs and to derive their probabilistic properties by extending the classical assertional style of programming [20]. Programs in pGCL are modelled (operationally) as functions (or transitions) which map *initial states* in S to (sets of) probability distributions over *final states* — the program at (1) for instance has a single transition which maps any initial state to a (single) final distribution; we represent that distribution as a function δ, evaluating to $2/3$ when $b = 1$ and to $1/3$ when $b = 0$.

Since properties are now quantitative we express them via a logic of *real-valued functions*, or *expectations*. For example the property "the final value of b is 1 with probability $2/3$" can be expressed as the *expected value* of the function $[b = 1]$ with respect to δ, which evaluates to $2/3 \times 1 + 1/3 \times 0 = 2/3$.

Direct appeal to the operational semantics quickly becomes impractical for all but the simplest programs — better is the equivalent transformer-style semantics which is obtained by rationalising the above calculation in terms of expected values rather than transitions, and the explanation runs as follows. Writing $\mathcal{E}S$ for the set of all functions from S to $\mathbb{R}^1$, which we call the set of *expectations*, we say that the expectation $[b = 1]$ has been transformed to the expectation $2/3$ by the program *coin* set out at (1) above so that they are in the relation "$2/3$ is the expected value of $[b = 1]$ with respect to the *coin*'s result distribution". More generally given a program *prog*, an expectation E in $\mathcal{E}S$ and a state $s \in S$, we define $Wp.prog.E.s$ to be the expected value of E with respect to the result distribution of program *prog* if executed initially from state s [19]. We say that $Wp.prog$ is the *expectation transformer* relative to *prog*. In our example that allows us to write

$$2/3 \quad = \quad Wp.(b\colon = 1 \ {}_{2/3}\oplus b\colon = 0).[b = 1] \ ,$$

where, as explained above, we use $2/3$ as a constant expectation. In the case that *nondeterminism* is present, execution of *prog* results in a *set* of possible distributions and we modify the definition of Wp to take account of this, so that it computes the maximum or minimum value (taken over the full set of result distributions), depending on whether the nondeterminism is angelic or demonic. More information of the expectation transformer semantics is set out elsewhere [19].

---

[1] Strictly speaking we also include ∞ and $-\infty$ for well-definedness of fixed points [10]. All expectations used in this paper are finitary.

At Fig. 1 we set out the details of pGCL, a variation of Dijkstra's GCL with probability [2]. All the programming features have been defined previously elsewhere, and (apart from probabilistic choice) have interpretations which are merely adapted to the real-valued context. For example demonic nondeterminism, can be thought of as being resolved by a "minimal-seeking demon", providing guarantees on all program behaviour, such as is expected for total correctness. Angelic nondeterminism, on the other hand, can be thought of as a maximal-seeking angel, and provides an upper bound on possible behaviours. Finally *probabilistic choice* selects the operands at random with weightings determined by the probability parameter p. We make use of the following definitions. The combination of the various choices allows us to model two player stochastic games; crucially however is that our definitions prevent the demon and angel from predicting the result of subsequent probabilistic choices, and we shall use that feature in our case study to come.

• Given a family $\mathcal{I}$ of commands we write $[]_{i:\,\mathcal{I}}C_i$ for the generalised demonic (nondeterministic) choice over the family, and $\sum_{i\in\mathcal{I}}C_i@p_i$ for the generalised probabilistic choice (where $\sum_{i\in\mathcal{I}}p_i\leq 1$).

• We say that a command is *normal* if it is of the form of a generalised probabilistic choice over standard (non-probabilistic) commands F_i only containing angelic nondeterminism, *i.e.* of the form $\sum_{i\in\mathcal{I}}F_i@p_i$, where the F_i are standard, possibly angelic (but nowhere demonic) commands.

• We say that a pair of states (s_0, s') are *related via (normal) command C* if it is possible to reach s' from initial s_0 via C with some non-zero probability. [3]

We shall need to be able to compose the effect of "running" commands simultaneosly, and the next definition sets out how to do it.

Definition 1. *Given normal guarded commands $C \hat{=} G \rightarrow prog$ and $C' \hat{=} G' \rightarrow prog'$, we define their* composition *as follows.*

$$C \otimes C' \quad \hat{=} \quad (G \wedge G') \rightarrow \sum_{(i,j)\in I\times J} (F_i \otimes F'_j)\,@(p_i\times p'_j)\ ,$$

where $prog = \sum_{i\in I}F_i@p_i$ and $prog' = \sum_{j\in J}F'_j@p'_j$, and $Wp.F\otimes F'$ is given by the fusion *operator of Back and Butler [5]. In the case that F and F' operate over distinct state spaces (as in our case study) $F \otimes F'$ is equivalent to $F\ ;\ F'$.*

2.1 Probabilistic Action Systems

Action systems [2] are a "state-based" formalism for describing so-called reactive systems, *viz.* systems that may execute indefinitely. Although others [8, 25] have added probability to action systems, our work is most closely related to Morgan's version of labelled probabilistic action systems [21], which have been extended in various ways [14] described below.

---

[2] The language also includes abortion, miracles and iteration, but we do not need them here.

[3] For total commands this condition is expressed as $Wp.C.[s = s'].s_0 > 0$.

Skip	$Wp.\mathsf{skip}.E \mathrel{\hat=} E$,
Assignment	$Wp.(x := f).E \mathrel{\hat=} E[f/x]$,
Sequential composition	$Wp.(r; r').E \mathrel{\hat=} Wp.r.(Wp.r'.E)$,
Probabilistic choice	$Wp.(r \mathbin{_p\oplus} r').E \mathrel{\hat=} p \times Wp.r.E + (1-p) \times Wp.r'.E$,
Demonic choice	$Wp.(r \sqcap r').E \mathrel{\hat=} Wp.r.E \sqcap Wp.r'.E$,
Angelic choice	$Wp.(r \sqcup r').E \mathrel{\hat=} Wp.r.E \sqcup Wp.r'.E$,
Boolean choice	$Wp.(r \lhd G \rhd r').E \mathrel{\hat=} \overline{G} \times Wp.r.E + \overline{\neg G} \times Wp.r'.E$,
Guarded command	$Wp.(G \rightarrow r).E \mathrel{\hat=} \overline{G} \times Wp.r.E + \overline{\neg G} \times \infty$,

E is an expectation in $\mathcal{E}S$, and f is a function of the state, $E[f/x]$ represents substitution of f for x in E, and $\sqcap$, $\sqcup$ are respectively the pointwise minimum and maximum in the interpretations on the right. The real p is restricted to lie between 0 and 1.

Fig. 1. Structural definitions of Wp for pGCL

A (probabilistic) action system consists of a (finite) set of labelled guarded commands, together with a distinguished command called an initialisation. An action system is said to *operate* over a state space S, meaning that the variables used in the system define its state space. Operationally an action system first executes its initialisation, after which any labelled action may "fire" if its guard is true by executing its body. Actions may continue to fire indefinitely until all the guards are false. If more than one guard is true then any one of those actions may fire, demonically.

In Fig. 2 we set out a small example of a probabilistic action system *Guesser* which operates over the state defined by its variables x, y, d and t. They are all initialised to 0 or 1, and then action a or b fires depending on whether d is 0 or 1; the random flipper used to govern the setting of d degrades over time so that it becomes more likely for d to change whenever an action fires. In terms of actions, *Guesser* executes strings of a's and b's, whose relative frequency depends on the probabilistic selection of d.

$$
Guesser \mathrel{\hat=} \left(
\begin{array}{l}
\textbf{var } x, y, d \colon \{0, 1\}, t \colon \mathbb{N} \\
\textbf{initially } x, d := 0 \; ; \; y, t := 1 \\
a \colon\; (d = 0) \rightarrow\; t := t + 1 \; ; \; x := 1 \mathbin{_{1/3}\oplus} x := 0 \; ; \\
\qquad\qquad\qquad d := 1 \mathbin{_{(t-1)/t}\oplus} d := 0 \\
b \colon\; (d = 1) \rightarrow\; t := t + 1 \; ; \; y := 1 \sqcup y := 0 \; ; \\
\qquad\qquad\qquad d := 1 \mathbin{_{1/t}\oplus} d := 0
\end{array}
\right)
$$

Fig. 2. Guessing a random number

For action system P and label a we write P_a for the generalised choice of all actions labelled with a, and P_i for its initialisation. The set of labels (labelling actions in P) is denoted $\alpha.P$, and called P's *alphabet*. The semantics of an action system is given by pGCL set out at Fig. 1, so that, for example, $Wp.P_a.E.s$ is the greatest guaranteed expected value of E from execution of P_a, when s satisfies the guard of P_a.

Action systems are normally constructed in a modular fashion from a set of separate *modules*. Each module is itself an action system, with (normally) a state space independent from that of the other modules. In the complete system however the modules operate essentially independently, except for having to synchronise on shared actions.

2.2 Synchronising Actions

Synchronisation is defined so that all action systems participating in a parallel composition simultaneously fire their shared actions — in this mode the demonic nondeterminism (arising from possibly overlapping guards) is resolved first, followed by any probability, and last of all any angelic nondeterminism (in the bodies). All other actions fire independently, interleaving with any others.

Definition 2. *Given action systems P and Q in which all actions are normal; we define their* parallel composition $P||Q$ *as follows.*

1. *$P||Q$ operates over the union of the two state spaces, and $\alpha.(P||Q) = \alpha.P \cup \alpha.Q$;*
2. *$(P||Q)_i \quad \hat{=} \quad P_i \otimes Q_i$;*
3. *$(P||Q)_b \quad \hat{=} \quad$ if $(b \in \alpha.P)$ then P_b else Q_b, for $b \in \alpha.(P||Q)\backslash(\alpha.P \cap \alpha.Q)$;*
4. *$(P||Q)_a \quad \hat{=} \quad \|_{\{P^a \in P, Q^a \in Q\}} P^a \otimes Q^a$, for $a \in \alpha.P \cap \alpha.Q$, where P^a and Q^a are the individual a-labelled actions belonging to P and Q respectively.*

Finally we also make use of the convenient message-passing syntax found elsewhere [9, 11] and set out at Fig. 3.

$$
\begin{array}{llll}
\textit{Sending } x & chan!x :\ G\ \rightarrow P & \hat{=} & \|_{(y:\ \mathcal{Y})} chan :\ G \wedge (x = y)\ \rightarrow P \\
\textit{Receiving } x & chan?x :\ G'\ \rightarrow Q(x) \hat{=} & & \|_{(y:\ \mathcal{Y})} chan :\ G' \wedge (x = y)\ \rightarrow Q(y)
\end{array}
$$

$\mathcal{Y}$ is the set of values over which x ranges.

Fig. 3. Message-passing

In this section we have described pGCL and action systems as a basis for describing probabilistic reactive systems. In the next section we consider how to specify and analyse quantitative performance-style properties of those systems.

2.3 Property Specification and Optimisation Problems

Probabilistic temporal logic [1] is the well-known generalisation of standard temporal logic for investigating properties such as "the system will eventually establish condition *Pred* with probability $1/2$", and indeed such properties can be readily expressed using the expectation-transformer semantics and pGCL [19]. Besides standard temporal logic however there other quantitative properties pertinent to the analysis of performance, and in this section we investigate one such example. To begin, we consider the expression

$$
\diamond A \quad \hat{=} \quad (\mu X \cdot A \sqcup Wp.System.X) , \tag{2}
$$

where A is an expectation, and *System* an action system. The term $(\mu X \dots)$ refers to the least fixed point of the expectation-to-expectation function $(\lambda X \cdot A \sqcup Wp.System.X)$ with respect to $\leq$, lifted pointwise to real-valued functions. If A is any expectation then the expression at (2) is well-defined for any action system *System* [22], since in this case the definitions set out at Fig. 1 guarantee a least fixed point. [4]

To understand the interpretation, consider for example when A is the expectation defined by the "random variable"

$$\text{if } (x = y \wedge d = 1 \wedge t < 5) \text{ then } 1 \text{ else } 1/8 \qquad (3)$$

and *System* is *Guesser*. Here (2) gives a numerical value which averages the possible outcomes of repeatedly executing *Guesser*, so that a payoff of 1 is given if ever $(x = y \wedge d = 1 \wedge t < 5)$ is established, and only 1/8 otherwise. To see that, we extend the basic idea of probabilistic temporal logic, which relies on the observation that a probabilistic (action) system generates (a set of) distributions[5] over so-called "computation paths", where a *computation path* is the sequence of states through which the computation passes. Since formulae such as the above define measurable functions over the space of path distributions, the expected value is well defined (for bounded expectations). We discuss the above interpretation in more detail below.

2.4   A Game View

In more complicated situations we sometimes combine both angelic and demonic nondeterminism with probabilistic choice in *System*. Here (2) is also well-defined, although the operational interpretation is now somewhat more involved.

When all three — demonic, angelic and probabilistic nondeterminism — are present, the formula on the right-hand side of (2) describes a game [17], in which two players *Max* and *Min* decide how to resolve respectively the angelic and demonic nondeterminism in *System*, and (in this particular game) *Max* also decides when to terminate for an immediate "payoff" defined by A. The aims of *Max* and *Min* are opposite [6] — as the ultimate payoff goes to *Max* he tries to maximise it, whereas *Min* tries to minimise it. We call the expected payoff the *value* of the game.

We call a particular resolution of the nondeterminism (by a player) to be a *strategy* (of that player), and it turns out that in this kind of game (where both players have full knowledge of the state) the *Wp*-semantics gives a quantitative result which may be interpreted as the optimal payoff which *Max* may achieve against any strategy played out by *Min* [17], and furthermore that strategy is equivalent to replacing all angelic choices with a Boolean choice which describes which branch *Max* should take from any particular state.

---

[4] The reals form a complete partial order if augmented with $+\infty$ [10] and, by Tarski's result [27], that is sufficient to guarantee a least fixed point.

[5] Usually called the Borel probability algebra over computation paths.

[6] This is effectively a *zero-sum* game.

More generally when A is a (fixed) bounded expectation, both players may find optimal strategies in their play *viz.* each nondeterministic choice (either angelic or demonic) in *System* may be replaced by a Boolean choice so that the resulting *System'* satisfies

$$(\mu X \cdot A \sqcup Wp.System.X) \quad = \quad (\mu X \cdot A \sqcup Wp.System'.X) \; .$$

The strategies are *memoryless*, only depending on the current state [17]. For example the command labelled b in Fig. 2 may be replaced by

$$b: \; (d = 1) \rightarrow \; t: \; = t + 1 \; ; \; y: \; = x \; ; \; d: \; = 1 \,_{1/t} \oplus d: \; = 0 \; , \qquad (4)$$

for if *Max* always sets his value to the current value of x, then his expected payoff is maximised when A is defined by (3).

The above facts may be applied to system design in the following way. Suppose that the design of a protocol, besides satisfying some qualitative specification, is also required to achieve some level of performance specified by (2), and that the performance may vary depending on how the identified parameter is set. We may determine the optimal value of the parameter relative to particular payoff A as follows. First, we model the protocol as an action system, using angelic choice to set the identified parameter. Next we compute the optimal cost relative to A by evaluating (2) for the various definitions, and the optimal value for the identified parameter may then be determined by, for example, using the "policy iteration method" [26].These ideas are illustrated in our case study below.

Thus far our comments only apply when A is a bounded expectation. In our case study however we are obliged to consider unbounded expectations A, to express expected times. In the next section we consider a variation of the game which applies to unbounded payoffs as well.

2.5   Discounted Games with Unbounded Payoffs

In some cases early payoffs are valued more highly over later ones, and in these situations a *discount* factor is usually applied at each iteration [4]. In wireless networks for example degrading battery lives mean that the results from later payoffs become insignificant.

Definition 3. *Given an action system System, the discounted game with discount factor $p \in (0, 1)$, is defined to be*[7]

$$\diamond_p A \quad \hat{=} \quad (\mu X \cdot A \; \sqcup \; p \times Wp.System.X) \; . \qquad (5)$$

Discounted games over finite state spaces enjoy a number of nice properties [16], which follow from standard results in real analysis; it turns out that the same properties hold even in infinite state spaces (and for essentially the same reasons) provided that the (possibly unbounded) payoff function is "well behaved" relative

---

[7] We shall also consider the slightly less general $(\mu X \cdot A \lhd G \rhd p \times Wp.System.X)$, where G is any predicate. We note that all the lemmas are still valid for this variation.

to the underlying *System*. We say that expectation A *grows linearly* relative to *System* if there is some fixed constant $K \geq 0$ such that for all pairs of states (s, s') related via *System*, the inequality $|A.s - A.s'| \leq K$ holds.

In the remainder of this section we shall show that, for these payoffs, the game is well-defined and the players still have optimal memoryless strategies. The proofs of all the results may be found in the appendix.[8]

Lemma 1. *Suppose that A grows linearly with respect to* System *in the expression $\diamond_p A$ set out at (5), and is bounded below. The least fixed point on the right hand side at (5) is well-defined (i.e. non-infinitary).*

It turns out that the optimal strategies of the players may be computed from the solution of the game at (5). We denote the optimal strategies of a single step of *System* relative to an immediate post-expectation E as follows. We define $System_E$ to be *System* with each nondeterministic choice (both angelic and demonic) is replaced by a Boolean choice such that

$$Wp.System.E \quad = \quad Wp.System_E.E \ .$$

(The revised *Guesser* given by (4) defines such a Boolean choice for expectation (2) and (3).) Note that such Boolean choices always exist if the nondeterminism has only a finite range of possibilities [28, 17]. With that notation we may now state a corollary of Lem. 1, that both players in (5) have optimal strategies.

Lemma 2. *The players of the game $\diamond_p A$ both have optimal strategies whenever A grows linearly with respect to System, and is bounded below.*

Computing the optimal strategies can be done using the well-known "value (policy) iteration method" [26]. The idea is that the optimal strategies may be improved at each iteration by solving the equations

$$A \sqcup Wp.System_{E_n}.F^n.A \quad = \quad F^{n+1}.A \ ,$$

where $F \mathrel{\hat{=}} (\lambda X \cdot A \sqcup Wp.System.X)$. Here $System_{E_0}$, $System_{E_1} \ldots$ define a sequence of strategies, which converges in finite state spaces [26], so that there is some $N > 0$ such that for all $n \geq N$ we have the equality $System_{E_n} = System_{E_N}$, and that $System_{E_N}$ is optimal. It turns out that the same idea works even for unbounded expectations, as the next lemma shows.

Lemma 3. *The value (policy) iteration method is a valid method for computing the optimal strategies under the assumptions of Lem. 2.*

In this section we have indicated how angelic nondeterminism may be used to optimise system design relative to a payoff function, even when that function is unbounded. In the next section we illustrate these ideas in an application for wireless communication.

---

[8] Found at http://www.comp.mq.edu.au/~anabel/ICTAC06.pdf.

3   A Sleep/Awake Protocol for Wireless Networks

A promising approach to conserving battery power in wireless networks is to allow nodes periodically to enter a "low power mode" at times when the network traffic is low. During a low power phase, nodes do not actively listen for network activity, thus power is conserved that would otherwise have been wasted on so-called "idle listening" [29]. The disadvantage of this approach however is that the throughput is (almost certainly) decreased since messages may be blocked temporarily en route as they are forced to wait until sleeping nodes wake up.

In this section we describe a protocol designed to manage the scheduling of low/high power modes in a wireless network, with the goal of analysing the sleeping time so that the optimal sleep schedule may be determined.

Our study is based on a protocol suggested by Wei Ye *et al.* [29] and is intended to reduce the effects of message delay by arranging neighbouring nodes to wake up at approximately the same time. Nodes do this by broadcasting a *synch packet* just before they go to sleep announcing when they will next wake. Any neighbour in receipt of the synch packet then knows when it should also be awake and listening for traffic.

The main events in the sleep/awake protocol are set out at Fig. 4; the general scheme is as follows. After waking from a low power mode, a node listens for a while, sending and receiving any data as necessary. It then broadcasts and/or receives a *synch* packet, before setting its internal timer to its next scheduled waking time; it then goes to sleep.

Although the overall scheme of the protocol is fixed, there are still some opportunities for fine-tuning. For example the synch packet informs a node only *approximately* (rather than exactly) when its neighbour will next wake, and therefore it may be better for the neighbour to become active at some slightly different time, one which takes into account the uncertainties caused by natural delays involved in wireless communication and "clock drift", both of which diminish the reliability of the information received in the *synch* packet. Here *clock drift* is a common phenomenon in distributed systems that cannot rely on a global clock. Wireless nodes, for instance, use their own internal clocks, and after some time (the order of tens of seconds [29]) nodes' internal timers will have drifted relative to others' in the network. The problem may be corrected by periodic time synchronisation, or (in some applications) the use of distributed global clocking schemes.

Our formal model is constructed from a number of *modules*, each one consisting of a set of labelled *actions* describing the underlying state changes incurred after each event. In Fig. 5 we set out an action system modelling the main events at Fig. 4 for a *Receiver* node. The *Sender$_i$* nodes are similar except that we use variables s_i, t_i and w_i instead of (respectively) r, t_r and w_r, and the commands labelled † and ‡ are replaced as follows. We replace the †'s respectively by

$$send!i : \ (s_i = listen) \ \rightarrow \ s_i : \ = \ ack_i$$
$$ack_i : \ (s_i = ack) \ \rightarrow \ s_i = listen$$

- *Wake*: If local timer exceeds the wake up deadline, then the mode changes from low to high power;
- *Listen*:   The node listens for a signal in the network;
- *Send/Receive(data)*: The node receives any data, and replies with an acknowledgement if necessary;
- *Send/Receive(synch)*: The node either receives or sends a "synch packet" announcing a sleep schedule.
- *Choose(w_r)* : If a synch packet has been received from a neighbour, it sets its own wake-up deadline by setting parameter w_r;
- *Sleep*: It reinitialises its local timer and changes the mode from awake to sleeping.

Fig. 4. The major events in the sleep/awake protocol

$$Receiver \mathrel{\hat{=}} \left(\begin{array}{ll} \mathbf{var}\ r\colon \{listen, sleep, ack_i\}, t_r, w_r : \mathbb{N} & \\ \mathbf{initially}\ r\colon\ =\ listen; & \\ \|_i\, send?i :\ (r = listen)\ \rightarrow\ r\colon\ =\ ack_i & \dagger \\ \|_i\, ack_i :\ (r = ack_i)\ \rightarrow\ r\colon\ =\ listen & \dagger \\ clash :\ (r = listen)\ \rightarrow\ \mathsf{skip} & \\ & \\ tick :\ (r = sleep \wedge t_r < w_r)\ \rightarrow\ t_r\colon\ =\ t_r + 1\ {}_d\oplus \mathsf{skip} & \\ tick :\ (r = sleep \wedge t_r \geq w_r)\ \rightarrow\ r\colon\ =\ listen & \\ tick :\ (r = listen \wedge (\forall i \cdot s_i = sleep))\ \rightarrow\ \mathsf{skip} & \ddagger \\ synch :\ (r = listen)\ \rightarrow\ r\colon\ =\ sleep\ ;\ t_r\colon\ =\ 0\ ;\ Choose(w_r) & \end{array} \right)$$

The function $Choose(w_r) \mathrel{\hat{=}} (w_r :\ =\ 1)\ \sqcup \ldots \sqcup\ (w_r :\ =\ T)$, for some fixed T; the probabilistic assignment to t_r indicates some clock drift with rate relative to d.

Fig. 5. Specification of a Receiver node

and ‡ by

$$tick :\ (s_i = listen \wedge (r = sleep))\ \rightarrow\ \mathsf{skip}\ .$$

Thus the exchange of data is indicated by the senders and receivers synchronising on $send_i$ and ack_i events. Additional delays on throughput can be due to messages colliding (event *clash* handled by module *Channel* set out in Fig. 6), or the time spent waiting for a node's neighbour to wake. The latter may routinely happen because of clock drift, and here we model that behaviour using a probabilistic increment for the internal timer variable.

The whole system is defined by the parallel composition of the senders, the receivers, the channel and a module *time* which provides a notion of the real passage of time so that statistics on the time spent in the sleep state and the delays in throughput may be gathered. In this small example, we only have two senders and a receiver.

$$Network\quad \mathrel{\hat{=}}\quad Sender_1\ \|\ Sender_2\ \|\ Channel\ \|\ Receiver\ \|\ RealTime$$

$$RealTime \,\hat{=}\, \begin{pmatrix} \textbf{var } t\colon \mathbb{N} \\ \textbf{initially } t\colon\, = 0 \\ \|_{(evt\colon\, \alpha)} \; evt\colon (t \geq 0) \rightarrow t\colon\, = t+1 \end{pmatrix} \qquad Channel \,\hat{=}\, \begin{pmatrix} \textbf{var } c\colon \{block, clear\} \\ \textbf{initially } c\colon\, = \; block\, ; \\ clash\colon (c = block) \rightarrow \textsf{skip }_q\oplus c\colon\, = \; clear \end{pmatrix}$$

The module *RealTime* is used to allow us to collect statistics for the performance analysis. Here α is the union of all the timing events defined by the *senders* and the *receivers*; specifically $\alpha \,\hat{=}\, \{tick, synch, clash\}$. The event *clash* signifies a collision between messages.

Fig. 6. Modelling the behaviour of real time and the channel

Our aim is to investigate how to choose the optimal sleeping schedule w_r, namely to resolve the angelic nondeterminism in $Choose(w_r)$, where w_r is chosen from some finite range of values on the firing of action *synch*. Note that this choice is made before going to sleep, *i.e.* at a time when the *Receiver effectively has no knowledge* of when the senders actually do wake, as it cannot predict the result of the subsequent random choices governing the clock-drift.

3.1   Optimal Behaviour of the Sleep/Awake Protocol

In this section we formalise a game in order to optimise $Choose(w_r)$ in Fig. 5 relative to an appropriate payoff function. The idea here is to optimise the payoff for saving battery power in the context of message delivery; thus our payoff function optimises time spent in the sleep state offset by the cost of possibly delaying messages. To estimate the latter cost, we assign a value to the messages according to the length of time they took to be delivered. For example if the contents of the messages quickly become out of date, then the longer they take to be delivered the less valuable they are.

$$(\mu X \; \cdot \; (a \times totalSleep - b \times totalDelay) \; \triangleleft G \triangleright \; (p \times Wp.System \; ; \; X)) \qquad (6)$$

totalSleep is the total time that the receiver has spent in the sleeping mode; *totalDelay* is the total message delay, and G is the termination condition, that all messages have been delivered. Constants a and b are determined by the application.

Fig. 7. The game for optimising the cost of sleeping offset by the throughput

An example of such a function is set out at Fig. 7, where *totalSleep* and *totalDelay* are statistics defining respectively the overall time spent in the low power mode, and the total time it takes to deliver messages. [9] We can collect those statistics from the formal model of *Network* as follows. To define the overall time spent in the *Receiver*'s low power state we augment the definition at Fig. 5

---

[9] We include the termination condition in Fig. 7 rather than use $\sqcup$ since we are only intending to optimise the selection of w_r.

with variables *SleepTime* and *totalSleep*. Thus on powering down *SleepTime* is set to the current value of the global time variable t, and on waking *totalSleep* is set to $totalSleep + t - SleepTime$. We measure the total additional time it takes to send a message, and store it in a variable called *totalDelay* by similarly augmenting the $Sender_i$'s.

When scalars a and b are set to 1, the problem does not articulate any constraint on message delay (and thus the optimal sleep schedule would be never to wake up!) A better variation is to include scalars a and b to express the relative importance between saving power and tolerance of message delay, depending on the application [29]. Thus a high value of b relative to a means that message delay costs more than power savings; for example if $a/b = 1/2$ then a delay of 1 second costs twice as much as the power saved by a low power interval of 1 second.[10]

Finally from Fig. 6 we see that time is incremented linearly with each execution of *Network*, and so (6) also only grows linearly with respect to *Network*, thus Lem. 1 and Lem. 2 implies that (6) is well-defined and the player *Max* choosing the schedule must have an optimal strategy.

3.2   Experimental Results

We used the PRISM model checker [24] to model *Network*, and to compute the various probability distributions over *totalSleep* and *totalDelay*. From those results we computed the expected optimal productive sleeping time. We assumed that the *Senders* always announced a fixed sleep schedule of 2 time steps, and based on that we computed *Receiver*'s optimal assignment to w_r. In our experiments we used parameters $a, b: = 1$ and also $a: = 1$ and $b: = 2$. As expected, the results show that in the former case, it is better for the *Receiver* to set its wait deadline greater than 2 time steps, whereas in the latter case, where throughput is more essential (comparatively) than saving power it is better for *Receiver* to wake up after 2.

4   Conclusions

We have proposed a stochastic parity game to investigate the tradeoff between power savings and message throughput in a wireless network. Our formalisation allows the use of standard value and policy iteration algorithms to compute the optimal sleep schedule, moreover having access to model checking allows the overall expected delays to be computed once the optimal sleep schedule has been determined.

An alternative approach would be to formalise the problem as a standard optimisation problem *viz.* to optimise the time spent in the low power mode constrained by an upper bound on throughput. There are several practical and theoretical drawbacks to this however. The first is that both the objective function,

---

[10] Note that the apparent unboundness (below) of (6) is not a problem — see *Lem. 6* in the appendix.

and the constraints in such a formalisation must be determined by expressions of the form (6), and need themselves to be computed using (for example) non-trivial probabilistic model-checking techniques. Furthermore there is an additional dependency between the contraint and the objective function due to the inherent nondeterminism, and this cannot be expressed straightforwardly. The use of our proposed game addresses the latter problem, as there is no separate constraint expression; moreover as there is only a single expression of the form (6) involved in the problem fomalisation its solution can be obtained more efficiently. A drawback is that it might be difficult to determine appropriate parameters a and b.

We are not the first to give a game interpretation of Action Systems [3]. Others have explored similar two-player "Markov Games" [13], and de Alfaro et $al.$ have studied the use of discounting in systems theory [7]. Formal models of power management have be investigated in other contexts [4, 23].

References

1. A. Aziz, V. Singhal, F. Balarinand R.K. Brayton, and A.L. Sangiovanni-Vincentelli. It usually works: The temporal logic of stochastic systems. In *Computer-Aided Verification, 7th Intl. Workshop*, volume 939 of *LNCS*, pages 155–65. Springer Verlag, 1995.
2. R.-J.R. Back. A calculus of refinements for program derivations. *Acta Informatica*, 25:593–624, 1988.
3. R.-J.R. Back and J. von Wright. *Refinement Calculus: A Systematic Introduction*. Springer Verlag, 1998.
4. Luca Benini, Alessandro Bogliolo, Giuseppe A. Paleologo, and Giovanni De Micheli. Policy optimization for dynamic power management. *IEEE Transactions of Computer-Aided Design of Integrated Systems and Circuits*, 18(6):813–834, 1999.
5. M.J. Butler and C.C. Morgan. Action systems, unbounded nondeterminism and infinite traces. *Formal Aspects of Computing*, 7(1):37–53, 1995.
6. K. Chatterjee, M. Jurdzinski, and T. Henzinger. Quantitative stochastic parity games.
7. Luca de Alfaro, Thomas A. Henzinger, and Rupak Majumdar. Discounting the future in systems theory. In *Proceedings of the 30th International Colloquium on Automata, Languages, and Programming (ICALP)*, LNCS, pages 1022–1037, 2003.
8. S. Hallerstede and M. Butler. Performance analysis of probabilistic action systems. *Formal Aspects of Computing*, 16(4):313–331, 2004.
9. C.A.R. Hoare. *Communicating Sequential Processes*. Prentice Hall International, 1985.
10. Joe Hurd, A.K. McIver, and C.C. Morgan. Probabilistic guarded commands mechanised in HOL. *Theoretical Computer Science*, pages 96–112, 2005.
11. G. Jones. *Programming In occam*. Prentice Hall International, 1988.
12. D. Kozen. Results on the propositional μ-calculus. *Theoretical Computer Science*, 27:333–54, 1983.
13. M.G. Lagoudakis and R. Parr. Value function approximation in zero-sum markov games. 2002. Available at
   citeseer.ist.psu.edu/article/lagoudakis02value.html.

14. A.K. McIver. Quantitative refinement and model checking for the analysis of probabilistic systems. Accepted for FM 2006.
15. A.K McIver and C.C. Morgan. Games, probability and the quantitative μ-calculus qMu. In *Proc. LPAR*, volume 2514 of *LNAI*, pages 292–310. Springer Verlag, 2002. Revised and expanded at [17].
16. AK McIver and CC Morgan. Memoryless strategies for stochastic games via domain theory. *ENTCS*, 130:23–37, 2005.
17. A.K. McIver and C.C. Morgan. Results on the quantitative μ-calculus $qM\mu$. To appear in *ACM TOCL*, 2006.
18. A.K. McIver, C.C. Morgan, J.W. Sanders, and K. Seidel. Probabilistic Systems Group: Collected reports.
    `web.comlab.ox.ac.uk/oucl/research/areas/probs`.
19. Annabelle McIver and Carroll Morgan. *Abstraction, Refinement and Proof for Probabilistic Systems*. Technical Monographs in Computer Science. Springer Verlag, New York, 2004.
20. C.C. Morgan. *Programming from Specifications*. Prentice-Hall, second edition, 1994.
21. C.C. Morgan. Of probabilistic Wp and CSP. *25 years of CSP*, 2005.
22. C.C. Morgan and A.K. McIver. *pGCL*: Formal reasoning for random algorithms. *South African Computer Journal*, 22, March 1999. Available at [18, key PGCL].
23. G. Norman, D. Parker, M. Kwiatkowska, S. Shukla, and R. Gupta. Using probabilistic model checking for dynamic power management. *Formal Aspects of Computing*, 17(2):160–176, 2005.
24. PRISM. Probabilistic symbolic model checker.
    `www.cs.bham.ac.uk/~dxp/prism`.
25. Kaisa Sere and Elena Troubitsyna. Probabilities in action systems. In *Proc. of the 8th Nordic Workshop on Programming Theory*, 1996.
26. RS Sutton and AG Barto. *Reinforcement Learning*. MIT Press, 1998.
27. A. Tarski. A lattice-theoretic fixpoint theorem and its applications. *Pacific Journal of Mathematics*, 5:285–309, 1955.
28. J. von Neumann and O. Morgenstern. *Theory of Games and Economic Behavior*. Princeton University Press, second edition, 1947.
29. Wei Ye, J. Heidemann, and D. Estrin. Medium access control with coordinated adaptive sleeping for wireless sensor networks. *IEEE/ACM Transactions on Networking*, (3), 2004.

Termination and Divergence Are Undecidable Under a Maximum Progress Multi-step Semantics for LinCa

Mila Majster-Cederbaum and Christoph Minnameier[*]

Institut für Informatik
Universität Mannheim, Germany
cmm@informatik.uni-mannheim.de

Abstract. We introduce a multi-step semantics $MTS\text{-}mp$ for $LinCa$ which demands *maximum progress* in each step, i.e. which will only allow transitions that are labeled with maximal (in terms of set inclusion) subsets of the set of enabled actions. We compare $MTS\text{-}mp$ with the original ITS-semantics for LinCa specified in [CJY94] and with a slight modification of the original MTS-semantics specified in [CJY94]. Given a $LinCa$-process and a *Tuple Space* configuration, the possible transitions under our $MTS\text{-}mp$-semantics are always a subset of the possible transitions under the presented MTS-semantics for $LinCa$.

We compare the original ITS-semantics and the presented MTS-semantics with our $MTS\text{-}mp$-semantics, and as a major result, we will show that under $MTS\text{-}mp$ neither termination nor divergence of $LinCa$ processes is decidable. In contrast to this [BGLZ04], in the original semantics for $LinCa$ [CJY94] termination is decidable.

1 Introduction

A Coordination Language is a language defined specifically to allow two or more parties (components) to communicate for the purpose of coordinating operations to accomplish some shared (computation) goal. *Linda* seems to be the mostly known Coordination Language. Ciancarini, Jensen and Yankelevich [CJY94] defined *LinCa*, the *Linda Calculus* and gave a single-step, as well as a multi-step semantics for *LinCa*.

A *Linda* process may contain several parallel subprocesses that communicate via a so called *Tuple Space*. The *Tuple Space* is some kind of global store, where tuples are stored. In *Linda*, a tuple is a vector consisting of variables and/or constants, and there is a matching relation that is similar to data type matching in common programming languages. For the purpose of investigating the properties of the coordination through the *Tuple Space* it is common practice to ignore the matching relation and internal propagation of tuples. Tuples are distinguished from each other by giving them unique names $(t_1, t_2, t_3, ...)$ and *LinCa* is based on a *Tuple Space* that is countably infinite.

---

[*] Corresponding author.

K. Barkaoui, A. Cavalcanti, and A. Cerone (Eds.): ICTAC 2006, LNCS 4281, pp. 65–79, 2006.
© Springer-Verlag Berlin Heidelberg 2006

As far as the semantics for $LinCa$ is concerned, the traditional interleaving point of view does not make any assumptions about the way concurrent actions are performed, i.e. for any number of processing units and independently of their speed all possible interleavings of actions are admitted. On the other hand, the traditional multi-step point of view allows actions to be carried out concurrently or interleaved.

Let us assume a system, where all processing units work at the same speed and where all of them are globally clocked. For such a system, we might demand *maximum progress*, i.e. as long as additional actions can be performed in the present step they must be. More formally, we consider only (set inclusion) maximal sets of actions for each step.

Consider, for example, a system where a number of workers (processes) have to perform different jobs (calculations) on some object (tuple). The objects are supplied sequentially by some environment, which is represented by the process foreman. (Readers that are familiar with $LinCa$ might want to have a look at the end of Section 3, where we model the example in $LinCa$.)

In a setting with a common clock for all processes where the workers' calculations (plus taking up the object) can always be finished within one clock cycle we would (for maximum efficiency) want the systems semantics to represent the actual proceeding as follows: All workers are idle while the foreman supplies an object. The foreman waits while all the workers read the object and perform their jobs simultaneously. All workers put their results into the tuple space simultaneously while the foreman deletes the object, and so on.

In this paper we study a MTS-mp (*Multi-Step Transition System* with *maximum progress*) semantics that models the specified behavior. As already implicitly stated in this example, we assume a data-base-like setting, where multiple read-operations may be performed on a single instance of a tuple (whereas this is not the case for in-operations). As a remark, we want to add, that this detail in design does however not affect the decidability results presented in Section 5 (this is obvious due to the fact that the given encoding of a RAM in LinCa doesn't include any rd-operation). The paper is organized as follows: In Section 2, we set up notation and terminology. In Section 3, we present the original interleaving semantics for $LinCa$ as well as a multi-step semantics and the MTS-mp semantics. In Section 4, we establish a relation between the non-maximum-progress semantics and MTS-mp. Finally, Section 5 includes the main purpose of this paper: i.e. termination and divergence are undecidable for $LinCa$ under MTS-mp. This is an interesting result as we do adopt the basic version of the $LinCa$ language used in [BGLZ04], where it is shown that termination is decidable for the traditional interleaving semantics. In particular, we do not apply the predicative operator $inp(t)?P\_Q$ (see, e.g. [BGM00]) that represents an "if-then-else-construct" and thereby makes it easy to give a deterministic simulation of a RAM.

2   Definitions

- Most sets in this paper represent multisets. Given a multiset M, we write $(a, k) \in M$ $(k \geq 0)$ iff M includes exactly k instances of the element a. We

will write $a \in M$ instead of $(a, 1) \in M$ and $a \notin M$, instead of $(a, 0) \in M$.
We will use the operators $\uplus, \setminus$ and $\subseteq$ on multisets in their intuitive meaning.
- Given a multiset M we denote by $set(M)$ the set derived from M by deleting every instance of each element except for one, i.e.
$set(M) = \{a \mid \exists i > 0 \in \mathbb{N} : (a, i) \in M\}$
- Given a set S we denote the *power-multiset* (that is the set of subsets that may include multiple instances of the same element of S) of S by $\wp(S)$.
- LinCa processes:
Note, that by *Tuple Space*, we denote the basic set from which *tuples* are chosen and by *Tuple Space* configuration we refer to the state of our store in the present computation, i.e. a *Tuple Space* configuration is a multiset over the *Tuple Space*, i.e. for each *Tuple Space* configuration M and the underlying *Tuple Space* TS, we have $M \in \wp(TS)$.

In order to show some properties of the introduced semantics, we will sometimes modify it slightly, by adding some extra tuples to TS. We will denote these extra tuples by c, d, e and we will write TS_{cde} for $TS \cup \{c, d, e\}$, where $TS \cap \{c, d, e\} = \emptyset$.

Given a fixed *Tuple Space* TS, we can define the set of processes $LinCa_{TS}$ as the set of processes derived from the grammar in Figure 1, where every time we apply one of the rules $\{P := in(t).P, P := out(t).P, P := rd(t).P, P :=! in(t).P\}$, t is substituted by an element of the *Tuple Space*. $in(t), out(t)$ and $rd(t)$ are called actions. If $t \in \{c, d, e\}$ then they are called *internal* actions, else *observable* actions. Trailing zeros (.0) will be dropped in examples.

$$P := 0 \mid in(t).P \mid out(t).P \mid rd(t).P \mid P \mid P \mid ! \, in(t).P$$

Fig. 1. LinCa

- $ea(P)$ with P a *LinCa*-process denotes the multiset of enabled actions of P, defined in Figure 2. We define a decomposition of (the tuples used in) $ea(P)$ into three subsets $ea_{IN}(P), ea_{OUT}(P), ea_{RD}(P)$ as given in Figure 3:

1) $ea(0) = \emptyset$
2) $ea(in(t).P) = \{in(t)\}$
3) $ea(out(t).P) = \{out(t)\}$
4) $ea(rd(t).P) = \{rd(t)\}$
5) $ea(! \, in(t).P) = \{(in(t), \infty)\}$
6) $ea(P \mid Q) = ea(P) \uplus ea(Q)$

Fig. 2. The set of enabled actions $ea(P)$ of a process $P \in LinCa$

$$\boxed{\begin{aligned} &ea_{IN}(P) = \{(t,i) \mid (in(t),i) \in ea(P)\} \\ &ea_{OUT}(P) \text{ analogously} \\ &ea_{RD}(P) \text{ analogously} \end{aligned}}$$

Fig. 3. The sets $ea_{IN}(P), ea_{OUT}(P), ea_{RD}(P)$ of a process $P \in LinCa$

The notions $(in(t), \infty) \in ea(P)$ and $(t, \infty) \in ea_{IN}(P)$ describe the fact, that infinitely many actions $in(t)$ are *enabled* in P. These notions will only be used for *enabled actions*, never for *Tuple Space* configurations, because (due to the *in-guardedness* of *replication*) all computed *Tuple Space* configurations remain finite.

- A Labeled Transition System is a triple $(S, Lab, \rightarrow)$, where S is the set of states, *Lab* is the set of labels and $\rightarrow \subseteq S \times Lab \times S$ is a ternary relation (of labeled transitions). If $p, q \in S$ and $a \in Lab$, $(p, a, q) \in \rightarrow$ is also denoted by: $p \xrightarrow{a} q$. This represents the fact that there is a transition from state p to state q with label a. We write $p \nrightarrow$ iff $\nexists a \in Lab, q \in S : p \xrightarrow{a} q$. In addition we often want to designate a starting state s_0, in this case we use the quadruple $(S, Lab, \rightarrow, s_0)$.

   In the Transition Systems describing the various semantics, states are pairs $< P, M >$ of *LinCa*-processes and *Tuple Space* configurations and labels are triples (I, O, R) of (possibly empty) multisets of tuples, where I represents the performed *in*-actions, O the performed *out*-actions and R the performed *rd*-actions. We write τ instead of (I, O, R) iff $I, O, R \in \wp(\{c, d, e\})$ and call τ *internal* label and a transition $s \xrightarrow{\tau} s'$ an *internal* transition. A label $a = (I, O, R) \neq \tau$ is called *observable* label and a transition $s \xrightarrow{a} s'$ is called *observable* transition.

- Let $SEM \in \{ITS, MTS, MTS\text{-}mp\}$ (see Section 3 for details). The *SEM*-semantics of $LinCa_{TS}$ is given by the Transition System $(S, Lab, \rightarrow)$, where:
   1. $S = LinCa_{TS} \times \wp(TS)$
   2. $Lab = \wp(TS) \times \wp(TS) \times \wp(TS)$
   3. $\rightarrow = \rightarrow_{SEM}$ (see Section 3)

   For a process $P \in LinCa_{TS}$ the *SEM*-semantics is considered as $(S, Lab, \rightarrow_{SEM}, < P, \emptyset >)$ and we denote it by $SEM[P]$.

- Given a LTS LTS_1 and nodes $s_1, s_1' \in S$ we define: $s_1 \xrightarrow{(I,O,R)}{}^+ s_1'$
   iff $\exists s_2, ..., s_n \in S$, such that: $s_1 \xrightarrow{\tau} s_2 \xrightarrow{\tau} ... \xrightarrow{\tau} s_n \xrightarrow{(I,O,R)} s_1'$

- Given a LTS LTS_1 with starting state s_0 we define its set of *traces* as follows:
   $$traces(LTS_1) := \{(a_1, a_2, ...) \in Tr_{Lab} \mid \exists s_1, s_2, ... \in S : s_0 \xrightarrow{a_1}{}^+ s_1 \xrightarrow{a_2}{}^+ s_2 ...\}$$
   where $Tr_{Lab} = (Lab \setminus \{\tau\})^* \cup (Lab \setminus \{\tau\})^\infty$ and $S^* (S^\infty)$ denotes the set of finite (infinite) sequences over a set S.

- a LTS LTS_1 with starting state s_0 terminates iff:
   $$\exists s_1, ..., s_n \in S, a_1, ..., a_n \in Lab : s_0 \xrightarrow{a_1} s_1 \xrightarrow{a_2} ... \xrightarrow{a_n} s_n \nrightarrow$$

- a LTS LTS_1 with starting state s_0 diverges iff it has at least one infinite transition sequence, i.e: $\exists s_i \in S, a_i \in Lab : s_0 \xrightarrow{a_1} s_1 \xrightarrow{a_2} ...$

- Let $LTS_1 = (S_1, Lab_1, \rightarrow_1, s_{01})$ and $LTS_2 = (S_2, Lab_2, \rightarrow_2, s_{02})$ be two Labeled Transition Systems. We write $LTS_1 \preceq LTS_2$ iff the following properties hold:
  1) $traces(LTS_1) = traces(LTS_2)$
  2) LTS_2 is able to weakly step simulate LTS_1, i.e. $\exists R \subseteq S_1 \times S_2$ such that:
     2.1) $(s_{01}, s_{02}) \in R$ and
     2.2) $(p, q) \in R \wedge p \stackrel{(I,O,R)}{\rightarrow} p' \Rightarrow \exists q' \in S_2 : q \stackrel{(I,O,R)}{\rightarrow}^+ q' \wedge (p', q') \in R.$

3 Semantics

In this section, we introduce the ITS-semantics for $LinCa$ based on the semantics given in [BGLZ04] and a MTS-semantics that we consider the natural extension of ITS. In the given MTS-semantics, we allow (in contrast to [CJY94]) an arbitrarily large number of rd-actions to be performed simultaneously on a single instance of a tuple.

To describe the various semantics, we split the semantic description in two parts: a set of rules for *potential* transitions of $LinCa$-processes (Figures 4 and 6) and an additional rule to establish the semantics in which we check if some *potential* transition is allowed under the present *Tuple Space* configuration (Figures 5, 7 and 9).

This allows us to reuse the rules in Figure 4 (henceforth called *pure syntax* rules) for the succeeding MTS and MTS-mp semantics. Choosing this representation makes it convenient to point out common features and differences of the discussed semantics.

In contrast to [BGLZ04] we label transitions. We have to do so to record which actions a step-transition performs in order to check if this is possible under the present *Tuple Space* configuration. The labels serve as a link between the rules of *pure syntax* and the semantic rule: For a *potential* transition $P \stackrel{(I,O,R)}{\rightarrow} P'$ the multisets $I/O/R$ contain the tuples on which we want to perform in/out/rd actions. In MTS (see Figure 7), such a *potential* transition is only valid for some *Tuple Space* configuration M, if $I \uplus set(R) \subseteq M$, i.e. M includes enough instances of each tuple to satisfy all performed *in*-actions and at least one additional instance for the performed *rd*-actions on that tuple (if any *rd*-actions are performed). For *out*-actions there is no such restriction.

In Figure 9 we use the notion of *maximality* of a *potential* transition for some *Tuple Space* configuration M. *Maximality* is given iff conditions 1) and 2) in Figure 8 hold, where 1) means, that all enabled out-actions have to be performed. 2) means, that as many of the *in* and *rd*-actions as possible have to be performed. More precisely 2.1) represents the case, that the number of instances of some tuple t in the present *Tuple Space* configuration M exceeds the number of enabled *in*-actions on that tuple. In this case all *in*-actions and all *rd*-actions have to be performed.

We define the relations $\rightarrow_{ITS}$, $\rightarrow_{MTS}$ and $\rightarrow_{MTS\text{-}mp}$ as the smallest relations satisfying the corresponding rule in Figure 5, 7 and 9, respectively.

$$
\begin{aligned}
&1)\ in(t).P \xrightarrow{(\{t\},\emptyset,\emptyset)} P \\
&2)\ out(t).P \xrightarrow{(\emptyset,\{t\},\emptyset)} P \\
&3)\ rd(t).P \xrightarrow{(\emptyset,\emptyset,\{t\})} P \\
&4)\ !\,in(t).P \xrightarrow{(\{t\},\emptyset,\emptyset)} P\ |\ !\,in(t).P \\
&5)\ \frac{P \xrightarrow{(I,O,R)} P'}{P\ |\ Q \xrightarrow{(I,O,R)} P'\ |\ Q}
\end{aligned}
$$

Fig. 4. ITS: pure syntax (symmetrical rule for 5 omitted)

$$
\frac{P \xrightarrow{(I,O,R)} P' \in \textit{ITS-Rules} \quad I \subseteq M \quad R \subseteq M}{<P,M> \xrightarrow{(I,O,R)}_{ITS} <P',(M\backslash I)\uplus O>}
$$

Fig. 5. ITS

ITS-Rules 1) - 5) (from Figure 4)

$$
6)\quad !\,in(t).P \xrightarrow{(\{(t,i)\},\emptyset,\emptyset)} \prod_i P\ |\ !\,in(t).P
$$

$$
7)\quad \frac{P \xrightarrow{(I_P,O_P,R_P)} P' \quad Q \xrightarrow{(I_Q,O_Q,R_Q)} Q'}{P\ |\ Q \xrightarrow{(I_P\uplus I_Q,\,O_P\uplus O_Q,\,R_P\uplus R_Q)} P'\ |\ Q'}
$$

Fig. 6. MTS: pure syntax

We end this Section by modeling[1] the example mentioned in the Introduction in *LinCa*. A foreman supplies a group of workers with jobs.

Let $P := foreman\ |\ worker_1\ |\ ...\ |\ worker_n$, where:

$foreman = out(object).wait.in(object).foreman$
$worker_i = rd(object).out(result_i).worker_i$

Ciancarini's original MTS semantics would allow P to evolve in a variety of ways. However, given a common clock and given that all workers can perform their rd-operations (as well as their internal calculation which we abstract from in LinCa) within one clock cycle, the expected/desired maximum-progress behavior of P (that has already been described in the introduction) corresponds to the one and only path in $MTS\text{-}mp[P]$.

---

[1] The *wait*-operator is used for ease of notation only, it is not part of the discussed language. For details on the usage of the *wait*-operator see Section 4.2.

$$\frac{P^{(I,O,R)}_{\rightarrow} P' \in MTS\text{-}Rules \quad (I \uplus Set(R)) \subseteq M}{<P,M> \overset{(I,O,R)}{\rightarrow}_{MTS} <P',(M\backslash I)\uplus O>}$$

Fig. 7. MTS

$$
\begin{aligned}
&1)\ (t,i) \in ea_{OUT}(P) \Rightarrow (t,i) \in O \\
\wedge\ &2)\ (t,i) \in M \wedge (t,j) \in ea_{IN}(P) \wedge (t,k) \in ea_{RD}(P) \Rightarrow \\
&(\quad 2.1)\ j < i \wedge (t,j) \in I \wedge (t,k) \in R \\
&\vee\ 2.2)\ j \geq i \wedge (t,i) \in I \wedge (t,0) \in R \\
&\vee\ 2.3)\ j \geq i \wedge (t,i-1) \in I \wedge (t,k) \in R \wedge k \geq 1\ )
\end{aligned}
$$

Fig. 8. Cond. for *Maximality* of a trans. $P \overset{(I,O,R)}{\rightarrow} P'$ for some *Tuple Space* config. M

$$\frac{P^{(I,O,R)}_{\rightarrow} P' \in MTS\text{-}Rules \quad P^{(I,O,R)}_{\rightarrow} P' \text{ is maximal for } M}{<P,M> \overset{(I,O,R)}{\rightarrow}_{MTS\text{-}mp} <P',(M\backslash I)\uplus O>}$$

Fig. 9. MTS-mp

4 Relations Between ITS, MTS, MTS-mp

For all $P \in LinCa$ the following properties hold for the defined semantics *ITS*, *MTS* and *MTS-mp*:

- *ITS*[P] is always a subgraph of *MTS*[P], as the *pure syntax* rules for *ITS* in Figure 4 are a subset of those for *MTS* in Figure 6 and the way the semantics are based on (Figures 5 and 7) the *pure syntax* rules is the same.
- *MTS-mp*[P] is always a subgraph of *MTS*[P], as the *pure syntax* rules for *MTS* and *MTS-mp* are the same but for the *MTS-mp* semantics in Figure 9 we apply a stronger precondition than for the *MTS* semantics in Figure 7.

By $LinCa_{cde}$ we denote the *LinCa* language based on an extended *Tuple Space*. That is, we assume the existence of 3 designated tuples *c,d,e* that are not elements of the original *LinCa Tuple Space*. We extend our *MTS-mp* semanics to treat actions on these tuples just like any other actions in the purely syntactic description. However in Transition Systems whenever (I, O, R) consists of nothing but designated tuples we replace it by τ, the *internal* label. Whenever some *internal* actions are performed concurrently with some *observable* actions, the label of the resulting transition will simply consist of the *observable* ones.

By $MTS\text{-}mp[P]$ where $P \in LinCa_{cde}$ we denote its semantics as described above.

4.1   The Relation Between *ITS* and *MTS-mp*

In this subsection we define an encoding $enc_{ITS}\colon LinCa \to LinCa_{cde}$ and prove that $ITS[P] \preceq MTS\text{-}mp[enc_{ITS}(P)]$ holds.

enc_{ITS} is composed of the main encoding $\widetilde{enc}_{ITS}$ and a parallel $out(c)$:

$\widetilde{enc}_{ITS}(0) = 0$
$\widetilde{enc}_{ITS}(act(t).P) = in(c).act(t).out(c).enc(P)$
$\widetilde{enc}_{ITS}(P \mid Q) = enc(P) \mid enc(Q)$
$\widetilde{enc}_{ITS}(!\, in(t).P) = !\, in(c).in(t).out(c).enc(P)$

$enc_{ITS}(P) = \widetilde{enc}_{ITS}(P) \mid out(c)$

Theorem 1. $ITS[P] \preceq MTS\text{-}mp[enc_{ITS}(P)]$

Proof.   1) *Weak Similarity*
$enc_{ITS}(P)$ puts a prefix $in(c)$ in front of and a suffix $out(c)$ behind every action in P. The weak step simulation deterministically starts by performing the *internal* action $out(c)$ and subsequently simulates every step of the ITS Transition System by performing three steps as follows:

First, we remove the encoding-produced guarding $in(c)$-prefix from the *observable* action we want to simulate (henceforth we call this *unlocking an action*) then we perform this action and finally we perform the suffix $out(c)$ to supply the *Tuple Space* configuration with the tuple c for the simulation of the next action. As all described steps are indeed maximal, the transitions are valid for *MTS-mp*.

2) *Equality of traces*
$traces(ITS[P]) \subseteq traces(MTS\text{-}mp[enc_{ITS}(P)])$ follows immediately from weak similarity. As for the reverse inclusion: $MTS\text{-}mp[enc_{ITS}(P)]$ can either unlock an action that can be performed under the present *Tuple Space* configuration then $ITS[P]$ can perform the same action directly. $MTS\text{-}mp[enc_{ITS}(P)]$ could also unlock an action that is blocked under the present *Tuple Space* configuration, but in this case the computation (and thus the trace) halts due to the total blocking of the process $enc_{ITS}(P)$ (as the single instance of tuple c has been consumed without leaving an opportunity to provide a new one).

4.2   The Relation Between *MTS* and *MTS-mp*

First, we introduce the basic encoding $enc\colon LinCa \to LinCa_{cde}$, that simply prefixes every action of a process with an additional blocking $in(c)$ action.

$enc(0) = 0$
$enc(act(t).P) = in(c).act(t).enc(P)$
$enc(P \mid Q) = enc(P) \mid enc(Q)$
$enc(!\, in(t).P) = !\, in(c).in(t).enc(P)$

Second, we introduce the encoding $\widetilde{enc}_{MTS}$ which encodes a process by enc and provides it with an additional parallel process $\tilde{P}$. All actions performed by $\tilde{P}$ are *internal* actions, and $\tilde{P}$ will be able to produce an arbitrary number of instances of the tuple c simultaneously.

We define: $\tilde{P} := \quad ! \, in(d).[rd(e).out(c) \mid out(d)]$
$$\mid \, ! \, in(d).out(e).wait.in(e).wait.out(d)$$
$\widetilde{enc}_{MTS}(P) := enc(P) \mid \tilde{P} \mid out(d)$

Strictly speaking the *wait*-operator used in $\tilde{P}$ is not included in $LinCa$. We nevertheless use it because a *wait*-action (which has no other effect on the rest of the process and is not *observable*) can be implemented by a rd-action in the following way. Let t^* be a designated tuple that is not used for other purposes. If P is a $LinCa$-process except for the fact, that it may contain some *wait*-actions then consider it as the process $P[wait/rd(t^*)] \mid out(t^*)$. However, we state that the *wait*-actions are not at all needed for the correctness of the encoding and we added them only for ease of proofs and understanding.

   We now define the final encoding enc_{MTS}, that adds the parallel process $out(d)$ with the single purpose to put a tuple d into the initially empty *Tuple Space* configuration to activate the process $\tilde{P}$.

Theorem 2. $MTS[P] \preceq MTS\text{-}mp[enc_{MTS}(P)]$

Proof. 1) *Weak similarity*
The proof is similar to that of Theorem 1. Whenever we want to simulate some step $< P, M >\overset{(I,O,R)}{\rightarrow}_{MTS}< P', M' >$ (where $|I|+|O|+|R| = z$) $\tilde{P}$ first produces z processes $rd(e).out(c)$ by subsequently performing z times $in(d)$ and $out(d)$ in line 1 of $\tilde{P}$. Then line 2 of $\tilde{P}$ is performed, i.e. the tuple e is provided and then read simultaneously by the z $rd(e).out(c)$-processes (and deleted by $in(e)$ immediately afterwards). This causes the simultaneous production of z instances of c, which are used to unlock the desired actions in $enc(P)$ in the subsequent step. As the step we want to simulate is valid in MTS and as all other actions (besides the second *internal* *wait*-action of $\tilde{P}$ that is in fact performed simultaneously) are still blocked by their prefixes $in(c)$ the step is also *maximal* and thus it is valid in $MTS\text{-}mp$.

          2) *Equality of traces*
Again, $traces(ITS[P]) \subseteq traces(MTS-mp[enc_{ITS}(P)])$ follows immediately from weak similarity. We give a sketch of the proof of the reverse inclusion:

   The process $\tilde{P}$ performs some kind of loop in which it continuously produces arbitrary numbers of instances of the tuple c (let the number of produced c's be z). In the subsequent step (due to our maximality-request) as many actions $in(c)$ as possible are performed. The actual number of these *unlockings* is restricted either by the number of enabled $in(c)$ processes (let this number be x, i.e. $(c, x) \in ea_{IN}(enc(P))$) in case $x \leq z$ or by the number of instances of c that we have produced in case $x > z$.

In the next step we perform as many unlocked actions as possible. That might be all of them, if the present *Tuple Space* configuration M allows for it, or a subset of them. In any of those cases, the same set of actions can instantly be performed in $MTS[P]$ and it simply remains to show that neither the overproduction of c's, nor the unlocking of more actions than we can simultaneously perform under M will ever enable any *observable* actions, that are not already enabled in $MTS[P]$. To show this, we define a relation R' that includes all pairs $(< P, M >, < enc_{MTS}(P), M \uplus \{d\} >)$ as well as any pair $(< P, M >, s')$ where s' is a derivation from $< enc_{MTS}(P), M \uplus \{d\} >$ by τ-steps, and show, that whenever $(s_1, s_2) \in R'$ and s_2 performs an *observable* step in $MTS\text{-}mp[enc_{MTS}(P)]$, s_1 will be ready to imitate it in $MTS[P]$.

5   Termination and Divergence Are Undecidable in MTS-mp-LinCa

5.1   RAMs

A Random Access Machine (RAM) $\hat{M}$ [SS63] consists of m registers, that may store arbitrarily large natural numbers and a program (i.e. sequence of n enumerated instructions) of the form:

$$I_1$$
$$I_2$$
$$\vdots$$
$$I_n$$

Each I_i is of one of the following types (where $1 \leq j \leq m, s \in \mathbb{N}$):

a) $i : Succ(r_j)$
b) $i : DecJump(r_j, s)$

A configuration of $\hat{M}$ can be represented by a tuple $< v_1, v_2, ..., v_m, k > \in N^{m+1}$, where v_i represents the value stored in r_i and k is the number of the command line that is to be computed next.

Let $\hat{M}$ be a RAM and $c =< v_1, v_2, ..., v_m, k >$ the present configuration of $\hat{M}$.

Then we distinguish the following three cases to describe the possible transitions:

1) $k > n$ means that $\hat{M}$ halts, because the instruction that should be computed next doesn't exist. This happens after computing instruction I_n and passing on to I_{n+1} or by simply jumping to a nonexistent instruction.

2) if $k \in \{1, ..., n\} \wedge I_k = Succ(r_j)$ then v_j and k are incremented, i.e. we increment the value in register r_j and succeed with the next instruction.

3) if $k \in \{1, ..., n\} \wedge I_k = DecJump(r_j, s)$ then $\hat{M}$ checks whether the value v_j of r_j is > 0. In that case, we decrement it and succeed with the next instruction (i.e. we increment k). Else (i.e. if $v_j = 0$) we simply jump to instruction I_s, (i.e. we assign $k := s$).

We say a RAM $\hat{M}$ with starting configuration $< v_1, v_2, ..., v_m, k >$ terminates if its (deterministic) computation reaches a configuration that belongs to case 1). If such a configuration is never reached, the computation never stops and we say that $\hat{M}$ diverges. It is well-known [M67] that the question whether a RAM diverges or terminates under a starting configuration $< 0, ..., 0, 1 >$ is undecidable for the class of all RAMs.

It is quite obvious, that for those *LinCa*-dialects that include a predicative *in*-operator $inp(t)?P\_Q$ (with semantical meaning *if* $t \in TS$ *then* P *else* Q, for details see e.g. [BGM00]) the questions of termination and divergence are undecidable (moreover those dialects are even Turing complete, as for any RAM there is an obvious deterministic encoding).

However neither the original *Linda Calculus* [CJY94] nor the discussed variant (adopted from [BGLZ04]) include such an operator and the proof that neither termination nor divergence are decidable under the *MTS-mp* semantics is more difficult.

We will define encodings *term* and *div* that map *RAMs* to *LinCa*-processes such that a *RAM* $\hat{M}$ terminates (diverges) iff the corresponding Transition System $MTS\text{-}mp[term(\hat{M})]$ ($MTS\text{-}mp[div(\hat{M})]$) terminates (diverges).

While the computation of $\hat{M}$ is completely deterministic, the transitions in the corresponding *LTS* given by our encoding may be nondeterministic. Note that every time a nondeterministic choice is made, there will be one transition describing the simulation of $\hat{M}$, and one transition that will compute something useless. For ease of explanations in Sections 5.2 and 5.3 we call the first one *right* and the second *wrong*.

To guarantee that the part of the *LTS* that is reached by a *wrong* transition (that deviates from the simulation) does not affect the question of termination (divergence) we will make sure that all traces of the corresponding subtree are infinite (finite). This approach guarantees that the whole *LTS* terminates (diverges) iff we reach a finite (an infinite) trace by keeping to the *right* transitions.

Our encodings establish a natural correspondence between *RAM* configurations and *Tuple Space* configurations, i.e. the *RAM*-configuration $< v_1, v_2, ..., v_m, k >$ belongs to the *Tuple Space* configuration $\{(r_1, v_1), ..., (r_m, v_m), p_k\}$. For a *RAM* configuration c we refer to the corresponding *Tuple Space* configuration by $TS(c)$.

Theorem 3 (RAM Simulation). *For every RAM $\hat{M}$ the Transition System $MTS\text{-}mp[term(\hat{M})]$ ($MTS\text{-}mp[div(\hat{M})]$) terminates (diverges) iff $\hat{M}$ terminates (diverges) under starting configuration $< 0, ..., 0, 1 >$.*

5.2 Termination Is Undecidable in MTS-mp-LinCa

Let *term*: $RAMs \to LinCa$ be the following mapping:

$$term(\hat{M}) = \prod_{i \in \{1, ..., n\}} [I_i] \mid !\, in(div).out(div) \mid in(loop).out(div) \mid out(p_1)$$

where the encoding $[I_i]$ of a *RAM*-Instruction in *LinCa* is:

$$[i : Succ(r_j)] \quad = \quad ! \, in(p_i).out(r_j).out(p_{i+1})$$
$$[i : DecJump(r_j, s)] = \quad ! \, in(p_i).[\, out(loop) \mid in(r_j).in(loop).out(p_{i+1})\,]$$
$$\mid \; ! \, in(p_i).[\, in(r_j).out(loop)$$
$$\mid wait.wait.out(r_j).in(loop).out(p_s)\,]$$

Note that the first (deterministic) step of $term(\hat{M})$ will be the initial $out(p_1)$. The resulting *Tuple Space* configuration is $\{p_1\} = TS(< 0, ..., 0, 1 >)$. For ease of notation, we will henceforth also denote the above defined process where $out(p_1)$ has already been executed by $term(\hat{M})$.

We now describe (given some RAM $\hat{M}$ and configuration c) the possible transition sequences from some state $< term(\hat{M}), TS(c) >$ in $MTS\text{-}mp[term(\hat{M})]$. In cases 1 and 2 the computation in our LTS is completely deterministic and performs the calculation of $\hat{M}$. In case 3 the transition sequence that simulates $DecJump(r_j,s)$ includes nondeterministic choice. As described in Subsection 5.1 performing only *right* choices (cases 3.1.1 and 4.1.1) results in an exact simulation of $\hat{M}$'s transition $c \to_{\hat{M}} c'$, i.e. the transition sequence leads to the corresponding state $< term(\hat{M}), TS(c') >$. Performing at least one *wrong* choice (cases 3.1.2, 3.2, 4.1.2 and 4.2) causes the subprocess $! \, in(div).out(div)$ to be activated, thus assuring that any computation in the corresponding subtree diverges (denoted by $\rightsquigarrow$). (In this case other subprocesses are not of concern because they can't interfere by removing the tuple div, so we substitute these subprocesses by "...".)

1. $k > n$, i.e. $\hat{M}$ has terminated. Then $<term(\hat{M}), TS(c)>$ is totally blocked.

2. $k \in \{1, ..., n\} \wedge I_k = k : Succ(r_j)$, then $\hat{M}$ increments both r_j and k. The corresponding transition sequence in $MTS\text{-}mp[term(\hat{M})]$ is:
$$<term(\hat{M}), TS(c)>$$
$$\to \; <term(\hat{M}) \mid out(r_j).out(p_{k+1}), TS(c) \setminus \{p_k\}>$$
$$\to \; <term(\hat{M}) \mid out(p_{k+1}), TS(c) \setminus \{p_k\} \uplus \{r_j\}>$$
$$\to \; <term(\hat{M}), TS(c) \setminus \{p_k\} \uplus \{r_j, p_{k+1}\}>$$
$$= \; <term(\hat{M}), TS(c')>$$

3. $k \in \{1, ..., n\} \wedge I_k = k : DecJump(r_j, s) \wedge v_j \neq 0$, then $\hat{M}$ decrements r_j and increments k. The possible transition sequences in $MTS\text{-}mp[term(\hat{M})]$ are:
$$<term(\hat{M}), TS(c)>^{\;nondet.}\to$$
   3.1 **right**:
$$<term(\hat{M}) \mid out(loop) \mid in(r_j).in(loop).out(p_{k+1}), TS(c) \setminus \{p_k\}>$$
$$\to \; <term(\hat{M}) \mid in(loop).out(p_{k+1}), TS(c) \setminus \{p_k, r_j\} \uplus \{loop\}>^{\;nondet.}\to$$

      3.1.1 **right - right**:
$$<term(\hat{M}) \mid out(p_{k+1}), TS(c) \setminus \{p_k, r_j\}>$$
$$\to \; <term(\hat{M}), TS(c) \setminus \{p_k, r_j\} \uplus \{p_{k+1}\}>$$
$$= \; <term(\hat{M}), TS(c')>$$

      3.1.2 **right - wrong**:
$$<term(\hat{M}) \mid in(loop).out(p_{k+1}), TS(c) \setminus \{p_k, r_j\} \uplus \{loop\}>$$
$$\to \; <... \mid out(div), TS(c) \setminus \{p_k, r_j\}>\rightsquigarrow$$

*3.2 **wrong***:

$<term(\hat{M}) \mid in(r_j).out(loop) \mid wait^2.out(r_j).in(loop).out(p_s), TS(c) \setminus \{p_k\}>$
$\rightarrow <term(\hat{M}) \mid out(loop) \mid wait.out(r_j).in(loop).out(p_s), TS(c) \setminus \{p_k, r_j\}>$
$\rightarrow <term(\hat{M}) \mid out(r_j).in(loop).out(p_s), TS(c) \setminus \{p_k, r_j\} \uplus \{loop\}>$
$\rightarrow <... \mid out(div), TS(c) \setminus \{p_k\}> \rightsquigarrow$

4. $k \in \{1, ..., n\} \wedge I_k = k : DecJump(r_j, s) \wedge v_j = 0$, then $\hat{M}$ assigns $k := s$
$<term(\hat{M}), TS(c)>^{\,nondet.}_{\rightarrow}$

*4.1 **right***:

$\rightarrow<term(\hat{M}) \mid in(r_j).out(loop) \mid wait^2.out(r_j).in(loop).out(p_s), TS(c) \setminus \{p_k\}>$
$\rightarrow<term(\hat{M}) \mid in(r_j).out(loop) \mid wait.out(r_j).in(loop).out(p_s), TS(c) \setminus \{p_k\}>$
$\rightarrow<term(\hat{M}) \mid in(r_j).out(loop) \mid out(r_j).in(loop).out(p_s), TS(c) \setminus \{p_k\}>$
$\rightarrow<term(\hat{M}) \mid in(r_j).out(loop) \mid in(loop).out(p_s), TS(c) \setminus \{p_k\} \uplus \{r_j\}>$
$\rightarrow<term(\hat{M}) \mid out(loop) \mid in(loop).out(p_s), TS(c) \setminus \{p_k\}>$
$\rightarrow<term(\hat{M}) \mid in(loop).out(p_s), TS(c) \setminus \{p_k\} \uplus \{loop\}>^{\,nondet.}_{\rightarrow}$

*4.1.1 **right - right***:

$<term(\hat{M}) \mid out(p_s), TS(c) \setminus \{p_k\}>$
$\rightarrow <term(\hat{M}), TS(c) \setminus \{p_k\} \uplus \{p_s\}>$
$= <term(\hat{M}), TS(c')>$

*4.1.2 **right - wrong***:

$<... \mid out(div), TS(c) \setminus \{p_k\}> \rightsquigarrow$

*4.2 **wrong***:

$<term(\hat{M}) \mid out(loop) \mid in(r_j).in(loop).out(p_{k+1}), TS(c) \setminus \{p_k\}>$
$\rightarrow <term(\hat{M}) \mid in(r_j).in(loop).out(p_{k+1}), TS(c) \setminus \{p_k\} \uplus \{loop\}>$
$\rightarrow <... \mid out(div), TS(c) \setminus \{p_k\}> \rightsquigarrow$

5.3   Divergence Is Undecidable in MTS-mp-LinCa

Let div: $RAMs \rightarrow LinCa$ be the following mapping:

$$div(\hat{M}) = \prod_{i\in\{1,...,n\}} [I_i] \mid in(flow) \mid out(p_1)$$

where the encoding $[I_i]$ of a RAM-Instruction in $LinCa$ is:

$$[i : Succ(r_j)] \quad = \quad !\, in(p_i).out(r_j).out(p_{i+1})$$
$$[i : DecJump(r_j, s)] = \quad !\, in(p_i).in(r_j).out(p_{i+1})$$
$$\mid \; !\, in(p_i).[\, in(r_j).out(flow)$$
$$\mid wait^2.out(r_j).in(flow).out(p_s)\,]$$

Note that the first (deterministic) step of $div(\hat{M})$ will be the initial $out(p_1)$. The resulting *Tuple Space* configuration is $\{p_1\} = TS(< 0, ..., 0, 1 >)$. For ease of notation, we will henceforth also denote the above defined process where $out(p_1)$ has already been executed by $div(\hat{M})$.

We now describe (given some RAM $\hat{M}$ and configuration c) the possible transition sequences from some state $< div(\hat{M}), TS(c) >$ in $MTS\text{-}mp[div(\hat{M})]$. In cases 1 and 2 the computation in our LTS is completely deterministic and performs the calculation of $\hat{M}$. In case 3 the transition sequence that simulates $DecJump(r_j,s)$ includes nondeterministic choice. As described in Subsection 5.1 performing only $right$ choices (cases 3.1 and 4.1.1) results in an exact simulation of $\hat{M}$s transition $c \to_{\hat{M}} c'$, i.e. the transition sequence leads to the corresponding state $< div(\hat{M}), TS(c') >$. Performing at least one $wrong$ choice (cases 3.2, 4.1.2 and 4.2) causes the tuple $flow$ to be removed from the $Tuple\ Space$ configuration, thus leading to some state $< P, M >$ where P is totally blocked under M, denoted by $< P, M > \nrightarrow$. For cases 1 and 2 see preceding subsection.

3. $k \in \{1,...,n\} \wedge I_k = k : DecJump(r_j, s) \wedge v_j \neq 0$, then $\hat{M}$ decrements r_j and
   increments k. The possible transition sequences in $MTS\text{-}mp[div(\hat{M})]$ are:
   $<div(\hat{M}), TS(c)>^{nondet.} \to$

   3.1 right:
   $<div(\hat{M}) \mid in(r_j).out(p_{k+1}), TS(c) \setminus \{p_k\}>$
   $\to <div(\hat{M}) \mid out(p_{k+1}), TS(c) \setminus \{p_k, r_j\}>$
   $\to <div(\hat{M}), TS(c) \setminus \{p_k, r_j\} \uplus \{p_{k+1}\}>$
   $= <div(\hat{M}), TS(c')>$

   3.2 wrong:
   $<div(\hat{M}) \mid in(r_j).out(flow) \mid wait^2.out(r_j).in(flow).out(p_s), TS(c) \setminus \{p_k\}>$
   $\to <div(\hat{M}) \mid out(flow) \mid wait.out(r_j).in(flow).out(p_s), TS(c) \setminus \{p_k, r_j\}>$
   $\to <div(\hat{M}) \mid out(r_j).in(flow).out(p_s), TS(c) \setminus \{p_k, r_j\} \uplus \{flow\}>$
   $\to <\Pi\ [I_i] \mid in(flow).out(p_s), TS(c) \setminus \{p_k\}> \nrightarrow$

4. $k \in \{1,...,n\} \wedge I_k = k : DecJump(r_j, s) \wedge v_j = 0$, then $\hat{M}$ assigns $k := s$
   $<div(\hat{M}), TS(c)>^{nondet.} \to$

   4.1 right:
   $<div(\hat{M}) \mid in(r_j).out(flow) \mid wait^2.out(r_j).in(flow).out(p_s), TS(c) \setminus \{p_k\}>$
   $\to <div(\hat{M}) \mid in(r_j).out(flow) \mid wait.out(r_j).in(flow).out(p_s), TS(c) \setminus \{p_k\}>$
   $\to <div(\hat{M}) \mid in(r_j).out(flow) \mid out(r_j).in(flow).out(p_s), TS(c) \setminus \{p_k\}>$
   $\to <div(\hat{M}) \mid in(r_j).out(flow) \mid in(flow).out(p_s), TS(c) \setminus \{p_k\} \uplus \{r_j\}>$
   $\to <div(\hat{M}) \mid out(flow) \mid in(flow).out(p_s), TS(c) \setminus \{p_k\}>$
   $\to <div(\hat{M}) \mid in(flow).out(p_s), TS(c) \setminus \{p_k\} \uplus \{flow\}>^{nondet.} \to$

   4.1.1 right - right:
   $<div(\hat{M}) \mid out(p_s), TS(c) \setminus \{p_k\}>$
   $\to <div(\hat{M}), TS(c) \setminus \{p_k\} \uplus \{p_s\}>$
   $= <div(\hat{M}), TS(c')>$

   4.1.2 right - wrong:
   $<\Pi\ [I_i] \mid in(flow).out(p_s), TS(c) \setminus \{p_k\}> \nrightarrow$

4.2 wrong:
$<div(\hat{M}) \mid in(r_j).out(p_{k+1}), TS(c) \setminus \{p_k\}> \nrightarrow$

6 Conclusion

In order to guarantee maximum utilization of processing units in a MIMD setting, we modified Ciancarini's MTS-semantics for LinCa. We restricted the valid paths of the Multi Step Transition System to those in which in each step there are performed as many actions as possible. Pursuing the aim of maximizing the resource utilization we found it astounding that the restriction to paths satisfying the maximum progress condition causes a change in expressiveness. The fact that a RAM can be simulated (nondeterministically) is non-trivial for two reasons: First, we are not able to implement an if-then-else construct (or at least there is no obvious way to do that) without the usage of *predicative* tuple space operators. Second, we do not even allow for a *choice*-operator and as a consequence we have to "neutralize" remaining process-artifacts in order to prevent them from interfering with the calculation at some time in the future.

We also discussed the relation between our semantics and ITS and MTS, respectively. The outcome of our analysis is that in all future approaches of maximizing the resource utilization for LinCa in a multiple-step scenario, one has to take into account that - unpleasantly - there are programs for which termination is undecidable. Nevertheless the existence of such programs does not mean that demanding maximum progress is not meaningful or useless.

References

[BGLZ04] Mario Bravetti, Roberto Gorrieri, Roberto Lucchi, Gianluigi Zavattaro. *Adding Quantitative Information to Tuple Space Coordination Languages*, Bologna, Italy, July 04.

[BGM00] Frank S. de Boer, Maurizio Gabbrielli, Maria Chiara Meo, *A Timed Linda Language*, Lecture Notes in Computer Science, Volume 1906, Pages 299-304, Jan 2000.

[BGZ00] Nadia Busi, Roberto Gorrieri, Gianluigi Zavattaro. *On the Expressiveness of Linda Coordination Primitives* Information and Computation Vol. 156(1-2), p.90-121, January 2000.

[BZ05] Nadia Busi, Gianluigi Zavattaro. *Prioritized and Parallel Reactions in Shared Data Space Coordination Languages*, COORD05. Namur, Belgium. LNCS 3454, p.204-219, 2005.

[CJY94] Paolo Ciancarini , Keld K. Jensen , Daniel Yankelevich. *On the Operational Semantics of a Coordination Language* Selected papers from the ECOOP'94 Workshop on Models and Languages for Coordination of Parallelism and Distribution, Object-Based Models and Languages for Concurrent Systems, p.77-106, 1994.

[M67] M.L.Minksy - *Computation: finite and infinite machines*, Prentice Hall, Englewoof Cliffs, 1967.

[SS63] J.C. Sheperdson, J.E. Sturgis. *Computability of recursive functions*. Journal of the ACM, Vol. 10, p. 217-255, 1963.

A Topological Approach of the Web Classification

Gabriel Ciobanu[1,2] and Dănuţ Rusu[1,3]

[1] Romanian Academy, Institute of Computer Science, Iaşi
[2] "A.I.Cuza" University of Iaşi, Faculty of Computer Science
gabriel@iit.tuiasi.ro
[3] "A.I.Cuza" University of Iaşi, Faculty of Mathematics
drusu@uaic.ro

Abstract. In this paper we study some topological aspects related to the important operations of searching and classification over the Web. Classification is dictated by some criteria, and these criteria can be defined as a classification operator. An interesting problem is to prove the existence of a stable classification with respect to a certain operator. In this context we provide a topological approach to describe the structure of the web based on the trips given by the links of the web documents, and present various topologies defined over the Web. Some results regarding the topological properties as connectivity, density and separation are presented. The Alexandrov topology plays a particular role, and we have a certain equivalence between this topology and the classification process.

1 Introduction

The World-Wide-Web is a large collection of accessible web pages. It is also a fast growing network. The web is becoming an important resource in our lives, and we use it mainly for finding information and communication. Nowadays our computers are used more for surfing the web in order to find desired information than to execute programs computing scientific or business information. This is done by direct navigation, where the users go directly to the web page they wish to see. Another possibility is given by *surfing* or navigating by following the links. In this case the user may start from a home page of a site, and then click on links following the direction given by link text. It is also possible to use a search engine, where the search engine holds the key to find the web pages the user wishes to see.

We consider the Web as a directed graph, with vertices represented by documents and arcs corresponding to the links between them. Due to its dynamics, namely that new web pages and links are created, we consider the World-Wide-Web as having potentially an infinite number of documents. The set of the documents at a certain moment is an *instance* of the Web. An instance is always finite. The dynamics of the Web can be described by its instances and their evolution in a discrete time. As a consequence, the Web can be interpreted as

K. Barkaoui, A. Cavalcanti, and A. Cerone (Eds.): ICTAC 2006, LNCS 4281, pp. 80–92, 2006.

a countable space. An important practical operation over this space is given by searching (search engine). Web searching is based on indexing. Due to a high dynamics, the Web indexing should be repeated periodically. We introduce here some theoretical aspects related to these important operations over the Web. Web indexing can be simplified by classification. Classification is dictated by some criteria. In order to define a classification, we should associate a set to each document, namely the set representing its class. Each document belongs to its class. Moreover, if a document x belongs to the class of a document y, then the class of x is a subset of the class of y. For instance, if x is a document containing information regarding differential geometry, and y is a document containing information regarding geometry (in general), then the class of x (differential geometry) is included in the class of y (general geometry). Classification criteria can be defined as a classification operator. Such an operator transforms usually a classification into a finer classification, i.e., a set of documents into a smaller set of documents. We say that a classification is stable with respect to a classification operator if the operator does not change it anymore. An interesting problem is to prove the existence of the stable classifications with respect to a certain operator.

Since we can associate an Alexandrov topology to each classification in a one-to-one manner, the study of these topologies is relevant to the Web classification. We introduce a preorder over the Web space given by the links between Web pages. For a given web document a, an important set denoted by In_a is the set of the documents having a link to a. Its cardinal could be a good indicator regarding the importance or the relevance of a. It is easy to note that $f(a) = In_a$ is a classification. We study this classification and the topological properties of the Web induced by it.

2   Web Classifications

Let $\mathcal{W}$ be the Web space.

Definition 1. *Let $f : \mathcal{W} \to \mathcal{P}(\mathcal{W})$ be a function.*

1. *The function f is called reflective if $x \in f(x)$, for all $x \in \mathcal{W}$.*
2. *The function f is called hereditary if $x \in f(y)$ implies $f(x) \subseteq f(y)$.*
3. *The function f is a (Web) classification of $\mathcal{W}$ if it is reflective and hereditary.*

If f is a Web classification, then $f(x)$ is called the class of the document x, and x is a generator of the class $f(x)$. A Web classification f is called *unambiguous* if every class has a unique generator. Therefore, a Web classification f is unambiguous iff f is injective.

Proposition 1. *A function $f : \mathcal{W} \to \mathcal{P}(\mathcal{W})$ is a classification iff ($x \in f(y)$ is equivalent with $f(x) \subseteq f(y)$).*

We denote by $\mathcal{C}(\mathcal{W})$ the set of all Web classifications, and by $\mathcal{C}_0(\mathcal{W})$ the set of all unambiguous Web classifications. We can define a relation over $\mathcal{C}(\mathcal{W})$ by

$f \leq g$ iff $f(x) \subseteq g(x)$ for all $x \in \mathcal{W}$. This is a partial order on $\mathcal{C}(\mathcal{W})$. Let $u : \mathcal{W} \to \mathcal{P}(\mathcal{W})$ defined by $u(x) = \{x\}$ for all $x \in \mathcal{W}$. Then u is the least element of the poset $(\mathcal{C}(\mathcal{W}), \leq)$. If $A \subseteq \mathcal{C}(\mathcal{W})$, then the function $g : \mathcal{W} \to \mathcal{P}(\mathcal{W})$ defined by $g(x) = \cap_{f \in A} f(x)$ for all $x \in \mathcal{W}$ is the infimum of the set A.

Definition 2.

1. A *Web classification* f is called *stable relative to the operator* $T : \mathcal{C}(\mathcal{W}) \to \mathcal{C}(\mathcal{W})$ if $T(f) = f$.
2. A *monotone operator* $T : (\mathcal{C}(\mathcal{W}), \leq) \to (\mathcal{C}(\mathcal{W}), \leq)$ is called *classification operator*.

Since every subset of $(\mathcal{C}(\mathcal{W}), \leq)$ has infimum, by using the fixpoint theorem of Knaster-Tarski[9], we get the following result:

Theorem 1. *If T is a classification operator, then there is a stable classification $f \in \mathcal{C}(\mathcal{W})$ with respect to the operator T. More, $f(x) = \cap_{g \in \mathcal{C}(\mathcal{W}), T(g) \leq g} g(x)$ for all $x \in \mathcal{W}$.*

3 Alexandrov Topology Associated to a Classification

In this section we devote a particular attention to the Alexandrov topology. More details on Alexandrov topologies are in [1,8].

Let $f : \mathcal{W} \to \mathcal{P}(\mathcal{W})$ be a function. We define the relation $\leq_f = \{(x, y) \in \mathcal{W} \times \mathcal{W} \mid x \in f(y)\}$. f is reflective iff $\leq_f$ is reflective, and f is hereditary iff $\leq_f$ is transitive. Also, if f is a classification, then f is unambiguous iff $\leq_f$ is anti-symmetric. Therefore defining a classification over $\mathcal{W}$ is equivalent to defining a preorder over the same space. Moreover, defining an unambiguous classification over $\mathcal{W}$ is equivalent to defining an order relation over $\mathcal{W}$. Each preorder corresponds one-to-one to an Alexandrov topology, and each partial order corresponds one-to-one to a T_0 Alexandrov topology [1]. We can establish similar correspondences between classifications and Alexandrov topologies. Then we can study the Web space using the topological terms of connectivity, compactness, density, continuity, etc., and we can use notions of neighbourhood, closure, frontier, open and close sets. For instance, the monotone operators over $(\mathcal{W}, \leq_f)$ are continuous functions with respect to the Alexandrov topology associated to f. We remind here some elementary notions.

A topology on the space $\mathcal{W}$ is a family τ of subsets of $\mathcal{W}$ such that:

1. $\emptyset, \mathcal{W} \in \tau$,
2. for each family $\{D_i\}_{i \in I} \subset \tau$ we have $\cup_{i \in I} D_i \in \tau$,
3. if $D_1, D_2 \in \tau$, then $D_1 \cap D_2 \in \tau$.

The sets of a topology τ are called τ-open sets [5]. A set $A \subset \mathcal{W}$ is τ-closed iff its complement $\mathcal{W} \setminus A$ is τ-open. A topology τ on $\mathcal{W}$ is called *Alexandrov topology* if the family of the τ-closed sets forms a topology. The family of the τ-closed sets forms also an Alexandrov topology called *the dual of the topology τ*.

A topology can be defined directly by means of its open sets, or it can be defined by means of a neighbourhood operator. A neighbourhood operator is a function $\mathcal{V} : \mathcal{W} \to \mathcal{P}(\mathcal{P}(\mathcal{W}))$ such that $\mathcal{V}(x)$ holds the following conditions for all $x \in \mathcal{W}$:

1. if $V \in \mathcal{V}(x)$, then $x \in V$;
2. if $V_1, V_2 \in \mathcal{V}(x)$, then $V_1 \cap V_2 \in \mathcal{V}(x)$;
3. if $V \in \mathcal{V}(x)$ and $V \subset U$, then $U \in \mathcal{V}(x)$;
4. for all $V \in \mathcal{V}(x)$, there is $W \in \mathcal{V}(x)$ such that $V \in \mathcal{V}(y)$ for all $y \in W$.

If τ is a topology on $\mathcal{W}$, then $\mathcal{V}_\tau : \mathcal{W} \to \mathcal{P}(\mathcal{P}(\mathcal{W}))$ defined by $\mathcal{V}_\tau(x) = \{V \subset \mathcal{W} \mid \exists D \in \tau$ such that $x \in D \subset V\}$ is a neighbourhood operator on $\mathcal{W}$. If $\mathcal{V}$ is a neighbourhood operator on $\mathcal{W}$, then $\tau_\mathcal{V} = \{D \subset \mathcal{W} \mid D \neq \emptyset$ and $D \in \mathcal{V}(x), \forall x \in D\} \cup \{\emptyset\}$ is a topology on $\mathcal{W}$. The notions of topology and neighbourhood operator are equivalent because $\tau_{\mathcal{V}_\tau} = \tau$ and $\mathcal{V}_{\tau_\mathcal{V}} = \mathcal{V}$ (see [2,5]).

We consider a function $f : \mathcal{W} \to \mathcal{P}(\mathcal{W})$, and define two topologies related to the classification process.

First we consider a classification $f : \mathcal{W} \to \mathcal{P}(\mathcal{W})$. Then the function $\mathcal{V}_f : \mathcal{W} \to \mathcal{P}(\mathcal{P}(\mathcal{W}))$ defined by $\mathcal{V}_f(x) = \{V \subseteq \mathcal{W} \mid f(x) \subseteq V\}$ for all $x \in \mathcal{W}$ is a neighbourhood operator on $\mathcal{W}$. Let $\tau_f = \{D \subset \mathcal{W} \mid D \neq \emptyset$ and $D \in \mathcal{V}_f(x), \forall x \in D\} \cup \{\emptyset\}$ be the topology generated by $\mathcal{V}_f$. Since every document $x \in \mathcal{W}$ has a minimal neighbourhood, it results that τ_f is an Alexandrov topology [1]. Let $\mathcal{A}(\mathcal{W})$ the set of the Alexandrov topologies on the space $\mathcal{W}$, and $\mathcal{A}_0(\mathcal{W})$ the set of the T_0 Alexandrov topologies on $\mathcal{W}$. Then we have:

Theorem 2.

1. $\varphi : (\mathcal{C}(\mathcal{W}), \leq) \to (\mathcal{A}(\mathcal{W}), \supseteq)$ defined by $\varphi(f) = \tau_f$ is a bijective and mono-tone operator;
2. $\varphi : (\mathcal{C}_0(\mathcal{W}), \leq) \to (\mathcal{A}_0(\mathcal{W}), \supseteq)$ defined by $\varphi(f) = \tau_f$ is a bijective and mono-tone operator.

Consequently, the study of Alexandrov topologies on $\mathcal{W}$ becomes relevant for the classifications and search process over the Web.

The second topology is built starting from a reflective function $f : \mathcal{W} \to \mathcal{P}(\mathcal{W})$. Then we can consider an extension $F : \mathcal{P}(\mathcal{W}) \to \mathcal{P}(\mathcal{W})$ defined by $F(A) = \cup_{x \in A} f(x)$ for all $A \in \mathcal{P}(\mathcal{W})$.

Proposition 2. $F : \mathcal{P}(\mathcal{W}) \to \mathcal{P}(\mathcal{W})$ defined above has the following properties:

1. $A \subseteq F(A)$, for all $A \in \mathcal{P}(\mathcal{W})$;
2. if $A \subseteq B$, then $F(A) \subseteq F(B)$;
3. $F(\emptyset) = \emptyset$, and $F(\mathcal{W}) = \mathcal{W}$;
4. $F(A \cup B) = F(A) \cup F(B)$, for all $A, B \in \mathcal{P}(\mathcal{W})$.

From these properties it follows that $\tau^f = \{D \subseteq \mathcal{W} \mid F(\mathcal{W} \setminus D) = \mathcal{W} \setminus D\}$ is a topology on $\mathcal{W}$. If $cl^f(A)$ is the τ^f-closure of A, then $F(A) \subseteq cl^f(A)$, for all $A \in \mathcal{P}(\mathcal{W})$. If A is a τ^f-closed set, then $F(A) = cl^f(A) = A$. It is easy to prove that if f is a classification on $\mathcal{W}$, then $F(F(A)) = F(A)$ for all $A \in \mathcal{P}(\mathcal{W})$, and then $F(A) = cl^f(A)$ for all $A \in \mathcal{P}(\mathcal{W})$. This means that τ^f is an Alexandrov topology, and it is the dual of the topology τ_f. Indeed, if $D \in \tau_f$, then $f(x) \subseteq D$ for all $x \in D$, and we have $D = \cup_{x \in D}\{x\} \subseteq \cup_{x \in D}f(x) \subseteq D$. Therefore $D = F(D)$, i.e., $W \setminus D \in \tau^f$.

4   Link-Based Classifications of the Web

In this section we introduce and study the Web classifications based on the links between the documents. The logic behind the classification based on links is given by the related contents of two linked documents. Since such a content-based relationship exists, the classifications based on links represent interesting candidates for our approach. We would also like to sustain formally the idea that the Web has a special kind of computability defined by travelling in search of information. This computability is rather content-oriented. We look at two entities composing the Web: the notion of page (document), and that of link. Especially the latter is to be looked at more carefully, since it is the one that provides the Web topologies. This section defines some topologies over the Web, making possible a formal description of the Web connectivity, topological density, and separation.

In the link-based ranking of the web pages there are two important algorithms: PageRank and the authority measures of the Hyperlink-Induced Topic Search (HITS) algorithm. PageRank is based on the probability of a random surfer to be visiting a page. This probability is modelled with two actions: the chance of the surfer to get bored and jump randomly to any page in the Web (with uniform probability), or to choose randomly one of the links in the page. This defines a Markov chain, that converges to a permanent state, where the probabilities are defined as $PR_i = \frac{q}{T} + (1-q)\sum_{j=1,\; j \neq i}^{k} \frac{PR_{m_j}}{L_{m_j}}$, where T is the total number of Web pages, q is the probability of getting bored (typically 0.15), m_j with $j \in (1,\ldots,k)$ are the pages that point to page i, and L_j is the number of outgoing links in page j. Consistently with PageRank algorithm, we focus on the process of surfing following the links in the page, and considering as relevant the links pointing to a page as well as the outgoing links in a page.

We consider the collection W of all pages available on-line. Due to its strongly dynamic structure, we consider W as being a potentially infinite set (somehow similar to the set of natural numbers). We define the links by a binary relation $\hookrightarrow : W \longrightarrow W$ called *points-to*; by $a \hookrightarrow b$ we denote that a document a contains a link to a document b. $\hookrightarrow$ is extended to the smallest preorder $\rightsquigarrow$ containing $\hookrightarrow$. We consider some topologies over W which are induced by this preorder $\rightsquigarrow$.

Thinking now in terms of Web navigation, we define first a surfing trip over the Web documents.

Definition 3. *Let $a, b \in W$ and $n \geq 0$. A n-trip from document a to document b is a function $f : \{1, ..., n+1\} \rightarrow W$ such that $a = f(1) \hookrightarrow f(2) \hookrightarrow \ldots \hookrightarrow f(n+1) = b$. In this case n is called the length of the trip, and it is denoted by $\lambda(f)$. The image of f is denoted by $Im(f)$.*

0-trips $f : \{1\} \rightarrow \{a\}$ with $f(1) = a$ are used as a notation for a page a. We denote by L_{ab} the set of all trips from document a to document b.

Definition 4. *Let $a, b \in \mathcal{W}$.*

1. *Let $k \geq 0$. We say that a is k-connected with b if there is a k-trip from a to b. We denote this by $a \leadsto_k b$.*
2. *We say that a is connected with b if there is a $k \geq 0$ such that a is k-connected with b. We denote this by $a \leadsto b$.*
3. *We say that a is biconnected with b if a is connected with b and b is connected with a; this is denoted by $a \longleftrightarrow b$.*

Proposition 3. *The relation $\leadsto$ is a preorder on $\mathcal{W}$ called the trip preorder. Moreover, $\longleftrightarrow$ is an equivalence over $\mathcal{W}$.*

Let $a \in \mathcal{W}$, and $A \subseteq \mathcal{W}$. We have the following notations:

$Out_a = \{x \in \mathcal{W} \mid a \leadsto x\}$,
$In_a = \{x \in \mathcal{W} \mid x \leadsto a\}$,
$Net_a = In_a \cup Out_a = \{x \in \mathcal{W} \mid a \leadsto x \text{ or } x \leadsto a\}$,
$R_a = In_a \cap Out_a = \{x \in \mathcal{W} \mid a \longleftrightarrow x\}$ – the *center* of Net_a,
$Out_A = \cup_{a \in A} Out_a$, $In_A = \cup_{a \in A} In_a$,
$Net_A = In_A \cup Out_A = \cup_{a \in A} Net_a$, $R_A = \cup_{a \in A} R_a$,
$I_a = \{(x, y) \in \mathcal{W} \times \mathcal{W} \mid y \leadsto a \Rightarrow x \leadsto a\}$,
$O_a = \{(x, y) \in \mathcal{W} \times \mathcal{W} \mid a \leadsto y \Rightarrow a \leadsto x\}$,
$\triangle = \{(x, x) \mid x \in \mathcal{W}\}$.

I_a and O_a define certain similarities regarding the contents of the documents based on the common links. We call both of them as content-based surroundings (entourages in topology, according to the notion introduced by Bourbaki).

Proposition 4. *Let $a, b \in \mathcal{W}$. Then we have*
1. *$b \in In_a$ iff $a \in Out_b$;*
2. *if $b \in In_a$, then $In_b \subseteq In_a$, and $Out_a \subseteq Out_b$;*
3. *if $b \in Out_a$, then $Out_b \subseteq Out_a$, and $In_a \subseteq In_b$;*
4. *if $b \in R_a$, then $In_b = In_a, Out_a = Out_b, Net_b = Net_a$;*
5. *$I_a = (\mathcal{W} \times (\mathcal{W} \backslash In_a)) \cup (In_a \times \mathcal{W})$;*
6. *$(\mathcal{W} \times \mathcal{W}) \backslash I_a = (\mathcal{W} \backslash In_a) \times In_a$;*
7. *$O_a = (\mathcal{W} \times (\mathcal{W} \backslash Out_a)) \cup (Out_a \times \mathcal{W})$;*
8. *$(\mathcal{W} \times \mathcal{W}) \backslash O_a = (\mathcal{W} \backslash Out_a) \times Out_a$;*
9. *$\triangle \subset O_a \cap I_a$;*
10. *O_a and I_a are transitive relations.*

Let $U \subset \mathcal{W} \times \mathcal{W}$, and $x \in \mathcal{W}$. We denote by $U[x]$ the section $\{y \in \mathcal{W} \mid (x, y) \in U\}$.

Proposition 5.
1. *$x \leadsto y \Rightarrow I_a[y] \subseteq I_a[x]$, and $O_a[x] \subseteq O_a[y]$, $\forall a \in \mathcal{W}$.*
2. *$x \leadsto y$ iff $y \in I_y[x]$ iff $x \in O_x[y]$.*

We consider an instance of the Web space, and use the notations $\preceq_i = \cap_{a \in \mathcal{W}} I_a$, and $\preceq_o = \cap_{a \in \mathcal{W}} O_a$.

As we already mentioned, we use an infinite $\mathcal{W}$ to express the dynamics of the Web. Here we define some operators. Let $\mathcal{V}_i : \mathcal{W} \to \mathcal{P}(\mathcal{P}(\mathcal{W}))$ given by $\mathcal{V}_i(x) = \{V \subset \mathcal{W} \mid$ there is a finite subset A of $\mathcal{W}$ such that $\cap_{a \in A} I_a[x] \subseteq V\}$. In a similar way, we can define $\mathcal{V}_o : \mathcal{W} \to \mathcal{P}(\mathcal{P}(\mathcal{W}))$ by $\mathcal{V}_o(x) = \{V \subset \mathcal{W} \mid$ there is a finite subset A of $\mathcal{W}$ such that $\cap_{a \in A} O_a[x] \subseteq V\}$.

Proposition 6. $\mathcal{V}_i$ and $\mathcal{V}_o$ are neighbourhood operators over $\mathcal{W}$.

Let $\tau_i = \{D \subset \mathcal{W} \mid D \neq \emptyset$ and $D \in \mathcal{V}_i(x), \forall x \in D\} \cup \{\emptyset\}$ be the topology generated by $\mathcal{V}_i$, and $\tau_o = \{D \subset \mathcal{W} \mid D \neq \emptyset$ and $D \in \mathcal{V}_o(x), \forall x \in D\} \cup \{\emptyset\}$ be the topology generated by $\mathcal{V}_o$. We call τ_i the *in-topology*, and τ_o the *out-topology*. It is easy to note that these topologies are dual, and the results in one of them are obtained by duality from the results in the other. Consequently we can restrict our study to only one of them, namely to τ_i. If $A \subseteq \mathcal{W}$, then $int_i A$, $cl_i A$, $Fr_i A$ are respectively the interior, the closure, and the frontier of A with respect to τ_i.

Theorem 3. Let $x, y \in \mathcal{W}$.

1. If $x \rightsquigarrow y$, then $\mathcal{V}_i(x) \subseteq \mathcal{V}_i(y)$.
2. $In_a = cl_i\{a\}$ for all $a \in \mathcal{W}$.
3. $x \rightsquigarrow y$ iff $x \preceq_i y$ iff $y \preceq_o x$ (expressing that $\preceq_i$ and $\preceq_o$ are dual).

Proof. 1. If $x \rightsquigarrow y$, then $I_a[y] \subseteq I_a[x]$ for all $a \in \mathcal{W}$. If $V \in \mathcal{V}_i(x)$, then there is a finite subset A of $\mathcal{W}$ such that $\cap_{a \in A} I_a[x] \subseteq V$. Since $\cap_{a \in A} I_a[y] \subseteq \cap_{a \in A} I_a[x]$, we have $\cap_{a \in A} I_a[y] \subseteq V$, and then $V \in \mathcal{V}_i(y)$. Therefore $\mathcal{V}_i(x) \subseteq \mathcal{V}_i(y)$.
2. If $x \in In_a$, then $x \rightsquigarrow a$. So $\mathcal{V}_i(x) \subseteq \mathcal{V}_i(a)$. Then $a \in V$, for all $V \in \mathcal{V}_i(x)$. Therefore $x \in cl_i\{a\}$. Now, let $x \in cl_i\{a\}$. Then $a \in I_b[x]$, for all $b \in \mathcal{W}$. So $a \in I_a[x]$. Then $x \rightsquigarrow a$, that is $x \in In_a$.
3. We have $x \rightsquigarrow y$ iff $x \in cl_i\{y\}$ iff $y \in I_a[x]$, for all $a \in \mathcal{W}$. Therefore $x \rightsquigarrow y$ iff $(x, y) \in \preceq_{\mathcal{I}}$, that is $x \preceq_{\mathcal{I}} y$. The equivalence $x \rightsquigarrow y$ iff $y \preceq_o x$ is proved analogous.

Consequently, $\preceq_i [x] = Out_x$, and $\preceq_o [x] = In_x$, for all $x \in \mathcal{W}$. Hence $\preceq_i [x]$ is a τ_o-closed set, and $\preceq_o [x]$ is a τ_i-closed set. According to Proposition 4(2), we can have a classification $f_i : \mathcal{W} \to \mathcal{P}(\mathcal{W})$ defined by $f_i(a) = In_a$, as well as a classification $f_o : \mathcal{W} \to \mathcal{P}(\mathcal{W})$ defined by $f_o(a) = Out_a$. We study the Alexandrov topologies associated to these classifications. In fact, we have $\tau_i = \tau_{f_o}$ and $\tau_o = \tau_{f_i}$. We remark that the specialization preorder (i.e., $x \leq y$ iff $x \in cl_i(\{y\})$) is identical to the trip preorder. τ_i topology is not the only topology satisfying this identity. The coarsest topology over $\mathcal{W}$ with this property is the upper topology, i.e., the topology within which all closed sets are the sets In_a, for all $a \in \mathcal{W}$. The finest topology with this property is the Alexandrov topology, i.e., the topology within which all closed sets are the sets In_A, for all $A \subseteq \mathcal{W}$. There is also another interesting topology between these two extremes, namely the Scott topology.

If $B \subseteq \mathcal{W}$, then $int_i B$, $cl_i B$ and $Fr_i B$ are respectively the interior, the closure, and the frontier of B with respect to τ_i. In an Alexandrov topology, the closure of every union of sets is equal to the union of their closures. Since $cl_i\{x\} = In_x$ for all $x \in W$, it follows that $cl_i A = In_A$, $int_i A = W \setminus In_{W \setminus A}$, and $Fr_i A = In_A \cap In_{W \setminus A}$ for all $A \subset W$. Since $cl_i A = A \cup Fr_i A$, we have $In_A = A \cup (In_A \cap In_{W \setminus A})$.

4.1 Content-Based Hierarchies

We define various topologies induced by the k-trip functions rather by the trip function. These topologies can be used to define a hierarchy of the possible trips over the web, and the Alexandrov topology τ_i is a lower limit of these topologies.

We use the relation $y \hookrightarrow_k x$ defined by a sequence $x_1, x_2, ..., x_{k+1} \in W$ such that $y = x_1 \hookrightarrow x_2 \hookrightarrow ... \hookrightarrow x_{k+1} = x$. We note that $z \hookrightarrow_k y$ and $y \hookrightarrow_k x$ implies $z \hookrightarrow_{2k} x$. Let $In_x^k = \{y \in W | y \hookrightarrow_k x\} \cup \{x\}$ and $In_x^{\leq k} = \cup_{j=1,k} In_x^j$, where $k \geq 1$.

We use a particular case for Proposition 2 by considering $h_k : \mathcal{P}(W) \to \mathcal{P}(W)$ defined by $h_k(A) = \cup_{x \in A} In_x^{\leq k}$ for all $A \in \mathcal{P}(W)$.

Proposition 7. *This operator has the following properties:*

1. *$A \subseteq h_k(A)$, for all $A \in \mathcal{P}(W)$;*
2. *$h_k(A \cup B) = h_k(A) \cup h_k(B)$, for all $A, B \in \mathcal{P}(W)$;*
3. *$h_k(\emptyset) = \emptyset$;*
4. *$h_k(h_k(A)) = h_{2k}(A)$, for all $A \in \mathcal{P}(W)$;*
5. *if $A \subseteq B$, then $h_k(A) \subseteq h_k(B)$;*
6. *$h_k(A) \subseteq h_{k+1}(A)$, for all $A \in \mathcal{P}(W)$;*

We remark that $h_k(\cup_{i \in I} A_i) = \cup_{i \in I} h_k(A_i)$ for every family of subsets $\{A_i\}_{i \in I} \subset \mathcal{P}(W)$. Since $h_k(h_k(A)) \neq h_k(A)$, the operator h_k is not a Kuratowski operator (i.e., satisfying (1), (2), (3) and $h_k(h_k(A)) = h_k(A)$, for all $A \in \mathcal{P}(W)$). However, we can consider that h_k is a weaker Kuratowski operator.

Definition 5. *A subset $A \in \mathcal{P}(W)$ is called k-closed iff $h_k(A) = A$.*

Let $\tau_k = \{D \subseteq W \mid W \setminus D$ is k-closed $\}$. ¿From the properties (1), (2), (3) and (5) of the previous proposition, it results that τ_k is a topology over the space W. Since $h_k(h_k(A)) \neq h_k(A)$, it results that $h_k(A) \subseteq cl_k(A)$, where $cl_k(A)$ is the closure of A in the topology τ_k. We also remark that $y \hookrightarrow_k x$ iff $y \in h_k(\{x\})$.

From (1) and (6) we can derive that if A is $k+1$-closed, then A is k-closed. Therefore $\tau_{k+1} \subseteq \tau_k$, for all $k \geq 1$. Since $In_A = \cup_{k \geq 1} h_k(A)$ and the operator $h(A) = In_A$ is a Kuratowski operator generating the Alexandrov topology, we have that $\tau_i = \lim_{k \to \infty} \tau_k = \cap_{k \geq 1} \tau_k$. Therefore we have the following hierarchy:

$$\tau_i \subseteq ... \subseteq \tau_{k+1} \subseteq \tau_k \subseteq ... \subseteq \tau_1$$

If we impose a bounded number n, then $h_n(h_n(A)) = h_n(A)$ for all $A \in \mathcal{P}(W)$. Then we have $h_n(A) = In_A$ for all $A \in \mathcal{P}(W)$, and $\tau_n = \tau_i$.

5   Topological Properties of the Web

Based on the topological notions presented in the previous sections, we present some results regarding the *connectivity, density* and *separation* of the Web. Many papers devoted to the Web structure focuses on the connectivity of the Web pages. We also start by studying the connectivity of our topologies.

Since $\{a\}$ is a τ_i-connected set, it results that $cl_i\{a\}$ is a τ_i-connected set. Therefore In_a is τ_i-connected. In a similar way, since $\{a\}$ is a τ_o-connected set, it results that $cl_o\{a\}$ is a τ_o-connected set, and Out_a is τ_o-connected. Moreover, considering $A \subset W$, if A is a τ_i-connected set, then In_A is a τ_i-connected set, and if A is a τ_o-connected set, then Out_A is a τ_o-connected set.

Let (X, τ) be a topological space, and $x_0, x_1 \in X$. A topological path in (X, τ) from x_0 to x_1 is a continuous function $g : [0, 1] \to (X, \tau)$ with $g(0) = x_0$, and $g(1) = x_1$.

If $g : [0, 1] \to (X, \tau)$ is a topological path from x_0 to x_1, then $g([0, 1])$ is a τ-connected set in X.

Theorem 4. *Let $f : \{1, ..., n\} \to W$ be a trip from a to b, and let the functions $g, h : [0, 1] \to W$ be defined by*

$$g(t) = \begin{cases} f(1), & t \in [0, \frac{1}{n}] \\ ... \\ f(k), & t \in (\frac{k-1}{n}, \frac{k}{n}] \\ ... \\ f(n), & t \in (\frac{n-1}{n}, 1] \end{cases}, \quad h(t) = \begin{cases} f(1), & t \in [0, \frac{1}{n}) \\ ... \\ f(k), & t \in [\frac{k-1}{n}, \frac{k}{n}) \\ ... \\ f(n), & t \in [\frac{n-1}{n}, 1] \end{cases}$$

Then g is a topological path in (X, τ_i) from a to b, and h is such a path in (X, τ_o) from a to b.

Proof. It is clear that g is continuous on $[0, \frac{1}{n}), (\frac{1}{n}, \frac{2}{n}), ..., (\frac{n-1}{n}, 1]$. We prove that g is continuous in $\frac{1}{n}, \frac{2}{n}, ..., \frac{n-1}{n}$. Let $t_0 = \frac{k}{n}$, $k \in \{1, .., n - 1\}$ and let $V \in \mathcal{V}_i(g(t_0))$. Then $\cap_{a \in W} I_a[g(t_0)] \subseteq V$. Let $\varepsilon \in (0, \frac{1}{2n})$ and $t \in (t_0 - \varepsilon, t_0 + \varepsilon)$. If $t \leq t_0$, then $(g(t_0), g(t)) = (f(k), f(k)) \in \cap_{a \in W} I_a \Rightarrow g(t) \in V$. If $t > t_0$, then $g(t) = f(k + 1)$. Because $f(k) \hookrightarrow f(k + 1)$, it results $f(k) \rightsquigarrow f(k + 1)$. So $(g(t_0), g(t)) = (f(k), f(k + 1)) \in \preceq_{\mathcal{I}} \Rightarrow g(t) \in V$. Therefore g is τ_i -continuous and $g(0) = a$ and $g(1) = b$.

Theorem 5. *If f is a trip from a to b, then $Im(f)$ is a τ_i-connected set, and also a τ_o-connected set.*

A web page $a \in W$ is called an α-*point* if $In_a \subseteq Out_a$. A web page $a \in W$ is called an ω-*point* if $Out_a \subseteq In_a$. It is obvious that a is an α-point iff $Net_a = Out_a$, and $a \in W$ is an ω-point iff $Net_a = In_a$. We denote by Γ the set of α-points, and by Ω the set of all ω-points. Considering $a \in W$ and $B \subseteq W$, we call B as an in-branch of a if there are $b \in \Gamma$, and $f \in L_{ba}$ such that $B = Im(f)$. In a similar way, B is an out-branch of a if there are $b \in \Omega$ and $f \in L_{ab}$ such that $B = Im(f)$. Finally, B is a branch of a if B is either an in-branch, or an out-branch of a. Every branch of a is a τ_i-connected set, as well as a τ_o-connected set. Let $\mathcal{B}_{i,a}$ be the set of all in-branches of a, $\mathcal{B}_{o,a}$ the set of all out-branches of a, and $\mathcal{B}_a = \mathcal{B}_{i,a} \cup \mathcal{B}_{o,a}$.

Theorem 6. *For all $a \in \mathcal{W}$, $In_a = \cup_{B \in \mathcal{B}_{i,a}} B$, $Out_a = \cup_{B \in \mathcal{B}_{o,a}} B$, and $Net_a = \cup_{B \in \mathcal{B}_a} B$.*

Proof. Let $a \in \mathcal{W}$. It is obvious that $\cup_{B \in \mathcal{B}_{i,a}} B \subseteq In_a$. Let now $x \in In_a$ and $x_1 = x$. We consider the following algorithm:

Step $(k \geq 1)$: If $x_k \in \Gamma$ break; else let $x_{k+1} \in In_{x_k}$ such that $x_{k+1} \notin Out_{x_k}$; $k++$; continue;

Because In_a is finite, there is $l \in N^*$ such that $x_l \in \Gamma$. Since $x_{k+1} \in In_{x_k}, \forall k \in \{1, .., l-1\}$, it results that $Out_{x_1} \subseteq Out_{x_2} \subseteq ... \subseteq Out_{x_l}$. So $x \in Out_{x_l}$. Because $x \in In_a$, $a \in Out_{x_l}$. Therefore, there is $f \in L_{x_l a}$ such that $x \in Im(f)$. It follows that $In_a \subset \cup_{B \in \mathcal{B}_{i,a}} B$.

The equality $Out_a = \cup_{B \in \mathcal{B}_{o,a}} B$ is proved by similar arguments.

Corollary 1. *In_a, Out_a and Net_a are τ_i, τ_o-connected sets.*

In general, with respect to a classification, the Web connectivity can be described in the following way [1]:

Theorem 7. *Let f be an unambiguous classification. Then $\mathcal{W}$ is connected with respect to τ_f iff for every $a, b \in \mathcal{W}$, there exist $a_0, \ldots, a_{n+1} \in \mathcal{W}$ such that $a = a_0$, $a_{n+1} = b$ and $f(a_i) \cap f(a_j) \neq \emptyset$ if $|i - j| \geq 1$.*

We work with instances of the Web, i.e., the sets of Web pages we consider at each moment are finite (even arbitrary large). The following result shows that α-points, as well as the ω-points, can generate the whole web space with respect to our topologies.

Theorem 8. *$\mathcal{W}$ is generated by Γ or by Ω:*
1. *Γ is a τ_o-dense set, i.e. $\mathcal{W} = cl_o(\Gamma) = Out_\Gamma$.*
2. *Ω is a τ_i-dense set, i.e., $\mathcal{W} = cl_i(\Omega) = In_\Omega$.*

Proof. Let $a \in \mathcal{W}$. Then $a \in In_a = \cup_{B \in \mathcal{B}_{i,a}} B$. Therefore, there is $B \in \mathcal{B}_{i,a}$ such that $a \in B$. Since $B \in \mathcal{B}_{i,a}$, there is $b \in \Gamma$ and $f \in L_{ba}$ such that $B = Im(f)$. It results that $B \subseteq Out_b$. Therefore $a \in Out_b$. We obtained that $\mathcal{W} = \cup_{b \in \Gamma} Out_b$. Then $\mathcal{W} = \cup_{b \in \Gamma} Out_b = \cup_{b \in \Gamma} cl_o\{b\} = cl_o(\cup_{b \in \Gamma}\{b\}) = cl_o(\Gamma)$.

We show that our topologies τ_i and τ_o are generated by quasi-pseudo-metrics. We remind that a quasi-pseudo-metric on $\mathcal{W}$ is a function $d : \mathcal{W} \times \mathcal{W} \to [0, \infty)$ which satisfies the following conditions: $d(x, x) = 0, \forall x \in \mathcal{W}$, and $d(x, y) \leq d(x, z) + d(z, y), \forall x, y, z \in \mathcal{W}$. A quasi-pseudo-metric d is pseudo-metric if $d(x, y) = d(y, x)$, for all $x, y \in \mathcal{W}$.

Proposition 8. *For all $a \in \mathcal{W}$, let $d_{i,a} : \mathcal{W} \times \mathcal{W} \to [0, \infty)$,*

$$d_{i,a}(x, y) = \begin{cases} 0, (x, y) \in I_a \\ 1, (x, y) \notin I_a \end{cases}$$

for all $(x, y) \in \mathcal{W} \times \mathcal{W}$. *Then* $d_i : \mathcal{W} \times \mathcal{W} \to [0, \infty)$ *defined by*

$$d_i(x, y) = \sum_{a \in \mathcal{W}} d_{i,a}(x, y)$$

is a quasi-pseudo-metric on $\mathcal{W}$, *and* $\preceq_i = \{(x, y) \in \mathcal{W} \times \mathcal{W} \mid d_i(x, y) < \varepsilon\}$, $\forall \varepsilon \in (0, 1)$.

Proposition 9. *For all* $a \in \mathcal{W}$, *let* $d_{o,a} : \mathcal{W} \times \mathcal{W} \to [0, \infty)$,

$$d_{o,a}(x, y) = \begin{cases} 0, (x, y) \in O_a \\ 1, (x, y) \notin O_a \end{cases}$$

for all $(x, y) \in \mathcal{W} \times \mathcal{W}$. *Then* $d_o : \mathcal{W} \times \mathcal{W} \to [0, \infty)$ *defined by*

$$d_o(x, y) = \sum_{a \in \mathcal{W}} d_{o,a}(x, y)$$

for all $(x, y) \in \mathcal{W} \times \mathcal{W}$ *is a quasi-pseudo-metric on* $\mathcal{W}$, *and* $\preceq_o = \{(x, y) \in \mathcal{W} \times \mathcal{W} \mid d_o(x, y) < \varepsilon\}$, $\forall \varepsilon \in (0, 1)$.

We note that $d_i(x, y) = card\{a \in \mathcal{W} \mid (x, y) \notin I_a\}$, and $d_o(x, y) = card\{a \in \mathcal{W} \mid (x, y) \notin O_a\}$. Moreover, $\tau_i = \tau_{d_i}$, and $\tau_o = \tau_{d_o}$, where τ_{d_i} is the topology generated by d_i, and τ_{d_o} is the topology generated by d_o [5]. This means that the topological notions can be described in terms of quasi-pseudo-metrics.

We can define another quasi-pseudo-metric able to give a better representation of R_a, the center of Net_a. The function is $d_M : \mathcal{W} \times \mathcal{W} \to [0, \infty)$ defined by

$$d_M(x, y) = \max\{d_i(x, y), d_o(x, y)\}$$

for all $(x, y) \in \mathcal{W} \times \mathcal{W}$. It is clear that $d_i, d_o \leq d_M$.

Proposition 10. d_M *is a quasi-pseudo-metric on* $\mathcal{W}$, *and* $\tau_i \cup \tau_o \subseteq \tau_M$, *where* τ_M *is the topology on* $\mathcal{W}$ *generated by* d_M.

Theorem 9. $cl_M\{a\} = R_a$ *for all* $a \in \mathcal{W}$, *and* $cl_M A = R_A$ *for all* $A \subseteq \mathcal{W}$, *where* $cl_M A$ *is the* τ_M-*closure of* A.

We can build now another set of generators for $\mathcal{W}$. Since $\mathcal{W}$ is a finite set, we suppose that $\mathcal{W} = \{x_1, ..., x_n\}$. Let $a_1 = x_1$. We consider the following algorithm: Step i $(i \geq 2)$: We already have the set $\{a_1, ..., a_k\}$. If $x_i \not\leftrightarrow a_j$ for $1 \leq j \leq k$, $a_{k+1} = x_i$; i++ and continue; otherwise i++ and continue. If $i > n$, then break. This algorithm builds the set $A = \{a_1, ..., a_m\} \subseteq \mathcal{W}$, where every pair of elements a_i and a_j are not biconnected, $\forall i, j$ with $i \neq j$. Hence $R_{a_i} \cap R_{a_j} = \emptyset$, $\forall i, j$ with $i \neq j$. Since $\leftrightarrow$ is an equivalence, it follows that $\mathcal{W} = \cup_{a \in A} R_a$. Therefore $\mathcal{W} = cl_M A = R_A$, and we have a new set A of generators.

According to some previous results, we have $\preceq_i \neq \triangle$ and $\preceq_o \neq \triangle$. Therefore $(\mathcal{W}, \tau_i)$ and $(\mathcal{W}, \tau_o)$ are not Hausdorff separate, i.e., they are not T_2 separate (see [5]). Since generally single point subsets of $\mathcal{W}$ are not τ_i (or τ_o) closed, the spaces $(\mathcal{W}, \tau_i)$ and $(\mathcal{W}, \tau_o)$ are not T_1 separate.

With respect to an arbitrary classification, we have the following results related to the Web separation according to [1]:

Theorem 10. *Let f be a classification. Then $(\mathcal{W}, \tau_f)$ is regular (see [5]) iff $f(x)$ is a τ_f-closed set for all $x \in \mathcal{W}$.*

Theorem 11. *Let f be a classification. Then $(\mathcal{W}, \tau_f)$ is pseudo-metrizable (see [5]) iff $f(x)$ is a finite τ_f-closed set for all $x \in \mathcal{W}$.*

The existence of a pseudo-metrics allows the quantitative evaluations with respect to a Web classification.

6   Conclusion

In this paper we consider the Web as a dynamic set of web pages together with a binary relation denoting that there is a link from a page to another. The complexity of this structure derives not only from the quantity, but mainly from its dynamics: new documents appear and disappear together with their links, cutting off all the corresponding nodes and arcs in the web topology.

An important practical operation over the Web is given by searching, and Web searching is based on indexing and classification. In this paper we introduce and study some topological aspects related to the important operations of searching and classification over the Web. Classification is dictated by some criteria. In order to define a classification, we associate a set to each document. Classification criteria can be defined as a classification operator. The Alexandrov topologies play an important role because they are equivalent to the Web classifications. We define and study the Alexandrov topologies associated to the Web classifications. This approach provides a suitable formal framework to express Web connectivity, density, and separation. As a consequence of investigating the relations between web pages and the dynamics of the Web documents, we can define a notion of Alexandrov computability for the web search and classification. We define a content-based hierarchy given by various topologies induced by the the finite trips over the web, and the Alexandrov topology τ_i is a lower limit of these topologies.

According to our knowledge, there are no similar topological approach to the problem of Web classification and computability. The further work consists in both defining some efficient operators for classification, and providing algorithms of building Web classifications.

References

1. F.G. Arenas, Alexandroff spaces, *Acta Math. Univ. Comenianae* vol.LXVIII, 17-25, 1999.
2. E. Cech. *Topological Spaces*. Publishing House of the Czechoslovak Academy of Sciences, Prague, 1966.

3. G. Ciobanu, D.Dumitriu. Space and Time Over the Web. *12th Int'l World Wide Web Conference*, Budapest, ACM, 2003.
4. G. Ciobanu, D.Rusu. Topological Spaces of the Web. *14th Int'l World Wide Web Conference*, Japan, 1112-1114, ACM Press, 2005.
5. R. Engelking. *General Topology*. 2nd edition. Sigma Series in Pure Mathematics 6, Heldermann, 1989.
6. J.L. Kelley. *General Topology*. van Nostrand, 1955.
7. D. Scott. Domains for Denotational Semantics. *Proceedings ICALP*, LNCS vol.140, Springer-Verlag, 577-613, 1982.
8. M.B. Smyth. Topology. *Handbook of Logic in Computer Science* vol.1, Oxford University Press, 641-761, 1992.
9. A. Tarski. A lattice-theoretical fixpoint theorem and its applications. *Pacific Journal of Mathematics* 5, 1955.

Bisimulation Congruences in the Calculus of Looping Sequences

Roberto Barbuti, Andrea Maggiolo-Schettini,
Paolo Milazzo, and Angelo Troina

Dipartimento di Informatica, Università di Pisa
Largo B. Pontecorvo 3, 56127 - Pisa, Italy
{barbuti, maggiolo, milazzo, troina}@di.unipi.it

Abstract. The Calculus of Looping Sequences (CLS) is a calculus suitable to describe biological systems and their evolution. CLS terms are constructed by starting from basic constituents and composing them by means of operators of concatenation, looping, containment and parallel composition. CLS terms can be transformed by applying rewrite rules. We give a labeled transition semantics for CLS by using, as labels, contexts in which rules can be applied. We define bisimulation relations that are congruences with respect to the operators on terms, and we show an application of CLS to the modeling of a biological system and we use bisimulations to reason about properties of the described system.

1 Introduction

In the last few years many formalisms originally developed by computer scientists to model systems of interacting components have been applied to Biology. Among these, there are Petri Nets [9], Hybrid Systems [1], and the π-calculus [6,12]. Moreover, some new formalisms have been proposed to describe biomolecular and membrane interactions [2,4,5,7,10,11]. The formal modeling of biological systems allows the development of simulators and the verification of properties of the described systems.

The π–calculus and new calculi based on it [10,11] have been particularly successful in the description of biological systems. Interactions of biological components are modeled as communications on channels whose names can be passed. Sharing names of private channels allows describing biological compartments, such as membranes. Calculi such as those proposed in [4,5,7] give an abstract description of systems and offer special biologically motivated operators.

In [3] we have presented a new calculus, called Calculus of Looping Sequences (CLS for short), for describing biological systems and their evolution, and we have shown how to use it for modeling interactions among bacteria and bacteriophage viruses as well as bacteria sporulation. In this paper we focus on semantic aspects of the formalism, in particular on bisimulation relations. We define a simplified variant of CLS (that we still call CLS in the following), we study bisimulations for it, and we apply such relations on the CLS model of a real example of gene regulation.

K. Barkaoui, A. Cavalcanti, and A. Cerone (Eds.): ICTAC 2006, LNCS 4281, pp. 93–107, 2006.
© Springer-Verlag Berlin Heidelberg 2006

The calculus we propose is more general than those in [4,5,7], which could be encoded into CLS (see [3] for an example), and with respect to the π–calculi and calculi based on the π–calculus [10,11], which are more expressive, it has the advantage of allowing the definition of bisimulations that are congruences.

The terms of our calculus are constructed by starting from basic constituent elements and composing them by means of operators of sequencing, looping, containment and parallel composition. Sequencing can be used to describe biological elements such as DNA fragments and proteins. DNA fragments can be modeled as sequences of nucleotides or as sequences of genes; proteins can be modeled as sequences of amino acids or as sequences of interaction sites. Looping allows tying up the ends of a sequence, thus creating a circular sequence of the constituent elements. We assume that the elements of a circular sequence can rotate, and this motivates the terminology of looping sequence. A looping sequence can represent a membrane. This description of membranes is finer than the one given in specialized membrane calculi (see e.g. [4,11]) as it allows representing interaction of membrane constituent elements. The containment operator can be used to represent that an element is inside the membrane, and parallel composition expresses juxtaposition of elements.

A structural congruence relation allows considering as equivalent terms that are intended to represent the same biological system. The evolution of a system is described by a set of rewrite rules to be applied to terms. The definition of the rewrite rules depends on the system and the evolution one wants to represent.

Bisimilarity is widely accepted as the finest extensional behavioural equivalence one may want to impose on systems. It may be used to verify a property of a system by assessing the bisimilarity of the considered system with a system one knows to enjoy that property. The notion of congruence is very important for a compositional account of behavioural equivalence. This is true, in particular, for complex systems such as biological ones.

To define bisimilarity of systems, these must have semantics based on labeled transition relations capturing potential external interactions between systems and their environment. A labeled transition semantics for CLS is derived from rewrite rules by using as labels contexts in which rules can be applied, in the style of Sewell [13] and Leifer and Milner [8]. We define bisimulation relations and we show them to be congruences with respect to the operators on terms.

The main difference between the definition of CLS we give in this paper with respect to the one in [3], is the presence of some constraints on the syntax of terms which simplifies the definition of the labeled transition relation for the calculus. We model an example of gene regulation, namely the regulation of the lactose operon in E. coli, to show that the new variant of the calculus, though simple, is expressive enough to model real systems. We use bisimulations to obtain an equivalent simplified model and to verify a property of the described system.

2 Calculus of Looping Sequences

In this section we introduce the Calculus of Looping Sequences (CLS).

Definition 1 (Terms). Terms T, looping sequences S_L, elementary sequences S, and elementary constituents E of CLS are given by the following grammar:

$$T \quad ::= \quad S \quad | \quad S_L \quad | \quad T \,|\, T \quad | \quad S_L \,\rfloor\, T$$
$$S_L \quad ::= \quad (S)^L$$
$$S \quad ::= \quad E \quad | \quad \epsilon \quad | \quad S \cdot S$$
$$E \quad ::= \quad a \quad | \quad b \quad | \quad c \quad | \quad \ldots$$

We denote with $\mathcal{E}$ the set of elementary constituents $a, b, c, \ldots$.

An elementary sequence S may be either an element in $\mathcal{E}$ or the empty sequence ϵ or a concatenation of elementary sequences. An example of elementary sequence is $a \cdot b \cdot c$. We denote with $\mathcal{S}$ the set of elementary sequences.

A looping sequence S_L is obtained by applying the looping operator $(\_)^L$ to an elementary sequence S. A term T may be either an elementary sequence S, or a looping sequence S_L, or the combination of a looping sequence and a term by means of the containment operator $\rfloor$, or the combination of two terms by means of the parallel composition operator $|$.

A looping sequence $(S)^L$ is a closed circular sequence of the elements constituting the elementary sequence S. Term $(S)^L \rfloor T$ represents the containment of term T in the looping sequence $(S)^L$. The set of all terms is denoted by $\mathcal{T}$.

Brackets can be used to indicate the order of application of the operators in a term. We assume that the $\rfloor$ operator has precedence over the $|$ operator, therefore $S \rfloor T_1 \,|\, T_2$ stands for $(S \rfloor T_1) \,|\, T_2$. Moreover, from the definition of CLS terms, the $\rfloor$ operator is right–associative, therefore $S_1 \rfloor S_2 \rfloor T$ denotes $S_1 \rfloor (S_2 \rfloor T)$. In Fig. 1 we show some examples of CLS terms and their visual representation.

Definition 2 (Structural Congruence). *The structural congruence relations $\equiv_S$ and $\equiv_T$ are the least congruence relations on elementary sequences and on terms, respectively, satisfying the following axioms:*

$$S_1 \cdot (S_2 \cdot S_3) \equiv_S (S_1 \cdot S_2) \cdot S_3 \qquad S \cdot \epsilon \equiv_S \epsilon \cdot S \equiv_S S$$

$$T_1 \,|\, T_2 \equiv_T T_2 \,|\, T_1 \qquad T_1 \,|\, (T_2 \,|\, T_3) \equiv_T (T_1 \,|\, T_2) \,|\, T_3 \qquad \epsilon \equiv_T (\epsilon)^L$$

$$T \,|\, \epsilon \equiv_T T \qquad (S)^L \rfloor \epsilon \equiv_T (S)^L \qquad (S_1 \cdot S_2)^L \rfloor T \equiv_T (S_2 \cdot S_1)^L \rfloor T$$

Axioms of the structural congruence state the associativity of $\cdot$ and $|$, the commutativity of the latter and the neutral role of ϵ and $(\epsilon)^L$. We remark that $(\epsilon)^L \rfloor T \not\equiv T$. Moreover, axiom $(S_1 \cdot S_2)^L \rfloor T \equiv_T (S_2 \cdot S_1)^L \rfloor T$ says that elementary sequences in a looping can rotate.

Note that $\equiv_S$ can be lifted to $\equiv_T$, in the sense that if $S \equiv_S S'$ then $S \equiv_T S'$. Moreover, note that the first operand of the $\rfloor$ operator is not a general term, but a looping sequence $(S)^L$, which is an element of S_L, hence $\equiv_T$ cannot be applied to it, but $\equiv_S$ can be applied to the sequence S. In the following, for simplicity, we will use $\equiv$ in place of $\equiv_T$.

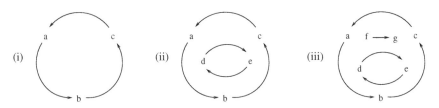

Fig. 1. (i) represents $(a \cdot b \cdot c)^L$; (ii) represents $(a \cdot b \cdot c)^L \rfloor (d \cdot e)^L$; (iii) represents $(a \cdot b \cdot c)^L \rfloor ((d \cdot e)^L \mid f \cdot g)$

Now, we define rewrite rules, which can be used to describe the transformation of terms by giving a transition relation as the semantics of rule applications. Let us consider a set of term variables TV ranged over by $X, Y, Z, \ldots$, a set of elementary sequence variables SV ranged over by $\widetilde{x}, \widetilde{y}, \widetilde{z}, \ldots$, and a set of element variables $\mathcal{X}$ ranged over by $x, y, z, \ldots$. All these sets are possibly infinite and pairwise disjoint. We denote by $\mathcal{V}$ the set of all variables, $\mathcal{V} = TV \cup SV \cup \mathcal{X}$.

An *instantiation* is a function $\sigma : \mathcal{V} \to \mathcal{T}$; let Σ be the set of all the possible instantiations. With $\mathcal{T}_\mathcal{V}$ we denote the set of CLS terms which may also contain variables in $\mathcal{V}$ and, given $T \in \mathcal{T}_\mathcal{V}$, with $T\sigma$ we denote the term obtained by replacing each occurrence of each variable $X_\mathcal{V} \in \mathcal{V}$ appearing in T with the corresponding term $\sigma(X_\mathcal{V})$. An instantiation σ must respect the type of variables, thus for $X \in TV$, $\widetilde{x} \in SV$ and $x \in \mathcal{X}$ we have $\sigma(X) \in \mathcal{T}$, $\sigma(\widetilde{x}) \in \mathcal{S}$ and $\sigma(x) \in \mathcal{E}$, respectively.

Definition 3 (Rewrite Rule). *A rewrite rule is a pair of terms (T, T'), denoted with $T \mapsto T'$, where $T, T' \in \mathcal{T}_\mathcal{V}$, $T \not\equiv \epsilon$ and such that $Var(T') \subseteq Var(T)$. We denote with $\mathfrak{R}$ the infinite set of all the possible rewrite rules.*

A rewrite rule (T, T') states that a ground term $T\sigma$, obtained by instantiating variables in T by some instantiation function σ, can be transformed into the ground term $T'\sigma$. The rewrite rules must be applied to terms only if they occur in a legal context. Contexts are defined as follows.

Definition 4 (Contexts). *Contexts $\mathcal{C}$ are given by the following grammar:*

$$\mathcal{C} ::= \square \quad | \quad \mathcal{C} \mid T \quad | \quad T \mid \mathcal{C} \quad | \quad (S)^L \rfloor \mathcal{C}$$

where $T \in \mathcal{T}$ and $S \in \mathcal{S}$. Context $\square$ is called the empty context.

By definition, every context contains a single $\square$.

Let us assume $C, C' \in \mathcal{C}$. With $C[T]$ we denote the term obtained by replacing $\square$ with T in C; with $C[C']$ we denote the context composition, whose result is the context obtained by replacing $\square$ with C' in C.

Definition 5 (Reduction Semantics). *Given a set of rewrite rules $\mathcal{R} \subseteq \mathfrak{R}$, the* reduction semantics *of CLS is the least relation closed wrt $\equiv$ and satisfying the following inference rule:*

$$\frac{T \mapsto T' \in \mathcal{R} \quad T\sigma \not\equiv \epsilon \quad \sigma \in \Sigma \quad C \in \mathcal{C}}{C[T\sigma] \to C[T'\sigma]}$$

Definition 6 (Parallel Contexts). *Parallel contexts $\mathcal{C}_P$ are a subset of contexts given by the following grammar, where $T \in \mathcal{T}$:*

$$\mathcal{C}_P ::= \square \quad | \quad \mathcal{C}_P \mid T \quad | \quad T \mid \mathcal{C}_P$$

Given $C_1, C_2 \in \mathcal{C}_P$, we write $C_1 \sqcap C_2$ if the two parallel contexts share some components, namely if $\exists T_1 \not\equiv \epsilon, T_2, T_3 \in \mathcal{T}.C_1[\epsilon] \equiv T_1 \mid T_2 \wedge C_2[\epsilon] \equiv T_1 \mid T_3$. We write $C_1 \not\sqcap C_2$ otherwise. Contexts are used in the labeled semantics of CLS.

Definition 7 (Labeled Semantics). *Given a set of rewrite rules $\mathcal{R} \subseteq \Re$, the labeled semantics of CLS is the labeled transition system given by the following inference rules:*

$$(\text{rule\_appl}) \; \frac{T \mapsto T' \in \mathcal{R} \quad C[T''] \equiv T\sigma \quad T'' \not\equiv \epsilon \quad \sigma \in \Sigma \quad C \in \mathcal{C}}{T'' \xrightarrow{C} T'\sigma}$$

$$(\text{cont}) \; \frac{T \xrightarrow{\square} T'}{T'' \rfloor T \xrightarrow{\square} T'' \rfloor T'} \qquad (\text{par}) \; \frac{T \xrightarrow{C} T' \quad C \in \mathcal{C}_P \quad C \not\sqcap \square \mid T''}{T \mid T'' \xrightarrow{C} T' \mid T''}$$

where the dual version of the (par) *rule is omitted.*

The labeled semantics is similar to the one in [13] for ground term rewriting. A transition $T \xrightarrow{C} T'$ indicates that the application of the context C to T creates an instance of the left part of a rewrite rule, with target instance T'. Intuitively, the transition makes observable the context C, which, when filled with the term T, can be reduced to T', namely $C[T] \mapsto T'$ is an instance of a rewrite rule. Note that, since in rule (rule_appl) $T'' \not\equiv \epsilon$, the context C used as label cannot provide completely the left part of the rule. Differently with respect to [13], we allow to observe the context in the reduction of a subterm of a parallel composition. Namely, if $C[T] \mapsto T'$ is an instance of a rewrite rule, then we have that $T|T'' \xrightarrow{C} T'|T''$ (rule (par)), under the condition that T'' does not provide part of the context C. In this manner we obtain that the context observed is the minimum necessary to apply a rule.

The following proposition states that the labeled semantics is equivalent to the reduction semantics when the context is empty. The proof is immediate.

Proposition 1. $T \to T' \iff T \xrightarrow{\square} T'$.

Lemma 1 gives a property of parallel contexts, and Lemma 2 gives the labeled semantics with respect to context composition.

Lemma 1. *Given $T, T' \in \mathcal{T}$ and a parallel context $C \in \mathcal{C}_P$, it holds that:* $C[T]|T' \equiv C[T|T']$.

Proof. Since $C \in \mathcal{C}_P$ there exists T_C such that $C[T] = T_C|T$, and moreover we have that $(T_C|T)|T' \equiv T_C|(T|T') = C[T|T']$.

Lemma 2. $T \xrightarrow{C[C']} T' \iff C'[T] \xrightarrow{C} T'$.

Proof. By induction on the depth of the derivation tree of $T \xrightarrow{C[C']} T'$.

- *Base.* Derivation trees of depth 1 are obtained by rule (rule_appl).
  $T \xrightarrow{C[C']} T' \iff$ there exists $T_1 \mapsto T_1' \in \mathcal{R}$ such that $T_1 \sigma = C[C'[T]]$ and $T_1' \sigma = T'$ for some instantiation function $\sigma \iff C'[T] \xrightarrow{C} T'$.
- *Induction step.* We assume that the thesis holds for depth n.
  - (par). We first prove the direction $\implies$. Let us assume $T = T_1 | T_2$; then $T' = T_1' | T_2$, $T_1 \xrightarrow{C[C']} T_1'$, $C[C'] \in \mathcal{C}_P$ and $C[C'] \nparallel \Box | T_2$ (which implies $C \nparallel \Box | T_2$). We have $C'[T_1] \xrightarrow{C} T_1'$ by induction hypothesis, which implies $C'[T_1] | T_2 \xrightarrow{C} T_1' | T_2$ (by applying rule (par)), and hence $C'[T] \xrightarrow{C} T'$, since $T' = T_1' | T_2$, $C' \in \mathcal{C}_P$ and by Lemma 1. The proof of $\impliedby$ is symmetric.
  - (cont). This case is trivial because $C[C'] = \Box$. $\qquad\square$

We introduce a notion of *strong bisimilarity* between CLS terms.

Definition 8 (Strong Bisimulation). *A binary relation R on terms is a strong bisimulation if, given T_1, T_2 such that $T_1 R T_2$, the two following conditions hold:*
$$T_1 \xrightarrow{C} T_1' \implies \exists T_2' \text{ such that } T_2 \xrightarrow{C} T_2' \text{ and } T_1' R T_2'$$
$$T_2 \xrightarrow{C} T_2' \implies \exists T_1' \text{ such that } T_1 \xrightarrow{C} T_1' \text{ and } T_2' R T_1'.$$
The strong bisimilarity $\sim$ is the largest of such relations.

The strong bisimilarity $\sim$ is a congruence with respect to CLS operators.

Proposition 2 (Strong Congruence). *The relation $\sim$ is a congruence.*

Proof. We show that $\mathcal{S} \overset{def}{=} \{ (C[T_1], C[T_2]) \mid T_1 \sim T_2 \text{ and } C \in \mathcal{C} \}$ is a bisimulation. In particular, we note that $\sim \subseteq \mathcal{S}$ and $T_1 \mathcal{S} T_2 \implies C[T_1] \mathcal{S} C[T_2]$. Finally, given $T_1 \sim T_2$, we prove by induction on the derivation of $C[T_1] \xrightarrow{C'} T_1'$ that $C[T_1] \xrightarrow{C'} T_1' \implies \exists T_2'. C[T_2] \xrightarrow{C'} T_2'$ and $T_1' \mathcal{S} T_2'$. A detailed proof can be found in Appendix A.1. $\qquad\square$

We denote with $\overset{\Box}{\implies}$ a sequence of zero or more transitions $\xrightarrow{\Box}$, and with $\overset{C}{\implies}$, where $C \neq \Box$, the sequence of transitions such that $T \overset{C}{\implies} T'$ if and only if there exist $T_1, T_2 \in \mathcal{T}$ such that $T \overset{\Box}{\implies} T_1 \xrightarrow{C} T_2 \overset{\Box}{\implies} T'$. We have two lemmas.

Lemma 3. *If one of the following two conditions holds: (i) $C, C' \in \mathcal{C}_P$ with $C \nparallel C'$, (ii) $C = \Box$, $C' \in \mathcal{C}$, then $T \overset{C}{\implies} T' \iff C'[T] \overset{C}{\implies} C'[T']$.*

Proof. By definition of $\overset{C}{\implies}$ and of the labeled semantics. $\qquad\square$

Lemma 4. $T \stackrel{C[C']}{\Longrightarrow} T' \iff C'[T] \stackrel{C}{\Longrightarrow} T'$.

Proof. First of all, it is worth noticing that, by Lemma 3, $T \stackrel{\square}{\Longrightarrow} T' \iff C[T] \stackrel{\square}{\Longrightarrow} C[T']$ for any context C. Now, $T \stackrel{C[C']}{\Longrightarrow} T' \iff$ there exist T_1, T_2 such that $T \stackrel{\square}{\Longrightarrow} T_1 \stackrel{C[C']}{\longrightarrow} T_2 \stackrel{\square}{\Longrightarrow} T'$. By Lemma 2, we have that $C'[T_1] \stackrel{C}{\longrightarrow} T_2$, and hence $C'[T] \stackrel{\square}{\Longrightarrow} C'[T_1] \stackrel{C}{\longrightarrow} T_2 \stackrel{\square}{\Longrightarrow} T'$, that is $C'[T] \stackrel{C}{\Longrightarrow} T'$. $\square$

Most of the time we want to consider bisimilarity without taking into account system internal moves. This relation is usually called *weak bisimilarity*.

Definition 9 (Weak Bisimulation). *A binary relation R on terms is a* weak bisimulation *if, given T_1, T_2 such that T_1RT_2, the two following conditions hold:*

$T_1 \stackrel{C}{\longrightarrow} T_1' \implies \exists T_2'$ *such that* $T_2 \stackrel{C}{\Longrightarrow} T_2'$ *and* $T_1'RT_2'$

$T_2 \stackrel{C}{\longrightarrow} T_2' \implies \exists T_1'$ *such that* $T_1 \stackrel{C}{\Longrightarrow} T_1'$ *and* $T_2'RT_1'$.

The weak bisimilarity $\approx$ *is the largest of such relations.*

Proposition 3 (Weak Congruence). *The relation $\approx$ is a congruence.*

Proof. Similar to the proof of Proposition 2, by using Lemmas 3 and 4. A detailed proof can be found in Appendix A.2. $\square$

Example 1. Consider the following set of rules:

$$\mathcal{R} = \{ \quad a \mid b \mapsto c \quad , \quad d \mid b \mapsto e \quad , \quad e \mapsto e \quad , \quad c \mapsto e \quad , \quad f \mapsto a \quad \}$$

We have that $a \sim d$, because $a \stackrel{\square|b}{\longrightarrow} c \stackrel{\square}{\longrightarrow} e \stackrel{\square}{\longrightarrow} e \stackrel{\square}{\longrightarrow} \ldots$ and $d \stackrel{\square|b}{\longrightarrow} e \stackrel{\square}{\longrightarrow} e \stackrel{\square}{\longrightarrow} \ldots$, and $f \approx d$, because $f \stackrel{\square}{\longrightarrow} a \stackrel{\square|b}{\longrightarrow} c \stackrel{\square}{\longrightarrow} e \stackrel{\square}{\longrightarrow} e \stackrel{\square}{\longrightarrow} \ldots$. On the other hand, $f \not\sim e$ and $f \not\approx e$.

One may also be interested in comparing the behaviour of terms whose evolution is given by the application of two possibly different sets of rewrite rules. To this aim we define *CLS systems* as pairs consisting of a CLS term and a set of rewrite rules.

Definition 10 (System). *A CLS System is a pair $\langle T, \mathcal{R} \rangle$ with $T \in \mathcal{T}$, $\mathcal{R} \subseteq \Re$.*

Given a system $\langle T, \mathcal{R} \rangle$, we write $\mathcal{R} : T \stackrel{C}{\longrightarrow} T'$ to mean that the transition $T \stackrel{C}{\longrightarrow} T'$ is performed by applying a rule in $\mathcal{R}$, and we write $\mathcal{R} : T \stackrel{C}{\Longrightarrow} T'$ to mean that the sequence of transitions $T \stackrel{C}{\Longrightarrow} T'$ is performed by applying rules in $\mathcal{R}$. Now, we introduce strong and weak bisimilarities between CLS systems. With abuse of notation we denote such relations with $\sim$ and $\approx$, respectively.

Definition 11 (Strong Bisimulation on Systems). *A binary relation R on CLS systems is a* strong bisimulation *if, given $\langle T_1, \mathcal{R}_1 \rangle$ and $\langle T_2, \mathcal{R}_2 \rangle$ such that $\langle T_1, \mathcal{R}_1 \rangle R \langle T_2, \mathcal{R}_2 \rangle$, the two following conditions hold:*

$\mathcal{R}_1 : T_1 \stackrel{C}{\longrightarrow} T_1' \implies \exists T_2'$ *such that* $\mathcal{R}_2 : T_2 \stackrel{C}{\longrightarrow} T_2'$ *and* $\langle T_1', \mathcal{R}_1 \rangle R \langle T_2', \mathcal{R}_2 \rangle$

$\mathcal{R}_2 : T_2 \stackrel{C}{\longrightarrow} T_2' \implies \exists T_1'$ *such that* $\mathcal{R}_1 : T_1 \stackrel{C}{\longrightarrow} T_1'$ *and* $\langle T_2', \mathcal{R}_2 \rangle R \langle T_1', \mathcal{R}_1 \rangle$.

The strong bisimilarity $\sim$ *is the largest of such relations.*

Definition 12 (Weak Bisimulation on Systems). *A binary relation R on CLS systems is a* weak bisimulation *if, given* $\langle T_1, \mathcal{R}_1 \rangle$ *and* $\langle T_2, \mathcal{R}_2 \rangle$ *such that* $\langle T_1, \mathcal{R}_1 \rangle R \langle T_2, \mathcal{R}_2 \rangle$, *the two following conditions hold:*

$$\mathcal{R}_1 : T_1 \xrightarrow{C} T_1' \implies \exists T_2' \text{ such that } \mathcal{R}_2 : T_2 \xRightarrow{C} T_2' \text{ and } \langle T_1', \mathcal{R}_1 \rangle R \langle T_2', \mathcal{R}_2 \rangle$$
$$\mathcal{R}_2 : T_2 \xrightarrow{C} T_2' \implies \exists T_1' \text{ such that } \mathcal{R}_1 : T_1 \xRightarrow{C} T_1' \text{ and } \langle T_2', \mathcal{R}_2 \rangle R \langle T_1', \mathcal{R}_1 \rangle.$$

The weak bisimilarity $\approx$ *is the largest of such relations.*

If we fix a set of rewrite rules, strong and weak bisimilarities on CLS systems correspond to strong and weak bisimilarities on terms, respectively. Namely, for a given $\mathcal{R} \in \Re$, $\langle T_1, \mathcal{R} \rangle \sim \langle T_2, \mathcal{R} \rangle$ if and only if $T_1 \sim T_2$ and $\langle T_1, \mathcal{R} \rangle \approx \langle T_2, \mathcal{R} \rangle$ if and only if $T_1 \approx T_2$. However, as we show in the following example, bisimilarity relations introduced for CLS systems are not congruences.

Example 2. Let $\mathcal{R}_1 = \{a \mid b \mapsto c\}$ and $\mathcal{R}_2 = \{a \mid d \mapsto c , \; b \mid e \mapsto c\}$. We have that $\langle a, \mathcal{R}_1 \rangle \approx \langle e, \mathcal{R}_2 \rangle$ and $\langle b, \mathcal{R}_1 \rangle \approx \langle d, \mathcal{R}_2 \rangle$, but $\langle a \mid b, \mathcal{R}_1 \rangle \not\approx \langle e \mid d, \mathcal{R}_2 \rangle$.

Even if bisimilarity on CLS systems are not congruences, they allow us to define equivalence relations on sets of rewrite rules.

Definition 13 (Rules Equivalence). *Two sets of rewrite rules* $\mathcal{R}_1$ *and* $\mathcal{R}_2$ *are strongly (resp. weakly) equivalent, denoted* $\mathcal{R}_1 \simeq \mathcal{R}_2$ *(resp.* $\mathcal{R}_1 \cong \mathcal{R}_2$*), if and only if for any term* $T \in \mathcal{T}$ *it holds* $\langle T, \mathcal{R}_1 \rangle \sim \langle T, \mathcal{R}_2 \rangle$ *(resp.* $\langle T, \mathcal{R}_1 \rangle \approx \langle T, \mathcal{R}_2 \rangle$*).*

Example 3. Given $\mathcal{R}_1 = \{a \mapsto c\}$, $\mathcal{R}_2 = \{a \mapsto f\}$ and $\mathcal{R}_3 = \{a \mapsto b , \; b \mapsto c\}$, we have that $\mathcal{R}_1 \simeq \mathcal{R}_2$, but $\mathcal{R}_1 \not\simeq \mathcal{R}_3$ and $\mathcal{R}_1 \cong \mathcal{R}_2$.

Now, if we resort to equivalent rules, we can prove congruence results on CLS systems.

Proposition 4 (Congruences on Systems). *Given* $\mathcal{R}_1 \simeq \mathcal{R}_2$ *(resp.* $\mathcal{R}_1 \cong \mathcal{R}_2$*) and* $\langle T, \mathcal{R}_1 \rangle \sim \langle T', \mathcal{R}_2 \rangle$ *(resp.* $\langle T, \mathcal{R}_1 \rangle \approx \langle T', \mathcal{R}_2 \rangle$*), for any* $C \in \mathcal{C}$ *we have* $\langle C[T], \mathcal{R}_1 \rangle \sim \langle C[T'], \mathcal{R}_2 \rangle$ *(resp.* $\langle C[T], \mathcal{R}_1 \rangle \approx \langle C[T'], \mathcal{R}_2 \rangle$*).*

Proof. Since $\mathcal{R}_1 \simeq \mathcal{R}_2$ we have that $\langle T, \mathcal{R}_1 \rangle \sim \langle T, \mathcal{R}_2 \rangle$; moreover, by hypothesis, $\langle T, \mathcal{R}_1 \rangle \sim \langle T', \mathcal{R}_2 \rangle$, and therefore $\langle T, \mathcal{R}_2 \rangle \sim \langle T', \mathcal{R}_2 \rangle$. Now, since the set of rewrite rules is the same ($\mathcal{R}_2$), by the congruence results for CLS terms, we have $\langle C[T], \mathcal{R}_2 \rangle \sim \langle C[T'], \mathcal{R}_2 \rangle$. Again, since $\mathcal{R}_1 \simeq \mathcal{R}_2$, we have $\langle C[T], \mathcal{R}_1 \rangle \sim \langle C[T], \mathcal{R}_2 \rangle$, and hence, $\langle C[T], \mathcal{R}_1 \rangle \sim \langle C[T'], \mathcal{R}_2 \rangle$. The proof is identical for $\cong$ and $\approx$ instead of $\simeq$ and $\sim$, respectively. $\qquad \square$

3 An Application to the Modeling of Gene Regulation

In this section we develop a CLS model of the regulation process of the lactose operon in E. coli (Escherichia coli), we use the weak bisimulation on terms to simplify the model and the weak bisimulation on systems to prove a property.

E. coli is a bacterium often present in the intestine of many animals. As most bacteria, it is often exposed to a constantly changing physical and chemical

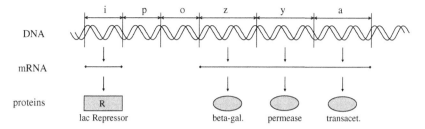

Fig. 2. The lactose operon

environment, and reacts to changes in its environment through changes in the kinds of proteins it produces.

In general, in order to save energy, bacteria do not synthesize degradative enzymes (which are proteins) unless the substrates for these enzymes are present in the environment. For example, E. coli does not synthesize the enzymes that degrade lactose (a sugar) unless lactose is in the environment. This phenomenon is called *enzyme induction* or, more generally, *gene regulation* since it is obtained by controlling the transcription of some genes into the corresponding proteins.

Let us consider the lactose degradation example in E. coli. Two enzymes are required to start the breaking process: the *lactose permease*, which is incorporated in the membrane of the bacterium and actively transports the sugar into the cell (without this enzyme lactose can enter the bacterium anyway, but much more slowly), and the *beta galactosidase*, which splits lactose into glucose and galactose. The bacterium produces also the *transacetylase* enzyme, whose function is less known, but is surely related with the usage of lactose.

The sequence of genes in the DNA of E. coli which produces the described enzymes, is known as the *lactose operon* (see Fig. 2). It is composed by six genes: the first three (i, p, o) regulate the production of the enzymes, and the last three (z, y, a), called *structural genes*, are transcribed (when allowed) into the mRNA for beta galactosidase, lactose permease and transacetylase, respectively[1].

The regulation process is as follows (see Fig. 3): gene i encodes the *lac Repressor*, which in the absence of lactose, binds to gene o (the *operator*). Transcription of structural genes into mRNA is performed by the RNA polymerase enzyme, which usually binds to gene p (the *promoter*) and scans the operon from left to right by transcribing the three structural genes z, y and a into a single mRNA fragment. When the lac Repressor is bound to gene o, it becomes an obstacle for the RNA polymerase, and transcription of the structural genes is not performed. On the other hand, when lactose is present inside the bacterium, it binds to the Repressor and this cannot stop any more the activity of the RNA polymerase. In this case transcription is performed and the three enzymes for lactose degradation are synthesized.

Now we describe how to model the gene regulation process with CLS. For the sake of simplicity we give a partial model, in the sense that we describe

---

[1] We recall that in protein synthesis first the DNA of one or more genes is transcribed into a piece of mRNA, then the mRNA is translated into one or more proteins.

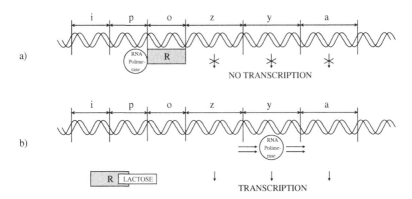

Fig. 3. The regulation process. In the absence of lactose (case a) the lac Repressor binds to gene o and precludes the RNA polymerase from transcribing genes z,y and a. When lactose is present (case b) it binds to and inactivates the lac Repressor.

how the transcription of the structural genes is activated when the lactose is in the environment, but we do not describe how the transcription of such genes is stopped when the lactose disappears. Moreover, in order to simplify the example, we assume that genes are transcribed directly into proteins (thus avoiding the modeling of the mRNA), that the lac Repressor is transcribed from gene i without the need of the RNA polymerase and that it can be produced only once. Finally, we assume that one RNA polymerase is present inside the bacterium.

We model the membrane of the bacterium as the looping sequence $(m)^L$, where the elementary constituent m generically denotes the whole membrane surface in normal conditions. Moreover, we model the lactose operon as the sequence $lacI \cdot lacP \cdot lacO \cdot lacZ \cdot lacY \cdot lacA$ ($lacI$–A for short), in which each element corresponds to a gene, and we replace $lacO$ with RO in the sequence when the lac Repressor is bound to gene o. When the lac Repressor is unbound, it is modeled by the elementary constituent $repr$. Finally, we model the RNA polymerase as the elementary constituent $polym$, a molecule of lactose as the elementary constituent $LACT$, and beta galactose, lactose permease and transacetylase enzymes as elementary constituents $betagal, perm$ and $transac$, respectively.

When no lactose is present the bacterium is modeled by the following term:

$$Ecoli ::= (m)^L \rfloor (lacI\text{–}A \mid polym)$$

The transcription of the DNA is modeled by the following set of rules:

$$
\begin{aligned}
lacI \cdot \widetilde{x} &\mapsto lacI' \cdot \widetilde{x} \mid repr & \text{(R1)} \\
polym \mid \widetilde{x} \cdot lacP \cdot \widetilde{y} &\mapsto \widetilde{x} \cdot PP \cdot \widetilde{y} & \text{(R2)} \\
\widetilde{x} \cdot PP \cdot lacO \cdot \widetilde{y} &\mapsto \widetilde{x} \cdot lacP \cdot PO \cdot \widetilde{y} & \text{(R3)} \\
\widetilde{x} \cdot PO \cdot lacZ \cdot \widetilde{y} &\mapsto \widetilde{x} \cdot lacO \cdot PZ \cdot \widetilde{y} & \text{(R4)} \\
\widetilde{x} \cdot PZ \cdot lacY \cdot \widetilde{y} &\mapsto \widetilde{x} \cdot lacZ \cdot PY \cdot \widetilde{y} \mid betagal & \text{(R5)} \\
\widetilde{x} \cdot PY \cdot lacA &\mapsto \widetilde{x} \cdot lacY \cdot PA \mid perm & \text{(R6)} \\
\widetilde{x} \cdot PA &\mapsto \widetilde{x} \cdot A \mid transac \mid polym & \text{(R7)}
\end{aligned}
$$

Rule (R1) describes the transcription of gene i into the lac Repressor. After transcription $lacI$ becomes $lacI'$ to avoid further productions of the lac Repressor. Rule (R2) describes the binding of the RNA polymerase to gene p. We denote the complex formed by the binding RNA polymerase to a gene lac_- with the elementary constituent P_-. Rules (R3)–(R6) describe the scanning of the DNA performed by the RNA polymerase and the consequent production of enzymes. Rule (R3) can be applied (and the scanning can be performed) only when the sequence contains $lacO$ instead of RO, that is when the lac Repressor is not bound to gene o. Finally, in rule (R7) the RNA polymerase terminates the scanning and releases the sequence.

The following rules describe the binding of the lac Repressor to gene o, and what happens when lactose is present in the environment of the bacterium:

$$repr \mid \widetilde{x} \cdot lacO \cdot \widetilde{y} \quad \mapsto \quad \widetilde{x} \cdot RO \cdot \widetilde{y} \tag{R8}$$

$$LACT \mid \left(m \cdot \widetilde{x}\right)^{L} \rfloor X \quad \mapsto \quad \left(m \cdot \widetilde{x}\right)^{L} \rfloor (X \mid LACT) \tag{R9}$$

$$\widetilde{x} \cdot RO \cdot \widetilde{y} \mid LACT \quad \mapsto \quad \widetilde{x} \cdot lacO \cdot \widetilde{y} \mid RLACT \tag{R10}$$

Rule (R8) describes the binding of the lac Repressor to gene o, rule (R9) models the passage of the lactose through the membrane of the bacterium and rule (R10) the removal of the lac Repressor from gene o operated by the lactose. In this rule the elementary constituent $RLACT$ denotes the binding of the lactose to the lac Repressor.

Finally, the following rules describe the behaviour of the enzymes synthesized when lactose is present, and their degradation:

$$\left(\widetilde{x}\right)^{L} \rfloor (perm \mid X) \quad \mapsto \quad \left(perm \cdot \widetilde{x}\right)^{L} \rfloor X \tag{R11}$$

$$LACT \mid \left(perm \cdot \widetilde{x}\right)^{L} \rfloor X \quad \mapsto \quad \left(perm \cdot \widetilde{x}\right)^{L} \rfloor (LACT \mid X) \tag{R12}$$

$$betagal \mid LACT \quad \mapsto \quad betagal \mid GLU \mid GAL \tag{R13}$$

$$perm \quad \mapsto \quad \epsilon \tag{R14}$$

$$betagal \quad \mapsto \quad \epsilon \tag{R15}$$

$$transac \quad \mapsto \quad \epsilon \tag{R16}$$

Rule (R11) describes the incorporation of the lactose permease in the membrane of the bacterium, rule (R12) the transportation of lactose from the environment to the interior performed by the lactose permease, and rule (R13) the decomposition of the lactose into glucose (denoted GLU) and galactose (denoted GAL) performed by the beta galactosidase. Finally, rules (R14),(R15) and (R16) describe degradation of the lactose permease, the beta galactosidase and the transacetylase enzymes, respectively.

Let us denote the set of rewrite rules $\{(R1), \ldots, (R16)\}$ as $\mathcal{R}_{lac}$, and the lactose operon $lacI' \cdot lacP \cdot lacO \cdot lacZ \cdot lacY \cdot lacA$, after the production of the lac Repressor, as $lacI'-A$. An example of possible sequence of transitions which can be performed by the term $Ecoli$ by applying rules in $\mathcal{R}_{lac}$ is the following:

$$Ecoli \quad \overset{\square}{\Longrightarrow} \quad (m)^L \rfloor (lacI' \cdot lacP \cdot RO \cdot lacZ \cdot lacY \cdot lacA \mid polym)$$

$$\overset{LACT|\square}{\Longrightarrow} \quad (m)^L \rfloor (lacI'-A|polym|RLACT)$$

$$\overset{\square}{\Longrightarrow} \quad (perm \cdot m)^L \rfloor (lacI'-A|betagal|transac|polym|RLACT)$$

$$\overset{LACT|\square}{\Longrightarrow} \quad (perm \cdot m)^L \rfloor (lacI'-A|betagal|transac|polym|RLACT|GLU|GAL)$$

In the example, by applying rules (R1) and (R8), *Ecoli* produces the lac Repressor, which binds to gene o in the lactose operon. Then, the bacterium interacts with an environment containing a molecule of lactose (represented by the context $LACT|\square$): by applying rule (R9) the lactose enters the membrane of the bacterium and by applying rule (R10) it binds to the lac Repressor. Then, a sequence of internal transitions are performed by applying rules (R2)–(R7) and (R11): the result is the transcription of the structural genes and the incorporation of the lactose permease in the membrane of the bacterium. Finally, the term interacts with an environment containing another molecule of lactose, which enters the bacterium and is decomposed into *GLU* and *GAL*. The rules applied in this phase are (R12) and (R13).

Note that, if one starts from *Ecoli*, every time (R12) can be applied, also (R9) can be applied giving the same results. Therefore, rule (R12) seems to be redundant. Nevertheless, rule (R12) describes a precise phenomenon, namely the action performed by the lactose permease, which is modeled by no other rule. The difference between rules (R9) and (R12) is that the latter describes a much faster event. However, since quantitative aspects are not considered in the calculus, the difference between the two rules does not appear.

The model can be simplified. Let us denote by T the term $lacP \cdot lacO \cdot lacZ \cdot lacY \cdot lacA \mid repr$. Note that T behaves as $lacI-A$ apart from the transcription of the lac Repressor, which is already present. Therefore, the transition system derived from T corresponds to the one derived form $lacI-A$ apart from some $\square$-labeled transitions obtained by the application of rule (R1). As a consequence, $T \approx lacI-A$. Now, since $\approx$ is a congruence, we may replace $lacI-A$ with T in *Ecoli*, thus obtaining an equivalent term.

Now we use the weak bisimulation defined on CLS systems to verify a simple property of the described system, namely that by starting from a situation in which the lac Repressor is bound to gene o, and none of the three enzymes produced by the lactose operon is present (which is a typical stable state of the system), production of such enzymes can start only if lactose appears.

In order to verify this property with the bisimulation relation we defined, we need to modify the rules of the model in such a way that the event of starting the production of the three enzymes becomes observable. We can obtain this result, for instance, by replacing rule (R10) with the rule

$$(\widetilde{w})^L \rfloor (\widetilde{x} \cdot RO \cdot \widetilde{y} \mid LACT \mid X) \mid START \quad \mapsto$$
$$(\widetilde{w})^L \rfloor (\widetilde{x} \cdot lacO \cdot \widetilde{y} \mid RLACT \mid X) \qquad \text{(R10bis)}$$

We choose to modify (R10) because we know that, after applying rule (R10), the three enzymes can be produced freely, and we add to the rule the interaction with the artificial element $START$ in the environment in order to obtain $\Box|START$ as a transition label every time the rule is applied to the term. The property we want to verify is satisfied, for some ground terms T_1, T_2 and T_3, by the system $\langle T_1, \mathcal{R} \rangle$, where $\mathcal{R}$ consists of the following four rules:

$$
\begin{array}{llll}
T_1 \mid LACT & \mapsto & T_2 & \text{(R1')} \\
T_2 \mid LACT & \mapsto & T_2 & \text{(R2')}
\end{array}
\qquad
\begin{array}{llll}
T_2 \mid START & \mapsto & T_3 & \text{(R3')} \\
T_3 \mid LACT & \mapsto & T_3 & \text{(R4')}
\end{array}
$$

It can be proved that the system $\langle T_1, \mathcal{R} \rangle$ is weakly bisimilar to the system $\langle EcoliRO, (\mathcal{R}_{lac} \setminus \{R_{10}\}) \cup \{(R_{10bis})\} \rangle$, where:

$$ EcoliRO = \left(m \right)^L \rfloor lacI' \cdot PP \cdot RO \cdot lacZ \cdot lacY \cdot lacA $$

In particular, the bisimulation relation associates (the system containing) term T_1 with (the system containing) term $EcoliRO$, term T_2 with all the terms representing a bacterium containing at least one molecule of lactose with the Lac repressor bound to gene o, and, finally, term T_3 with all the terms in which the repressor has left gene o and is bound to the lactose.

4   Conclusions

We have presented a variant of CLS, we have given the calculus a labeled semantics and we have defined bisimulation relations on terms and on systems of the calculus. We have proved bisimilarities to be congruences and shown an example of application of CLS to the modeling of a biological system.

Bisimulations permit studying systems by comparison, and in this case they could be used for making predictions on the modeled biological phenomenon. However, as we have pointed out before, the framework we have developed in this paper does not deal with speed of events, hence we cannot prove properties depending on time and perform simulations. As future work, we plan to develop a quantitative extension of the calculus in which speed of events are modeled as rates of rewrite rule applications. This will increase significantly the complexity of the semantics of the calculus. In fact, in biological systems the speed of an event depends on the total number of entities that may cause that event, and hence the rate of application of a rule will depend on the number of different positions in a term where the rule can be applied.

References

1. R. Alur, C. Belta, F. Ivancic, V. Kumar, M. Mintz, G.J. Pappas, H. Rubin and J. Schug. "Hybrid Modeling and Simulation of Biomolecular Networks". Hybrid Systems: Computation and Control, LNCS 2034, pages 19–32, Springer, 2001.
2. R. Barbuti, S. Cataudella, A. Maggiolo-Schettini, P. Milazzo and A. Troina. "A Probabilistic Model for Molecular Systems". Fundamenta Informaticae, volume 67, pages 13–27, 2005.

3. R. Barbuti, A. Maggiolo-Schettini, P. Milazzo and A. Troina. "A Calculus of Looping Sequences for Modelling Microbiological Systems". Fundamenta Informaticae, volume 72, pages 1–15, 2006.
4. L. Cardelli. "Brane Calculi. Interactions of Biological Membranes". CMSB'04, LNCS 3082, pages 257–280, Springer, 2005.
5. N. Chabrier-Rivier, M. Chiaverini, V. Danos, F. Fages and V. Schachter. "Modeling and Querying Biomolecular Interaction Networks". Theoretical Computer Science, volume 325, number 1, pages 25-44, 2004.
6. M. Curti, P. Degano, C. Priami and C.T. Baldari. "Modelling Biochemical Pathways through Enhanced pi-calculus". Theoretical Computer Science, volume 325, number 1, pages 111–140, 2004.
7. V. Danos and C. Laneve. "Formal Molecular Biology". Theoretical Computer Science, volume 325, number 1, pages 69–110, 2004.
8. J. Leifer and R. Milner. "Deriving Bisimulation Congruences for Reactive Systems". CONCUR'00, LNCS 1877, pages 243–258, Springer, 2000.
9. H. Matsuno, A. Doi, M. Nagasaki and S. Miyano. "Hybrid Petri Net Representation of Gene Regulatory Network". Pacific Symposium on Biocomputing, World Scientific Press, pages 341–352, 2000.
10. C. Priami and P. Quaglia "Beta Binders for Biological Interactions". CMSB'04, LNCS 3082, pages 20–33, Springer, 2005.
11. A. Regev, E.M. Panina, W. Silverman, L. Cardelli and E. Shapiro. "BioAmbients: An Abstraction for Biological Compartments". Theoretical Computer Science, volume 325, number 1, pages 141–167, 2004.
12. A. Regev, W. Silverman and E.Y. Shapiro. "Representation and Simulation of Biochemical Processes Using the pi-calculus Process Algebra". Pacific Symposium on Biocomputing, World Scientific Press, pages 459–470, 2001.
13. P. Sewell. "From Rewrite Rules to Bisimulation Congruences". Theoretical Computer Science, volume 274, pages 183–230, 2002.

A   Proofs

A.1   Proof of Proposition 2

We show that $\mathcal{S} \overset{def}{=} \{ (C[T_1], C[T_2]) \mid T_1 \sim T_2$ and C is a context$\}$ is a bisimulation. First of all, it is worth noting that $\mathcal{S}$ includes $\sim$ because $C[T_1] = T_1$ when $C = \square$. Moreover, the following implication holds:

$$T_1 \mathcal{S} T_2 \implies C[T_1] \mathcal{S} C[T_2] \tag{1}$$

because $T_1 \mathcal{S} T_2$ implies $\exists C'. T_1 = C'[T_1'], T_2 = C'[T_2']$ for some $T_1', T_2' \in \mathcal{T}$ such that $T_1' \sim T_2'$. Hence $C[C'[T_1']] \mathcal{S} C[C'[T_2']]$, that is $C[T_1] \mathcal{S} C[T_2]$.

Now, since $\sim$ is a symmetric relation, we have only to show that given $T_1 \sim T_2$ it holds that: $C[T_1] \xrightarrow{C'} T_1' \implies \exists T_2'. C[T_2] \xrightarrow{C'} T_2'$ and $T_1' \mathcal{S} T_2'$.

We prove this by induction on the depth of the derivation tree of $C[T_1] \xrightarrow{C'} T_1'$:

– *Base case* (rule_appl). There exists $T \mapsto T_1' \in \mathcal{R}$ such that $C'[C[T_1]] \equiv T\sigma$ for some instantiation function σ. This implies $T_1 \xrightarrow{C'[C]} T_1'$ and, since $T_1 \sim T_2$, there exists T_2' such that $T_2 \xrightarrow{C'[C]} T_2'$ with $T_1' \sim T_2'$. Finally, $T_2 \xrightarrow{C'[C]} T_2'$ implies $C[T_2] \xrightarrow{C'} T_2'$ by Lemma 2 and $T_1' \sim T_2'$ implies $T_1' \mathcal{S} T_2'$.

– *Induction step* (par). In this case $C = C_1[C_2]$ for some C_2 and where $C_1 = \square \,|\, T$ for some T. Hence, $C[T_1] = C_1[C_2[T_1]]$ and by the premise of the inference rule we obtain $C_2[T_1] \xrightarrow{C'} T_1''$ with $C_1 \not\pitchfork C'$. It follows that $T_1' = C_1[T_1'']$. By the induction hypothesis we have that $\exists T_2''.C_2[T_2] \xrightarrow{C'} T_2'' \wedge T_1''ST_2''$, hence, by applying the (par) rule, $C_1[C_2[T_2]] \xrightarrow{C'} C_1[T_2'']$, that is $C[T_2] \xrightarrow{C'} T_2'$. By the closure of $\mathcal{S}$ to contexts given in (1), we have $C_1[T_1'']SC_1[T_2'']$, that is $T_1'ST_2'$.

– *Induction step* (cont). In this case $C' = \square$ and $C = C_1[C_2]$ for some C_2 and where $C_1 = T \,\rfloor\, \square$ for some T. Hence, $C[T_1] = C_1[C_2[T_1]]$ and by the premise of the inference rule we obtain $C_2[T_1] \xrightarrow{\square} T_1''$. It follows that $T_1' = C_1[T_1'']$. By the induction hypothesis we have that $\exists T_2''.C_2[T_2] \xrightarrow{C'} T_2'' \wedge T_1''ST_2''$, hence, by applying the (cont) rule, $C_1[C_2[T_2]] \xrightarrow{\square} C_1[T_2'']$, that is $C[T_2] \xrightarrow{\square} T_2'$. By the closure of $\mathcal{S}$ to contexts given in (1), we have $C_1[T_1'']SC_1[T_2'']$, that is $T_1'ST_2'$. $\square$

A.2   Proof of Proposition 3

We show that $\mathcal{S} \overset{def}{=} \{\, (C[T_1], C[T_2]) \mid T_1 \approx T_2 \text{ and } C \text{ is a context}\}$ is a weak bisimulation. Similarly as in the proof of Proposition 2 we have that $\mathcal{S}$ includes $\approx$, and that the following implication holds:

$$T_1ST_2 \implies C[T_1]SC[T_2] \qquad (2)$$

and we have only to show that given $T_1 \approx T_2$ it holds that: $C[T_1] \xrightarrow{C'} T_1' \implies \exists T_2'.C[T_2] \overset{C'}{\Longrightarrow} T_2'$ and $T_1'ST_2'$.

We prove this by induction on the depth of the derivation tree of $C[T_1] \xrightarrow{C'} T_1'$:

– *Base case* (rule_appl). There exists $T \mapsto T_1' \in \mathcal{R}$ such that $C'[C[T_1]] \equiv T\sigma$ for some instantiation function σ. This implies $T_1 \xrightarrow{C'[C]} T_1'$ and, since $T_1 \approx T_2$, there exists T_2' such that $T_2 \overset{C'[C]}{\Longrightarrow} T_2'$ with $T_1' \approx T_2'$. Finally, $T_2 \overset{C'[C]}{\Longrightarrow} T_2'$ implies $C[T_2] \overset{C'}{\Longrightarrow} T_2'$ by Lemma 4 and $T_1' \approx T_2'$ implies $T_1'ST_2'$.

– *Induction step* (par). In this case $C = C_1[C_2]$ for some C_2 and where $C_1 = \square \,|\, T$ for some T. Hence, $C[T_1] = C_1[C_2[T_1]]$ and by the premise of the inference rule we obtain $C_2[T_1] \xrightarrow{C'} T_1''$ with $C_1 \not\pitchfork C'$. It follows $T_1' = C_1[T_1'']$. By the induction hypothesis we have that $\exists T_2''.C_2[T_2] \overset{C'}{\Longrightarrow} T_2'' \wedge T_1''ST_2''$, hence, by Lemma 3, $C_1[C_2[T_2]] \overset{C'}{\Longrightarrow} C_1[T_2'']$, that is $C[T_2] \overset{C'}{\Longrightarrow} T_2'$. By the closure of $\mathcal{S}$ to contexts given in (2), we have $C_1[T_1'']SC_1[T_2'']$, that is $T_1'ST_2'$.

– *Induction step* (cont). In this case $C' = \square$ and $C = C_1[C_2]$ for some C_2 and where $C_1 = T \,\rfloor\, \square$ for some T. Hence, $C[T_1] = C_1[C_2[T_1]]$ and by the premise of the inference rule we obtain $C_2[T_1] \xrightarrow{\square} T_1''$. It follows that $T_1' = C_1[T_1'']$. By the induction hypothesis we have that $\exists T_2''.C_2[T_2] \overset{C'}{\Longrightarrow} T_2'' \wedge T_1''ST_2''$, hence, by Lemma 3, $C_1[C_2[T_2]] \overset{\square}{\Longrightarrow} C_1[T_2'']$, that is $C[T_2] \overset{C'}{\Longrightarrow} T_2'$. By the closure of $\mathcal{S}$ to contexts given in (2), we have $C_1[T_1'']SC_1[T_2'']$, that is $T_1'ST_2'$. $\square$

Stronger Reduction Criteria for
Local First Search

Marcos E. Kurbán[1], Peter Niebert[2], Hongyang Qu[2], and Walter Vogler[3]

[1] Formal Methods and Tools Group, University of Twente, EWI INF - PO Box 217,
7500 AE, Enschede, The Netherlands
mkurban@cs.utwente.nl
[2] Laboratoire d'Informatique Fondamentale de Marseille, Université de Provence
39, rue Joliot-Curie / F-13453 Marseille Cedex 13,
{niebert, hongyang}@cmi.univ-mrs.fr
[3] Institut für Informatik, Universität Augsburg, D-86135 Augsburg
Walter.Vogler@Informatik.Uni-Augsburg.DE

Abstract. Local First Search (LFS) is a partial order technique for
reducing the number of states to be explored when trying to decide
reachability of a local (component) property in a parallel system; it is
based on an analysis of the structure of the partial orders of executions
in such systems. Intuitively, LFS is based on a criterion that allows to
guide the search for such local properties by limiting the "concurrent
progress" of components.

In this paper, we elaborate the analysis of the partial orders in question and obtain related but significantly stronger criteria for reductions,
show their relation to the previously established criterion, and discuss
the algorithmics of the proposed improvement. Our contribution is both
fundamental in providing better insights into LFS and practical in providing an improvement of high potential, as is illustrated by experimental
results.

1   Introduction

Partial order methods [16,5,8,7,13,17,9,10,14,4,6] exploit the structural property
of independence that occurs naturally in asynchronous parallel systems. The basic observation exploited by partial order methods is the commutation of pairs
of independent transitions which, by definition, lead to the same state independently of the order of execution. This structural information can be applied in
order to remove redundant transitions or, if the property in question permits,
even states, without changing the validity of the property. Independence is typically derived from distribution, i.e. transitions of distinct processes in a system
may commute (unless they access shared variables or synchronize). This commutation of independent transitions gives rise to a notion of equivalent executions,
and the equivalence classes are called *Mazurkiewicz traces*.

Among these methods, *Local First Search* (LFS) [11,1] is specialized for the
complete search for *local properties*, i.e. properties that can only be modified by

K. Barkaoui, A. Cavalcanti, and A. Cerone (Eds.): ICTAC 2006, LNCS 4281, pp. 108–122, 2006.
© Springer-Verlag Berlin Heidelberg 2006

dependent transitions. The definition and justification of LFS highly depend on the characterization of equivalent executions as labelled partial orders. In [11], it is shown that *prime traces*, i.e. partial orders with a single maximal element, suffice to search for local properties; in turn, to approximate all prime traces, it suffices to consider only traces (partial orders) with a logarithmic number of maximal elements (compared to the overall parallelism in the system); this number is called *LFS*-bound.

In [11], a first method for exploiting this criterion was given, which however did not guarantee that the number of states actually explored would be inferior to the global number of states. In [1] in contrast, the LFS-bound is combined with ideas from McMillan unfoldings [4] to obtain a breadth first search based algorithm that is complete and never explores the same state twice. For a number of benchmarks, it was observed that (asymptotically) LFS with the unfolding approach gives decent reductions where the stubborn set method [17], the ample set [13] and related methods give only very weak reductions.

In the current work, we revisit the LFS correctness theorem and derive a hierarchy of criteria, *peak rest compliance* (pr-compliance), *peak width sequence compliance* (pws-compliance), a *recursive LFS-bound* and finally the previously published *logarithmic LFS-bound*. These criteria characterize subsets of traces, ordered by inclusion: *pr-compliance* defines the smallest set of traces and the *logarithmic LFS-bound* the biggest. We prove that any prime trace can be reached through a sequence of prefixes such that each one is pr-compliant, and for that matter pws-compliant, and satisfies the LFS-bounds. On the whole, we thus obtain a modular proof of the original theorem and stronger reduction criteria. Efficient exploration algorithms have been implemented using the technique from [1].

The paper is structured as follows. Section 2 presents the necessary background on Marzurkiewicz trace theory. Section 3 explains the basic concepts of the LFS technique. Section 4 introduces *pr-compliance* based on a tree like recursive decomposition of traces, and a proof of the preservation of local properties is given. In Section 5, we derive a simplified version of pr-compliance, *pws-compliance*, which is computationally less expensive. In Section 6 in turn, we derive a *recursive LFS-bound* from pws-compliance and the previously published logarithmic bound from the recursive bound. In Section 7, we explain the complexity and steps needed to implement a pws-compliance procedure. In Section 8, we report experimental results obtained with our prototype implementation and conclude in Section 9.

2   Basic Concepts

The theory of Marzurkiewicz traces is built on the concept of a *concurrent alphabet*, which is a tuple (Σ, I) with Σ a finite set of *actions* and I an irreflexive symmetric binary relation on Σ. I is called the *independence relation* of the alphabet, and we will refer to $D = (\Sigma \times \Sigma) \setminus I$ as the *dependence relation* of such an alphabet. We will assume that (Σ, I) is fixed for this paper.

A transition system over Σ is a triple $T = (S, \rightarrow, s_0)$ with S a set of states, $s_0 \in S$ the initial state, and $\rightarrow \subseteq S \times \Sigma \times S$ a transition relation. For $(s, a, s') \in \rightarrow$ we also write $s \xrightarrow{a} s'$. We only consider deterministic transition systems, i.e. systems such that $s \xrightarrow{a} s_1$ and $s \xrightarrow{a} s_2$ implies $s_1 = s_2$. Moreover, we only consider systems that respect the independence relation in the following way: If $s \xrightarrow{a} s_1 \xrightarrow{b} s_2$ and $a \, I \, b$ then there exists s_1' with $s \xrightarrow{b} s_1' \xrightarrow{a} s_2$.

A word over Σ is a – possibly empty – finite sequence of symbols from Σ; the set of words is Σ^*, ranged over by u, v, w, etc.; the empty sequence will be denoted by ε. When used on words, $\preceq$ will denote the usual prefix ordering on words.

Let $\equiv_I$ be the least congruence on the monoid generated by Σ^* and concatenation such that $\forall a, b \in \Sigma : (a, b) \in I \Rightarrow ab \equiv_I ba$. The equivalence classes of $\equiv_I$ will be called *traces*, the equivalence class of u will be denoted by $[u]$ and the set of all traces by $[\Sigma^*]$. Since $\equiv_I$ is a congruence, concatenation carries over to traces: $[u][v] = [uv]$ is well-defined. Similarly, the *prefix relation* $\preceq$ carries over, i.e. $[u] \preceq [v]$ iff there exists $[w]$ with $[u][w] = [v]$.

For a transition system T, let $L(T) \subseteq \Sigma^*$ denote the words $u = a_1 \ldots a_n$ such that there exists a path $s_0 \xrightarrow{a_1} s_1 \ldots s_{n-1} \xrightarrow{a_n} s_n$ and let $\sigma(u) = s_n$ denote the state reached by the word. Obviously, if $u \in L(T)$ and $u \equiv_I u'$ then $u' \in L(T)$ and $\sigma(u) = \sigma(u')$. We therefore also write $\sigma([u]) := \sigma(u)$.

A *property* of a transition system T is a subset $P \subseteq S$. An action a is *visible for P* iff there exist $s_1 \in P$ and $s_2 \in S \setminus P$ such that $s_1 \xrightarrow{a} s_2$ or $s_2 \xrightarrow{a} s_1$ (i.e. a may "change" the validity of P). A property P is a *local property* iff, for all pairs of actions a and b both visible for P, we have $a \, D \, b$. Typically, a local property is a property of a single variable or a single process in a parallel product.

Local properties have an interesting link with traces, as has been observed in [11]: if some state satisfies local property P, then such a state can be reached by a trace which seen as a partial order has exactly one maximal element; cf. Section 3.

3   Local First Search

The aim of "Local First Search" is to optimize the search for local properties in transition systems. It is based on the following parameters of a concurrent alphabet.

Definition 1. *We say that (Σ, I) has parallel degree m if m is the maximal number of pairwise independent actions in Σ, i.e.*

$$m = \max\{|A| \mid A \subseteq \Sigma \text{ and } a, b \in A, a \neq b \Rightarrow aIb\}.$$

We say that (Σ, I) has communication degree cd if cd is the maximal number of pairwise independent actions such that all of them depend on a common action, i.e.

$$cd = \max\{|B| \mid B \subseteq \Sigma, \exists c \in \Sigma : (\forall b \in B : \neg cIb) \text{ and } (\forall b, b' \in B : b \neq b' \Rightarrow bIb')\}.$$

Intuitively, the parallel degree might correspond to the number of processes of a concurrent system, whereas the communication degree is related to synchronisation, e.g. systems based on binary channels have a communication degree 2.

The main idea of *Local First Search* (*LFS*) is better understood by viewing traces as partial orders. This is based on the well known one-to-one correspondence [3, Chapter 2] between traces and the class of finite Σ-labeled partial orders $(E, \leq, \lambda)$ such that

(1) For any $e, f \in E$ with $\lambda(e) \, D \, \lambda(f)$ we have $e \leq f$ or $f \leq e$.
(2) $\leq$ is equal to the transitive closure of $\leq \cap \{(e, f) \mid \lambda(e) \, D \, \lambda(f)\}$.

We will refer to such partial orders as a (Σ, I)-*lpo* or *lpo* for short. Any of them can be seen as an abstract representation of an execution. In this representation, two elements are unordered if and only if the actions labelling them could have occurred in any relative order (or in parallel). Correspondingly, any two such elements are labeled with independent actions.

By a *linearisation* we mean a word over E which contains each element of E once and where an element e occurs before f whenever $e < f$. We obtain a *labeled linearisation* from such a word, if we replace each element by its label. The relation between traces and lpo's is simply that the set of all labelled linearisations of an lpo is a trace and each trace, as described above, induces such a lpo.

If we have an lpo $(E, \leq, \lambda)$, we call subset F of E an *interval* iff for all $e, f \in F$ and $g \in E$ with $e \leq g \leq f$ also $g \in F$. We identify an interval F with the labeled partial order it induces by restricting $\leq$ and λ appropriately. Note that F is a (Σ, I)-lpo again. For a linearisation v of F we define $set(v)$ by $set(v) = F$.

The *downward closure* of $F \subseteq E$ is $\downarrow F = \{e \in E \mid \exists f \in F : e \leq f\}$, and we write $\downarrow f$ if $F = \{f\}$.

Element e of an lpo is an *immediate predecessor* of f and f an *immediate successor* of e iff $e < f$ and $\forall g : \; e \leq g \leq f \implies g = e$ or $g = f$. We now define notions for $(E, \leq, \lambda)$ some of which correspond to the parallel and the communication degree of a concurrent alphabet.

Definition 2. *Let $(E, \leq, \lambda)$ be an lpo. An element $e \in E$ is* maximal *if there is no $f \in E$ such that $e < f$. We define* $\max(E)$ *as the set of maximal elements of E and call E* prime, *if $\max(E)$ has just one element.*

The width *of E (denoted by $width(E)$) is the maximal number of pairwise incomparable elements, i.e. $max\{|A| \mid A \subseteq E \wedge \forall e, f \in A : e \leq f \Rightarrow e = f\}$.*

The communication degree *of E is the maximal number of immediate predecessors of an element of E.*

The following proposition first relates these notions to the concurrent alphabet; the proof of this relation can be found in [11]. The last claim is easy to see.

Proposition 3. *Let $(E, \leq, \lambda)$ be an lpo.*
Then $|max(E)| \leq width(E)$ and $width(E)$ is at most the parallel degree of (Σ, I) and the communication degree of E is at most cd.
For an interval $F \subseteq E$ we have $width(F) \leq width(E)$.

From the definition of local properties, one gets immediately the following: If a system can reach a state satisfying such a property, then a satisfying state can be reached with a prime trace corresponding to a prime lpo (the proof can be seen in [1]). The following fundamental result of LFS shows that one can construct all prime lpo's by restricting attention to lpo's with a bounded number of maximal elements; this implies that checking for satisfaction of a local property can be performed on a restricted state space.

Theorem 4 (LFS theorem [11]). *Let* $(E, \leq, \lambda)$ *be an lpo of width* m *with at most* cd *maximal elements. Then there exists a linearisation* w *of* E *such that, for every prefix* v *of* w, $set(v)$ *has at most* 1 *maximal element if* $cd = 1$, *and at most* $\lfloor (cd - 1)log_{cd}(m) + 1 \rfloor$ *maximal elements if* $cd > 1$.

This theorem provides a filter for excluding traces in the search of states satisfying local properties. The best known way of exploiting this filter in a search procedure is given in [1]. For guidance purposes, it is also outlined below. Let us first consider a kind of "unfolding" of transition system T that respects traces, the trace system of T:

Definition 5 (Trace system). *Let* $T = (S, \rightarrow, s_0)$ *be a transition system respecting* (Σ, I). *Then the* trace system *of* T *is the transition system* $TS(T)$ *whose states are the traces associated to words in* $L(T)$, *with the empty trace* $[\varepsilon]$ *as initial state and such that the transition relation is* $\rightarrow = \{([u], a, [ua]) \mid ua \in L(T)\}$.

Based on $\sigma([u])$ we can lift properties of T to properties of $TS(T)$, and we can restrict the test for a local property to the search for a suitable prime trace.

The next notion, originating from McMillan prefixes [10], is needed to avoid the exploration of an infinite number of traces.

Definition 6 (Adequate order). *A partial order* $\sqsubseteq$ *on the whole set of traces is called* adequate *if*

(Ad$_1$) *it is well-founded;*
(Ad$_2$) *it refines the prefix order, i.e.* $[u] \preceq [v]$ *implies* $[u] \sqsubseteq [v]$;
(Ad$_3$) *it is a right congruence, i.e.* $[u] \sqsubseteq [v]$ *implies* $[u.z] \sqsubseteq [v.z]$ *for any* $z \in \Sigma^*$.

In practice, only adequate orders that refine the length order, i.e. $|u| < |v|$ implies $[u] \sqsubseteq [v]$, are used. Together with the filter of Theorem 4, adequate orders are used to *cut* the search in the state space, as is shown in the following algorithm that refines breadth first search.

Algorithm 1 guarantees that each state of the system is explored at most once (i.e. for at most one Mazurkiewicz trace leading to it), while preserving reachability of local properties. In practice, it considerably reduces the set of states explored. The correctness proof of the algorithm and a detailed explanation was presented in [1], and this proof relies on Theorem 4 as a module. What is important here is the consequence that the LFS-criterion in the algorithm, which is "bounding the set of maximal elements of trace $[ua]$ by $\lfloor (cd - 1)log_{cd}(m) + 1 \rfloor$", can be replaced by other criteria similar to Theorem 4 without changing the correct functioning. The aim of this paper is to provide more restrictive criteria or tighter filters for lpo's that suffice to guarantee reachability of all prime lpo's but exclude a lot of traces or lpo's violating the criterion.

Algorithm 1. Computation of a finite locally complete subsystem

Table $\leftarrow \{(s_0, [\varepsilon])\}$, Next_Level $\leftarrow \{(s_0, [\varepsilon])\}$
while Next_Level $\neq \emptyset$ **do**
  Current_Level $\leftarrow$ Next_Level; Next_Level $\leftarrow \emptyset$
  for all $(s, [u]) \in$ Current_Level, $a \in \Sigma$, $s' \in S$ such that $s \xrightarrow{a} s'$ **do**
    if $s' \in P$ **then**
      Return(ua)
    else
      if $[ua]$ respects LFS-criterion **then**
        if $(s', [v]) \in$ Table **then**
          if $|ua| = |v|$ and $(s', [v]) \in$ Next_Level and $[ua] \sqsubset [v]$ **then**
            Table $\leftarrow$ (Table $\setminus \{(s', [v])\}) \cup \{(s', [ua])\}$
            Next_Level $\leftarrow$ (Next_Level $\setminus \{(s', [v])\}) \cup \{(s', [ua])\}$
          end if
        else
          Table $\leftarrow$ Table $\cup \{(s', [ua])\}$
          Next_Level $\leftarrow$ Next_Level $\cup \{(s', [ua])\}$
        end if
      end if
    end if
  end for
end while
Return unreachable

---

4   A New Approach for Tighter Constraints

We will show in this section that, for building up prime lpo's, it is sufficient to consider peak-rest-compliant lpo's, which we define below. We will discuss in the succeeding sections in some detail how one can check this condition, and how one can weaken it to make the check more efficient; in the course of this discussion we will also prove that each peak-rest-compliant lpo obeys the bound on the number of maximal elements given in Theorem 4.

Definition 7. *Let* $(E, \leq, \lambda)$ *be an lpo. Let* $e_1, \ldots, e_k \in \max(E)$ *be different,* $k \geq 0$, *and* $F = \max(E) \setminus \{e_1, \ldots, e_k\}$ *with* $F \neq \emptyset$. *Define* $E_i = (\downarrow e_i) \setminus \bigcup\{\downarrow f \mid e_i \neq f \in \max(E)\}$ *for* $i = 1, \ldots, k$ *and* $E_{k+1} = (\downarrow F) \setminus \bigcup\{\downarrow e_i \mid i = 1, \ldots, k\}$.

Then $(E_1, \ldots, E_{k+1})$ *is a* peak-rest-decomposition *of* E, *and in case that* F *is a singleton a* peak-decomposition. *We call* $E_1, \ldots, E_k$, *and also* E_{k+1} *in the latter case,* peaks *of* E.

A peak is defined by a maximal element e; it consists of all elements that are below e, but not below any other maximal element. From this, it is clear that there exists a peak-decomposition, which is unique up to the ordering of its components; further, peaks are disjoint, elements of different peaks are unordered and a label appearing in one peak is independent of any label appearing in another peak – and this even holds for $E_1, \ldots, E_{k+1}$ in the general case. From this, we see that the sum over the $width(E_i)$ is at most $width(E)$.

Note that, in the general case, E_{k+1} could contain more elements than just the union of the peaks of the maximal elements in F, namely some elements that are below more than one maximal element of F.

Definition 8. *An lpo $(E, \leq, \lambda)$ is called* peak-rest-compliant *or* pr-compliant *for short if it has at most cd maximal elements or it has a peak-rest-decomposition $(E_1, \ldots, E_{k+1})$ with $1 \leq k < cd$ such that $width(E_{k+1}) \leq width(E_i)$ for $i = 1, \ldots, k$ and E_{k+1} is pr-compliant as well.*

Intuitively, a pr-compliant lpo has at most cd maximal elements or it is an initial part of an lpo with at most cd maximal elements and needed to build up the latter lpo; in the latter case, the idea is that k of the peaks of the latter lpo have already been built and that E_{k+1} will lead to the next peak. This idea will be formalized in the proof of our first main theorem, which we present now.

Theorem 9. *Let $(E, \leq, \lambda)$ be an lpo with at most cd maximal elements. Then there exists a linearisation w of E such that for each prefix v of w, $set(v)$ is pr-compliant.*

Proof. The proof will be by induction on the size of E, the case of $E = \emptyset$ being trivial. We assume that the claim has been shown for all smaller lpo's and make the following distinction of cases.

i) E has just one maximal element e. Then by Proposition 3, $E \setminus \{e\}$ has at most cd maximal elements, namely the immediate predecessors of e. Choose a suitable linearisation u of $E \setminus \{e\}$ by induction, and then we are done by setting $w = ue$.

ii) Let $\max(E) = \{e_1, \ldots, e_{k+1}\}$ with $1 \leq k < cd$. Let $(E_1, \ldots, E_{k+1})$ be the peak-decomposition of E ordered according to decreasing width. Choose linearisations u for $\downarrow (E_1 \cup \ldots \cup E_k)$ and u' for E_{k+1} by induction. Since these sets are a partition of E with no element of the latter below any element of the first, $w = uu'$ is a linearisation of E; we have to check all prefixes of w.

Let v be a prefix of w; if v is a prefix of u, we are done by induction, otherwise $v = uv'$ with v' a prefix of u'. Let $F = set(uv')$. Clearly, $e_1, \ldots, e_k \in F$ are still maximal; so let $\max(F) = \{e_1, \ldots, e_k, f_1, \ldots, f_l\}$, where $l \geq 1$ and $\max(set(v')) = \{f_1, \ldots, f_l\}$. Let $(F_1, \ldots, F_{k+1})$ be the peak-rest-decomposition of F induced by the maximal elements $e_1, \ldots, e_k$ and the set $\{f_1, \ldots, f_l\}$.

Since each $e \leq e_i$ for some $i \in \{1, \ldots, k\}$ occurs in u, we have $F_{k+1} \subseteq set(v') \subseteq E_{k+1}$, which implies $width(F_{k+1}) \leq width(E_{k+1})$ by Proposition 3. Vice versa, for each $f \in set(v') \subseteq E_{k+1}$, we cannot have $f \leq e_i$ for any $i \in \{1, \ldots, k\}$, hence we must have $F_{k+1} = set(v')$, which implies that F_{k+1} is pr-compliant by choice of u'.

For $i = 1, \ldots, k$, we have $E_i \subseteq F_i$: any $e \in E_i$ occurs in u, hence $e \in F$; we do not have $e \leq e_j$ for $j \neq i$ and we cannot have $e \leq f_j$ for some $j = 1, \ldots, l$ since $f_j \leq e_{k+1}$. Thus, we have $width(E_i) \leq width(F_i)$ by Proposition 3.

Hence, due to the chosen ordering of the E_i, we have $width(F_{k+1}) \leq width(E_{k+1}) \leq width(E_i) \leq width(F_i)$ for all $i = 1, \ldots, k$, and we are done.

$\square$

5 The Peak-Width-Sequence Criterion

In this section, we present a criterion that is slightly weaker than pr-conformance but avoids the recursive checks of the rest in a peak-rest-decomposition for pr-conformance. For this, we need the following notion for sequences of numbers, which is rather technical but easy to check.

Definition 10 (n-cumulative sequence). *For $n \geq 2$, a decreasing sequence of natural numbers $m_1 \geq m_2 \geq \ldots \geq m_l$ with $m_i \geq 1$ is called n-cumulative, if $l < n$ or there exists a j with $1 < j \leq n$ such that $m_{j-1} \geq \sum_{k=j}^{l} m_k$ and $m_j, \ldots, m_l$ is n-cumulative.*

Definition 11. *Let $m_1 \geq m_2 \geq \ldots \geq m_l$ be the widths of the peaks of an lpo $(E, \leq, \lambda)$; then the lpo is called* peak-width-sequence-compliant *or* pws-compliant *for short if this sequence is cd-cumulative.*

Together with Theorem 9, the following theorem demonstrates that we can restrict ourselves to pws-compliant lpo's if we want to build up all lpo's with at most cd maximal elements incrementally.

Theorem 12. *Each pr-compliant lpo is pws-compliant.*

Proof. Let $(E, \leq, \lambda)$ be a pr-compliant lpo and $(E_1, \ldots, E_{k+1})$ the respective peak-rest-decomposition with the peaks ordered by decreasing size. The proof is by induction on the size of E. Let $(F_{k+1}, \ldots, F_l)$ be the peak-decomposition of E_{k+1}, again with the peaks ordered by decreasing size. Since no element of E_{k+1} is below any element outside of E_{k+1}, $(E_1, \ldots, E_k, F_{k+1}, \ldots, F_l)$ is the peak-decomposition of E. Since $(F_{k+1}, \ldots, F_l)$ is cd-cumulative by induction and $k < cd$, it remains to check that $width(E_k) \geq \sum_{j=k+1}^{l} width(F_j)$. This follows from $\sum_{j=k+1}^{l} width(F_j) \leq width(E_{k+1})$, which is satisfied since the F_j are the peaks of E_{k+1}, and $width(E_{k+1}) \leq width(E_k)$ according to Definition 8. $\square$

The difference between pws-compliance and pr-compliance is that the width of the rest in a peak-rest-decomposition might be larger than the sum of the peak widths for the peaks in this rest; in such case, the lpo could be pws-compliant without being pr-compliant. Hence, pr-conformance may give a stronger restriction of the visited part of the state space. But algorithmically, checking for pr-conformance requires to identify the rest of a suitable peak-rest-decomposition, and this would presumably involve to determine all peaks and their widths first. Then one has additionally to compute the width of the rest, where the latter might be even larger than the union of the respective peaks. For the recursive checks for pr-conformance, the peaks of the rest and their widths are already given, but the problems with finding and checking a suitable peak-rest-decomposition of the rest occur repeatedly.

To test pws-compliance, we have to construct the peaks of the given lpo and to determine their widths $m_1 \geq m_2 \geq \ldots \geq m_l$; this sequence is cd-cumulative if – viewed from the end – there are never $cd-1$ indices in a row where the cumulative sum is larger than the next (smaller) number. It is easy to check this in linear time by one scan from right to left, building the cumulative sums on the way.

6   Deriving the LFS Bounds

In this section, we derive the classical LFS-bound as presented in [11], as well as some slight improvements, from the pws-criterion. Moreover, this is the first published proof of the LFS-bound for the general case (communication degree not limited to 2).

We begin by introducing a recursive formula for the bound that gives a relation of length and sum of n-cumulative sequences. Then, we derive the previously published logarithmic bound for the recursive formula.

Definition 13 (recursive bound). *For $n \geq 2$ and $m \geq 1$ let $L(n,m)$ be inductively defined by*

$$L(n,m) = \qquad m \qquad \text{for } m \leq n$$
$$L(n,m) = n - 1 + L(n, \lfloor \tfrac{m}{n} \rfloor) \quad \text{for } m > n$$

Lemma 14.
For $1 \leq k \leq n$ and $m \geq 1$ we have $k + L(n, \lfloor \tfrac{m}{k} \rfloor) \leq n + L(n, \lfloor \tfrac{m}{n} \rfloor)$.

Proof. By induction on m. We assume that the statement is already proven for all $m' < m$ with $m' \geq 1$. For an easier case analysis observe that $L(n,m) = n - 1 + L(n, \lfloor \tfrac{m}{n} \rfloor)$ also for $m = n$. This allows us to distinguish the following three cases: (a) $\lfloor \tfrac{m}{n} \rfloor \leq \lfloor \tfrac{m}{k} \rfloor < n$, (b) $\lfloor \tfrac{m}{n} \rfloor < n \leq \lfloor \tfrac{m}{k} \rfloor$ and (c) $n \leq \lfloor \tfrac{m}{n} \rfloor \leq \lfloor \tfrac{m}{k} \rfloor$.

For (a), we have to show that $k + \lfloor \tfrac{m}{k} \rfloor \leq n + \lfloor \tfrac{m}{n} \rfloor$. Due to properties of $\lfloor . \rfloor$ this follows from $k + \tfrac{m}{k} \leq n + \tfrac{m}{n}$ or equivalently $nk + n\tfrac{m}{k} \leq n^2 + k\tfrac{m}{n}$ or $\tfrac{m}{k}(n - k) \leq n(n - k)$. This follows, since $k \leq n$ and $\tfrac{m}{k} \leq n$ by $\lfloor \tfrac{m}{k} \rfloor < n$.

For (b), we have that $\lfloor \tfrac{\lfloor \frac{m}{k} \rfloor}{n} \rfloor = \lfloor \tfrac{m}{kn} \rfloor < n \leq \lfloor \tfrac{m}{k} \rfloor$. Therefore, we have to show that $k + n - 1 + \lfloor \tfrac{m}{kn} \rfloor \leq n + \lfloor \tfrac{m}{n} \rfloor$ which follows from $k - 1 + \tfrac{m}{kn} \leq \tfrac{m}{n}$. This is equivalent to $n(k - 1) + \tfrac{m}{k} \leq k\tfrac{m}{k}$ or $n(k - 1) \leq \tfrac{m}{k}(k - 1)$. The latter follows since $k \geq 1$ and $n \leq \tfrac{m}{k}$ by the assumption $n \leq \lfloor \tfrac{m}{k} \rfloor$.

For (c), we have to show that $k+n-1+L(n, \lfloor \tfrac{\lfloor \frac{m}{k} \rfloor}{n} \rfloor) \leq n+n-1+L(n, \lfloor \tfrac{\lfloor \frac{m}{n} \rfloor}{n} \rfloor)$. Since $\lfloor \tfrac{\lfloor \frac{m}{n} \rfloor}{n} \rfloor = \lfloor \tfrac{m}{kn} \rfloor = \lfloor \tfrac{\lfloor \frac{m}{k} \rfloor}{n} \rfloor$, this follows immediately from induction for $m' = \lfloor \tfrac{m}{n} \rfloor < m$. $\qquad\square$

Proposition 15. *Let $m_1 \geq m_2 \geq \ldots \geq m_l$ be n-cumulative $(n \geq 2)$ and $m = \sum_{i=1}^{l} m_i$. Then for the length l of the sequence we have $l \leq L(n, m)$.*

Proof. The proof is by induction on l.

For the case $m \leq n$ (in accordance with the first defining equation of L), we use $l \leq m$ (since $m_i \geq 1$ for each of the l summands m_i) and $m = L(m, n)$.

Now, for $m > n$, let j be the first position in the sequence, such that $m_{j-1} \geq \sum_{k=j}^{l} m_k =: m'$. Then $j \leq n$. Since $m_j \geq \ldots \geq m_l$ (as a suffix of an n-cumulative sequence) is itself n-cumulative of length $l' = l - (j-1)$, it holds by induction that $l' \leq L(n, m')$ and consequently $l \leq j - 1 + L(n, m')$. Since $m' \leq m_{j-1} \leq \ldots \leq m_1$, we have that $m' \leq \lfloor \frac{m}{j} \rfloor$. By Lemma 14 and the monotonicity of L in the second argument, we finally obtain $l \leq n - 1 + L(n, \lfloor \frac{m}{n} \rfloor) = L(n, m)$ as desired.   □

Corollary 16. *Let $(E, \leq, \lambda)$ be an lpo of width m with at most $cd \geq 2$ maximal elements. Then there exists an linearisation w of E such that, for every prefix v of w, $set(v)$ has at most $L(cd, m)$ maximal elements.*

Proof. We choose w as linearisation according to Theorem 9. Let v be a prefix of w; then $set(v)$ is by choice pr-compliant and according to Theorem 12 also pws-compliant, and $width(set(v)) \leq width(E) = m$ (Proposition 3). The peaks of $set(v)$ are mutually independent and hence the sum of their widths is bounded by m (antichains of the peaks freely combine to antichains of $set(v)$). Hence, the number of peaks of $set(v)$ is bounded by $L(cd, m)$ according to Proposition 15 and monotonicity of $L(n, m)$ in m.   □

The recursive formula L is an improvement over the originally published bound of Theorem 4, as shown by the following statement.

Proposition 17.
For $2 \leq n$ and $1 \leq m$ we have $L(n, m) \leq \lfloor (n-1) \log_n m \rfloor + 1$.

Proof. By induction on m. For $m \leq n$ by definition $L(n, m) = m$. Observe that $\log_n m$ is concave in m and has for $m = 1$ and $m = n$ the same value as $\frac{m-1}{n-1}$, thus $\frac{m-1}{n-1} \leq \log_n m$ for $1 \leq m \leq n$. Hence, $m \leq (n-1) \log_n m + 1$ which implies $m \leq \lfloor (n-1) \log_n m \rfloor + 1$ and we are done.

Now for $m > n$ we get $L(n, m) = n - 1 + L(n, \lfloor \frac{m}{n} \rfloor)$. By induction, we obtain that $L(n, m) \leq (n-1) + \lfloor (n-1)(log_n \lfloor \frac{m}{n} \rfloor) \rfloor + 1 = \lfloor (n-1)(1 + log_n \lfloor \frac{m}{n} \rfloor) \rfloor + 1 = \lfloor (n-1)(log_n n \lfloor \frac{m}{n} \rfloor) \rfloor + 1 \leq \lfloor (n-1)(log_n m) \rfloor + 1$, as desired.   □

Now, we can see how the original Theorem 4 is the end of a chain of reasoning in our present paper: We simply have to combine Corollary 16 with Proposition 17.

Concluding, we have seen how pr-compliance implies pws-compliance and pws-compliance induces a new recursive bound, which itself implies the original logarithmic bound.

7 Complexity and Algorithmics of Pws-Compliance

Pws-compliance may filter out significantly more traces than the LFS-bound, which means less states need to be stored. But its overhead, i.e. the cost of testing pws-compliance of each explored trace, has an impact on execution time.

The test for pws-compliance of a trace can be decomposed as follows:

- At first, the peaks need to be extracted as subtraces of the trace. Due to the characterization of dependency graphs at the beginning of Section 3, this task can be carried out in time at most $O(m^2)$, where m is the length of the trace. In the case of dependency based on reading and writing of shared variables, this can be improved to $O(m \cdot n)$ where n is the number of shared variables. The computation of the partial order for a peak, the transitive closure of the dependency relation of (ordered) occurrences of actions, can be performed in $O(m^3)$, but again this can be improved to $O(m^2n)$ where n is the number of shared variables.
- Then, for the partial order of each peak, its width has to be computed. Computing the width of a partial order is a problem that is known to be equivalent to that of finding a maximal matching in a bipartite graph [15]. The matching problem can then be solved with Hopcroft and Karp's algorithm [2] in $O(n^{\frac{5}{2}})$, where n is the size of the bipartite graph. This is in turn, twice the size of the peak.
- At last, the resulting widths have to be ordered and the test for an n-decreasing sequence has to be done. This is largely subsumed in the complexity of the previous task.

On the whole, the worst-case complexity of the pws-compliance test is thus subsumed by the $O(n^{\frac{5}{2}})$ of the matching algorithm in case of shared variable dependency. Profiling has shown that in practice the matching algorithm dominates in the computation time. We therefore opted for reuse of computed peak widths as much as possible which greatly improved the performance: Very often, only few peaks need to be recomputed under extension of a trace $[u]$ by an action a.

- Suppose that the subtrace $[vb]$ corresponding to a peak of $[u]$ is completely independent of a, then this peak is also a peak of $[ua]$.
- If a is dependent only of one peak with subtrace $[vb]$ and in addition $a \, D \, b$, then all peak widths are preserved.
- Otherwise, the peaks with subtrace $[vb]$ such that a depends on v are not preserved and must be "recomputed", whereas the peak of a is necessarily a singleton peak of with.

The optimization indicated by these observations allowed us to speed up our prototype significantly (for the examples in the next sections 4 to 15 times faster).

Still, exploring a transition system that has very long paths to some state is costly, the time complexity can only be limited by $O(n^{\frac{7}{2}})$ where n is the number of actually visited states (after reduction). On the other hand, our filtering may lead to an exponential reduction of the size of the state space; in such cases, this at first sight high complexity pays well off with a significant speed up and even with dramatic space savings, as the experiments of the next section suggest.

8   First Experimental Results

We have conducted first experiments with a new prototype using Algorithm 1. In one version, we use the bound of Proposition 15, which is slightly tighter than the previously published bound of Theorem 4. In another version, we use pws-compliance according to Theorem 12. We also did less systematic experiments with an implementation of pr-compliance (cf. Section 5). Without figures, we report qualitatively that pr-compliance offered little extra reduction compared to pws-compliance and our prototype implementation obviously took much more computation time.

In each parametric experiment, we compare the number of states, the memory consumption and the running time for exhaustive exploration on a machine with 2GB memory. We only give data for cases not running out of memory, which sometimes means that we can treat bigger problem instances with one or the other reduction method.

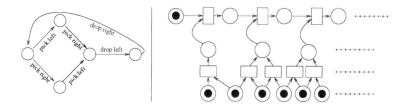

Fig. 1. An instance of the philosophers / the "comb" process as Petri net

The first experiment concerns a version of Dijkstra's dining philosophers with 5 states, which each choose nondeterministically, which fork they pick up first (Figure 1 at left). This is an example, where typical partial order techniques like stubborn sets [17] or ample sets [13] fail to achieve significant reduction; in fact, experimentally, Spin's partial order reduction does not remove any state. Moreover, we ran the experiment on a partial order package (PO-PACAKGE) based on Spin 1.6.5, which was developed in the University of Liege. This package supports stubborn-set-like techniques and does better reduction than Spin. Indeed, it works very well, i.e. generates very small state spaces, on lefthanded dining philosophers, which always try to first pick up forks on their left, and Sieve of Erastosthenes, the third example in this section. The data in parentheses, numbers of states visited by the package, are the evidence that supports our claim. Finally, it turns out that already the bound-based algorithm obtains a decent reduction, while the pws-compliant based reduction has an advantage in states, time and memory on this series. Observe the sub-exponential growth with reduction, whereas growth is cleanly exponential without reduction.

The second example "comb" (indicated as a Petri net in Figure 1 at right) is an artificial series of "best-case reductions" for the pws-criterion. While exponential without reduction, and while Spin's partial order reduction does fail to eliminate any state, it is clearly sub-exponential using the LFS-bound and it is

N	No reduction			LFS bound			PWS compliant			SPIN PO red		
	states	time (s)	memory (m)	states	time (s)	memory (m)	states	time (s)	memory (m)	states	time (s)	memory (m)
2	13	0.01	4.1	13	0.01	4.6	13	0.01	4.8	13(13)	0.00	2.6
3	51	0.01	4.1	49	0.01	4.7	49	0.01	4.8	51(50)	0.00	2.6
4	193	0.01	4.1	191	0.01	4.7	147	0.01	4.9	193(183)	0.01	2.6
5	723	0.01	4.1	651	0.01	4.7	441	0.01	4.9	723(631)	0.02	2.6
6	2701	0.02	4.4	1937	0.02	4.8	1552	0.02	5.0	2701(2207)	0.02	2.7
7	10083	0.05	5.4	5041	0.05	5.4	4694	0.05	5.4	10083(7564)	0.09	3.1
8	37633	0.22	9.3	25939	0.25	8.8	11825	0.12	5.5	37633(26369)	0.35	7.9
9	140451	1.02	25.6	70225	0.76	17.3	26269	0.32	9.3	140451(91202)	1.59	43.8
10	524173	4.52	91.6	173031	2.13	38.1	63561	0.84	16.5	524173(322163)	7.03	74.1
11	1956243	21.06	357.5	392701	5.28	84.9	139788	1.96	32.6	1956243(1128208)	31.03	325.1
12	7300801	106.49	1422.5	830145	12.33	183.5	340179	5.06	79.5	7300801(3950372)	127.40	1030.1
13	—	—	—	1652587	26.99	378.3	808390	12.56	191.8	—	—	—
14	—	—	—	3121147	56.44	743.9	1817375	29.39	441.5	—	—	—
15	—	—	—	5633381	111.55	1399.0	3815044	67.35	948.4	—	—	—
16	—	—	—	—	—	—	7492734	240.85	1911.7	—	—	—

Fig. 2. Results of the philosophers example

« Comb »

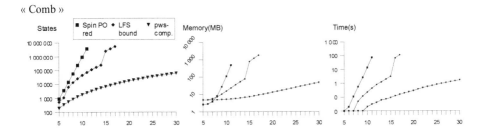

Fig. 3. Results of the comb example

not difficult to understand that it has cubic growth under pws-compliant reduction. Observe the jumps in state memory and time for the LFS-bound reduction: They occur when the LFS-bound increases.

The third example is a series of instances of an asynchronous version[1] of the Sieve of Erastosthenes, where N is the number of iterations of the sieve. This is an example where the partial order methods like the ample set method are good at. Indeed, PO-PACKAGE visited quite few states (see the numbers in parentheses), which are far less than those by pws-compliance. However, pws-compliance gives a significantly better reduction with respect to both memory and time than LFS-bound and Spin.

A natural question to ask is the performance of the LFS reduction compared to McMillan unfoldings [4]. Without going into all details, by nature, the latter only consider traces with a single maximal element (the events of the event structure) and thus produce significantly smaller structures than LFS (which generates also states from certain interleavings). The academic examples presented are naturally modeled as Petri nets and decend unfolders easily outperform LFS. However, unfoldings use the operation of combining traces for "possible extensions", an operation that may not always be feasible, where LFS just computes successors.

---

[1] Our prototype does not allow rendezvous yet, so to compare, we had to modify this example for Promela/Spin.

N	No reduction			LFS bound			PWS compliant			SPIN PO red		
	states	time (s)	memory (m)	states	time (s)	memory (m)	states	time (s)	memory (m)	states	time (s)	memory (m)
1	340	0.01	4.1	198	0.01	4.7	198	0.01	4.8	188(41)	0.00	2.3
2	1912	0.01	4.3	1456	0.01	4.8	910	0.02	4.9	630(77)	0.00	2.3
3	8632	0.04	5.4	4560	0.05	5.5	2874	0.04	5.2	2134(121)	0.00	2.5
4	63984	0.39	15.5	18252	0.19	8.5	14392	0.27	7.5	10599(203)	0.04	3.6
5	178432	1.30	40.7	35072	0.46	12.9	26644	0.67	10.5	25048(263)	0.13	6.2
6	1097296	10.31	259.2	361736	9.10	99.8	63212	3.64	20.3	109880(361)	0.70	21.7
7	2978208	34.12	772.2	707120	19.75	206.7	112964	10.23	35.2	1076639(437)	9.32	243.5
8	—	—	—	2072162	75.71	650.1	304386	37.85	95.0	4311167(551)	86.52	1801.0
9	—	—	—	—	—	—	1158208	166.24	395.1	—(711)	—	—
10	—	—	—	—	—	—	1858340	308.54	654.2	—(811)	—	—

Fig. 4. Results of the sieve example

9 Conclusions and Future Work

In this paper, we report on an improvement concerning both the theoretical basis and practice of Local First Search, a recent partial order reduction technique. The theory not only gives a better insight into previously published results, but in particular yields a stronger reduction method than previously known, using *peak-width-sequence* compliance. Concerning the previously published "LFS-bound", pws-compliance can be used in a chain of reasoning that derives it.

We have also built an ambitious prototype implementation of the algorithm that starts to yield results. The prototype uses an implementation of traces and a new adequate order described in [12]. Already for a version of Local First Search according to [1], the results reported here are more conclusive and show that the latter method scales and is a serious partial order reduction method, and although simple often superiour to the one implemented in Spin.

However, the new pws-compliance test resulting in stronger reductions gives reductions of a new quality to a point which surprised the authors. The latter reduction is more complicated to implement efficiently and we gave a few hints on how this can be done. The first observations reported here show that the pws-compliance provides a model checking algorithm that is competitive with state of the art partial order reduction techniques, and can give significantly stronger reductions depending on the model. In the future, we will experiment on realistic applications rather than benchmarks. We believe that in particular applications in the field of AI planning should be an interesting domain of application due to the goal oriented nature of LFS.

An open theoretical question of practical interest remains whether the approach of using adequate orders as in [1] is avoidable while maintaining exhaustive exploration using the LFS reduction criteria. The importance of this question lies in the fact that the adequate orders known (and the one we use) implicitely force a breadth first search order, which is not optimal for all applications.

References

1. BORNOT, S., MORIN, R., NIEBERT, P., AND ZENNOU, S. Black box unfolding with local first search. In *TACAS* (2002), LNCS 2280, pp. 386–400.
2. CORMEN, T., LEISERSON, C., AND RIVEST, R. *Introduction to Algorithms.* MIT Press, 1990.

3. DIEKERT, V., AND ROZEMBERG, G., Eds. *The Book of Traces*. World Scientific Publishing Co. Pte. Ltd., 1995.

4. ESPARZA, J., ROMER, S., AND VOGLER, W. An improvement of McMillan's unfolding algorithm. In *TACAS* (1996), pp. 87–106.

5. GODEFROID, P. Using partial orders to improve automatic verification methods. In *CAV* (London, UK, 1990), Springer-Verlag, pp. 176–185.

6. GODEFROID, P., PELED, D., AND STASKAUSKAS, M. Using partial-order methods in the formal validation of industrial concurrent programs. *IEEE Trans. Softw. Eng. 22*, 7 (1996), 496–507.

7. GODEFROID, P., AND PIROTTIN, D. Refining dependencies improves partial-order verification methods (extended abstract). In *CAV* (Berlin, Heidelberg, 1993), C. Courcoubetis, Ed., Springer, pp. 438–449.

8. GODEFROID, P., AND WOLPER, P. A partial approach to model checking. In *Logic in Computer Science* (1991), pp. 406–415.

9. HOLZMANN, G., AND PELED, D. Partial order reduction of the state space. In *First SPIN Workshop* (Montrèal, Quebec, 1995).

10. MCMILLAN, K. L. A technique of state space search based on unfolding. *Form. Methods Syst. Des. 6*, 1 (1995), 45–65.

11. NIEBERT, P., HUHN, M., ZENNOU, S., AND LUGIEZ, D. Local first search: a new paradigm in partial order reductions. In *CONCUR* (2001), LNCS 2154, pp. 396–410.

12. NIEBERT, P. AND QU, H. The Implementation of Mazurkiewicz Traces in POEM In *ATVA* (2006), LNCS, to appear

13. PELED, D. All from one, one for all: on model checking using representatives. In *CAV* (1993), pp. 409–423.

14. PENCZEK, W., AND KUIPER, R. Traces and logic. In Diekert and Rozemberg [3].

15. REICHMEIDER, P. F. *The Equivalence of Some Combinatorial Matching Theorems*. Polygonal Pub House, 1985.

16. VALMARI, A. Stubborn sets for reduced state space generation. In *Applications and Theory of Petri Nets* (1989), pp. 491–515.

17. VALMARI, A. On-the-fly verification with stubborn sets. In *CAV* (1993), pp. 397–408.

A Lattice-Theoretic Model for an Algebra of Communicating Sequential Processes

Malcolm Tyrrell[1,3], Joseph M. Morris[1,3],
Andrew Butterfield[2,3], and Arthur Hughes[2]

[1] School of Computing, Dublin City University, Dublin 9, Ireland
{Malcolm.Tyrrell, Joseph.Morris}@computing.dcu.ie
[2] Department of Computer Science, Trinity College, Dublin 2, Ireland
{Andrew.Butterfield, Arthur.Hughes}@cs.tcd.ie
[3] Lero, the Irish Software Engineering Research Centre

Abstract. We present a new lattice-theoretic model for communicating sequential processes. The model underpins a process algebra that is very close to CSP. It differs from CSP "at the edges" for the purposes of creating an elegant algebra of communicating processes. The one significant difference is that we postulate additional distributive properties for external choice. The shape of the algebra that emerges suggests a lattice-theoretic model, in contrast to traditional trace-theoretic models. We show how to build the new model in a mathematically clean step-by-step process. The essence of our approach is to model simple processes (i.e. those without choice, parallelism, or recursion) as a poset S of sequences, and then order-embed S into a complete (and completely distributive) lattice called the *free completely distributive lattice* over S. We explain the technique in detail and show that the resulting model does indeed capture our algebra of communicating sequential processes. The focus of the paper is not on the algebra per se, but on the model and the soundness of the algebra.

Keywords: communicating sequential processes, denotational models, nondeterminacy.

1 Introduction

Process algebras are formally defined languages for the study of fundamental concepts in concurrent processes, including communication, synchronisation, nondeterminacy, abstraction, recursion, divergence, and deadlock. Among the best-known is CSP (*Communicating Sequential Processes*). Although CSP satisfies a large body of laws, the laws are not intended to be sufficient for everyday formal reasoning. Rather they "provide a useful way of gaining understanding and intuition about the intended meaning of constructs [and can] be useful in proofs about CSP processes" [6]. In fact, practitioners do not typically use algebraic means to reason about CSP code, but instead rely on model-checking approaches.

K. Barkaoui, A. Cavalcanti, and A. Cerone (Eds.): ICTAC 2006, LNCS 4281, pp. 123–137, 2006.
© Springer-Verlag Berlin Heidelberg 2006

We embarked on constructing a practically useful algebra for communicating sequential processes that would be as CSP-like as we could make it, but which might depart from CSP "at the edges" if the algebra demanded it. We have constructed what seems to us to be a satisfactory algebra for a language that differs from CSP in one significant respect: we postulate that external choice enjoys the same distributive properties as internal choice. In contrast, external choice is somewhat less distributive in classical CSP. We speculate that this change does not impact significantly on the practice of writing CSP code, and that any drawbacks will be more than compensated for by the usefulness of the new algebra. However, the pros and cons of this are not the subject of the present paper. Our purpose here is to present a new model for an algebra of communicating sequential processes and show that the algebra is sound.

CSP has various models, all based on trace theory [6]. We have not adopted them because a more mathematically appealing approach suggested itself. In our algebra, internal and external choice are mathematical duals of one another, and so one would expect that they could be modelled by some lattice in which lattice meets and joins model internal and external choice, respectively. The creative part of our work lies in discovering this lattice and mapping all the terms and operators of communicating sequential processes into it. We think our model-building technique is sufficiently general to be useful in other contexts, in particular wherever nondeterministic choice is employed.

We construct the model, and show that the axioms of our algebra hold in it. Although it is not our purpose here to discuss our algebra per se, we will describe it to the extent that the reader needs to follow the soundness argument.

The model-building strategy can be broken into six steps, which we outline briefly:

Step 1. In the first step we model simple processes (or *proper* processes as we shall prefer to call them). These consist of processes that do not employ choice, parallelism, or recursion. Such processes are trivially modelled as sequences. The operations that apply to proper processes are easily modelled as operations on sequences. For example, sequential composition of processes is modelled more or less as sequence concatenation.

Step 2. Next we impose a partial ordering on the set of sequences. Our model building technique is indifferent as to how one chooses this ordering. One simply chooses it so that it captures the mathematical properties we want to hold, such as yielding the desired least fixpoint when modelling recursion, and ensuring that parallelism will have the properties we want.

Step 3. Next we introduce choice. We do so by finding an order-embedding of the sequence poset into some complete (and completely distributive) lattice such that lattice meets and joins model internal and external choice, respectively. The lattice we want turns out to be what is called the *free completely distributive (FCD) lattice* over the sequence poset.

Step 4. We have to "lift" the poset operators into the lattice. For example, sequence concatenation in the poset must be lifted into a similar operator in the lattice such that it preserves its behaviour. In addition, we have to give the lifted operator additional behaviour to cater for the new lattice elements (these represent processes with choice). We develop a small suite of higher-order "lifting" devices that lift operators from a poset to the FCD lattice. For each operator on the sequence poset, we select an appropriate lifting into the lattice. *Step 5.* In Step 5 we add parallelism. This has to be treated separately since unlike the other operators, parallelism can give rise to choice even when applied to proper processes.

Step 6. In the final step, we model recursively defined processes using completely standard fixed-point theory.

The rest of the paper is organised as follows:

Section 2. We describe the process algebra, and give its axioms.

Section 3. We give a poset model for proper processes.

Section 4. We show how to model choice using the FCD lattice construction.

Section 5. We give the model for the full language, and give the soundness result for the algebra.

Section 6. We give our conclusions and discuss related work.

2   The Process Algebra

Our language is based on that of CSP [6]. For brevity we will not consider all of the constructs of CSP. The subset we deal with is given in Table 1. Actually we will write $\bigsqcup$ rather than $\Box$ to emphasise the fact that our two choices are duals of one another. We will henceforth refer to our two choices as *demonic* and *angelic* choice instead of the traditional *internal* and *external* choice, respectively. Internal choice in CSP is precisely demonic choice as it occurs in other contexts (such as the refinement calculus [1]), and so the two names are interchangeable. The dual of demonic choice is typically called angelic choice in the literature, and so our terminology is in this regard consistent with established usage. However, we caution the reader against associating any "badness" with demonic choice, or any "goodness" with angelic choice. They are simply two choice operators that are mathematically dual. Henceforth, "external choice" will refer to CSP's version, and "angelic choice" will refer to ours. Angelic nondeterminacy is often associated with backtracking. However, our use of the term should not be taken to imply that an implementation is necessarily backtracking.

2.1   Proper Processes

We assume an alphabet of events denoted by Σ. There are two primitive processes: *SKIP* and *STOP*. *SKIP* denotes a process that has terminated successfully, and *STOP* denotes a process which has failed in some respect. We construct other simple processes from these base cases by *prefixing*, as in $a \to b \to c \to SKIP$ and $a \to b \to STOP$, where a, b and c are drawn from the alphabet of events.

For a set of events $A \subseteq \Sigma$, we define $\mathrm{Proc}(A)$ to be the set of processes constructed from *SKIP*, *STOP* and prefixing by events in A. We abbreviate $\mathrm{Proc}(\Sigma)$ by Proc. We call these simple processes *proper processes* and denote them by p, q, r.

Table 1. CSP

Σ	universal set of events
$STOP$	deadlocked process
$SKIP$	terminated process
$a \to P$	process P prefixed by event a
$\sqcap S$	internal choice of the terms in set S
$P \square Q$	external choice of processes P and Q
$P \restriction A$	restriction of P to the events in A
$P_A \|_B Q$	alphabetised parallel composition of P and Q with alphabets A and B
$\mu N.P$	recursively defined process

We partially order Proc by the *refinement order*, denoted by $\sqsubseteq$, and defined by the following axioms:

$$\text{(A1)} \quad \sqsubseteq \text{ is a partial order}$$
$$\text{(A2)} \quad STOP \sqsubseteq p$$
$$\text{(A3)} \quad a \to p \sqsubseteq b \to q \iff (a = b) \wedge (p \sqsubseteq q)$$

where p, q denote proper processes and a, b denote (possibly equal) events. Actually, we need to assert that $p \sqsubseteq q$ does not hold unless it follows from the preceding axioms, and so we postulate in addition:

$$\text{(A4)} \quad a \to p \not\sqsubseteq SKIP \not\sqsubseteq a \to p$$

(Note: We label the axioms of our algebra (A1), (A2), etc., and the theorems (other than axioms) by (T1), (T2), etc.)

It follows from (A1)–(A4) that $SKIP$ and all proper processes ending in $SKIP$ are maximal in the refinement order. A process which fails is refined by a process which can engage in the same events and then terminate, or one which can engage in the same events and then some further events. Otherwise processes are incomparable. Note that the refinement order is quite different from the common prefix order.

There are two operators which act on proper processes: restriction $p \restriction A$ and sequential composition $p ; q$. They are defined by the following axioms:

$$\text{(A5)} \quad SKIP \restriction A = SKIP$$
$$\text{(A6)} \quad STOP \restriction A = STOP$$
$$\text{(A7)} \quad (a \to p) \restriction A = \begin{cases} a \to (p \restriction A) & \text{if } a \in A \\ p \restriction A & \text{otherwise} \end{cases}$$

$$\text{(A8)} \quad SKIP ; p = p$$
$$\text{(A9)} \quad STOP ; p = STOP$$
$$\text{(A10)} \quad (a \to p) ; q = a \to (p ; q)$$

where A is a set of events, a is an event, and p, q are proper processes.

2.2   Choice Operators

For S a set of process terms, the term $\bigsqcap S$ denotes the demonic (or internal) choice of processes in S, and $\bigsqcup S$ denotes the angelic choice. We write $\sqcap$ and $\sqcup$ for the binary infix versions of $\bigsqcap$ and $\bigsqcup$, respectively. They are governed by the following axioms:

$$(\text{A11})\quad P \sqsubseteq Q \;\Leftrightarrow\; (\forall X \subseteq \text{Proc} \cdot \bigsqcap X \sqsubseteq P \Rightarrow \bigsqcap X \sqsubseteq Q)$$

$$(\text{A12})\quad P \sqsubseteq Q \;\Leftrightarrow\; (\forall X \subseteq \text{Proc} \cdot Q \sqsubseteq \bigsqcup X \Rightarrow P \sqsubseteq \bigsqcup X)$$

$$(\text{A13})\quad \bigsqcap S \sqsubseteq \bigsqcup X \;\Leftrightarrow\; (\exists P \in S \cdot P \sqsubseteq \bigsqcup X)$$

$$(\text{A14})\quad \bigsqcap X \sqsubseteq \bigsqcup S \;\Leftrightarrow\; (\exists P \in S \cdot \bigsqcap X \sqsubseteq P)$$

where P, Q are process terms, X is a set of proper processes, and S is a set of process terms. It is not easy to put an intuitive interpretation on these, and we suggest the reader does not try to do so. They have little role in the practical use of the algebra, but rather are used to establish a body of more practical theorems.

The preceding axioms also extend the refinement relation from proper to arbitrary processes, except that we need to postulate antisymmetry of refinement for arbitrary processes:

$$(\text{A15})\quad (P \sqsubseteq Q \wedge Q \sqsubseteq P) \;\Leftrightarrow\; P = Q$$

We can infer that if $R \subseteq S$ then $\bigsqcap S \sqsubseteq \bigsqcap R$, i.e. that refinement allows reduction in demonic choice (and dually an increase in angelic choice). We can also establish the classic lattice-theoretic relationship $P \sqsubseteq Q \Leftrightarrow P \sqcap Q = P \Leftrightarrow P \sqcup Q = Q$ where P and Q denote processes.

For empty choices, we define the abbreviations $\bot$ and $\top$ for $\bigsqcup \emptyset$ and $\bigsqcap \emptyset$, respectively. These satisfy $\bot \sqsubseteq P \sqsubseteq \top$ for all processes P; also $\sqcup$ and $\sqcap$ have units and zeros among $\bot$ and $\top$.

One of the most significant theorems of the algebra is that all processes can be expressed in a simple normal form. Before stating it, we introduce some additional notation: To express complex sets of process terms, we employ the set comprehension notation $\{x \in T \mid R \cdot P\}$, where R denotes a predicate and P denotes a term, in each of which x may occur free as a term of type T. This denotes the set of P's for each x in T that satisfy R. We write $\{x \in T \mid R\}$ as an abbreviation for $\{x \in T \mid R \cdot x\}$ and $\{x \in T \cdot P\}$ as an abbreviation for $\{x \in T \mid \text{true} \cdot P\}$.

Let us say that a term is *angelically proper* if it can be expressed as the angelic choice of a set of proper processes. It turns out that every process term can be expressed as the demonic choice of a set of angelically proper terms:

$$(\text{T1})\quad P = \bigsqcap \Big\{ X \subseteq \text{Proc} \;\Big|\; P \sqsubseteq \bigsqcup X \cdot \bigsqcup X \Big\}$$

for any process term P. (T1) says that any process P is equivalent to the demonic choice over all $\bigsqcup X$ where X ranges over those subsets of Proc satisfying $P \sqsubseteq$

$\bigsqcup X$. A term written this way is said to be in *demonic normal form* (there is also a dual *angelic normal form* which needn't concern us here).

2.3 Distribution Properties

We define prefixing and restriction to distribute over choice in their process arguments:

$$(A16) \quad a \to \left(\bigsqcap S\right) = \bigsqcap \{P \in S \cdot a \to P\}$$

$$(A17) \quad a \to \left(\bigsqcup S\right) = \bigsqcup \{P \in S \cdot a \to P\}$$

$$(A18) \quad \left(\bigsqcap S\right) {\upharpoonright} A = \bigsqcap \{P \in S \cdot P {\upharpoonright} A\}$$

$$(A19) \quad \left(\bigsqcup S\right) {\upharpoonright} A = \bigsqcup \{P \in S \cdot P {\upharpoonright} A\}$$

where a denotes an event, S a set of process terms and A a set of events. For sequential composition, which has two process arguments, we assert that it distributes over choice on the left:

$$(A20) \quad \left(\bigsqcap S\right); P = \bigsqcap \{Q \in S \cdot Q; P\}$$

$$(A21) \quad \left(\bigsqcup S\right); P = \bigsqcup \{Q \in S \cdot Q; P\}$$

where S is a set of process terms and P a process term. We also assert that it distributes over choice on the right, provided the left argument is proper:

$$(A22) \quad p; \left(\bigsqcap S\right) = \bigsqcap \{P \in S \cdot p; P\}$$

$$(A23) \quad p; \left(\bigsqcup S\right) = \bigsqcup \{P \in S \cdot p; P\}$$

where p is a proper process and S is a set of process terms. The requirement that the left argument in (A22) and (A23) be proper is a formal way of expressing that if both arguments of a sequential composition contain choice, distribution should happen on the left first and then on the right. Bearing in mind that the arguments can be expressed in normal form, (A20) to (A23) suffice to eliminate all choice from the arguments of a sequential composition, after which we can apply (A8) to (A10).

2.4 Alphabetised Parallel

There are several parallel operators in CSP, for example synchronising parallel, alphabetised parallel, interleaving, interface parallel, etc. We will describe the alphabetised parallel operator here, as it is typical. We give the operator three axioms, the first of which applies to angelically proper terms:

$$(A24) \quad P \underset{A}{\parallel}_{B} Q = \bigsqcup \{p \in \mathrm{Proc}(A \cup B) \mid p {\upharpoonright} A \sqsubseteq P \land p {\upharpoonright} B \sqsubseteq Q\}$$

where P, Q are angelically proper and A, B are sets of events. Its other two axioms assert that it distributes over demonic choice:

$$(A25) \quad \sqcap S_A \|_B Q \ = \ \sqcap \Big\{ P \in S \ \cdot \ P_A \|_B Q \Big\}$$

$$(A26) \quad P_A \|_B \sqcap S \ = \ \sqcap \Big\{ Q \in S \ \cdot \ P_A \|_B Q \Big\}$$

where S is a set of process terms, P, Q are arbitrary process terms and A, B are sets of events. The axioms are sufficient to prove that the operator is symmetric, associative (with appropriate alphabet adjustment) and satisfies a useful step law.

2.5 Recursively Defined Processes

Processes may be defined recursively, as in for example:

$$N \ = \ a \rightarrow N \ \sqcup \ SKIP$$

A recursive process definition is written $N = P$ where P is a process term which may contain free occurrences of N. The definition is *well-formed* only if P is monotonic in N and $P[STOP/N] \neq \bot$. ($P[Q/N]$ denotes the substitution of term Q for all free occurrences of N in P.) The monotonicity requirement excludes some unusual uses of the choice operators.

A well-formed recursive process definition $N = P$ defines a process $\mu N.P$ which satisfies the following axioms:

$$(A27) \quad \mu N.P \ = \ P[(\mu N.P)/N]$$
$$(A28) \quad P[Q/N] \sqsubseteq Q \ \Rightarrow \ (\mu N.P) \sqsubseteq Q$$
$$(A29) \quad \mu N.P \neq \bot$$

where Q is a process such that $Q \neq \bot$.

An example of a recursively defined process is $\mu N.(a \rightarrow N)$. We can prove that it equals $\bigsqcup_{n \in \mathbb{N}} (a^n \rightarrow STOP)$ where a^n abbreviates a sequence of n as. Another example is $\mu N.(a \rightarrow N \sqcup SKIP)$ which can be shown to equal $\bigsqcup_{n \in \mathbb{N}} (a^n \rightarrow SKIP)$. We don't distinguish between deadlock and divergence in our model: the divergent process $\mu N.N$ equals $STOP$.

A recursive process definition may also involve an argument, as in for example:

$$COUNT = \lambda n \colon \mathbb{N}. \ up \rightarrow COUNT(n+1)$$
$$\sqcup \mathbf{if} \ n > 0 \ \mathbf{then} \ down \rightarrow COUNT(n-1) \ \mathbf{else} \ STOP \ \mathbf{fi}$$

A parametrised recursive process definition is written $N = E$ where E is an abstracted process $(\lambda x \colon T.P)$ and T is some simple type (such as $\mathbb{N}$). The definition is *well-formed* only if N occurs in monotonic positions in P and for all $x \in T$, $E[(\lambda y \colon T \cdot STOP)/N](x) \neq \bot$. The defined process is written $(\mu N.E)$ and it satisfies the following axioms:

$$(A30) \quad \mu N.E \ = \ E[(\mu N.E)/N]$$
$$(A31) \quad (\forall x \colon T \cdot E[F/N](x) \sqsubseteq F(x)) \ \Rightarrow \ (\forall x \colon T \cdot (\mu N.E)(x) \sqsubseteq F(x))$$
$$(A32) \quad \forall x \colon T \cdot (\mu N.E)(x) \ \neq \ \bot$$

where F is any function of type $T \rightarrow Proc$ such that $(\forall x \colon T \cdot F(x) \neq \bot)$.

3   Modelling Proper Processes

Our first step in giving the semantics of our process algebra is to model the collection of proper processes as a poset.

Semantically, we won't distinguish between the type of events, Σ, and the set we use to model it. Similarly, we will allow an event a to model itself.

We model proper processes with a partially-ordered set denoted [Proc]. This consists of finite sequences of events which terminate in one of two ways: $\langle\rangle$ or Ω. Proper processes p have an interpretation in [Proc] which we denote $[p]$. They are interpreted as follows:

$$
\begin{aligned}
[SKIP] &\triangleq \langle\rangle \\
[STOP] &\triangleq \Omega \\
[a \rightarrow p] &\triangleq a{:}[p]
\end{aligned}
$$

where a is an event, p is a proper process and : is the cons operator on sequences. Let $\leq$ be the smallest partial order on [Proc] such that:

$$
\begin{aligned}
&(\forall\, u \in [\text{Proc}] \cdot \Omega \leq u) \\
&(\forall\, a \in \Sigma, u, v \in [\text{Proc}] \cdot a{:}u \leq a{:}v \Leftrightarrow u \leq v)
\end{aligned}
$$

We use $\leq$ to model the refinement relation on proper processes.

The operators on proper processes are given meanings as monotonic operators on the poset [Proc]. Restriction is interpreted as:

$$
[\upharpoonright] \qquad : \quad [\text{Proc}] \times \mathbb{P}\Sigma \rightarrow [\text{Proc}]
$$

$$
[\upharpoonright](u, A) \triangleq
\begin{cases}
a{:}([\upharpoonright](u', A)) & \text{if } u = a{:}u',\ a \in A \\
[\upharpoonright](u', A) & \text{if } u = a{:}u',\ a \notin A \\
\langle\rangle & \text{if } u = \langle\rangle \\
\Omega & \text{if } u = \Omega
\end{cases}
$$

for all $u \in [\text{Proc}]$ and $A \subseteq \Sigma$.

Sequential composition is interpreted as:

$$
[;] \qquad : \quad [\text{Proc}] \times [\text{Proc}] \rightarrow [\text{Proc}]
$$

$$
[;](u, v) \triangleq
\begin{cases}
a{:}([;](u', v)) & \text{if } u = a{:}u' \\
v & \text{if } u = \langle\rangle \\
\Omega & \text{if } u = \Omega
\end{cases}
$$

for all $u, v \in [\text{Proc}]$.

We can use $[\upharpoonright]$ to give the interpretation of $\text{Proc}(A)$:

$$
[\text{Proc}(A)] \triangleq \{x \in [\text{Proc}] \mid [\upharpoonright](x, A) = x\}
$$

We have shown that the definitions we give for the poset and its operations are well-defined [8].

4   Modelling Unbounded Demonic and Angelic Choice

To model the choice operators, we will embed the poset in a complete lattice. There are many ways to embed a poset in a complete lattice, but the one we want is what's known as the *free completely distributive lattice* over a poset (FCD). The FCD lattice preserves the order of the original poset, is completely distributive, and has meets and joins that capture demonic and angelic choice, respectively.

4.1   Lattice Theory

Everything in this subsection is standard and is available in more detail in any standard text (such as [3,2]).

A *complete lattice* is a partially ordered set L such that every subset of L has a least upper bound and greatest lower bound. We will denote the order on the lattice by $\leq$. We denote the least upper bound of $S \subseteq L$ by $\bigvee S$ and the greatest lower bound by $\bigwedge S$. Least upper bounds are also called *joins* and greatest lower bounds are also called *meets*. A complete lattice is *completely distributive* iff joins distribute over meets and vice versa.

A function f from poset C to poset D is *monotonic* iff $x \leq_C y \Rightarrow f\,x \leq_D f\,y$ for all $x, y \in C$, and an *order-embedding* iff $x \leq_C y \Leftrightarrow f\,x \leq_D f\,y$ for all $x, y \in C$. An order-embedding from a poset C to a complete lattice is said to be a *completion* of C. We write $C \to D$ to denote the *space of monotonic functions* from C to D, which is a poset under the pointwise order. If L and M are complete lattices, then a function $f : L \to M$ is a *complete homomorphism* iff it preserves joins and meets, i.e. $f(\bigvee S) = \bigvee (fS)$ and $f(\bigwedge S) = \bigwedge (fS)$ for all $S \subseteq L$.

4.2   The Free Completely Distributive Lattice over a Poset

A completely distributive lattice L is called the *free completely distributive lattice over a poset* C iff there is a completion $\phi : C \to L$ such that for every completely distributive lattice M and function $f : C \to M$, there is a unique function $\phi_M^* f : L \to M$ which is a complete homomorphism and satisfies $\phi_M^* f \circ \phi = f$.

For any poset C, the free completely distributive lattice over C exists and is unique up to isomorphism [5]. It is written $\mathrm{FCD}(C)$. The completions $\phi : C \to \mathrm{FCD}(C)$ involved in the definition are not necessarily unique, but for each poset C, we assume that some such completion has been chosen.

We briefly offer some insight into the properties of FCD lattices. One of their most useful features is that each element of $\mathrm{FCD}(C)$ can be described as the meet of joins of subsets of ϕC, or the join of meets of subsets of ϕC. Another property of FCD lattices is that their bottom and/or their top element can be removed and the resulting structure is still a complete lattice. We will make use of this property when we model recursion.

Theorem 1. *Let ϕ be the FCD completion of C in $\mathrm{FCD}(C)$. Then, for all $x \in \mathrm{FCD}(C)$:*

$$x \;=\; \bigwedge \{X \subseteq \phi C \mid x \leq \bigvee X \;\cdot\; \bigvee X\} \;=\; \bigvee \{X \subseteq \phi C \mid \bigwedge X \leq x \;\cdot\; \bigwedge X\}$$

Proof. This is proved in [5].

Theorem 2. $\{x \in \mathrm{FCD}(C) \mid x \neq \bot\}$ *is a complete lattice under the inherited order from* $\mathrm{FCD}(C)$.

Proof. This is proved in [8].

4.3 Lifting Operators

Suppose that ϕ completes poset C in $\mathrm{FCD}(C)$. For each of the operators on C, we will want to lift them to corresponding operators on $\mathrm{FCD}(C)$. Since $\mathrm{FCD}(C)$ is a much richer space than C, it turns out that there are several options for how an operator is lifted.

To lift a unary operator $f : C \to C$, we define:

$$\mathcal{U} \quad : (C \to C) \to (\mathrm{FCD}(C) \to \mathrm{FCD}(C))$$
$$\mathcal{U} f \triangleq \phi^*(\phi \circ f)$$

As the following theorem shows, $\mathcal{U}f$'s behaviour on ϕC corresponds to f's behaviour on C. Its behaviour outside ϕC is determined by the fact that it distributes over meets and joins.

Theorem 3. *For all* $f : C \to C$, $x \in C$ *and* $X \subseteq \mathrm{FCD}(C)$:

$$(\mathcal{U} f)(\phi x) = \phi(f x)$$
$$(\mathcal{U} f)(\bigwedge X) = \bigwedge \{y \in X \cdot (\mathcal{U} f) y\}$$
$$(\mathcal{U} f)(\bigvee X) = \bigvee \{y \in X \cdot (\mathcal{U} f) y\}$$

We define the following two functions for when only one of the arguments of a binary operator is lifted to an FCD:

$$\mathcal{R} \quad : (D \times C \to C) \to (D \times \mathrm{FCD}(C) \to \mathrm{FCD}(C))$$
$$\mathcal{R} f \triangleq \mathrm{uncurry}\,(\mathcal{U} \circ \mathrm{curry}\, f)$$

$$\mathcal{L} \quad : (C \times D \to C) \to (\mathrm{FCD}(C) \times D \to \mathrm{FCD}(C))$$
$$\mathcal{L} \quad \triangleq \mathrm{swap} \circ \mathcal{R} \circ \mathrm{swap}$$

where curry, uncurry and swap are defined:

$$\mathrm{curry} \quad = \lambda f : C \times D \to B \cdot \lambda x : C \cdot \lambda y : D \cdot f(x, y)$$
$$\mathrm{uncurry} = \lambda f : C \to D \to B \cdot \lambda(x, y) : C \times D \cdot f\,x\,y$$
$$\mathrm{swap} \quad = \lambda f : C \times D \to B \cdot \lambda(x, y) : D \times C \cdot f(y, x)$$

Theorem 4. *For all* $f : D \times C \to C$, $g : C \times D \to C$, $x \in C$, $y \in D$ *and* $X \subseteq \mathrm{FCD}(C)$:

$$(\mathcal{R} f)(y, \phi x) = \phi(f(y, x))$$
$$(\mathcal{R} f)(y, \bigwedge X) = \bigwedge \{z \in X \cdot (\mathcal{R} f)(y, z)\}$$
$$(\mathcal{R} f)(y, \bigvee X) = \bigvee \{z \in X \cdot (\mathcal{R} f)(y, z)\}$$

$$(\mathcal{L} g)(\phi x, y) = \phi(g(x, y))$$
$$(\mathcal{L} g)(\bigwedge X, y) = \bigwedge \{z \in X \cdot (\mathcal{L} g)(z, y)\}$$
$$(\mathcal{L} g)(\bigvee X, y) = \bigvee \{z \in X \cdot (\mathcal{L} g)(z, y)\}$$

If both arguments of a binary operator are lifted to an FCD, one way of lifting the operator is called *left-first lifting*. Define the left-first lifting operator:

$$\mathcal{B} \;\; : \; (C \times C \to C) \to (\text{FCD}(C) \times \text{FCD}(C) \to \text{FCD}(C))$$
$$\mathcal{B} f \triangleq \text{uncurry}(\phi^*(\mathcal{U} \circ (\text{curry} f)))$$

$\mathcal{B} f$ distributes over meets and joins on its left-hand argument first, and then on its right-hand argument.

Theorem 5. *For all* $x, y \in C$, $X \subseteq \text{FCD}(C)$ *and* $z \in \text{FCD}(C)$:

$$
\begin{aligned}
(\mathcal{B} f)(\phi x , \phi y) &= \phi (f(x , y)) \\
(\mathcal{B} f)(\bigwedge X , z) &= \bigwedge \{w \in X \; \cdot \; (\mathcal{B} f)(w , z)\} \\
(\mathcal{B} f)(\bigvee X , z) &= \bigvee \{w \in X \; \cdot \; (\mathcal{B} f)(w , z)\} \\
(\mathcal{B} f)(\phi x , \bigwedge X) &= \bigwedge \{w \in X \; \cdot \; (\mathcal{B} f)(\phi x , w)\} \\
(\mathcal{B} f)(\phi x , \bigvee X) &= \bigvee \{w \in X \; \cdot \; (\mathcal{B} f)(\phi x , w)\}
\end{aligned}
$$

As well as left-first lifting, there are also right-first, meet-first and join-first lifting operators. These are not needed for the material considered here.

The theorems in this section are proved in [8].

5   The Model

The interpretation of the type Proc is given as:

$$[\![\text{Proc}]\!] \triangleq \text{FCD}([\text{Proc}])$$

Let ϕ complete $[\text{Proc}]$ in $[\![\text{Proc}]\!]$. Each process term P has an interpretation $[\![P]\!] \in [\![\text{Proc}]\!]$. Strictly, the interpretation is evaluated in an environment which assigns values to free variables. For the sake of readability, we will leave environments implicit whenever possible.

The constructors and operators of proper processes are interpreted as:

$$
\begin{aligned}
[\![SKIP]\!] &\triangleq \phi \langle \rangle \\
[\![STOP]\!] &\triangleq \phi \Omega \\
[\![a \to P]\!] &\triangleq [\![\to]\!](a, [\![P]\!]) \\
[\![P \restriction A]\!] &\triangleq [\![\restriction]\!]([\![P]\!], A) \\
[\![P ; Q]\!] &\triangleq [\![;]\!]([\![P]\!], [\![Q]\!])
\end{aligned}
$$

where a is an event, P, Q are process terms, A is a set of events and $[\![\to]\!]$, $[\![\restriction]\!]$ and $[\![;]\!]$ are liftings of prefixing, restriction and sequential composition, respectively, defined as follows:

$$
\begin{aligned}
[\![\to]\!] &\; : \; \Sigma \times [\![\text{Proc}]\!] \to [\![\text{Proc}]\!] \\
[\![\to]\!] &\triangleq \mathcal{R} (:)
\end{aligned}
$$

$$
\begin{aligned}
[\![\restriction]\!] &\; : \; [\![\text{Proc}]\!] \times \mathbb{P}\Sigma \to [\![\text{Proc}]\!] \\
[\![\restriction]\!] &\triangleq \mathcal{L} [\restriction]
\end{aligned}
$$

$$
\begin{aligned}
[\![;]\!] &\; : \; [\![\text{Proc}]\!] \times [\![\text{Proc}]\!] \to [\![\text{Proc}]\!] \\
[\![;]\!] &\triangleq \mathcal{B}[;]
\end{aligned}
$$

where, in the definition of $[\![\to]\!]$, $(:)$ is the cons operator $:$ on [Proc] in prefix form.

The interpretation of a proper process lies in ϕ[Proc]. We interpret demonic and angelic choice as meet and join in the lattice, respectively.

5.1 Alphabetised Parallel Operator

To give the interpretation of the alphabetised parallel operator, we start with its behaviour on angelically proper processes. An angelically proper process can be represented by a set of elements of ϕ[Proc]. We define an operator $\langle\|\rangle$ which takes subsets of ϕ[Proc] as arguments. $\langle\|\rangle$ is defined as:

$$\langle\|\rangle \;:\; (\mathbb{P}(\phi[\mathrm{Proc}]) \times \mathbb{P}\Sigma) \times (\mathbb{P}(\phi[\mathrm{Proc}]) \times \mathbb{P}\Sigma) \to [\![\mathrm{Proc}]\!]$$

$$\langle\|\rangle\,((X, A), (Y, B))$$
$$\triangleq \bigvee \{y \in \phi[\mathrm{Proc}(A \cup B)] \mid [\![\uparrow]\!](y, A) \le \bigvee X \wedge [\![\uparrow]\!](y, B) \le \bigvee Y\}$$

We now give the denotation of $\|$ on $[\![\mathrm{Proc}]\!]$:

$$[\![\,\|\,]\!] \;:\; ([\![\mathrm{Proc}]\!] \times \mathbb{P}\Sigma) \times ([\![\mathrm{Proc}]\!] \times \mathbb{P}\Sigma) \to [\![\mathrm{Proc}]\!]$$

$$[\![\,\|\,]\!]\,((x, A), (y, B))$$
$$\triangleq \bigwedge\{X, Y \subseteq \phi[\mathrm{Proc}] \mid x \le \bigvee X \wedge y \le \bigvee X \;\cdot\; \langle\|\rangle\,((X, A), (Y, B))\}$$

The interpretation of parallel compositions is as follows:

$$[\![P \;{}_A\|_B\; Q]\!] \;\triangleq\; [\![\,\|\,]\!]\,(([\![P]\!], A), ([\![Q]\!], B))$$

5.2 Recursive Process Definitions

Let $[\![\mathrm{Proc}]\!]^-$ be $[\![\mathrm{Proc}]\!]$ with $\bot$ removed. By Theorem 2, $[\![\mathrm{Proc}]\!]^-$ is a complete lattice. Given a recursive process definition $N = P$, define f to be the following function:

$$f \;:\; [\![\mathrm{Proc}]\!]^- \to [\![\mathrm{Proc}]\!]^-$$
$$f \triangleq \lambda x \colon [\![\mathrm{Proc}]\!]^- \;\cdot\; [\![P]\!]^x_N$$

where $[\![P]\!]^x_N$ denotes the interpretation of P when the environment associates x with N. For well-formed definitions, this is a well-defined monotonic function on the complete lattice $[\![\mathrm{Proc}]\!]^-$. Therefore, by the standard Knaster-Tarski theory [7], generalised by Park [4], it has a least fixpoint μf. We define $[\![\mu N.P]\!] = \mu f$.

Given a parametrised recursive process definition $N = E$ where E has the form $(\lambda x \colon T.P)$, define f as follows:

$$f \;:\; ([\![T]\!] \to [\![\mathrm{Proc}]\!]^-) \to ([\![T]\!] \to [\![\mathrm{Proc}]\!]^-)$$
$$f \triangleq \lambda g \colon [\![T]\!] \to [\![\mathrm{Proc}]\!]^- \;\cdot\; \lambda y \colon [\![T]\!] \;\cdot\; [\![P]\!]^{y\;g}_{x\;N}$$

For well-formed definitions, this is a well-defined monotonic function on the complete lattice $[\![T]\!] \to [\![\mathrm{Proc}]\!]^-$. Therefore, it has a least fixpoint μf. We define $[\![\mu N.E]\!] \triangleq \mu f$.

5.3   Soundness

The soundness of the axioms is a corollary of the following two theorems. Each statement of the theorems justify a single axiom. The statements are marked with the corresponding axiom number.

Theorem 6. *For all* $z, w \in [\![\text{Proc}]\!]$, $X \subseteq \phi\,[\text{Proc}]$ *and* $S \subseteq [\![\text{Proc}]\!]$:

$$(A11)\ \ z \le w \ \Leftrightarrow\ (\forall X \subseteq \phi\,[\text{Proc}] \cdot \bigwedge X \le z \Rightarrow \bigwedge X \le w)$$

$$(A12)\ \ z \le w \ \Leftrightarrow\ (\forall X \subseteq \phi\,[\text{Proc}] \cdot w \le \bigvee X \Rightarrow z \le \bigvee X)$$

$$(A13)\ \ \bigwedge S \le \bigvee X \ \Leftrightarrow\ (\exists z \in S \cdot z \le \bigwedge X)$$

$$(A14)\ \ \bigwedge X \le \bigvee S \ \Leftrightarrow\ (\exists z \in S \cdot \bigwedge X \le z)$$

$$(A15)\ \ \le\ \text{is a partial order}$$

Proof. This follows from results in [5].

Theorem 7. *For all* $a, b \in \Sigma$, $x, y \in \phi\,[\text{Proc}]$, $A, B \subseteq \Sigma$, $S \subseteq [\![\text{Proc}]\!]$, $z \in [\![\text{Proc}]\!]$, $X, Y \subseteq \phi\,[\text{Proc}]$, $f \in [\![\text{Proc}]\!]^- \to [\![\text{Proc}]\!]^-$, $g \in ([\![T]\!] \to [\![\text{Proc}]\!]^-) \to ([\![T]\!] \to [\![\text{Proc}]\!]^-)$, *and* $h \in [\![T]\!] \to [\![\text{Proc}]\!]^-$:

$(A1)\ \ \le\ \text{is a partial order}$

$(A2)\ \ \phi\Omega \ \le\ x$

$(A3)\ \ [\![\rightarrow]\!](a, x) \le [\![\rightarrow]\!](b, y) \ \Leftrightarrow\ (a = b) \wedge (x \le y)$

$(A4)\ \ [\![\rightarrow]\!](a, x) \not\le \phi\langle\rangle \not\le [\![\rightarrow]\!](a, x)$

$(A5)\ \ [\![\uparrow]\!](\phi\langle\rangle, A) \ =\ \phi\langle\rangle$

$(A6)\ \ [\![\uparrow]\!](\phi\Omega, A) \ =\ \phi\Omega$

$(A7)\ \ [\![\uparrow]\!]([\![\rightarrow]\!](a, x), A) \ =\ \begin{cases} [\![\rightarrow]\!](a, [\![\uparrow]\!](x, A)) & \text{if } a \in A \\ [\![\uparrow]\!](x, A) & \text{otherwise} \end{cases}$

$(A8)\ \ [\![;]\!](\phi\langle\rangle, x) \ =\ x$

$(A9)\ \ [\![;]\!](\phi\Omega, x) \ =\ \phi\Omega$

$(A10)\ \ [\![;]\!]([\![\rightarrow]\!](a, x), y) \ =\ [\![\rightarrow]\!](a, [\![;]\!](x, y))$

$(A16)\ \ [\![\rightarrow]\!](a, \bigwedge S) \ =\ \bigwedge\{w \in S \cdot [\![\rightarrow]\!](a, w)\}$

$(A17)\ \ [\![\rightarrow]\!](a, \bigvee S) \ =\ \bigvee\{w \in S \cdot [\![\rightarrow]\!](a, w)\}$

$(A18)\ \ [\![\uparrow]\!](\bigwedge S, A) \ =\ \bigwedge\{w \in S \cdot [\![\uparrow]\!](w, A)\}$

$(A19)\ \ [\![\uparrow]\!](\bigvee S, A) \ =\ \bigvee\{w \in S \cdot [\![\uparrow]\!](w, A)\}$

$(A20)\ \ [\![;]\!](\bigwedge S, z) \ =\ \bigwedge\{w \in S \cdot [\![;]\!](w, z)\}$

$(A21)\ \ [\![;]\!](\bigvee S, z) \ =\ \bigvee\{w \in S \cdot [\![;]\!](w, z)\}$

$(A22)\ \ [\![;]\!](x, \bigwedge S) \ =\ \bigwedge\{w \in S \cdot [\![;]\!](x, w)\}$

(A23) $[\![\,;\,]\!](x, \bigvee S) \;=\; \bigvee \{w \in S \cdot [\![\,;\,]\!](x, w)\}$

(A24) $[\![\,\|\,]\!]((\bigvee X, A), (\bigvee Y, B)) \;=\; \bigvee \{x \in \phi[\mathrm{Proc}(A \cup B)] \mid$
$$[\![\uparrow]\!](x, A) \le \bigvee X \;\wedge\; [\![\uparrow]\!](x, B) \le \bigvee Y\}$$

(A25) $[\![\,\|\,]\!]((\bigwedge S, A), (z, B)) \;=\; \bigwedge \{w \in S \cdot [\![\,\|\,]\!]((w, A), (z, B))\}$

(A26) $[\![\,\|\,]\!]((z, A), (\bigwedge S, B)) \;=\; \bigwedge \{w \in S \cdot [\![\,\|\,]\!]((z, A), (w, B))\}$

(A27) $\mu f \;=\; f(\mu f)$

(A28) $z \ne \bot \;\wedge\; f z \le z \;\Rightarrow\; \mu f \le z$

(A29) $\mu f \;\ne\; \bot$

(A30) $\mu g \;=\; g(\mu g)$

(A31) $(\forall w \in [\![T]\!] \cdot g h w \le h w) \;\Rightarrow\; (\forall w \in [\![T]\!] \cdot (\mu g) w \le h w)$

(A32) $(\forall w \in [\![T]\!] \cdot (\mu g) w \;\ne\; \bot)$

Proof. These results are proven in [8].

6 Conclusions

We have shown how to construct a model for an algebra of communicating sequential processes. The approach follows a mathematically clean step-by-step process which we speculate will apply whenever languages with choice are modelled. We first provide a poset which models the subset of the language without choice, parallelism or recursion. To model the whole language, we use the free completely distributive lattice over that poset. This is a suitable model for the choice operators, permits a very general model of the alphabetised parallel composition, and a natural definition of recursion. We have shown the algebra is sound by proving that the axioms hold in the model.

The algebra of communicating sequential processes we describe is very close to CSP: it differs mainly in the distributive properties of external choice. The model, however, is quite different from those of CSP and, in comparison, possesses some appealing qualities.

There exist several models for CSP [6], for example the failures-divergences model and the stable-failures model, all of which are based on trace theory. From a mathematical perspective, a complete, completely distributive lattice is a preferable structure to work with than the sets of pairs of traces employed by the standard CSP models, not least because it allows us to apply the tools of established lattice-theory.

Our prime motivation is the construction an algebra for communicating sequential processes which supports algebraic intuition and reasoning. The role a model plays in this context is to guarantee the soundness of the axioms. For this purpose, a single canonical model is desirable. This is what we have provided.

References

1. Ralph-Johan Back and Joakim von Wright. *Refinement Calculus — a systematic introduction.* Springer-Verlag, 1998.
2. Garrett Birkhoff. *Lattice Theory*, volume 25. American Mathematical Society, 1995.
3. B. A. Davey and H. A. Priestley. *Introduction to Lattices and Order.* Cambridge University Press, 1990.
4. P. Hitchcock and D. Park. Induction rules and termination proofs. In *IRIA Conference on Automata, Languages, and Programming Theory*, pages 225–251. North-Holland, Amsterdam, 1972.
5. Joseph M. Morris. Augmenting types with unbounded demonic and angelic nondeterminacy. In *Proceedings of the Seventh International Conference on Mathematics of Program Construction*, volume 3125, pages 274–288. Springer Verlag, 2004.
6. A. W. Roscoe. *The Theory and Practice of Concurrency.* Prentice Hall, 1998.
7. A. Tarski. A lattice-theoretical fixed point theorem and its applications. *Pacific Journal of Mathematics*, 5(2):285–309, 1955.
8. Malcolm Tyrrell, Joseph M. Morris, Andrew Butterfield, Arthur Hughes, and Wendy Verbruggen. A lattice-theoretic model for an algebra of communicating sequential processes: Definitions and proofs. Technical Report CA0206, School of Computing, Dublin City University, Dublin 9, Ireland, August 2006.

A Petri Net Translation of π-Calculus Terms

Raymond Devillers[1], Hanna Klaudel[2], and Maciej Koutny[3]

[1] Département d'Informatique, Université Libre de Bruxelles
CP212, B-1050 Bruxelles, Belgium
rdevil@ulb.ac.be
[2] IBISC, FRE 2873 CNRS, Université d'Evry, 91000 Evry, France
klaudel@ibisc.univ-evry.fr
[3] School of Computing Science, University of Newcastle
Newcastle upon Tyne, NE1 7RU, United Kingdom
maciej.koutny@newcastle.ac.uk

Abstract. In this paper, we propose a finite structural translation of possibly recursive π-calculus terms into Petri nets. This is achieved by using high level nets together with an equivalence on markings in order to model entering into recursive calls, which do not need to be guarded.

Keywords: mobility, process algebra, π-calculus, Petri nets, compositional translation, behavioural consistency.

1 Introduction

In our previous paper [8], we devised a structural way of translating terms from the finite fragment of the π-calculus into finite Petri nets. This translation relies on a combination of PBC [1] and M-net [2,10,11] features and its result is a Petri net whose semantics in terms of a labelled transition system is strongly bisimilar [17], and often even isomorphic, to that of the original π-term.

The translation in [8] only concerned terms without recursion (and replication, but the latter is equivalent to recursion), and in this paper we will show how to remove this restriction. The standard way of incorporating recursion in a PBC-like framework is to rely on net refinement and a fixpoint approach [1]. However, in the π-calculus framework, successive refinements would generally need to apply (somewhat arbitrary) alpha-conversions in order to keep the well-formedness of process expressions, making fixpoint approach much more complicated.

An alternative could be to use recursive Petri nets [14], but this would lead to a formalism, which in our view would be difficult to lift to the high level nets and to the specific framework needed to deal with recursive π-calculus terms (in particular, it is far from clear how one could support communications between different levels of recursion). Moreover, the various kinds of causality and concurrency semantics are not currently available in the recursive Petri net theory. We therefore decided to use instead a simpler and more direct approach inspired by [7] and used in the context of PBC.

We assume that the reader is familiar with the basics concepts of π-calculus and high-level Petri nets (all formal definitions and proofs can be found in [9]).

K. Barkaoui, A. Cavalcanti, and A. Cerone (Eds.): ICTAC 2006, LNCS 4281, pp. 138–152, 2006.
© Springer-Verlag Berlin Heidelberg 2006

2   The π-Calculus and Its Indexed Operational Semantics

We start by recalling the syntax and semantics of the π-calculus [18], assuming that $\mathbb{C}$ is a countably infinite set of *channels* ranged over by the first few lower case Roman letters; and that $\mathbb{X} = \{X_1, \ldots, X_m\}$ is a finite set of *process variables*, each variable $X \in \mathbb{X}$ having a finite arity n_X. The concrete syntax we use is given below, where P denotes an *agent* (or π-expression).

$$\ell ::= \bar{a}b \;\mid\; ac \;\mid\; \tau \qquad\qquad\qquad\qquad \text{(output/input/internal prefixes)}$$
$$P ::= 0 \;\mid\; \ell.P \;\mid\; P + P \;\mid\; P|P \;\mid\; (\boldsymbol{\nu}c)P \;\mid\; X(a_1, \ldots, a_{n_X}) \qquad\quad \text{(agents)}$$

The constructs $ac.P$ (input) and $(\boldsymbol{\nu}c)P$ (restriction) *bind* the channel c in P, and we denote by $fn(P)$ the free channels of P. For each process variable $X \in \mathbb{X}$, there is exactly one definition D_X of the form $X(a_1, \ldots, a_{n_X}) \stackrel{\text{df}}{=} P_X$, where $a_i \neq a_j$ for $i \neq j$. We assume that $fn(P_X) \subseteq \{a_1, \ldots, a_{n_X}\}$, so that the free channels of P_X are *parameter bound*. Agents are defined up to the *alpha-conversion*, meaning that bound channels may be coherently renamed avoiding potential clashes. Moreover, $\{b/c, \ldots\}P$ will denote the agent obtained from P by replacing all free occurrences of c by b, etc, possibly after alpha-converting P in order to avoid name clashes; for example $\{b/c, f/a\}ab.\bar{g}b.X(d,c) = fe.\bar{g}e.X(d,b)$.

The semantical treatment of the π-calculus adopted in this paper is that expounded by Cattani and Sewell [5], where the usual transition steps are augmented with an explicit information about unrestricted channels:

$$A \vdash P \stackrel{\ell}{\longrightarrow} B \vdash Q$$

where ℓ is a prefix and $A, B \subset \mathbb{C}$ are finite sets of *indexing* channels such that $fn(P) \subseteq A \subseteq B \supseteq fn(Q)$. Its intuitive meaning is that

> "in a state where the channels A may be known by agent P and by its environment, P can do ℓ to become agent Q and the channels B may be known to Q and its environment".

As a result, Q may know more channels than P as an input $\ell = ab$ adds b whenever $b \notin A$ (intuitively, such a b is a new channel communicated by the outside world – see the IN rule in table 1), and an output $\ell = \bar{a}b$ adds b whenever $b \notin A$ (intuitively, such a b is a channel restricted in P which becomes a new known channel in Q – see the OPEN rule in table 1).

The operational semantics rules for the *indexed* π-expressions are shown in table 1 (in [5], the '$B \vdash$' parts of the rules are implicit). The complete behaviour of an expression $A \vdash P$, where $fn(P) \subseteq A$, is then given by a labelled transition system derived using these rules, and denoted $\mathsf{lts}_{A \vdash P}$.

As a running example, consider an expression $\{a\} \vdash X(a) + \tau.0$ with X defined by $X(e) \stackrel{\text{df}}{=} ec.\bar{c}e.0 + (\nu d)(X(d)|\bar{d}e.0)$. It admits, e.g., the following executions:

$$\{a\} \vdash X(a) + \tau.0 \stackrel{\tau}{\longrightarrow} \{a\} \vdash (\nu d)((\bar{a}d.0)|0)$$
$$\{a\} \vdash X(a) + \tau.0 \stackrel{\tau}{\longrightarrow} \{a\} \vdash 0 \;.$$

Table 1. Operational semantics of π-calculus, where: $ns(\tau) \stackrel{df}{=} \varnothing$; $ns(ab) = ns(\overline{a}b) \stackrel{df}{=} \{a,b\}$; the notation A,c stands for the disjoint union $A \uplus \{c\}$; and $(\nu c \setminus A)P$ is P if $c \in A$ and $(\nu c)P$ otherwise. Symmetric versions of SUM, PAR and COM are omitted.

$$\text{TAU} \quad \frac{}{A \vdash \tau . P \stackrel{\tau}{\longrightarrow} A \vdash P} \qquad\qquad \frac{}{A \vdash ac . P \stackrel{ab}{\longrightarrow} A \cup \{b\} \vdash \{b/c\}P} \quad \text{IN}$$

$$\text{OUT} \quad \frac{}{A \vdash \overline{a}b . P \stackrel{\overline{a}b}{\longrightarrow} A \vdash P} \qquad\qquad \frac{A,c \vdash P \stackrel{\overline{a}c}{\longrightarrow} A,c \vdash P' \quad a \neq c}{A \vdash (\nu c)P \stackrel{\overline{a}c}{\longrightarrow} A \cup \{c\} \vdash P'} \quad \text{OPEN}$$

$$\text{PAR} \quad \frac{A \vdash P \stackrel{\ell}{\longrightarrow} A' \vdash P'}{A \vdash P|Q \stackrel{\ell}{\longrightarrow} A' \vdash P'|Q} \qquad\qquad \frac{A,c \vdash P \stackrel{\ell}{\longrightarrow} A',c \vdash P' \quad c \notin ns(\ell)}{A \vdash (\nu c)P \stackrel{\ell}{\longrightarrow} A' \vdash (\nu c)P'} \quad \text{RES}$$

$$\text{SUM} \quad \frac{A \vdash P \stackrel{\ell}{\longrightarrow} A' \vdash P'}{A \vdash P+Q \stackrel{\ell}{\longrightarrow} A' \vdash P'} \qquad \frac{A \vdash P \stackrel{\overline{a}c}{\longrightarrow} A' \vdash P' \quad A \vdash Q \stackrel{ac}{\longrightarrow} A'' \vdash Q'}{A \vdash P|Q \stackrel{\tau}{\longrightarrow} A \vdash (\nu c \setminus A)(P'|Q')} \quad \text{COM}$$

$$\text{PROCDEF} \quad \frac{A \vdash \{b_1/a_1, \ldots, b_{n_X}/a_{n_X}\}P \stackrel{\ell}{\longrightarrow} A' \vdash P' \quad X(a_1, \ldots, a_{n_X}) \stackrel{df}{=} P}{A \vdash X(b_1, \ldots, b_{n_X}) \stackrel{\ell}{\longrightarrow} A' \vdash P'}$$

Given an indexed π-expression $A \vdash P$, it is always possible to apply alpha-conversions to P and the process definitions so that no channel across $P, D_{X_1}, \ldots, D_{X_m}$ is both free and bound, no such channel generates more than one binding, and no restricted channel occurs in A. Such an indexed π-expression will be called *well-formed*. We fix such a well-formed $A \vdash P$ for the rest of this paper.

Context-based representation. Before translating to nets, we give a term a presentation which separates its structure from the specific channels used to express what is visible from the outside and which channels are (input or parameter) bound or restricted. This also involves separating the features related to control flow of the term from those related to channel substitution and binding. For the resulting context based representation we need two fresh countably infinite sets of *restricted channels* $\mathbb{R}$ ranged over by the upper case Greek letters, and *channel holders* $\mathbb{H}$ ranged over by the first few lower case Greek letters. A *context* itself is a partial mapping $\varsigma : \mathbb{H} \to \mathbb{C} \uplus \mathbb{R}$ with a finite domain.

The aim is to represent an expression like $\{b,d\} \vdash ba . (\nu c)\overline{a}c . \overline{c}b . 0$ as a context based expression $\mathcal{P}{:}\varsigma$, where $\mathcal{P} \stackrel{df}{=} \beta\alpha . \overline{\alpha}\gamma . \overline{\gamma}\beta . 0$ is a *restriction-free* agent based solely on channel holders and $\varsigma \stackrel{df}{=} [\beta \mapsto b, \delta \mapsto d, \gamma \mapsto \Delta]$ is a context allowing their interpretation. In this particular case ς implies that: (i) α is a channel holder bound by an input prefix (since α is not in the domain of the context mapping though it occurs in $\mathcal{P}$); (ii) β and δ correspond respectively to the known channels b and d; and (iii) γ is a channel holder corresponding to the restricted channel Δ, the detailed identity of this restricted channel being irrelevant.

Now, given our well-formed indexed expression $A \vdash P$ together with process definitions $D_{X_1}, \ldots, D_{X_m}$, we proceed as follows. For each channel name c

occurring in the indexed expression or process definitions, we choose a *distinct* channel holder α_c. The bodies of $P, D_{X_1}, \ldots, D_{X_m}$ are then transformed by first deleting all the instances of the restriction operator, and then replacing each occurrence of each channel by the corresponding channel holder, resulting in new holder-based terms: $\mathcal{P}, \mathcal{D}_{X_1}, \ldots, \mathcal{D}_{X_m}$.

We then construct contexts, $\varsigma, \varsigma_1, \ldots, \varsigma_m$. The context ς maps every α_c used in the body of P for which c was restriction bound into a distinct restricted channel Δ_c, and every α_c for which $c \in A$ into c. Each ς_i simply maps every α_c which is restriction bound in the body of D_{X_i} into a distinct Δ_c. We finally obtain a *main* expression $\mathcal{H} = \mathcal{P}{:}[\varsigma]$ and the modified definitions $\mathcal{D}_{X_1}{:}[\varsigma_1], \ldots, \mathcal{D}_{X_m}{:}[\varsigma_m]$, which will be used as an input to our translation into Petri nets.

For example, our running example can be rendered in the context-based scheme as: $X(\alpha) + \tau . 0 : [\alpha \mapsto a]$ with $X(\epsilon) \overset{\text{df}}{=} \epsilon\gamma . \overline{\gamma}\epsilon . 0 + (X(\delta)|\overline{\delta}\epsilon . 0) : [\delta \mapsto \Delta]$.

3   An Algebra of Nets

The development of our Petri net model, called *rp-nets*, has been inspired by the box algebra [1,2,10] and by the p-net algebra used in [8] to model the finite fragment of π-calculus. In particular, we shall use coloured tokens and read-arcs (allowing any number of transitions to simultaneously check for the presence of a resource stored in a place [6]). Transitions in rp-nets will have four different kinds of labels:

- UV, Uv and $\overline{U}V$ (where U, V and v are net variables) to specify communication with the external environment.
- τ to represent internal actions.
- rcv and snd to effect internal process communication.
- $X(\alpha_1, \ldots, \alpha_{n_X})$ to identify hierarchical transitions supporting recursion (we use gray rectangles to represent such transitions).

A key idea behind our translation of a context-based expression using a set of process definitions is to view this system as consisting of a main program together with a number of procedure declarations. We then represent the control structure of the main program and the procedures using disjoint unmarked nets, one for the main program and one for each of the procedure declarations. The program is executed once, while each procedure can be invoked several times (even concurrently), each such invocation being uniquely identified by structured tokens which correspond to the sequence of recursive calls along the execution path leading to that invocation.[1] With this in mind, we will use the notion of a *trail* σ to denote a finite (possibly empty) sequence of hierarchical transitions of an rp-net. The places of the nets which are responsible for control flow will carry tokens which are simply trails. (The empty trail will be treated as the usual

---

[1] That this sequence is sufficient to identify an invocation will follow from the fact that a given hierarchical transition may be activated many times, but each time with a different sequence.

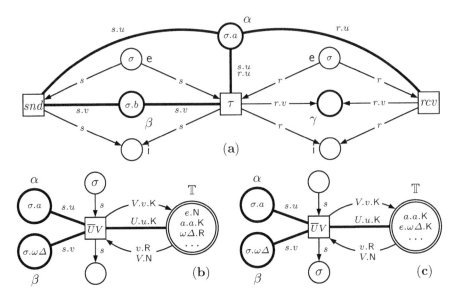

Fig. 1. Holder places and read arcs (**a**), and the usage of the tag-place (**b, c**), where K, R, N are constants, while the other symbols in arc inscriptions are net variables

'black' token.) Procedure invocation is then possible if each of the input places of a hierarchical transition t labelled with $X(\dots)$ contains the same trail token σ, and it results in removing these tokens and inserting a new token σt in each initial (entry) place of the net corresponding to the definition of X.

Trailed channels and holder places. Places in rp-nets are labelled in ways reflecting their intended role. Those used to model control flow are labelled by their status symbols (*internal* places by i, and *interface* places by e and x, for entry and exit, respectively), and the tokens they carry are simply the trails σ. Another kind of places, called *holder* places, carry structured tokens representing channels used by different procedure invocations. Each such token, called a *trailed channel*, is of the form $\sigma.\xi$ where σ is a trail and ξ is a known channel in $\mathbb{C}$, or a restricted channel $\omega\Delta$ (ω is a trail and $\Delta \in \mathbb{R}$). Intuitively, its first part, σ, identifies the invocation in which the token is used, while the second part, a or $\omega\Delta$, provides its value. In the diagrams, holder places are labelled by the elements of $\mathbb{H}$ and have thick borders. (A third kind of places will be introduced later on.)

Referring to figure 1(a), a holder place can be accessed by directed arcs, which can deposit or remove tokens, as well as by read arcs (drawn as thick undirected edges), which *test* for the presence of specific tokens. The net itself may be seen as a fragment of the translation of a context-based process definition, $Y(\alpha, \beta) \overset{\text{df}}{=} (\overline{a}\beta \dots | a\gamma \dots) : [\ ]$, where the channel holders α, β and γ are represented by the corresponding holder places. The depicted procedure invocation has been activated by the trail σ, and two trailed channels, $\sigma.a$ and $\sigma.b$, have been inserted as actual parameters into the holder places labelled by α and β, respectively. On the other hand, the γ-labelled holder place, corresponding to an input bound channel holder, remains empty until a communication or input action inserts a trailed channel into it.

Control flow places are connected using directed arcs, labelled with trail variables, s or r, while the holder places are connected using directed arcs and read arcs labelled with structured annotations, like $s.u$, with two variables directly matching the type of tokens allowed in holder places. To interpret arcs annotations, we use *bindings* $\flat$ assigning concrete values to the variables occurring there as well as those appearing in transition labels. In our setting, $\flat(s)$ and $\flat(r)$ return trails, $\flat(u)$ and $\flat(v)$ return channels (or trailing restricted channels), whereas $\flat(U)$ and $\flat(V)$ return channels. As usual in high-level Petri nets, bindings will yield tokens transferred/tested along arcs adjacent to executed transitions as well as the visible labels of the latter.

For the net depicted in figure 1(a), the rcv-labelled transition is enabled if the right entry place contains a trail (in our case, σ) and the α-labelled place contains a trailed channel with precisely the same 'trail' part (in our case, $\sigma.a$). More formally, there must be a binding $\flat$ such that $\flat(r)$ evaluates to σ and $\flat(r.u) \stackrel{\mathrm{df}}{=} \flat(r).\flat(u)$ evaluates to $\sigma.a$. Indeed, such a binding can be constructed, by setting $\flat(r) = \sigma$ and $\flat(u) = a$. The firing of the rcv-labelled transition transforms the current marking in the following way: σ is removed from the right entry place and deposited in the right internal place, the token in the α-labelled place is left unchanged, and a trailed channel $\flat(r.v)$ (e.g., $\sigma.e$ or $\sigma.b$, depending on the choice of the binding which in this case is not unique) is inserted into the γ-labelled holder place. Similarly, the firing of the snd-labelled transition is also possible and results in a transfer of the trail σ from the left entry place to the left internal place. Now, if we look at the firing of the τ-labelled transition, which corresponds to the fusion of the two transitions considered previously, the binding with $\flat(v) = e$ is inconsistent with the only binding option for v (i.e., $\flat(v) = b$), and so a unique internal communication is possible through which the γ-labelled holder place acquires the trailed channel $\sigma.b$.

Tag-places. The third, and last, kind of node in a rp-net is a special holder place, called the *tag-place*, which is always present and unique; it is $\mathbb{T}$-labelled and indicated in the diagrams by a double border. The tokens, called *bookkeeping tokens*, stored in this place are structured by being *tagged* with a member of the set $\mathbb{T} \stackrel{\mathrm{df}}{=} \{\mathsf{K}, \mathsf{N}, \mathsf{R}\}$. The first tag, K, will be used to indicate the known channels (initially, those in $\varsigma(\mathbb{H}) \cap \mathbb{C}$). The second tag, N, will be used to indicate the new, yet unknown channels (initially, those in $\mathbb{C} \setminus \varsigma(\mathbb{H})$), and the third tag, R, will be used to indicate the restricted channels. The first case is slightly more complicated than the remaining two, for a restricted $\omega\Delta$ may be present with different preceding trails σ's in holder places, due to internal communications.[2] Now, if the restriction has been *opened*, $\omega\Delta$ should become a newly known channel c, but it is not possible to replace $\omega\Delta$ by c in all the relevant holder places

---

[2] More precisely, we may have various $\omega\Delta$'s in various holder places with the same trail σ due to internal communications, and with different σ's due to parameter passing.

without some global transformation of the net. Instead, we will indicate this fact by inserting a bookkeeping token $c.\omega\Delta.\mathsf{K}$ into the tag-place, and then consulting it whenever necessary (i.e., whenever we need to establish whether a restricted channel has been opened and what is its actual known value). Moreover, to keep the notation uniform, we shall use bookkeeping tokens $a.a.\mathsf{K}$ to denote all those known channels which were never restricted. To summarise, a bookkeeping token in the tag-place may be of the form:

- $a.\mathsf{N}$ meaning that a is a new channel.
- $\omega\Delta.\mathsf{R}$ meaning that Δ is a restricted channel for the incarnation of its defining process corresponding to trail ω.
- $a.a.\mathsf{K}$ meaning that a is a known channel (either a has always been known or a was initially new and then became known).
- $a.\omega\Delta.\mathsf{K}$ meaning that the restricted $\omega\Delta$ has become known as a.

The arcs adjacent to the tag-place (both directed and read ones) are labelled with annotations which are evaluated through bindings so that the tags are left intact; e.g., $\flat(V.\mathsf{N}) \stackrel{\mathrm{df}}{=} \flat(V).\mathsf{N}$ and $\flat(U.u.\mathsf{K}) \stackrel{\mathrm{df}}{=} \flat(U).\flat(u).\mathsf{K}$.

To explain the way a tag-place is used, we consider an rp-net fragment in figure 1(b), where the (irrelevant) labels of the two control flow places have been omitted. The marking in the tag-place indicates that $\omega\Delta$ is a restricted channel in the incarnation of some procedure definition identified by ω. Moreover, e is a new unknown channel, and a is a known one. The transition is enabled with the binding $\flat(u) = \flat(U) = a$, $\flat(v) = \omega\Delta$, $\flat(V) = e$ and $\flat(s) = \sigma$. Its firing produces the visible action $\flat(\overline{U}V) \stackrel{\mathrm{df}}{=} \overline{\flat(U)}\flat(V) = \overline{a}e$ and leads to the marking in figure 1(c). This firing illustrates how a restricted channel becomes known (which is represented by the insertion of the bookkeeping token $e.\omega\Delta.\mathsf{K}$ in the tag-place), and corresponds to the OPEN rule in table 1.

Composing rp-nets. The operators we shall use to combine rp-nets can be seen as suitably adapted instances of those defined within PBC and its various extensions [1,10]. In particular, the way in which the holder places are handled when composing nets is directly inspired by the asynchronous communication construct of APBC [10].

The rp-net composition operators that we need are *prefixing*, $N.N'$, *choice*, $N + N'$, *parallel composition*, $N|N'$, and *scoping*, $\mathrm{sco}(N)$. The first three operators merge the tag-places, as well as the corresponding holder places (i.e., labelled by the same channel holder). This corresponds to the asynchronous links used in [10], and will allow one to mimic the standard rewriting mechanism of the π-calculus. For two operand nets, their transitions and control flow places are made disjoint before applying a composition operator in order to allow to properly handle the cases when, for example, $N = N'$.

- In the choice composition, the entry and exit places of N and N' are combined through a cartesian product together. This has the following effect: if we start from a situation where each entry place contains a copy of a common token σ, then either N or N' can be executed, mimicking the SUM rule and its symmetric counterpart.

– The prefixing operator combines the exit place (it will always be unique) of the prefix N with the entry places of N' into internal places, and the effect is that the execution of N after reaching the terminal marking, where the only exit place is marked, is followed by that of N'. Such a behaviour mimics the TAU, IN and OUT rules.

– The parallel composition of N and N' puts them side by side, allowing to execute both parts in parallel, as in the PAR rule and its symmetric counterpart; and then merges all pairs of transitions labelled rcv and snd, resulting in τ-labelled transitions: the connectivity of the new transition is the combination of those of the composed transitions. This merging is illustrated in the middle of figure 1; it has an effect similar to the COM rule.

– Finally, the scoping operation erases all the rcv- and snd-labelled transitions.

4   Translating Context-Based Expressions into Rp-Nets

We now come back to our context-based expression $\mathcal{H} = \mathcal{P}{:}[\varsigma]$ and the process definitions $\mathcal{D}_{X_1}{:}[\varsigma_1], \ldots, \mathcal{D}_{X_m}{:}[\varsigma_m]$. The proposed rendering of $\mathcal{H}$ in terms of rp-nets is obtained in three phases. First, we compositionally translate $\mathcal{P}$ and each $\mathcal{D}_{X_i}$ into disjoint unmarked rp-nets $\mathbb{K}(\mathcal{P}), \mathbb{K}(\mathcal{D}_{X_1}), \ldots, \mathbb{K}(\mathcal{D}_{X_m})$. The resulting nets are then combined using parallel composition and scoping. Finally, using the contexts $\varsigma, \varsigma_1, \ldots, \varsigma_m$, we construct an initial marking, which results in the target rp-net $\mathbb{PN}(\mathcal{H})$.

Phase I. The translation $\mathbb{K}(\mathcal{P})$ (resp. $\mathbb{K}(\mathcal{P}_X)$), guided by the syntax tree of $\mathcal{P}$, consists in first giving the translation for the basic sub-terms (i.e., the basic process 0, the process calls, and the internal, input and output prefixes) shown in figure 2, and then applying rp-net operators following the syntax.

The translations of the basic process 0 and the internal prefix τ are very simple (they do not involve any manipulation on channels). The same is true of a process call $X(\alpha_1, \ldots, \alpha_{n_X})$, but the result employs a hierarchical transition, which will never fire but rather contribute to a marking equivalence.

Each output prefix $\overline{\alpha}\beta$, for $\alpha \neq \beta$, is translated into the rp-net $\mathbb{K}(\overline{\alpha}\beta)$ which may exhibit three kinds of behaviours, corresponding to the firing, under some binding $\flat$, of three specific transitions:

– t^k: *known output.* A known channel $\flat(V)$ is sent through a channel $\flat(U)$. The actual values of U and V are provided by the bookkeeping tokens present in the tag-place matching those in the holder places α and β, accessed through u and v and preceded by a trail which corresponds, thanks to the common annotation s, to a token in the entry place. This corresponds to the OUT rule. That the channels $\flat(U)$ and $\flat(V)$ are known is determined by the presence in the tag-place of bookkeeping tokens tagged with K.

– t^n: *new output.* A new channel $\flat(V)$ is sent through a known channel $\flat(U)$, for some trail token, $\flat(s)$ as before. That the channels $\flat(v)$ and $\flat(V)$ are respectively restricted and new is determined by the presence in the tag-place of a bookkeeping token tagged with R for $\flat(v)$, and a bookkeeping

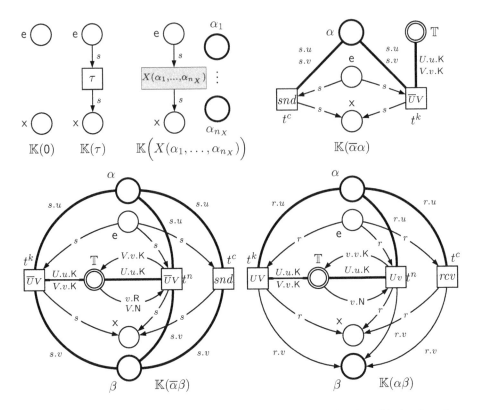

Fig. 2. The unmarked rp-nets for 0, τ, the process call and the three kinds of prefixes (the tag-place is omitted when disconnected)

token tagged with N for $\flat(V)$. After the firing of this transition, the restricted channel represented by v becomes known; this is indicated by inserting a bookkeeping token of the form $\flat(V.v.\mathsf{K})$ into the tag-place which now replaces $\flat(v.\mathsf{R})$ and $\flat(V.\mathsf{N})$. This corresponds to the OPEN rule.

- t^c: *communicating output.* It is intended to synchronise with a corresponding communication input in order to provide the transfer of a channel $\flat(v)$ through the channel $\flat(u)$, be it known or restricted. This models one of the main features of the π-calculus which is the ability of *passing* the channels around.

The special case of the output prefix $\overline{a}a$ has a simpler translation, since a may not be both known and restricted, so that t^n is irrelevant in this case. Even though the a-labelled holder place will never contain more than one token with the same trail part, it is not a problem to have two variables on the arcs adjacent to it since these are read arcs, and so transitions will be enabled by simply identifying $s.u$ and $s.v$ with the same token in the a-labelled place.

For an input prefix $a\beta$, the translation is broadly the same as for the output prefix (notice that prefixes of the form aa are excluded by the well-formedness assumption). In particular, the known, new and communicating inputs should be interpreted in a similar way. Simply, $\flat(r.v)$ is now inserted into β instead of being checked, t^k corresponds to the rule IN when b is already known (including the case of a previously restricted channel), and t^n to the same rule when b is new (it may not be restricted here). In the latter case, the variable V is not involved, and the transition is labelled Uv rather than UV. Notice also that, for t^k, while $\flat(v)$ is known as $\flat(V)$, it is the possibly restricted original value $\flat(v)$ which is written (together with the trailed token $\flat(s)$) into β, and not the corresponding known value for V. This is important in order to allow subsequent synchronisations between rcv (with $\flat(u)$) coming from β and snd (with $\flat(u)$) coming from another holder place and containing a copy of the original token.

For the compound sub-terms, we proceed compositionally: $\mathbb{K}(\mathcal{P}' \; op \; \mathcal{P}'') \stackrel{\mathrm{df}}{=} \mathbb{K}(\mathcal{P}') \; op \; \mathbb{K}(\mathcal{P}'')$, where $op \in \{|, +, .\}$. There is however a simplification which may be applied to the above translation rule, which amounts to throwing away useless instances of the translation for 0. One simply has to first apply the following simplifications: $\mathbb{K}(P|0) = \mathbb{K}(0|P) \rightsquigarrow \mathbb{K}(P)$ and $\mathbb{K}(a.0) \rightsquigarrow \mathbb{K}(a)$ (notice that we already have that $\mathbb{K}(P + 0) = \mathbb{K}(0 + P) = \mathbb{K}(P)$). Finally, we add a holder place for each channel holder occurring in the domain of ς but not in $\mathcal{P}$.

The translation of process definitions proceeds similarly. Assuming that $\mathcal{D}_X$ is of the form $X(\kappa_1^X, \ldots, \kappa_{n_X}^X) \stackrel{\mathrm{df}}{=} \mathcal{P}_X$, we derive $\mathbb{K}(\mathcal{P}_X)$ following the scheme just described, and then add a holder place for each channel holder κ_i^X which does not occur in $\mathcal{P}_X$.

Phase II. The various components are then connected by constructing the net $\mathbf{sc}\left(\mathbb{K}(\mathcal{P})|\mathbb{K}(\mathcal{D}_{X_1})|\ldots|\mathbb{K}(\mathcal{D}_{X_m})\right)$. This merges the various tag places and the pairs of snd- and rcv-labelled transitions, possibly from different components. All the rcv- and snd-labelled transitions are erased after that.

Phase III. Having applied the parallel composition and scoping, we add the initial marking, leading to the full translation $\mathbb{PN}(\mathcal{H})$, in the following way:

- An empty trail token $\bullet$ is inserted in each entry place of $\mathbb{K}(\mathcal{P})$.
- $\bullet.\varsigma(\alpha)$ trailed channel (in the diagrams represented as $\varsigma(\alpha)$, $\bullet$ representing the empty trail) is inserted into each α-labelled holder place, for $\alpha \in dom(\varsigma)$.
- $\omega.\omega\varsigma_i(\alpha)$ trailed channel is inserted into the α-labelled holder place, and $\omega\varsigma_i(\alpha).R$ bookkeeping token is inserted into the tag-place, for each trail ω and $\alpha \in dom(\varsigma_i)$ $(1 \le i \le m)$.
- $a.a.K$ bookkeeping token is inserted into the tag-place, for $a \in \varsigma(\mathbb{H}) \cap \mathbb{C}$.
- $e.N$ bookkeeping token is inserted into the tag-place, for $e \in \mathbb{C} \setminus \varsigma(\mathbb{H})$.
- $\Delta.R$ bookkeeping token is inserted into the tag-place, for $\Delta \in \varsigma(\mathbb{H}) \cap \mathbb{R}$.

Figure 3 (top) shows the rp-net resulting from the translation where, for clarity, all the arcs adjacent to the tag-place and holder places are omitted and arc annotations have been shortened or omitted.

5   Firing Rule and Marking Equivalence

To define the semantics of the resulting rp-net $\mathbb{PN}(\mathcal{H})$, we need to introduce the firing rule for non-hierarchical transitions, which may use a combination of annotated standard (oriented) arcs and read-arcs, and a marking equivalence corresponding to procedure calls.

For each transition t, we denote by $\iota(t)$ its label (a term with variables), by $\iota(s,t)$, $\iota(t,s)$ and $\iota(\{s,t\})$ the labels (sets of terms with variables) of its incoming arcs, out-going arcs and read-arcs, respectively. We shall assume that each variable has an associated domain of possible values, for instance, the domain of u, v, U and V is $\mathbb{C} \cup \{\omega\Gamma \mid \omega \text{ is a trail}, \Gamma \in \mathbb{R}\}$ and that of r and s is $\{\omega \mid \omega \text{ is a trail}\}$. For each transition t, if $\{u_1, ..., u_n\}$ denotes the variables occurring in the label of t and on the arcs adjacent to t, we shall denote by $\flat$ a binding assigning to each variable u_i a value in its domain. We shall only consider legal bindings, i.e., such that for each arc $\mathfrak{A}$ between t and an adjacent place s, if $\hbar$ is a function in $\iota(\mathfrak{A})$, the evaluation of $\hbar$ under the binding $\flat$ (denoted $\flat(\hbar)$) will deliver a value allowed in s. Moreover, the observed label of a transition fired under binding $\flat$ will be denoted by $\flat(\iota(t))$.

A *marking* $\mathcal{M}$ of a rp-net N is a function assigning to each place s a multiset of tokens belonging to its type. A marked rp-net will be denoted by $(N, \mathcal{M})$. Below we use $\oplus$ and $\ominus$ to denote respectively multiset sum and difference. Moreover, if $\mathcal{M}$ and $\mathcal{M}'$ are multisets over the same set of elements Z then $\mathcal{M} \geq \mathcal{M}'$ will mean that $\mathcal{M}(z) \geq \mathcal{M}'(z)$, for all $z \in Z$. We shall also denote by $z \in \mathcal{M}$ the fact that $\mathcal{M}(z) > 0$.

Let $\mathcal{M}$ be a marking of $\mathbb{PN}(\mathcal{H})$, t be any of its non–hierarchical transitions, and $\flat$ be a binding for t. Then we denote by $\mathcal{M}^{\flat}_{t,in}$ and $\mathcal{M}^{\flat}_{t,out}$ the two markings such that, for every place s,

$$\mathcal{M}^{\flat}_{t,in}(s) \overset{\text{df}}{=} \bigoplus_{\hbar \in \iota((s,t))} \{\flat(\hbar)\} \quad \text{and} \quad \mathcal{M}^{\flat}_{t,out}(s) \overset{\text{df}}{=} \bigoplus_{\hbar \in \iota((t,s))} \{\flat(\hbar)\} \,.$$

A non-hierarchical transition t will be *enabled* (i.e., allowed to be fired) under the binding $\flat$ and the marking $\mathcal{M}$ if, for every place s, $\mathcal{M}(s) \geq \mathcal{M}^{\flat}_{t,in}(s)$ and, moreover[3], $\flat(\hbar) \in \mathcal{M}(s)$ for every $\hbar \in \iota(\{s,t\})$. An enabled t may then be *fired*, which transforms the current marking $\mathcal{M}$ into a new marking $\mathcal{M}'$ in such a way that, for every place s:

$$\mathcal{M}'(s) = \mathcal{M}(s) \ominus \mathcal{M}^{\flat}_{t,in}(s) \oplus \mathcal{M}^{\flat}_{t,out}(s) \,.$$

This will be denoted by $(N, \mathcal{M}) \xrightarrow{\flat(\iota(t))} (N, \mathcal{M}')$ and moves of this type will be used in the definition of labelled transition systems generated by rp-nets.

As already mentioned, hierarchical transitions do not fire; instead, they drive a marking equivalence $\equiv$ corresponding to procedure calls (this resembles to certain extent the approach presented in [16]). This relation is defined as the

---

[3] Notice that this allows to have $\mathcal{M}(z) = 1$ and $\hbar_1, \hbar_2 \in \iota(\{s,t\})$ with $\flat(\hbar_1) = z = \flat(\hbar_2)$.

smallest equivalence such that, for each transition t labelled $X(\alpha_1, \ldots, \alpha_{n_X})$ with a definition $X(\kappa_1^X, \ldots, \kappa_{n_X}^X) \stackrel{\text{df}}{=} \mathcal{P}_X : \varsigma_X$, and for each trailed channel $\sigma.\xi_i$ (for $1 \leq i \leq n_X$), we have

$$\mathcal{M} \oplus \mathcal{M}_t^\sigma \oplus \mathcal{M}_\alpha^{\sigma.\xi} \equiv \mathcal{M} \oplus \mathcal{M}_X^{\sigma t} \oplus \mathcal{M}_\alpha^{\sigma.\xi} \oplus \mathcal{M}_\kappa^{\sigma t.\xi}, \text{ where:} \qquad (1)$$

- $\mathcal{M}_t^\sigma$ is the marking with a trail σ in each place s such that there is a directed arc from s to t (note that hierarchical transitions are only connected to control flow places), and nothing else.
- $\mathcal{M}_X^{\sigma t}$ is the marking with a trail σt in each entry place of $\mathbb{K}(\mathcal{P}_X)$, and nothing else.
- $\mathcal{M}_\alpha^{\sigma.\xi}$ (and $\mathcal{M}_\kappa^{\sigma t.\xi}$) is the marking with a trailed channel $\sigma.\xi_i$ (resp. $\sigma t.\xi_i$) in the holder place for α_i (resp. κ_i), for $i = 1 \ldots n_X$, and nothing else.

The complete behaviour of the rp-net $\mathbb{PN}(\mathcal{H})$, is then given by a labelled transition system derived using the above rules (the nodes of this system are $\equiv$-equivalence classes of net markings, and $(N, [\mathcal{M}_1]_\equiv) \xrightarrow{act} (N, [\mathcal{M}_2]_\equiv)$ iff there are $\mathcal{M}_1'$ and $\mathcal{M}_2'$ such that $\mathcal{M}_1 \equiv \mathcal{M}_1' \xrightarrow{act} \mathcal{M}_2' \equiv \mathcal{M}_2$), and denoted $\mathsf{lts}_{\mathbb{PN}(\mathcal{H})}$.

For the running example, a double application of the rule (1) above leads, from the initial marking shown in figure 3(a) to that in figure 3(b) (for clarity, we omitted all the arcs linking the transitions of the process definition part with the holder places). From there, the rightmost τ-transition may be fired, with the binding $\flat = \{r \mapsto tz, s \mapsto t, u \mapsto t\Delta, v \mapsto a\}$. The resulting marking is illustrated in figure 3(c), where all the arcs linking the executed transition with the holder places are shown and, for clarity, the other transitions appearing in the part of the net corresponding to the process definition have been left out.

6   Main Results

We proposed in this paper a translation from finite π-calculus specifications to rp-nets with finite structure, i.e., $\mathbb{PN}(\mathcal{H})$ is a net with finitely many places, transitions and arcs. Even though its marking is not finite, a closer examination of the possible reachable markings can reveal that they all may be obtained from a finite *condensed* form. For instance, in the rp-net for the running example, the marking of the holder place δ is constant and each token $\sigma.\sigma\Delta$ in it only becomes checkable if we enter a process instance corresponding to the trail σ, while the marking of the tag-place $\mathbb{T}$ is constantly such that the N-tagged and R-tagged tokens may be deduced from the K-tagged ones, which are a finite number. In other words, only a finite number of tokens is relevant at any given stage of evolution, and one can keep adding new tokens 'on demand' as the new instantiations of procedure calls are entered, and as new channels become known. Crucially, the proposed translation is *sound*. This means that, for every well-formed indexed π-expression $A \vdash P$, its labelled transition system $\mathsf{lts}_{A \vdash P}$ is strongly bisimilar [17] to the labelled transition system $\mathsf{lts}_{\mathbb{PN}(\mathcal{H})}$ of the corresponding rp-net.

Theorem 1. $\mathbb{PN}(\mathcal{H})$ *is an rp-net with finitely many places and transitions such that* $\mathsf{lts}_{A \vdash P}$ *and* $\mathsf{lts}_{\mathbb{PN}(\mathcal{H})}$ *are strongly bisimilar transition systems.*

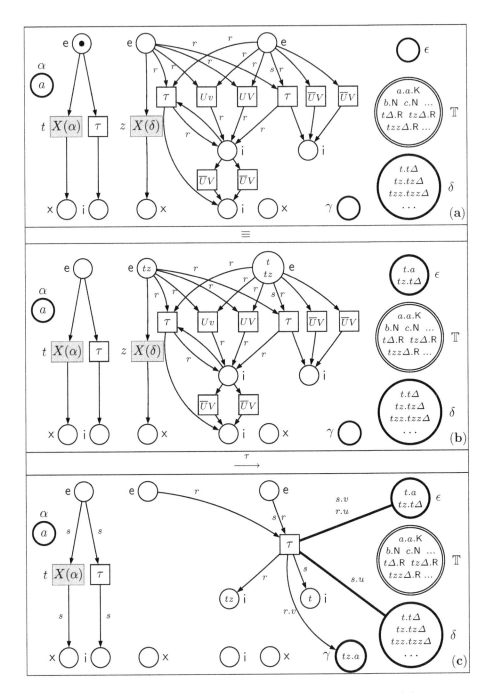

Fig. 3. Translation of the running example (**a**); marking transformation (**b**); and transition firing (**c**). For clarity, in (**a,b**), all the directed arcs annotated with s only are shown unannotated.

The above theorem yields a bisimilarity property between the labelled transition systems of the original π-agents and their Petri net translations. That the result is not formulated in terms of isomorphism is due to the *amnesia* feature of the SUM rule, complemented by a similar phenomenon for the prefix rules (TAU, IN and OUT). The loss of the past in the prefix rules is not essential by itself, since it corresponds to the progression of the control flow token(s) in the corresponding net. However, when combined with the SUM rule, which completely forgets the non-chosen branch, this may lead to differences in the labelled transition systems. Indeed, if we have a choice between two branches with a reachable common suffix then, after some time, the two branches will lead to the same intermediate expression in the π-semantics, while this never happens in the Petri net semantics, where the two branches correspond to two disjoint subnets, hence two different markings depending on which branch has been chosen.

The proposed translation is also a conservative extension of that in [8].

Theorem 2. *If the indexed π-expression $A \vdash P$ is recursion-free (i.e., $m = 0$) then $\mathbb{PN}(\mathcal{H})$ is the same as that in [8] up to some dead transitions and the suppression of all trails and trail variables.*

7   Related Work and Concluding Remarks

A first paper giving a Petri net semantics for the π-calculus is [12]. However, it only considers the so-called 'small' π-calculus (without the choice composition) provided with the reduction semantics (addressing only the communications between parallel components). Due to these limited aims, the problem is greatly simplified as restrictions may be managed syntactically. While not based on nets, [3] already considers the causality structures of the π-calculus, and distinguishes structural and link dependencies (the former mainly due to prefixing and communications, and the latter due to extrusion). A graph-rewriting system is proposed in [19] as a semantic model for a fragment of the π-calculus mainly addressing the concurrency feature of systems. Although it is not the objective of the present paper, we intend to look at concurrency issues, and in this respect we may notice a discrepancy between our approach and [19] in the handling of restriction. More precisely, [19] allows parallel opening for expressions like $(\nu y)(\overline{x}y|P|\overline{z}y)$ by letting the actions $\overline{x}y$ and $\overline{z}y$ to occur in parallel, while in our approach they must in some sense agree on their common exportation, so that only one of them is in fact an opening. The translation of π-terms into Petri nets of [4] uses (low-level) labelled Petri nets extended with inhibitor arcs, while we use high-level nets with read-arcs. Moreover, the way compositionality is obtained is different from that used in our approach, relying to a construction of a general infrastructure, with places corresponding to all the possible sequential π-terms with all possible transitions between those places, and a compositionally defined initial marking corresponding to each π-term.

We outlined a translation of recursive π-calculus process expressions into high-level Petri domain. The next step is to incorporate it into suitable computer aided tools, such as PEP [13], to allow the verification and simulation of π-calculus specifications using techniques found in the Petri net domain (for the finite π-calculus translation of [8] this has been already been done in [15]).

Acknowledgements. We thank the anonymous referees for their helpful comments. This research was supported by the EC IST grant 511599 (RODIN).

References

1. Best, E., Devillers, R., Koutny, M.: Petri Net Algebra. EATCS Monographs on TCS, Springer (2001).
2. Best, E., Fraczak, W., Hopkins, R.P., Klaudel, H., Pelz, E.: M-nets: an Algebra of High Level Petri Nets, with an Application to the Semantics of Concurrent Programming Languages. Acta Informatica **35** (1998) 813–857
3. Boreale, M., Sangiorgi, D.: A Fully Abstract Semantics for Causality in the π-calculus. Proc. of STACS'95, Springer, LNCS 900 (1995) 243–254
4. Busi, N., Gorrieri, R.: A Petri net Semantics for π-calculus. Proc. of CONCUR'95, LNCS 962 (1995) 145–159
5. Cattani, G.L., Sewell, P.: Models for Name-Passing Processes: Interleaving and Causal. Proc. of LICS'2000, IEEE CS Press (2000) 322–333
6. Christensen, S., Hansen, N.D.: Coloured Petri Nets Extended with Place Capacities, Test Arcs and Inhibitor Arcs. Proc. of ICATPN'93, Springer, LNCS 691 (1993) 186–205
7. Devillers, R., Klaudel, H.: Solving Petri Net Recursions through Finite Representation. Proc. of IASTED'04, ACTA Press (2004) 145–150
8. Devillers, R., Klaudel, H., Koutny, M.: Petri Net Semantics of the Finite π-Calculus Terms. Fundamenta Informaticae **70** (2006) 1–24
9. Devillers, R., Klaudel, H., Koutny, M.: A Petri Net Translation of pi-calculus Terms. Report CS-TR 887, University of Newcastle (2005)
10. Devillers, R., Klaudel, H., Koutny, M., Pommereau, F.: Asynchronous Box Calculus. Fundamenta Informaticae **54** (2003) 295–344
11. Devillers, R., Klaudel, H., Riemann, R.-C.: General Parameterised Refinement and Recursion for the M-net Calculus. Theoretical Comp. Sci. **300** (2003) 235–258
12. Engelfriet, J.: A Multiset Semantics for the π-calculus with Replication. Theoretical Comp. Sci. **153** (1996) 65–94
13. Grahlmann, B., Best, E.: PEP - More than a Petri net tool. Proc. of TACAS'96, Springer, LNCS 1055 (1996) 397–401
14. Haddad, S., Poitrenaud, D.: Modelling and Analyzing Systems with Recursive Petri Nets. Proc. of WODES'00, Kluwer Academics Publishers (2000) 449–458
15. Khomenko, V., Koutny, M., Niaouris, A.: Applying Petri Net Unfoldings for Verification of Mobile Systems. Report CS-TR 953, University of Newcastle (2006)
16. Kiehn, A.: Petri Net Systems and their Closure Properties. In: Advances in Petri Nets 1989, Rozenberg, G (Ed.). Springer, LNCS 424 (1990) 306–328
17. Milner, R.: Communication and Concurrency. Prentice Hall (1989).
18. Milner, R., Parrow, J., Walker, D.: A Calculus of Mobile Processes. Information and Computation **100** (1992) 1–77
19. Montanari, U., Pistore, M.: Concurrent Semantics for the π-calculus. Proc. of MFPS'95, Electronic Notes in Computer Science 1, Elsevier (1995) 1–19

Handling Algebraic Properties in Automatic Analysis of Security Protocols[*]

Y. Boichut, P.-C. Héam, and O. Kouchnarenko

LIFC, FRE 2661 CNRS, Besançon, France, INRIA/CASSIS
{boichut, heampc, kouchna}@lifc.univ-fcomte.fr

Abstract. In this paper we extend the approximation based theoretical framework in which the security problem – secrecy preservation against an intruder – may be semi-decided through a reachability verification.

We explain how to cope with algebraic properties for an automatic approximation-based analysis of security protocols. We prove that if the initial knowledge of the intruder is a regular tree language, then the security problem may by semi-decided for protocols using cryptographic primitives with algebraic properties. More precisely, an automatically generated approximation function enables us 1) an automatic normalization of transitions, and 2) an automatic completion procedure. The main advantage of our approach is that the approximation function makes it possible to verify security protocols with an arbitrary number of sessions.

The concepts are illustrated on an example of the *view-only* protocol using a cryptographic primitive with the exclusive or algebraic property.

Keywords: Security protocol, algebraic properties, automatic verification, approximation.

1 Introduction

Cryptographic protocols are widely used to secure the exchange of information over open modern networks. It is now widely accepted that formal analysis can provide the level of assurance required by both the developers and the users of the protocols. However, whatever formal model one uses, analyzing cryptographic protocols is a complex task because the set of configurations to consider is very large, and can even be infinite. Indeed, any number of sessions (sequential or parallel executions) of protocols, sessions interleaving, any size of messages, algebraic properties of encryption or data structures give rise to infinite-state systems.

Our main objective is to automate in so far as possible the analysis of protocols. More precisely, we are interested in a fully automatic method to (semi)decide the *security* problem. In the context of the verification of protocols, the security problem consists of deciding whether a protocol preserves secrecy against an intruder, or not.

---

[*] This work has been supported by the European project AVISPA IST-2001-39252 and the French projects RNTL PROUVE and ACI SATIN.

K. Barkaoui, A. Cavalcanti, and A. Cerone (Eds.): ICTAC 2006, LNCS 4281, pp. 153–167, 2006.
© Springer-Verlag Berlin Heidelberg 2006

For this problem, current verification methods based on model-checking can be applied whenever the number of participants and the number of sessions between the agents are bounded. In this case, the protocol security problem is co-NP-complete [21]. The recent work [22] presents new decidability results for a bounded number of sessions, when the initial knowledge of the intruder is a regular language under the assumption that the keys used in protocols are atomic.

When the number of sessions is unbounded, the security problem of cryptographic protocols becomes undecidable, even when the length of the messages is bounded [15]. Decidability can be recovered by adding restrictions as in [13] where tree automata with one memory are applied to decide secrecy for cryptographic protocols with single blind copying.

Another way to circumvent the problem is to employ abstraction-based approximation methods [19, 17]. In fact, these methods use regular tree languages to approximate the set of messages that the intruder might have acquired during an unbounded number of sessions of protocols. In this framework, the security problem may be semi-decided through a reachability verification. The finite tree automata permit to ensure that some states are unreachable, and hence that the intruder will never be able to know certain terms.

To achieve the goal of an automatic analysis of protocols, we have investigated, improved [7] and extended [6] the semi-algorithmic method by Genet and Klay. The main advantage of our approach is that the automatically generated symbolic approximation function makes it possible to automatically verify security protocols while considering an unbounded number of sessions. The efficiency and usefulness of our approach have been confirmed by the tool TA4SP (Tree Automata based on Automatic Approximations for the Analysis of Security Protocols), which has already been used for analyzing many real Internet security protocols as exemplified in the European Union project AVISPA [1] [2].

However, for some cryptographic protocols, the secrecy is not preserved even when used with strong encryption algorithms. The purpose of the work we present in this paper is to extend the symbolic approximation-based theoretical framework defined in [6] to security protocols using cryptographic primitives with algebraic properties. To be more precise, the goal is to relax the perfect cryptography assumption in our symbolic approximation-based method. As explained in [14], such an assumption is too strong in general since some attacks are built using the interaction between protocol rules and properties of cryptographic operators.

The main contribution of this paper consists of showing the feasibility of the automatic analysis of secrecy properties of protocols where the number of sessions is unbounded and some algebraic properties of the cryptographic primitives – e.g. the exclusive or – are taken into account.

The main result of the paper is that the automatically generated approximation function allows us to over-approximate the knowledge of the intruder. For obtaining experimental results we have used the tool TA4SP. The most important

---

[1] http://www.avispa-project.org/

new feature is the exclusive or algebraic property, XOR for short, modulo which the protocol analysis is performed. The feasibility of our approach is illustrated on the example of the *view-only* protocol.

Related Work. In [20] it has been shown that using equational tree automata under associativity and/or commutativity is relevant for security problems of cryptographic protocols with an equational property. For protocols modeled by associative-commutative TRSs, the authors announce the possibility for the analysis to be done automatically thanks to the tool ACTAS manipulating associative-commutative tree automata and using approximation algorithms. However, the engine has still room to be modified and optimized to support an automated verification.

In [23], the authors investigate algebraic properties and timestamps in the approximation-based protocol analysis. Like in [6], there is no left-linearity condition on TRSs modeling protocols. However, the weakness of the work is that no tool is mentioned in [23].

In the recent survey [14], the authors give an overview of the existing methods in formal approaches to analyze cryptographic protocols. In the same work, a list of some relevant algebraic properties of cryptographic operators is established, and for each of them, the authors provide examples of protocols or attacks using these properties.

This survey lists two drawbacks with the recent results aiming at the analysis of protocols with algebraic properties. First, in most of the papers a particular decision procedure is proposed for a particular property. Second, the authors emphasize the fact that the results remain theoretical, and very few implementations automatically verify protocols with algebraic properties.

Following the result presented in [10], the authors have prototyped a new feature to handle the XOR operator in CL-AtSe (Constraint Logic based Attack Searcher), one of the four official tools of the AVISPA tool-set [2].

Layout of the paper. The paper is organized as follows. After giving preliminary notions on tree-automata and term rewriting systems (TRSs), we introduce in Section 2 a substitution notion depending on rules of a TRS, and a notion of compatibility between that substitutions and finite tree-automata, both suitable for our work. Section 3 presents the completion theorem making the completion procedure stop even when protocols – modeled by non left-linear TRSs – use cryptographic primitives with algebraic properties. The main result is then a consequence of the completion theorem allowing us to use an approximation function to obtain an over-approximation of the knowledge of the intruder. In Section 4, we explain how to apply the main theorem to verify the *view-only* protocol using a cryptographic primitive with the exclusive or algebraic property.

2   Background and Notation

In this section basic notions on finite tree automata, term rewriting systems and approximations are reminded. The reader is refereed to [12] for more detail.

2.1 Notations

We denote by $\mathbb{N}$ the set of natural integers and $\mathbb{N}^*$ denotes the finite strings over $\mathbb{N}$.

Let $\mathcal{F}$ be a finite set of symbols with their arities. The set of symbols of $\mathcal{F}$ of arity i is denoted $\mathcal{F}_i$. Let $\mathcal{X}$ be a finite set whose elements are variables. We assume that $\mathcal{X} \cap \mathcal{F} = \emptyset$.

A finite ordered tree t over a set of labels $(\mathcal{F}, \mathcal{X})$ is a function from a prefix-closed set $\mathcal{P}os(t) \subseteq \mathbb{N}^*$ to $\mathcal{F} \cup \mathcal{X}$. A term t over $\mathcal{F} \cup \mathcal{X}$ is a labeled tree whose domain $\mathcal{P}os(t)$ satisfies the following properties:

- $\mathcal{P}os(t)$ is non-empty and prefix closed,
- For each $p \in \mathcal{P}os(t)$, if $t(p) \in \mathcal{F}_n$ (with $n \neq 0$), then $\{i \mid p.i \in \mathcal{P}os(t)\} = \{1, \ldots, n\}$,
- For each $p \in \mathcal{P}os(t)$, if $t(p) \in \mathcal{X}$ or $t(p) \in \mathcal{F}_0$, then $\{i \mid p.i \in \mathcal{P}os(t)\} = \emptyset$.

Each element of $\mathcal{P}os(t)$ is called a position of t. For each subset $\mathcal{K}$ of $\mathcal{X} \cup \mathcal{F}$ and each term t we denote by $\mathcal{P}os_{\mathcal{K}}(t)$ the subset of positions p's of t such that $t(p) \in \mathcal{K}$. Each position p of t such that $t(p) \in \mathcal{F}$, is called a functional position. The set of terms over $(\mathcal{F}, \mathcal{X})$ is denoted $\mathcal{T}(\mathcal{F}, \mathcal{X})$. A ground term is a term t such that $\mathcal{P}os(t) = \mathcal{P}os_{\mathcal{F}}(t)$ (i.e. such that $\mathcal{P}os_{\mathcal{X}}(t) = \emptyset$). The set of ground terms is denoted $\mathcal{T}(\mathcal{F})$.

A subterm $t_{|p}$ of $t \in \mathcal{T}(\mathcal{F}, \mathcal{X})$ at position p is defined by the following:

- $\mathcal{P}os(t_{|p}) = \{i \mid p.i \in \mathcal{P}os(t)\}$,
- For all $j \in \mathcal{P}os(t_{|p})$, $t_{|p}(j) = t(p.j)$.

We denote by $t[s]_p$ the term obtained by replacing in t the subterm $t_{|p}$ by s.

For all sets A and B, we denote by $\Sigma(A, B)$ the set of functions from A to B. If $\sigma \in \Sigma(\mathcal{X}, B)$, then for each term $t \in \mathcal{T}(\mathcal{F}, \mathcal{X})$, we denote by $t\sigma$ the term obtained from t by replacing for each $x \in \mathcal{X}$, the variable x by $\sigma(x)$.

A term rewriting system $\mathcal{R}$ (TRS for short) over $\mathcal{T}(\mathcal{F}, \mathcal{X})$ is a finite set of pairs (l, r) from $\mathcal{T}(\mathcal{F}, \mathcal{X}) \times \mathcal{T}(\mathcal{F}, \mathcal{X})$, denoted $l \to r$, such that the set of variables occurring in r is included in the set of variables of l. A term rewriting system is left-linear if for each rule $l \to r$, every variable occurring in l occurs at most once. For each ground term t, we denote by $\mathcal{R}(t)$ the set of ground terms t' such that there exist a rule $l \to r$ of $\mathcal{R}$, a function $\mu \in \Sigma(\mathcal{X}, \mathcal{T}(\mathcal{F}))$ and a position p of t satisfying $t_{|p} = l\mu$ and $t' = t[r\mu]_p$. The relation $\{(t, t') \mid t' \in \mathcal{R}(t)\}$ is classically denoted $\to_{\mathcal{R}}$. For each set of ground terms B we denote by $\mathcal{R}^*(B)$ the set of ground terms related to an element of B modulo the reflexive-transitive closure of $\to_{\mathcal{R}}$.

A tree automaton $\mathcal{A}$ is a tuple $(\mathcal{Q}, \Delta, F)$, where $\mathcal{Q}$ is the set of states, Δ the set of transitions, and F the set of final states. Transitions are rewriting rules of the form $f(q_1, \ldots, q_k) \to q$, where $f \in \mathcal{F}_k$ and the q_i's are in $\mathcal{Q}$. A term $t \in \mathcal{T}(\mathcal{F})$ is accepted or recognized by $\mathcal{A}$ if there exists $q \in F$ such that $t \to_{\Delta}^* q$ (we also write $t \to_{\mathcal{A}}^* q$). The set of terms accepted by $\mathcal{A}$ is denoted $\mathcal{L}(\mathcal{A})$. For each state $q \in \mathcal{Q}$, we write $\mathcal{L}(\mathcal{A}, q)$ for the tree language $\mathcal{L}((\mathcal{Q}, \Delta, \{q\}))$. A tree automaton is finite if its set of transitions is finite.

2.2   Approximations to Handle Algebraic Properties

This section recalls the approximation-based framework we have been developing, and explains our objectives from a formal point of view.

Given a tree automaton $\mathcal{A}$ and a TRS $\mathcal{R}$ (for several classes of automata and TRSs), the tree automata completion [17, 16] algorithm computes a tree automaton $\mathcal{A}_k$ such that $\mathcal{L}(\mathcal{A}_k) = \mathcal{R}^*(\mathcal{L}(\mathcal{A}))$ when it is possible (for the classes of TRSs covered by this algorithm see [16]), and such that $\mathcal{L}(\mathcal{A}_k) \supseteq \mathcal{R}^*(\mathcal{L}(\mathcal{A}))$ otherwise.

The tree automata completion works as follows. From $\mathcal{A} = \mathcal{A}_0$ completion builds a sequence $\mathcal{A}_0, \mathcal{A}_1, \ldots, \mathcal{A}_k$ of automata such that if $s \in \mathcal{L}(\mathcal{A}_i)$ and $s \to_{\mathcal{R}} t$ then $t \in \mathcal{L}(\mathcal{A}_{i+1})$. If we find a fixpoint automaton $\mathcal{A}_k$ such that $\mathcal{R}^*(\mathcal{L}(\mathcal{A}_k)) = \mathcal{L}(\mathcal{A}_k)$, then we have $\mathcal{L}(\mathcal{A}_k) = \mathcal{R}^*(\mathcal{L}(\mathcal{A}_0))$ (or $\mathcal{L}(\mathcal{A}_k) \supseteq \mathcal{R}^*(\mathcal{L}(\mathcal{A}))$ if $\mathcal{R}$ is not in one class of [16]). To build $\mathcal{A}_{i+1}$ from $\mathcal{A}_i$, we achieve a *completion step* which consists of finding *critical pairs* between $\to_{\mathcal{R}}$ and $\to_{\mathcal{A}_i}$. For a substitution σ : $\mathcal{X} \mapsto \mathcal{Q}$ and a rule $l \to r \in \mathcal{R}$, a critical pair is an instance $l\sigma$ of l such that there exists $q \in \mathcal{Q}$ satisfying $l\sigma \to^*_{\mathcal{A}_i} q$ and $r\sigma \not\to^*_{\mathcal{A}_i} q$. For every critical pair $l\sigma \to^*_{\mathcal{A}_i} q$ and $r\sigma \not\to^*_{\mathcal{A}_i} q$ detected between $\mathcal{R}$ and $\mathcal{A}_i$, $\mathcal{A}_{i+1}$ is constructed by adding new transitions to $\mathcal{A}_i$ such that it recognizes $r\sigma$ in q, i.e. $r\sigma \to_{\mathcal{A}_{i+1}} q$.

However, the transition $r\sigma \to q$ is not necessarily a normalized transition of the form $f(q_1, \ldots, q_n) \to q'$ and so has to be normalized first. For example, to normalize a transition of the form $f(g(a), h(q')) \to q$, we need to find some states q_1, q_2, q_3 and replace the previous transition by a set of normalized transitions: $\{a \to q_1, g(q_1) \to q_2, h(q') \to q_3, f(q_2, q_3) \to q\}$.

Assume that q_1, q_2, q_3 are new states, then adding the transition itself or its normalized form does not make any difference. Now, assume that $q_1 = q_2$, the normalized form becomes $\{a \to q_1, g(q_1) \to q_1, h(q') \to q_3, f(q_1, q_3) \to q\}$. This set of normalized transitions represents the regular set of non normalized transitions of the form $f(g^\star(a), h(q')) \to q$; which contains the transition initially we wanted to add amongst many others. Hence, this is an over-approximation. We could have made an even more drastic approximation by identifying q_1, q_2, q_3 with q, for instance.

The above method does not work for all TRSs. For instance, consider a constant A and the tree automaton $\mathcal{A} = (\{q_1, q_2, q_f\}, \{A \to q_1, A \to q_2, f(q_1, q_2) \to q_f\}, \{q_f\})$ and the TRS $\mathcal{R} = \{f(x, x) \to g(x)\}$. There is no substitution σ such that $l\sigma \to^*_{\mathcal{A}} q$, for a q in $\{q_1, q_2, q_f\}$. Thus, following the procedure, there is no transition to add. But $f(A, A) \in \mathcal{L}(\mathcal{A})$. Thus $g(A) \in \mathcal{R}(L(\mathcal{A}))$. Since $g(A) \notin \mathcal{L}(\mathcal{A})$, the procedure stops (in fact does not begin) before providing an over-approximation of $\mathcal{R}^*(\mathcal{L}(\mathcal{A}))$.

The TRSs used in the security protocol context are often non left-linear. Indeed, there are a lot of protocols that cannot be modeled by left-linear TRSs.

Unfortunately, to be sound, the approximation-based analysis described in [17] requires the use of left-linear TRSs. Nevertheless, this method can still be applied to some non left-linear TRSs, which satisfy some weaker conditions. In [16] the authors propose new linearity conditions. However, these new conditions are not well-adapted to be automatically checked.

In our previous work [6] we explain how to define a criterion on $\mathcal{R}$ and $\mathcal{A}$ to make the procedure automatically work for industrial protocols analysis. This criterion ensures the soundness of the method described in [17, 16].

However, to handle protocols the approach in [6] is based on a kind of constant typing. In this paper we go further and propose a procedure supporting a fully automatic analysis and handling – without typing – algebraic properties like XOR presented in Fig. 1.

Let us remark first that the criterion defined in [16] does not allow managing the above rule IV. Second, in [6] we have to restrict XOR operations to typed terms to deal with the rule IV.

However, some protocols are known to be flawed by type confusing attacks [14, 8, 11]. In order to cope with these protocols, a new kind of substitution is defined in Section 2.3, and a new left-linear like criterion is introduced in Section 3.

Notice that following and extending [6], our approach can be applied for any kinds of TRSs. Moreover, it can cope with exponentiation algebraic properties and this way analyse Diffie-Hellman based protocols.

$$
\begin{array}{ll}
\texttt{xor(x,y)} \longrightarrow \texttt{xor(y,x)} & \text{I.} \\
\texttt{xor(xor(x,y),z)} \longrightarrow \texttt{xor(x,xor(y,z))} & \text{II.} \\
\texttt{xor(x,0)} \longrightarrow \texttt{x} & \text{III.} \\
\texttt{xor(x,x)} \longrightarrow \texttt{0} & \text{IV.}
\end{array}
$$

Fig. 1. XOR properties

2.3 $(l \rightarrow r)$-Substitutions

In this technical subsection, we define the notion of a $(l \rightarrow r)$-substitution suitable for the present work.

Definition 1. *Let $\mathcal{R}$ be a term rewriting system and $l \rightarrow r \in \mathcal{R}$. A $(l \rightarrow r)$-substitution is an application from $\mathcal{P}os_{\mathcal{X}}(l)$ into $\mathcal{Q}$.*

Let $l \rightarrow r \in \mathcal{R}$ and σ be a $(l \rightarrow r)$-substitution. We denote by $l\sigma$ the term of $\mathcal{T}(\mathcal{F}, \mathcal{Q})$ defined as follows:

- $\mathcal{P}os(l\sigma) = \mathcal{P}os(l)$,
- for each $p \in \mathcal{P}os(l)$, if $p \in \mathcal{P}os_{\mathcal{X}}(l)$ then $l\sigma(p) = \sigma(l(p))$, otherwise $l\sigma(p) = l(p)$.

Similarly, we denote by $r\sigma$ the term of $\mathcal{T}(\mathcal{F}, \mathcal{Q})$ defined by:

- $\mathcal{P}os(r\sigma) = \mathcal{P}os(r)$,
- for each $p \in \mathcal{P}os(r)$, if $p \notin \mathcal{P}os_{\mathcal{X}}(r)$ then $r\sigma(p) = r(p)$ and $r\sigma(p) = \sigma(l(p'))$ otherwise, where $p' = \min \mathcal{P}os_{r(p)}(l)$ (positions are lexicographically ordered).

Example 1. *Let us consider $l = f(g(x), h(x, f(y, y)))$ and $r = f(h(x, y), h(y, x))$ represented by the following trees (elements after the comma are the positions in the term; l is represented on the left and r on the right):*

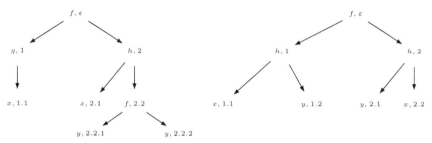

Variable positions of l are 1.1 and 2.1 for x, and 2.2.1 and 2.2.2 for y. Let $\sigma(1.1) = q_1$, $\sigma(2.1) = q_2$, $\sigma(2.2.1) = q_3$ and $\sigma(2.2.2) = q_4$; σ is a $(l \to r)$-substitution and

$$l\sigma = f(g(q_1), h(q_2, f(q_3, q_4)))$$

is the term obtained from l by substituting the variable in position p by $\sigma(p)$. Now we explain how to compute $r\sigma$. The minimal position where x [resp. y] occurs in l is 1.1 [resp. 2.2.1]. Thus $r\sigma$ is obtained from r by substituting all x's in r by $\sigma(1.1) = q_1$ and all y's by $\sigma(2.2.1) = q_3$. Thus

$$r\sigma = f(h(q_1, q_3), h(q_3, q_1)).$$

As mentioned in Section 2.2, the completion procedure does not work for all tree automata and TRSs. That is why we introduce the notion of compatibility between finite tree-automata and $(l \to r)$-substitutions. The intuition behind the next definition is that different occurences of a variable may be substitute by different states if there exists a term recognized by all of these states, at least. Notice that the condition required below is weaker than the conditions in [16]. Moreover, it is more general and can be applied to a larger class of applications.

Definition 2. *Let $\mathcal{A}$ be a finite tree automaton. We say that a $(l \to r)$-substitution σ is $\mathcal{A}$-compatible if for each $x \in \mathcal{V}ar(l)$,*

$$\bigcap_{p \in \mathcal{P}os_{\{x\}}(l)} \mathcal{L}(\mathcal{A}, \sigma(p)) \neq \emptyset.$$

Example 2. *Let $\mathcal{A}_{\mathrm{exe}} = (\{q_0, q_f\}, \Delta_{\mathrm{exe}}, \{q_f\})$ with the set of transitions $\Delta_{\mathrm{exe}} = \{A \to q_0, A \to q_f, f(q_f, q_0) \to q_f, h(q_0, q_0) \to q_0\}$. Let $\mathcal{R}_{\mathrm{exe}} = \{f(x, h(x, y)) \to h(A, x)\}$. The automaton $\mathcal{A}_{\mathrm{exe}}$ recognizes the set of trees such that every path* *from the root to a leaf is of the form f^*h^*A. Let us consider the substitution σ_{exe} defined by $\sigma_{\text{exe}}(1) = q_f$, $\sigma_{\text{exe}}(2.1) = q_0$ and $\sigma_{\text{exe}}(2.2) = q_0$. The tree $t = A$ can be reduced to q_f and belongs to $\mathcal{L}(\mathcal{A}, \sigma_{\text{exe}}(1))$. Furthermore $t \to q_0$, so $t \in \mathcal{L}(\mathcal{A}, \sigma_{\text{exe}}(2.2))$. Therefore σ_{exe} is $\mathcal{A}$-compatible.*

3   Approximations for Non-left Linear TRSs

In this section $\mathcal{R}$ denotes a fixed term rewriting system and $\mathcal{Q}$ an infinite set of states. We first introduce the notion of normalization associated with $(l \to r)$-substitutions. Secondly, we give the main result – consequence of the completion theorem – allowing us to over-approximate the descendants of regular sets.

3.1   Normalizations

The notion of normalization is common. The definitions below are simply a-dapted to our notion of $(l \to r)$-substitutions.

Definition 3. *Let $\mathcal{A}$ be a finite tree automaton. An approximation function (for $\mathcal{A}$) is a function which associates to each tuple $(l \to r, \sigma, q)$, where $l \to r \in \mathcal{R}$, σ is an $\mathcal{A}$-compatible $(l \to r)$-substitution and q a state of $\mathcal{A}$, a function from $\mathcal{P}os(r)$ to $\mathcal{Q}$.*

Example 3. *Consider the automaton $\mathcal{A}_{\text{exe}}$, the term rewriting system $\mathcal{R}_{\text{exe}}$ and the substitution σ_{exe} defined in Example 2. For σ_{exe}, an approximation function γ_{exe} may be defined by*

$$\gamma_{\text{exe}}(l \to r, \sigma_{\text{exe}}, q_f) : \begin{cases} \varepsilon \mapsto & q_1 \\ 1 \mapsto & q_0 \\ 2 \mapsto & q_1 \end{cases}.$$

To totally define γ_{exe}, the others (finitely many) $\mathcal{A}_{\text{exe}}$-compatible substitutions should be considered too.

The notion of normalization below is classical. The definition takes our notion of $(l \to r)$-substitutions into account only.

Definition 4. *Let $\mathcal{A} = (\mathcal{Q}_0, \Delta, F_0)$ be a finite tree automaton, γ an approxima-tion function for $\mathcal{A}$, $l \to r \in \mathcal{R}$, σ an $\mathcal{A}$-compatible $(l \to r)$-substitution, and q a state of $\mathcal{A}$. We denote by $\text{Norm}_\gamma(l \to r, \sigma, q)$ the following set of transitions, called normalization of $(l \to r, \sigma, q)$:*

$$\{f(q_1, \ldots, q_k) \to q' \,|\, p \in \mathcal{P}os_{\mathcal{F}}(r), \; t(p) = f,$$
$$q' = q \text{ if } p = \varepsilon \text{ otherwise } q' = \gamma(l \to r, \sigma, q)(p)$$
$$q_i = \gamma(l \to r, \sigma, q)(p.i) \text{ if } p.i \notin \mathcal{P}os_{\mathcal{X}}(r),$$
$$q_i = \sigma(\min\{p' \in \mathcal{P}os_{\mathcal{X}}(l) \mid l(p') = r(p.i)\}) otherwise\}$$

The min is computed for the lexical order.

Notice that the set $\{p' \in \mathcal{P}os_{\mathcal{X}}(l) \mid l(p') = r(p.i)\}$ used in the above definition is not empty. Indeed, in a term rewriting system variables occurring in the right-hand side must, by definition, occur in the left-hand side too.

Example 4. *Following Example 3, ε is the unique functional position of $r = h(A, y)$. We set q' of the definition to be equal to q_f. Consequently the set $\mathrm{Norm}_{\gamma_{\mathrm{exe}}}(l \rightarrow r, \sigma_{\mathrm{exe}}, q_f)$ is of the form $\{A \rightarrow q?, h(q?, q??) \rightarrow q_f\}$. Since for r, the position 1 is a functional position and 2 is in $\mathcal{P}os_{\mathcal{X}}(r)$, we use the last line of the definition to compute $q??$ and $q?$ is defined by the approximation function γ_{exe}. Finally we obtain:*

$$\mathrm{Norm}_{\gamma_{\mathrm{exe}}}(l \rightarrow r, \sigma_{\mathrm{exe}}, q_f) = \{r(1) \rightarrow \gamma_{\mathrm{exe}}(1), r(\varepsilon)(\gamma_{\mathrm{exe}}(1), \sigma_{\mathrm{exe}}(1)) \rightarrow q_f\}$$
$$= \{A \rightarrow q_0, h(q_0, q_f) \rightarrow q_f\}.$$

Lemma 1. *Let $\mathcal{A} = (\mathcal{Q}_0, \Delta, F_0)$ be a finite tree automaton, γ an approximation function, $l \rightarrow r \in \mathcal{R}$, σ an $\mathcal{A}$-compatible $(l \rightarrow r)$-substitution, and q a state of $\mathcal{A}$. If $l\sigma \rightarrow^*_{\mathcal{A}_0} q$ then*

$$r\sigma \rightarrow^*_{\mathrm{Norm}_\gamma(l \rightarrow r, \sigma, q)} q.$$

Proof is obvious. The transitions in Norm_γ are precisely added to reduce $r\sigma$ to q.

3.2   Completions

This section is dedicated to the proof of the main result: how to build a regular over-approximation of $\mathcal{R}^*(\mathcal{A})$? The above lemma shows how to over-approximate one rewriting step.

Lemma 2. *Let $\mathcal{A}_0 = (\mathcal{Q}_0, \Delta_0, F_0)$ be a finite tree automaton and γ an approximation function for $\mathcal{A}_0$. The automaton $\mathcal{C}_\gamma(\mathcal{A}_0) = (\mathcal{Q}_1, \Delta_1, F_1)$ is defined by:*

$$\Delta_1 = \Delta \cup \bigcup \mathrm{Norm}_\gamma(l \rightarrow r, \sigma, q)$$

where the union involves all rules $l \rightarrow r \in \mathcal{R}$, all states $q \in \mathcal{Q}_0$, all $\mathcal{A}_0$-compatible $(l \rightarrow r)$-substitutions σ such that $l\sigma \rightarrow^*_{\mathcal{A}_0} q$ and $r\sigma \not\rightarrow^*_{\mathcal{A}_0} q$,

$$F_1 = F_0 \quad and \quad \mathcal{Q}_1 = \mathcal{Q}_0 \cup \mathcal{Q}_2,$$

where $\mathcal{Q}_2$ denotes the set of states occurring in left or right-hand sides of transitions of Δ_1. One has

$$\mathcal{L}(\mathcal{A}_0) \cup \mathcal{R}(\mathcal{L}(\mathcal{A}_0)) \subseteq \mathcal{L}(\mathcal{C}_\gamma(\mathcal{A}_0)).$$

Proof. Let $t \in \mathcal{L}(\mathcal{A}_0) \cup \mathcal{R}(\mathcal{L}(\mathcal{A}_0))$. By definition of $\mathcal{C}_\gamma(\mathcal{A}_0)$, $\mathcal{L}(\mathcal{A}_0) \subseteq \mathcal{L}(\mathcal{C}_\gamma(\mathcal{A}_0))$. Consequently, if $t \in \mathcal{L}(\mathcal{A}_0)$, one has $t \in \mathcal{L}(\mathcal{C}_\gamma(\mathcal{A}_0))$. Thus we may now assume that $t \in \mathcal{R}(\mathcal{L}(\mathcal{A}_0))$. Thus there exists a rule $l \rightarrow r \in \mathcal{R}$ a term t_0 in $\mathcal{L}(\mathcal{A}_0)$, a position p of t_0 and a substitution μ in $\Sigma(\mathcal{X}, \mathcal{T}(\mathcal{F}))$ such that

$$t_{0|p} = l\mu \quad and \quad t = t_0[r\mu]_p. \tag{1}$$

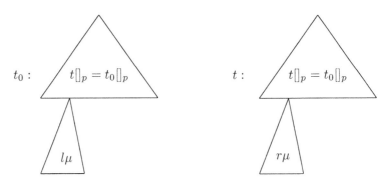

Since $t_0 \in \mathcal{L}(\mathcal{A}_0)$, there exists a state $q \in \mathcal{Q}_0$ and a state $q_f \in F_0$ such that

$$l\mu \to^*_{\mathcal{A}_0} q \quad \text{and} \quad t_0[q]_p \to^*_{\mathcal{A}_0} q_f. \tag{2}$$

Since $l\mu \to^*_{\mathcal{A}_0} q$ there exists an $(l \to r)$-substitution σ such that $l\mu \to_{\mathcal{A}_0} l\sigma$. Furthermore, for each $x \in \mathcal{V}ar(l)$,

$$\mu(x) \in \bigcap_{p \in \mathcal{P}os_{\{x\}}(l)} \mathcal{L}(\mathcal{A}, \sigma(p)),$$

thus the $(l \to r)$-substitution σ is $\mathcal{A}_0$ compatible. Therefore , using Lemma 1 (by hypothesis, $l\sigma \to^*_{\mathcal{A}_0} q$), one has

$$r\sigma \to^*_{\mathcal{C}_\gamma(\mathcal{A}_0)} q. \tag{3}$$

For each variable x occurring in l and all positions p of x in l one has $\mu(x) \to^*_{\mathcal{A}_0} \sigma(p)$. In particular, for each variable x occurring in l, $\mu(x) \to^*_{\mathcal{A}_0} \sigma(p')$, where p' is the minimal position where x occurs in l. Consequently and by definition of $r\sigma$, one has

$$r\mu \to^*_{\mathcal{A}_0} r\sigma. \tag{4}$$

We are now able to conclude.

$$\begin{aligned} t = &\quad t_0[r\mu]_p &&\text{using (1)} \\ \to^*_{\mathcal{A}_0} &\quad t_0[r\sigma]_p &&\text{using (4)} \\ \to^*_{\mathcal{C}_\gamma(\mathcal{A}_0)} &\quad t_0[q]_p &&\text{using (3)} \\ \to^*_{\mathcal{A}_0} &\quad q_f &&\text{using (2)} \end{aligned}$$

Thus $t \in \mathcal{L}(\mathcal{C}_\gamma(\mathcal{A}_0))$, proving the theorem.

Let us remark that using well chosen approximation functions may iteratively lead to a fixpoint automaton which recognizes an over-approximation of $\mathcal{R}^*(\mathcal{A}_0)$. One can formally express this by the following (soundness) main theorem.

Theorem 5. *Let $(\mathcal{A}_n)$ and (γ_n) be respectively a sequence of finite tree automata and a sequence of approximation functions defined by: for each integer n, γ_n is an approximation function for $\mathcal{A}_n$ and*

$$\mathcal{A}_{n+1} = \mathcal{C}_{\gamma_n}(\mathcal{A}_n).$$

If there exists a positive integer N, such that for every $n \geq N$ $\mathcal{A}_n = \mathcal{A}_N$, then

$$\mathcal{R}^*(\mathcal{L}(\mathcal{A}_0)) \subseteq \mathcal{L}(\mathcal{A}_N).$$

The proof is immediate by a simple induction using Lemma 2. Notice that in [6], we have defined a family of approximation functions which can be automatically generated. Another advantage is that they can be easily adapted to the present construction as explained in the next section. Furthermore using appropriate approximation functions may lead to a proof of the non-reachability of a term. However, these methods don't provide a way to prove that a particular term is reachable, since we compute an over-approximation of reachable terms (the method is not complete).

An example is given in Appendix A.

4   Application to the *View-Only* Protocol

In this section we illustrate the main concepts on the example of the *view-only* protocol, and we explain how to manipulate the tool TA4SP supporting an automated verification.

4.1   The *View-Only* Protocol

Before describing the protocol, notice that encoding security protocols and secrecy properties with tree automata and term rewriting systems is classical [17].

The *View-Only* protocol (Fig. 2) is a component of the *Smartright* system [1]. In the context of home digital network, this system prevents users from unlawfully copying movie broadcasts on the network. The *view-only* participants are a decoder (DC) and a digital TV set (TVS). They share a secret key Kab securely sealed in both of them. The goal of this protocol is to periodically change a secret control word (CW) enabling to decode the current broadcast program. As seen in Fig. 2, the properties of the XOR operator allow to establish the sharing of CW between the participants.

The data VoKey, VoR and VoRi are randomly generated numbers. The functional symbol h represents a one-way function, meaning that no-one can guess x from h(x), unless he already knows x.

Let us explain how this protocol works.

- **Step 1:** DC sends a message containing xor(CW,VoR) and VoKey to TVS. This message is encoded by the private shared key Kab. The data VoKey is a fresh symmetric key used along the session. At this stage, TVS can extract neither CW nor VoR from xor(CW,VoR) since TVS knows neither CW nor VoR.
- **Step 2:** TVS sends in return a random challenge VoRi whose goal is to identify DC.
- **Step 3:** DC replies by sending VoR.{h(VoRi)}$_{VoKey}$. Receiving this message, TVS both checks whether the challenge's answer is correct (by comparing the hashed value h(VoRi) with its own value), and extracts CW from the datum

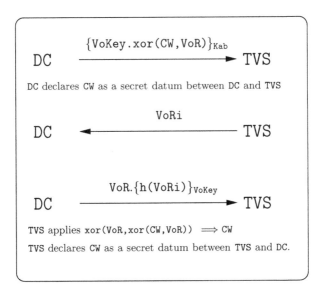

Fig. 2. The *"view-only"* Protocol

`xor(CW,VoR)` received at step 1 and using `VoR`.

This is done by computing `xor(xor(CW,VoR),VoR)`, and by applying sequentially rules **II.**, **IV.** and **III.** of Fig. 1 to it, TVS obtains: `xor(xor(CW,VoR),VoR)` $\overset{II.}{\to}$ `xor(CW,xor(VoR,VoR))` $\overset{IV.}{\to}$ `xor(CW,0)` $\overset{III.}{\to}$ `CW`.

Notice that Rule **IV.** of Fig. 1 is crucial at Step 3 of this protocol.

We have implemented our approach within the TA4SP tool presented in the following subsection.

4.2   Using TA4SP

This tool, whose method is detailed in [6], is one of the four official tools of the AVISPA tool-set [2]. The particularity of this tool is verifying of secrecy properties for an unbounded number of sessions.

The structure of the TA4SP tool is detailed in Fig. 3.

The language IF is a low level specification language automatically generated from HLPSL (High Level Protocol Specification Language) [9] in the AVISPA toolset.

The TA4SP tool is made up of:

- IF2TIF, a translator from IF to a specification well-adapted to TIMBUK+, and
- TIMBUK+,[2] a collection of tools for achieving proofs of reachability over term rewriting systems and for manipulating tree automata. This tool has been initially developed by Th. Genet (IRISA/ INRIA-Rennes, FRANCE) and improved to handle our approximation functions.

---

[2] Timbuk is available at http://www.irisa.fr/lande/genet/timbuk/.

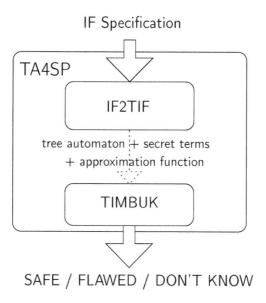

Fig. 3. TA4SP tool

Note that the tool TA4SPmay also answer "FLAWED" while performing under-approximations. Let us remark that the available version of TA4SP at http://www.avispa-project.org used in the framework of the AVISPA project is not yet updated with the XOR features. It is intended that this be updated in the near future.

4.3   Verifying the *View-Only* Protocol

In [18], the authors verified that no old value of CW can be reused. Indeed, if the freshness of CW was not satisfied then we can imagine that the copy-protection would become obsolete. By storing all control words and by reusing them, an unethical individual could for instance decrypt the broadcasted program without paying the amount. However, the model considered is strongly typed in the sense that the authors handle the XOR operator only for terms satisfying a particular given form.

In order to consider type confusing attacks, we have succeeded in verifying the secrecy of CW on an untyped model for the XOR algebraic properties, using the method developed in this paper. Furthermore, using the family of approximation functions defined in [6] we have succeeded in verifying it automatically.

Time computation of the verification is about one hundred minutes on a classical laptop, but we hope to manage to have a faster computation by removing some redundant calculus. The computed fixed point automaton (encoding an over-approximation of intruder's knowledge) has 203 states and 583 transitions. Some technical details (HLPSL specification, input/output automata, etc), on this verification are given in Appendix B.

5   Conclusion

This paper shows that the symbolic approximation-based approach we have been developing is well-adapted for analyzing security protocols using algebraic properties while considering an unbounded number of sessions. Indeed, the automatically generated symbolic approximation function enables us 1) an automated normalization of transitions, and 2) an automated completion procedure. Notice that the variables used to manipulate algebraic properties are not typed, like in [23]. Our symbolic approximation-based framework allowing us to handle algebraic properties does not deal with timestamps.

The tool TA4SP has been updated to take the exclusive or algebraic property of cryptographic primitives into account. This way the feasibility of the analysis has been confirmed by the experimentation on the *view-only* protocol. Future development concerns the implementation optimization.

We intend to investigate further algebraic properties that can be handled in practice. We anticipate that it could be carried out for algebraic properties expressed by quadratic rules. At this stage, experiments should be performed again.

To the best of our knowledge, this is the first attempt to automatically handle a large class of algebraic properties used in cryptographic protocols. Indeed, we wish to emphasize the fact that our theoretical framework is supported by a *push-button* tool TA4SP [3, 5]. Moreover, TA4SP is used for protocols specified in the standard High Level Protocol Specification Language (HLPSL) [9, 4]. This language is known to be suitable for industrial users.

These two significant advantages make it possible to use our framework and the fully automatic tool in the industrial context.

References

1. Smartright technical white paper v1.0. Technical report, Thomson, http://www.smartright.org, October 2001.
2. A. Armando, D. Basin, Y. Boichut, Y. Chevalier, L. Compagna, J. Cuellar, P. Hankes Drielsma, P.-C. Héam, O. Kouchnarenko, J. Mantovani, S. Mödersheim, D. von Oheimb, M. Rusinowitch, J. Santos Santiago, M. Turuani, L. Viganò, and L. Vigneron. The AVISPA Tool for the automated validation of internet security protocols and applications. In K. Etessami and S. Rajamani, editors, *CAV'2005*, volume 3576 of *LNCS*, pages 281–285, Edinburgh, Scotland, 2005. Springer.
3. A. Armando, D. Basin, M. Bouallagui, Y. Chevalier, L. Compagna, S. Mödersheim, M. Rusinowitch, M. Turuani, L. Viganò, and L. Vigneron. The AVISS Security Protocol Analysis Tool. In *Proceedings of CAV'02*, LNCS 2404, pages 349–354. Springer, 2002.
4. AVISPA. Deliverable 2.1: The High-Level Protocol Specification Language. Available at *http://www.avispa-project.org*, 2003.
5. AVISPA. Deliverable 7.2: Assessment of the AVISPA tool v.1. Available at *http://www.avispa-project.org*, 2003.
6. Y. Boichut, P.-C. Héam, and O. Kouchnarenko. Automatic Verification of Security Protocols Using Approximations. Research Report RR-5727, INRIA-CASSIS Project, October 2005.

7. Y. Boichut, P.-C. Héam, O. Kouchnarenko, and F. Oehl. Improvements on the Genet and Klay technique to automatically verify security protocols. In *Proc. AVIS'2004, joint to ETAPS'04*, pages 1–11, April 2004. To appear in ENTCS.

8. L. Bozga, Y. Lakhnech, and M. Perin. HERMES: An automatic tool for verification of secrecy in security protocols. In *CAV: International Conference on Computer Aided Verification*, 2003.

9. Y. Chevalier, L. Compagna, J. Cuellar, P. Hankes Drielsma, J. Mantovani, S. Mödersheim, and L. Vigneron. A high level protocol specification language for industrial security-sensitive protocols. In *Proceedings of SAPS 04*, volume 180, Linz, Austria, September 2004.

10. Y. Chevalier, R. Kusters, M. Rusinowitch, and M. Turuani. An NP decision procedure for protocol insecurity with XOR. *Theoretical Computer Science*, 338, 2005.

11. I. Cibrario, L. Durante, R. Sisto, and A. Valenzano. Automatic detection of attacks on cryptographic protocols: A case study. In Christopher Kruegel Klaus Julisch, editor, *Intrusion and Malware Detection and Vulnerability Assessment: Second International Conference*, volume 3548 of *LNCS*, Vienna, 2005.

12. H. Comon, M. Dauchet, R. Gilleron, F. Jacquemard, D. Lugiez, S. Tison, and M. Tommasi. Tree automata techniques and applications, 2002. http://www.grappa.univ-lille3.fr/tata/.

13. H. Comon-Lundh and V. Cortier. Tree automata with one memory, set constraints and cryptographic protocols. *Theoretical Computer Science*, 331(1):143–214, February 2005.

14. V. Cortier, S. Delaune, and P. Lafourcade. A survey of algebraic properties used in cryptographic protocols. *Journal of Computer Security*, 2005.

15. N. A. Durgin, P. D. Lincoln, J. C. Mitchell, and A. Scedrov. Undecidability of bounded security protocols. In *Proc. FMSP'99*, Italy, Trento, August 1999.

16. G. Feuillade, Th. Genet, and V. Viet Triem Tong. Reachability analysis of term rewriting systems. *Journal of Automated Reasonning*, 33, 2004.

17. Th. Genet and F. Klay. Rewriting for cryptographic protocol verification. In *Proc. Int. Conf. CADE'00*, LNCS 1831, pages 271–290. Springer-Verlag, 2000.

18. Th. Genet, Y.-M. Tang-Talpin, and V. Viet Triem Tong. Verification of copy-protection cryptographic protocol using approximations of term rewriting systems. In *Proc. of WITS'03*, 2003.

19. D. Monniaux. Abstracting cryptographic protocols with tree automata. In *SAS'99*, number 1694 in LNCS. Springer-Verlag, 1999.

20. H. Ohsaki and T. Takai. Actas: A system design for associative and commutative tree automata theory. In *Proc. of RULE'2004*, June 2004. To appear in ENTCS.

21. M. Rusinowitch and M. Turuani. Protocol insecurity with finite number of sessions is NP-complete. In *Proc of CSFW'01*, pages 174–190. IEEE, June 2001.

22. T. Truderung. Regular protocols and attacks with regular knowledge. In *Proc. of CADE'05*, volume 3632 of *LNCS*, pages 377–391. Springer, 2005.

23. R. Zunino and P. Degano. Handling exp, x (and timestamps) in protocol analysis. In *Proc. of Int. Conf. FOSSACS'06*, volume 3921 of *LNCS*, 2006.

A Compositional Algorithm for Parallel Model Checking of Polygonal Hybrid Systems

Gordon Pace[1] and Gerardo Schneider[2]

[1] Dept. of Computer Science and AI, University of Malta, Msida, Malta
[2] Dept. of Informatics, University of Oslo, Oslo, Norway
gordon.pace@um.edu.mt, gerardo@ifi.uio.no

Abstract. The reachability problem as well as the computation of the phase portrait for the class of planar hybrid systems defined by constant differential inclusions (SPDI), has been shown to be decidable. The existing reachability algorithm is based on the exploitation of topological properties of the plane which are used to accelerate certain kind of cycles. The complexity of the algorithm makes the analysis of large systems generally unfeasible. In this paper we present a compositional parallel algorithm for reachability analysis of SPDIs. The parallelization is based on the qualitative information obtained from the phase portrait of an SPDI, in particular the controllability kernel.

1 Introduction

Hybrid systems are systems in which the discrete and the continuous worlds co-exist. Examples can be found in avionics, robotics, bioinformatics and highway systems. For the majority of non trivial systems, reachability and most verification questions are undecidable. Various decidable subclasses have, subsequently, been identified, including timed [AD94] and rectangular automata [HKPV95], hybrid automata with linear vector fields [LPY01], piecewise constant derivative systems (PCDs) [MP93] and polygonal differential inclusion systems[1] (SPDIs) [ASY01], just to mention a few. From the practical point of view, a proof of decidability of reachability is only useful if accompanied with a decision procedure for effectively computing it, which is the case in the above-mentioned examples. Also of importance is the complexity of the algorithm: How expensive is it to compute reachability? Is it feasible with reasonable memory and time requirements? How large are the systems we can treat? Only in a few cases have the algorithms found scaled up to large industrial systems, and obtaining faster and cheaper algorithms is still an ongoing research challenge. One approach is the identification of smart ways of parallelizing and distributing reachability algorithms.

Reduction of memory and time requirements are the main reasons for seeking parallelization. In verification, in particular, the main bottleneck is usually memory. The effort in distributed programming is usually put on finding good ways

---

[1] In the literature the name *simple planar differential inclusion* has been used to describe the same class of systems.

K. Barkaoui, A. Cavalcanti, and A. Cerone (Eds.): ICTAC 2006, LNCS 4281, pp. 168–182, 2006.

of partitioning the task among different processes in order to keep a balanced distribution of the use of memory and execution time. An important issue is the communication cost; it is desirable to have a good ratio between process computation and communication time, where the communication cost should not be much greater than the analysis cost of the original system without parallelization. One way of reducing communication cost in distributed algorithms in general, is *compositionality*, that is dividing the problem in independent smaller ones. The partial results are then combined in order to exactly answer the original question. This approach reduces communication between processes to a minimum — communication is only carried out at instantiation and when returning the result.

Given the non-compositional nature of hybrid systems, obtaining distributed reachability algorithms for hybrid systems is a challenging task. A qualitative analysis of hybrid systems may, however, provide useful information for partitioning the state-space in independent subspaces, thus helping in achieving compositional analysis.

In this paper we present a compositional algorithm for parallel reachability analysis of polygonal differential inclusion systems. The identification and computation of controllability kernels is the core of our algorithm and the main reason for compositionality. We also give a lower bound for the number of parallel processes which may be launched for computing reachability in an independent way, each one operating in smaller state spaces than the original, and we prove soundness and completeness of our algorithm.

2   Preliminaries

A (positive) *affine* function $f : \mathbb{R} \to \mathbb{R}$ is such that $f(x) = ax + b$ with $a > 0$. An *affine multivalued* function $F : \mathbb{R} \to 2^{\mathbb{R}}$, denoted $F = \langle f_l, f_u \rangle$, is defined by $F(x) = \langle f_l(x), f_u(x) \rangle$ where f_l and f_u are affine and $\langle \cdot, \cdot \rangle$ denotes an interval. For notational convenience, we do not make explicit whether intervals are open, closed, left-open or right-open, unless required for comprehension. For an interval $I = \langle l, u \rangle$ we have that $F(\langle l, u \rangle) = \langle f_l(l), f_u(u) \rangle$. The *inverse* of F is defined by $F^{-1}(x) = \{y \mid x \in F(y)\}$. It is not difficult to show that $F^{-1} = \langle f_u^{-1}, f_l^{-1} \rangle$.

A *truncated affine multivalued* function (TAMF) $\mathcal{F} : \mathbb{R} \to 2^{\mathbb{R}}$ is defined by an affine multivalued function F and intervals $S \subseteq \mathbb{R}^+$ and $J \subseteq \mathbb{R}^+$ as follows: $\mathcal{F}(x) = F(x) \cap J$ if $x \in S$, otherwise $\mathcal{F}(x) = \emptyset$. For convenience we write $\mathcal{F}(x) = F(\{x\} \cap S) \cap J$. For an interval I, $\mathcal{F}(I) = F(I \cap S) \cap J$ and $\mathcal{F}^{-1}(I) = F^{-1}(I \cap J) \cap S$. We say that $\mathcal{F}$ is *normalized* if $S = \mathsf{Dom}(\mathcal{F}) = \{x \mid F(x) \cap J \neq \emptyset\}$ (thus, $S \subseteq F^{-1}(J)$) and $J = \mathsf{Im}(\mathcal{F}) = \mathcal{F}(S)$. TAMFs are closed under composition:

Theorem 1 ([ASY01]). The composition of two TAMFs $\mathcal{F}_1(I) = F_1(I \cap S_1) \cap J_1$ and $\mathcal{F}_2(I) = F_2(I \cap S_2) \cap J_2$, is the TAMF $(\mathcal{F}_2 \circ \mathcal{F}_1)(I) = \mathcal{F}(I) = F(I \cap S) \cap J$, where $F = F_2 \circ F_1$, $S = S_1 \cap F_1^{-1}(J_1 \cap S_2)$ and $J = J_2 \cap F_2(J_1 \cap S_2)$. □

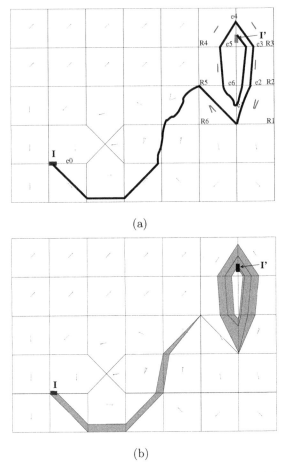

(a)

(b)

Fig. 1. (a) An SPDI and its trajectory segment; (b) Reachability analysis

2.1 SPDIs

An *angle* $\angle_\mathbf{a}^\mathbf{b}$ on the plane, defined by two non-zero vectors $\mathbf{a}, \mathbf{b}$ is the set of all positive linear combinations $\mathbf{x} = \alpha\,\mathbf{a} + \beta\,\mathbf{b}$, with $\alpha, \beta \geq 0$, and $\alpha + \beta > 0$. We can always assume that $\mathbf{b}$ is situated in the counter-clockwise direction from $\mathbf{a}$.

A *polygonal differential inclusion system* (SPDI) is defined by giving a finite partition[2] $\mathbb{P}$ of the plane into convex polygonal sets, and associating with each $P \in \mathbb{P}$ a couple of vectors $\mathbf{a}_P$ and $\mathbf{b}_P$. Let $\phi(P) = \angle_{\mathbf{a}_P}^{\mathbf{b}_P}$. The SPDI's behavior at a point $\mathbf{x} \in P$ is expressed by the differential inclusion $\dot{\mathbf{x}} \in \phi(P)$.

Let $E(P)$ be the set of edges of P. We say that e is an *entry* of P if for all $\mathbf{x} \in e$ (considering only interior points of e) and for all $\mathbf{c} \in \phi(P)$, $\mathbf{x} + \mathbf{c}\epsilon \in P$ for some $\epsilon > 0$. We say that e is an *exit* of P if the same condition holds for

---

[2] Since the edges of the adjacent polygons are shared, more precisely it is a closed cover with disjoint interiors.

some $\epsilon < 0$. We denote by $in(P) \subseteq E(P)$ the set of all entries of P and by $out(P) \subseteq E(P)$ the set of all exits of P.

Assumption 1. *All the edges in $E(P)$ are either entries or exits, that is, $E(P)= in(P) \cup out(P)$.*

Reachability for SPDIs is decidable provided the above assumption holds [ASY01]; without such assumption it is not known whether reachability is decidable.

A *trajectory segment* over $T \in \mathbb{R}$ of an SPDI is a continuous function $\xi : [0, T] \to \mathbb{R}^2$ which is smooth everywhere except in a discrete set of points, and such that for all $t \in [0, T]$, if $\xi(t) \in P$ and $\dot{\xi}(t)$ is defined then $\dot{\xi}(t) \in \phi(P)$. The *signature*, denoted $\mathsf{Sig}(\xi)$, is the ordered sequence of edges traversed by the trajectory segment, that is, $e_1, e_2, \ldots$, where $\xi(t_i) \in e_i$ and $t_i < t_{i+1}$. If $T = \infty$, a trajectory segment is called a *trajectory*.

Example 1. Consider the SPDI illustrated in Fig. 1-(a). For sake of simplicity we will only show the dynamics associated to regions R_1 to R_6 in the picture. For each region R_i, $1 \le i \le 6$, there is a pair of vectors $(\mathbf{a}_i, \mathbf{b}_i)$, where: $\mathbf{a}_1 = (45, 100)$, $\mathbf{b}_1 = (1, 4)$, $\mathbf{a}_2 = \mathbf{b}_2 = (1, 10)$, $\mathbf{a}_3 = \mathbf{b}_3 = (-2, 3)$, $\mathbf{a}_4 = \mathbf{b}_4 = (-2, -3)$, $\mathbf{a}_5 = \mathbf{b}_5 = (1, -15)$, $\mathbf{a}_6 = (1, -2)$, $\mathbf{b}_6 = (1, -1)$. A trajectory segment starting on interval $I \subset e_0$ and finishing in interval $I' \subset e_4$ is depicted.   ∎

We say that a signature σ is *feasible* if and only if there exists a trajectory segment ξ with signature σ, i.e., $\mathsf{Sig}(\xi) = \sigma$. From this definition, it immediately follows that extending an unfeasible signature, can never make it feasible.

Successors and Predecessors. Given an SPDI, we fix a one-dimensional co-ordinate system on each edge to represent points laying on edges [ASY01]. For notational convenience, we indistinctly use letter e to denote the edge or its one-dimensional representation. Accordingly, we write $\mathbf{x} \in e$ or $x \in e$, to mean "point $\mathbf{x}$ in edge e with coordinate x in the one-dimensional coordinate system of e". The same convention is applied to sets of points of e represented as intervals (e.g., $\mathbf{x} \in I$ or $x \in I$, where $I \subseteq e$) and to trajectories (e.g., "ξ starting in x" or "ξ starting in $\mathbf{x}$").

Now, let $P \in \mathbb{P}$, $e \in in(P)$ and $e' \in out(P)$. For $I \subseteq e$, $\mathsf{Succ}_{e,e'}(I)$ is the set of all points in e' reachable from some point in I by a trajectory segment $\xi : [0, t] \to \mathbb{R}^2$ in P (i.e., $\xi(0) \in I \wedge \xi(t) \in e' \wedge \mathsf{Sig}(\xi) = ee'$). $\mathsf{Succ}_{e,e'}$ is a TAMF [ASY01].

Example 2. Let $e_1, \ldots, e_6$ be as in Fig. 1-(a) and $I = [l, u]$. We assume a one-dimensional coordinate system. We show only the first and last edge-to-edge TAMF of the cycle:

$$F_{e_1 e_2}(I) = \left[\tfrac{l}{4}, \tfrac{9}{20}u \right], \quad S_1 = [0, 10], \quad J_1 = \left[0, \tfrac{9}{2} \right]$$
$$F_{e_6 e_1}(I) = [l, 2u], \quad S_6 = [0, 10], \quad J_6 = [0, 10]$$

with $\mathsf{Succ}_{e_i e_{i+1}}(I) = F_{e_i e_{i+1}}(I \cap S_i) \cap J_i$, for $1 \le i \le 6$; S_i and J_i are computed as shown in Theorem 1.   ∎

Given a sequence $w = e_1, e_2, \ldots, e_n$, the successor of I along w defined as $\mathsf{Succ}_w(I) = \mathsf{Succ}_{e_{n-1}, e_n} \circ \ldots \circ \mathsf{Succ}_{e_1, e_2}(I)$ is a TAMF.

Example 3. Let $\sigma = e_1 \cdots e_6 e_1$. We have that $\mathsf{Succ}_\sigma(I) = F(I \cap S_\sigma) \cap J_\sigma$, where: $F(I) = [\frac{l}{4} + \frac{1}{3}, \frac{9}{10}u + \frac{2}{3}]$, with $S_\sigma = [0, 10]$ and $J_\sigma = [\frac{1}{3}, \frac{29}{3}]$.   ∎

For $I \subseteq e'$, $\mathsf{Pre}_{e,e'}(I)$ is the set of points in e that can reach a point in I by a trajectory segment in P. The definition can be extended straightforwardly to signatures $\sigma = e_1 \cdots e_n$, $\mathsf{Pre}_\sigma(I)$.

Qualitative Analysis of Simple Edge-Cycles. Let $\sigma = e_1 \cdots e_k e_1$ be a simple edge-cycle, i.e., $e_i \neq e_j$ for all $1 \leq i \neq j \leq k$. Let $\mathsf{Succ}_\sigma(I) = F(I \cap S_\sigma) \cap J_\sigma$ with $F = \langle f_l, f_u \rangle$ (we suppose that this representation is normalized). We denote by $\mathcal{D}_\sigma$ the one-dimensional discrete-time dynamical system defined by Succ_σ, that is $x_{n+1} \in \mathsf{Succ}_\sigma(x_n)$.

Assumption 2. *None of the two functions f_l, f_u is the identity.*

Let l^* and u^* be the fix-points[3] of f_l and f_u, respectively, and $S_\sigma \cap J_\sigma = \langle L, U \rangle$. A simple cycle is of one of the following types [ASY01]: STAY, the cycle is not abandoned neither by the leftmost nor the rightmost trajectory, that is, $L \leq l^* \leq u^* \leq U$; DIE, the rightmost trajectory exits the cycle through the left (consequently the leftmost one also exits) or the leftmost trajectory exits the cycle through the right (consequently the rightmost one also exits), that is, $u^* < L \vee l^* > U$; EXIT-BOTH, the leftmost trajectory exits the cycle through the left and the rightmost one through the right, that is, $l^* < L \wedge u^* > U$; EXIT-LEFT, the leftmost trajectory exits the cycle (through the left) but the rightmost one stays inside, that is, $l^* < L \leq u^* \leq U$; EXIT-RIGHT, the rightmost trajectory exits the cycle (through the right) but the leftmost one stays inside, that is, $L \leq l^* \leq U < u^*$.

Example 4. Let $\sigma = e_1 \cdots e_6 e_1$. We have that $S_\sigma \cap J_\sigma = \langle L, U \rangle = [\frac{1}{3}, \frac{29}{3}]$. The fix-points of the Eq. given in Example 3 are such that $\frac{1}{3} < l^* = \frac{11}{25} < u^* = \frac{20}{3} < \frac{29}{3}$. Thus, σ is a STAY.   ∎

Any trajectory that enters a cycle of type DIE will eventually quit it after a finite number of turns. If the cycle is of type STAY, all trajectories that happen to enter it will keep turning inside it forever. In all other cases, some trajectories will turn for a while and then exit, and others will continue turning forever. This information is crucial for proving decidability of the reachability problem.

Reachability Analysis. It has been shown that reachability is decidable for SPDIs. Proof of the decidability result is constructive, giving an algorithmic procedure $Reach(\mathcal{S}, e, e')$ based on a depth-first search algorithm. An alternative breadth-first search algorithm which can deal with multiple edges has been presented in [PS03].

---

[3] The fix-point x^* is computed by solving the equation $f(x^*) = x^*$, where $f(\cdot)$ is positive affine.

Theorem 2 ([ASY01]). *The reachability problem for SPDIs is decidable.*   □

An edgelist is a set of intervals of edges. Given edgelists I and I', we denote the reachability of (some part of) I' from (some part of) I as $Reach(\mathcal{S}, I, I')$. Clearly, using the decidability result on edge intervals, reachability between edgelists is decidable. Although decidability may be point-to-point, edge-to-edge, edgelist-to-edgelist and region-to-region, in the rest of this paper, we will only talk about edgelist reachability. We define the following predicate: $I \xrightarrow{\mathcal{S}} I'$ $\equiv Reach(\mathcal{S}, I, I')$.

Example 5. Consider the SPDI of Fig. 1-(a). Fig. 1-(b) shows part of the reach set of the interval $[8, 10] \subset e_0$, answering positively to the reachability question: Is $[1, 2] \subset e_4$ reachable from $[8, 10] \subset e_0$? Fig. 1-(b) has been automatically generated by the SPeeDI toolbox [APSY02] we have developed for reachability analysis of SPDIs based on the results of [ASY01].   ■

2.2 Controllability and Viability Kernels

We recall the definition of controllability and viability kernels of an SPDI and we show how to obtain such kernels — proofs are omitted and for further details, refer to [ASY02]. In the following, given σ a cyclic signature, we define K_σ as follows: $K_\sigma = \bigcup_{i=1}^{k}(int(P_i) \cup e_i)$ where P_i is such that $e_{i-1} \in in(P_i)$, $e_i \in out(P_i)$ and $int(P_i)$ is P_i's interior.

We say that K, a subset of $\mathbb{R}^2$, is *controllable* if for any two points $\mathbf{x}$ and $\mathbf{y}$ in K there exists a trajectory segment ξ starting in $\mathbf{x}$ that reaches an arbitrarily small neighborhood of $\mathbf{y}$ without leaving K. More formally: A set K is controllable if $\forall \mathbf{x}, \mathbf{y} \in K, \forall \delta > 0, \exists \xi : [0, t] \rightarrow \mathbb{R}^2, t > 0 \,.\, (\xi(0) = \mathbf{x} \wedge |\xi(t) - \mathbf{y}| < \delta \wedge \forall t' \in [0, t] \,.\, \xi(t') \in K)$. The *controllability kernel* of K, denoted $\mathsf{Cntr}(K)$, is the largest controllable subset of K.

For $I \subseteq e_1$ we define $\overline{\mathsf{Pre}}_\sigma(I)$ to be the set of all $\mathbf{x} \in \mathbb{R}^2$ for which there exists a trajectory segment ξ starting in $\mathbf{x}$, that reaches some point in I, such that $\mathsf{Sig}(\xi)$ is a suffix of $e_2 \ldots e_k e_1$. It is easy to see that $\overline{\mathsf{Pre}}_\sigma(I)$ is a polygonal subset of the plane which can be calculated using the following procedure. We start by defining: $\overline{\mathsf{Pre}}_e(I) = \{\mathbf{x} \mid \exists \xi : [0, t] \rightarrow \mathbb{R}^2, t > 0 \,.\, \xi(0) = \mathbf{x} \wedge \xi(t) \in I \wedge \mathsf{Sig}(\xi) = e\}$ and apply this operation k times: $\overline{\mathsf{Pre}}_\sigma(I) = \bigcup_{i=1}^{k} \overline{\mathsf{Pre}}_{e_i}(I_i)$ with $I_1 = I$, $I_k = \mathsf{Pre}_{e_k, e_1}(I_1)$ and $I_i = \mathsf{Pre}_{e_i, e_{i+1}}(I_{i+1})$, for $2 \leq i \leq k - 1$.

For $I \subseteq e_1$ let us define $\overline{\mathsf{Succ}}_\sigma(I)$ as the set of all points $\mathbf{y} \in \mathbb{R}^2$ for which there exists a trajectory segment ξ starting in some point $\mathbf{x} \in I$, that reaches $\mathbf{y}$, such that $\mathsf{Sig}(\xi)$ is a prefix of $e_1 \ldots e_k$. The successor $\overline{\mathsf{Succ}}_\sigma(I)$ is a polygonal subset of the plane which can be computed similarly to $\overline{\mathsf{Pre}}_\sigma(I)$.

For a given cyclic signature σ, we define $\mathcal{C}_\mathcal{D}(\sigma)$ as follows:

$$\mathcal{C}_\mathcal{D}(\sigma) = \begin{cases} \langle L, U \rangle & \text{if } \sigma \text{ is EXIT-BOTH} \\ \langle L, u^* \rangle & \text{if } \sigma \text{ is EXIT-LEFT} \\ \langle l^*, U \rangle & \text{if } \sigma \text{ is EXIT-RIGHT} \\ \langle l^*, u^* \rangle & \text{if } \sigma \text{ is STAY} \\ \emptyset & \text{if } \sigma \text{ is DIE} \end{cases} \qquad (1)$$

$\mathcal{C}_\mathcal{D}(\sigma)$ is an interval on the first edge of the signature σ with the property that any point on such interval is reachable from any other point in the interval, and conversely. We compute the controllability kernel of K_σ as follows:

Theorem 3 ([ASY02]). $\mathsf{Cntr}(K_\sigma) = (\overline{\mathsf{Succ}_\sigma} \cap \overline{\mathsf{Pre}_\sigma})(\mathcal{C}_\mathcal{D}(\sigma))$. □

In what follows we present some definitions and a result which are crucial for obtaining a compositional algorithm for reachability analysis of SPDIs. See [PS06] for proofs and more details.

Let $\mathsf{Cntr}^l(K_\sigma)$ be the closed curve obtained by taking the leftmost trajectory and $\mathsf{Cntr}^u(K_\sigma)$ be the closed curve obtained by taking the rightmost trajectory which can remain inside the controllability kernel. In other words, $\mathsf{Cntr}^l(K_\sigma)$ and $\mathsf{Cntr}^u(K_\sigma)$ are the two polygons defining the controllability kernel.

A non-empty controllability kernel $\mathsf{Cntr}(K_\sigma)$ of a given cyclic signature σ partitions the plane into three disjoint subsets: (1) the controllability kernel itself, (2) the set of points limited by $\mathsf{Cntr}^l(K_\sigma)$ (and not including $\mathsf{Cntr}^l(K_\sigma)$) and (3) the set of points limited by $\mathsf{Cntr}^u(K_\sigma)$ (and not including $\mathsf{Cntr}^u(K_\sigma)$).

We define the *inner* of $\mathsf{Cntr}(K_\sigma)$ (denoted by $\mathsf{Cntr}_{in}(K_\sigma)$) to be the subset defined by (2) above if the cycle is counter-clockwise or to be the subset defined by (3) if it is clockwise. The *outer* of $\mathsf{Cntr}(K_\sigma)$ (denoted by $\mathsf{Cntr}_{out}(K_\sigma)$) is defined to be the subset which is not the inner nor the controllability itself.

We proceed now by defining and stating the computability result of viability kernels. A trajectory ξ is *viable* in K if $\xi(t) \in K$ for all $t \geq 0$. K is a *viability domain* if for every $\mathbf{x} \in K$, there exists at least one trajectory ξ, with $\xi(0) = \mathbf{x}$, which is viable in K. The *viability kernel* of K, denoted $\mathsf{Viab}(K)$, is the largest viability domain contained in K.

The following result provides a non-iterative algorithmic procedure for computing the viability kernel of K_σ on an SPDI:

Theorem 4 ([ASY02]). *If σ is DIE, $\mathsf{Viab}(K_\sigma) = \emptyset$, otherwise $\mathsf{Viab}(K_\sigma) = \overline{\mathsf{Pre}_\sigma}(S_\sigma)$.* □

Note that an edge in the SPDI may intersect a kernel. In such cases, we can generate a different SPDI, with the same dynamics but with the edge split into parts, such that each part is completely inside, on or outside the kernel. Although the signatures will obviously change, it is easy to prove that the behavior of the SPDI remains identical to the original. In the rest of the paper, we will assume that all edges are either completely inside, on or completely outside the kernels. We note that in practice splitting is not necessary since we can just consider parts of edges.

Example 6. Fig. 2 shows all the controllability and viability kernels of the SPDI given in Example 1. There are 4 cycles with controllability and viability kernels — in the picture two of the kernels are overlapping. ∎

Properties of the Kernels. Before stating two results relating controllability and viability kernels, we need the following definition:

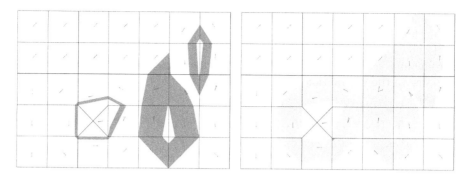

(a) Controllability kernels   (b) Viability kernels

Fig. 2. Kernels of the SPDI in Fig. 1

Definition 1. *Given a controllability kernel C (of a loop σ — $C = \mathsf{Cntr}(K_\sigma)$), then let C^+ be the related viability kernel ($C^+ = \mathsf{Viab}(K_\sigma)$), C_{in} be the inside of the kernel, and C_{out} be the outside.*

Proposition 3 in [PS06] gives conditions for feasible trajectories traversing controllability kernels. The following is a generalization of such result:

Proposition 1. *Given two edges e and e', one lying completely inside a kernel, and the other outside or on the same kernel, such that ee' is feasible, then there exists a point on the kernel, which is reachable from e and from which e' is reachable.*   □

The following corollary follows from [PS06, Proposition 2], asserting that the controllability kernel is the local basin of attraction of the viability kernel:

Corollary 1. *Given an controllability kernel C, and related viability kernel C^+, then for any $e \subseteq C^+$, $e' \subseteq C$, there exists a feasible path $e\sigma e'$.*   □

3 Independent Questions and Parallelization

3.1 SPDI Decomposition

In this section, we propose a number of theorems which, given an SPDI and a reachability question, for each controllability kernel, allow us to either (i) answer the reachability question without any further analysis; or (ii) reduce the state space necessary for reachability analysis; or (iii) decompose the reachability question into two smaller, and independent reachability questions.

The following theorem enables us to answer certain reachability questions without any analysis, other than the identification of controllability and viability kernels. This result is based on two properties, that within the controllability kernel of a loop, any two points are mutually reachable, and that any point on the viability kernel of the same loop can eventually reach the controllability kernel. Therefore if the source edgelist lies (possibly partially) within the viability kernel of a loop, and the destination edgelist lies (possibly partially) within the controllability kernel of the same loop, then, there must exist a trajectory from the source to the destination edgelist. The full proof of this result can be found in [PS06].

Theorem 5. *Given an SPDI S, two edgelists I and I' and a controllability kernel C, then if $I \subseteq C^+$ and $I' \subseteq C$, then $I \overset{S}{\longrightarrow} I'$.* □

The following theorem allows us to reduce the state space based on controllability kernels. If both the source and destination edgelists lie on the same side of a controllability kernel, then we can disregard all edges on the other side of the kernel. The full proof of this result can be found in [PS06].

Theorem 6. *Given an SPDI S, two edgelists I and I' and a controllability kernel C, then if $I \subseteq C_{in}$ and $I' \subseteq C_{in}$, then $I \overset{S}{\longrightarrow} I'$ if and only if $I \overset{S \backslash C_{out}}{\longrightarrow} I'$. Similarly, if $I \subseteq C_{out}$ and $I' \subseteq C_{out}$, then $I \overset{S}{\longrightarrow} I'$ if and only if $I \overset{S \backslash C_{in}}{\longrightarrow} I'$.* □

Finally, the following new result allows us to decompose a reachability question into two smaller questions independent of each other. The theorem states that if the source and destination edgelists lie on opposite sides of a controllability kernel, then we can try (i) to reach the related viability kernel from the source edgelist, and (ii) to reach the destination from the controllability kernel. The original reachability question can be answered affirmatively if and only if both these questions are answered affirmatively.

Theorem 7. *Given an SPDI S, two edgelists I and I' and a controllability kernel C, then if $I \subseteq C_{in}$ and $I' \subseteq C_{out}$, then $I \overset{S}{\longrightarrow} I'$ if and only if $I \overset{S \backslash C_{out}}{\longrightarrow} C^+ \wedge C \overset{S \backslash C_{in}}{\longrightarrow} I'$. Similarly, if $I \subseteq C_{out}$ and $I' \subseteq C_{in}$, then $I \overset{S}{\longrightarrow} I'$ if and only if $I \overset{S \backslash C_{in}}{\longrightarrow} C^+ \wedge C \overset{S \backslash C_{out}}{\longrightarrow} I'$.*

Proof. Without loss of generality, let $I \subseteq C_{in}$ and $I' \subseteq C_{out}$.

Soundness of Decomposition. Let us assume that $I \overset{S \backslash C_{in}}{\longrightarrow} C^+$ and $C \overset{S \backslash C_{out}}{\longrightarrow} I'$. From $I \overset{S \backslash C_{in}}{\longrightarrow} C^+$ we can conclude that there are partial edges $e_0 \subseteq I$ and $e_m \subseteq C^+$, and a path σ in $(S \backslash C_{out})$, such that $e_0 \sigma e_m$ is a feasible path.

Similarly, from $C \overset{S \backslash C_{out}}{\longrightarrow} I'$ we can conclude that there are partial edges $e_{m'} \subseteq C$ and $e_f \subseteq I'$, and a path σ' in $(S \backslash C_{in})$, such that $e_{m'} \sigma' e_f$ is a feasible path. However, since $e_{m'}$ is in a controllability kernel, and e_m is in the related viability kernel, then by corollary 1, there exists a feasible path $e_m \sigma'' e_{m'}$ in S. Therefore, $e_0 \sigma e_m \sigma'' e_{m'} \sigma' e_f$ is a feasible path in S. Since $e_0 \subseteq I$ and $e_f \subseteq I'$, we can conclude that $I \overset{S}{\longrightarrow} I'$.

Completeness of Decomposition. Conversely, let us assume that $I \overset{S}{\longrightarrow} I'$. Then, there must be edges $e_0 \subseteq I$ and $e_f \subseteq I'$ such that $e_0 \sigma e_f$ is feasible in S.

By the Jordan curve theorem [Hen79], the trajectory must cross $\mathsf{Cntr}^l(K_\sigma)$ or $\mathsf{Cntr}^u(K_\sigma)$ at least once, meaning that there exists a partial edge e_m in the controllability kernel C such that $e_0\sigma_1 e_m \sigma_2 e_f$ is feasible. But every subpath of a feasible path is itself feasible, meaning that both $e_0\sigma_1 e_m$ and $e_m\sigma_2 e_f$ are feasible in $\mathcal{S}$, implying that $I \xrightarrow{\mathcal{S}} C^+$ and $C \xrightarrow{\mathcal{S}} I'$. Consider the feasible path $e_0\sigma_1 e_m$. Recall that $I \subseteq C_{in}$, and that $e_0 \subseteq I$, hence $e_0 \subseteq C_{in}$. Assume that σ_1 contains some edges in C_{out}, and let f be the first such edge. The path is thus: $e_0\sigma_a f \sigma_b e_m$. Since f is the first edge inside the kernel, it follows that the last element of σ_a is outside the kernel. Using proposition 1, it follows that there exists a point p on the kernel reachable from the last element of σ_a. We have thus obtained a shorter discrete path $e_0\sigma_a p$ which is feasible and no point of which lies inside the kernel. Therefore, $I \xrightarrow{\mathcal{S}\backslash C_{in}} C^+$. Similarly, we can prove that $C \xrightarrow{\mathcal{S}\backslash C_{out}} I'$.   □

3.2   Unavoidable Kernels

Unavoidable kernels are defined geometrically to be kernels which a straight line from the source interval to the destination interval 'intersects' an odd number of times. We call the kernel unavoidable since it can be proved that any path from the source to the destination will have to pass through the kernel.

Definition 2. *Given an SPDI $\mathcal{S}$ and two edgelists I and I', we say that a controllability kernel $\mathsf{Cntr}(K_\sigma)$ is unavoidable if any segment of line with extremes on points lying on I and I' intersects with both the edges of $\mathsf{Cntr}^l(K_\sigma)$ and those of $\mathsf{Cntr}^u(K_\sigma)$ an odd number of times (disregarding tangential intersections with vertices).*

The following theorem enables us to discover separating controllability kernels using a simple geometric test.

Theorem 8. *Given an SPDI $\mathcal{S}$, two edgelists I and I', and a controllability kernel $C = \mathsf{Cntr}(K_\sigma)$, then C is an unavoidable kernel if and only if one of the following conditions holds (i) $I \subseteq C_{in}$ and $I' \subseteq C_{out}$; or (ii) $I \subseteq C_{out}$ and $I' \subseteq C_{in}$.*

Proof. This theorem is a standard geometrical technique frequently used in computer graphics [FvDFH96] (referred to as the odd-parity test).   □

Corollary 2. *Given an SPDI $\mathcal{S}$, two edgelists I and I', and an unavoidable controllability kernel $C = \mathsf{Cntr}(K_\sigma)$, then $I \xrightarrow{\mathcal{S}} I'$ if and only if $I \xrightarrow{\mathcal{S}} C$ and $C \xrightarrow{\mathcal{S}} I'$.*

Proof. This follows directly from theorems 6 and 8.   □

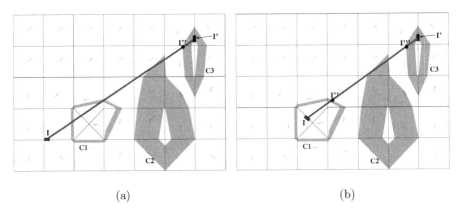

(a)   (b)

Fig. 3. Unavoidable kernels and independent reachability questions

The following result relates unavoidable kernels between each other:

Proposition 2. *Given two disjoint controllability kernels C and C', both unavoidable from I to I', then either C' is unavoidable from I to C or C' is unavoidable from C to I', but not both.*

Proof. This follows directly from definition of unavoidable kernel, the disjointness assumption and theorem 8.   □

3.3   Counting Sub-problems

The following theorem bounds the number of times a reachability question may be decomposed into independent sub-questions using theorem 7. We will consider a collection of mutually disjoint controllability kernels.

Theorem 9. *Given an SPDI S and two edgelists I and I', the question $I \xrightarrow{S} I'$ can be split into no more than k reachability questions, k is the number of mutually-disjoint controllability kernels.*

Proof. We note that whenever we decompose an SPDI, the source and destination intervals are always within the sub-SPDI under consideration.

Now consider a reachability question $I \xrightarrow{S} I'$, and a controllability kernel C upon which we can branch. Without loss of generality, we assume $I \subseteq C_{in}$ and $I' \subseteq C_{out}$. The question is thus decomposed into two questions: $I \xrightarrow{S \setminus C_{in}} C^+$ (question a) and $C \xrightarrow{S \setminus C_{out}} I'$ (question b).

Now consider another controllability kernel C'. We now have two possible cases: (i) $C' \subseteq C_{in}$; (ii) $C' \subseteq C_{out}$. Note that by the Jordan curve theorem, C' cannot be partially in and partially out of C without intersecting C.

In the first case (i), we note that since all edges in $S \setminus C_{out}$ lie outside or inside C', this new kernel cannot be be used to split question (b) or any question derived from it. Therefore, C' can only induce a split in question (a). Case (ii), is the mirror case and the argument follows identically.

Therefore, each controllability kernel can contribute at one extra process, bounding the number of reachability questions to k. □

We now give a lower bound on the number of independent questions induced by theorem 7 in terms of the number of mutually-disjoint unavoidable controllability kernels.

Theorem 10. *Given an SPDI S and two edgelists I and I', the question $I \xrightarrow{S} I'$ can be split into at least $u + 1$ reachability questions, u is the number of mutually-disjoint unavoidable controllability kernels.*

Proof. We prove this by induction on the number of mutually-disjoint unavoidable controllability kernels.

With $u = 0$, the number of questions is clearly at least $u + 1$.

Now consider the unavoidable controllability kernel C, and the question $I \xrightarrow{S} I'$. By theorem 8, it follows that I and I' are on opposite sides of C. The reachability question can be thus decomposed to $I \xrightarrow{S \setminus C_{in}} C^+$ (question a) and $C \xrightarrow{S \setminus C_{out}} I'$ (question b) by theorem 7. Also, by proposition 2, we known that any other unavoidable controllability kernel C' from I to I', is also an unavoidable controllability kernel from either I to C or from C to I' (but not both). In both cases we obtain a decomposition of the reachability question into $I \xrightarrow{S \setminus C_{out}} C$ and $C \xrightarrow{S \setminus C_{in}} C'$ (or, $I \xrightarrow{S \setminus C'_{out}} C$ and $C' \xrightarrow{S \setminus C'_{in}} C$). Splitting the kernels into the relevant ones to the two questions (u_1 kernels relevant to question a and u_2 relevant to question b — $u = u_1 + u_2 + 1$), we can conclude that the number of questions we get is $(u_1 + 1) + (u_2 + 1)$ which is $u + 1$. □

We have thus given lower and upper bounds on the the number of independent questions generated by applying theorem 7 over a number of mutually disjoint unavoidable controllability kernels. The results may be extended to work with overlapping kernels.

Example 7. Let us consider again the SPDI defined in Example 1 and the same intervals I and I'. In Fig. 3-(a) we show the unavoidable kernels. The segment of line from I to I' traverses C_1 and C_2 twice and C_3 exactly once (an odd number of times). Thus, only C_3 is an unavoidable kernel. The reachability question can be split into at least 2 independent questions: $I \xrightarrow{S \setminus C3_{in}} I''$ and $I'' \xrightarrow{S \setminus C3_{out}} I'$.

As another example let us consider I and I' as in Fig. 3-(b). The segment of line from I to I' traverses C_1 and C_3 exactly once (an odd number of times), while C_2 is traversed twice. Thus, there are two unavoidable kernels, namely C_1 and C_3. In this case the reachability question can be split into at least 3 independent questions: $I \xrightarrow{S \setminus C1_{out}} I''$, $I'' \xrightarrow{S \setminus (C1_{in} \cup C3_{in})} I'''$, and $I''' \xrightarrow{S \setminus C3_{out}} I'$. ■

4   Parallel Reachability Algorithm

In Fig. 4 we give an algorithm for parallel reachability analysis of SPDIs using parallel recursive calls corresponding to independent reachability questions.

```
function ReachPar(S, I, I') =
  ReachParKernels (S, ControllabilityKernels(S), I, I')

function ReachParKernels(S, [], I, I') =
  Reach(S, I, I');

function ReachParKernels(S, k:ks, I, I') =
  if (ImmedieteAnswer(S, I, I')) then
     True;
  elsif (SameSideOfKernel(S, k, I, I')) then
     S_I := S \ EdgesOnOtherSideOf(S, k, I');
     ReachParKernels(S_I, ks, I, I');
  else
     S_I := S \ EdgesOnOtherSideOf(S, k, I);
     S_I' := S \ EdgesOnOtherSideOf(S k, I');
     parbegin
        r1 := ReachParKernels(S_I, ks, I, viability(k));
        r2 := ReachParKernels(S_I', ks, k, I');
     parend;
     return (r1 and r2);
```

Fig. 4. Parallel algorithm for reachability of SPDIs

The function ReachParKernels is called with the SPDI to consider, a list of kernels still to be used for reduction, and the source and destination edgelists. With no kernels to consider, the algorithm simply calls the standard sequential algorithm (Reach). Otherwise, one of the kernels is analyzed, with three possible cases:

1. If the source lies (possibly partially) on the extended kernel, and the destination lies (possibly partially) on the kernel, then we can give an immediate answer (using theorem 5).
2. If both the edgelists lie on the same side of the kernel, then we simply eliminate redundant parts of the SPDI — anything on the other side of the kernel (theorem 6).
3. Otherwise, if the edgelists both lie on opposite sides of the kernel, we can split the problem into two independent questions (reaching the kernel from the source, and the destination from the kernel) which can be run in parallel (theorem 7). An affirmative answer from both these subquestions is equivalent to an affirmative answer to the original question.

Note that the function ReachParKernels is compositional in the sense that each recursive call launch a process which operates in (most cases in) disjoint state spaces which are smaller than the original one (S). The final answer is the composition of the partial reachability questions.

Given two edgelists I and I', we define the following predicate $I \xrightarrow{S}_{\parallel} I' \equiv$ ReachPar(S, I, I'). The following theorem states that the (compositional) parallel algorithm exactly answers the reachability question, also giving a soundness and completeness proof of the algorithm:

Theorem 11. *Given an SPDI S and two intervals $I \subseteq e$ and $I' \subseteq e'$, $I \xrightarrow{S} I'$ if and only if $I \xrightarrow{S}_{\parallel} I'$.*

Proof. The proof follows from theorems 5, 6 and 7 and induction on ks. $\square$

5   Concluding Remarks

We have shown how answering reachability on an SPDI can be reduced to a number of smaller reachability questions. Moreover, our algorithm can be combined with recent optimizations developed for the reachability analysis of SPDIs [PS06] in order to optimize each local reachability question.

We note that due to the fact that we present the algorithm working on edge-lists, the breadth-first-search algorithm we present in [PS03] is better adapted than the original algorithm [ASY01] to be used in this context. The algorithm consists essentially in partitioning[4] the state space into parts, discarding some of these partitions and performing reachability analysis on others. Furthermore, as long as separate reachability analysis of two disjoint state spaces is not more expensive than performing reachability analysis on the state spaces merged together (which is true for any reachability algorithm with complexity worse than linear) the state space partitioning provides a speedup over global model checking.

Part of our algorithm is based on certain geometric tests (e.g., theorem 8) which may be avoided if we consider a more abstract approach by enriching the reachability graph with information about the order among edges of each SPDI region. This is part of our on-going work, as well as the study of a variant of the algorithm which executes exactly $u + 1$ parallel processes, u being the number of unavoidable kernels.

Another natural question that arises is whether this can somehow be applicable to model checking of other models. To attempt to partially answer this question, we identify the properties of SPDIs that were used in the system decomposition. The property depends on the ability to identify subsets of the state space such that each such subset (i) is a strongly connected set (in terms of reachability); and (ii) partitions the state space into two — such that any state on one side that can reach states on the other side can do so via an intermediate state within the subset. These conditions are satisfied thanks to the planarity of SPDIs. In fact, the conditions can possibly be applied to systems with a planar state graph. The application and generalization of the results presented here remains an open research area.

One current research direction is to apply our results to semi-decide the reachability question for SPDIs defined on 2-dimensional manifolds, for which the decidability of reachability remains unresolved [AS02]. Maybe the most prominent

---

[4] The division is *almost* a partition, since the controllability kernels may be shared between parts.

application of SPDIs is for approximating complex non-linear differential equations on the plane, for which an exact solution is not known. The decidability of SPDI's reachability and of its phase portrait construction would be of invaluable help for the qualitative analysis of such equations. The challenge would be to find an "intelligent" partition of the plane in order to get an optimal approximation of the equations. Since such partition might produce a high number of regions, our parallel algorithm might be extremely useful here.

References

[AD94]   R. Alur and D.L. Dill. A theory of timed automata. *Theoretical Computer Science*, 126:183–235, 1994.

[APSY02]   E. Asarin, G. Pace, G. Schneider, and S. Yovine. SPeeDI: a verification tool for polygonal hybrid systems. In *CAV'2002*, volume 2404 of *LNCS*, pages 354–358, 2002.

[AS02]   E. Asarin and G. Schneider. Widening the boundary between decidable and undecidable hybrid systems. In *CONCUR'2002*, volume 2421 of *LNCS*, pages 193–208, 2002.

[ASY01]   E. Asarin, G. Schneider, and S. Yovine. On the decidability of the reachability problem for planar differential inclusions. In *HSCC'2001*, number 2034 in LNCS, pages 89–104, 2001.

[ASY02]   E. Asarin, G. Schneider, and S. Yovine. Towards computing phase portraits of polygonal differential inclusions. In *HSCC'02*, volume LNCS 2289, 2002.

[FvDFH96]   J.D. Foley, A. van Dam, S.K. Feiner, and J.F. Hughes. *Computer graphics (2nd ed. in C): principles and practice*. Addison-Wesley Longman Publishing Co., Inc., Boston, MA, USA, 1996.

[Hen79]   M. Henle. *A combinatorial introduction to topology*. Dover publications, Inc., 1979.

[HKPV95]   T.A. Henzinger, P.W. Kopke, A. Puri, and P. Varaiya. What's decidable about hybrid automata? In *STOC'95*, pages 373–382. ACM Press, 1995.

[LPY01]   G. Lafferriere, G. Pappas, and S. Yovine. Symbolic reachability computation of families of linear vector fields. *Journal of Symbolic Computation*, 32(3):231–253, September 2001.

[MP93]   O. Maler and A. Pnueli. Reachability analysis of planar multi-linear systems. In *CAV'93*, pages 194–209. LNCS 697, Springer Verlag, July 1993.

[PS03]   G. Pace and G. Schneider. Model checking polygonal differential inclusions using invariance kernels. In *VMCAI'04*, number 2937 in LNCS, pages 110–121. Springer Verlag, December 2003.

[PS06]   G. Pace and G. Schneider. Static analysis of SPDIs for state-space reduction. Technical Report 336, Department of Informatics, University of Oslo, PO Box 1080 Blindern, N-0316 Oslo, Norway, April 2006.

Thread-Modular Verification Is Cartesian Abstract Interpretation

Alexander Malkis[1], Andreas Podelski[1,2], and Andrey Rybalchenko[1,3]

[1] Max-Planck Institut für Informatik, Saarbrücken
[2] Albert-Ludwigs-Universität Freiburg
[3] EPFL IC IIF MTC, Lausanne
{malkis, podelski, rybal}@mpi-sb.mpg.de

Abstract. Verification of multithreaded programs is difficult. It requires reasoning about state spaces that grow exponentially in the number of concurrent threads. Successful verification techniques based on modular composition of over-approximations of thread behaviors have been designed for this task. These techniques have been traditionally described in assume-guarantee style, which does not admit reasoning about the abstraction properties of the involved compositional argument. Flanagan and Qadeer thread-modular algorithm is a characteristic representative of such techniques. In this paper, we investigate the formalization of this algorithm in the framework of abstract interpretation. We identify the abstraction that the algorithm implements; its definition involves Cartesian products of sets. Our result provides a basis for the systematic study of similar abstractions for dealing with the state explosion problem. As a first step in this direction, our result provides a characterization of a minimal increase in the precision of the Flanagan and Qadeer algorithm that leads to the loss of its polynomial complexity.

1 Introduction

Multithreaded software is everywhere. Verifying multithreaded software is an important and difficult task. The worst-case runtime of every existing verification algorithm is exponential in the number of threads. Due to inherent theoretical restrictions (see [9]) this is unlikely to change in the future.

However there are many successful algorithms and tools for different types of communication between components of a concurrent system. One can mention algorithms in SPIN (see [8]) and BLAST (see [7]) model-checkers. The main challenge for any verification algorithm is to reason modularly, avoiding explicit products of states and state spaces, which lead to combinatorial explosion. Such algorithms are called thread-modular.

Assume-guarantee reasoning offers a prominent approach to devise thread-modular algorithms. The behavior of each thread with respect to global variables is described by its guarantee. You can view this guarantee as a transition relation. For each thread, the model-checking procedure is applied to a parallel composition of the thread's transition relation and guarantees of other threads.

K. Barkaoui, A. Cavalcanti, and A. Cerone (Eds.): ICTAC 2006, LNCS 4281, pp. 183–197, 2006.

In this way the thread assumes that its environment sticks to the guarantees of other threads. Thus the guarantees of other threads represent the environment assumption. During model-checking of the parallel composition, the behavior of each thread is checked to stick to its own guarantee.

However, assume-guarantee reasoning doesn't provide an insight about the abstraction process involved. All that is known about precision loss during search in a thread's state space is that during discovering states of the thread, the behavior of all other threads is reduced to their action on global variables. Nothing was known about the loss of precision for the program as a whole. It was unclear whether or how is it possible to represent thread-modular reasoning in the standard framework of abstract interpretation.

As soon as the abstraction is identified, it provides additional insight into the algorithms. For instance, one could try to increase precision of the abstraction, to try to adapt the precision to a verification task, to optimize the algorithms, to combine with other abstractions or add refinement and create a counterexample-guided abstraction refinement loop. One could construct modifications of the abstraction, derive the corresponding algorithms and look at their runtime and precision.

We study the Flanagan-Qadeer algorithm for thread-modular verification (from now - FQ-algorithm). The distinguishing property of this algorithm lies in its low complexity. It is polynomial in the number of threads. The low complexity has its price: the algorithm is incomplete. The algorithm is also of the assume-guarantee type. Each computed guarantee is a set of pairs of valuations of unprimed and primed global variables (g, g'). While model-checking a thread, each time a thread state is discovered, we allow the global variables to be changed according to the guarantees of other threads. Each time the thread itself changes global variables from a discovered state, the corresponding pair of valuations of global variables before and after the step is added to the guarantee. Upon convergence, the environment assumptions are devised and the discovered states of each threads include the reachable thread states.

We would like to identify the abstraction used by the FQ-algorithm to be able to reason about the algorithm. In particular, we would like to know how far one can push the FQ-algorithm while still being polynomial in time and space.

In this paper we study the abstraction used in FQ-algorithm and identify the boundary. Our result is that FQ-algorithm implements Cartesian abstraction in special setting with threads (a so-called local Cartesian abstraction).

This insight allows us to find the "least modification" of the FQ-algorithm that leads to the loss of polynomial complexity. Thus, the identification of the abstraction provides the insight into the algorithm itself.

Local Cartesian abstraction formulation does not immediately provide a basis for complexity analysis, since the concrete domain (which is both the domain and the range of local Cartesian abstraction) admits exponentially long chains. Since local Cartesian abstraction is "the what" of FQ-algorithm, we obtain a polynomial time algorithm for reachability under local Cartesian abstraction.

Cartesian abstraction in program analysis is also known as "independent attribute method" (see [10]). There has been a lot of research since then, but to our best knowledge the method has not been applied to multithreaded programs yet. So our work is the first attempt to develop the theory of Cartesian abstraction for multithreaded programs.

Outline of the paper: First we define our program model.

Then we explain the algorithm. We provide a small example.

After that we define a concrete and an abstract domain and a corresponding Galois-connection that involve Cartesian products of sets. We state our first theorem saying how the output of the FQ-algorithm is expressible in the standard framework of abstract interpretation. We prove this theorem.

Then we define local Cartesian abstraction of multithreaded programs. We state our second theorem which says that the algorithm implements local Cartesian abstraction: the output of the algorithm represents local Cartesian abstraction of the program. We demonstrate the theorem on our example and prove it in general.

At last, we give a boundary of the abstraction, namely, an optimizing modification that works for many other verification methods but immediately breaks the polynomial-time border of the FQ-algorithm.

2   Preliminaries

2.1   Programs with Threads

We are interested in proving safety properties of multithreaded programs. Each safety property can be encoded as a reachability property. Simplifying, we consider programs consisting of only two threads communicating via shared variables.

A two-threaded *program* is given by a tuple

$$(\text{Glob}, \text{Loc}_1, \text{Loc}_2, \rightarrow_1, \rightarrow_2, \text{init})$$

where
- Loc_1 and Loc_2 contain valuations of local variables of the first and second threads, we call them the *local stores* of the first and second thread;
- Glob contains valuations of shared variables, we call it the *global store*;
- the elements of States = $\text{Glob} \times \text{Loc}_1 \times \text{Loc}_2$ are called *program states*, the elements of $Q_1 = \text{Glob} \times \text{Loc}_1$ and $Q_2 = \text{Glob} \times \text{Loc}_2$ are called *thread states*;
- the relation $\rightarrow_1$ (resp. $\rightarrow_2$) is a binary transition relation on the states of the first (resp. second) thread;
- init $\subseteq$ States is a set of initial states.

The program is equipped with the interleaving semantics. If a thread makes a step, then it may change its own local variables and the global variables but may not change the local variables of another thread; a step of the whole program is either a step of the first or a step of the second thread. The following successor operator maps a set of program states to the set of their successors:

$$\text{post} : 2^{\text{States}} \to 2^{\text{States}}$$

$$S \mapsto \{(g', l_1', l_2') \mid \exists (g, l_1, l_2) \in S : \quad (g, l_1) \to_1 (g', l_1') \text{ and } l_2 = l_2'$$
$$\text{or } (g, l_2) \to_2 (g', l_2') \text{ and } l_1 = l_1'\}.$$

We are interested whether there is a computation of any length $k \geq 0$ that starts in an initial state and ends in a single user-given error state f, formally:

$$\exists k \geq 0 : \ f \in \text{post}^k(\text{init}).$$

2.2   Flanagan-Qadeer Algorithm

The FQ-algorithm from [6] tests whether a given bad state f is reachable from an initial state. The test says "no" or "don't know".

The algorithm computes sets $\mathcal{R}_i \subseteq \text{Glob} \times \text{Loc}_i$ and $\mathcal{G}_i \subseteq \text{Glob} \times \text{Glob}$ ($i = 1, 2$) defined by the least fixed point of the following inference rules:

$$\text{INIT} \ \frac{}{\text{init}_i \in \mathcal{R}_i} \qquad \text{STEP} \ \frac{(g, l) \in \mathcal{R}_i \quad (g, l) \to_i (g', l')}{(g', l') \in \mathcal{R}_i \quad (g, g') \in \mathcal{G}_i}$$

$$\text{ENV} \ \frac{(g, l) \in \mathcal{R}_i \quad (g, g') \in \mathcal{G}_j}{(g', l) \in \mathcal{R}_i} \ i \neq j$$

Here, $\text{init}_1 = \{(g, l_1) \mid (g, l_1, \_) \in \text{init}\}$, similarly $\text{init}_2 = \{(g, l_2) \mid (g, \_, l_2) \in \text{init}\}$. (The underscore means "anything", i.e. an existentially quantified variable. The quantification is innermost, so in a formula, two underscores at different places denote different existentially quantified variables.) If $f \in \{(g, l_1, l_2) \mid (g, l_1) \in \mathcal{R}_1 \text{ and } (g, l_2) \in \mathcal{R}_2\}$, the algorithm says "don't know", otherwise it says "no".

The rules work as follows. The STEP rule discovers successors of a state of a thread that result due to a step of the same thread. Further, it stores the information about how the step changed the globals in the sets $\mathcal{G}_i$. The ENV rule uses this information to discover successors of a state of a thread that result due to communication between threads via globals. After the fixed point is reached, the set $\mathcal{R}_1$ (resp. $\mathcal{R}_2$) contains those states of the first (resp. second) thread that the algorithm discovers. The discovered thread states contain those thread states that occur in computations.

3   Represented Program States

The inference rules of the FQ-algorithm define the sets $\mathcal{R}_1, \mathcal{R}_2$ of "discovered" thread states. These sets represent those program states, whose globals and locals of the first thread are in $\mathcal{R}_1$ and globals and locals of the second thread are in $\mathcal{R}_2$, namely $\{(g, l_1, l_2) \mid (g, l_1) \in \mathcal{R}_1 \text{ and } (g, l_2) \in \mathcal{R}_2\}$.

Here is a small example. The program below has one global variable g that can take values 0 or 1, the first (resp. second) thread has a single local variable pc_1 (resp. pc_2), representing the program counter.

$$\text{Initially } g = 0$$

$$A: \quad g := 0; \qquad\qquad\qquad C: \quad g := 1;$$
$$B: \qquad\qquad\qquad\qquad\qquad D:$$

The algorithm discovers the following thread states:

$$\mathcal{R}_1 = \{(0, A), (0, B), (1, A), (1, B)\}, \quad \mathcal{R}_2 = \{(0, C), (0, D), (1, D)\},$$

where (x, Y) is a shorthand for the the pair of two maps $([g \mapsto x], [pc_i \mapsto Y])$. These two sets represent the set of program states

$$\{(g, l_1, l_2) \mid (g, l_1) \in \mathcal{R}_1 \text{ and } (g, l_2) \in \mathcal{R}_2\} =$$
$$\{(0, A, C), (0, A, D), (0, B, C), (0, B, D), (1, A, D), (1, B, D)\},$$

where (x, Y, Z) means the triple of maps $([g \mapsto x], [pc_1 \mapsto Y], [pc_2 \mapsto Z])$.

4   Cartesian Abstract Interpretation

In order to characterize the FQ-algorithm in the abstract interpretation framework, we first need a concrete domain, an abstract domain and a Galois connection between them:

$D = 2^{\text{States}}$ is the set underlying the concrete lattice,
$D^{\#} = 2^{Q_1} \times 2^{Q_2}$ is the set underlying the abstract lattice,
$\alpha_{\text{cart}} : D \to D^{\#}, \quad S \mapsto (T_1, T_2)$ where $T_1 = \{(g, l) \mid (g, l, \_) \in S\}$
$\qquad\qquad\qquad\qquad\qquad\qquad\qquad\quad T_2 = \{(g, l) \mid (g, \_, l) \in S\},$
$\gamma_{\text{cart}} : D^{\#} \to D, \quad (T_1, T_2) \mapsto \{(g, l_1, l_2) \mid (g, l_1) \in T_1 \text{ and } (g, l_2) \in T_2\}.$

The ordering on the concrete lattice D is inclusion, the least upper bound is the union $\cup$, the greatest lower bound is the intersection $\cap$.

The ordering on the abstract lattice $D^{\#}$ is the product ordering, i.e. $(T_1, T_2) \sqsubseteq (T_1', T_2')$ if and only if $T_1 \subseteq T_1'$ and $T_2 \subseteq T_2'$. The least upper bound $\sqcup$ is componentwise union, the greatest lower bound $\sqcap$ is componentwise intersection.

Remark that the image of the abstraction map α_{cart} is always contained in

$$D^{\#+} = \{(T_1, T_2) \in D^{\#} \mid \forall g \in \text{Glob} : (g, \_) \in T_1 \Leftrightarrow (g, \_) \in T_2\}.$$

Now we show that for the finite-state case the maximal chain length of the abstract domain is in general smaller than that of the concrete domain.

Proposition 1. *Let* $\text{Glob}, \text{Loc}_1, \text{Loc}_2$ *be finite. Let* $G := |\text{Glob}| \geq 1$ *be the cardinality of the global store and* $L_1 := |\text{Loc}_1|, L_2 := |\text{Loc}_2|$ *be the cardinalities of the local stores, both at least 2 and* $l := \min\{L_1, L_2\}$. *Then the maximal chain length of abstract domain is smaller and also asymptotically smaller than the maximal chain length of the concrete domain. Formally:*

a) (maximal chain length of $D^{\#}$) $\leq$ (maximal chain length of D);

b) $\lim_{l\to\infty} \dfrac{\text{maximal chain length of } D^{\#}}{\text{maximal chain length of } D} = 0$.

Proof. a) Consider any longest chain in D and any adjacent elements $A \subset B$ in the chain. Then $A \mathbin{\dot{\cup}} \{\_\} = B$ (otherwise the chain could be lengthened). So if $\emptyset$ is the 0th element of the chain, then its ith element from the bottom has size i. The maximal element is States, so the chain has $1 + |\text{States}| = 1 + GL_1L_2$ elements.

Consider any longest chain in $D^{\#}$ and any two adjacent elements $(A_1, A_2) \sqsubset (B_1, B_2)$ in the chain. Then either $A_1 = B_1$ and $A_2 \mathbin{\dot{\cup}} \{\_\} = B_2$ or $A_2 = B_2$ and $A_1 \mathbin{\dot{\cup}} \{\_\} = B_1$ (otherwise the chain could be lengthened). So one can construct the chain by starting with $(\emptyset, \emptyset)$ and adding elements one by one in some order to the first or to the second component. The number of such additions is bounded by the maximal sizes of the components $|Q_1|$ and $|Q_2|$. Totally $|Q_1| + |Q_2|$ additions can be performed, so the chain has $1 + |Q_1| + |Q_2| = 1 + GL_1 + GL_2$ elements.

b)

$$\lim_{l\to\infty} \frac{\text{maximal chain length of } D^{\#}}{\text{maximal chain length of } D} = \lim_{l\to\infty} \frac{1 + G(L_1 + L_2)}{1 + GL_1L_2} =$$

$$\underbrace{\lim_{l\to\infty} \frac{1}{1 + GL_1L_2}}_{0} + \lim_{l\to\infty} \frac{G(L_1 + L_2)}{1 + GL_1L_2} = \lim_{l\to\infty} \frac{1}{\frac{1}{GL_1} + L_2} + \lim_{l\to\infty} \frac{1}{\frac{1}{GL_2} + L_1} = 0.$$

$\square$

Two remarks should be made. First, if only one local store grows but the other remains constant-size, then the quotient $\frac{\text{maximal chain length of } D^{\#}}{\text{maximal chain length of } D}$ approaches some small positive value between 0 and 1. In case the number of threads is not two, but variable (say, n), we get similar asymptotic results for $n \to \infty$.

From now on, we sometimes omit the parentheses around the argument of a map, writing, e.g. fx for $f(x)$.

A pair of maps (α, γ) with $\alpha : D \to D^{\#}$ and $\gamma : D^{\#} \to D$ is called a *Galois connection* if for all $S \in D, T \in D^{\#}$ we have: $\alpha S \subseteq T$ iff $S \sqsubseteq \gamma T$.

Proposition 2. *The pair of maps $(\alpha_{\text{cart}}, \gamma_{\text{cart}})$ is a Galois connection, formally:*

$$\forall S \in D, (T_1, T_2) \in D^{\#} : \quad \alpha_{\text{cart}} S \sqsubseteq (T_1, T_2) \text{ iff } S \subseteq \gamma_{\text{cart}}(T_1, T_2).$$

Proof. "$\Rightarrow$": Let $(g, l_1, l_2) \in S$. Let $(T_1', T_2') = \alpha_{\text{cart}} S$. Then by definition of α_{cart} we have $(g, l_1) \in T_1' \subseteq T_1$ and $(g, l_2) \in T_2' \subseteq T_2$. So $(g, l_1, l_2) \in \gamma_{\text{cart}}(T_1, T_2)$ by definition of γ_{cart}.

"$\Leftarrow$": Let $(T_1', T_2') = \alpha_{\text{cart}} S$. Let $(g, l_1) \in T_1'$. By definition of α_{cart} there is an l_2 with $(g, l_1, l_2) \in S \subseteq \gamma_{\text{cart}}(T_1, T_2)$. By definition of γ_{cart} we have $(g, l_1) \in T_1$. So $T_1' \subseteq T_1$. Analogously we get $T_2' \subseteq T_2$. $\square$

5 Flanagan-Qadeer Algorithm Implements Cartesian Abstract Fixpoint Checking

Given a Galois connection (α, γ) between an abstract and a concrete domain, the abstraction of the program is defined as the least fixed point of $\lambda T.\alpha(\text{init} \cup \text{post}\gamma T)$ (see e.g. [5]). Recall that the FQ-algorithm computes $\mathcal{R}_1$ and $\mathcal{R}_2$, the sets of "discovered" states of the first and second thread.

Theorem 3. *[Thread-Modular Model Checking is Cartesian Abstract Interpretation]*

The output of the FQ-algorithm is the least fixed point of the abstract fixpoint checking operator with the abstraction map α_{cart} and concretization map γ_{cart}. Formally:

$$(\mathcal{R}_1, \mathcal{R}_2) \;=\; \text{lfp } \lambda T. \, \alpha_{\text{cart}}(\text{init} \cup \text{post}\gamma_{\text{cart}}T) \,.$$

It is not clear why this is so and how the assumptions are connected. For our tiny example, the right hand of the above equation (i.e. the least fixed point) is

$$(\{(0, A), (0, B), (1, A), (1, B)\}, \; \{(0, C), (0, D), (1, D)\}) \,,$$

which coincides with $(\mathcal{R}_1, \mathcal{R}_2)$ computed by the algorithm. We prove that the left and right hand side always coincide in the next section.

6 Proof

First we transform the inference rules of the FQ-algorithm by getting rid of the sets $\mathcal{G}_1$ and $\mathcal{G}_2$. We get an equivalent system of inference rules

$$\text{INIT}'_1 \; \frac{}{\text{init}_1 \in \mathcal{R}_1} \qquad\qquad \text{STEP}'_1 \; \frac{(g, l) \in \mathcal{R}_1 \qquad (g, l) \to_1 (g', l')}{(g', l') \in \mathcal{R}_1}$$

$$\text{ENV}'_1 \; \frac{(g, l) \in \mathcal{R}_1 \qquad (g, l_2) \in \mathcal{R}_2 \qquad (g, l_2) \to_2 (g', \_)}{(g', l) \in \mathcal{R}_1}$$

The rules INIT'_2, STEP'_2 and ENV'_2 are accordingly to INIT'_1, STEP'_1 and ENV'_1 where the indices 1 and 2 are exchanged. Remark that init_1 and init_2 contain thread states with the same global parts. Also remark that whenever $(g, l) \in \mathcal{R}_1$ and $(g, l) \to_1 (g', \_)$ and there is some thread state $(g, \_)$ in $\mathcal{R}_2$, then both rules STEP'_1 and ENV'_2 apply, giving two thread states for $\mathcal{R}_1$ and $\mathcal{R}_2$ with the same global part g'. Similarly, whenever $(g, l) \in \mathcal{R}_2$ and $(g, l) \to_2 (g', \_)$ and there is some thread state $(g, \_)$ in $\mathcal{R}_1$, then both rules STEP'_2 and ENV'_1 apply, giving two thread states for $\mathcal{R}_2$ and $\mathcal{R}_1$ with the same global part g'. By induction follows that whenever there is a thread state in $\mathcal{R}_i$ with some global part g, there is a thread state in $\mathcal{R}_j$ with the same global part g $(i \neq j)$.

This means that we can replace the STEP' and ENV' rules by one rule. The following system of inference rules is equivalent to the system above.

$$\text{INIT}'_1 \; \overline{\text{init}_1 \in \mathcal{R}_1} \qquad\qquad \text{INIT}'_2 \; \overline{\text{init}_2 \in \mathcal{R}_2}$$

$$\text{POST}^\#_1 \; \frac{(g, l_1) \in \mathcal{R}_1 \quad (g, l_2) \in \mathcal{R}_2 \quad (g, l_2) \to_2 (g', l'_2)}{(g', l_1) \in \mathcal{R}_1 \quad (g', l'_2) \in \mathcal{R}_2}$$

$$\text{POST}^\#_2 \; \frac{(g, l_2) \in \mathcal{R}_2 \quad (g, l_1) \in \mathcal{R}_1 \quad (g, l_1) \to_1 (g', l'_1)}{(g', l_2) \in \mathcal{R}_2 \quad (g', l'_1) \in \mathcal{R}_1}$$

Each POST$^\#$ rule takes two sets (called $\mathcal{R}_1$ and $\mathcal{R}_2$ above) and gives new elements for the first and new elements for the second set. All possible applications of the POST$^\#$ rules on a fixed pair of sets (T_1, T_2) can be expressed as computing

$$p^\#(T_1, T_2) = \{((g', l'_1), (g', l'_2)) \mid \exists ((g, l_1), (g, l_2)) \in T_1 \times T_2 :$$
$$(g, l_1) \to_1 (g', l'_1) \text{ and } l_2 = l'_2$$
$$\text{or } (g, l_2) \to_2 (g', l'_2) \text{ and } l_1 = l'_1\},$$

the new elements being the first and second projection of the result. Thus, applying the POST$^\#$ rules corresponds to applying the map post$^\# : D^\# \to D^\#$,

$$(T_1, T_2) \mapsto (\pi_1 p^\#(T_1, T_2), \pi_2 p^\#(T_1, T_2)),$$

where π_i is the projection on the ith component ($i = 1, 2$). Notice: $(\text{init}_1, \text{init}_2) = \alpha_{\text{cart}}\text{init}$. Then the pair of computed sets $(\mathcal{R}_1, \mathcal{R}_2)$ is the least fixed point of

$$\lambda T . \; \alpha_{\text{cart}}\text{init} \sqcup \text{post}^\# T .$$

The abstract successor map post$^\#$ can be expressed in terms of post and the abstraction/concretization maps:

Proposition 4. *For any $T \in D^\#$ holds:*

$$\text{post}^\# T = \alpha_{\text{cart}} \text{post} \gamma_{\text{cart}} T .$$

Proof. Let $(T_1, T_2) := T$.
"$\sqsubseteq$":
Let $(g', l'_1) \in \pi_1 p^\# T$. Then there is an l'_2 so that the pair $((g', l'_1), (g', l'_2)) \in p^\# T$. Then there are g, l_1, l_2 with $(g, l_1) \in T_1$, $(g, l_2) \in T_2$ and

$$(g, l_1) \to_1 (g', l'_1) \text{ and } l_2 = l'_2$$
$$\text{or } (g, l_2) \to_2 (g', l'_2) \text{ and } l_1 = l'_1 .$$

Then $(g, l_1, l_2) \in \gamma_{\text{cart}}(T_1, T_2) = \gamma_{\text{cart}} T$ by definition of γ_{cart}. So $(g', l'_1, l'_2) \in \text{post}\gamma_{\text{cart}} T$ by definition of the successor map post and thus (g', l'_1) is in the first component of $\alpha_{\text{cart}}\text{post}\gamma_{\text{cart}} T$. So $\pi_1 p^\# T$ is contained in the first component of $\alpha_{\text{cart}}\text{post}\gamma_{\text{cart}} T$. That $\pi_2 p^\# T$ is contained in the second component of $\alpha_{\text{cart}}\text{post}\gamma_{\text{cart}} T$ can be proven analogously.
"$\sqsupseteq$":
Let (g', l'_1) be in the first component of $\alpha_{\text{cart}}\text{post}\gamma_{\text{cart}} T$. Then there is an l'_2 with $(g', l'_1, l'_2) \in \text{post}\gamma_{\text{cart}} T$. So there are g, l_1, l_2 with $(g, l_1, l_2) \in \gamma_{\text{cart}} T$ and

$$(g, l_1) \to_1 (g', l'_1) \text{ and } l_2 = l'_2$$
$$\text{or } (g, l_2) \to_2 (g', l'_2) \text{ and } l_1 = l'_1 .$$

From $(g, l_1, l_2) \in \gamma_{\text{cart}} T$ we know that $(g, l_1) \in T_1$ and $(g, l_2) \in T_2$. By definition of $p^\#$ we have $((g', l_1'), (g', l_2')) \in p^\#(T_1, T_2)$. So $(g', l_1') \in \pi_1 p^\# T$. We have shown that the first component of $\alpha_{\text{cart}} \text{post} \gamma_{\text{cart}} T$ is included in $\pi_1 p^\# T$. Analogously one can show that the second component of $\alpha_{\text{cart}} \text{post} \gamma_{\text{cart}} T$ is included in $\pi_2 p^\# T$.

$\square$

So the algorithm computes the least fixed point of

$$\lambda T \cdot \alpha_{\text{cart}} \text{init} \sqcup \alpha_{\text{cart}} \text{post} \gamma_{\text{cart}} T = \lambda T \cdot \alpha_{\text{cart}} (\text{init} \cup \text{post} \gamma_{\text{cart}} T).$$

7 Local Cartesian Abstraction

Up to now we identified the FQ-algorithm as abstract fixpoint checking on an abstract domain. However, it turns out that the output of the FQ-algorithm can also be characterized by a very simple abstraction of multithreaded programs which is defined on the concrete domain. Now we define this abstraction.

Recall that the *Cartesian abstraction of a set of pairs* is the smallest Cartesian product containing this subset. We define it formally as

$$\mathcal{C}^\# : 2^{Q_1 \times Q_2} \to 2^{Q_1 \times Q_2},$$
$$P \mapsto \{(s_1, s_2) \mid (s_1, \_) \in P \text{ and } (\_, s_2) \in P\},$$

We have $\mathcal{C}^\# P = \pi_1 P \times \pi_2 P$. An analog of Cartesian abstraction on the concrete domain is

$$\mathcal{C} : D \to D$$
$$S \mapsto \{(g, l_1, l_2) \mid (g, l_1, \_) \in S \text{ and } (g, \_, l_2) \in S\}.$$

We call this map *local Cartesian abstraction* of a set of program states since it simplifies to the Cartesian abstraction of a set of pairs if Glob is a singleton.

It turns out that local Cartesian abstraction is representable in the abstract interpretation framework.

Proposition 5. *Local Cartesian abstraction is overapproximation with the abstraction map α_{cart} and the concretization map γ_{cart}. Formally:*

$$\mathcal{C} = \gamma_{\text{cart}} \alpha_{\text{cart}}$$

Proof. Let $S \subseteq$ States. We show that $\mathcal{C}S = \gamma_{\text{cart}} \alpha_{\text{cart}} S$. Let $(T_1, T_2) = \alpha_{\text{cart}} S$. We have
$(g, l_1, l_2) \in \mathcal{C}S \overset{\text{def. of } \mathcal{C}}{\Leftrightarrow} (g, l_1, \_) \in S \text{ and } (g, \_, l_2) \in S \overset{\text{def. of } \alpha_{\text{cart}}}{\Leftrightarrow} (g, l_1) \in T_1$
and $(g, l_2) \in T_2 \overset{\text{definition of } \gamma_{\text{cart}}}{\Leftrightarrow} (g, l_1, l_2) \in \gamma_{\text{cart}}(T_1, T_2) = \gamma_{\text{cart}} \alpha_{\text{cart}} S.$ $\square$

8 Thread-Modular Model-Checking as Local Cartesian Abstraction

Given an abstraction map α and a concretization map γ between an abstract and a concrete domain, we can alternatively perform the abstract fixed point checking in the concrete domain. Then the least fixed point of $\lambda S.\gamma\alpha(\text{init}\cup\text{post}S)$ is computed.

For our special Galois connection $(\alpha_{\text{cart}}, \gamma_{\text{cart}})$ we can discover the states of the program by iterative successor computation and at each step overapproximate by local Cartesian abstraction. Naively implemented, this algorithm would require exponential time (in number of threads, if it is not constant). It turns out that the FQ-algorithm solves the same problem in polynomial time.

Theorem 6 (Thread-Modular Model-Checking as Local Cartesian abstraction). *The concretization of the output of the FQ-algorithm is equal to the result of abstract fixpoint checking with local Cartesian abstraction. Formally:*

$$\gamma(\mathcal{R}_1, \mathcal{R}_2) \; = \; \text{lfp } \lambda S. \; \mathcal{C}(\text{init} \cup \text{post}S). \tag{1}$$

For our tiny example, let us compute the least fixed point of $\lambda S.\mathcal{C}(\text{init} \cup \text{post}S)$ by definition. The corresponding chain is

$$\{(0, A, C)\} \sqsubseteq \{(0, A, C), (0, B, C), (1, A, D)\} \sqsubseteq$$
$$\sqsubseteq \{(0, A, C), (0, B, C), (1, A, D), (1, B, D), (0, B, D), (0, A, D)\} \quad \text{(fixed point)},$$

the last term being the right hand side of (1). The left and the right hand side coincide in this example. We prove that they always coincide in the next section.

9   Proof

9.1   Preparations

Before we start proving the theorem, let's prove a basic fact about the abstract fixpoint checking.

Let D be a complete lattice with ordering $\subseteq$, bottom element $\emptyset$, join $\cup$, meet $\cap$ (concrete lattice). Further, let $D^{\#}$ be a complete lattice with ordering $\sqsubseteq$, bottom element $\bot$, join $\sqcup$ and meet $\sqcap$ (abstract lattice). Let a pair of maps $\alpha : D \to D^{\#}$ and $\gamma : D^{\#} \to D$ be a Galois connection between the concrete and abstract lattices. Let $F : D \to D$ be any monotone map and init $\in D$ any concrete element. Further, we call $\rho := \gamma\alpha : D \to D$ the *overapproximation* operator.

One way to perform abstract fixpoint checking is to compute the least fixed point of $G^{\#} = \lambda T. \; \alpha(\text{init} \cup F\gamma T)$ in the abstract lattice. The other way is to compute the least fixed point of $G = \lambda S. \; \gamma\alpha(\text{init} \cup FS)$ in the concrete lattice.

One would expect that these two fixed points are the same up to abstraction/concretization. Now we show that this is indeed the case if we assume the following

Hypothesis. The concretization map γ is semi-continuous, i.e. for all ascending chains $X \subseteq D^{\#}$ we have $\gamma(\sqcup X) = \cup\gamma X$.

This hypothesis is especially satisfied for a continuous γ, i.e. when for all chains $X \subseteq D^{\#}$ we have $\gamma(\sqcup X) = \cup\gamma X$.

Let μ be any ordinal whose cardinality (the cardinality of the class of ordinals smaller than μ) is greater than the cardinalities of D and $D^{\#}$. Let's define two sequences with indices from μ:

$$T^0 = \alpha \operatorname{init} \qquad S^0 = \rho \operatorname{init} \qquad\qquad\qquad \text{for } k = 0\,,$$
$$T^{k+1} = G^{\#} T^k \qquad S^{k+1} = G S^k \qquad \text{for successor ordinals } k+1 \in \mu\,,$$
$$T^k = \bigsqcup_{k' < k} T^{k'} \qquad S^k = \bigcup_{k' < k} S^{k'} \qquad \text{for limit ordinals } k \in \mu\,.$$

From [3] Cor 3.3 we know that the sequences $(S^k)_k$, $(T^k)_k$ are stationary increasing chains and the limits are the least fixed points over $\alpha \operatorname{init}$ and $\rho \operatorname{init}$, respectively. One can show that if we start the sequences $(T^k)_k$ and $(S^k)_k$ with the bottom elements $\bot$ and $\emptyset$ (instead of $\alpha \operatorname{init}$ and $\rho \operatorname{init}$), the limits would be the same, respectively. So the limits are the least fixed points (over $\bot$ and $\emptyset$). The hypothesis immediately implies that for each limit ordinal $k \in \mu$ holds

$$\gamma \bigsqcup_{k' < k} T^{k'} = \bigcup_{k' < k} \gamma T^{k'} \quad \text{and} \quad \gamma \bigsqcup_{k' < k} \alpha S^{k'} = \bigcup_{k' < k} \gamma \alpha S^{k'}\,. \tag{2}$$

We need some basic facts about Galois connections and about the overapproximation operator (see e.g. [2], [4]). From the definition of Galois connection one can prove that the abstraction and concretization maps α and γ are monotone. Further overapproximation map ρ is idempotent. Further, overapproximating and then abstracting is the same as abstracting: $\alpha\rho = \alpha$.

First we show that overapproximating S^k doesn't change it.

Proposition 7. *Each S^k is invariant under overapproximation. Formally:*

$$\forall k \in \mu : \quad \rho S^k = S^k\,.$$

Proof. We use transfinite induction.

For $k = 0$, we have $\rho S^0 = \rho \rho \operatorname{init} \overset{\rho \text{ idempotent}}{=} \rho \operatorname{init} = S^0$.

For a successor ordinal $k + 1$, we have $\rho S^{k+1} = \rho \rho (\operatorname{init} \cup F S^k) \overset{\rho \text{ idempotent}}{=} \rho (\operatorname{init} \cup F S^k) = S^{k+1}$.

If k is a limit ordinal, $\rho S^k = \gamma \alpha \bigcup_{k'<k} S^{k'} \overset{\alpha \text{ complete join morphism}}{=} \gamma \bigsqcup_{k'<k} \alpha S^{k'} \overset{\text{formula}(2)}{=} \bigcup_{k'<k} \gamma \alpha S^{k'} \overset{\rho = \gamma\alpha}{=} \bigcup_{k'<k} \rho S^{k'} \overset{\text{induction assumption}}{=} \bigcup_{k'<k} S^{k'} = S^k$. $\square$

Proposition 8. *Each T^k is the abstraction of S^k. Formally:*

$$\forall k \in \mu : \quad T^k = \alpha S^k\,.$$

Proof. Transfinite induction.

For $k = 0$ we have $T^0 = \alpha \operatorname{init} \overset{\alpha = \alpha\rho}{=} \alpha \rho \operatorname{init} = \alpha S^0$.

For a successor ordinal $k + 1$ we have $T^{k+1} = \alpha(\operatorname{init} \cup F \gamma T^k) \overset{\text{induction assumption}}{=} \alpha(\operatorname{init} \cup F \gamma \alpha S^k) \overset{\gamma\alpha = \rho}{=} \alpha(\operatorname{init} \cup F \rho S^k) \overset{\rho S^k = S^k}{=} \alpha(\operatorname{init} \cup F S^k) \overset{\alpha = \alpha\rho}{=} \alpha \rho(\operatorname{init} \cup F S^k) = \alpha S^{k+1}$.

For a limit ordinal k holds $T^k = \bigsqcup_{k'<k} T^{k'} \overset{\text{induction assumption}}{=} \bigsqcup_{k'<k} \alpha S^{k'} \overset{\alpha \text{ complete join morphism}}{=} \alpha \bigcup_{k'<k} S^{k'} = \alpha S^k$. $\square$

Proposition 9. *Each S^k is the concretization of T^k. Formally:*

$$\forall\, k \in \mu \,: \quad \gamma T^k = S^k\,.$$

Proof. Transfinite induction.
For $k = 0$ we have $\gamma T^0 = \gamma\alpha\text{init} = \rho\text{init} = S^0$.
For a successor ordinal $k + 1$ we have $\gamma T^{k+1} = \gamma\alpha(\text{init} \cup F\gamma T^k) = \rho(\text{init} \cup F\gamma T^k) \overset{\text{induction assumption}}{=} \rho(\text{init} \cup FS^k) = S^{k+1}$.
If k is a limit ordinal, $\gamma T^k = \gamma\bigsqcup_{k'<k} T^{k'} \overset{\text{formula(2)}}{=} \bigcup_{k'<k}\gamma T^{k'} \overset{\text{induction assumption}}{=} \bigcup_{k'<k} S^{k'} = S^k$. $\qquad\square$

Let $\lambda \in \mu$ be any ordinal at which both sequences are stationary, i.e. $S^\lambda = S^{\lambda+1}$ and $T^\lambda = T^{\lambda+1}$. Then the least fixed point of G is S^λ and the least fixed point of $G^\#$ is T^λ. Propositions 8 and 9 imply the following

Theorem 10. *Let the concretization map be semi-continuous. Then the least fixed points of G and $G^\#$ coincide up to abstraction and concretization:*

$$\gamma\,\text{lfp}\,G^\# = \text{lfp}\,G \quad and \quad \text{lfp}\,G^\# = \alpha\,\text{lfp}\,G\,.$$

9.2 Applying the Theory

We now show that for our Galois connection $(\alpha_\text{cart}, \gamma_\text{cart})$ the hypothesis holds.

Proposition 11. γ_cart *is continuous, i.e. for all chains $X \subseteq D^\#$ holds:*

$$\gamma_\text{cart}(\sqcup X) \;=\; \cup\gamma_\text{cart}X\,.$$

Proof. "$\subseteq$". Let $(g, l_1, l_2) \in \gamma_\text{cart}(\sqcup X)$. Then (g, l_1) (resp. (g, l_2)) is in the first (resp. second) component of $\sqcup X$. Then there are (T_1, T_2) and (T_1', T_2') in X with $(g, l_1) \in T_1$ and $(g, l_2) \in T_2'$. Since X is a chain, we have either $(T_1, T_2) \sqsupseteq (T_1', T_2')$ or $(T_1, T_2) \sqsubseteq (T_1', T_2')$. Without loss of generality let $(T_1, T_2) \sqsupseteq (T_1', T_2')$. Then $(g, l_2) \in T_2$, so $(g, l_1, l_2) \in \gamma_\text{cart}(T_1, T_2) \subseteq \cup\gamma_\text{cart}X$.
"$\supseteq$" holds by monotonicity of γ_cart and definition of the least upper bound. $\quad\square$

The map post $: D \rightarrow D$ is monotone. Proposition 5 and Theorems 3 and 10 imply

$$\gamma(\mathcal{R}_1, \mathcal{R}_2) \;=\; \text{lfp}\,\lambda S.\,\mathcal{C}(\text{init} \cup \text{post}S)\,.$$

10 Boundary of the Flanagan-Qadeer Algorithm

Now we try to push the FQ-algorithm to increase precision without losing polynomial complexity and show where this fails. For speaking about runtime, let's assume that all the domains are finite. The definitions of the multithreaded program, of the concrete and the abstract domain, of abstraction/concretization maps and the corresponding theorems extend to n threads in a natural way.

A usual way to gain more precision is to abstract not all states, but only the recently discovered states:

$$T^0 = \alpha_{\text{cart}}\text{init} \quad \text{and} \quad T^{i+1} = \text{post}^{\#}T^i \quad (i \geq 0).$$

The sequence stops for $k \geq 0$ with $\gamma_{\text{cart}}T^{k+1} \subseteq \cup_{i=0}^{k}\gamma_{\text{cart}}T^i$. Then $X :=$ $\cup_{i=0}^{k}\gamma_{\text{cart}}T^k$ is an inductive invariant, i.e. init $\subseteq X$ and post$X \subseteq X$.

We can implement this iteration in the abstract domain $D^{\#}$ by the following inference rule:

$$\text{POST}_{ij}^{\#} \frac{(g,l_i) \in \mathcal{R}_i \quad (g,l_j) \in \mathcal{R}_j \quad (g,l_j) \to_j (g',l_j')}{(g',l_i) \in \mathcal{R}_i' \quad (g',l_j') \in \mathcal{R}_j'} \, i \neq j.$$

Except for the primed versions $\mathcal{R}_i'$ and $\mathcal{R}_j'$ in the conclusion of the rule, this is the same rule that is used in the reformulation of the FQ-algorithm. As before we have $(\mathcal{R}_1', ..., \mathcal{R}_n') = \text{post}^{\#}(\mathcal{R}_1, ..., \mathcal{R}_n)$. So each steps of the new iteration scheme is polynomial. But it turns out that number of steps can be exponential:

Theorem 12. *Frontier search with Cartesian abstraction has exponential worst-case runtime in the number of threads.*

Proof. It suffices to present a family of multithreaded programs so that:

1. the nth program in the family has n threads;
2. the sizes of the global store and local stores are polynomial in n;
3. each program of the family has exactly one run of exponential length in n.

Assume such a program with a single initial state is given. If for some $i \geq 0$ the components of the tuple T^i contain at most one element each, then $\gamma_{\text{cart}}T^i$ contains at most one element, and hence post$\gamma_{\text{cart}}T^i$ is a singleton or empty, so $T^{i+1} = \alpha_{\text{cart}}\text{post}\gamma_{\text{cart}}T^i$ is a tuple of singletons or empty sets. Since $\gamma_{\text{cart}}T^i$ contains post^i(init), we inductively follow that $\gamma_{\text{cart}}T^i = \text{post}^i(\text{init})$ for all $i \geq 0$, i.e. no approximation happens. Especially the sequence $(T^i)_{0 \leq i \leq k}$ is exponentially long.

Now we give a family of programs satisfying the conditions above.

Example 13. [Binary Counter] The statements in brackets $<>$ are atomic. Global boolean variable with initial value:
$t = 1$ (takes values from $\{0, ..., n\}$)
Thread 1:
`0: wait until` $t = 1$`;`
`1: <`$t := 2$`;    goto 0;>`
Thread i $(1 < i < n)$**:**
`0: <wait until` $t = i$`;    ` $t := 1$`;>`
`1: <wait until` $t = i$`;    ` $t := i+1$`;    goto 0;>`
Thread n**:**
`0: <wait until` $t = n$`;    ` $t := 1$`;>`
`1: <wait until` $t = n$`;    ` $t := 0$`;    goto 0;>`
The program implements a binary counter with the school addition method. The local store of the ith thread represents the position $i - 1$ of the number

196 A. Malkis, A. Podelski, and A. Rybalchenko

$(1 \leq i \leq n)$. The carry position is stored in the global variable t. The value $t = 0$ means the carry is nowhere.

Below is the single run for $n = 3$ where pc_i is the program counter of the ith thread. Each column represents a state of the whole program, a successor state is to the right of its predecessor:

variable	* *	* *		* *	* *	
t	1 1 2 1 1 2 3 1 1 2 1 1 2 3 0					
pc_1	0 1 0 0 1 0 0 0 1 0 0 1 0 0 0					
pc_2	0 0 0 1 1 1 0 0 0 0 1 1 1 0 0					
pc_3	0 0 0 0 0 0 0 1 1 1 1 1 1 1 0					

Let us look at the columns marked by the star (*), i.e where carry is above the 0th position. The values of the program counters (pc_3, pc_2, pc_1) evolve like a binary counter. □

So frontier search breaks the polynomial time border of Cartesian Abstraction.

Another interesting property of the binary counter is that the set of reachable states is so big that the output of the FQ-algorithm is exact:

$$\begin{aligned}
\mathcal{R}_1 &= \{(1,0),(1,1),(2,0), & (3,0), & (0,0)\}, \\
\mathcal{R}_2 &= \{(1,0),(1,1),(2,0),(2,1), & (3,0), & (0,0)\}, \\
\mathcal{R}_3 &= \{(1,0),(1,1),(2,0),(2,1), & (3,0),(3,1), & (0,0)\}.
\end{aligned}$$

Namely, $\gamma_{\text{cart}}(\mathcal{R}_1, \mathcal{R}_2, \mathcal{R}_3)$ is exactly the set of reachable states. So no more precision can be regained.

The binary counter has a property that the size of the global store grows linearly with n and the transition graph has exponential diameter. Can one get exponential diameter with a sublinear or even constant global store size? We pose the following open

Problem 14. Prove or give a counterexample. There is no family $(P_n)_{n \geq 1}$ of multithreaded programs so that

1. the nth program P_n consists of n threads;
2. the global and local stores are constant throughout the family;
3. there is a constant $c > 1$ so that for almost all $n \in \mathbb{N}$ the diameter of the transition graph of P_n exceeds c^n.

We do not see how to solve this problem at the moment.

11 Summary

We have examined an approach for verifying concurrent programs.

On one side, we have examined the FQ-algorithm for checking safety of multithreaded programs. We have characterized it in a well-known framework of abstract interpretation. Using this characterization, we have shown the boundary of this algorithm.

On the other side, we have started developing the theory of Cartesian abstraction for multithreaded programs. We have shown two equivalent approaches for abstract fixpoint checking on the abstract and the concrete domain. We have seen that local Cartesian abstraction is polynomial in the number of threads.

Both contributions seem to be first steps in a systematic study of similar abstractions of the state explosion problem.

Acknowledgements

We would like to thank Springer-Verlag for editorial assistance.

References

1. Birkhoff, G., *Lattice Theory*, 3rd ed., Providence, Rhode Island: Amer. Math. Soc., 1967.
2. Blanchet, B., Introduction to Abstract Interpretation, 2002, lecture script, `http://www.di.ens.fr/~blanchet/absint.pdf`
3. Cousot, P., Cousot, R., *Constructive versions of Tarski's fixed point theorems*, Pacific Journal of Mathematics, Vol. 82, No. 1, 1979.
4. Cousot, P., Cousot, R., *Systematic design of program analysis frameworks*, 6th annual ACM symposium on principles of program languages, 1979.
5. Cousot, P., *Partial Completeness of the Abstract Fixpoint checking*, SARA 2000, LNAI 1864, pp. 1-25, 2000.
6. Flanagan, C., Qadeer, S., *Thread-Modular Model Checking*, in T.Ball and S.K. Rajamani (Eds.): SPIN 2003, LNCS 2648, pp. 213-224, 2003, Springer-Verlag Berlin Heidelberg 2003
7. Henzinger, T. A., Jhala, R., Majumdar, R., Qadeer, S., *Thread-modular Abstraction Refinement*, Proceedings of the 15th International Conference on Computer-Aided Verification (CAV), LNCS 2725, Springer-Verlag, pages 262-274, 2003.
8. Holzmann, G. J., *The model checker SPIN*, IEEE Transactions on Software Engineering, 23(5):279–295, May 1997.
9. Kozen, D., *Lower Bounds for Natural Proof Systems*. FOCS 1977, pp.261-262.
10. Muchnik, S. S., Jones, N. D., *Program Flow Analysis: Theory and Applications*, Prentice-Hall, Inc., Englewood Cliffs, New Jersey 07632

Capture-Avoiding Substitution
as a Nominal Algebra

Murdoch J. Gabbay[1] and Aad Mathijssen[2]

[1] School of Mathematical and Computer Sciences, Heriot-Watt University,
Edinburgh EH14 4AS, Scotland, Great Britain
murdoch.gabbay@gmail.com
[2] Department of Mathematics and Computer Science, Eindhoven University of
Technology, P.O. Box 513, 5600 MB Eindhoven, The Netherlands
A.H.J.Mathijssen@tue.nl

Abstract. Substitution is fundamental to computer science, underlying for example quantifiers in predicate logic and beta-reduction in the lambda-calculus. So is substitution something we define on syntax on a case-by-case basis, or can we turn the idea of 'substitution' into a mathematical object?

We exploit the new framework of Nominal Algebra to axiomatise substitution. We prove our axioms sound and complete with respect to a canonical model; this turns out to be quite hard, involving subtle use of results of rewriting and algebra.

1 Introduction

Substitution is intuitively the operation $v[a \mapsto t]$ meaning:

Replace the variable a by t in v.

Is there an algebra which describes exactly the properties of $v[a \mapsto t]$ independently of what v and t are (λ-terms, formulae of a logic, or any mixture or variation thereof)?

Consider by way of analogy the notion of 'a field'. This has an algebraic characterisation which tells us what properties 'a field' must have, independently of *which* field it is, or *how* it may be implemented (if we are programming). This is useful; for example the definition of 'vector space' is parametric over fields, and this step requires a characterisation of what fields are [1].

When we begin to algebraically axiomatise substitution some unusual difficulties present themselves. Consider the following informally expressed candidate property of substitution:

$$v[a \mapsto t][b \mapsto u] = v[b \mapsto u][a \mapsto t[b \mapsto u]] \qquad \text{provided } a \notin fv(u).$$

This is not algebraic, because of the side-condition $a \notin fv(u)$. Here $fv(u)$ is 'the free variables of u', which is a property of the syntax of u.

So is it the case that substitution *cannot* be axiomatised, and only exists as an incidental property of syntax used to talk about 'real' mathematical objects?

K. Barkaoui, A. Cavalcanti, and A. Cerone (Eds.): ICTAC 2006, LNCS 4281, pp. 198–212, 2006.

But in that case, what is the status of the intuition which makes us agree that the property above should be satisfied by any self-respecting substitution action?

We shall argue that the following properties axiomatise substitution, all of substitution, and nothing but substitution. We express them in Nominal Algebra (given formal meaning in the rest of this paper):

$$
\begin{array}{lll}
(\mathbf{var} \mapsto) & \vdash \mathsf{var}(a)[a \mapsto T] & = T \\
(\# \mapsto) & a\#X \vdash X[a \mapsto T] & = X \\
(\mathbf{f} \mapsto) & \vdash \mathsf{f}(X_1, \ldots, X_n)[a \mapsto T] & = \mathsf{f}(X_1[a \mapsto T], \ldots, X_n[a \mapsto T]) \quad (\mathsf{f} \neq \mathsf{var}) \\
(\mathbf{abs} \mapsto) & b\#T \vdash ([b]X)[a \mapsto T] & = [b](X[a \mapsto T]) \\
(\mathbf{ren} \mapsto) & b\#X \vdash X[a \mapsto \mathsf{var}(b)] & = (b\ a) \cdot X
\end{array}
$$

Fig. 1. Axioms of SUB

For convenience we now give an *informal* reading:

($\mathbf{var} \mapsto$): If a is a variable then a with a replaced by T, is T.

($\# \mapsto$): If a is fresh for X then X with a replaced by T is X.

($\mathbf{f} \mapsto$): Substitution distributes through term-formers (we can have as many as we like); f ranges over them.

($\mathbf{abs} \mapsto$): Substitution distributes under abstraction, provided an 'accidental capture-avoidance' condition holds (b is fresh for T).

($\mathbf{ren} \mapsto$): If b is fresh for X then X with a replaced by b is identical to X with a replaced by b and *simultaneously* b replaced by a.

Formally, Fig. 1 uses nominal terms [2] as a syntax, and nominal algebra [3] as an algebraic framework.

A number of questions now arise: a) Is this substitution? In what sense; are the axioms sound, and for what model? b) Are the axioms complete for that model? c) Do other (perhaps unexpected) models exist of the same axioms? d) Can the axioms be used to found theories of predicate logic, λ-calculus, unification, and so on?

Sections 2 and 3 define nominal terms and nominal algebra. Section 4 defines substitution as a nominal algebraic theory. Section 5 develops some highly non-trivial technical results. Section 6 answers a) by showing that on a canonical model, our axioms for substitution give rise to something which is recognisably substitution as we might expect it to behave. Section 7 further shows the harder property mentioned in b) that our axioms for substitution precisely characterise what is true of that concrete model. The Conclusions then describes related and future work. Questions c) and d) are answered positively in other papers [4, 5].

2   Nominal Terms

We define a syntax of nominal terms. For simplicity fix a **sort of atoms** $\mathbb{A}$ and a **(base) sort of terms** $\mathbb{T}$. Then **sorts** τ are inductively defined by:[1]

---

[1] So sorts are just $\mathbb{T}$, $[\mathbb{A}]\mathbb{T}$, $[\mathbb{A}][\mathbb{A}]\mathbb{T}$, and so on, and similarly $\mathbb{A}$, $[\mathbb{A}]\mathbb{A}$, and so on.

$$\tau ::= \mathbb{T} \mid \mathbb{A} \mid [\mathbb{A}]\tau$$

We could admit more sorts of atoms, and base sorts other than $\mathbb{T}$, if we wished.

Our syntax has term-formers: Fix **term-formers** f_ρ to each of which is associated some unique **arity** $\rho = (\tau_1, \ldots, \tau_n)\tau$. We may write $f : \rho$ for 'f, which has arity ρ'. We assume term-formers:

$$\mathsf{sub} : ([\mathbb{A}]\tau, \mathbb{T})\tau \ \ (\tau \in \{\mathbb{T}, [\mathbb{A}]\mathbb{T}\}) \ \ \ \mathsf{var} : (\mathbb{A})\mathbb{T} \ \ \ \mathsf{pair} : (\mathbb{T}, \mathbb{T})\mathbb{T} \ \ \ \mathsf{binder} : ([\mathbb{A}]\mathbb{T})\mathbb{T}$$

The two subs will be used to represent the substitutions from Fig. 1; the condition on τ is for simplicity only.

var, pair, and binder define a sufficiently rich language for our axioms of substitution to have an interesting action, but as mentioned in the Introduction *almost anything else would do* (e.g. see example signatures in [6]).

Finally, we can define the sorted syntax itself:

Fix some countably infinite set of **atoms** $a, b, c, \ldots \in \mathbb{A}$. These model object-level variable symbols (the ones we axiomatise substitution for).

Fix a countably infinite collection of **unknowns** $X, Y, Z, T, U, \ldots$.[2] Intuitively these represent unknown terms. We assume unknowns are inherently sorted and infinitely many populate each sort: so X is shorthand for X_τ, and $X_\mathbb{A}$ and $X_\mathbb{T}$ are two *different* unknowns with confusingly similar names.

Terms t, u, v are inductively defined by the following grammar:

$$t \ ::= \ a_\mathbb{A} \mid (\pi \cdot X_\tau)_\tau \mid ([a_\mathbb{A}]t_\tau)_{[\mathbb{A}]\tau} \mid (f_{(\tau_1, \ldots, \tau_n)\tau}(t^1_{\tau_1}, \ldots, t^n_{\tau_n}))_\tau$$

Here we call $(\pi \cdot X_\tau)_\tau$ a **moderated unknown**; π is described below. We have indicated sorts with a subscript but we shall usually omit them; we repeat the definition above without subscripts, for clarity:

$$t \ ::= \ a \mid \pi \cdot X \mid [a]t \mid f(t_1, \ldots, t_n).$$

A **permutation** π of atoms is a bijection on $\mathbb{A}$ with **finite support** meaning that for some finite set of atoms $\pi(a) \neq a$, and for all other atoms $\pi(a) = a$; in other words, for 'most' atoms π is the identity. As usual write **Id** for the **identity** permutation, π^{-1} for the **inverse** of π, and $\pi \circ \pi'$ for the **composition** of π and π', i.e. $(\pi \circ \pi')(a) = \pi(\pi'(a))$. **Id** is also the identity of composition, i.e. **Id** $\circ \pi = \pi$ and $\pi \circ$ **Id** $= \pi$. We may abbreviate **Id** $\cdot X$ to X. Importantly, we shall write $(a\ b)$ for the permutation which maps a to b and vice versa, and maps all other c to themselves.

In Fig. 1 we have sugared $\mathsf{sub}([a]u, t)$ to $u[a{\mapsto}t]$. We suggestively name a term of this form an **explicit substitution**.

A few more simple notations are useful for later: We call the **size of** t its *inductive rank*.[3] Write $a \in t$ (or $X \in t$) for 'a (or X) **occurs in (the syntax of)** t'. Occurrence is literal, e.g. $a \in [a]a$ and $a \in \pi \cdot X$ when $\pi(a) \neq a$. Similarly

---

[2] Unknowns, atoms, and term-formers, are assumed *disjoint*.

[3] In plain english: the depth of a proof that t *is* in the set of terms, using the inductive definition above.

write $a \notin t$ and $X \notin t$ for 'does not occur in the syntax of t'. Write **syntactic identity** of terms t, u as $t \equiv u$ to distinguish it from provable equality. *Important: we do not quotient terms in any way.*

It may help to show how nominal terms relate to 'ordinary' syntax. For convenience identify atoms with *variable symbols*, then the syntax of the untyped λ-calculus is inductively defined by $e ::= a \mid ee \mid \lambda a.e$. We define a map $(-)'$ to nominal terms by: $a' = \mathsf{var}(a)$, $(e_1 e_2)' = \mathsf{pair}(e_1', e_2')$, $(\lambda a.e)' = \mathsf{binder}([a](e'))$. Even for this simple signature of var, pair, and binder, there are interesting things to say. For example we shall see that $\mathsf{binder}([a]X)$ behaves much like the λ-context $\lambda a.-$ where - is a 'hole', and of course sub will allow us to state (and prove!) nontrivial properties of substitution in the presence of those holes. Example 4.1 gives three such properties; there are many more and our main result Theorem 7.5 asserts that we can prove all of them from our axioms.

3   Nominal Algebra

We can now do algebra. For us, algebra is the *logic of equality* (no implication, no quantification). We consider a canonical syntax-based model later in Section 6 and find much of interest to say about it in Section 7 — other models of our axioms are the topic of other work [4].

A **freshness (assertion)** is a pair $a\#t$ of an atom and a term. Call a freshness of the form $a\#X$ (so $t \equiv X$) **primitive**. Write Δ for a (possibly infinite) set of *primitive* freshnesses and call it a **freshness context**. We may drop set brackets in freshness contexts, e.g. writing $a\#X, b\#Y$ for $\{a\#X, b\#Y\}$. Also, we may write $a, b\#X$ for $a\#X, b\#X$. Define **derivability** on freshnesses in natural deduction style by:

$$\frac{}{a\#b}(\#\mathbf{ab}) \quad \frac{a\#t_1 \ \cdots \ a\#t_n}{a\#\mathsf{f}(t_1,\ldots,t_n)}(\#\mathbf{f}) \quad \frac{}{a\#[a]t}(\#[]\mathbf{a}) \quad \frac{a\#t}{a\#[b]t}(\#[]\mathbf{b}) \quad \frac{\pi^{-1}(a)\#X}{a\#\pi \cdot X}(\#\mathbf{X})$$

Here f ranges over term-formers,[4] t and $t_1,\ldots,t_n$ range over terms, X ranges over unknowns, and a and b *permutatively* range over atoms, i.e. a and b represent any two *distinct* atoms. We use similar conventions henceforth.

Write $\Delta \vdash a\#t$ when a derivation of $a\#t$ exists using the elements of Δ as assumptions. Say that Δ **entails** $a\#t$ or $a\#t$ **is derivable from** Δ; call this a **freshness judgement**.

An **equality (assertion)** is a pair $t = u$ where t and u are terms of the same sort. Define **derivability** on equalities in natural deduction style by:

$$\frac{}{t=t}(\mathbf{refl}) \quad \frac{t=u}{u=t}(\mathbf{symm}) \quad \frac{t=u \quad u=v}{t=v}(\mathbf{tran}) \quad \frac{t_1=u_1 \cdots t_n=u_n}{\mathsf{f}(t_1,\ldots,t_n)=\mathsf{f}(u_1,\ldots,u_n)}(\mathbf{congf})$$

$$\frac{t=u}{[a]t=[a]u}(\mathbf{cong}[]) \quad \frac{a\#t \quad b\#t}{(a\ b)\cdot t=t}(\mathbf{perm}) \quad \frac{\begin{array}{cc}[a\#X_1,\ldots,a\#X_n] & \Delta \\ \vdots & \\ t=u\end{array}}{t=u}(\mathbf{fr}) \quad (a \notin t,u,\Delta)$$

---

[4] More precisely, f is a *meta-variable* ranging over term-formers.

We may call this the **core theory** and refer to it as CORE. We may write $\Delta \vdash_{\mathsf{CORE}} t = u$ for '$t = u$ is derivable from assumptions Δ in the core theory'; call this an **equality judgement**.

In (**fr**) square brackets denote *discharge* in the sense of natural deduction, as in implication introduction [7]; Δ denotes the other assumptions of the derivation of $t = u$.[5] This is useful because unknowns in a derivation intuitively represent unknown terms, but any finite collection of such terms can mention only finitely many atoms; (**fr**) expresses that we can always find a fresh one.

In (**perm**) read $(a\ b) \cdot t$ as 'swap a and b in t'. It is defined on syntax by:

$$\pi \cdot a \equiv \pi(a) \qquad \pi \cdot (\pi' \cdot X) \equiv (\pi \circ \pi') \cdot X \qquad \pi \cdot [a]t \equiv [\pi(a)](\pi \cdot t)$$
$$\pi \cdot \mathsf{f}(t_1, \ldots, t_n) \equiv \mathsf{f}(\pi \cdot t_1, \ldots, \pi \cdot t_n)$$

So π propagates through the structure of t until it reaches an atom or a moderated unknown. We can easily verify that $(\pi \circ \pi') \cdot t \equiv \pi \cdot (\pi' \cdot t)$ and $\mathbf{Id} \cdot t \equiv t$. Here is an example derivation, using the fact that $[a]a \equiv (a\ b) \cdot [b]b$:

$$\cfrac{\cfrac{\cfrac{}{a\#b}\,(\#\mathbf{ab})}{a\#[b]b}\,(\#[]\mathbf{b}) \qquad \cfrac{}{b\#[b]b}\,(\#[]\mathbf{a})}{[a]a = [b]b}\,(\mathbf{perm})$$

Provable equality in CORE coincides with provable equality on nominal terms in the sense of nominal unification [2], for details see elsewhere [3]. This corresponds in a suitable sense to α-equivalence, though in a non-trivial way since $\vdash_{\mathsf{CORE}} [a]X = [b]X$ does not hold — but $b\#X \vdash_{\mathsf{CORE}} [a]X = [b](b\ a) \cdot X$ does [2].

Nominal Algebra (**NA**) is the theory outlined above, along with the ability to impose axioms. Call a triple $\Delta \vdash t = u$ where Δ is finite an **axiom**. We may write $\vdash t = u$ when Δ **is empty** (the empty set). Call an **instance** of an axiom a step in a derivation where the conclusion is obtained from an axiom by instantiating unknowns by terms,[6] and permutatively renaming atoms, such that the hypotheses are corresponding instances of freshness conditions of the axiom.

4   SUB: The Theory of Explicit Substitution

NA substitution allows the axioms in Fig. 1. Here (**f↦**) represents a schema of axioms, one for each term-former other than var; one particular example is (**sub↦**). We make *concrete* choices of atoms a and b, of an unknown T of sort $\mathbb{T}$, and of unknowns $X, X_1, \ldots, X_n$ of appropriate sorts. We call the axioms and the resulting equality a **theory of substitution** and write it SUB.

---

[5] In sequent style, (**fr**) would be $\cfrac{\Delta, a\#X_1, \ldots, a\#X_n \vdash t = u}{\Delta \vdash t = u}\ (a \notin t, u, \Delta)$.

[6] Instantiation of unknowns is mostly what the reader would expect: textual replacement of X by t. See Sect. 7.1 for the formal definition.

Example 4.1. The following judgements are derivable in SUB:

1. $a\#Y \vdash_{\mathsf{SUB}} Z[a \mapsto X][b \mapsto Y] = Z[b \mapsto Y][a \mapsto X[b \mapsto Y]]$
2. $b\#Z \vdash_{\mathsf{SUB}} Z[a \mapsto X] = ((b\ a) \cdot Z)[b \mapsto X]$
3. $\vdash_{\mathsf{SUB}} X[a \mapsto \mathsf{var}(a)] = X$

We give only the first derivation in full. We write σ for $[b \mapsto Y]$ and we use the unsugared syntax for the other substitutions.

$$\cfrac{}{\mathsf{sub}([a]Z, X)\sigma = \mathsf{sub}(([a]Z)\sigma, X\sigma)}\ (\mathbf{f}\mapsto) \qquad \cfrac{\cfrac{\cfrac{a\#Y}{([a]Z)\sigma = [a](Z\sigma)}\ (\mathbf{abs}\mapsto) \quad \cfrac{}{X\sigma = X\sigma}\ (\mathbf{refl})}{\mathsf{sub}(([a]Z)\sigma, X\sigma) = \mathsf{sub}([a](Z\sigma), X\sigma)}\ (\mathbf{congf})}{}$$

$$\cfrac{}{\mathsf{sub}([a]Z, X)\sigma = \mathsf{sub}([a](Z\sigma), X\sigma)}\ (\mathbf{tran})$$

For part 2: We must prove $b\#Z \vdash_{\mathsf{SUB}} \mathsf{sub}([a]Z, X) = \mathsf{sub}([b](b\ a) \cdot Z, X)$. By (**congf**), (**refl**), and (**symm**), it suffices to derive $[b](a\ b) \cdot Z = [a]Z$. Using (**perm**) it suffices to derive $a, b\#[a]Z$, which is easy.

For part 3: By (**fr**) we may assume $b\#X$ for some $b \notin X, X[a \mapsto \mathsf{var}(a)]$, i.e. $b \neq a$. By (**tran**) it suffices to derive $X[a \mapsto \mathsf{var}(a)] = ((b\ a) \cdot X)[b \mapsto \mathsf{var}(a)]$ and $((b\ a) \cdot X)[b \mapsto \mathsf{var}(a)] = X$. The former is an instance of part 2 of this example. For the latter it suffices to derive $a\#(b\ a) \cdot X$, by axiom (**ren** $\mapsto$) and $X \equiv (a\ b) \cdot (b\ a) \cdot X$. By (**#X**), this follows from the assumption $b\#X$.

5   SUBfr: Explicit Substitution Rewritten

Equality has no algorithmic content so we have specified *what* is equal, but not *how* to verify it. Rewriting is algorithmic in that sense, given confluence. It is useful to give a rewrite system for SUB.

Nominal rewriting is like nominal algebra, but with a directed notion of equality; terms are taken up to equality in CORE. A rewrite rule $\nabla \vdash l \to r$ may trigger a rewrite in a term t when (an instance of) l is provably equal in CORE to some subterm of t, and the corresponding instance of ∇ is derivable using the ambient context of freshness assumptions Δ (so ∇ is *freshness conditions* on the rewrite rule) [8, 9, 10]. Rewrite rules are given in Fig. 2. Write $\to_\Delta$ for the rewrite relation induced by rewrites in CORE, given Δ.

Say a freshness context Δ' **freshly extends** Δ when $\Delta' = \Delta \cup \Delta''$ where Δ'' may be empty, but if $a\#X \in \Delta''$ then $a \notin \Delta$. Note that the rule (**fr**) precisely 'introduces a Δ''. So $b\#X, a\#X$ freshly extends $a\#X$ but $a\#Y, a\#X$ does not.

Lemma 5.1 (Rewriting *is* equality). *$\Delta \vdash_{\mathsf{SUB}} t = u$ is derivable if and only if t is related to u by the symmetric transitive reflexive closure of $\to_{\Delta'}$ for some Δ' freshly extending Δ.*

Say a property holds of a triple (Δ, t, u) '**provided Δ has sufficient freshnesses**' when that property holds of some (Δ', t, u) for Δ' freshly extending Δ. So for Δ, t, and u, equality between t and u SUB coincides with rewritability between them in SUBfr, provided that Δ has sufficient freshnesses.

(**Rvar**)	$\vdash \mathsf{var}(a)[a \mapsto X]$	$\to X$
(**R#**)	$a\#Z \vdash Z[a \mapsto X]$	$\to Z$
(**Rf**)	$\vdash \mathsf{f}(Z_1, \dots, Z_n)[a \mapsto X]$	$\to \mathsf{f}(Z_1[a \mapsto X], \dots, Z_n[a \mapsto X])$ (f$\neq$var, sub)
(**Rsub**)	$a\#Y \vdash Z[a \mapsto X][b \mapsto Y]$	$\to Z[b \mapsto Y][a \mapsto X[b \mapsto Y]]$
(**Rabs**)	$c\#X \vdash ([c]Z)[a \mapsto X]$	$\to [c](Z[a \mapsto X])$
(**Rren**)	$b\#Z \vdash Z[a \mapsto \mathsf{var}(b)]$	$\to (b\ a) \cdot Z$

Fig. 2. Substitution as a rewrite system SUBfr

5.1 SUBe and Strong Normalisation Up to SUBe

Substitution has the character of a computation and our re-casting SUB as a rewrite system recognises this. However substitutions also have an awkward 'simultaneous' character. For example

$$\vdash_{\mathsf{SUB}} X[a \mapsto \mathsf{var}(a')][b \mapsto \mathsf{var}(b')][c \mapsto \mathsf{var}(c')] = X[c \mapsto \mathsf{var}(c')][b \mapsto \mathsf{var}(b')][a \mapsto \mathsf{var}(a')]$$

is derivable but there is no obvious direction to the equality and SUBfr does not strongly normalise on the terms.

Call a binary relation (by incredible coincidence write it $\to$) **strongly normalising** when if for $t_1, t_2, \dots$ we have $t_1 \to t_2 \to t_3 \to \dots$ then i exists such that if $j \geq i$ then $t_i = t_j$. Clearly this is not the case of any $\to_\Delta$ from SUBfr.

Let SUBe be the NA theory with axioms in Fig. 3.

(**Eswap**)	$a\#Y, b\#X \vdash Z[a \mapsto X][b \mapsto Y]$	$= Z[b \mapsto Y][a \mapsto X]$
(**Egarbage**)	$a\#Z \vdash Z[a \mapsto X]$	$= Z$

Fig. 3. The theory SUBe

Lemma 5.2. *The rules obtained from directing the equalities from* SUBe, *are admissible in* SUBfr, *i.e. every instance of the following can be obtained in* SUBfr:

(**Rswap**)	$a\#Y, b\#X \vdash Z[a \mapsto X][b \mapsto Y]$	$\to Z[b \mapsto Y][a \mapsto X]$
(**Rgarbage**)	$a\#Z \vdash Z[a \mapsto X]$	$\to Z$

As a corollary, provable equality in SUBe *implies provable equality in* SUB.

We will show that $\to$ of SUBfr is strongly normalising *up to* provable equality in SUBe. Some auxiliary functions and notations are needed.

Fix Δ and write $a\#v$ for $\Delta \vdash a\#v$ and $\neg a\#v$ for $\Delta \nvdash a\#v$. Let f range over all term-formers excluding sub (but including var), and let . denote the arithmetic product. Define $|v|_b$ by $|v|_b = 0$ if $b\#v$ and *only otherwise* by:

$$|a|_a = 1 \qquad |v[a \mapsto t]|_a = |t|_a + 1 \qquad |v[a \mapsto t]|_b = |v|_b \quad (a\#v)$$

$$|v[a \mapsto t]|_b = |v|_b \quad (\neg a\#v, b\#t) \qquad |v[a \mapsto t]|_b = |v|_b + |t|_b . |v|_a + 1 \quad (\neg a\#v, \neg b\#t)$$

$$|\mathsf{f}(v_1, \dots, v_n)|_b = |v_1|_b + \dots + |v_n|_b + 1 \qquad |[a]v|_b = |v|_b + 1 \qquad |\pi \cdot X|_a = 1$$

Then the following inductive definition makes Theorem 5.3 a matter of easy arithmetic:

$$|\mathsf{f}(v_1, \ldots, v_n)| = |v_1| + \cdots + |v_n| \quad (n > 0) \qquad |\mathsf{f}()| = 1 \qquad |[a]v| = |v|$$
$$|\pi \cdot X| = 1 \qquad |a| = 1 \qquad |v[a \mapsto t]| = |t|.|v|_a + |v|$$

Theorem 5.3. *If $t \to_\Delta t'$ then either $\Delta \vdash_{\mathsf{SUBe}} t = t'$ or $|t|^\Delta > |t'|^\Delta$. As a result* SUBfr *is strongly normalising up to provable equality in* SUBe.

Write $\to_\Delta^*$ for the transitive reflexive (but not symmetric) closure of $\to_\Delta$. We note that $\Delta \vdash_{\mathsf{SUBe}} t = u$ does *not* imply $t \to_\Delta^* u$ or $u \to_\Delta^* t$. For a counterexample consider $t \equiv \mathsf{var}(a)[b \mapsto \mathsf{var}(c)]$ and $u \equiv \mathsf{var}(a)[b \mapsto \mathsf{var}(c')]$.

5.2   Garbage and Garbage-Collection

Call the pair $\Delta \vdash t$ a (nominal) **term-in-context**. Equalities, and rewrites, are on terms *in context*. Only if t is closed is context irrelevant.

Say that a term-in-context $\Delta \vdash t$ has **garbage** when:

- for some subterm $t'[a \mapsto u]$ it is the case that $\Delta \vdash a\#t'$, or
- for some subterm of the form $\pi \cdot X$ and some $a \in \pi \cdot X$, it is the case that both $\Delta \vdash a\#X$ and $\Delta \vdash \pi(a)\#X$ hold.

Otherwise say $\Delta \vdash t$ has **no garbage**.

Example 5.4. Terms in the top line have no garbage, the others do:

$$\vdash \mathsf{var}(a)[a \mapsto X] \qquad \vdash X[a \mapsto Y] \qquad a\#X \vdash (a\,b) \cdot X$$
$$\vdash \mathsf{var}(a)[b \mapsto X] \quad a\#X \vdash X[a \mapsto Y] \quad a, b\#X \vdash (a\,b) \cdot X \quad a, b\#X \vdash ((a\,b) \cdot X)[c \mapsto \mathsf{var}(c')].$$

Alas the rewrite rule (**Rsub**) in SUBfr may introduce garbage (the innermost $[b \mapsto Y]$ acting on X). Alas also, α-equivalence (provable equality in CORE) may introduce garbage, for example $a, b\#X \vdash_{\mathsf{CORE}} (a\,b) \cdot X = X$.[7]

Say that $\Delta \vdash t$ is a SUBfr-**normal form** when $\Delta \vdash_{\mathsf{SUBe}} t = t'$ for all t' with $t \to_\Delta t'$. So a SUBfr-normal form may still rewrite with a rule from SUBfr ((**R#**) and (**Rsub**) to be precise) but that rewrite just has no effect up to provable equality in SUBe.

Lemma 5.5 (Garbage collection). *For any $\Delta \vdash t$ there is some t' a* SUBfr-*normal form with no garbage such that $t \to_\Delta^* t'$. Furthermore, if $\Delta \vdash_{\mathsf{SUBe}} t = u$ is derivable then there is some* SUBfr-*normal form v with no garbage such that $t \to_\Delta^* v$ and $u \to_\Delta^* v$.*

5.3   Confluence

A standard way to prove confluence is to prove *local* confluence and strong normalisation. But SUBfr is not strongly normalising, see the example of Sect. 5.1. The interest of this proof is that we use SUBe to 'cancel that out'.

Lemma 5.6. *Rewrites of $\Delta \vdash t$ in the nominal rewrite system* SUBfr *are locally confluent in a context with sufficient freshnesses, up to provable equivalence in* CORE.

---

[7] This is one reason SUB is a difficult beast to handle, and it took us quite a while to decide to split it up as a rewrite system over a provable equality, and then which provable equality to use.

(Recall that the restriction on contexts is not a 'real' one, because we have (**fr**).)

Theorem 5.7. SUBfr *is confluent in a context with sufficient freshnesses.*

Proof. SUBfr is strongly normalising up to provable equality in SUBe by Theorem 5.3. It is locally confluent (in a context with sufficient freshnesses) by Lemma 5.6. By Newman's Lemma [11] it is confluent up to provable equality in SUBe. Finally, we use the second part of Lemma 5.5.   □

From this follow:

Theorem 5.8. SUB *is conservative over* CORE. *That is,* $\Delta \vdash_{SUB} t = u$ *if and only if* $\Delta \vdash_{CORE} t = u$, *assuming that neither* t *nor* u *mention explicit substitution.*

Corollary 5.9 (Consistency). *For all* Δ *there are* t, u *such that* $\Delta \not\vdash_{SUB} t = u$.

6   Ground Terms

Call terms g and h **ground terms** when they do not mention unknowns or explicit substitutions. These are inductively characterised by

$$g ::= a \mid \mathsf{f}(g, \ldots, g) \mid [a]g$$

where f ranges over all term-formers except for sub.

We consider the **meaning of explicit substitution** on ground terms (making a connection between $[a \mapsto t]$ and actual capture-avoiding substitution on syntax).

Define a 'free atoms of' function $fa(g)$ on ground terms inductively as follows:

$$fa(a) = \{a\} \quad fa(\mathsf{f}(g_1, \ldots, g_n)) = \bigcup_{1 \le i \le n} fa(g_i) \quad fa([a]g) = fa(g) \setminus \{a\}$$

Define the **support** of g by $\mathrm{supp}(g) = \{a \mid \not\vdash a\#g\}$.

Lemma 6.1. $fa(g) = \mathrm{supp}(g)$.

For each finite set of atoms arbitrarily choose some canonical 'fresh' atom not in that finite set. Then define a **ground substitution action** $g[h/a]$ on ground terms of sort $\mathbb{T}$ and $[\mathbb{A}]\mathbb{T}$ by

$$\mathsf{var}(b)[h/a] \equiv \mathsf{var}(b) \quad \mathsf{var}(a)[h/a] \equiv h \quad \mathsf{f}(g_1, \ldots, g_n)[h/a] \equiv \mathsf{f}(g_1[h/a], \ldots, g_n[h/a])$$
$$([a]g)[h/a] \equiv [a]g \quad ([b]g)[h/a] \equiv [b](g[h/a]) \quad (b \notin fa(h))$$
$$([b]g)[h/a] \equiv [c](g[\mathsf{var}(c)/b][h/a]) \quad (b \in fa(h), \ c \text{ fresh}),$$

where f ranges over all term-formers excluding var (and sub of course), and 'c fresh' means c is fresh for $\{a, b\} \cup fa(g) \cup fa(h)$ according to our arbitrary choice.

Theorem 6.2. $\vdash_{SUB} g[h/a] = g[a \mapsto h]$ *is always derivable.*

Proof. By straightforward induction on the structure of g, using Lemma 6.1.   □

Define an α-equivalence relation $g =_\alpha h$ inductively by:

$$a =_\alpha a \qquad \frac{g_1 =_\alpha h_1 \cdots g_n =_\alpha h_n}{\mathsf{f}(g_1, \ldots, g_n) =_\alpha \mathsf{f}(h_1, \ldots, h_n)} \qquad \frac{g =_\alpha h}{[a]g =_\alpha [a]h} \qquad \frac{g[\mathsf{var}(c)/a] =_\alpha h[\mathsf{var}(c)/b]}{[a]g =_\alpha [b]h} \ (c \text{ fresh})$$

Here 'c fresh' means c fresh for $\{a, b\} \cup fa(g) \cup fa(h)$.

Theorem 6.3. *$g =_\alpha h$ if and only if $\vdash_{\mathsf{SUB}} g = h$ is derivable.*

Proof. By Theorem 5.8 $\vdash_{\mathsf{SUB}} g = h$ is equivalent to $\vdash_{\mathsf{CORE}} g = h$. By results about nominal terms [2, 3] this happens *precisely* when $g =_\alpha h$. □

So intuitively: *On ground terms $\vdash_{\mathsf{SUB}} g = h$ is α-equivalence and explicit substitution is capture-avoiding substitution.*

7 ω-Completeness

How do we know that SUB *really is* an axiomatisation of substitution? We now give a soundness and completeness result. ω-completeness (notation from [12]) is 'soundness and completeness with respect to the closed term model'.

We need a number of technical definitions and lemmas.

7.1 Meta-level Substitution

Call a **substitution** σ a finitely supported function from unknowns to terms of the same sort. Here, finite support means that $\sigma(X) \equiv \mathbf{Id} \cdot X$ for all but finitely many unknowns X, i.e. for 'most' X.

Write $[t/X]$ for σ defined by $\sigma(X) \equiv t$ and $\sigma(Y) \equiv \mathbf{Id} \cdot Y$, for all $Y \not\equiv X$.

Let $t\sigma$ ('σ **applied to** t') be inductively defined by:

$$a\sigma \equiv a \quad (\pi \cdot X)\sigma \equiv \pi \cdot \sigma(X) \quad ([a]t)\sigma \equiv [a](t\sigma) \quad \mathsf{f}(t_1, \ldots, t_n)\sigma \equiv \mathsf{f}(t_1\sigma, \ldots, t_n\sigma)$$

We may call $t\sigma$ an **instance** of t. The substitution action extends to freshness assertions, equalities, and so on. We extend notations and terminologies silently. Note that this does not avoid capture; $([a]X)[a/X] \equiv [a]a$ and in this formal sense X is 'meta' and really does represent an unknown *term*.

Call σ **nontrivial on** X when $\sigma(X) \not\equiv \mathbf{Id} \cdot X$. By assumption σ is nontrivial for only finitely many unknowns. Say that σ' **extends** σ when $\sigma'(X) \equiv \sigma(X)$ whenever σ is nontrivial on X. Call σ **closing** for some collection of freshness and equality assertions S when $\sigma(X)$ is a closed term for every $X \in S$. We will not mention S when it is clear from the context.

Say a closing σ is Δ-**consistent** when $\vdash a\#\sigma(X)$ for all $a\#X \in \Delta$.

Lemma 7.1. *Fix Δ, X, and closed term v. If $\vdash a\#v$ for every $a\#X \in \Delta$ then there is a Δ-consistent closing σ which extends $[v/X]$.*

7.2 Suspended Explicit Substitutions

Suppose a term-in-context $\Delta \vdash t \equiv (\pi \cdot t')[a_1 \mapsto t_1] \ldots [a_m \mapsto t_m]$ is such that $\Delta \vdash a_i\#t_j$ for all $1 \leq i, j \leq m$. Here m may equal 0, in which case $t \equiv (\pi \cdot t')$.

Then call the partial syntax $(\pi \cdot -)[a_1 \mapsto t_1] \ldots [a_m \mapsto t_m]$ a **suspended substitution**; we generally let α and β vary over suspended substitutions. β will typically be $(\pi' \cdot -)[b_1 \mapsto u_1] \ldots [b_n \mapsto u_n]$. Suspended substitutions have a natural action on terms $t'\alpha$ given by replacing - by t'.

Lemma 7.2. *Assuming sufficient freshnesses, if $\Delta \vdash t$ is a SUBfr-normal form with no garbage then every explicit substitution t mentions is in a subterm u such that $\Delta \vdash_{\mathsf{CORE}} u = X\alpha$ and $\Delta \vdash X\alpha$ has no garbage.*

Proof. Otherwise there is a rewrite such that $\Delta \vdash t \to t'$ where $\Delta \nvdash_{\mathsf{SUBe}} t = t'$. □

Lemma 7.3. *Suppose t and u are SUBfr-normal forms with no garbage. Then $\Delta \vdash_{\mathsf{SUBe}} t = u$ precisely when one of the following hold:*

1. $t \equiv a$ *and* $u \equiv a$.
2. $t \equiv \pi \cdot X$ *and* $u \equiv \pi \cdot X$.
3. $t \equiv [a]t'$ *and* $u \equiv [a]u'$ *and* $\Delta \vdash_{\mathsf{SUBe}} t' = u'$.
4. $t \equiv [a]t'$ *and* $u \equiv [b]u'$ *and* $\Delta \vdash_{\mathsf{SUBe}} (b\ a) \cdot t' = u'$ *and* $\Delta \vdash b \# t'$.
5. $t \equiv \mathsf{f}(t_1, \ldots, t_n)$ *and* $u \equiv \mathsf{f}(u_1, \ldots, u_n)$ *and* $\Delta \vdash_{\mathsf{SUBe}} t_i = u_i$ *for* $1 \le i \le n$
   ($\mathsf{f} \ne \mathsf{sub}$).
6. $t \equiv t'\alpha$ *and* $u \equiv u'\beta$ *and* $m = n > 0$ *and* $\Delta \vdash_{\mathsf{SUBe}} t' = u'$, *and for every i there
   is a unique j such that* $\pi^{-1}(a_i) = \pi'^{-1}(b_j)$ *and* $\Delta \vdash_{\mathsf{SUBe}} t_i = u_j$ — *and similarly
   for every j.*

Theorem 7.4. *Equality in SUB is decidable.*

Proof. Given Δ, t and u, we can calculate whether $\Delta \vdash_{\mathsf{SUB}} t = u$ is derivable:

1. Rewrite t and u to SUBfr-normal forms t' and u', using Theorem 5.3.
2. Remove garbage from t' and u', using Lemma 5.5.
3. Check if the top-level term-formers of t' and u' satisfy the criteria stated
   in Lemma 7.3; for each of the new proof obligations $\Delta \vdash_{\mathsf{SUBe}} t'' = u''$ go to
   step 2.[8]
4. If all criteria checks were successful, return true; otherwise false.   □

7.3 ω-Completeness

ω-completeness is soundness and completeness with respect to a model made
out of closed terms (terms which do not mention unknowns X); since syntax *is* the canonical example on which substitution is defined, soundness *and*
completeness with respect to this model is a powerful argument that in theory SUB, we got it right. An NA judgement $\Delta \vdash_{\mathsf{SUB}} t = u$ has the flavour of
a universal quantification over the unknowns it mentions. Soundness for the
closed terms model means: if $\Delta \vdash_{\mathsf{SUB}} t = u$ is derivable then all *instances* of
this equality (subject to Δ) on closed terms are derivable. Much harder to
prove is that furthermore if all instances are derivable (subject to Δ), then
so is $\Delta \vdash_{\mathsf{SUB}} t = u$.

Call SUB ω-**complete** when if $\vdash_{\mathsf{SUB}} t\sigma = u\sigma$ is derivable for all Δ-consistent
closing substitutions σ (for Δ, t and u), then $\Delta \vdash_{\mathsf{SUB}} t = u$ is derivable.

---

[8] Garbage could be introduced by case 4 of Lemma 7.3, so we must remove it.

Theorem 7.5. SUB *is ω-complete.*

Proof. By contraposition. Suppose *not* $\Delta \vdash_{\mathsf{SUB}} t = u$. We construct Δ-consistent σ such that *not* $\vdash_{\mathsf{SUB}} t\sigma = u\sigma$. It suffices to do this for some Δ' which freshly extends Δ; for convenience assume $\Delta = \Delta'$. By the first part of Lemma 5.5 and by Lemma 5.1 we may suppose t and u are SUBfr-normal forms with no garbage. By Lemma 7.2 further assume they have the particular form mentioned in that result. By Lemma 5.2 also $\Delta \vdash_{\mathsf{SUBe}} t = u$ is not derivable. So now we must prove

$$\left(\Delta \nvdash_{\mathsf{SUBe}} t = u\right) \quad \text{implies} \quad \left(\exists \sigma \text{ closing and } \Delta\text{-consistent. } \nvdash_{\mathsf{SUB}} t\sigma = u\sigma\right),$$

where t and u have the structure as described above.

We work by induction on the size of t and u. We proceed by case distinction (we omit routine cases, and calculations concerning size):

- $t \equiv a$ and $u \equiv b$.   By Theorem 6.3.
- $t \equiv \mathsf{f}(t_1, \ldots, t_m)$ and $u \equiv \mathsf{g}(u_1, \ldots, u_n)$ ($\mathsf{f}, \mathsf{g} \neq \mathsf{sub}$).   Apply *any* closing Δ-consistent σ (easy to manufacture), use Theorem 6.2 to remove all explicit substitutions, and then use Theorem 6.3 to conclude $\nvdash_{\mathsf{SUB}} t\sigma = u\sigma$.
- $t \equiv \mathsf{f}(t_1, \ldots, t_m)$ and $u \equiv \mathsf{f}(u_1, \ldots, u_m)$ ($\mathsf{f} \neq \mathsf{sub}$).   By part 5 of Lemma 7.3 $\Delta \nvdash_{\mathsf{SUBe}} t_i = u_i$ for some i. We use the inductive hypothesis and Theorems 6.2 and 6.3.
- $t \equiv [a]t'$ and $u \equiv [b]u'$.   Using Lemma 7.3 $\Delta \nvdash_{\mathsf{SUBe}} (b\ a) \cdot t' = u'$ or $\Delta \nvdash b\#t'$. If $\Delta \nvdash b\#t'$, then choose appropriate σ and use Theorems 6.2 and 6.3. If $\Delta \nvdash_{\mathsf{SUBe}} (b\ a) \cdot t' = u'$ then we can remove possible garbage from $(b\ a) \cdot t'$ without increasing size, apply the inductive hypothesis, and finally use Theorems 6.2 and 6.3.
- $t \equiv X\alpha$ and $u \equiv X\beta$ and $m = n > 0$.   Using Lemma 7.3 and notation from that result, $\Delta \vdash_{\mathsf{SUBe}} t = u$ precisely when $\Delta \vdash_{\mathsf{SUBe}} t_i = u_j$ for every i, j such that $\pi^{-1}(a_i) = \pi'^{-1}(b_j)$. So suppose i and j are such that $\Delta \nvdash_{\mathsf{SUBe}} t_i = u_j$. Now using pair, var, and binder, generate v such that $a_i \in \mathrm{supp}(v)$ and $\mathrm{supp}(v)$ is otherwise fresh (thus, disjoint from atoms mentioned in t and u). Choose Δ-consistent closing σ extending $[v/X]$ using Lemma 7.1. Then by Theorems 6.2 and 6.3 we see that $\nvdash_{\mathsf{SUB}} t\sigma = u\sigma$.   □

8   Conclusions

Substitution underlies quantifiers in predicate logics, the λ-binder of the λ-calculus, unification, and lots more besides. It is a *central*, not incidental, feature of these systems. This paper throws a new and unexpected light on this profoundly important common denominator.

Future work on nominal techniques needs a *nominal* axiomatisation of substitution. This paper provides that and the work has already found application in concurrent work; we use it to 'power' a nominal axiomatisation of first-order logic [5], and we develop abstract (non-term-based) models of SUB in [4]. Such enterprises would not be mathematically secure without Theorem 7.5 to tell us that we got our foundations right.

We have considered *one* substitution and Theorem 7.5 tells us it is capture-avoiding substitution. We can think of other kinds of substitution, for example context substitution which does not avoid capture; the basic principles are clear in this paper and there are a great many possibilities for applying them elsewhere.

Note how we decompose an equational system into a rewrite system over a simpler equational system, and we fully exploit results of nominal rewriting and nominal algebra as well as detailed calculations on terms (such as the notion of measure we use to prove confluence). Similar techniques may be useful for other systems; they seemed to arise in our treatment of first-order logic [5].

We find the nominal terms treatment of binding pleasingly clean; a nominal term such as $\lambda[a]X$ or $\forall[a]X$ corresponds *exactly* and *syntax-for-syntax* to what we intend when we write $\lambda a.t$ and $\forall a.\phi$, right down to the way in which t and ϕ are instantiated. Other approaches to binding involve some degree of emulation (index lifting in de Bruijn [13], type-raising in type-based techniques [14]). Thus a *nominal* treatment of substitution is worthwhile to investigate in itself.

8.1   Related Work

Crabbé [15, 16] axiomatises substitution much like us and shares (in our terminology) atoms and freshness conditions. Crabbé does not treat binding.[9] So our substitution is *capture-avoiding*. Also, for us atoms and freshness side-conditions are parts of a broader nominal framework whereas Crabbé expresses them in first-order logic; we feel that nominal techniques have given us a cleaner separation of the layers of complexity hidden in these deceptively simple ideas.

Feldman [17] gives an algebraic axiomatisation inspired by a concrete model of functions/evaluations. His axioms are closer in spirit to Cylindric Algebras [1] and Lambda Abstraction Algebras [18, 19]. The three approaches share an infinity of term-formers which are 'morally' precisely $\lambda[a]$, $-[a \mapsto -]$, and $\exists[a]$. We see the advantage of our treatment as systematising and formalising precisely what rôle the atoms really have. In any case the approaches above *cannot directly express* (**ren**$\mapsto$), (#$\mapsto$), and (**abs**$\mapsto$), even though instantiations are derivable for closed terms by calculations parametric over their specific structure.

Combinatory Algebra (CA) [20] and related systems implement substitution by 'pipes' (e.g. the translation of λ-terms into CA [20]). General truths such as (#$\mapsto$) are only provable for fixed closed terms by calculations parametric over its specific structure.

Lescanne's classic survey [13] and the thesis of Bloo [21] chart a vast literature on λ-calculi with explicit substitutions. These decompose β-reduction as a rule to introduce explicit substitution ($(\lambda a.u)t \rightarrow u[a \mapsto t]$), and explicit rules for that substitution's subsequent behaviour (which is to substitute, of course). These calculi are designed to measure the cost of a β-reduction (in an implementation, which may be based on de Bruijn indexes [22] or on named variable

---

[9] He declares as much: '... we are not concerned with the notion of bound variable' [16, page 2]. See also the axioms (there is no (**abs**$\mapsto$)) and the soundness and completeness result — Crabbé's model is based on (in our notation) var and pair, whereas we consider a model based on var, pair, binder, and sub.

symbols). They do not *axiomatise* substitution, they *implement* it. For example, 'confluence' is a typical correctness criterion for a calculus, and 'ω-completeness' is not.

8.2   Future Work

Nominal unification [2] is 'merely' unification of nominal terms up to CORE. Our confluence results are a step towards unification up to SUB. Nominal Unification is to be compared (in a sense we do not discuss here) with higher-order patterns [23]; we now suggest that unification up to SUB is to be compared with higher-order unification [24] — with the difference that SUB is weaker, because there is no λ and application, only their combination as 'substitution'.

There is no obstacle to taking SUB *over itself* — that is, to taking what we write in this paper as, say, $(X[a \mapsto Y])[t/X]$ and expressing it in a stronger axiom system as $(X[a \mapsto Y])[X \mapsto T]$ where T is a 'stronger' meta-variable. This relates to the NEW calculus of contexts [25] and hierarchical nominal rewriting [26] investigated by the first author, but much more is possible and there are many substitutions out there which we could axiomatise.

Armed with SUB and the knowledge that it is correct in the sense of Theorem 7.5 we hope to develop logics and λ-calculi with a fundamentally new, beautiful, and mathematically advantageous, way of treating substitution and more generally internalising the meta-level.

References

[1] Burris, S., Sankappanavar, H.: A Course in Universal Algebra. Springer (1981) Available online.
[2] Urban, C., Pitts, A.M., Gabbay, M.J.: Nominal unification. Theoretical Computer Science **323**(1–3) (2004) 473–497
[3] Gabbay, M.J., Mathijssen, A.: Nominal algebra. Submitted STACS'07 (2006)
[4] Gabbay, M.J., Bulò, S.R., Marin, A.: Substitution as an abstract notion: holy functions! Submitted STACS'07 (2006)
[5] Gabbay, M.J., Mathijssen, A.: One-and-a-halfth-order logic. In: PPDP '06: Proceedings of the 8th ACM SIGPLAN symposium on Principles and practice of declarative programming, New York, NY, USA, ACM Press (2006) 189–200
[6] Gabbay, M.J., Pitts, A.M.: A new approach to abstract syntax with variable binding. Formal Aspects of Computing **13**(3–5) (2001) 341–363
[7] Hodges, W.: Elementary predicate logic. In Gabbay, D., Guenthner, F., eds.: Handbook of Philosophical Logic, 2nd Edition. Volume 1. Kluwer (2001) 1–131
[8] Fernández, M., Gabbay, M.J., Mackie, I.: Nominal rewriting systems. In: Proc. 6th Int. ACM SIGPLAN Conf. on Principles and Practice of Declarative Programming (PPDP'2004), ACM (2004) 108–119
[9] Fernández, M., Gabbay, M.J.: Nominal rewriting. Journal version, submitted Information and Computation (2005)
[10] Fernández, M., Gabbay, M.J.: Nominal rewriting with name generation: abstraction vs. locality. In: Proc. 7th Int. ACM SIGPLAN Conf. on Principles and Practice of Declarative Programming (PPDP'2005), ACM (2005) 47–58

[11] Newman, M.: On theories with a combinatorial definition of equivalence. Annals of Mathematics **43**(2) (1942) 223–243

[12] Groote, J.F.: A new strategy for proving omega-completeness applied to process algebra. In Baeten, J., Klop, J., eds.: CONCUR '90: Proceedings of the Theories of Concurrency: Unification and Extension. Volume 458 of LNCS., London, UK, Springer-Verlag (1990) 314–331

[13] Lescanne, P.: From lambda-sigma to lambda-upsilon a journey through calculi of explicit substitutions. In: POPL '94: Proc. 21st ACM SIGPLAN-SIGACT Symposium on Principles of Programming Languages, ACM Press (1994) 60–69

[14] Paulson, L.C.: The foundation of a generic theorem prover. Journal of Automated Reasoning **5**(3) (1989) 363–397

[15] Crabbé, M.: Une axiomatisation de la substitution. Comptes rendus de l'Académie des Sciences de Paris, Série I **338** (2004) 433–436

[16] Crabbé, M.: On the notion of substitution. Logic Journal of the IGPL **12 n.2** (2004) 111–124

[17] Feldman, N.: Axiomatization of polynomial substitution algebras. Journal of Symbolic Logic **47**(3) (1982) 481–492

[18] Lusin, S., Salibra, A.: The lattice of lambda theories. Journal of Logic and Computation **14 n.3** (2004) 373–394

[19] Salibra, A.: On the algebraic models of lambda calculus. Theoretical Computer Science **249**(1) (2000) 197–240

[20] Barendregt, H.P.: The Lambda Calculus: its Syntax and Semantics (revised ed.). Volume 103 of Studies in Logic and the Foundations of Mathematics. North-Holland (1984)

[21] Bloo, R.: Preservation of Termination for Explicit Substitution. PhD thesis, Eindhoven University of Technology, Eindhoven (1997)

[22] de Bruijn, N.G.: Lambda calculus notation with nameless dummies, a tool for automatic formula manipulation, with application to the church-rosser theorem. Indagationes Mathematicae **5**(34) (1972) 381–392

[23] Miller, D.: A logic programming language with lambda-abstraction, function variables, and simple unification. Extensions of Logic Programming **475** (1991) 253–281

[24] Huet, G.: Higher order unification 30 years later. In: TPHOL 2002. Number 2410 in LNCS (2002) 3–12

[25] Gabbay, M.J.: A new calculus of contexts. In: Proc. 7th Int. ACM SIGPLAN Conf. on Principles and Practice of Declarative Programming (PPDP'2005), ACM (2005)

[26] Gabbay, M.J.: Hierarchical nominal rewriting. In: LFMTP'2006. (2006) 32–47

Prime Decomposition Problem for Several Kinds of Regular Codes

Kieu Van Hung and Do Long Van

[1] Hanoi Pedagogical University No. 2, Vietnam
hungkv@hn.vnn.vn
[2] Institute of Mathematics, VAST, Vietnam
dlvan@math.ac.vn

Abstract. Given a class C of codes. A regular code in C is called prime if it cannot be decomposed as a catenation of at least two non-trivial regular codes in C. The prime decomposition problem for the class C of codes consists in decomposing regular codes in C into prime factors in C. In this paper, a general approach to this problem is proposed, by means of which solutions for the prime decomposition problem are obtained, in a unified way, for several classes of codes. These classes are all subclasses of prefix codes and can be defined by binary relations.

Keywords: Code, invariant relation, prime decomposition problem.

1 Introduction

Throughout the paper about codes we mean length-variable codes whose theory has been initiated by M. P. Schützenberger and then developed by many others. Codes are closely related to formal languages. A code is a language such that every text encoded by words of the language can be decoded in a unique way or, in other words, every encoded message admits only one factorization into code-words. For background of the theory of codes we refer to [1,12,15].

Codes are useful in many areas of application such as information processing, data compression, cryptography, information transmission and so on (see [12]). A prefix code (suffix code) is a language such that no word is a prefix (suffix, resp.) of another word in it. Prefix codes and suffix codes play a fundamental role in the theory of codes as well as in applications. They are classified by means of different relations on code-words such as being prefix (suffix, infix, outfix, ...) of each other. These relations define different classes of prefix codes (suffix codes), such as those of bifix codes [1], infix codes, outfix codes [10,11], hypercodes [15], subinfix codes [6,7], supercodes [16] and so on.

A. Mateescu, A. Salomaa, and S. Yu [13,14] examined prime decompositions for regular languages and showed that it is decidable whether or not a given regular language has a decomposition and that, in general, the prime decomposition is not unique. J. Czyzowicz et al. [2] studied the prime decomposition problem for the class of prefix codes and proved that the prime decomposition of a regular prefix code is unique. They also demonstrated the importance of

K. Barkaoui, A. Cavalcanti, and A. Cerone (Eds.): ICTAC 2006, LNCS 4281, pp. 213–227, 2006.

the prime decomposition for prefix codes in practice. Recently, Y. -S. Han et al. [3] examined the prime decomposition problem for regular infix codes and showed that the prime decomposition in this case is not unique. An algorithm for testing the primality of regular infix codes was designed. Also, it was shown that the prime decomposition can be computed in polynomial time. Then, in [4] these authors demonstrated the uniqueness of the prime decomposition for regular outfix codes. A linear-time algorithm to compute the prime decomposition for regular outfix codes was designed.

In this paper, a general approach to the prime decomposition problem is proposed. As applications, solutions for the prime decomposition problem are obtained, in a unified way, for several classes of codes. These classes are all subclasses of prefix codes and can be defined by binary relations. In Section 2 necessary definitions are recalled, and several facts useful in the sequel are shown. Section 3 presents a general approach to the prime decomposition problem which consists of several general prime decomposition theorems (Theorems 1-3). This is based mainly on the notion of (strong) bridge states in the minimal finite-state automata recognizing codes. In Section 4 the general approach is used to consider the prime decomposition problem for several classes of codes, namely those of bifix codes, infix codes, subinfix codes, outfix codes, hypercodes, supercodes and uniform codes. We show that the minimal finite-state automaton recognizing a code in each of these classes of codes has k strong bridge states if and only if the code can be decomposed uniquely into $k+1$ prime factors in the corresponding class of codes (Theorem 6). Moreover, for regular outfix codes, hypercodes, supercodes and uniform codes, the primality can be tested and the unique prime decomposition can be computed in $O(\mu)$ time, where μ is the size of the minimal finite-state automaton recognizing the corresponding code (Theorem 7). For regular bifix codes it takes $O(m^3)$, where m is the number of states (Theorem 8). Note that, the prime decomposition problem for finite codes is not trivial at all because the primality test for finite languages is believed to be NP-complete [14]. Our work is motivated by the idea to define codes as independent sets with respect to a binary relation [10,15], and the way to solve the prime decomposition problem for regular infix codes [3] and regular outfix codes [4].

2   Preliminaries

Let A throughout be a finite alphabet and A^* the set of all the words over A. The empty word is denoted by 1 and A^+ stands for $A^* - \{1\}$. The number of all the occurrences of letters in a word u is the *length* of u, denoted by $|u|$. Any subset of A^* is a *language* over A. A language X is a *code* if for any $n, m \geq 1$ and any $x_1, \ldots, x_n, y_1, \ldots, y_m \in X$, the condition

$$x_1 x_2 \ldots x_n = y_1 y_2 \ldots y_m$$

implies $n = m$ and $x_i = y_i$ for $i = 1, \ldots, n$. Since $1.1 = 1$, a code never contains the empty word 1. It is clear that, the empty set is a code and called a *trivial* code.

Given a binary relation $\prec$ on A^*. A subset X in A^* is an *independent set* with respect to the relation $\prec$ if any two elements of X are not in this relation. A class C of codes is said to be *defined by* $\prec$ if these codes are exactly the independent sets w.r.t. $\prec$. The class C is then denoted by $C_\prec$. When the relation $\prec$ characterizes some property α of words, instead of $\prec$ we write $\prec_\alpha$, and also C_α stands for $C_{\prec_\alpha}$. We denote by $\preceq$ the reflexive closure of $\prec$, i.e. for any $u, v \in A^*, u \preceq v$ iff $u = v$ or $u \prec v$.

A word u is called an *infix* (a *prefix*, a *suffix*) of a word v if there exist words x, y such that $v = xuy$ ($v = uy$, $v = xu$, resp.). The infix (prefix, suffix) is *proper* if $xy \neq 1$ ($y \neq 1$, $x \neq 1$, resp.). A word u is called an *outfix* of a word v if there exists word x such that $u = u_1u_2$ and $v = u_1xu_2$. If $x \neq 1$ then u is a *proper outfix* of v. A word u is a *subword* of a word v if, for some $n \geq 1, u = u_1 \dots u_n, v = x_0u_1x_1 \dots u_nx_n$ with $u_1, \dots, u_n, x_0, \dots, x_n \in A^*$. If $x_0 \dots x_n \neq 1$ then u is called a *proper subword* of v. A word u is called a *permutation* of a word v if $|u|_a = |v|_a$ for all $a \in A$, where $|u|_a$ denotes the number of occurrences of the letter a in u.

Definition 1. *Let A be an alphabet and $X \subseteq A^+$.*

(i)   *X is a prefix code (suffix code) if no word in X is a proper prefix (proper suffix, resp.) of another word in X;*
(ii) *X is a bifix code if it is both a prefix code and a suffix code;*
(iii) *X is an infix code if no word in X is a proper infix of another word in X;*
(iv) *X is an outfix code if no word in X is a proper outfix of another word in X;*
(v)   *X is a hypercode if no word in X is a proper subword of another word in X;*
(vi) *X is a subinfix code if no word in X is a subword of a proper infix of another word in X;*
(vii) *X is a supercode if no word in X is a proper subword of a permutation of another word in X;*
(viii)*X is a uniform code if it consists of elements of equal length.*

The classes of prefix codes, suffix codes, bifix codes, infix codes, outfix codes, hypercodes, subinfix codes, supercodes and uniform codes are denoted respectively by C_p, C_s, C_b, C_i, C_o, C_h, C_{si}, C_{sp} and C_u. It is easy to see that these classes of codes are defined respectively by the relations which satisfy, for any $u, v \in A^*$, the following corresponding conditions:

$$u \prec_p v \Leftrightarrow v = ux, \text{ with } x \neq 1;$$
$$u \prec_s v \Leftrightarrow v = xu, \text{ with } x \neq 1;$$
$$u \prec_b v \Leftrightarrow (u \prec_p v) \vee (u \prec_s v);$$
$$u \prec_i v \Leftrightarrow v = xuy, \text{ with } xy \neq 1;$$
$$u \prec_o v \Leftrightarrow u = u_1u_2, v = u_1xu_2, \text{ with } x \neq 1;$$
$$u \prec_h v \Leftrightarrow \exists n \geq 1 : u = u_1 \dots u_n \wedge v = x_0u_1x_1 \dots u_nx_n, \text{ with } x_0 \dots x_n \neq 1;$$
$$u \prec_{si} v \Leftrightarrow \exists w \in A^* : w \prec_i v \wedge u \preceq_h w;$$
$$u \prec_{sp} v \Leftrightarrow \exists v' \in \pi(v) : u \prec_h v';$$
$$u \prec_u v \Leftrightarrow |u| < |v|;$$

where $\pi(v)$ is the set of all permutations of v.

Prefix codes, suffix codes and bifix codes play a fundamental role in the theory of codes (see [1,15]). For details about infix codes and outfix codes we refer to [10,15]. Hypercodes, a special kind of infix codes, have some interesting properties, especially, all hypercodes are finite (see [15]). Subinfix codes and supercodes were introduced and considered in [5,6,7,8,16,17,18] (see also [19]).

Now we formulate, in the form of lemmas, several facts which will be useful in the sequel.

Lemma 1 ([1,7,10]). *The classes C_b of bifix codes, C_i of infix codes and C_{si} of subinfix codes are closed under catenation.*

A finite automaton $\mathcal{A}$ is specified by a tuple (Q, A, δ, s, F), where Q is a finite set of states, A is an input alphabet, $\delta \subseteq Q \times A \times Q$ is a (finite) set of transitions, $s \in Q$ is the start state and $F \subseteq Q$ is a set of final states. Let $|Q|$ denote the number of states and $|\delta|$ the number of transitions in of $\mathcal{A}$. Then, the size $|\mathcal{A}|$ of $\mathcal{A}$ is defined as $|Q| + |\delta|$. If $t = (p, a, q)$ is a transition, where $p, q \in Q$ and $a \in A$, then we say that t is an *out-transition* of p and an *in-transition* of q. Also, p is called a *source state* of q and q a *target state* of p. Instead of writing $(p, a, q) \in \delta$, we often write also $\delta(p, a) = q$. Then δ is extended to a mapping from $Q \times A^*$ to Q in a normal way. A word w over A is accepted by $\mathcal{A}$ if there is a labeled path from s to a state in F, called a *successful path* in $\mathcal{A}$, which spells out the word w. Thus, the language recognized by $\mathcal{A}$, denoted by $L(\mathcal{A})$, is the set of the labels of all the successful paths in $\mathcal{A}$. The languages recognized by finite-state automata are called regular languages.

Lemma 2. *Given prefix (suffix) codes L, L_1, L_2, ..., L_k, $k \geq 2$, such that $L = L_1.L_2.....L_k$. Then L is regular iff so are L_1, L_2, ..., L_k.*

Proof. It is easily proved for $k = 2$ (see for example [2]). With the remark that the class C_p (C_s, resp.) is closed under catenation, the assertion can be proved easily by induction.   □

We say that the automaton $\mathcal{A}$ is *non-returning* if the start state of $\mathcal{A}$ has no any in-transitions, and that $\mathcal{A}$ is *non-exiting* if no final state of $\mathcal{A}$ has out-transitions. Clearly, if $\mathcal{A}$ is non-exiting then we may always assume that $\mathcal{A}$ has only one final state. Moreover, we always assume that $\mathcal{A}$ has only useful states, that is each state of $\mathcal{A}$ must appears on at least one successful path in $\mathcal{A}$. In this paper, we restrict ourselves to consider only deterministic finite automata, which are non-returning and non-exiting, denoted by N-DFAs, for short.

Lemma 3. *For every regular code in C_b there exists an N-DFA recognizing L.*

Proof. Suppose L is a regular code in C_b. There is then a deterministic finite-state automaton $\mathcal{A}$ recognizing L, $L = L(\mathcal{A})$. It is easy to see that if the start state of $\mathcal{A}$ has an in-transition then L cannot be a suffix code, and if a final state of $\mathcal{A}$ has an out-transition then L cannot be a prefix code. Thus, $\mathcal{A}$ must be both non-returning and non-exiting, i.e. $\mathcal{A}$ is an N-DFA.   □

Let $\mathcal{A} = (Q, A, \delta, s, F)$ be a deterministic finite-state automaton recognizing a language L, $L = L(\mathcal{A})$. Let $\equiv_A$ be the equivalence relation on the states of $\mathcal{A}$ such that $p \equiv_A q$ iff, for any input string w, $\delta(p, w)$ is in F iff so is $\delta(q, w)$. As well known (see [9]), $\mathcal{A}$ is a minimal deterministic automaton recognizing L iff, for any two different states p, q in Q, $p \not\equiv_A q$. Note that the minimal deterministic finite-state automaton recognizing a language L is unique up to an isomorphism. Let $\mathcal{A}_1$ and $\mathcal{A}_2$ be two N-DFAs with the start states s_1, s_2 and the unique final states f_1, f_2 respectively. The N-DFA $\mathcal{A}$ obtained from $\mathcal{A}_1$ and $\mathcal{A}_2$ by identifying f_1 with s_2 is called the composition of $\mathcal{A}_1$ and $\mathcal{A}_2$ and denoted by $\mathcal{A}_1 \circ \mathcal{A}_2$. Note that the composition operation is associative.

Lemma 4. *If $\mathcal{A}_1, \mathcal{A}_2, \ldots, \mathcal{A}_k$, $k \geq 2$, are minimal N-DFAs recognizing the bifix codes $L_1, L_2, \ldots, L_k$, respectively, then $\mathcal{A} = \mathcal{A}_1 \circ \mathcal{A}_2 \circ \cdots \circ \mathcal{A}_k$ is a minimal N-DFA recognizing the bifix code $L = L_1.L_2 \ldots L_k$.*

Proof. Because the class of bifix codes is closed under catenation, it suffices to prove for $k = 2$. Let $\mathcal{A}_1 = (Q_1, A, \delta_1, s_1, f_1)$, $\mathcal{A}_2 = (Q_2, A, \delta_2, s_2, f_2)$, and $\mathcal{A} = \mathcal{A}_1 \circ \mathcal{A}_2$. Thus, $\mathcal{A} = (Q = Q_1 \cup Q_2, A, \delta, s_1, f_2)$, where δ coincides with δ_1 on Q_1 and with δ_2 on Q_2. Let denote by r the state of $\mathcal{A}$ which is f_1 identified with s_2. Clearly, $\mathcal{A}$ is an N-DFA recognizing $L = L_1.L_2$. We prove that $\mathcal{A}$ is minimal among such automata. It suffices to prove that for any $p, q \in Q$, $p \neq q$, $p \not\equiv_A q$. We consider separately three possible cases.

Case 1: $p, q \in Q_1$. The minimality of $\mathcal{A}_1$ implies $p \not\equiv_{A_1} q$. There exists a word w_1 in A^* such that one and only one among $\delta_1(p, w_1)$ and $\delta_1(q, w_1)$ is equal to r, say $\delta_1(p, w_1) = p' \neq r$ with $p' \in Q_1$, and $\delta_1(q, w_1) = r$. Choose a word w_2 such that $\delta_2(r, w_2) = f_2$. Putting $w = w_1 w_2$ we have $\delta(q, w) = \delta(q, w_1 w_2) = \delta_2(\delta_1(q, w_1), w_2) = \delta_2(r, w_2) = f_2$. Assume $\delta(p, w) = f_2$ too, we have $\delta(p, w) = \delta(\delta_1(p, w_1), w_2) = \delta(p', w_2) = f_2$. It follows that $w_2 = w_2' w_2''$ with $w_2' \neq 1$ such that $\delta(p', w_2') = r$ and $\delta(r, w_2'') = f_2$. Thus $\delta_2(r, w_2) = \delta_2(r, w_2'') = f_2$, i.e. $w_2, w_2'' \in L_2$, which is impossible because L_2 is bifix. So we have $\delta(p, w) \neq f_2$ whereas $\delta(q, w) = f_2$, which means $p \not\equiv_A q$.

Case 2: $p, q \in Q_2$. By the minimality of $\mathcal{A}_2$, there must exist a word w in A^* such that one and only one among $\delta_2(p, w)$ and $\delta_2(q, w)$ is equal to f_2. This implies evidently that one and only one among $\delta(p, w)$ and $\delta(q, w)$ is equal to f_2. Thus we have again $p \not\equiv_A p$.

Case 3: $p \in Q_1, q \in Q_2$ with $p, q \neq r$. If $q = f_2$ then by taking $w = 1$ we have $\delta(p, w) = p \neq f_2$ whereas $\delta(q, w) = q = f_2$, which implies $p \not\equiv_A q$. Suppose $q \neq f_2$. There must exist a word $v \neq 1$ such that $\delta_2(q, v) = f_2$. Choose a word u such that $\delta_2(r, u) = q$. Put $w = uv$, we have $\delta(r, w) = \delta_2(r, w) = \delta_2(\delta_2(r, u), v) = \delta_2(q, v) = f_2$. It follows $w \in L_2$. Assume that $\delta(p, v) = f_2$ too. There must exist v', v'' with $v' \neq 1$ such that $v = v'v''$ and such that $\delta(p, v') = r$ and $\delta(r, v'') = f_2$. This implies $\delta_2(r, v'') = f_2$, i.e. $v'' \in L_2$. Thus we have $w, v'' \in L_2$ with v'' is a proper suffix of w, a contradiction. Thus $\delta(p, v) \neq f_2$ whereas $\delta(q, v) = f_2$, which imply $p \not\equiv_A q$.

So, in all the cases we have proved that whenever $p \neq q$, $p \not\equiv_A q$. By this the minimality of $\mathcal{A}$ is confirmed. □

3   General Prime Decomposition Theorems

In this section we present several general prime decomposition theorems. For this we need some more definitions and notations.

Definition 2. *Given a class C of codes. A regular code L in C is* prime *in C if L cannot be decomposed into at least two non-trivial regular codes in C. Clearly, if C is closed under catenation then L is prime iff it cannot be decomposed into two non-trivial regular codes in C.*

Definition 3. *A state b in an N-DFA $\mathcal{A}$ is called a* bridge state *of $\mathcal{A}$ if hold the following conditions:*

(i) *The state b is neither the start state nor a final state;*
(ii) *Every successful path in $\mathcal{A}$ must pass through b;*
(iii) *The state b does not belong to any cycle in $\mathcal{A}$.*

Thus, if b is a bridge state in the N-DFA $\mathcal{A}$, then we can partition $\mathcal{A}$ into two subautomata $\mathcal{A}_1$ and $\mathcal{A}_2$ such that $\mathcal{A}_1$ consists of all the states incomming to b, b including, and $\mathcal{A}_2$ consists of all the states outgoing from b, b including. Such a partition, denoted by $(\mathcal{A}_1, \mathcal{A}_2)_b$ or simply $(\mathcal{A}_1, \mathcal{A}_2)$ when there is no confusion, is called the partition of $\mathcal{A}$ at the bridge state b. The subautomata $\mathcal{A}_1$ and $\mathcal{A}_2$ are called components of the partition.

Definition 4. *Let C be a class of bifix codes, let $\mathcal{A}$ be an N-DFA recognizing a code in C. Let b be a bridge state of $\mathcal{A}$ and $(\mathcal{A}_1, \mathcal{A}_2)$ be the partition of $\mathcal{A}$ at b. The bridge state b is called a* strong bridge state *of $\mathcal{A}$ w.r.t. C (or simply a strong bridge state of $\mathcal{A}$, if no any confusion may arise) if $L(\mathcal{A}_1), L(\mathcal{A}_2) \in C$.*

Clearly, if $(\mathcal{A}_1, \mathcal{A}_2)$ is the partition of an N-DFA $\mathcal{A}$ at a bridge state then, by (ii) in Definition 3, we have $L(\mathcal{A}) = L(\mathcal{A}_1).L(\mathcal{A}_2)$. If moreover $L(\mathcal{A})$ is in a class C of codes and b is a strong bridge state of $\mathcal{A}$ w.r.t. C then $L(\mathcal{A}_1).L(\mathcal{A}_2)$ becomes a decomposition of $L(\mathcal{A})$ into regular codes in C.

Lemma 5. *Let C be a class of bifix codes which is closed under catenation. Let $\mathcal{A}$ be a minimal N-DFA recognizing a regular code in C. Let j be a strong bridge state of $\mathcal{A}$ w.r.t. C. Let $(\mathcal{A}_1, \mathcal{A}_2)$ be the partition of $\mathcal{A}$ at j. Then, if i is a state of $\mathcal{A}$ not being a strong bridge state of $\mathcal{A}$, then i cannot be a strong bridge state of any among $\mathcal{A}_1$ and $\mathcal{A}_2$.*

Proof. Suppose that i is not a strong bridge state of $\mathcal{A}$ but it becomes a strong bridge state of one of the components of the given partition $(\mathcal{A}_1, \mathcal{A}_2)$, say $\mathcal{A}_1$ (see Fig. 1). We may assume that i is a bridge state of $\mathcal{A}$, otherwise, as easily verified, it cannot be a bridge state of $\mathcal{A}_1$ neither, and therefore cannot be a strong bridge state of $\mathcal{A}_1$.

   Let $L'_j.L''_j$ be the decomposition of $L(\mathcal{A})$ corresponding to the partition of $\mathcal{A}$ at the state j, and $L'_i.L''_i$ the decomposition of $L(\mathcal{A}_1)$ corresponding to the partition of $\mathcal{A}_1$ at i. Then, we have $L'_j, L''_j, L'_i, L''_i \in C$ because j and i are strong bridge states of $\mathcal{A}$ and $\mathcal{A}_1$, respectively. From $L''_i \in C$ and $L''_j \in C$ it follow $L''_i.L''_j \in C$ since the class C is closed under catenation. Therefore, $L(\mathcal{A}) = L'_i.L''_i.L''_j$, which means that i is also a strong bridge state of $\mathcal{A}$, a contradiction.   □

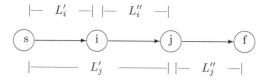

Fig. 1. Decomposing $\mathcal{A}$ at j and $\mathcal{A}_1$ at i

Lemma 6. *Let L be a regular code in a class C of bifix codes, and let $\mathcal{A}$ be a minimal N-DFA $\mathcal{A}$ recognizing L. Then,*

(i) *If L is prime then $\mathcal{A}$ has no any strong bridge state;*
(ii) *If $\mathcal{A}$ has no strong bridge states then L is prime.*

Proof. (i) Let denote by s and f the start state and the final state in $\mathcal{A}$, respectively. Suppose L is prime in C but $\mathcal{A}$ has a strong bridge state q. Let $(\mathcal{A}_1, \mathcal{A}_2)$ be the partition of $\mathcal{A}$ at q. Then, $\mathcal{A}_1$ has s as the start state and q as its unique final state while $\mathcal{A}_2$ has q as the start state and f as its unique final state. Therefore, $L = L(\mathcal{A}_1).L(\mathcal{A}_2)$ with $L(\mathcal{A}_1), L(\mathcal{A}_2) \in C$, which contradicts the primality of L. Thus $\mathcal{A}$ must have no any strong bridge state.

(ii) Suppose the contrary that L is not prime. Then, $L = L_1.L_2 \ldots L_k$ with $k \geq 2$, where $L_1, L_2, \ldots, L_k$ are non-trivial codes in C which are all bifix. Moreover, because L is regular, by Lemma 2, $L_1, L_2, \ldots, L_k$ are all regular bifix codes. Hence, by Lemma 3, $L_1, L_2, \ldots, L_k$ can be recognized by N-DFAs. Let $\mathcal{A}_1, \mathcal{A}_2, \ldots, \mathcal{A}_k$ be minimal N-DFAs recognizing $L_1, L_2, \ldots, L_k$, respectively. By Lemma 4, $\mathcal{A}' = \mathcal{A}_1 \circ \mathcal{A}_2 \circ \cdots \circ \mathcal{A}_k$ is a minimal N-DFA recognizing $L_1.L_2 \ldots L_k = L$. Thus $\mathcal{A}'$ is isomorphic to $\mathcal{A}$. But $\mathcal{A}'$ has strong bridge states, namely the final states of $\mathcal{A}_1, \mathcal{A}_2, \ldots, \mathcal{A}_{k-1}$, a contradiction. So L must be prime. □

Theorem 1. *Let C be a subclass of C_b which is closed under catenation. Let $\mathcal{A}$ be a minimal N-DFA recognizing a regular code L in C. If $\mathcal{A}$ has k strong bridge states, $k \geq 1$, then L can be decomposed into t prime regular codes in C, $L = L_1.L_2 \ldots L_t$, with $t \leq k + 1$. Conversely, if L can be decomposed into $k + 1$ prime regular codes in C, $k \geq 1$, then $\mathcal{A}$ has k strong bridge states.*

Proof. Consider a successful path p in $\mathcal{A}$. By (ii) of Definition 3, all the strong bridge states of $\mathcal{A}$ must appear on p. Let denote by $b_1, b_2, \ldots, b_k$ all these strong bridge states in the order we meet them on p when going from the starting state to the final state of $\mathcal{A}$. Note that, by (iii) of Definition 3, this order does not depend on the choice of p. Now we prove the assertion of the theorem by induction on k. With $k = 1$ we consider the partition $(\mathcal{A}_1, \mathcal{A}_2)$ of $\mathcal{A}$ at b_1. We have $L = L(\mathcal{A}) = L(\mathcal{A}_1).L(\mathcal{A}_2)$. By the definition of strong bridge states, $L(\mathcal{A}_1)$ and $L(\mathcal{A}_2)$ are regular codes in C. By Lemma 5, $\mathcal{A}_1$ and $\mathcal{A}_2$ have no any strong bridge states. Therefore, by Lemma 6, $L_1 = L(\mathcal{A}_1)$ and $L_2 = L(\mathcal{A}_2)$ are both prime, and hence $L_1.L_2$ is a prime decomposition of L, $L = L_1.L_2$, where $t = 2 = k + 1$. Suppose now $k > 1$ and that the assertion is already true for all $k' < k$. Let $(\mathcal{A}_1, \mathcal{A}_2)$ be the partition of $\mathcal{A}$ at b_1. We have $L = L(\mathcal{A}_1).L(\mathcal{A}_2)$. By

Lemma 5, $\mathcal{A}_1$ has no strong bridge states. Therefore, by Lemma 6, $L_1 = L(\mathcal{A}_1)$ is prime. Again by Lemma 5, all the strong bridge states of $\mathcal{A}_2$ must be among $b_2, \ldots, b_k$, whose number is $k - 1 < k$. By the induction hypothesis, $L(\mathcal{A}_2)$ can be decomposed into t' prime regular codes in C, $L(\mathcal{A}_2) = L_2 \ldots L_{t'+1}$, with $t' \leq k-1+1 = k$. Put $t = t'+1$ we obtain $L = L_1.L_2 \ldots L_t$, with $t = t'+1 \leq k+1$, where all L_i, $1 \leq i \leq t$, are prime regular codes in C. The rest of the proof is immediate from Lemma 4.   □

Definition 5. *A binary relation $\prec$ on A^* is called* invariant *if, for any $u, v \in A^*$, $u \prec v$ implies either $uw \prec vw$ or $wu \prec wv$ each $w \neq 1$. Especially, if it implies both $uw \prec vw$ and $wu \prec wv$ instead, for all $w \neq 1$, then the relation $\prec$ is called* strictly invariant.

Lemma 7. *Let $\prec$ be an invariant binary relation on A^* which defines a class $C_\prec$ of bifix codes. Let $\mathcal{A}$ be a minimal N-DFA recognizing a regular code in $C_\prec$ which has strong bridge states. Let j be an arbitrary strong bridge state of $\mathcal{A}$. Then, every strong bridge state i of $\mathcal{A}$, $i \neq j$, must be a strong bridge state of one of the components of the partition of $\mathcal{A}$ at j.*

Proof. Let $(\mathcal{A}_1, \mathcal{A}_2)$ be the partition of $\mathcal{A}$ at j. The state i must be in one and only one of the components of this partition, say $\mathcal{A}_1$. Assume that i is not a strong bridge state of $\mathcal{A}_1$ (see Fig. 2). By the definition of strong bridge states, we have $L_i', L_i'', L_j', L_j'' \in C_\prec$. Evidently, i must be a bridge state of $\mathcal{A}_1$. Since i is not a strong bridge state in $\mathcal{A}_1$, it follows that $L_{ij} \notin C_\prec$. Then, there exist two words $u, v \in L_{ij}$ such that $u \prec v$. Since the relation $\prec$ is invariant, either $uw \prec vw$ or $wu \prec wv$, for any $w \neq 1$. For the first case, choosing w as a word in L_j'', we have $uw \prec vw$ with $uw, vw \in L_i''$, which contradicts the fact that $L_i'' \in C_\prec$. Similarly, for the second case, taking w as a word in L_i', we have $wu \prec wv$ with $wu, wv \in L_j'$, again a contradiction. Thus, i must be a strong bridge state of $\mathcal{A}_1$. For the case when i is in $\mathcal{A}_2$ the argument is similar.   □

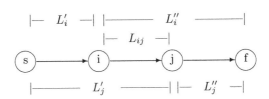

Fig. 2. Decompositions of $L(\mathcal{A})$ corresponding to the strong bridge states i and j

Theorem 2. *Let $\prec$ be an invariant binary relation on A^* which defines a class $C_\prec$ of codes. Let $C_\prec$ be a subclass of C_b which is closed under catenation. Let $\mathcal{A}$ be a minimal N-DFA recognizing a regular code L in $C_\prec$. Then $\mathcal{A}$ has exactly k strong bridge states, $k \geq 1$, if and only if L can be decomposed uniquely into $k + 1$ prime factors, namely, $L = L_1.L_2 \ldots L_{k+1}$ where $L_1, L_2, \ldots, L_{k+1}$ are all prime regular codes in $C_\prec$.*

Proof. Let $b_1, b_2, \ldots, b_k$ be the strong bridge states of $\mathcal{A}$ ordered as in the proof of Theorem 1. We prove the existence of a prime decomposition by induction on k. It is sufficient to show that $L(\mathcal{A}) = L'.L''$ such that L' is accepted by an N-DFA $\mathcal{A}'$ with $k-1$ strong bridge states and L'' is a prime regular code in $C_\prec$.

Indeed, let $(\mathcal{A}', \mathcal{A}'')$ be the partition of $\mathcal{A}$ at b_k. By the definition of strong bridge states, $L(\mathcal{A}')$ and $L(\mathcal{A}'')$ are regular codes in $C_\prec$. By Lemma 5, $\mathcal{A}''$ has no strong bridge states. Therefore, $L'' = L(\mathcal{A}'')$ is prime by Lemma 6. Next, by Lemmas 5 and 7, $\mathcal{A}'$ has exactly $k-1$ strong bridge states which are $b_1, b_2, \ldots, b_{k-1}$. Thus, by using induction hypothesis, we can conclude that L can be decomposed into $k+1$ prime regular codes in $C_\prec$.

Suppose $L = L'_1.L'_2 \ldots L'_{l+1}$ be an arbitrary prime decomposition of L. Since $L \in C_\prec$ and $C_\prec \subseteq C_b$, the languages $L'_1, L'_2, \ldots, L'_{l+1}$ are all bifix codes in $C_\prec$. By Lemma 2, they are all regular too. Let $\mathcal{A}'_1, \mathcal{A}'_2, \ldots, \mathcal{A}'_{l+1}$ be minimal N-DFAs recognizing $L'_1, L'_2, \ldots, L'_{l+1}$, respectively. By Lemma 4, the automaton $\mathcal{A}' = \mathcal{A}'_1 \circ \mathcal{A}'_2 \circ \cdots \circ \mathcal{A}'_{l+1}$ is a minimal N-DFA recognizing L. Evidently, $\mathcal{A}'$ has exactly l strong bridge states. Let $b'_1, b'_2, \ldots, b'_l$ be these strong bridge states in the order we meet them on one (and therefore on any) successful path in $\mathcal{A}'$. Because $\mathcal{A}'$ is isomorphic to $\mathcal{A}$, we must have $l = k$ and for any isomorphism ϕ between $\mathcal{A}$ and $\mathcal{A}'$, b'_i corresponds to b_i, $\phi(b_i) = b'_i$, $1 \le i \le k$. It follows that for all i, $1 \le i \le k+1$, $\mathcal{A}'_i$ is isomorphic to $\mathcal{A}_i$, where $\mathcal{A}_i$ is a minimal N-DFA recognizing L_i, that implies $L_i = L'_i$. Thus, we have proved that the prime decomposition of L is unique.

Conversely, suppose L can be decomposed uniquely into $k+1$ prime regular factors, $L = L_1.L_2 \ldots L_{k+1}$. By Lemma 4, $\mathcal{A} = \mathcal{A}_1 \circ \mathcal{A}_2 \circ \cdots \circ \mathcal{A}_{k+1}$, where $\mathcal{A}_i$ is the minimal N-DFA recognizing L_i ($i = 1, \ldots, k+1$). Evidently $\mathcal{A}$ has k bridge states. They are strong because $C_\prec$ is closed under catenation. The uniqueness of the prime decomposition of L implies that $\mathcal{A}$ has no more than k strong bridge states mentioned above. $\qquad\square$

Lemma 8. *Let $\prec$ be a strictly invariant binary relation on A^* which defines the class $C_\prec$ of bifix codes. Suppose that $\mathcal{A}$ is a minimal N-DFA recognizing a regular code in $C_\prec$. Then,*

(i) *All bridge states in $\mathcal{A}$ are strong bridge states in $\mathcal{A}$;*
(ii) *If i is not a strong bridge state in $\mathcal{A}$, and j, $j \ne i$, is a strong bridge state in $\mathcal{A}$ then i cannot be a strong bridge state of any component of the partition of $\mathcal{A}$ at j.*

Proof. (i) Suppose that b is a bridge state in $\mathcal{A}$. We prove that b must be a strong bridge state in $\mathcal{A}$. It suffices to show that $L(\mathcal{A}_1)$ and $L(\mathcal{A}_2)$ are in $C_\prec$, where $(\mathcal{A}_1, \mathcal{A}_2)$ is the partition of $\mathcal{A}$ at b. Clearly, we have $L(\mathcal{A}) = L(\mathcal{A}_1).L(\mathcal{A}_2)$. Assume that $L(\mathcal{A}_1)$ is not in $C_\prec$. Then, there exist two words $u, v \in L(\mathcal{A}_1)$ such that $u \prec v$. Since $\prec$ is strictly invariant, both $uw \prec vw$ and $wu \prec wv$ hold, for all $w \ne 1$. Therefore, taking w as any word in $L(\mathcal{A}_2)$, we have $uw \prec vw$ with $uw, vw \in L(\mathcal{A})$, a contradiction with $L(\mathcal{A}) \in C_\prec$. Thus $L(\mathcal{A}_1)$ must be in $C_\prec$. A similar argument shows that $L(\mathcal{A}_2) \in C_\prec$.

(ii) Let $(\mathcal{A}_1, \mathcal{A}_2)$ be the partition of $\mathcal{A}$ at j. Assume that i is a strong bridge state in a component of the partition of $\mathcal{A}$ at j, say $\mathcal{A}_1$. Clearly, i is not neither the starting state nor the final state of $\mathcal{A}$. By the definition of strong bridge states in $\mathcal{A}_1$, all successful paths in $\mathcal{A}_1$ and therefore all the successful paths in $\mathcal{A}$ must pass through i. If i is not in any cycle in $\mathcal{A}$ then i is a bridge state of $\mathcal{A}$, and therefore, by (i), it is also a strong bridge state of $\mathcal{A}$, a contradiction. Thus there must exist a cycle V in $\mathcal{A}$ containing i. Since i is a strong bridge state of $\mathcal{A}_1$, the cycle V cannot belong entirely to $\mathcal{A}_1$. So V contains at least one state in $\mathcal{A}_2$. It follows that V must contain j, which is impossible because j is a strong bridge state of $\mathcal{A}$. We conclude that i cannot be a strong bridge state of $\mathcal{A}_1$. For the case when i is a strong bridge state of $\mathcal{A}_2$, the argument is similar.   □

Theorem 3. *Let $\prec$ be a strictly invariant binary relation on A^* which defines a class $C_\prec$ of codes, and let $C_\prec$ be a subclass of C_b. Let $\mathcal{A}$ be a minimal N-DFA recognizing a regular code L in $C_\prec$. Then $\mathcal{A}$ has exactly k strong bridge states w.r.t. $C_\prec$, $k \geq 1$, if and only if L can be decomposed uniquely into $k+1$ prime factors, namely, $L = L_1.L_2 \ldots L_{k+1}$ where $L_1, L_2, \ldots, L_{k+1}$ are all prime regular codes in $C_\prec$.*

Proof. The proof is quite similar to that of Theorem 2, where Lemma 8 is used instead of Lemma 5, and therefore we don't need the requirement that $C_\prec$ is closed under catenation.   □

Now we consider how to verify the primality and how to compute a prime decomposition. Let C be a subclass of C_b. Suppose moreover that either C is closed under catenation or C can be defined by a strictly invariant binary relation $\prec$, $C = C_\prec$. Then, by Lemma 3, every regular code L in C is recognized by a minimal N-DFA $\mathcal{A}$, $L = L(\mathcal{A})$. By Theorem 2 and Theorem 3, if $\mathcal{A}$ has k strong bridge states w.r.t. C then L can be decomposed into $k+1$ prime factors in C.

Given L, to verify the primality of L it suffices to verify whether $\mathcal{A}$ has strong bridge states or not. If not, then L is prime and is a prime decomposition of itself. If yes, we partition $\mathcal{A}$ at a strong bridge state into two subautomata $\mathcal{A}_1$ and $\mathcal{A}_2$. If both of $L(\mathcal{A}_1)$ and $L(\mathcal{A}_2)$ are prime then $L(\mathcal{A}_1).L(\mathcal{A}_2)$ is a prime decomposition of L. Otherwise, the above procedure is repeated for one among $L(\mathcal{A}_1)$ and $L(\mathcal{A}_2)$ or both of them according to the case.

Let B denote the set of strong bridge states of the given minimal N-DFA $\mathcal{A}$. Clearly, the number of states in B is at most m, where m is the number of states in $\mathcal{A}$. Note that every time we partition $\mathcal{A}$ at a strong bridge state $b \in B$ into $\mathcal{A}_1$ and $\mathcal{A}_2$, then only states in $B \setminus \{b\}$ can be strong bridge states of $\mathcal{A}_1$ and $\mathcal{A}_2$ (by virtue of Lemmas 5 and 8). Therefore, we can determine the primality of $L(\mathcal{A})$ by checking whether $\mathcal{A}$ has strong bridge states or not and compute a prime decomposition of $L(\mathcal{A})$ using only these strong bridge states. Since there are at most m strong bridge states in an N-DFA for a regular code in $C_\prec$, we can obtain a prime decomposition of $L(\mathcal{A})$ after a finite number times, no more than m, of partitioning component automata at the strong bridge states in B.

The following result is due to Y. -S. Han, Y. Wang and D. Wood.

Lemma 9 ([3]). *We can compute the set of bridge states for a given N-DFA* $\mathcal{A} = (Q, A, \delta, s, f)$ *in* $O(|Q| + |\delta|)$ *worst-case time using DFS (depth-first search).*

Using this result we obtain the following theorem.

Theorem 4. *Let* $\prec$ *be a strictly invariant binary relation on* A^* *which defines the class* $C_\prec$ *of codes, and let* $C_\prec$ *be a subclass of* C_b. *Let* $\mathcal{A}$ *be a minimal N-DFA recognizing a regular code in* $C_\prec$.

(i) *We can determine the primality of* $L(\mathcal{A})$ *in* $O(\mu)$ *time;*
(ii) *We can compute the unique prime decomposition of* $L(\mathcal{A})$ *in* $O(\mu)$ *time if* $L(\mathcal{A})$ *is not prime;*

where μ *is the size of* $\mathcal{A}$.

Proof. By (i) of Lemma 8, all bridge states in $\mathcal{A}$ become strong bridge states in $\mathcal{A}$. Then, by Lemma 9, the set of strong bridge states in $\mathcal{A}$ can be computed in $O(\mu)$ worst-case time. Therefore, if $\mathcal{A}$ has no strong bridge states then $L(\mathcal{A})$ is prime. Otherwise, by Theorem 3, we can compute the unique prime decomposition of $L(\mathcal{A})$ using strong bridge states in $O(\mu)$ time. □

4   Applications

In this section we apply the general prime decomposition theorems to solve the prime decomposition problem for the classes of codes introduced in Sec. 2.

Firstly, note that, by Lemma 1, the class C_i of infix codes is closed under catenation. Therefore, as an immediate consequence of Theorem 1, we obtain again the following result the first part of which has been proved in [3].

Theorem 5 ([3]). *Let* $\mathcal{A}$ *be a minimal N-DFA recognizing a regular infix code* L. *If* $\mathcal{A}$ *has* k *strong bridge states,* $k \geq 1$, *then* L *can be decomposed into* t *prime regular infix codes,* $L = L_1.L_2 \ldots L_t$, *with* $t \leq k + 1$. *Conversely, if* L *can be decomposed into* $k + 1$ *prime regular infix codes,* $k \geq 1$, *then* $\mathcal{A}$ *has exactly* k *strong bridge states.*

Furthermore, we need some more lemmas.

Lemma 10. *The relations* $\prec_b$ *and* $\prec_{si}$ *are invariant on* A^*.

Proof. Let $u \prec_b v$ for some $u, v \in A^*$. Then, by the definition of $\prec_b$, either $u \prec_p v$ or $u \prec_s v$. Therefore, for any $w \neq 1$, either $uw \prec_s vw$ or $wu \prec_p wv$. This means either $uw \prec_b vw$ or $wu \prec_b wv$.

Now let $u \prec_{si} v$. Then $\exists n \geq 1 : u = u_1 \ldots u_n \wedge v = x_0 u_1 x_1 \ldots u_n x_n$, with $x_0 x_n \neq 1$. It is easy to check that, for any $w \neq 1$, either $uw \prec_{si} vw$ or $wu \prec_{si} wv$ according as $x_0 \neq 1$ or $x_n \neq 1$. □

Lemma 11. *The relations* $\prec_o$, $\prec_h$, $\prec_{sp}$ *and* $\prec_u$ *are strictly invariant on* A^*.

Proof. It can be easily verified from the corresponding definitions. □

As a consequence of Theorems 2 and 3 we have.

Theorem 6. *Let A be a minimal N-DFA recognizing a regular code L in C_α, $\alpha \in \{b, si, o, h, sp, u\}$. Then, A has exactly k strong bridge states, $k \geq 1$, if and only if L can be decomposed uniquely into $k + 1$ prime factors, namely, $L = L_1.L_2 \ldots L_{k+1}$ where $L_1, L_2, \ldots, L_{k+1}$ are all prime regular codes in C_α.*

Proof. It follows immediately from Lemmas 1, 10, 11 and Theorems 2, 3.   □

Let's take some examples.

Example 1. Consider the language $L = \{aaab, ab^+abab\}$ over $A = \{a, b\}$. It easy to see that L is both a regular infix code and a regular subinfix code.

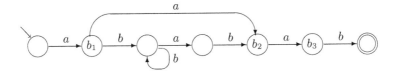

Fig. 3. The minimal N-DFA A for $L = \{aaab, ab^+abab\}$

• The minimal N-DFA A recognizing L has 3 strong bridge states w.r.t C_i which are b_1, b_2 and b_3 (see Fig. 3). However, if (A_1, A_2) is the partition of A at b_2, then b_1 is no longer a strong bridge state of A_1 w.r.t. C_i. Similarly, if (A'_1, A'_2) is the partition of A at b_1, then b_2 is no longer a strong bridge state of A'_2 w.r.t. C_i. Thus, by Theorem 5, L has two different prime decompositions

$$L = \{a\}.\{aa, b^+aba\}.\{b\} = \{aa, ab^+ab\}.\{a\}.\{b\}$$

where $\{a\}, \{b\}, \{aa, b^+aba\}$ and $\{aa, ab^+ab\}$ are prime regular infix codes.
• Considering X as a regular subinfix code, A has the only strong bridge state w.r.t. C_{si} which is b_3. Therefore, by Theorem 6, L can be decomposed uniquely into two prime factors in C_{si}, namely

$$L = \{aaa, ab^+aba\}.\{b\},$$

where $\{aaa, ab^+aba\}$ and $\{b\}$ are prime regular subinfix codes.

Example 2. Consider the regular bifix code $L = \{aabbaa^+b^+a, abaa^+b^+a, aabbab, abab\}$ over $A = \{a, b\}$. It is easy to see that the minimal N-DFA A recognizing L has b_1 and b_2 as strong bridge states w.r.t C_b and b_0 as a bridge state (see Fig. 4). Thus, by Theorem 6, L can be decomposed uniquely into three prime factors in C_b, namely

$$L = \{ab, aabb\}.\{a\}.\{b, a^+b^+a\},$$

where $\{ab, aabb\}, \{a\}$ and $\{b, a^+b^+a\}$ are prime regular bifix codes.

Example 3. Consider the supercode $L = \{a^2b^2c, a^2bc^4, ab^5c, ab^4c^4\}$ over $A = \{a, b, c\}$. The minimal N-DFA $\mathcal{A}$ for L has 4 (strong) bridge states which are b_1, b_2, b_3 and b_4 (see Fig. 5). By Theorem 6, L may be decomposed uniquely into 5 prime factors in C_{sp}, namely

$$L = \{a\}.\{a, b^3\}.\{b\}.\{b, c^3\}.\{c\}$$

where $\{a\}, \{b\}, \{c\}, \{a, b^3\}$ and $\{b, c^3\}$ are prime supercodes.

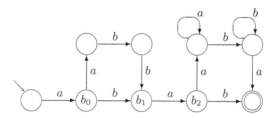

Fig. 4. The minimal N-DFA $\mathcal{A}$ for $L = \{aabbaa^+b^+a, abaa^+b^+a, aabbab, abab\}$

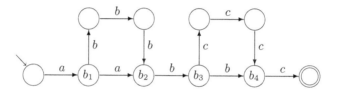

Fig. 5. The minimal N-DFA $\mathcal{A}$ for $L = \{a^2b^2c, a^2bc^4, ab^5c, ab^4c^4\}$

The following result is a consequence of Lemma 11 and Theorem 4.

Theorem 7. *Given a minimal N-DFA $\mathcal{A}$ recognizing a regular code in C_α, with $\alpha \in \{o, h, sp, u\}$.*

(i) *We can determine the primality of $L(\mathcal{A})$ in $O(\mu)$ time;*
(ii) *We can compute the unique prime decomposition of $L(\mathcal{A})$ in $O(\mu)$ time if $L(\mathcal{A})$ is not prime;*

where μ is the size of $\mathcal{A}$.

In [3], Y. -S. Han et al. showed that given an NFA $\mathcal{A} = (Q, A, \delta, s, f)$, we can determine whether or not $L(\mathcal{A})$ is a bifix code in $O(|Q|^2 + |\delta|^2)$ worst-case time. Therefore, using Thompson automata (see [3,9]), we obtain the following result for checking whether or not a regular expression defines a bifix code.

Lemma 12. *Given a regular expression E, we can determine whether or not $L(E)$ is a bifix code in $O(|E|^2)$ worst-case time.*

Theorem 8. *Given a minimal N-DFA $\mathcal{A} = (Q, A, \delta, s, f)$ recognizing a bifix regular code $L(\mathcal{A})$, we can determine the primality of $L(\mathcal{A})$ in $O(m^3)$ worst-case* *time and compute the unique prime decomposition of $L(\mathcal{A})$ in $O(m^3)$ worst-case, where m is the number of states in $\mathcal{A}$.*

Proof. Denote by B the set of all the bridge states of $\mathcal{A}$. There can be at most m bridge states after DFS. Then, by Lemma 12, it takes $O(m^2)$ time, for each bridge state, to determine whether or not $L(\mathcal{A}_1)$ and $L(\mathcal{A}_2)$ are bifix codes. Therefore, the total running time for determining the primality of $L(\mathcal{A})$ is $O(m).O(m^2) = O(m^3)$ in the worst-case.

If a state $b \in B$ is not a strong bridge state, then we remove b from B because, by Lemma 5, it can never be a strong bridge state of any component. Furthermore, each time we find a strong bridge state b', then we partition $\mathcal{A}$ at b' into two components $\mathcal{A}_1$ and $\mathcal{A}_2$, and then repeat the procedure for $L(\mathcal{A}_1)$ and $L(\mathcal{A}_2)$, respectively, using the remaining bridge states in B. Since each bridge state in B can contribute at most one time in partitioning, it takes $O(m^3)$ worst-case time to compute the unique prime decomposition for $L(\mathcal{A})$. $\square$

Acknowledgement. The authors would like to thank their colleagues in Seminar "Mathematical Foundation of Computer Science" at Hanoi Institute of Mathematics for useful discussions and attention to the work. Especially, we express our sincere thanks to Professor Derick Wood and Professor Yo-Sub Han for providing us with their papers. Our sincere thanks are due to the referees whose valuable comments and suggestions helped very much in improving this final version of the paper.

References

1. J. BERSTEL, D. PERRIN, *Theory of Codes.* Academic Press, New York, 1985.
2. J. CZYZOWICZ, W. FRACZAK, A. PELC, W. RYTTER, Linear-time prime decomposition of regular prefix codes. *Int. J. Found. Comput. Sci.* **14** (2003), 1019–1032.
3. Y. -S. HAN, Y. WANG, D. WOOD, Infix-free regular expressions and languages. *Int. J. Found. Comput. Sci.* **17** (2006), 379–394.
4. Y. -S. HAN, D. WOOD, Outfix-free regular languages and prime outfix-free decomposition. *LNCS* 3722, Springer, NJ, 2005, 96–109.
5. K. V. HUNG, On maximality for some kinds of codes over two-letter alphabets. *Acta Math. Vietnam.* **31** (2006), 17–30.
6. K. V. HUNG, P. T. HUY, D. L. VAN, On some classes of codes defined by binary relations. *Acta Math. Vietnam.* **29** (2004), 163–176.
7. K. V. HUNG, P. T. HUY, D. L. VAN, Codes concerning roots of words. *Vietnam J. Math.* **32** (2004), 345–359.
8. K. V. HUNG, N. Q. KHANG, An embedding algorithm for supercodes and sucypercodes. *Vietnam J. Math.* **33** (2005), 119–206.
9. J. HOPCROFT, J. ULLMAN, *Formal Languages and Their Relation to Automata.* Addison-Wesley Publishing Company, MA, 1969.
10. M. ITO, H. JÜRGENSEN, H. SHYR, G. THIERRIN, Outfix and infix codes and related classes of languages. *J. Comput., Syst. Sci.* **43** (1991), 484–508.
11. M. ITO, G. THIERRIN, Congruences, infix and cohesive prefix codes. *Theoret. Comput. Sci.* **136** (1994), 471–485.

12. H. JÜRGENSEN, S. KONSTANTINIDIS, Codes. In: G. ROZENBERG, A. SALOMAA (eds.), *Handbook of Formal Languages*. Springer, Berlin, 1997, 511–607.

13. A. MATEESCU, A. SALOMAA, S. YU, On the decomposition of finite languages, *Technical Report* **222**, TUCS, 1998.

14. A. MATEESCU, A. SALOMAA, S. YU, Factorizations of languages and commutativity conditions, *Acta Cyber.* **15** (2002), 339–351.

15. H. SHYR, *Free Monoids and Languages*. Hon Min Book Company, Taichung, 1991.

16. D. L. VAN, On a class of hypercodes. In: M. ITO, T. IMAOKA (eds.), *Words, Languages and Combinatorics III*. World Scientific, 2003, 171–183.

17. D. L. VAN, K. V. HUNG, An approach to the embedding problem for codes defined by binary relations. In: *Proceedings of CAI*, Greece, 2005, 111–127.

18. D. L. VAN, K. V. HUNG, Characterizations of some classes of codes defined by binary relations. In: K. G. SUBRAMANIAN, K. RANGARAJAN, M. MUKUND (eds.), *Formal Models, Languages and Applications Vol. 66*. World Scientific, 2006, 391–410.

19. D. L. VAN, K. V. HUNG, P. T. HUY, Codes and length-increasing transitive binary relations, *LNCS* 3722, Springer, NJ, 2005, 29–48.

A New Approach to Determinisation Using Bit-Parallelism[*]

Jan Šupol and Bořivoj Melichar

Department of Computer Science & Engineering
Faculty of Electrical Engineering
Czech Technical University in Prague
Karlovo nám. 13, 121 35 Prague 2
jan.supol@gmail.com, melichar@fel.cvut.cz

Abstract. We present a new approach to the determinisation process of specified types of automata using bit-parallel algorithms. We present the determinisation of nondeterministic pattern matching automata (PMA) for approximate pattern matching and we introduce the determinisation of suffix automata. This new approach speeds the determinisation up to m times, where m is the length of the pattern searched by PMA, or accepted by the suffix automaton, respectively.

1 Introduction

The determinisation process is a key process for many automata-based applications. The subset construction algorithm is the most popular algorithm for solving the determinisation issue and it has been explained e.g. in [HMU01]. The time complexity of the algorithm is known to be at worst $\mathcal{O}(2^{|Q|} \times |Q|^2 \times |A|)$ in the general case, where Q is the set of states of the nondeterministic finite automaton (NFA) and $A = a_1, a_2, \ldots, a_{|A|}$ is the input alphabet. The time complexity is lower for the pattern matching automaton, where the number of states of the NFA is linear with the length of matching pattern $P = p_1 p_2 \ldots p_m$, $|Q| = \mathcal{O}(m)$. Thus the time complexity is $\mathcal{O}(|Q_D| \times |Q| \times \mathcal{C} \times |A| + \tau)$, where Q_D is the set of states of the deterministic finite automaton (DFA), $\mathcal{C}$ is the average number of transitions from one state and τ is the time needed to verify the uniqueness of the newly constructed deterministic states (d-subsets). The transition table of DFA has $|Q_D|$ rows, each for a unique d-subset and each d-subset has an average length $|Q|$. Thus the subset construction has to compute a new d-subset by a union of all transitions from all approximately $|Q|$ states in each of $|Q_D|$ d-subsets for each symbol of the alphabet. Note that for exact PMA there is only a constant number of transitions for each state, with the exception of the initial state, which makes the final time complexity of the determinisation

---

[*] This research has been partially supported by the Ministry of Education, Youth, and Sport of the Czech Republic under research program MSM6840770014, by the Czech Science Foundation as project No. 201/06/1039, and by the Czech Technical University as project No. CTU0609613.

K. Barkaoui, A. Cavalcanti, and A. Cerone (Eds.): ICTAC 2006, LNCS 4281, pp. 228–241, 2006.

no different. For Levenshtein distance (see definition lower), however, there are $\mathcal{O}(k)$ transitions (because of the ε-transitions) from one state. Our idea is to compute all of the approximately $|Q|$ states in one d-subset at a time and to do so we use the bit-parallel simulation technique. This technique has been introduced in [Döm64](the "shift-and" variation), and improved in [BYG92, WM92] (the "shift-or" variation used in this paper). It has been shown [Hol00], that the bit-parallel algorithms simulate NFA and we modify them for the determinisation of PMA and suffix automata. Note that simulation of the suffix automata was introduced in [NR98].

We now introduce some notation. A finite automaton is a quintuple (Q, A, δ, I, F) where Q is a finite set of states, A is a finite input alphabet, $F \subseteq Q$ is a set of final states. If FA is nondeterministic (NFA), then δ is a mapping $Q \times (A \cup \{\varepsilon\}) \mapsto P(Q)$ and $I \subseteq Q$ is a set of initial states. If $FA = (Q, A, \delta, q_0, F)$ is deterministic (DFA), then δ is a (partial) function $Q \times A \mapsto Q$ and q_0 is the only initial state. We refer to NFA used for pattern matching as the pattern matching automaton (PMA). A suffix automaton is an automaton accepting all the suffixes of pattern x defined as $Suff(x) = \{y : x = uy, u, x \in A^*, y \in A^+\}, x \in A^*$.

The Hamming distance $H(x, y) \leq k$ is maximum k substitutions (replace operations) required to transform string x into string y (see [Ham86]). The Levenshtein distance $L(x, y) \leq k$ is maximum k operations "replace", "insert", or "delete" required to transform string x into string y. PMA for pattern P using the Hamming distance k is a pattern matching automaton that matches any pattern x, such that $H(P, x) \leq k$. PMA for pattern P using the Levenshtein distance k is a pattern matching automaton that matches any pattern x, such that $L(P, x) \leq k$. A suffix automaton for pattern P using the Hamming distance k is a suffix automaton that accepts any pattern x, such that $H(y, x) \leq k$, $y \in suff(P)$.

We use some bitwise operation in the following text. Operation **or** is a standard bitwise OR operation and operation **and** is a standard bitwise AND operation. Operation **shl** is a standard shift-left bitwise operation, and the right-most (the top-most when depicted) bit is set to 0. We use operation **shl1**, which is a shift-left bitwise operation, but the right-most bit is set to 1, $\mathbf{shl1}(x) \equiv \mathbf{shl}(x)$ **or** 1.

This paper is organized as follows. Section 2 explains the "shift-or" variation of a bit-parallel algorithm. Section 3 presents the "shift-or" modification for the determinisation of PMA and Section 4 presents a modification for determinisation of the suffix automaton. Section 5 provides a conclusion.

2   Bit-Parallelism

Here we explain the "shift-or" variation of the bit-parallel algorithms for the simulation of PMA. It uses matrices $R^l, 0 \leq l \leq k$ of size $m \times (n + 1)$, and matrix D of size $m \times |A|$, where k is the maximum number of edit operations in pattern P. Each element $r^l_{j,i}, 0 \leq i \leq n$ contains 0, if the edit distance between string $p_1 p_2 \ldots p_j$ and string ending at position i in text $T = t_1 t_2 \ldots t_n$ is $\leq l$, or

1, otherwise. Each element $d_{j,x}, 0 < j \leq m, x \in A$, contains 0, if $p_j = x$, or 1, otherwise.

In exact pattern matching, vectors $R_i^0, 0 \leq i \leq n$, are computed as follows:

$$
\begin{aligned}
r_{j,0}^0 &= 1, & 0 < j \leq m \\
R_i^0 &= \mathbf{shl}(R_{i-1}^0) \text{ or } D[t_i], \; 0 < i \leq n
\end{aligned} \tag{1}
$$

In approximate pattern matching using the Hamming distance, vectors $R_i^l, 0 \leq l \leq k, 0 \leq i \leq n$, are computed as follows:

$$
\begin{aligned}
r_{j,0}^l &= 1, & 0 < j \leq m, 0 \leq l \leq k \\
R_i^0 &= \mathbf{shl}(R_{i-1}^0) \text{ or } D[t_i], & 0 < i \leq n \\
R_i^l &= (\mathbf{shl}(R_{i-1}^l) \text{ or } D[t_i]) \text{ and } \mathbf{shl}(R_{i-1}^{l-1}), \; 0 < i \leq n, 0 < l \leq k
\end{aligned} \tag{2}
$$

In approximate pattern matching using the Levenshtein distance, vectors $R_i^l, 0 \leq l \leq k, 0 \leq i \leq n$, are computed as follows:

$$
\begin{aligned}
r_{j,0}^l &= 0, & 0 < j \leq l, 0 < l \leq k \\
r_{j,0}^l &= 1, & l < j \leq m, 0 \leq l \leq k \\
R_i^0 &= \mathbf{shl}(R_{i-1}^0) \text{ or } D[t_i], & 0 < i \leq n \\
R_i^l &= (\mathbf{shl}(R_{i-1}^l) \text{ or } D[t_i]) \\
& \quad \text{and } \mathbf{shl}(R_{i-1}^{l-1} \text{ and } R_i^{l-1}) \\
& \quad \text{and } (R_{i-1}^{l-1} \text{ or } V), & 0 < i \leq n, 0 < l \leq k
\end{aligned} \tag{3}
$$

The auxiliary vector V is computed as follows:

$$
V = \begin{bmatrix} v_1 \\ v_2 \\ \vdots \\ v_m \end{bmatrix}, \text{ where } v_m = 1 \text{ and } v_j = 0, \forall j, 1 \leq j < m. \tag{4}
$$

The term $\mathbf{shl}(R_{i-1}^l)$ or $D[t_i]$) represents matching – position i in text T is increased, the position in pattern P is increased by operation $\mathbf{shl}$, and the positions corresponding to the input symbol t_i are selected by the term or $D[t_i]$. The term $\mathbf{shl}(R_{i-1}^{l-1})$ represents edit operation "replace" – position i in text T is increased, the position in pattern P is increased, and edit distance l is increased. The term $\mathbf{shl}(R_i^{l-1})$ represents edit operation "delete" – the position in the pattern is increased, the position in the text is not increased, and edit distance l is increased. The term R_{i-1}^{l-1} represents edit operation "insert" – position in pattern is not increased, position in the text is increased, and edit distance l is increased. The term or V provides that no "insert" transition leads from any final state.

3   Determinisation of Pattern Matching Automata

The idea of determinisation is simple. The bit-parallel formulas represent the transitions from a set of states (d-subset). Thus we use them to compute the transition table of the *DFA* and we do not need any transition table of the *NFA* at all. This section shows the determinisation of *PMA* for exact and approximate string matching. For the example pattern we use "adbb", because the *DFA* ("Hamming" and "Levensthein" *PMA*, $k = 1$) has only 15 states after the determinisation.

3.1   Exact and "Hamming" Pattern Matching Automata

The nondeterministic and deterministic transition table for exact *PMA* is shown in Table 1. We do not highlight initial and final states in this paper, because this is not fundamental for the explanation.

Table 1. Transition table of the exact nondeterministic and deterministic pattern-matching automaton for the pattern $P = adbb$

NFA	a	b	d
0^0	$0^0 1^0$	0^0	0^0
1^0			2^0
2^0		3^0	
3^0		4^0	
4^0			

DFA	a	b	d
0^0	$0^0 1^0$	0^0	0^0
$0^0 1^0$	$0^0 1^0$	0^0	$0^0 2^0$
$0^0 2^0$	$0^0 1^0$	$0^0 3^0$	0^0
$0^0 3^0$	$0^0 1^0$	$0^0 4^0$	0^0
$0^0 4^0$	$0^0 1^0$	0^0	0^0

Using bit-parallelism for the determinisation, we need a bit-mask matrix D, which is partially different from the matrix for the pattern matching simulation defined in Section 2, and it is shown in Table 2. We will deal with the matrix $\overline{D}$ later when speaking about the Hamming distance. The first row for ε refers to the self-loop of *PMA*. The "shift-or" algorithm starts with vector $r_{j,0}^0 = 1, 0 < j \le m$ and therefore we need some initial vector too. This vector refers to the initial state and it has the following form: $r_{1,1}^0[\varepsilon] = 0, r_{j,1}^0[\varepsilon] = 1, 1 < j \le m + 1$. This vector has the length $m+1$, in spite of the pattern matching "shift-or" algorithm, due to the number of states of *NFA*.

Table 2. Matrices D and $\overline{D}$ for the pattern $P = adbb$

D	a	b	d	$A \setminus \{a, b, d\}$
ε	0	0	0	0
a	0	1	1	1
d	1	1	0	1
b	1	0	1	1
b	1	0	1	1

$\overline{D}$	a	b	d	$A \setminus \{a, b, d\}$
ε	1	1	1	1
a	1	0	0	0
d	0	0	1	0
b	0	1	0	0
b	0	1	0	0

The determinisation of exact *PMA* is very similar to pattern matching (1). The initial vector is left-shifted and new states are selected by the term **or** $D[x]$, where each symbol from the alphabet A is taken as symbol x. These new bit-vectors (see Table 3) refer to the deterministic states (d-subsets), and the bit-vectors are pushed in a queue. All zeros in a bit-vector correspond to the states of NFA. As we can see, the first four bit-vectors correspond to the first row of the transition table of DFA in Table 1. Already processed bit-vectors (referring to the d-subsets) are stored. In this case the initial bit-vector is stored, and later all already non-stored bit-vectors popped from the queue are also stored, after processing. The computation ends when the queue is empty.

Table 3. Matrix R^0 for determinisation of exact PMA for the pattern $P = adbb$

R^0	ε	a	b	d	ε	a	b	d	ε	a	b	d	ε	a	b	d	ε	a	b	d
0	0	0	0	0	0	0	0	0	0	0	0	0	0	0	0	0	0	0	0	0
1	1	0	1	1	0	0	1	1	1	0	1	1	1	0	1	1	1	0	1	1
2	1	1	1	1	1	1	1	0	0	1	1	1	1	1	1	1	1	1	1	1
3	1	1	1	1	1	1	1	1	1	1	0	1	0	1	1	1	1	1	1	1
4	1	1	1	1	1	1	1	1	1	1	1	1	1	1	0	1	0	1	1	1
d-subset	$\emptyset^0$	0^0_1	$\emptyset^0$	$\emptyset^0$	0^0_1	0^0_1	$\emptyset^0$	0^0_2	0^0_2	0^0_1	0^0_3	$\emptyset^0$	0^0_3	0^0_1	0^0_4	$\emptyset^0$	0^0_4	0^0_1	$\emptyset^0$	$\emptyset^0$

The determinisation is shown in Table 3. Each bit in the vector corresponds to one of the states (0-4) and the bit-vector popped from the queue is labeled with symbol "ε" in the header of the table. There follow all three symbols of the alphabet and the new bit-vectors pushed to queue. Each such quadruple is delimited by a double line.

Before formalizing these ideas, we prefer to look at the example of determinisation using Hamming distance $k=1$. The transition tables of both the NFA and DFA pattern-matching automaton for pattern $P = adbb$ using Hamming distance $k = 1$ are depicted in Table 4.

Using the Hamming distance k, four main changes have to be made in the algorithm to the original Formula (2). The first change is to the initial bit-vector. Because there is no state $0^l, 0 < l \le k$, we set $r^l_{j,1}[\varepsilon] = 1, 0 < j \le m+1, 0 \le l < k$, and the bit-vector $R^0_1[\varepsilon]$ remains.

The second change is to the computation style. In determinisation we need to know the exact level of the state, the number of mismatches. This level is given by index l of table R^l. Therefore in table R^0 there are bit-vectors corresponding to the deterministic states with upper index 0, in table R^1 corresponding to states with index 1 and so on. The d-subset is then merged from all $k + 1$ bit-vectors, therefore all $k + 1$ bit-vectors are computed together. The $(k + 1)$-tuple of the bit-vectors is pushed to and popped from the queue together.

The third change is to the algorithm. The idea of the "shift-or" algorithm is "when I found a pattern without mismatches I had to find it using mismatches too". However, this idea is wrong when dealing with determinisation, because it is originally implemented as "replace a symbol with any symbol, even with the same one". Since we need to know the exact level of the state, the number

Table 4. Transition table of the nondeterministic and deterministic pattern-matching automaton for the pattern $P = adbb$ and the Hamming distance $k=1$

DFA	a	b	d
0^0	$0^0 1^0$	$0^0 1^1$	$0^0 1^1$
$0^0 1^0$	$0^0 1^0 2^1$	$0^0 1^1 2^1$	$0^0 2^0 1^1$
$0^0 1^1$	$0^0 1^0$	$0^0 1^1$	$0^0 1^1 2^1$
$0^0 1^0 2^1$	$0^0 1^0 2^1$	$0^0 1^1 2^1 3^1$	$0^0 2^0 1^1$
$0^0 1^0 3^1$	$0^0 1^0 2^1$	$0^0 1^1 2^1 4^1$	$0^0 2^0 1^1$
$0^0 1^0 4^1$	$0^0 1^0 2^1$	$0^0 1^1 2^1$	$0^0 2^0 1^1$
$0^0 2^0 1^1$	$0^0 1^0 3^1$	$0^0 3^0 1^1$	$0^0 1^1 2^1 3^1$
$0^0 3^0 1^1$	$0^0 1^0 4^1$	$0^0 4^0 1^1$	$0^0 1^1 2^1 4^1$
$0^0 4^0 1^1$	$0^0 1^0$	$0^0 1^1$	$0^0 1^1 2^1$
$0^0 1^1 2^1$	$0^0 1^0$	$0^0 1^1 3^1$	$0^0 1^1 2^1$
$0^0 1^1 3^1$	$0^0 1^0$	$0^0 1^1 4^1$	$0^0 1^1 2^1$
$0^0 1^1 4^1$	$0^0 1^0$	$0^0 1^1$	$0^0 1^1 2^1$
$0^0 1^1 2^1 3^1$	$0^0 1^0$	$0^0 1^1 3^1 4^1$	$0^0 1^1 2^1$
$0^0 1^1 2^1 4^1$	$0^0 1^0$	$0^0 1^1 3^1$	$0^0 1^1 2^1$
$0^0 1^1 3^1 4^1$	$0^0 1^0$	$0^0 1^1 4^1$	$0^0 1^1 2^1$

NFA	a	b	d
0^0	$0^0 1^0$	$0^0 1^1$	$0^0 1^1$
1^0	2^1	2^1	2^0
2^0	3^1	3^0	3^1
3^0	4^1	4^0	4^1
4^0			
1^1			2^1
2^1		3^1	
3^1		4^1	
4^1			

of mismatches, the replace term $\mathbf{shl}(R_{i-1}^{l-1})$ in the table $R^l, l > 0$ is only used when there really is the replace transition in the automaton for that symbol. This means that we deselect states without these replace transitions and thus change the "replace" term to $(\mathbf{shl}(R_{i-1}^{l-1})$ **or** $\overline{D}[t_i])$.

The last change is to operation $\mathbf{shl}$. Any time when computing the table $R^l, l > 0$, we use operation $\mathbf{shl1}$ instead of operation $\mathbf{shl}$. This is because there is only one self-loop, exactly in state 0^0 and the right-most 0 in the operation $\mathbf{shl}$ refers exactly to it.

Table 5 shows an example of the determinisation of PMA for the pattern $P = adbb$ using the Hamming distance $k = 1$. The DFA contains 15 states, and for this reason both tables R^0 and R^1 are split into two parts, one above the other, to fit these tables on the page.

Here we formalise the "shift-or" determinisation algorithm. It uses sets $R^l, 0 \le l \le k$ of size $(m + 1) \times (|Q_D| \times (|A| + 1))$, where k is the maximum number of edit operations in pattern P of length m, and Q_D is the set of states of the deterministic PMA automaton. It also uses matrix D of size $(m + 1) \times |A|$, and, for the Hamming and Levenshtein distance, matrix $\overline{D}$ of size $(m + 1) \times |A|$.

Each element $r_{j,i}^l[x]$, $0 < j \le (m + 1)$, $0 < i \le |Q_D|$, $0 \le l \le k$, $x \in \{A \cup \varepsilon\}$ contains 0, if the d-subset corresponding to the vector $R_i^l[x]$ contains state j^l, or 1, otherwise. Each element $d_{j,x}$, $0 < j \le (m+1)$, $x \in A$, contains 0, if $p_j = x$ or $j = 1$, or 1, otherwise. Element $\overline{d}_{j,x}$ is bit-negated $d_{j,x}$.

In determinisation of exact PMA, vectors $R_i^0, 1 \le i \le |Q_D|$, are computed as follows:

$$
\begin{aligned}
r_{1,1}^0[\varepsilon] &= 0 \\
r_{j,1}^0[\varepsilon] &= 1, & 1 < j \le (m + 1) \\
R_i^0[x] &= \mathbf{shl}(R_i^0[\varepsilon]) \text{ \textbf{or} } D[x], & x \in A, 1 < i \le |Q_D|
\end{aligned}
\tag{5}
$$

Table 5. Matrices R^0 and R^1 for determinisation of PMA using the Hamming distance $k = 1$, $p = adbb$

R^0	ε	a	b	d	ε	a	b	d	ε	a	b	d	ε	a	b	d	ε	a	b	d	ε	a	b	d	ε	a	b	d	ε	a	b	d
0	0	0	0	0	0	0	0	0	0	0	0	0	0	0	0	0	0	0	0	0	0	0	0	0	0	0	0	0	0	0	0	0
1	1	0	1	1	0	0	1	1	1	0	1	1	0	0	1	1	1	0	1	1	1	0	1	1	1	0	1	1	1	0	1	1
2	1	1	1	1	1	1	1	0	1	1	1	1	1	1	1	0	1	1	1	1	0	1	1	1	1	1	1	1	1	1	1	1
3	1	1	1	1	1	1	1	1	1	1	1	1	1	1	1	1	1	1	1	1	1	1	0	1	1	1	1	1	1	1	1	1
4	1	1	1	1	1	1	1	1	1	1	1	1	1	1	1	1	1	1	1	1	1	1	1	1	1	1	1	1	1	1	1	1

R^1	ε	a	b	d	ε	a	b	d	ε	a	b	d	ε	a	b	d	ε	a	b	d	ε	a	b	d	ε	a	b	d	ε	a	b	d
0	1	1	1	1	1	1	1	1	1	1	1	1	1	1	1	1	1	1	1	1	1	1	1	1	1	1	1	1	1	1	1	1
1	1	1	0	0	1	1	0	0	0	1	0	0	1	1	0	0	0	1	0	0	0	1	0	0	0	1	0	0	0	1	0	0
2	1	1	1	1	1	0	0	1	1	1	1	0	0	0	0	1	0	1	1	0	1	1	1	0	0	1	1	0	1	1	1	0
3	1	1	1	1	1	1	1	1	1	1	1	1	1	1	0	1	1	1	0	1	1	0	1	0	0	1	0	1	0	1	1	1
4	1	1	1	1	1	1	1	1	1	1	1	1	1	1	1	1	1	1	1	1	1	1	0	1	1	1	0	1	1	1	0	1
d-subset	0^0				$0^0 1^0$				$0^0 1^1$				$0^0 1^0$				$0^0 1^0 2^1$				$0^0 1^2 1^1$				$0^0 2^0 1^1$				$0^0 1^1$			

R^0					ε	a	b	d	ε	a	b	d	ε	a	b	d	ε	a	b	d	ε	a	b	d	ε	a	b	d	ε	a	b	d
0					0	0	0	0	0	0	0	0	0	0	0	0	0	0	0	0	0	0	0	0	0	0	0	0	0	0	0	0
1					0	0	1	1	1	0	1	1	1	0	1	1	1	0	1	1	0	0	1	1	1	0	1	1	1	0	1	1
2	cont.				1	1	1	0	1	1	1	1	1	1	1	1	1	1	1	1	1	1	1	0	1	1	1	1	1	1	1	1
3					1	1	1	1	0	1	1	1	1	1	1	1	1	1	1	1	1	1	1	1	1	1	1	1	1	1	1	1
4					1	1	1	1	1	1	0	1	1	1	1	1	1	1	1	1	1	1	1	1	1	1	1	1	0	1	1	1

R^1					ε	a	b	d	ε	a	b	d	ε	a	b	d	ε	a	b	d	ε	a	b	d	ε	a	b	d	ε	a	b	d
0					1	1	1	1	1	1	1	1	1	1	1	1	1	1	1	1	1	1	1	1	1	1	1	1	1	1	1	1
1					1	1	0	0	0	1	0	0	0	1	0	0	1	1	0	0	0	1	0	0	0	1	0	0	0	1	0	0
2	cont.				1	0	0	1	1	1	1	0	1	1	1	0	1	0	0	1	0	1	1	0	1	1	1	0
3					0	1	1	1	1	1	1	1	0	1	1	1	1	1	1	1	1	1	1	1	1	0	1	1	1	1	1
4					1	1	0	1	1	0	1	0	0	1	0	1	0	1	1	1	0	1	1	1	0	1	1	1	1	1	1	1
d-subset					$0^0 1^0 3^1$ $0^0 1^0 2^1$				$0^0 3^0 1^1$ $0^0 1^0 4^1$				$0^0 1^1 3^1 4^1$ $0^0 1^1$				$0^0 1^0 2^1$ $0^0 1^1$				$0^0 1^1 4^1$ $0^0 1^0 2^1$				$0^0 1^0 4^1$ $0^0 2^0 1^1$				$0^0 1^2 1^4 1$ $0^0 1^0$				$0^0 1^0 3^1$ $0^0 1^0 2^1$			

In determinisation of approximate PMA using the Hamming distance, vectors $R_i^l, 0 \leq l \leq k, 1 \leq i \leq |Q_D|$, are computed as follows:

$$
\begin{aligned}
r_{1,1}^0[\varepsilon] &= 0 \\
r_{j,1}^0[\varepsilon] &= 1, & 1 < j \leq (m+1) \\
r_{j,1}^l[\varepsilon] &= 1, & 0 < j \leq (m+1), 1 \leq l \leq k \\
R_i^0[x] &= \mathbf{shl}(R_i^0[\varepsilon]) \text{ or } D[x], & x \in A, 1 < i \leq |Q_D| \\
R_i^l[x] &= (\mathbf{shl1}(R_i^l[\varepsilon]) \text{ or } D[x]) \\
&\quad \text{and } (\mathbf{shl1}(R_i^{l-1}[\varepsilon]) \text{ or } \overline{D}[x]), & 1 < i \leq |Q_D|, 0 < l \leq k, x \in A
\end{aligned}
\tag{6}
$$

Each bit-vector $R_i^l[\varepsilon]$ in Formulas (5) and (6) is exactly the bit-vector popped from the queue. The complete algorithm is then as follows:

Algorithm 1. Determinisation of the nondeterministic pattern-matching automaton using the "shift-or" algorithm.
Input: Pattern P, allowed number of mismatches k, an empty queue
Output: Deterministic pattern-matching automaton
Method:

```
 1 Create matrices D and D̄ for pattern P.
 2 Set step-counter i ← 1
 3 Create initial vectors R₁ˡ[ε], 0 ≤ l ≤ k.
 4 queue.push(R₁⁰[ε], R₁¹[ε], ..., R₁ᵏ[ε]).
 5 while not queue.empty()
 6 │  Rᵢ⁰[ε], Rᵢ¹[ε], ..., Rᵢᵏ[ε] ← queue.pop()
 7 │  for each x ∈ A do
 8 │  │  Compute Rᵢ⁰[x], Rᵢ¹[x], ..., Rᵢᵏ[x] using Formula(6)
 9 │  │  queue.push(Rᵢ⁰[x], Rᵢ¹[x], ..., Rᵢᵏ[x])
10 │  endfor
11 │  i ← i+1
12 endwhile
```

$\square$

Algorithm 1 remains unchanged for determinisation of both exact and Hamming NFA. It also assumes an intelligent queue, which pushes only new bit-vectors.

3.2 "Levenshtein" Pattern Matching Automata

The transition tables of both nondeterministic and deterministic PMA using the Levenshtein distance for the pattern $adbb$, $k = 1$ is shown in Table 6.

We have three edit operations using the Levenshtein distance and one "match" operation. The problem is the operation "delete". The idea from Formula (3) cannot be used, and we have to invent a new term representing this operation. The new idea follows the transitions in the automaton, where the operation "delete" is implemented by ε-transitions along the "replace" transitions. Hence, we have two types of sequences of transitions. The first is the transition labeled by a symbol followed by a sequence of ε-transitions. The second is a sequence of ε-transitions followed by the transition labeled by a symbol.

Both cases need special bit-vectors computed along with bit-vectors R_i^l. We use bit-vectors $E_i^l[x]$ for the first case defined as follows:

$$
\begin{aligned}
E_i^0[x] &= R_i^0[x], & 1 \leq i \leq (m+1) \\
E_i^l[x] &= \mathbf{shl1}(E_i^{l-1}[x]) \text{ and } R_i^l[x], & l < i \leq (m+1), 1 \leq l \leq k
\end{aligned}
\tag{7}
$$

The bit-vector $E_i^{l-1}[x]$ represents states accessible by the transition x followed by ε-transitions (operation "delete"). We define bit-vectors $E_i^l[\varepsilon]$ for the second case as follows:

$$
\begin{aligned}
E_i^0[\varepsilon] &= R_i^0[\varepsilon], & 1 \leq i \leq (m+1) \\
E_i^l[\varepsilon] &= \mathbf{shl1}(E_i^{l-1}[\varepsilon]) \text{ and } R_i^l[\varepsilon], & l < i \leq (m+1), 1 \leq l \leq k
\end{aligned}
\tag{8}
$$

Table 6. Transition table of the nondeterministic and deterministic pattern-matching automaton for the pattern $P = adbb$ and the Levenshtein distance $k=1$

DFA	a	b	d
0^0	$0^0 1^0$	$0^0 1^1$	$0^0 1^1 2^1$
$0^0 1^0$	$0^0 1^0 1^1 2^1$	$0^0 1^1 2^1 3^1$	$0^0 2^0 1^1 2^1$
$0^0 1^1$	$0^0 1^0$	$0^0 1^1$	$0^0 1^1 2^1$
$0^0 1^1 2^1$	$0^0 1^0$	$0^0 1^1 3^1$	$0^0 1^1 2^1$
$0^0 1^1 3^1$	$0^0 1^0$	$0^0 1^1 4^1$	$0^0 1^1 2^1$
$0^0 1^1 4^1$	$0^0 1^0$	$0^0 1^1$	$0^0 1^1 2^1$
$0^0 1^0 1^1 2^1$	$0^0 1^0 1^1 2^1$	$0^0 1^1 2^1 3^1$	$0^0 2^0 1^1 2^1$
$0^0 1^0 2^1 3^1$	$0^0 1^0 1^1 2^1$	$0^0 1^1 2^1 3^1 4^1$	$0^0 2^0 1^1 2^1$
$0^0 1^0 3^1 4^1$	$0^0 1^0 1^1 2^1$	$0^0 1^1 2^1 3^1 4^1$	$0^0 2^0 1^1 2^1$
$0^0 2^0 1^1 2^1$	$0^0 1^0 2^1 3^1$	$0^0 3^0 1^1 2^1 3^1 4^1$	$0^0 1^1 2^1 3^1$
$0^0 1^1 2^1 3^1$	$0^0 1^0$	$0^0 1^1 3^1 4^1$	$0^0 1^1 2^1$
$0^0 1^1 3^1 4^1$	$0^0 1^0$	$0^0 1^1 4^1$	$0^0 1^1 2^1$
$0^0 4^0 1^1 3^1 4^1$	$0^0 1^0$	$0^0 1^1 4^1$	$0^0 1^1 2^1$
$0^0 1^1 2^1 3^1 4^1$	$0^0 1^0$	$0^0 1^1 3^1 4^1$	$0^0 1^1 2^1$
$0^0 3^0 1^1 2^1 3^1 4^1$	$0^0 1^0 3^1 4^1$	$0^0 4^0 1^1 3^1 4^1$	$0^0 1^1 2^1 3^1 4^1$

NFA	a	b	d
0^0	$0^0 1^0$	$0^0 1^1$	$0^0 1^1 2^1$
1^0	$1^1 2^1$	$1^1 2^1 3^1$	$2^0 1^1$
2^0	$2^1 3^1$	$3^0 2^1 4^1$	$2^1 3^1$
3^0	$3^1 4^1$	$4^0 3^1$	$3^1 4^1$
4^0			
1^1			2^1
2^1		3^1	
3^1		4^1	
4^1			

The operations "match", "replace", and "insert" use the second case and thus the bit-vectors $E_i^l[\varepsilon]$. Operation "delete" following a non-ε-transition uses the bit-vectors $E_i^l[x]$ and it is represented by the term: $(\mathbf{shl1}(E_i^{l-1}[x]))$.

For the operation "match" and "replace" we use Formula (6), but we have to count with the ε-transitions. Therefore these operations are represented by the terms $(\mathbf{shl1}(E_i^l[\varepsilon])$ **or** $D[x])$ and $(\mathbf{shl1}(E_i^{l-1}[\varepsilon])$ **or** $\overline{D}[x])$, respectively.

The operation "insert" is similar to the operation "insert" in Formula (3) and it is represented by the term $R_i^{l-1}[\varepsilon]$. Of course, we have to count with the ε-transitions, and the automaton does not have states $0^l, 1 \leq l \leq k$, $1^l, 2 \leq l \leq k, \ldots, (k-1)^k$, and this is different from a pattern matching issue, which might contain them for simplicity in the bit-parallel algorithms. Therefore we use auxiliary vectors Z^l defined as follows:

$$\begin{aligned} z_i^l &= 1, \quad 1 \leq i \leq l, 1 \leq l \leq k \\ z_i^l &= 0, \quad l < i \leq (m+1), 1 \leq l \leq k \end{aligned} \tag{9}$$

and the "insert" term has the form: $(E_i^{l-1}[\varepsilon]$ **or** Z^l **or** $V)$, where V is defined as Formula (4).

Now we might define the exact formula for determinisation using the Levenshtein distance as follows:

$$\begin{aligned} r_{1,1}^0[\varepsilon] &= 0 \\ r_{j,1}^0[\varepsilon] &= 1, & 1 < j \leq (m+1) \\ r_{j,1}^l[\varepsilon] &= 1, & 0 < j \leq (m+1), 1 \leq l \leq k \\ R_i^0[x] &= \mathbf{shl}(R_i^0[\varepsilon])\ \textbf{or}\ D[x], & x \in A, 1 < i \leq |Q_D| \\ R_i^l[x] &= (\mathbf{shl1}(E_i^l[\varepsilon])\ \textbf{or}\ D[x]) \\ & \quad \textbf{and}\ (\mathbf{shl1}(E_i^{l-1}[\varepsilon])\ \textbf{or}\ \overline{D}[x]) \\ & \quad \textbf{and}\ (E_i^{l-1}[\varepsilon]\ \textbf{or}\ Z^l\ \textbf{or}\ V) \\ & \quad \textbf{and}\ (\mathbf{shl1}(E_i^{l-1}[x])), & 1 < i \leq |Q_D|, 0 < l \leq k, x \in A \end{aligned} \tag{10}$$

Table 7. Matrices R^0 and R^1 for determinisation of PMA using the Levenshtein distance $k = 1$, $P = adbb$

R^0	ε	a	b	d	ε	a	b	d	ε	a	b	d	ε	a	b	d	ε	a	b	d	ε	a	b	d		a	b	d	ε	a	b	d
0	0	0	0	0	0	0	0	0	0	0	0	0	0	0	0	0	0	0	0	0	0	0	0	0	0	0	0	0	0	0	0	0
1	1	0	1	1	0	0	1	1	1	0	1	1	1	0	1	1	0	0	1	1	1	0	1	1	1	0	1	1	1	0	1	1
2	1	1	1	1	1	1	1	0	1	1	1	1	1	1	1	1	1	1	1	0	1	1	1	1	0	1	1	1	1	1	1	1
3	1	1	1	1	1	1	1	1	1	1	1	1	1	1	1	1	1	1	1	1	1	1	1	1	1	1	0	1	1	1	1	1
4	1	1	1	1	1	1	1	1	1	1	1	1	1	1	1	1	1	1	1	1	1	1	1	1	1	1	1	1	1	1	1	1

R^1	ε	a	b	d	ε	a	b	d	ε	a	b	d	ε	a	b	d	ε	a	b	d	ε	a	b	d	ε	a	b	d	ε	a	b	d
0	1	1	1	1	1	1	1	1	1	1	1	1	1	1	1	1	1	1	1	1	1	1	1	1	1	1	1	1	1	1	1	1
1	1	1	0	0	1	0	0	0	0	1	0	0	0	1	0	0	0	0	0	0	0	1	0	0	0	1	0	0	0	1	0	1
2	1	1	1	0	1	0	0	0	1	1	1	0	0	1	1	0	0	0	0	0	0	1	1	0	0	0	0	0	1	1	1	0
3	1	1	1	1	1	1	0	1	1	1	1	1	1	1	0	1	1	1	0	1	0	1	0	1	1	0	0	0	0	1	1	1
4	1	1	1	1	1	1	1	1	1	1	1	1	1	1	1	1	1	1	1	1	1	1	0	1	1	1	0	1	1	1	0	1

| d-subset | 0^0 | $0^0 1^0$ | $0^0 1^1$ | $0^0 1^1 2^1$ | $0^0 1^0$ | $0^0 1^0 1^2 1^1$ · $0^0 1^2 3^1 1^2$ · $0^0 2^0 1^2 1^2$ | $0^0 1^1$ · $0^0 1^0$ · $0^0 1^1$ · $0^0 1^1 2^1$ | $0^0 1^2 1^2$ · $0^0 1^0$ · $0^0 1^3 1^1$ · $0^0 1^2 1^2$ |

R^0				ε	a	b	d	ε	a	b	d	ε	a	b	d	ε	a	b	d	ε	a	b	d	ε	a	b	d	ε	a	b	d
0				0	0	0	0	0	0	0	0	0	0	0	0	0	0	0	0	0	0	0	0	0	0	0	0	0	0	0	0
1				1	0	1	1	0	0	1	1	1	0	1	1	1	0	1	1	1	0	1	1	0	0	1	1	1	0	1	1
2		*cont.*		1	1	1	1	1	1	1	0	1	1	1	1	1	1	1	1	1	1	1	1	1	1	1	0	1	1	1	1
3				1	1	1	1	1	1	1	1	0	1	1	1	1	1	1	1	1	1	1	1	1	1	1	1	1	1	1	1
4				1	1	1	1	1	1	1	1	1	1	0	1	1	1	1	1	1	1	1	1	1	1	1	1	0	1	1	1

R^1				ε	a	b	d	ε	a	b	d	ε	a	b	d	ε	a	b	d	ε	a	b	d	ε	a	b	d	ε	a	b	d
0				1	1	1	1	1	1	1	1	1	1	1	1	1	1	1	1	1	1	1	1	1	1	1	1	1	1	1	1
1				0	1	0	0	1	0	0	0	0	1	0	0	0	1	0	0	0	1	0	0	1	0	0	0	0	1	0	0
2		*cont.*		1	1	1	0	0	0	0	0	0	1	1	0	1	1	1	0	0	1	1	0	1	0	0	0	1	1	1	0
3				0	1	1	1	0	1	0	1	0	0	0	0	1	1	1	1	0	1	0	1	0	1	0	1	0	1	1	1
4				0	1	0	1	1	1	0	1	0	0	0	0	0	1	1	1	0	1	0	1	0	1	0	1	0	1	0	1

| d-subset | | | | $0^0 1^3 1^4$ · $0^0 1^4$ | $0^0 1^4 1^2$ | $0^0 1^2 1^2$ · $0^0 1^0 1^2$ · $0^0 1^2 3^1 4^1$ · $0^0 2^0 1^2 1^2$ | $0^3 3^1 1^2 1^3 4^1$ · $0^0 1^0 3^1 4^1$ · $0^0 4^1 1^3 4^1$ · $0^0 1^2 3^1 4^1$ | $0^0 1^4 1^2$ · $0^0 1^0$ · $0^0 1^{-1}$ · $0^0 1^2 1^2$ | $0^0 1^2 3^1 4^1$ · $0^0 1^0$ · $0^0 1^3 1^2$ · $0^0 1^2 1^2$ | $0^0 1^3 4^1$ · $0^0 1^0 1^2$ · $0^0 1^2 3^1 4^1$ · $0^0 2^1 1^2$ | $0^0 1^4 1^3 4^1$ · $0^0 1^0$ · $0^0 1^4 1^1$ · $0^0 1^2 1^2$ |

The example for pattern *adbb* is shown in Table 7. Algorithm 1 holds even with the Levenshtein distance, with one exception. The Formula 10 is used instead of Formula 6.

Each bit-vector $E_i^l[\varepsilon], l > 0$ is in fact computed twice. Once as $E_i^l[x]$ and then once more, after the bit-vectors $R_i^l[\varepsilon]$ are popped from the queue. To avoid this, the bit-vectors $E_i^l[x]$ can be pushed to the queue with the bit-vectors $R_i^l[x]$ and popped as the bit-vectors $E_j^l[\varepsilon], j > i$.

4   Determinisation of Suffix Automata

Determinisation of suffix automata is easier than determinisation of PMA, mainly because of the missing self-loop. However, it is more complicated to establish the initial bit-vectors. When they have been established, the determinisation is very similar to the determinisation of PMA and therefore we explain the process on an example using the Hamming distance $k = 1$ without bothering with an exact case. Once more we use the pattern $P = adbb$, and the transition table of the suffix automaton for this pattern using the Hamming distance $k = 1$ is given in Table 8.

Table 8. Transition table of the deterministic and nondeterministic suffix automaton for the pattern $P = adbb$ using the Hamming distance $k = 1$

DFA	a	b	d
0^0	$1^0 2^1 3^1 4^1$	$3^0 4^0 1^1 2^1$	$2^0 1^1 3^1 4^1$
2^0	3^1	3^0	3^1
3^0	4^1	4^0	4^1
4^0			
2^1		3^1	
3^1		4^1	
4^1			
$3^0 4^1$	4^1	4^0	4^1
$4^0 3^1$		4^1	
$2^1 3^1$		$3^1 4^1$	
$2^1 4^1$		3^1	
$3^1 4^1$		4^1	
$2^1 3^1 4^1$		$3^1 4^1$	
$1^0 2^1 3^1 4^1$	2^1	$2^1 3^1 4^1$	2^0
$2^0 1^1 3^1 4^1$	3^1	$3^0 4^1$	$2^1 3^1$
$3^0 4^0 1^1 2^1$	4^1	$4^0 3^1$	$2^1 4^1$

NFA	a	b	d
0^0	$1^0 2^1 3^1 4^1$	$3^0 4^0 1^1 2^1$	$2^0 1^1 3^1 4^1$
1^0	2^1	2^1	2^0
2^0	3^1	3^0	3^1
3^0	4^1	4^0	4^1
4^0			
1^1			2^1
2^1		3^1	
3^1		4^1	
4^1			

We explain the determinisation using the "shift-or" algorithm. First we need the initial bit-vectors. They are obtained from the first row of the transition table of NFA by converting the d-subsets into bit-vectors. These bit-vectors are the first four bit-vectors in the set R^0 in Table 10. The initial bit-vectors and no other bit-vectors derived from them refers to the initial state 0^0 of the NFA, and therefore matrices D and $\overline{D}$ no longer contain the row for symbol ε and these matrices are shown in Table 9.

Table 9. Matrices D and $\overline{D}$ for the pattern $P = adbb$

D	a	b	d	$A \setminus \{a,b,d\}$
a	0	1	1	1
d	1	1	0	1
b	1	0	1	1
b	1	0	1	1

$\overline{D}$	a	b	d	$A \setminus \{a,b,d\}$
a	1	0	0	0
d	0	0	1	0
b	0	1	0	0
b	0	1	0	0

The determinisation is shown in Table 10, and it is processed using the same rules as in Formula (6) except for two changes. The first change is to the initial vectors $R_1^l[\varepsilon]$ and $R_1^l[x]$, $x \in A$ as we have already explained. The second change

Table 10. Matrices R^0 and R^1 for determinisation of the suffix automata using the Hamming distance $k = 1$, $P = adbb$

R^0	ε	a	b	d	ε	a	b	d	ε	a	b	d	ε	a	b	d	ε	a	b	d	ε	a	b	d	ε	a	b	d	ε	a	b	d
1	0	0	1	1	0	1	1	1	1	1	1	1	1	1	1	1	1	1	1	1	1	1	1	1	1	1	1	1	1	1	1	1
2	1	1	1	0	1	1	1	0	1	1	1	1	0	1	1	1	1	1	1	1	1	1	1	1	0	1	1	1	1	1	1	1
3	1	1	0	1	1	1	1	1	0	1	1	1	1	1	0	1	1	1	1	1	1	1	1	1	1	1	0	1	1	1	1	1
4	1	1	0	1	1	1	1	1	0	1	0	1	1	1	1	1	1	1	1	1	1	1	1	1	1	1	1	1	1	1	1	1

R^1	ε	a	b	d	ε	a	b	d	ε	a	b	d	ε	a	b	d	ε	a	b	d	ε	a	b	d	ε	a	b	d	ε	a	b	d
1	1	1	0	0	1	1	1	1	0	1	1	1	0	1	1	1	1	1	1	1	1	1	1	1	1	1	1	1	1	1	1	1
2	1	0	0	1	0	0	0	1	0	1	1	0	1	1	1	0	0	1	1	1	0	1	1	1	1	1	1	1	1	1	1	1
3	1	0	1	0	0	1	0	1	1	1	0	1	0	0	1	0	1	1	0	1	0	1	0	1	1	0	1	0	1	1	1	1
4	1	0	1	0	0	1	0	1	1	0	1	0	0	1	0	1	1	1	1	1	0	1	0	1	1	0	1	0	0	1	1	1

d-subset labels (in reading order): 1^0, $1^0 2^1 3^1 4^1$, $3^0 4^0 1^2 4^1$, $2^0 1^3 3^1 4^1$, $1^0 2^1 3^1 4^1$, 2^1, $2^1 3^1 4^1$, 2^0, $3^0 4^0 1^2 1$, 4^1, $4^0 3^1$, $2^1 4^1$, $2^0 1^3 3^1 4^1$, 3^1, $3^0 4^1$, $2^1 3^1$, 2^1, 3^1, $2^1 3^1 4^1$, $3^1 4^1$, 2^0, 3^1, 3^0, 3^1, 4^1

R^0	ε	a	b	d	ε	a	b	d	ε	a	b	d	ε	a	b	d	ε	a	b	d	ε	a	b	d	ε	a	b	d	ε	a	b	d
1	1	1	1	1	1	1	1	1	1	1	1	1	1	1	1	1	1	1	1	1	1	1	1	1	1	1	1	1	1	1	1	1
2	1	1	1	1	1	1	1	1	1	1	1	1	1	1	1	1	1	1	1	1	1	1	1	1	1	1	1	1	1	1	1	1
3	1	1	1	1	1	1	1	1	1	1	1	1	0	1	1	1	1	1	1	1	1	1	1	1	0	1	1	1	1	1	1	1
4	0	1	1	1	1	1	1	1	1	1	1	1	1	1	0	1	1	1	1	1	1	1	1	1	1	1	0	1	0	1	1	1

R^1	ε	a	b	d	ε	a	b	d	ε	a	b	d	ε	a	b	d	ε	a	b	d	ε	a	b	d	ε	a	b	d	ε	a	b	d
1	1	1	1	1	1	1	1	1	1	1	1	1	1	1	1	1	1	1	1	1	1	1	1	1	1	1	1	1	1	1	1	1
2	1	1	1	1	0	1	1	1	1	1	1	1	1	1	1	1	0	1	1	1	1	1	1	1	1	1	1	1	1	1	1	1
3	0	1	1	1	1	1	0	1	0	1	1	1	1	1	1	1	0	1	0	1	0	1	1	1	1	1	1	1	1	1	1	1
4	1	1	0	1	0	1	1	1	1	1	0	1	0	0	1	0	1	1	0	1	0	1	0	1	1	0	1	0	1	1	1	1

d-subset labels (in reading order): $4^0 3^1$, 4^1, $2^1 4^1$, 3^1, 3^1, 4^1, $3^0 4^1$, 4^1, $4^1 3^0$, $2^1 3^1$, $3^1 4^1$, $3^1 4^1$, 4^1, 3^0, 4^1, 4^0, 4^1, 4^0

is to the **shl** operation. Because there is no self-loop, every **shl** operation in Formula (6) is rather operation **shl1**. Since there is no self-loop, the bit-vectors R may be one-bit shorter.

Now we can define the formal formulas of computation. The initial bit-vectors for $R_1^0[\varepsilon]$ are exactly the bit-vectors from matrix D. This is because all states were active due to the ε-transitions at the beginning – vector $(00\ldots0)$ – and a move using symbol $x \in A$ is performed as $\mathbf{shl}(00\ldots0)$ or $D[x]$. The initial bit-vectors for $R_1^1[\varepsilon]$ are exactly the bit-vectors from matrix $\overline{D}$, because the "replace" transitions are used. Other initial bit-vectors $R_{j,1}^l[\varepsilon] = 1$ for all $l \leq 2 \leq k, 1 \leq j \leq m$.

In the determinisation of the exact suffix automaton, vectors $R_i^0, 0 \leq i \leq |Q_D|$, are computed as follows:

$$
\begin{aligned}
r_{1,1}^0[\varepsilon] &= 0 \\
r_{j,1}^0[\varepsilon] &= 1, & 1 &< j \leq m \\
R_1^0[x] &= D[x], & x &\in A \\
R_i^0[x] &= \mathbf{shl1}(R_i^0[\varepsilon]) \text{ or } D[x], & x &\in A, 1 < i \leq |Q_D|
\end{aligned}
\tag{11}
$$

In the determinisation of the approximate suffix automaton using the Hamming distance, vectors $R_i^l, 0 \leq l \leq k, 0 \leq i \leq |Q_D|$, are computed as follows:

$$
\begin{aligned}
r_{1,1}^0[\varepsilon] &= 0 \\
r_{j,1}^0[\varepsilon] &= 1, & 1 &< j \leq m \\
R_1^0[x] &= D[x], & x &\in A \\
R_1^1[x] &= \overline{D}[x], & x &\in A \\
r_{j,1}^l[\varepsilon] &= 1, & 0 &< j \leq m, 0 < l \leq k \\
R_i^0[x] &= \mathbf{shl1}(R_i^0[\varepsilon]) \text{ or } D[x], & x &\in A, 1 < i \leq |Q_D| \\
R_i^l[x] &= (\mathbf{shl1}(R_i^l[\varepsilon]) \text{ or } D[x]) \\
&\quad \text{and } (\mathbf{shl1}(R_i^{l-1}[\varepsilon]) \text{ or } \overline{D}[x]), & 1 &< i \leq |Q_D|, 0 < l \leq k, x \in A
\end{aligned}
\tag{12}
$$

The complete Algorithm 1 still holds, except that Formula (12) is used instead of Formula (6). Of course, the initial bit-vectors $R_1^0[x]$ have to be pushed to the queue instead of $R_1^0[\varepsilon]$.

5 Conclusion

We have presented algorithms for simulation of the determinisation of special types of finite automata, pattern-matching automata and suffix automata.

The algorithms take $\mathcal{O}(|Q_D| \times |A| \times (k+1) + \tau)$ time, where Q_D is the set of states after the determinisation, A is the input alphabet, k is the number of allowed edit operations, and τ is the time needed to search among the already existing d-subsets to verify the uniqueness of the d-subset. The standard subset construction takes $\mathcal{O}(|Q_D| \times |Q| \times \mathcal{C} \times |A| + \tau)$, where $\mathcal{C}$ is the number of transitions from one state. Since $\mathcal{C}$ is $\mathcal{O}(1)$ for exact automata and $\mathcal{O}(k)$ for approximate automata using the Levenshtein distance, our algorithm is $|Q| = \mathcal{O}(m)$ times faster for these automata. Since $\mathcal{C} = \mathcal{O}(1)$ for the Hamming distance, our algorithm is $\mathcal{O}(\frac{m}{k})$ times faster for this case. This result is valid for both the *PMA* and suffix automaton.

It is interesting that the determinisation process does not need any transition table, even a nondeterministic table. The determinisation is driven only by the formulas of the "shift-or" algorithm.

References

[BYG92] Ricardo A. Baeza-Yates and Gaston H. Gonnet. A new approach to text searching. *Commun. ACM*, 35(10):74–82, 1992.

[Döm64] B. Dömölki. An algorithm for syntactic analysis. *Computational Linguistics*, 8:29–46, 1964.

[Ham86] Richard W. Hamming. *Coding and information theory (2nd ed.)*. Prentice-Hall, Inc., Upper Saddle River, NJ, USA, 1986.

[HMU01] J. E. Hopcroft, R. Motwani, and J. D. Ulman. *Introduction to Automata Theory, Languages, and Computation (2nd ed.)*. Addison-Wesley, 2001.

[Hol00]   J. Holub. *Simulation of Nondeterministic Finite Automata in Pattern Matching*. Ph.D. Thesis, Czech Technical University in Prague, February 2000.

[NR98]   G. Navarro and M. Raffinot. A bit-parallel approach to suffix automata: Fast extended string matching. In M. Farach-Colton, editor, *Proceedings of the 9th Annual Symposium on Combinatorial Pattern Matching*, number 1448, pages 14–33, Piscataway, NJ, 1998. Springer-Verlag, Berlin.

[WM92]   Sun Wu and Udi Manber. Fast text searching allowing errors. *Commun. ACM*, 35(10):83–91, 1992.

Proving ATL* Properties of Infinite-State Systems

Matteo Slanina, Henny B. Sipma, and Zohar Manna*

Stanford University
{matteo, sipma, manna}@cs.stanford.edu

Abstract. Alternating temporal logic (ATL*) was introduced to prove properties of multi-agent systems in which the agents have different objectives and may collaborate to achieve them. Examples include (distributed) controlled systems, security protocols, and contract-signing protocols. Proving ATL* properties over finite-state systems was shown decidable by Alur et al., and a model checker for the sublanguage ATL implemented in MOCHA.

In this paper we present a sound and complete proof system for proving ATL* properties over infinite-state systems. The proof system reduces proofs of ATL* properties over systems to first-order verification conditions in the underlying assertion language. The verification conditions make use of predicate transformers that depend on the system structure, so that proofs over systems with a simpler structure, e.g., turn-based systems, directly result in simpler verification conditions. We illustrate the use of the proof system on a small example.

1 Introduction

ATL* [1] is a logic used to specify properties of computing systems in which different agents have different goals. It allows reasoning about temporal properties that players can achieve in cooperation or competition with each other.

Alur et al. [1] showed that the verification of ATL* properties over *finite-state* systems is decidable, and they proposed several model-checking algorithms. Model checking of ATL (a restricted form of ATL*) properties over finite-state alternating systems was implemented in MOCHA [2]. MOCHA has since been applied to the analysis of a wide variety of systems, extending to such diverse realms as security and contract-signing protocols [3, 4, 5], or mechanism design [6]. Although in some of these analyses the restriction to finite-state systems was not a problem, in general this is not the case. For example, the analysis of the multi-party contract-signing protocol of [4, 5], which is parameterized by the number of participating parties, was limited to small instances with three or four parties. Thus there is a need for methods for verifying ATL properties over infinite-state systems.

---

* This research was supported in part by NSF grants CCR-01-21403, CCR-02-20134, CCR-02-09237, CNS-0411363, and CCF-0430102, by ARO grant DAAD19-01-1-0723, and by NAVY/ONR contract N00014-03-1-0939.

K. Barkaoui, A. Cavalcanti, and A. Cerone (Eds.): ICTAC 2006, LNCS 4281, pp. 242–256, 2006.

In this paper we present a sound and complete proof system for proving ATL* properties over infinite-state alternating systems.

Proof systems for program logics come in two flavors. The first approach [7] reduces proofs of system properties to proofs of validities in the program logic. To prove a property φ over a system $\mathcal{S}$, the system is encoded in a formula $\Phi_{\mathcal{S}}$ in the program logic, and $\Phi_{\mathcal{S}} \rightarrow \varphi$ is proved valid. A complete proof system of this kind for propositional ATL was developed by Goranko & al. [8]. The second approach [9, 10, 11] reduces proofs of system properties to proofs of first-order validities by means of rules that act on the system representation directly. The proof system proposed in this paper follows the second approach.

Our proof system consists of proof rules that reduce the verification of an ATL* property over an alternating system to a set of first-order *verification conditions* in the underlying assertion language of the system. The verification conditions are expressed in terms of a *controllable predecessor* predicate transformer (cpre). The advantage of parameterizing the proof rules by cpre is that the rules are independent of the system structure, but the resulting verification conditions for different types of systems – e.g., turn-based systems – can be simplified by instantiating cpre with the version that exploits the more constrained system structure. The proof rules are constructive: a proof of the verification conditions can be used to construct controllers for the original property proved.

Our proof system incrementally converts temporal formulas into finite automata that are then composed with the system. This technique of lifting automata-theoretic results to proof systems was first proposed by Vardi and applied to LTL [12]. Later a similar approach was applied to CTL [13] and CTL* [11]. Our approach is most closely related to that in [11].

The rest of the paper is organized as follows. Section 2 presents our model of computation. Section 3 defines ATL*. Section 4 describes the proof system and Section 5 concludes. The models and proof rules are illustrated with a small example. Proofs of soundness and completeness can be found in [14].

2   Alternating Discrete Systems

As computational model we use *alternating discrete systems* (ADS), based on the fair discrete systems of Kesten and Pnueli [11]. An ADS is a general first-order representation of alternating structures, that generalizes turn-based, synchronous and asynchronous concurrency models of [1] and recursive programming languages. States and fairness conditions are represented as value assignments to a finite set of typed variables. To enable a first-order representation of the next-state relation, the player's available actions are represented by special *action variables*. The formal definitions are as follows.

An alternating discrete system (ADS) is a tuple

$$\mathcal{S} = \langle \Omega, V_S, V_\Omega, \xi, \chi, \mathcal{F} \rangle ,$$

where:

- Ω is a finite set of players.
- V_S is a finite set of typed system variables; a *state* is a typed value assignment to the variables in V_S; the set of all states is denoted by Σ.
- $V_\Omega = \langle V_a \mid a \in \Omega \rangle$ provides each player with a finite set of typed action variables. An a-action is a typed value assignment to the variables in V_a; the set of all a-actions is denoted by Γ_a. An A-action for a set of players $A \subseteq \Omega$ is a typed value assignment to the variables in $V_A = \bigcup_{a \in A} V_a$; the set of all A-actions is denoted by Γ_A. We write Γ for Γ_Ω.
- $\xi = \langle \xi_a \mid a \in \Omega \rangle$ associates to each player a a first-order formula over variables V_S and V_a that restricts the actions player a can choose at each state: at state V_S, player a can choose only actions such that $\xi_a(V_S, V_a)$ holds. The extension of ξ to a set of players $A \subseteq \Omega$ is defined as $\xi_A(V_S, V_A) \equiv \bigwedge_{a \in A} \xi_a(V_S, V_a)$.
- χ is a first-order formula over V_S, V_Ω, V_S'; χ represents the game matrix: $\chi(V_S, V_\Omega, V_S')$ expresses that the system can move from state V_S to state V_S' when the players' choices are V_Ω.
- $\mathcal{F} : \Omega \rightarrow \mathbb{B}(\infty \operatorname{QF}(V_S))$ assigns to each player a fairness condition, represented as a Boolean formula over atoms of the form ∞p (read "infinitely many times p"), where p is an assertion (quantifier-free formula) over V_S. For example, $\infty(x = 2 \land y > x) \rightarrow \infty(y \geq z^2)$.

We assume that an ADS has no blocking states, i.e., states from which a player has no legal action, or from which there is no available successor state for certain choices of the players. Clearly, the property of being non-blocking can be expressed by a simple set of verification conditions, of the following forms:

$$\forall V_S \exists V_a. \xi_a(V_S, V_a) \text{ for all } a \in \Omega, \text{ and}$$
$$\forall V_S \forall V_\Omega. \xi_\Omega(V_S, V_\Omega) \rightarrow \exists V_S'. \chi(V_S, V_\Omega, V_S') \ .$$

The non-blocking assumption is not restrictive, since we can add a new state and make all previously blocking actions move to it; from there, all actions would then lead back to the same state. Thus we can assume without mentioning that these conditions hold in any system under consideration.

Some of the proof rules that we shall describe modify the underlying ADS. In those cases, if the original ADS is non-blocking, then the modified one is non-blocking too.

Example 1. As an illustration of the computational model of ADS, consider the model of PROCESSOR, a simple system consisting of a processor that must be scheduled to execute multiple processes, shown in Fig. 1. In the model, processes are stored in a queue, represented by the system variable qu, and the processor is either active or not active, represented by the boolean system variable pa. When the processor is inactive, a new process, represented by the environment action variable np, can enter and is inserted at the end of the queue. The environment may choose not to enter a new process by setting np to $\bot$. When the processor becomes active, the process at the head of the queue is therefrom

$$\Omega : \quad \{Env, Sched\}$$
$$V_S : \quad \{qu : \text{list of process}, pa : boolean, xp : \text{process}_\perp\}$$
$$V_{Env} : \quad \{np : \text{process}_\perp, te : \{no, yes, cont\}\}$$
$$V_{Sched} : \{pos : \mathbb{N}\}$$
$$\xi_{Env} : \quad \text{T}$$
$$\xi_{Sched} : \quad pa \rightarrow (0 \le pos \le |qu|)$$

$$\chi : \quad \begin{array}{ll}
(\neg pa \wedge np = \perp \wedge pres\{pa, xp, qu\}) & \vee \\
(\neg pa \wedge np \neq \perp \wedge qu' = append(qu, np) \wedge pres\{pa, xp\}) & \vee \\
(\neg pa \wedge np = \perp \wedge qu \neq empty \wedge pa' \wedge qu = cons(xp', qu')) & \vee \\
(pa \wedge te = no \wedge pres\{pa, xp\}) & \vee \\
(pa \wedge te = yes \wedge \neg pa' \wedge xp' = \perp \wedge pres\{qu\}) & \vee \\
(pa \wedge te = cont \wedge \neg pa' \wedge xp' = \perp \wedge qu' = insert(qu, pos, xp))
\end{array}$$

$$\mathcal{F}_{Env} : \quad \infty \neg pa \wedge \infty pa$$
$$\mathcal{F}_{Sched} : \text{T}$$

Fig. 1. ADS for PROCESSOR: $pres\{\dots\}$ means the values are preserved by the transition; *append* adds an element to the end of a list, *insert* adds an element at a certain position, &c

removed and becomes the *executing process*, represented by the system variable xp. When the process releases the processor, it may or may not need to continue later, represented by the environment action variable te. If it needs to continue, the scheduler reinserts it in the queue at the position determined by its action variable pos. It is assumed that all executing processes eventually release the processor and that there is an unlimited supply of processes to be executed, represented by the environment fairness condition. An informal representation of the model is shown in Fig. 2.

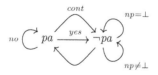

Fig. 2. Informal representation of ADS for PROCESSOR

Given an ADS $\mathcal{S}$, a run consists of the following game played ad infinitum: At each state $s \in \Sigma$ assigning values to variables V_S, every player $a \in \Omega$, independently of the others, picks an action by choosing values for the local variables V_a so that $\xi_a(V_S, V_a)$ holds. Then, the next state is nondeterministically chosen among the assignments to V_S' such that $\chi(V_S, V_\Omega, V_S')$ holds. Notice that our assumption of non-blocking guarantees that such an assignment always exists. The formal definitions are as follows.

A sequence $\pi \in \Sigma^\omega$ is a *run* of $\mathcal{S}$ from $s \in \Sigma$, with *choices* $\rho \in \Gamma^\omega$, if $\pi[0] = s$ and

$$\xi_a(\pi[n], \rho[n]_a) \qquad\qquad \chi(\pi[n], \rho[n], \pi[n+1])$$

for all $n < \omega$ and $a \in \Omega$. A run from $X \subseteq \Sigma$ is a run from any state $s \in X$. We omit the initial state if it is irrelevant or clear from the context. A run π is *fair* to player a, written $\pi \models \mathcal{F}_a$, if $\mathcal{F}_a$ evaluates to true under the interpretation of atoms ∞p as "p holds at $\pi[n]$ for infinitely many n".

A player $a \in \Omega$ can make its choices ρ in accordance with a *strategy*, a function

$$f_a : \Sigma^+ \to \Gamma_a$$

such that $\xi_a(s, f_a(ws))$ holds for all $w \in \Sigma^*$ and $s \in \Sigma$. A run π is *compatible* with strategy f_a for player a if its choices ρ satisfy

$$\rho[n]_a = f_a(\pi[0 \ldots n])$$

for all $n < \omega$. A run is compatible with strategies f_A (denoting the sequence $\langle f_a \mid a \in A \rangle$), for $A \subseteq \Omega$, if it is compatible with f_a for all $a \in A$. The set of all runs compatible with f_A starting at a certain state $s \in \Sigma$ is called the set of *outcomes* of f_A from s and denoted

$$out_S(s, f_A) \ ,$$

or $out(s, f_A)$ when S is clear from the context.

The fundamental operator to describe properties of discrete structures is the *controllable predecessors* operator cpre_A. Given a set of states $X \subseteq \Sigma$ and a set of players $A \subseteq \Omega$, $\mathrm{cpre}_A(X)$ denotes the set of states from which the players in A have a collaborative action with which they can ensure that the game will be in X at the next state. Formally,

$$\mathrm{cpre}_A(\varphi)(V_S) \equiv \exists V_A. \, \xi_A(V_S, V_A) \wedge$$
$$\forall V_{\Omega \setminus A}. \, \xi_{\Omega \setminus A} \to \forall V_S'. \, \chi(V_S, V_\Omega, V_S') \to \varphi(V_S') \ . \quad (1)$$

Dual to cpre_A is the *uncontrollable predecessors* operator upre_A, defined as

$$\mathrm{upre}_A(X) = \Sigma \setminus \mathrm{cpre}_A(\Sigma \setminus X) \ ,$$

or, explicitly, as

$$\mathrm{upre}_A(\varphi)(V_S) \equiv \forall V_A. \, \xi_A(V_S, V_A) \to$$
$$\exists V_{\Omega \setminus A}. \, \xi_{\Omega \setminus A} \wedge \exists V_S'. \, \chi(V_S, V_\Omega, V_S') \wedge \varphi(V_S') \ . \quad (2)$$

For classes of ADS with special properties, the cpre transformers have simpler forms [1, 15]. To take advantage of these simpler forms, we express our verification conditions in terms of these transformers as much as possible.

Example 2. As an illustration of how the cpre operator is affected by the system structure, consider the following asynchronous game structure $\mathcal{S}$, consisting of two agents a and b. The state space of $\mathcal{S}$ is partitioned so that, from any given state, either a or b has complete control of the next state, represented by the formulas $turn_a(V_S)$ and $turn_b(V_S) \equiv \neg turn_a(V_S)$. Furthermore, the next-state relation is represented by the formulas $\chi_a(V_S, V_S')$ and $\chi_b(V_S, V_S')$, meaning when it is a's turn, agent a can choose any state in V_S' such that $\xi_a(V_S, V_S')$ holds, and similarly for agent b. For this game structure, $\mathrm{cpre}_a(\varphi)$ can be simplified to

$$
\mathrm{cpre}_a(\varphi)(V_S) \;\equiv\; \left(\begin{array}{c} turn_a(V_S) \to \exists V_S'.\, \chi_a(V_S, V_S') \wedge \varphi(V_S) \\ \wedge \\ \neg turn_a(V_S) \to \forall V_S'.\, \chi_b(V_S, V_S') \to \varphi(V_S') \end{array} \right)
$$

As we shall see, cpre always appears in verification conditions in the consequent of a universally quantified implication, and thus the corresponding verification conditions for this game structure can always be split into two simpler ones.

3   The Logic ATL*

ATL* (Alternating Temporal Logic) was proposed by Alur & al. to allow selective quantification over runs that are the possible outcomes of games [1]. For convenience we use a version of ATL* with a few more connectives. (The expressive power is not affected.)

3.1   Syntax

ATL* formulas come in two types, state formulas and path formulas, defined by mutual induction.
   A *(state) formula* is one of:

- an assertion (first-order formula) in the underlying state language,
- a Boolean combination of state formulas,
- $\langle\!\langle A \rangle\!\rangle \varphi$, $[\![A]\!] \varphi$, $\langle\!\langle A \rangle\!\rangle_f \varphi$, or $[\![A]\!]_f \varphi$, for A a set of players and φ a path formula.

A *path formula* is one of:

- a state formula,
- a Boolean combination of path formulas, or
- an LTL temporal operator applied to path formulas.

For LTL operators we use the notation of [9, 10]: $\square$ for *always in the future*, $\diamondsuit$ for *eventually in the future*, &c.
   The operators $\langle\!\langle A \rangle\!\rangle$, $[\![A]\!]$, $\langle\!\langle A \rangle\!\rangle_f$, $[\![A]\!]_f$ are called *alternating quantifiers*. The most basic one is $\langle\!\langle A \rangle\!\rangle$, stating that A have a strategy to make a path formula true in all runs starting in the current state. The dual operator $[\![A]\!]$ is defined as $[\![A]\!]\varphi \equiv \neg\langle\!\langle A \rangle\!\rangle \neg\varphi$: we usually say that A *cannot avoid* φ from happening. The *fair* alternating quantifiers $\langle\!\langle A \rangle\!\rangle_f$ and $[\![A]\!]_f$ are similar, but interpreted over all fair runs instead of all runs.

3.2   Semantics

Let $\mathcal{S}$ be an ADS. We define truth relations

$$\mathcal{S}, s \vDash \varphi \qquad\qquad \mathcal{S}, \pi \vDash \psi$$

for a state formula φ at a state s and for a path formula ψ over a path π, by mutual induction on the structure of the formula. Recall that $out_{\mathcal{S}}(s, f_A)$ denotes the set of runs of $\mathcal{S}$ starting at s and compatible with strategies f_A.

- $\mathcal{S}, s \vDash p$, for p an assertion, if $s \vDash p$ in the assertion language;
- Boolean operators distribute over $\vDash$ in the natural way, both for state and path formulas;
- $\mathcal{S}, s \vDash \langle\!\langle A \rangle\!\rangle \psi$ if there exist strategies f_A such that, for all $\pi \in out(s, f_A)$, we have $\mathcal{S}, \pi \vDash \psi$;
- $\mathcal{S}, s \vDash [\![A]\!]\psi$ if, for all strategies f_A, there exists an outcome $\pi \in out(s, f_A)$ such that $\mathcal{S}, \pi \vDash \psi$ holds;
- $\mathcal{S}, s \vDash \langle\!\langle A \rangle\!\rangle_f \psi$ if there exist strategies f_A such that, for all outcomes $\pi \in out(s, f_A)$ such that $\pi \vDash \mathcal{F}_{\Omega \setminus A}$, we have also $\pi \vDash \mathcal{F}_A$ and $\mathcal{S}, \pi \vDash \psi$;
- $\mathcal{S}, s \vDash [\![A]\!]_f \psi$ if, for all strategies f_A, there is at least an outcome $\pi \in out(s, f_A)$ such that $\pi \vDash \mathcal{F}_{\Omega \setminus A}$ and, if $\pi \vDash \mathcal{F}_A$, then also $\mathcal{S}, \pi \vDash \psi$;
- LTL operators are evaluated over path formulas in the usual way.

When $\mathcal{S}$ is clear from the context, we simply write $s \vDash \varphi$ and $\pi \vDash \psi$. We say that

$$\mathcal{S} \vDash p \Rightarrow \varphi$$

when $\mathcal{S}, s \vDash \varphi$ for all states $s \in \Sigma$ satisfying p.

Example 3. Reconsider the system modeled in Example 1. We want to prove that the scheduler has a strategy that allows it to be fair: from a state where a process x is in the queue, the scheduler can play its choices in such a way that x will eventually be executed. We model this requirement with the ATL* formula

$$x \in qu \Rightarrow \langle\!\langle Sched \rangle\!\rangle_f \Diamond exec(x) \ ,$$

where x is a free variable and $exec(x)$ is an abbreviation for $pa \wedge xp = x$.

4   Proof System

4.1   Overview

Our proof system operates on statements of the form

$$\mathcal{S} \vDash p \Rightarrow (\!(A)\!)\varphi \ ,$$

where $\mathcal{S}$ is an ADS, p is an assertion, $(\!(A)\!)$ is an alternating quantifier, and φ is a path formula in positive normal form. (Every ATL* formula can be put in positive normal form, where all negations have been pushed to the assertion level, in the same way used for propositional logic and LTL, and rewriting $\neg\langle\!\langle A \rangle\!\rangle\varphi$ to $[\![A]\!]\neg\varphi$ &c.) When clear from the context, we omit $\mathcal{S}$ and simply write $p \Rightarrow (\!(A)\!)\varphi$. The rules of the proof system can be classified into four groups:

1. A basic state rule, which reduces all statements to the form $p \Rightarrow \langle\!\langle A \rangle\!\rangle \varphi$, where φ is an LTL formula.
2. A basic path rule, which reduces φ (an LTL formula) to an assertion while extending the system S by synchronously composing it with an automaton for φ.
3. A history rule, which augments the system with extra history variables such that, in the new system, A can win φ with memoryless strategies from its winning set.
4. Assertion rules, which reduce the validity of statements about winnability with memoryless strategies to assertional verification conditions.

The application of these rules results in a set of verification conditions to be proved in the underlying theory of the system plus the cpre predicate transformers. The advantage of parameterizing the underlying language to the cpre's is that, as illustrated in Example 2, in most practical cases the alternating system has specific properties that can be exploited by defining a simpler version of cpre than the generic form for ADS's shown in (1).

Completeness of the proof system is relative to validities in the first-order logic, with fixpoints and cpre, of the underlying theory – the same as required for relative completeness for LTL, or program termination, proof systems [9]. Proofs of soundness and completeness of all proof rules can be found in [14].

4.2   Basic State Rule

For ψ a state formula appearing with positive polarity in $\varphi(\psi)$,

$$
\begin{array}{l}
\text{BASIC-STATE:} \\
p \Rightarrow \varphi(q) \\
q \Rightarrow \psi \\
\hline
p \Rightarrow \varphi(\psi)
\end{array}
$$

This rule says that, in order to prove $p \Rightarrow \varphi(\psi)$, where ψ is a state formula appearing with positive polarity in φ, we guess an assertion q underapproximating the set of states on which ψ holds and substitute q for ψ in φ. The two premises require us to prove that q is indeed an underapproximation ($q \Rightarrow \psi$) and that the formula after the substitution holds in the system ($p \Rightarrow \varphi(q)$). Notice that there is an implicit "$S \models$" at the left of every line in the rule.

Example 4. Reconsider the system from Example 1. In trying to prove

$$\neg pa \Rightarrow \langle\!\langle Env \rangle\!\rangle \Diamond \langle\!\langle Sched \rangle\!\rangle_f \Diamond exec(x)$$

over this system, we can apply rule BASIC-STATE with $\psi \equiv \langle\!\langle Sched \rangle\!\rangle_f \Diamond exec(x)$ and $q \equiv x \in qu$ to obtain the subgoals $\neg pa \Rightarrow \langle\!\langle Env \rangle\!\rangle \Diamond (x \in qu)$ and $x \in qu \Rightarrow \langle\!\langle Sched \rangle\!\rangle_f \Diamond exec(x)$.

4.3   Basic Path Rule

Augmentation. The Basic Path Rule applies to statements of the form $S \models p \Rightarrow ((A))\varphi$ where φ is an LTL formula. The first step in the application of this rule is the synchronous composition of an automaton for φ with S [12, 11].

Let φ be a (quantifier-free) LTL formula over variables V_S. Let

$$\mathcal{A}_\varphi = \langle Q, q_0, \delta, \mathcal{F} \rangle$$

be a deterministic Muller automaton accepting the language of φ, where:

- Q is a finite set of states;
- $q_0 \in Q$ is the initial state;
- $\delta : Q \times \Sigma \to Q$ is a full deterministic transition function;
- $\mathcal{F} \in 2^{2^Q}$ is the Muller acceptance condition.

The definition suggests that the alphabet of $\mathcal{A}_\varphi$ is Σ, the – generally infinite – set of states of the underlying ADS. Only a finite quotient of Σ, however, is necessary, determined by the values assumed by the states on the atoms of φ. We use Muller acceptance condition for simplicity of notation. In practice, Streett is of course preferable (or, if possible, an even simpler acceptance condition).

The role of $\mathcal{A}_\varphi$ is to act as a temporal tester [11], that is, to observe the evolution of φ on the ADS. To achieve this, we construct a synchronous composition of $\mathcal{A}_\varphi$ and the ADS S and introduce a new player a_φ with the fairness conditions of $\mathcal{A}_\varphi$. The requirement that $\mathcal{A}_\varphi$ be deterministic ensures that no player gains power by the composition with $\mathcal{A}_\varphi$. In particular, the new player a_φ has only one choice of action at all times. The formal definition is as follows.

Let $S = \langle \Omega, V_S, V_\Omega, \xi, \chi, \mathcal{F} \rangle$ be an ADS, and $\mathcal{A} = \langle Q, q_0, \delta, \mathcal{F}_\mathcal{A} \rangle$ a deterministic Muller (or Büchi, or Streett ...) automaton on alphabet Σ, as defined above. The *synchronous composition* of S and $\mathcal{A}$, denoted $S \,|||\, \mathcal{A}$, is the ADS

$$\hat{S} = \langle \hat{\Omega}, \hat{V}_S, \hat{V}_\Omega, \hat{\xi}, \hat{\chi}, \hat{\mathcal{F}} \rangle \ ,$$

where:

- $\hat{\Omega} = \Omega \cup \{a_\mathcal{A}\}$, where $a_\mathcal{A}$ is a new player;
- $\hat{V}_S = V_S \cup \{q\}$, where q is a new variable of type Q;
- $\hat{V}_a = V_a$ if $a \in \Omega$;
  $\hat{V}_{a_\mathcal{A}} = \emptyset$;
- $\hat{\xi}_a(\hat{V}_S, V_a) \equiv \xi_a(V_S, V_a)$ if $a \in \Omega$;
  $\hat{\xi}_{a_\mathcal{A}}(\hat{V}_S, \emptyset) \equiv \mathrm{T}$;
- $\hat{\chi}(\hat{V}_S, \hat{V}_\Omega, \hat{V}'_S) \equiv \chi(V_S, V_\Omega, V'_S) \wedge q' = \delta(q, V_S)$;
- $\hat{\mathcal{F}} \equiv \mathcal{F} \wedge \mathcal{F}_\mathcal{A}$, where $\mathcal{F}_\mathcal{A}$ is an expression of $\mathcal{A}$'s acceptance condition.

The Basic-Path Rule. For an LTL formula φ,

BASIC-PATH:

$$\frac{S \,|||\, \mathcal{A}_\varphi \models p \wedge q = q_0 \Rightarrow ((A, a_\varphi))_f \mathrm{T}}{S \models \qquad p \Rightarrow ((A))_f \varphi}$$

where $\mathcal{A}_\varphi$ is a deterministic automaton on infinite words accepting φ, $\parallel\!\parallel$ is synchronous composition, $\langle\!\langle A\rangle\!\rangle_f$ is either $\langle\!\langle A\rangle\!\rangle_f$ or $[\![A]\!]_f$, and a_φ stands for $a_{\mathcal{A}_\varphi}$. Notice that we require the alternating quantifiers to be fair. If this is not the case, we simply remove all fairness conditions from the system before applying the rule.

Example 5. Returning to our example, we apply BASIC-PATH using the following deterministic automaton $\mathcal{A}$ for $\Diamond exec(x)$:

$$\neg exec(x) \;\;\bigcirc\;\; q_0 \xrightarrow{\;exec(x)\;} q_1 \;\bigcirc\; \text{T}$$

with initial state q_0 and fairness condition ∞q_1. Then $\mathcal{S} \parallel\!\parallel \mathcal{A}$ becomes:

$$\hat{\Omega} : \{Env, Sched, a\} \qquad \hat{V}_S : V_S \cup \{q : \{q_0, q_1\}\}$$
$$\hat{V}_{Env} : V_{Env} \qquad \hat{V}_{Sched} : V_{Sched} \qquad \hat{V}_a : \varnothing$$
$$\hat{\xi}_{Env} : \xi_{Env} \qquad \hat{\xi}_{Sched} : \xi_{Sched} \qquad \hat{\xi}_a : \text{T}$$
$$\hat{\chi} : \chi \wedge \big((q = q_0 \wedge \neg exec(x) \to q' = q_0) \wedge (q = q_1 \vee exec(x) \to q' = q_1)\big)$$
$$\hat{\mathcal{F}}_{Env} : \infty pa \wedge \infty \neg pa \qquad \hat{\mathcal{F}}_{Sched} : \text{T} \qquad \hat{\mathcal{F}}_a : \infty(q = q_1)$$

The following picture summarizes the game matrix $\hat{\chi}$ for the augmented ADS:

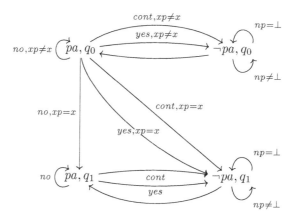

The property to prove on this system is now

$$x \in qu \wedge q = q_0 \Rightarrow \langle\!\langle Sched, a\rangle\!\rangle_f \text{T} \;. \tag{3}$$

4.4 History Rule

The purpose of the history rule is to allow for memoryless strategies in all the games of interest. Consider a property of the form $\mathcal{S} \vDash p \Rightarrow \langle\!\langle A\rangle\!\rangle\varphi$, where φ is an LTL property. It is known (see, for example, [16]) that if we partition the states of $\mathcal{S}$ into two sets, W_1 and W_2, such that players A have a winning strategy (can ensure φ) from every state in W_1, but not from any state in W_2, then players A have a *finite memory* winning strategy from every state in W_1.

The application of the assertion rules requires that A have a *memoryless* strategy. To achieve this, we add to the structure some new variables, called *history variables*, and a new player h (for *history*). We let h play in coalition with A and give it the task of maintaining the history variables: at every step, h will make a deterministic choice for the history variables, and the game matrix χ will simply copy these choices into the next stage of the game.

History Augmentations. Let h be a new player and V_h a new set of *history* variables. We define the history augmentation of S with history V_h, denoted $S[h, V_h]$, to be the ADS

$$\hat{S} = \langle \hat{\Omega}, \hat{V}_S, \hat{V}_\Omega, \hat{\xi}, \hat{\chi}, \hat{\mathcal{F}} \rangle \ ,$$

where:

- $\hat{\Omega} = \Omega \cup \{h\}$;
- $\hat{V}_S = V_S \cup V_h^*$, where V_h^* is a copy of V_h;
- $\hat{V}_a = V_a$ if $a \in \Omega$;
  $\hat{V}_h = V_h$;
- $\hat{\xi}_a(\hat{V}_S, V_a) \equiv \xi_a(V_S, V_a)$ if $a \in \Omega$;
  $\hat{\xi}_h(\hat{V}_S, V_h) \equiv \mathrm{T}$;
- $\hat{\chi}(\hat{V}_S, \hat{V}_\Omega, \hat{V}_S') \equiv \chi(V_S, V_\Omega, V_S') \wedge V_h^{*\prime} = V_h$;
- $\hat{\mathcal{F}} \equiv \mathcal{F}$.

The History Rule. For an LTL formula φ,

$$\begin{array}{c} \text{HISTORY:} \\ \dfrac{S[h, V_h] \models p \Rightarrow (\!(A, h)\!)\varphi}{S \models p \Rightarrow (\!(A)\!)\varphi} \end{array}$$

where $S[h, V_h]$ is a history augmentation of S.

4.5   Assertion Rules

After applying the previous rules as much as possible, we are left with a set of statements of the form

$$S \models p \Rightarrow (\!(A)\!)q \ ,$$

where S is an ADS, p and q are assertions, and $(\!(A)\!)$ is one of the four alternating quantifiers $\langle\!\langle A \rangle\!\rangle$, $[\![A]\!]$, $\langle\!\langle A \rangle\!\rangle_f$, $[\![A]\!]_f$. In this section we show how to reduce each of these to first-order validities. First, we transform the fair quantifiers into unfair ones by making the fairness conditions explicit. This reintroduces temporal operators in the scope of the alternating quantifier. The resulting temporal formula, however, is of a special form that is dealt with directly by the assertion rule.

Making Fairness Conditions Explicit. Recall that every fairness condition $\mathcal{F}_a$ is a Boolean combination of atoms of the form ∞p, where p is an assertion. We write ∞p instead of $\square\lozenge p$ to make it clear that we are now dealing with a special case and not with arbitrary LTL formulas.

From the definitions of the semantics of the alternating quantifiers it follows that $p \Rightarrow \langle\!\langle A \rangle\!\rangle_f q$ can be rewritten as the conjunction of the two statements

$$p \wedge q \Rightarrow \langle\!\langle A \rangle\!\rangle (\mathcal{F}_{\Omega \setminus A} \to \mathcal{F}_A) \qquad\qquad p \wedge \neg q \Rightarrow \langle\!\langle A \rangle\!\rangle \neg \mathcal{F}_{\Omega \setminus A}$$

and $p \Rightarrow [\![A]\!]_f q$ as the conjunction of

$$p \wedge q \Rightarrow [\![A]\!] \mathcal{F}_{\Omega \setminus A} \qquad\qquad p \wedge \neg q \Rightarrow [\![A]\!] (\mathcal{F}_{\Omega \setminus A} \wedge \neg \mathcal{F}_A)$$

These statements are all of the form

$$p \Rightarrow (\!(A)\!) \mathcal{F} \ ,$$

where $(\!(A)\!)$ is either $\langle\!\langle A \rangle\!\rangle$ or $[\![A]\!]$ and $\mathcal{F}$ is a Boolean combination of ∞ atoms, and can be rewritten as

$$\mathcal{S} \models p \Rightarrow (\!(A)\!) \bigwedge_i \left(\infty J_1^i \wedge \ldots \wedge \infty J_k^i \to \infty q_i \right) \ .$$

(Technically, the number k of antecedents is different for every i. Without loss of generality, we drop this distinction to lighten the notation.) Below we present proof rules to reduce these particular forms to assertional verification conditions.

The Positive Assertion Rule. This rule applies to formulas of the form

$$p \Rightarrow \langle\!\langle A \rangle\!\rangle \bigwedge_i \left(\infty J_1^i \wedge \ldots \wedge \infty J_k^i \to \infty q_i \right) \ . \tag{4}$$

To apply the rule, we guess intermediate assertions r^i and r_i^j (for $i \in \{1, \ldots, n\}$ and $j \in \{1, \ldots, k\}$) and ranking functions δ_i^j on a well-founded domain $\langle A, \prec \rangle$.

POS-ASSERTION:

$$p \Rightarrow \bigwedge_{i=1}^n r^i$$

For every $i \in \{1, \ldots, n\}$:

$$r^i \Rightarrow \bigvee_{j=1}^k r_j^i$$

For every choice of $\{j_i \mid i \in \{1, \ldots, n\}\}$:

$$\frac{\bigwedge_{i=1}^n (r_{j_i}^i \wedge \delta_{j_i}^i = a_i) \Rightarrow \mathrm{cpre}_A \bigwedge_{i=1}^n \begin{bmatrix} (r^i \wedge q_i) \\ \vee \\ \bigvee_{l=1}^k (r_l^i \wedge \delta_l^i \prec a_i) \\ \vee \\ (r_{j_i}^i \wedge \delta_{j_i}^i \preceq a_i \wedge \neg J_{j_i}^i) \end{bmatrix}}{p \Rightarrow \langle\!\langle A \rangle\!\rangle \bigwedge_{i=1}^n \left(\infty J_1^i \wedge \ldots \wedge \infty J_k^i \to \infty q_i \right)}$$

The intuition behind this rule is similar to that for the analogous rules for LTL [9]. The ranking functions enforce progress towards realizing the q_i, and the

r_i^j denote regions inside which the ranking functions are constant. The verification conditions assure that, assuming fairness of the adversaries, the players A can eventually force the game out of these regions, and thus decrease the ranking.

This proof rule is sound and relatively complete to prove properties of the form (4). Relative completeness means that, if (4) holds of a system, then there exist assertions r^i, r_j^i, δ_j^i that are expressible in the language and satisfy the premises.

Example 6. Returning to our running example, making the fairness conditions of (3) explicit results in

$$x \in qu \wedge q_0 \Rightarrow \langle\!\langle Sched, a \rangle\!\rangle (\hat{\mathcal{F}}_{Env} \rightarrow \hat{\mathcal{F}}_{Sched} \wedge \hat{\mathcal{F}}_a) \ ,$$

or, equivalently

$$x \in qu \wedge q_0 \Rightarrow \langle\!\langle Sched, a \rangle\!\rangle (\infty\neg pa \wedge \infty pa \rightarrow \infty q_1) \ ,$$

where we abbreviate $q = q_0$ with q_0 and $q = q_1$ with q_1.

To apply rule POS-ASSERTION, with $n = 1$ and $k = 2$ (since $n = 1$, we drop the superscripts), we need to find assertions r, r_1, r_2 and ranking functions δ_1, δ_2 (index 1 corresponds to the $\infty\neg pa$ requirement, index 2 to ∞pa) and then prove the following verification conditions:

$$x \in qu \wedge q_0 \rightarrow r$$

$$r \rightarrow r_1 \vee r_2$$

$$r_1 \wedge \delta_1 = d \rightarrow \text{cpre}_{Sched,a} \left[\begin{array}{l} (r \wedge q_1) \vee (r_1 \wedge \delta_1 \prec d) \\ \vee (r_2 \wedge \delta_2 \prec d) \vee (r_1 \wedge \delta_1 \preceq d \wedge pa) \end{array} \right]$$

$$r_2 \wedge \delta_2 = d \rightarrow \text{cpre}_{Sched,a} \left[\begin{array}{l} (r \wedge q_1) \vee (r_1 \wedge \delta_1 \prec d) \\ \vee (r_2 \wedge \delta_2 \prec d) \vee (r_2 \wedge \delta_2 \preceq d \wedge \neg pa) \end{array} \right]$$

We choose the following:

$$r : ((x \in qu \vee x = xp) \wedge q_0) \vee q_1$$

$$r_1 : r \wedge pa \qquad\qquad r_2 : r \wedge \neg pa$$

$$\delta_1 : \langle g, depth(x, qu), 1 \rangle \qquad \delta_2 : \langle g, depth(x, qu), 0 \rangle$$

where

$$g = \begin{cases} 0 & \text{if } x = xp \ , \\ 1 & \text{otherwise} \end{cases}$$

and $depth(x, qu)$ is the distance from the head of the first occurrence of x in qu, or 0 if x is not in qu. The domain of the ranking functions is $\{0, 1\} \times \mathbb{N} \times \{0, 1\}$ with the standard lexicographic order. The main part of the ranking functions is the $depth$ term – its value decreases as we remove items from the head of qu, provided the scheduler reinserts processes far enough back in the queue. The other two components are adjustments needed for the cases of going from active to not active (third component) and for the boundary case of x having left the queue and being executed (first component).

The Negative Assertion Rule. The negative assertion rule is used for formulas of the form

$$p \Rightarrow [\![A]\!] \bigwedge_i (\infty J_1^i \wedge \ldots \wedge \infty J_k^i \to \infty q_i) \ .$$

The rule and its properties are identical to the positive version, except that it uses the predicate transformer upre instead of cpre.

5   Conclusions and Future Work

We have presented a sound and complete proof system for proving ATL* properties over infinite-state alternating structures. The proof system can be used as a basis for the construction of special-purpose proof systems for alternating systems with a specific structure, e.g., turn-based or lock-step [1], or for proving specific properties, e.g., invariants or reachability. We expect that our proof system will be particularly beneficial in the verification of security and contract-signing protocols, which often have a very specific structure that can be exploited to simplify the cpre predicate transformers.

Our proof system may also contribute to the construction of abstraction-based verification methods. The foundations for proving ATL* properties over infinite-state alternating systems using abstraction were laid in [17]. However, methods for finding a suitable abstraction function and proving its correctness, which for infinite-state systems must necessarily rely on deduction, still require investigation. We expect that the proof rules presented here will provide valuable insights in proving that a proposed abstraction is sound, since the corresponding verification conditions are of the same form as those generated by our proof system.

Other areas for further investigation include the development of approximations and heuristics for special cases, e.g., automatic generation of ranking functions; the construction of efficient decision procedures, tailored to the verification conditions produced, e.g., for simple $\forall \exists$ formulas over program types; and the representation of proofs by diagrams, similar to verification diagrams [18], which allow to reduce the complexity of the premises of the assertion rules, by making use of user-provided structure.

Acknowledgments

We thank Aaron Bradley and the anonymous referees for their comments on a previous draft of this paper.

References

1. Alur, R., Henzinger, T.A., Kupferman, O.: Alternating-time temporal logic. Journal of the ACM **49**(5) (2002) 672–713
2. Alur, R., Henzinger, T., Mang, F., Qadeer, S., Rajamani, S., Tasiran, S.: MOCHA: Modularity in model checking. In: Proc. 10th Intl. Conference on Computer Aided Verification. Volume 1427 of LNCS., Springer (1998) 516–520

3. Kremer, S., Raskin, J.F.: A game-based verification of non-repudiation and fair exchange protocols. Journal of Computer Security **11**(3) (2003) 399–429
4. Kremer, S., Raskin, J.F.: Game analysis of abuse-free contract signing. In: Computer Security Foundations Workshop (CSFW), IEEE Computer Society (2002)
5. Chadha, R., Kremer, S., Scedrov, A.: Formal analysis of multi-party contract signing. Journal of Automated Reasoning (2006) To appear.
6. Pauly, M., Wooldridge, M.: Logic for mechanism design—A manifesto. In: Proceedings of the 2003 Workshop on Game Theory and Decision Theory in Agent-Based Systems (GTDT-2003), Melbourne, Australia (2003)
7. Lamport, L.: Specifying Systems. Addison-Wesley (2002)
8. Goranko, V., van Drimmelen, G.: Complete axiomatization and decidability of alternating-time temporal logic. Theoretical Computer Science **353**(1–3) (2006) 93–117
9. Manna, Z., Pnueli, A.: Completing the temporal picture. In Ausiello, G., Dezani-Ciancaglini, M., Ronchi Della Rocca, S., eds.: 16th International Colloquium on Automata, Languages, and Programming. Volume 372 of LNCS., Springer (1989) 534–558
10. Manna, Z., Pnueli, A.: Temporal Verification of Reactive Systems: Safety. Springer (1995)
11. Kesten, Y., Pnueli, A.: A compositional approach to CTL* verification. Theoretical Computer Science **331** (2005) 397–428
12. Vardi, M.Y.: Verification of concurrent programs: The automata-theoretic framework. Journal of Pure and Applied Logic **51**(1–2) (1991) 79–98
13. Fix, L., Grumberg, O.: Verification of temporal properties. J. Logic Computat. **6**(3) (1996) 343–361
14. Slanina, M., Sipma, H.B., Manna, Z.: Proving ATL* properties of infinite-state systems. Technical Report REACT-TR-2006-02, Stanford University, Computer Science Department, REACT Group (2006) Avaliable at http://react.stanford.edu/TR/.
15. Slanina, M.: Control rules for reactive system games. In Fischer, B., Smith, D.R., eds.: Logic-Based Program Synthesis: State of the Art and Future Trends. AAAI Spring Symposium, The American Association for Artificial Intelligence, AAAI Press (2002) 95–104 Available from AAAI as Technical Report SS-02-05.
16. Zielonka, W.: Infinite games on finitely coloured graphs with applications to automata on infinite trees. Theoretical Computer Science **200** (1998) 135–183
17. Henzinger, T.A., Majumdar, R., Mang, F., Raskin, J.F.: Abstract interpretation of game properties. In: Proc. 7th Intern. Static Analysis Symp. (SAS). Volume 1824 of LNCS., Springer (2000) 220–239
18. Manna, Z., Pnueli, A.: Temporal verification diagrams. In: Proc. International Symposium on Theoretical Aspects of Computer Software. Volume 789 of LNCS., Springer (1994) 726–765

Type Safety for FJ and FGJ[*]

Shuling Wang[1], Quan Long[1,2], and Zongyan Qiu[1]

[1] LMAM and Department of Informatics, School of Math., Peking University, Beijing, China
[2] IBM China Research Laboratory
{joycy, qzy}@math.pku.edu.cn, longquan@cn.ibm.com

Abstract. Mainly concerned with type safety, Featherweight Java, or FJ, is a well known minimal core for Java and Generic Java. However, in the type system of FJ, the treatment of downcast is omitted. In this paper we propose a stronger type system for FJ and FGJ. In order to deal with the cast problems, we introduce some special techniques for types, and also strengthen the types for expressions and methods in terms of the type declaration notations. Supported by the type system and our techniques, we can ensure properties stronger than the ones proved in Igarashi *et al*'s original FJ paper. Examples making the above mentioned contributions clear are illustrated throughout this paper. Furthermore a case study on design patterns showing the advantages of our results is given.

Keywords: Featherweight Java, Downcast, Type Safety, Observer Pattern.

1 Introduction

To understand the design of programming languages, a common practise is to develop a formal model which defines lightweight fragments as a minimal core of the original language. It is helpful to prove the key properties of languages.

Igarashi *et al.* presented a minimal core for Java: Featherweight Java, or FJ for short [9]. FJ is a functional language which excludes not only complex features like threads, exception handling, but also most basic features of Java, such as assignments. With such a small language, rigorous proofs about the key property concerned — *type safety* — can be clearly carried. In the paper, Igarashi *et al.* built a typing environment for FJ and proved the main theorem, the *type soundness* theorem which ensues their *type safety* for casts: a well-typed program is *cast-safe* if it includes only upcasts.

This minimal core is a significant attempt for static checking for Java programs. However, the result is not precise enough in the sense that it says nothing about *downcast*s which are frequently used in software development. For instance, many design patterns [6] involve downcast, thus can not be analyzed in FJ framework. Although sometimes the generic classes [1, 2] can be used to reduce the occurrences of downcast, resulting a more complex system, the downcast can not be eliminated entirely. This problem motivates this work, while we build another typing environment to capture the essential of *cast*s in the programs, to distinguish *correct* downcast, *wrong* downcast, as well as *suspicious* downcast. In contrast to the main theorems in [9], our typing environment permits *correct* downcast, rejects *wrong* downcast, and leaves the least of

---

[*] Supported by NNSF of China (No. 605730081).

K. Barkaoui, A. Cavalcanti, and A. Cerone (Eds.): ICTAC 2006, LNCS 4281, pp. 257–271, 2006.
© Springer-Verlag Berlin Heidelberg 2006

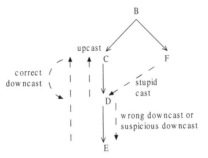

Fig. 1. The Inheritant Tree for Classes

suspicious downcast to the run-time checking. To intuitively illustrate the problem and our approach, we consider a simple example as follows.

Suppose B is a well defined FJ class, we consider the following class declarations[1]:

```
class C extends B {...}
class D extends C {...}
class E extends D {...
    C m(D x){ return (C)x; }            // upcast
    D q(){ return (D)new C(); }         // wrong downcast
}
class F extends B {...
    C m(D x){ return (E)x; }            // suspicious downcast
    C n(){ return (C)new D(); }         // upcast
    D p(){ return (D)(C)new E(); }      // correct downcast
    F r(){ return (F)new D(); }         // stupid cast
}
(E)(new F().m(new D()))                 // suspicious downcast
```

Thus (E $\preceq$ D stands for that E is a subclass of D),

$$E \preceq D \preceq C \preceq B, \quad F \preceq B$$

Figure 1 shows the class hierarchy defined by these class declarations, with the casts presented in the definition by dashed arrows. We classify them into five cases:

- *Upcast*, e. g., (C) new D() or (C) x in the body of m in class E
- *Wrong downcast*, e. g., (D) new C(). The expression is *wrong* because it attempts to cast an object to its subtype. It is wrong in any OO language.
- *Correct downcast*, e. g., (D) ((C) new E()). We see that (D) (C)... is a downcast. But the object upcasted by (C) has the original type E. So it is a correct downcast which will not cause any execution error for sure.
- *Suspicious downcast*, e. g., "(E) x" in the body of m in F. The expression attempts to cast a variable of type D to its subtype E. It seems not safe. But please notice that, the real object type of x (of its value) is determined by the actual arguments

---

[1] The syntax of FJ is given in Section 2. Readers could consider the programs as in general Java.

during the execution. It is too early to sentence this expression to death at the static checking phase. In our model, we will deal with this kind of downcast statically to the full extent, and leave other non-determined ones to dynamic checking.

– *Stupid cast*, e. g., "(F) new D()" attempts to cast an object to a type without any inheritance relationship.

In [9], the main theorem only ensures that when the type derivations of the whole class table and the well-typed expression contain neither downcast nor stupid cast, the expression can reduce to a final expression. This leaves too many cases with correct and wrong casts to dynamic checking (Figure 2, left), thus makes a very weak type system. This weakness is what we are going to remedy.

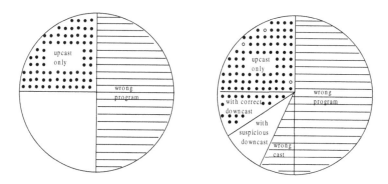

Fig. 2. The Effect Graph of [9] (left) vs The Effect Graph of Our Type System (right)

Inspired by [7], in this paper, we propose a stronger type system with an extended typing environment. For expression e, we define its type as a pair (T_1, T_2), where T_1 is called the expression type, *etype*(e), and T_2 the object type, *otype*(e), to indicate the type information known already about the real object. For instances, expression (C) new E() has the type (C, E); and the type of new C() is (C, C). When a downcast appears, we can validate it by comparing the casting type with the *otype* of the expression. For instances, *type*((D)(C) new E()) = (D, E) because E $\preceq$ D; but (D) new C() is not well-typed because the *otype* of new C() is not a subclass of D.

To distinguish *suspicious* downcast from *wrong* downcast, we use two additional forms of *otype*: ☐ and $C^\top$. Informally, ☐ indicates that the validity of the cast is not sure, while $C^\top$ indicates that the *otype* of the expression might be some subtype of C. Another important technique used here is to strengthen types for methods. From the application, it can reduce the non-determinism (☐) to some extent in static time.

Supported by these techniques, we can give better typing results than the ones given in [9]. Figure 2 illustrates our contribution explicitly: The dashed region denotes the programs which can not pass static type checking and dotted region for type safe programs. Our model admits more "good" programs and rejects more "bad" ones. While paper [9] leaves all programs including downcast to the run-time checking, our model reduces the white area to include only the programs with *suspicious* downcast.

Another important point is that our typing environment adopts a denotational style. The *typing rules* and *reduction rules* in [9] are defined by operational transition rules

Table 1. The Syntax of FJ

```
L ::= class C extends D {C̄ f̄; K M̄}
K ::= C(C̄ f̄){super(f̄); this.f̄=f̄}
M ::= C m(C̄ x̄){return e;}
e ::= x|e.f|e.m(ē)| new C(ē)|(C)e
```

Table 2. The Syntax of FGJ

```
T ::= X|N
N ::= C⟨T̄⟩
L ::= class C⟨X̄ ◁ N̄⟩◁ N{T̄ f̄; K M̄}
K ::= C(T̄ f̄){super(f̄); this.f̄ = f̄;}
M ::= ⟨X̄ ◁ N̄⟩ T m(T̄ x̄){return e;}
e ::= x|e.f|e.m ⟨T̄⟩(ē)| new N(ē)|(N)e
```

which are non-deterministic. But the corresponding rules in this paper are defined in the form of deterministic functions of *type* and *eval*.

The page limitation prevents us to include all the details of our work about FJ and FGJ (a generic extension of FJ, Featherweight Generic Java), as well as the soundness proofs in this paper. We will present the details of the FJ part here and leave some details of the other half (about FGJ) to our research report [11].

The remainder of this paper is organized as follows. An overview of FJ and FGJ is given in Section 2. Our typing system, evaluation function, and main results about type safety are presented in Section 3. The overview of parallel results on FGJ is in Section 4. In Section 5, we consider a case study about the Observer Pattern, and deal with its cast problems with our type system. Then we have a conclusion.

2   A Brief Overview of FJ and FGJ

FJ [9] is a pure *functional* minimal core calculus of Java. This makes the property of FJ easy to prove, and the proof may remain manageable for significant extensions. The abstract syntax of FJ is listed in Table 1. It includes only five forms of expressions (e): variables, field access, method invocation, object creation, and casting. A class declaration (L) consists of names of the new class and its super class, a sequence of field declarations $\bar{C}\ \bar{f}$, a constructor K, and a sequence of method declarations $\bar{M}$. The attributes and methods are both public. We use $\bar{C}$ to denote a possibly empty sequence $C_1, C_2, \cdots, C_n$, also the same in $\bar{f}, \bar{e}$, etc. FJ contains only expressions without side effects, which makes the semantics of the language more concise to describe. A program in FJ is a sequence of class declarations plus an expression e to be evaluated.

The main property investigated in [9] is the *type safety*. A type system is built to analyze FJ expressions statically. The model ensures that, for an expression e, if the type derivation of the whole class table and the expression contains no downcasts or stupid casts, then it is type safe.

Paper [9] presented also the corresponding minimal part of Generic Java as given in [2], called Featherweight Generic Java (FGJ for short), which adds generic types to FJ. The syntax for FGJ is in Table 2. In FGJ, both classes and methods may have generic type parameters. The relation extends is abbreviated to the symbol $\lhd$ for convenience. In the table, X over type variables, T ranges over types, representing both non-variable types and type variables. For uniforming the definition of classes and methods, as in [9], $C\langle\rangle, m\langle\rangle$ can be regarded as C, m respectively. Obviously, FJ is a proper subset of FGJ. Also, [9] proved the type safety property for FGJ.

3   Semantic Model for FJ

Now we present the semantic model of FJ. We consider the static structures of a program as its *static semantics*, while the evaluation of a program as *dynamic semantics*.

3.1   Static Semantics

Class Declaration. We denote the class declarations section as *cdecls*. The typing environment extracted from *cdecls* is denoted by Γ_{cdecls}, which records the typing information of methods and attributes, and the inheritant structures presented in *cdecls*. Γ_{cdecls} includes four fields: $\langle$*cnames, superclass, attr, op*$\rangle$, with the details as follows.

- *cnames*: the set of class names declared in *cdecls* plus the particular class Object, which is the superclass of all classes. Object has no fields or methods.
- *superclass*: a partial relation between classes. $C \mapsto D$ holds iff the declaration class C extends D$\{\cdots\}$ is in *cdecls*, i.e., D is the direct superclass of C. Each declared class has a direct superclass. We define *subtype* relation $\preceq$ as the reflective and transitive closure of $\mapsto$. If $C \preceq D$, we call C the *subtype* of D.
- *attr*: a partial function from *cnames* to their attributes, defined as:
  $$attr(C) \stackrel{def}{=} \{\langle C_i\ f_i\rangle | C_i\ f_i \text{ is declared as an attribute of } C\}$$
  $$\cup \{attr(D) | D \text{ is the direct superclass of } C\}$$
  The field *attr* records the names and types of all declared and inherited attributes of every declared class. The predicate $f \in attr(C)$ is used for brevity to denote that $\exists C' \in$ *cnames*, $\langle C'\ f\rangle \in attr(C)$ holds.
- *op*: a partial function from *cnames* to signatures and bodies of methods, defined as:
  $$op(C) \stackrel{def}{=} op(D) \oplus \{m \mapsto \langle(\overline{E} \to E), \lambda\overline{x} \cdot e\rangle \mid In(C, m(E, \overline{E}), \lambda\overline{x} \cdot e)\}$$
  where
  - D is the direct superclass of C.
  - $In(C, m(E, \overline{E}), \lambda\overline{x} \cdot e)$ means that m is a method of class C, with the declaration of the form E m($\overline{E}\ \overline{x}$)$\{$return e; $\}$.

Some notations used in the semantics definitions are introduced for simplifying the description. Suppose the current typing environment is Γ,

- If $\Gamma.op(C)(m) = \langle(\overline{E} \to E), \lambda\overline{x} \cdot e\rangle$, then we have:
  $$sign(C, m) \stackrel{def}{=} \overline{E} \to E, \quad mbody(C, m) \stackrel{def}{=} \lambda\overline{x} \cdot e$$
- We use *etype*() to denote the initial declared type of class attributes or method parameters. If $\Gamma.attr(C) = \{\langle\overline{C}\ \overline{f}\rangle\}$, then we have:
  $$etype(C.f_i) \stackrel{def}{=} C_i$$

And if the parameter list of m is $\overline{E}\,\overline{x}$, then

$$paras(C,m) \stackrel{def}{=} \overline{x} \qquad and \qquad etype(x_i) \stackrel{def}{=} E_i$$

Also, we will use $etype(e)$ to denote the expression type of e, which will be explained below.

Type Language. For simplicity, FJ doesn't have primitive types, thus each expression is of some class type C. The type of a method, including the constructor, is a pair written as $\overline{C} \rightarrow D$, where $\overline{C}$ is a sequence of parameter types and D is the return type. In our model, in order to solve the problem of cast, we introduce a new type language for expressions and methods in FJ, defined as follows. We use μ, ν to range over expression types and method types respectively.

Expression types

$\mu ::= (C, \tau), \qquad \tau ::= D \mid D^\top \mid \boxed{?}$

where $C, D \in \Gamma.cnames$ are valid class names.

Method types

$\nu ::= (\overline{C}, \overline{C'}) \rightarrow (D, \tau)$

where $\overline{C}, \overline{C'}, D \in \Gamma.cnames$ are valid class names, and τ is defined as above.

The type of an expression in FJ is a pair (C, τ), where τ has three forms: a valid class name D, or $D^\top$, or $\boxed{?}$. In the type, C is the static type of the expression, which is the same as in [9], denoted by $etype(e)$, while τ represents our knowledge about the real type of the object that expression e refers, denoted by $otype(e)$. The three forms of τ represent three possibilities of the type of the object denoted by e: a class name D, a subtype of a class D, or unknown $\boxed{?}$, which can not be determined until the execution.

The type of a method is of the form $(\overline{C}, \overline{C'}) \rightarrow (D, \tau)$. $\overline{C}$ and D are the corresponding sequence of types of parameters and the return type in the method definition respectively, while $\overline{C'}$ are the types for the arguments computed from the body of the method, which are subtype to $\overline{C}$. We use $\overline{C'}$ to record the fact that, the arguments of a method may have further restriction than what in the declaration of the method. Sometimes the arguments must have the stronger types than the types of formal parameter, to guarantee that the execution of the method body will not stuck. However, we may not get the just required types statically for arguments to guarantee the execution. Here we would like to get the most requirement for method arguments by static analyzing to the full extent.

Types for Methods in FJ. Now we show how to compute the types for the methods, i.e., the values of $\overline{C'}, \tau$ above. Suppose we have a method m defined in class A (we assume the method m has only one parameter for simplicity):

```
class A ···{··· D m(C x){return e;} ··· }
```

We compute the *least type* required of the argument for x of method m. The *least type* means that values of supertypes of it are definitely wrong for instantiating x in execution. It is determined by the body e of m, denoted by $rtype_e(x)$. Before giving the definition of *rtype*, we first classify a set of expressions $cast(e)$ coming from e after zero or more casts (here C ranges over valid class names in the environment Γ).

$$cast(e) ::= e \mid (C)cast(e)$$

Table 3. Definition of $rtype_e(x)$

$$rtype_e(x) \stackrel{\text{def}}{=} \begin{cases} etype(x) & \text{if } x \text{ is not included in } e \\ etype(x) & \text{if } e = x \\ rtype_{e_1}(x) & \text{if } e = e_1.f_i \\ \wedge_{i=0}^{n}(rtype_{e_i}(x)) \wedge rtype_g(x_i) \\ \quad \text{if } e = e_0.m_1(\overline{e}) \wedge x = e_i \wedge \exists D \bullet otype(e_0) = D \\ \quad\quad \wedge \Gamma.op(D)(m_1) = \langle(\overline{E} \to E), \lambda\overline{x}.g\rangle \\ \wedge_{i=0}^{n}(rtype_{e_i}(x)) \\ \quad \text{if } e = e_0.m_1(\overline{e}) \wedge (x \neq e_i \vee \neg\exists D \bullet otype(e_0) = D) \\ \wedge_{i=1}^{n}(rtype_{e_i}(x)) \\ \quad \text{if } e = \text{new } C(\overline{e}) \\ C & \text{if } e = (C)cast(x) \wedge C \preceq rtype_{cast(x)}(x) \\ rtype_{e_1}(x) & \text{if } e = (C)e_1 \wedge (e \neq (C)cast(x) \\ \quad\quad \vee C \npreceq rtype_{cast(x)}(x)) \end{cases}$$

$rtype_e(x)$ is defined by induction on the structure of e (Table 3, suppose $\overline{e} = e_1, \cdots, e_n$), where $C_1 \wedge C_2$ returns the smaller type between C_1 and C_2. In a context without confusion, we write $rtype(x)$ instead of $rtype_e(x)$ for convenience. Now we can see that we get the further required restriction for the argument for x. τ is the $otype$ of the expression body e of the method m, but on the premise that the type of the parameter x is $(etype(x), rtype(x)^{\top})$. The computation of $otype(e)$ will be defined next in Table 4. Please note that, there are three forms of τ as defined above. Therefore, the type of method m in class A is: $type_A(m) = (C, rtype(x)) \to (D, \tau)$. We denote the above four types that constitute $type_A(m)$ as $type_A(m)_i$ ($i=1,2,3,4$) respectively.

Now we illustrate the computation of method type by a simple example. The important thing is that, it makes great sense to reduce the cases of *suspicious* downcast. That is, it can determine statically some *suspicious* downcasts whether correct or wrong.

```
class C extends D {···}
class E extends F {  ··· D m(D x) {return (C)x;} }
```

The declared type of m in E is $D \to D$. When m is invoked, we can not determine whether the invocation is cast-safe statically, in general. For instance, `new E().m(new D())` is not cast-safe; while `new E().m(new C())` is cast-safe. The new form of method type solves the problem. It advances some checking of the arguments from execution time to static time. It rejects the first instance above. From the rules, the type of m is $(D, C) \to (D, C^{\top})$. Note C and $C^{\top}$ are both better than the original types (D and D here). From the typing rules defined later for expressions, `new E().m(new D())` is not well-typed because of the fact $D \npreceq type_E(m)_2$. It turns the originally *suspicious* downcast to *wrong* downcast statically.

Construction of Γ_{cdecls}. Now we show the construction of the typing environment from a sequence of class declarations. Suppose the sequence *cdecls* considered is of the form:

cds1   `class C extends D {` $\overline{C}\,\overline{f};$ `K` $E\,m(\overline{E}\,\overline{x})\{$ `return` $e;$ `} }`   *cds2* where *cds1* and *cds2* are two declaration sequences, which can both be empty. Here class C (we will call the declaration *cdec* in the follows) includes just one method m for simplicity, while its generalization to a class with an arbitrary number of methods is rather longer, but trivial. Typing environment Γ is constructed and used to check the class declared in progress. It is defined on induction with the initial value:

$$\Gamma_\varnothing = \langle \{\texttt{Object}\}, \{\texttt{Object} \mapsto \texttt{Object}\}, \{\texttt{Object} \mapsto \varnothing\}, \{\texttt{Object} \mapsto \varnothing\}\rangle$$

Suppose we have built Γ_{cds1}, and also computed the type for method m: $type_C(\texttt{m})$ in class C. Before adding corresponding information for *cdec* to the typing environment, we must check whether the following condition, denoted by $wt(cdec)$, holds in Γ_{cds1},

$$wt(cdec) \overset{\text{def}}{=} \texttt{C} \overline{\in} \Gamma_{cds1}.cnames \wedge \texttt{D} \in \Gamma_{cds1}.cnames \wedge wt(\texttt{K}) \wedge wt(\texttt{m}) \wedge wt(\overline{\texttt{f}})$$

$$wt(\texttt{m}) \overset{\text{def}}{=} \texttt{E} \in \Gamma_{cds1}.cnames \cup \{\texttt{C}\} \wedge \overline{\texttt{E}} \in \Gamma_{cds1}.cnames \cup \{\texttt{C}\}$$
$$\wedge \texttt{m} \in \Gamma_{cds1}.op(\texttt{D}) \Rightarrow sign(\texttt{C},\ \texttt{m}) = sign(\texttt{D},\texttt{m})$$
$$\wedge (wt(\texttt{e}) \wedge etype(\texttt{e}) \preceq \texttt{E}),$$
$$\text{where } etype(\overline{\texttt{x}}) = \overline{\texttt{E}}, otype(\overline{\texttt{x}}) = \overline{\texttt{E}}^{\top}$$
$$\text{and} \quad etype(\texttt{this}) = otype(\texttt{this}) = \texttt{C}.$$

$$wt(\overline{\texttt{f}}) \overset{\text{def}}{=} \overline{\texttt{C}} \in \Gamma_{cds1}.cnames \cup \{\texttt{C}\} \wedge \overline{\texttt{f}} \overline{\in} \Gamma_{cds1}.attr(\texttt{D})$$

In case of overriding, if a method with the same name is declared in a subclass, then it must have the same signature as its superclass. This is embodied in the definition of $wt(\texttt{m})$. In any method body, we always have the fact that $wt(\texttt{this}) = \textbf{true}$. On the premise of the typing information of method parameters $\overline{\texttt{x}}$ and the variable $\texttt{this}$, $wt(\texttt{m})$ also checks whether the body of m is well-typed, i. e., $wt(\texttt{e})$ to be defined in the sequel, and whether the method body type is the subtype of the return type.

The condition $wt(\texttt{K})$ checks that the constructor must first apply the corresponding constructor of the superclass to the fields of the superclass and then initialize the fields declared in this class, as showed in the syntax of FJ in Table 1. Here we omit the trivial formalization. Predicate $wt(\overline{\texttt{f}})$ states that the fields can not be redefined in subclass.

If $wt(cdec)$ holds, we will continue to construct $\Gamma_{cds1 \cup cdec}$ as follows; otherwise, we will define $\Gamma_{cdecls} \overset{\text{def}}{=} \boxtimes$, which means that the typing environment fails to be built.

$$\Gamma_{cds1 \cup cdec} = \langle\ \Gamma_{cds1}.cnames \cup \{\texttt{C}\}, \Gamma_{cds1}.superclass \cup \{\texttt{C} \mapsto \texttt{D}\},$$
$$\Gamma_{cds1}.attr \cup \{\texttt{C} \mapsto \{\langle\overline{\texttt{C}}\ \overline{\texttt{f}}\rangle\} \cup \Gamma_{cds1}.attr(\texttt{D})\},$$
$$\Gamma_{cds1}.op \cup \{\texttt{C} \mapsto \Gamma_{cds1}.op(\texttt{D}) \oplus \{\texttt{m} \mapsto \langle type_C(\texttt{m}), \lambda\overline{\texttt{x}} \cdot \texttt{e}\rangle\}\}\rangle$$

Typing FJ. The typing rules for FJ are given in Table 4. Γ_{cdecls} is the typing environment defined above. The typing rule for expression e consists of two parts: $wt_{\Gamma_{cdecls}}(\texttt{e})$ and $type_{\Gamma_{cdecls}}(\texttt{e})$, where the predicate $wt_{\Gamma_{cdecls}}(\texttt{e})$ checks whether e is well-typed in the environment Γ_{cdecls}, and when it holds, $type_{\Gamma_{cdecls}}(\texttt{e})$ records the type of e. From now on, on the premise of no confusion, we will omit the environment Γ_{cdecls} and write $wt(\texttt{e}), type(\texttt{e})$ and *cnames, superclass, attr, op* instead.

In order to solve the downcast problem, we use a pair (T_1, T_2) to represent the type of expression e, where T_1 is the static type of e denoted by $etype(\texttt{e})$, and T_2 is the type of the object that e refers in the run-time, denoted by $otype(\texttt{e})$. For example, if $\texttt{e} = (\texttt{C})\texttt{new D}(\overline{\texttt{v}})$ is well-typed, then $etype(\texttt{e}) = \texttt{C}$, while $otype(\texttt{e}) = \texttt{D}$.

Table 4. Typing FJ

Expr.	Typing Rules
x	$wt(x) \overset{\text{def}}{=} etype(x) \in cnames$ $type(x) \overset{\text{def}}{=} (etype(x), etype(x)^\top)$
$e.f_i$	$wt(e.f_i) \overset{\text{def}}{=} wt(e) \wedge f_i \in attr(etype(e))$ $type(e.f_i) \overset{\text{def}}{=} \begin{cases} (etype(etype(e).f_i), \boxdot) & \text{if } otype(e) = \boxdot \\ (etype(etype(e).f_i), etype(etype(e).f_i)^\top) & \text{otehwise} \end{cases}$
$e_0.m(\overline{e})$	Suppose that $sign(etype(e_0), m) = \overline{D} \to C$, $wt(e_0.m(\overline{e})) \overset{\text{def}}{=} \begin{cases} wt(e_0) \wedge wt(\overline{e}) \wedge (m \in op(etype(e_0))) \wedge etype(\overline{e}) \preceq \overline{D} \wedge \\ \bigwedge_{i=1}^{n} (\exists E_i \bullet otype(e_i) = E_i \Rightarrow E_i \preceq (type_{E_0}(m)_2)_i)) \\ \qquad\qquad \text{if } \exists E_0 \bullet otype(e_0) = E_0 \\ wt(e_0) \wedge wt(\overline{e}) \wedge (m \in op(etype(e_0))) \wedge etype(\overline{e}) \preceq \overline{D}) \\ \qquad\qquad \text{otherwise} \end{cases}$ $type(e_0.m(\overline{e})) \overset{\text{def}}{=} \begin{cases} (C, type_{E_0}(m)_4) \\ \quad \text{if for } i = 0, 1, \cdots, n, \exists E_i \bullet otype(e_i) = E_i \\ (C, otype(mbody(E_0, m))) \\ \quad \text{if } \exists E_0 \bullet otype(e_0) = E_0 \wedge (\neg \exists i \in 1..n \bullet otype(e_i) = \boxdot) \\ (C, \bigvee_{\forall i \bullet F_i \preceq E} (otype(mbody(F_i, m)))) \\ \quad \text{if } \exists E \bullet otype(e_0) = E^\top \wedge (\neg \exists i \in 1..n \bullet otype(e_i) = \boxdot) \\ (C, \boxdot) \qquad\qquad \text{otherwise} \end{cases}$
new $C(\overline{e})$	$wt(\text{new } C(\overline{e})) \overset{\text{def}}{=} C \in cnames \wedge wt(\overline{e}) \wedge etype(\overline{e}) \preceq etype(C.\overline{f})$ $type(\text{new } C(\overline{e})) \overset{\text{def}}{=} \begin{cases} (C, \boxdot) & \text{if } \exists e_i \in \overline{e}, otype(e_i) = \boxdot \\ (C, C) & \text{otherwise} \end{cases}$
$(C)e$	$wt((C)e) \overset{\text{def}}{=} C \in cnames \wedge wt(e)$ $\wedge\ (etype(e) \preceq C \vee (C \preceq etype(e) \wedge otype(e) \preceq C)$ $\vee\ (C \preceq otype(e) \wedge \exists E \bullet otype(e) = E^\top)$ $\vee\ (C \preceq etype(e) \wedge otype(e) = \boxdot))$ $type((C)e) \overset{\text{def}}{=} \begin{cases} (C, \boxdot) & \text{if } \exists E \bullet otype(e) = E^\top \wedge C \prec otype(e) \\ (C, otype(e)) & \text{otherwise} \end{cases}$

As stated before, we will distinguish two different kinds of casts: *wrong* downcast and *suspicious* downcast. The key point lies in the fact that the *otype* of the entity for *wrong* downcast and that for *suspicious* downcast are different: It is known for the first kind of cases; however, only the upper bound of it is known for the second. There are two other forms of the *otype* except the normal class type. As listed in Table 4, the *otype*s of x and e.f_i can be $C^\top$ for some C, to mean that the type of the objects referred by the expression is of some subtype of a known C. When a downcast applied to an expression e with its *otype* of the form $C^\top$, the cast is *suspicious*, and the expression is treated as a well-typed one with *otype* assigned to $\boxdot$. On the other side, expressions containing *wrong* downcast are not considered as well-typed. Except for this case, type $C^\top$ acts the same as C. The type $\boxdot$ shows that the object type of the expression can not be determined before the execution. From Table 4, we can see that $\boxdot$ occurs only as values of *otype* and will spread over expressions containing *suspicious* downcast. $T_1 \vee T_2$ returns the greater type between them. We define for each T, $T \vee \boxdot = \boxdot$.

Table 5. Evaluation of Expressions in FJ

Expression	Evaluation		
$e.f_i$	$eval(e.f_i)$	$\overset{\text{def}}{=}$	$\begin{cases} eval(e_i) & \text{if } e{=}\text{new } C(\overline{e}) \\ eval(eval(e).f_i) & \text{otherwise} \end{cases}$
$e_0.m(\overline{e})$	$eval(e_0.m(\overline{e}))$	$\overset{\text{def}}{=}$	$\begin{cases} eval([\overline{e}/\overline{x}, \text{new } C(\overline{d})/\text{this}]mbody(C, m)) \\ \qquad\qquad\qquad \text{if } e_0 = \text{new } C(\overline{d}) \\ eval(eval(e_0).m(\overline{e})) \quad \text{otherwise} \end{cases}$
new $C(\overline{e})$	$eval(\text{new } C(\overline{e}))$	$\overset{\text{def}}{=}$	$\begin{cases} \text{new } C(\overline{e}) & \text{if new } C(\overline{e}) \in V \\ eval(\text{new } C(eval(\overline{e}))) & \text{otherwise} \end{cases}$
$(C)e$	$eval((C)e)$	$\overset{\text{def}}{=}$	$\begin{cases} eval(e) & \text{if } e = \text{new } D(\overline{e}) \wedge D \preceq C \\ eval((C)eval(e)) & \text{if } e \neq \text{new } D(\overline{e}) \end{cases}$

3.2   Dynamic Semantics of FJ

The evaluation rules for expressions are given in Table 5, which are similar to reduction rules in [9]. The value of expression e is denoted as $eval_\Gamma(e)$. To state the evaluation rules formally, we give the definition of the set of *values*, V, as the final normal form[2] of the evaluated expressions as follows:

$$V ::= \text{new } C() \,|\, \text{new } C(\overline{V}) \qquad \text{where } C \in \Gamma.cnames$$

A program in FJ is of the form $cdecls \bullet e$, where e is the main expression to be evaluated. Now we can define the semantics of the whole program easily:

Definition 3.1. For a program $cdecls \bullet e$, suppose the typing environment built from $cdecls$ is Γ_{cdecls}, then the semantics of the program is defined as:

$$[\![cdecls \bullet e]\!] \overset{\text{def}}{=} eval_{\Gamma_{cdecls}}(e)$$

3.3   Properties

Now we are ready to give the type soundness results. First, three lemmas are introduced.

Lemma 3.2 (Subject Evaluation). Suppose e is a well-typed expression in typing environment Γ. According to the evaluation rules in Table 5, if we have $eval(e) = eval(e')$, and e' is well-typed, then $etype(e') \preceq etype(e)$. So particularly, if $eval(e) \in V_\Gamma$, then we have $etype(eval(e)) \preceq etype(e)$.

Proof. See our report [11] for details.   □

Lemma 3.3 (Progress). Suppose e is a well-typed expression in Γ, then:

- If e includes new $C(\overline{e}).f_i$ as a subexpression, then $\Gamma.attr(C) = \{\langle \overline{C}\ \overline{f}\rangle\}$ and $f_i \in \overline{f}$.
- If e includes new $C(\overline{d}).m(\overline{e})$ as a subexpression, then $mbody(C, m)$ is well-typed, and $|\overline{x}| = |\overline{e}|$.

Proof. Immediate from the typing rules in Table 4 based on the structure of e.   □

---

[2] In [9], it is not clearly defined.

Lemma 3.4 (Stuck). Suppose e is a closed well-typed expression in typing environment Γ. If e is evaluated to e' containing as a subexpression (C) new $D(\bar{e})$ where $C \prec D$, then $otype(e) = \boxed{?}$.

Proof. See our report [11] for details.   □

Theorem 3.5 (Typing Soundness). Suppose e is a closed well-typed FJ expression in typing environment Γ, i.e., $wt_\Gamma(e)$ holds, then $eval(e)$ is either a value in V_Γ with $etype(eval(e)) \preceq etype(e)$, or an expression containing (C) new $D(\bar{e})$ where $C \prec D$. Particularly, the former holds if $otype(e) \neq \boxed{?}$.

Proof. Immediate from **Lemma** 3.2, 3.3 and 3.4.   □

From **Theorem** 3.5, a well-typed expression e is *cast-safe*, if $otype(e) \neq \boxed{?}$, i.e., e contains no *suspicious* cast. Programs containing *wrong* downcast are not well-typed in our system, while programs including only *upcasts* and *correct* downcasts are *cast-safe*. Furthermore, some *suspicious* casts are determined actually wrong (not well-typed) or correct statically. The results are more precise and much better than what of [9].

3.4 Examples

We give some examples here to illustrate the properties stated above.

Example 3.1. Look at the class declarations sequence listed in the introduction. In the following, we check expressions containing various casts occurring in those class declarations in our type system to show the better results than in [9].

- Expressions containing upcast:
  $e_1 = (C) x$ in the body of m in E or $e_2 = (C)$ new $D()$
  $Typing: wt(e_1) = (C \in \Gamma.cnames \wedge etype(x) \preceq C) = (true \wedge D \preceq C) = true$
  $\qquad\qquad type(e_1) = (C, D^\top)$
  $\qquad\qquad wt(e_2) = (C \in \Gamma.cnames \wedge wt(new\ D()) \wedge etype(new\ D()) \preceq C)$
  $\qquad\qquad\qquad\quad = true$
  $\qquad\qquad type(e_2) = (C, \ D)$
  $Eval.: \quad eval(e_2) = eval(new\ D()) = new\ D() \in V_\Gamma$

- Expressions containing *wrong* downcast: $e = (D)$ new $C()$
  $Typing: wt(e) = D \in \Gamma.cnames \wedge wt(new\ C())$
  $\qquad\qquad\qquad\quad \wedge((etype(new\ C()) \preceq D) \vee (otype(new\ C()) \preceq D)$
  $\qquad\qquad\qquad\qquad \vee (otype(e) = T^\top) \vee (otype(e) = \boxed{?}))$
  $\qquad\qquad\quad = false$

- Expressions containing *correct* downcast: $e = (D)((C)$ new $E())$
  $Typing: wt(e) = (D \in \Gamma.cnames \wedge wt((C)new\ E())$
  $\qquad\qquad\qquad\quad \wedge(otype((C)new\ E()) \preceq D)) = true$
  $\qquad\qquad type(e) = (D, \ E)$
  $Eval.: \quad eval(e) = eval((D)eval((C)new\ E())) = eval((D)new\ E())$
  $\qquad\qquad\qquad = eval(new\ E()) = new\ E() \in V_\Gamma$

- Expressions containing *suspicious* downcast: $e_1 = $ (E) x in the body of m in F, or
  $e_2 = $ (E) new F() .m(new D())
  Typing : From the fact that $type(x) = (D, D^\top)$,

$$
\begin{aligned}
wt(e_1) &= \text{E} \in \Gamma.cnames \wedge wt(x) \wedge ((etype(x) \preceq \text{E}) \vee (otype(x) \preceq \text{E}) \vee \\
&\quad (\text{E} \preceq otype(x) \wedge otype(x) = \text{T}^\top) \vee otype(x) = \boxed{?}) \\
&= \texttt{true} \\
type(e_1) &= (\text{E}, \boxed{?})
\end{aligned}
$$

However, we can determine statically that the suspicious downcast in e_2 is actually a wrong downcast.

Typing : $wt(e_2) = otype(\text{new D()}) \preceq type_F(m)_2 \wedge \cdots = \texttt{false}$

- Expressions containing *stupid* cast: e= (F) new D()
  Typing : $wt(e) = \text{F} \in \Gamma.cnames \wedge wt(\text{new D()})$

$$
\begin{aligned}
&\wedge ((etype(\text{new D()}) \preceq \text{F}) \vee (otype(\text{new D()}) \preceq \text{F}) \\
&\quad \vee (otype(\text{new D()}) = \text{T}^\top) \vee (otype(\text{new D()}) = \boxed{?})) \\
&= \texttt{false}
\end{aligned}
$$

4 Parallel Results for FGJ

In the case of Featherweight Generic Java (FGJ), the situation is more complicated due to the fact that many accessorial techniques to deal with *type variables* are involved. However, we also obtained the parallel results for FGJ. In [11], we in detail present our formalisms for FGJ including the static semantics, dynamic semantics and type systems. We reached the property of *Type Soundness* which is better than that in [9], as similar to the case of FJ. Our FGJ type model can also distinguish the *correct*, *wrong* and *suspicious* downcasts statically and effectively. As in [9], We have also the *Backward Compatibility* property, which says that a well-typed FJ program is always a well-typed FGJ program, and that FJ and FGJ evaluations correspond. For the page limitation, we omit the detailed content in this paper. Please see [11] for the techniques as well as the proofs.

5 A Case Study

In this section, we consider a frequently used design pattern, *Observer Pattern* [6] and deal with the corresponding cast problems. The whole program is written in FJ extended

Table 6. The Observer Pattern

```
class Observer extends Object { ··· }
class Subject extends Object {
private:
  List observers;  ··· ;
protected:
  Object Attach(Observer o);  // add observer o to the list of the subject
  Object Notify();  ···
}
```

Table 7. Example Client for the Observer Pattern

```
class Screen extends Observer {
  ...
  Object display(string s) { ... } }
class Point extends Subject {
  ...
  Object Notify(){
    ListIterator i=new ListIterator(observers);
    for(i.First(); !i.IsDone(); i.Next()){
      this.updateObserver((Observer)i.CurrentItem());
    }             }
  Object updateObserver(Observer o) {
    ((Screen)o).display("Color change.");
  }
}

class Main extends Object {
  Object main(){
    List obl=nil;  Point p=new Point(obl);
    p.attach(new Screeen());  p.Notify();
  }
}
```

with some other common language features. For example, we have used the **sequential composition** and **for** command, and a method without return value is considered as with return type Object. However, with respect to the type issues, these are not essential. We can also check the program using the type system we built above.

Table 6 shows the Observer Pattern. A subject role maintains a list of observers ("views") to be notified when some event occurs. Method Attach provides a mean to add new observer, while notify represents the event of interest. Table 7 shows example client classes Screen, Point, and Main. Method main constructs and initializes a Subject, installs an Observer, and invokes Notify. In the process of the type derivations of the class table CT [9] and Main, there are two places involving downcast: (Observer)i.CurrentItem() and (Screen)o. As a result, the cast-safety of this program can not be determined by the type system in [9]. Our type system can determine that the program is well-typed and cast-safe.

We should build the environment Γ for the program first, and then check the main method (corresponding to the closed expression to be evaluated in FJ). We can know that the environment Γ is well-built. We omit the detailed form of Γ here. The main method is also well-typed by our typing rules. We focus on the cast problems now, and investigate the two downcasts here:

- (Screen)o
  Note that the method type has the form $(\overline{C}, \overline{C'}) \rightarrow (D, \tau)$. We can compute that the type for method updateObserver is

  $$(\text{Observer, Screen}) \rightarrow (\text{Object, Object})$$

- `(Observer)i.CurrentItem()`
  Because $type(\texttt{i.CurrentItem()}) = (\texttt{Object}, \texttt{Object}^\top)$, so according to the typing rules, $type((\texttt{Observer})\texttt{i.CurrentItem()}) = (\texttt{Observer}, ⧄)$. This kind of downcast problem lies in the use of the container class `List` and its iterator `ListIterator`, whose element types are both `Object`. It can be solved easily by the addition of *generic classes* in FGJ. So the program itself can have a little modification, which leads to the deletion of the downcast without change of the semantics. Then we make use of the corresponding typing rules and theorems in our FGJ system. We can see that our FGJ system solves this kind of downcasts entirely (The original downcast is deleted!):

```
class Subject extends Object {
  List⟨Screen⟩ observers;
     ...      // same as above
}
class Point extends Subject {
  Object Notify() {
    ListIterator⟨Screen⟩i=new ListIterator⟨Screen⟩(observers);
    for(i.First(); !i.IsDone(); i.Next()) {
      updateObserver(i.CurrentItem⟨Screen⟩());
      // note the deletion of the downcast
    }
... }
class Main extends Object {
  Object main(){ List⟨Screen⟩ obl=nil;  ...  //same as above
  }}
```

- In the end, from the typing rules, $otype(\texttt{main()}) = \texttt{Object} \neq ⧄$. We take the type of the last non-structural command as the type of the whole **sequential**.

According to the type soundness theorem in FGJ, the program is cast-safe.

6   Conclusions and Future Work

In this paper, we build a type system for FJ and FGJ. Supported by this model and some special techniques, such as paired types for expressions and methods, "$c^\top$" type, and "⧄" type, we proved similar, but stronger results than the ones in [9]. Using our results, the system can ensure more programs to be type safe and reject more incorrect programs during the static checking, and further, leave only the really suspicious ones to the dynamic checking, which are also plausibly correct programs.

Nipkow et. al [10] presented Java$_{light}$-a large subset of the sequential part of Java. They gave the type soundness theorem, and prove it in the theorem prover Isabelle/HOL, which makes machine-checked language design become a reality. Many core calculi for Java language, such as [3, 4, 5], are proposed. The authors gave proofs of type soundness in their subsets of Java. But all of these work did not precisely describe the cast cases as what we do here. In [7], J. He *et al.* proposed a denotational semantics for OO programs using *Unifying Theories of Programming* [8]. The idea of *etype* and *otype* used here is enlightened by that work. One can see that our *wt*() seems similar to their D().

However, there are clear differences between our work and theirs: Firstly, we focus on a different language and different problems. Secondly, they used $D()$ to denote the precondition of *design*s, and made not distinction of dynamic checking from static checking. The last, but not the least, we propose the $\boxed{?}$ and $C^\top$ as *otype* in the typing environment. We have not found literature with such notations in the type systems.

As for the future work, we will continue to investigate the properties of FJ and FGJ using our framework. In order to reason across the programs in different languages, we want to define a linking function between programs of FJ and FGJ. Hopefully, this linking can preserve some properties such as type safety, evaluation results, etc. Another future work is to extend our results for FJ (and FGJ) to more fully-fledged OO languages, to connect the results to the practical programming.

Acknowledgement. Quan Long would like to show his great appreciations to Jifeng He and Zhiming Liu for introducing him [7] and the knowledge of denotational models.

References

1. Ole Agesen, Stephen Freund, and John C. Mitchell. Adding type parameterization to the java language. In *Proceedings of OOPSLA'97*, pages 49–65. ACM Press, Atlanta, GA, 1997.
2. Gilad Bracha, Martin Odersky, David Stoutamire, and Philip Wadler. Making the future safe for the past: Adding genericity to the Java™ programming language. In *Proceedings of OOPSLA'98*, pages 183–200. ACM Press, New York, NY, 1998.
3. Sophia Drossopoulou, Susan Eisenbach, and Sarfraz Khurshid. Is the java type system sound? In *Theory and Practice of Object Systems*, volume 5(1), pages 3–24, 1999.
4. Matthew Flatt, Shriram Krishnamurthi, and Matthias Felleisen. Classes and mixins. In *Proceedings of POPL'98*, pages 171–183. ACM Press, New York, NY, 1998.
5. Matthew Flatt, Shriram Krishnamurthi, and Matthias Felleisen. A programmer's reduction semantics for classes and mixins. Technical Report 97-293, Computer Science Dept., Rice University, Corrected version in June, 1999.
6. Erich Gamma, Richard Helm, Ralph Johnson, and John Vlissides. *Design Patterns: Elements of Reusable Object-Oriented Software*. Addison-Wesley, 1995.
7. Jifeng He, Zhiming Liu, Xiaoshan Li, and Shengchao Qin. A relational model for object-oriented designs. In *Lecture Notes on Computer Science 3302, Proceedings of APLAS'04*, pages 415–436. Springer, 2004.
8. C.A.R. Hoare and Jifeng He. *Unifying Theories of Programming*. Prentice-Hall, 1998.
9. Atsushi Igarashi, Benjamin C.Pierce, and Philip Wadler. Featherweight java: A minimal core calculus for Java and GJ. In *Proceedings of OOPSLA'99*, pages 132–146. ACM Press, New York, NY, 1999.
10. Tobias Nipkow and David von Oheimb. Java$_{light}$ is type-safe-definitely. In *Proceedings of POPL'98*, pages 161–170. ACM Press, New York, NY, 1998.
11. Wang Shuling, Quan Long, and Qiu Zongyan. Type safety for FJ and FGJ. Technical Report 2005-40, Inst. of Math., Peking Univ., www.math.pku.edu.cn:8000/en/preindex.php, Corrected version in August, 2006.

Partizan Games in Isabelle/HOLZF

Steven Obua[*]

Technische Universität München
D-85748 Garching, Boltzmannstr. 3, Germany
obua@in.tum.de
http://www4.in.tum.de/~obua

Abstract. *Partizan Games* (PGs) were invented by John H. Conway and are described in his book *On Numbers and Games*. We formalize PGs in Higher Order Logic extended with ZF axioms (HOLZF) using Isabelle, a mechanical proof assistant. We show that PGs can be defined as the unique fixpoint of a function that arises naturally from Conway's original definition. While the construction of PGs in HOLZF relies heavily on the ZF axioms, operations on PGs are defined on a game type that hides its set theoretic origins. A polymorphic type of sets that are not bigger than ZF sets facilitates this. We formalize the induction principle that Conway uses throughout his proofs about games, and prove its correctness. For these purposes we examine how the notions of well-foundedness in HOL and ZF are related in HOLZF. Finally, games (modulo equality) are added to Isabelle's numeric types by showing that they are an instance of the axiomatic type class of partially ordered abelian groups.

1 Introduction

Partizan Games are extensively and beautifully described in Conway's book ONAG [1]. In this paper, we will instead focus on the issues that arise when representing and reasoning about PGs in the mechanical theorem proving assistant Isabelle[1]. For PGs we improve on the methods of Mamane, who has formalized PGs and surreal numbers, which are a special kind of PGs, in Coq [2]. Especially, our constructions and proofs are in direct relation to the ones found in ONAG and therefore short. The proofs in [2] often deviate from the original proofs and are (much) longer. This difference has two major reasons:

1. We use a logic / axiom system, *HOLZF*, that is very suitable for formalizing set-theoretic notions but still offers the advantages of Higher Order Logic, so that we can define our own type of games. Mamane uses the Calculus of Inductive Constructions (CIC).
2. We have formalized the induction principle that Conway uses, and proved its correctness once and for all. Actual inductions in the proofs about games are simple instantiations of this general induction principle.

---

[*] Supported by the Ph.D. program "Logik in der Informatik" of the "Deutsche Forschungsgemeinschaft."
[1] The theory files can be downloaded from [14].

K. Barkaoui, A. Cavalcanti, and A. Cerone (Eds.): ICTAC 2006, LNCS 4281, pp. 272–286, 2006.

Mamane has identified this induction principle and calls it *permuting induction* (and so will we) but has neither proven nor formalized it [2]. We show that also Conway's transitivity proof is perfectly correct according to this principle, contrary to what Mamane [2] states. On the other hand we have discovered a true flaw in one of Conway's proofs.

This paper can be seen from two points of view. One is that this paper is about formalizing PGs, and in order to achieve this, we will introduce Isabelle/HOLZF and some properties of it. The other point of view is that it really is about Isabelle/HOLZF, a logic that extends both Higher Order Logic (HOL) and Zermelo-Fraenkel set theory (ZF), and about the first application of it, namely formalizing games, that neither Isabelle/HOL nor Isabelle/ZF is suitable for.

2   Which Axiom System Suits Partizan Games?

Conway defines Partizan Games inductively:

> If L and R are any two sets of games, there is a game $G = \{L \mid R\}$. All games are constructed this way. The *left options* of G are the elements of L, and R is the set of *right options* of G. Two games G and H are called *identical* if they have the same left and right options.

Underlying this definition is the idea that every game has certain positions and is played by two players, Left and Right. Every position is characterized by the moves that either of both players could make if it were his turn. Each such move leads to a new position. In a given position G a move is identified with the position it leads to. The moves of Left are called the left options of G, the moves of Right are called the right options of G. Identifying a game with its starting position we arrive at the above definition of games.

There is a restriction on PGs that Conway demands: There is no infinite sequence of games $(G_i)_{i \in \mathbb{N}}$ such that G_{i+1} is an option (left or right) of G_i. This restriction is contained in the definition of PGs if *set* is understood in the sense of Zermelo-Fraenkel set theory.

Isabelle is a generic theorem prover [8]. Its meta logic is intuitionistic higher order logic, on top of which other logics can be built by asserting axioms and declaring types. Two such extensions of pure Isabelle are in more widespread use and we argue that neither of them is suitable for mechanizing Partizan Games:

Isabelle/HOL [8] is the Isabelle implementation of Higher Order Logic. It features packages for defining datatypes and general recursive functions. We might be tempted to use the datatype package to define the *game* type:

$$\textbf{datatype } game = \text{Game (game set) (game set)}. \tag{1}$$

If admissible, this statement would define a new type *game* that has one constructor *Game* that takes as arguments a *game set*, the left options of the game, and a further *game set*, the right options. But this statement is not admissible because *Game L* needs to be an injective function for any fixed *L* but cannot be; as a consequence of the Schroeder-Bernstein theorem one can prove in HOL that no function of type $'a\ set \Rightarrow 'a$ is possibly injective.

Isabelle/ZF [6,7] is based on classical first-order logic and the axioms of ZF set theory. Here we might try to use the provided facilities to define fixpoints; let us define a function *h* by

$$h\ A = \{(L,\ R) \mid L \subseteq A \wedge R \subseteq A\}. \tag{2}$$

Any set *G* that fulfills the fixpoint equation $h\ G = G$ would be a good candidate for a set of Partizan Games. But the cardinality of hA is greater than that of *A* for all sets *A* and therefore there is no such candidate. Therefore, Partizan Games do not form a set but rather a proper class.

In Isabelle/HOLZF we can solve all these problems; the next section introduces and describes Isabelle/HOLZF.

3   HOLZF = HOL + ZF

We obtain Isabelle/HOLZF by starting from Isabelle/HOL and introducing a new type *ZF* and a relation *Elem* of type $ZF \Rightarrow ZF \Rightarrow bool$ on it; we then make this type into the universe of ZF sets by postulating the ZF axioms.

That something like Isabelle/HOLZF could be possible was suspected by Tjark Weber and the author when they tried to formalize the semantics of the λ-calculus in Isabelle/HOL (and failed). The actual viability and how-to of the approach was brought to the attention of the author by Bob Solovay who outlined HOLZF on the Isabelle mailing list and claimed that "for certain reasons he needed such a monster", opposing Larry Paulson's remark that HOLZF might be "too much of a good thing". Bob Solovay also provided a proof of the consistency of HOLZF relative to the consistency of ZFC + 'there is an inaccessible cardinal'. Mike Gordon has worked on HOLZF already ten years ago [3]. He uses the name HOL-ST instead of HOLZF. Also, Sten Agerholm has used HOL-ST to formalize the inverse limit construction of domain theory to build a model of the λ-calculus [4].

We use the same axioms as Gordon in [3] with one exception; his axiom of separation is superfluous if one is willing to apply the axiom of choice which HOL provides via the Hilbert choice operator.

We first declare the new type *ZF* and introduce six new constants denoting the empty set (*Empty*), the element relation (*Elem*), the sum or union operator (*Sum*), the power set operator (*Power*), the replacement operator (*Repl*) and an infinite set (*Inf*):

typedecl *ZF*

consts
   Empty :: *ZF*
   Elem :: $ZF \Rightarrow ZF \Rightarrow bool$

$Sum :: ZF \Rightarrow ZF$
$Power :: ZF \Rightarrow ZF$
$Repl :: ZF \Rightarrow (ZF \Rightarrow ZF) \Rightarrow ZF$
$Inf :: ZF$

Standard constructions like unordered pairs (*Upair*), the singleton set (*Singleton*) and the union of two sets (*union*) are defined in terms of the new constants. We also need the function *SucNat* which just encodes the successor of a natural number as a set in the standard way.

Our seven axioms can now be expressed as follows:

axioms
  Empty: $\neg \, (Elem \; x \; Empty)$
  Ext: $(x = y) = (\forall z. \; Elem \; z \; x = Elem \; z \; y)$
  Sum: $Elem \; z \; (Sum \; x) = (\exists y. \; Elem \; z \; y \wedge Elem \; y \; x)$
  Power: $Elem \; y \; (Power \; x) = (\forall z. \; Elem \; z \; y \longrightarrow Elem \; z \; x)$
  Repl: $Elem \; b \; (Repl \; A \; f) = (\exists a. \; Elem \; a \; A \wedge b = f \; a)$
  Regularity: $A \neq Empty \longrightarrow (\exists x. \; Elem \; x \; A \wedge (\forall y. \; Elem \; y \; x \longrightarrow \neg \, (Elem \; y \; A)))$
  Infinity: $Elem \; Empty \; Inf \wedge (\forall x. \; Elem \; x \; Inf \longrightarrow Elem \; (SucNat \; x) \; Inf)$

As mentioned, separation (*Sep*) can be defined in terms of replacement and does not need an extra axiom.

constdefs
  $Sep :: ZF \Rightarrow (ZF \Rightarrow bool) \Rightarrow ZF$
  $Sep \; A \; p \equiv (if \; (\forall x. \; Elem \; x \; A \longrightarrow \neg \, (p \; x)) \; then \; Empty \; else$
  $(let \; z = (\epsilon x. \; Elem \; x \; A \wedge p \; x) \; in$
  $let \; f = \lambda \; x. \; (if \; p \; x \; then \; x \; else \; z) \; in \; Repl \; A \; f))$

We also define ordered pairs (*Opair*):

constdefs
  $Opair :: ZF \Rightarrow ZF \Rightarrow ZF$
  $Opair \; a \; b \equiv Upair \; (Upair \; a \; a) \; (Upair \; a \; b)$
  $Fst :: ZF \Rightarrow ZF$
  $Fst \; q \equiv \epsilon x. \; \exists y. \; q = Opair \; x \; y$
  $Snd :: ZF \Rightarrow ZF$
  $Snd \; q \equiv \epsilon y. \; \exists x. \; q = Opair \; x \; y$

The reasoning about these constants is easy if one can prove an equation for the constant that is characteristic for it and has the form of a simple logical equivalence so that the constant does not appear any more on the right hand side. In that way the actual work can be delegated to the classical reasoner and to the simplifier of Isabelle/HOL. The characteristic equations for *Upair*, *Singleton, union, Sep, Opair, Fst* and *Snd* are:

$$\begin{aligned}
Elem \; x \; (Upair \; a \; b) &\equiv x = a \vee x = b, \\
Elem \; x \; (Singleton \; y) &\equiv x = y, \\
Elem \; x \; (union \; A \; B) &\equiv Elem \; x \; A \vee Elem \; x \; B, \\
Elem \; b \; (Sep \; A \; p) &\equiv Elem \; b \; A \wedge p \; b, \\
Opair \; a \; b = Opair \; c \; d &\equiv a = c \wedge b = d, \\
Fst \; (Opair \; x \; y) &\equiv x, \\
Snd \; (Opair \; x \; y) &\equiv y.
\end{aligned}$$

The development of set theory proceeds along the same lines as in Isabelle/ZF [6]. We have not developed the whole theory but at least the pieces that are necessary to later construct Partizan Games. Paulson goes on building up an infrastructure for inductive definition and recursion within set theory [7]. This machinery is not sufficient in order to deal with Partizan Games as we have seen before. But this is no problem anyway because we can rely on the machinery of fixpoints, primitive and well-founded recursion that already exists in HOL instead of replicating the mechanisms of ZF! Before delving into that let us first construct Partizan Games in HOLZF.

4   Constructing Partizan Games

Partizan Games do not form a ZF set but, if they exist at all, only a proper class as we have explained earlier. Intuitively, a proper class is a collection of elements that is too 'big' to form a ZF set but which is rather defined by a property which all elements of the class, and only those, share. In HOL we have the polymorphic type of sets at our disposal which is just an abbreviation for a predicate / property:

$$\alpha \; set = \alpha \Rightarrow bool. \tag{3}$$

Therefore we call an object of type *ZF set* a *class*. When we discuss well-foundedness we will see that this is the right intuition. An object of type *ZF* is referred to as *set*. If we are talking about an object of type α *set* and we do not have necessarily $\alpha = ZF$ then we use the expression *HOL set*.

For each set there is a corresponding class which we obtain by applying the *explode* function to the set.

constdefs
  explode :: *ZF* $\Rightarrow$ *ZF set*
  explode $z \equiv \{\ x.\ Elem\ x\ z\ \}$
  implode :: *ZF set* $\Rightarrow$ *ZF*
  implode $\equiv inv\ explode$

Obviously we have the characteristic equations

$$(x \in explode\ X) = Elem\ x\ X, \quad implode\ (explode\ x) = x. \tag{4}$$

The empty set corresponds to the empty class $\emptyset$:

$$explode\ Empty = \emptyset. \tag{5}$$

What about the universal class *UNIV*? Russell's Paradox allows us to prove that there is no set which corresponds to the universal class:

$$explode\ z \neq UNIV. \tag{6}$$

Classes without a corresponding set are called *proper*.

We are now able to fix (2) by defining the function whose fixpoint we are interested in not on sets but on classes:

constdefs

fixgames :: *ZF set* ⇒ *ZF set*
fixgames A ≡ { *Opair l r* | *l r. explode l* ⊆ *A* ∧ *explode r* ⊆ *A*}

It is easy to see that *fixgames* is a monotone function,

$$mono\ fixgames, \tag{7}$$

where *mono* is defined by

$$mono\ f \equiv \forall A\ B.\ A \leq B \longrightarrow f\ A \leq f\ B. \tag{8}$$

Note that for HOL sets ≤ is just ⊆. The Knaster-Tarski theorem is already available in Isabelle/HOL for the complete lattice of HOL sets:

$$mono\ f \Longrightarrow lfp\ f = f\ (lfp\ f), \quad mono\ f \Longrightarrow gfp\ f = f\ (gfp\ f), \tag{9}$$

where *lfp* is the least and *gfp* the greatest fixpoint operator. Therefore we know that *fixgames* has a fixpoint. Every such fixpoint would be acceptable as a sensible definition for Partizan Games so we pick the least and the greatest.

constdefs

games-lfp :: *ZF set*
games-lfp ≡ *lfp fixgames*
games-gfp :: *ZF set*
games-gfp ≡ *gfp fixgames*

From (9) we deduce

$$games\text{-}lfp = fixgames\ games\text{-}lfp, \quad games\text{-}gfp = fixgames\ games\text{-}gfp. \tag{10}$$

Every fixpoint *G* of *fixgames* is bounded by *games-lfp* and *games-gfp*:

$$G = fixgames\ G \Longrightarrow games\text{-}lfp \subseteq G \land G \subseteq games\text{-}gfp. \tag{11}$$

So it seems that we can choose among several, maybe infinitely many definitions for Partizan Games! Fortunately, there is only one fixpoint of *fixgames*:

$$games\text{-}lfp = games\text{-}gfp. \tag{12}$$

To see why, we first define the options of a game.

constdefs

left-option :: *ZF* ⇒ *ZF* ⇒ *bool*
left-option g opt ≡ (*Elem opt* (*Fst g*))
right-option :: *ZF* ⇒ *ZF* ⇒ *bool*
right-option g opt ≡ (*Elem opt* (*Snd g*))
is-option-of :: (*ZF* × *ZF*) *set*
is-option-of ≡ {(*opt, g*) . *g* ∈ *games-gfp* ∧ (*left-option g opt* ∨ *right-option g opt*)}

We prove

$$g \in games\text{-}gfp \longrightarrow g \in games\text{-}lfp \tag{13}$$

by induction over *g*.

Proof. Let us assume that (13) holds for all options of g, that is for all *opt* such that $(opt, g) \in$ *is-option-of*. Let us further assume $g \in$ *games-gfp*. Because of *games-gfp* = *fixgames games-gfp* there are L and R such that

$$g = Opair\ L\ R, \quad explode\ L \subseteq games\text{-}gfp, \quad explode\ R \subseteq games\text{-}gfp. \quad (14)$$

All elements of *explode L* and *explode R* are options of g. Applying the induction hypothesis yields *explode* $L \subseteq$ *games-lfp* and *explode* $R \subseteq$ *games-lfp*. Because of *fixgames games-lfp* = *games-lfp* we deduce $g \in$ *games-lfp*.   □

Therefore (12) holds.

The alert reader might not be entirely convinced. And rightly so! Above proof only holds up if *is-option-of* is a well-founded relation. So it is time now to turn to well-founded relations in HOLZF.

5   Well-Foundedness and Induction in HOLZF

In Isabelle/HOL a relation is called *well-founded* (*wf*) if it comes with an induction principle:

$$wf\ r \equiv \forall P.\ (\forall x.\ (\forall y.\ (y, x) \in r \longrightarrow P\ y) \longrightarrow P\ x) \longrightarrow (\forall x.\ P\ x). \quad (15)$$

The predicate *wf* has type $(\alpha \times \alpha)\ set \Rightarrow bool$. Equivalent to (15) is that every non-empty HOL set has a minimal element with respect to the relation:

$$wf\ r = (\forall\, Q\ x.\ x \in Q \longrightarrow (\exists z {\in} Q.\ \forall y.\ (y, z) \in r \longrightarrow y \notin Q)). \quad (16)$$

In order to complete our above proof that *fixgames* has a unique fixpoint we have to show:
$$wf\ \textit{is-option-of}. \quad (17)$$

But *is-option-of* is already a fairly complicated relation; we have to consider both left and right options. Looking around we discover a more basic relation:

constdefs
  is-Elem-of :: $(ZF \times ZF)\ set$
  is-Elem-of $\equiv \{(a,b)\ .\ Elem\ a\ b\}$

Because of the way we constructed ordered pairs we can derive

$$\exists z.\ Elem\ x\ z \wedge Elem\ y\ z \wedge Elem\ z\ (Opair\ x\ y). \quad (18)$$

Now assume $(opt, g) \in$ *is-option-of*. This implies $g \in$ *games-gfp* = *fixgames games-gfp* and therefore we know that there exist sets L and R such that $g = Opair\ L\ R$ and *Elem opt L* $\vee$ *Elem opt R*. Together with (18) follows

$$(opt, g) \in \textit{is-option-of} \implies \exists u\ v.\ Elem\ opt\ u \wedge Elem\ u\ v \wedge Elem\ v\ g, \quad (19)$$

and further
$$\textit{is-option-of} \subseteq \textit{is-Elem-of}^{+}. \quad (20)$$

Here r^+ denotes the transitive closure of the relation r which is of course well-founded if r is. Therefore we are left with the proof obligation

$$wf\ is\text{-}Elem\text{-}of. \tag{21}$$

It is not exaggerated to call (21) the main theorem of well-foundedness in HOLZF. Despite that, to the author's knowledge it has neither been considered nor proven in previous work on HOLZF/HOL-ST.

Of course the *Elem* relation is well-founded on every *set* P; for every nonempty subset K of P there is a such that *Elem* a K and $\forall x.\ Elem\ x\ a \longrightarrow \neg\ Elem\ x\ K$ hold. This is a direct consequence of the axiom of regularity. Considering (16), what (21) says is that *Elem* is also well-founded on every *class* P!

Once this is understood, standard literature on set theory tells us how to proceed [10, ch. 6]. We introduce the notion of ZF-well-foundedness (*wfzf*):

constdefs
> $Ext :: ('\alpha \times '\beta)\ set \Rightarrow '\beta \Rightarrow '\alpha\ set$
> $Ext\ R\ y \equiv \{x\ .\ (x,\ y) \in R\}$

> $regular :: (ZF \times ZF)\ set \Rightarrow bool$
> $regular\ R \equiv \forall A.\ A \neq Empty \longrightarrow$
> $\qquad (\exists x.\ Elem\ x\ A \land (\forall y.\ (y,\ x) \in R \longrightarrow \neg\ (Elem\ y\ A)))$

> $set\text{-}like :: (ZF \times ZF)\ set \Rightarrow bool$
> $set\text{-}like\ R \equiv \forall y.\ \exists z.\ Ext\ R\ y = explode\ z$

> $wfzf :: (ZF \times ZF)\ set \Rightarrow bool$
> $wfzf\ R \equiv regular\ R \land set\text{-}like\ R$

A ZF-well-founded relation is therefore a relation R that is

1. *regular*, that is it is well-founded on every set, and
2. *set-like*, that is for any x the class $Ext\ R\ x$ of all predecessors of x is a set.

Because of the axiom of regularity we have *regular is-Elem-of*. Obviously

$$Ext\ is\text{-}Elem\text{-}of = explode \tag{22}$$

holds, therefore we also know *set-like is-Elem-of*. Finally we deduce

$$wfzf\ is\text{-}Elem\text{-}of. \tag{23}$$

Thus the main theorem (21) can be reformulated as

$$wfzf\ R \implies wf\ R. \tag{24}$$

The proof of (24) is quite involved, at least if one needs to build all the tools from scratch. We refer the reader who is interested in the details to the set theory literature [10, ch. 6] or the Isabelle theory files themselves [14].

6   The Type of Games

So there is a unique class of Partizan Games. If we carefully listen to Conway's 'cry for a Mathematician's liberation movement', also known as Appendix to Part Zero of ONAG, we might hear that it is desirable to package this class as a type so that we can forget about its set-theoretic origin. Software engineers call this approach data abstraction.

Defining the type is easy enough:

typedef *game = games-lfp*

The next item on our wish list is to have a function *Game* that takes the left and right options of a game as arguments and constructs a game out of them. But what type should the left and right options have, maybe *game set*? We have seen earlier that this does not work; we would want *Game* to be injective, but there is no injective function of type

$$Game :: (game\ set) \Rightarrow (game\ set) \Rightarrow game. \tag{25}$$

A solution to this problem would be not only to introduce the type of games, but also the type *gameset* of sets of games.

But this would entail the dreary definition of element relation, union operator and so on just for this one type.

There is a better solution; we still introduce a new type and we still have to define a third suit of operators on 'sets', but we do it in a general way. This new type is a natural addition to the types already available in HOL which is definable only in HOLZF:

typedef $'\alpha\ zet = \{A :: '\alpha\ set\ .\ \exists f\ z.\ inj\text{-}on\ f\ A \wedge f\ `\ A \subseteq explode\ z\}$

We define a polymorphic type *zet* of 'sets' that are 'not bigger' than some set of type *ZF*. We need a new name for them in order to not confuse them with our other notions class, set and HOL set. We will call them zets. A zet of type $\alpha\ zet$ corresponds to an HOL set A of type $\alpha\ set$ such that there is a set z and a mapping f from α to *ZF* such that the image of A under f is contained in the class that corresponds to z. We ensure that f preserves the size of A by requiring f to be injective on A.

We then define operators on zets that mimic those available on sets. We will not bother the reader with details here; we just state the names of the functions that are used frequently and also their characteristic property:

name :: type	characteristic property
$zin :: \alpha \Rightarrow \alpha\ zet \Rightarrow bool$	
$zempty :: \alpha\ zet$	$\neg\ zin\ x\ zempty$
$zimage$ $:: (\alpha \Rightarrow \beta) \Rightarrow \alpha\ zet \Rightarrow \beta\ zet$	$zin\ y\ (zimage\ f\ A) = (\exists x.\ zin\ x\ A \wedge y = f\ x)$
$zunion :: \alpha\ zet \Rightarrow \alpha\ zet \Rightarrow \alpha\ zet$	$zin\ x\ (zunion\ a\ b) = (zin\ x\ a \vee zin\ x\ b)$

Now we are equipped with the tools to introduce the left and right options of a game; we also introduce the *Game* constructor we wanted all along.

consts
  left-options :: *game* ⇒ *game zet*
  right-options :: *game* ⇒ *game zet*
  options :: *game* ⇒ *game zet*
  option-of :: (*game* × *game*) *set*
  Game :: *game zet* ⇒ *game zet* ⇒ *game*

Again, we do not give definitions here; the curious reader is referred to the Isabelle theory file. All that matters are the characteristic properties which have been proven from the definitions:

$$(Game\ L1\ R1\ =\ Game\ L2\ R2) = (L1 = L2 \land R1 = R2), \qquad (26)$$

$$g = Game\ (left\text{-}options\ g)\ (right\text{-}options\ g), \qquad (27)$$

$$zin\ opt\ (left\text{-}options\ g) \implies zin\ opt\ (options\ g), \qquad (28)$$

$$zin\ opt\ (right\text{-}options\ g) \implies zin\ opt\ (options\ g), \qquad (29)$$

$$((opt,\ g) \in option\text{-}of) = zin\ opt\ (options\ g). \qquad (30)$$

The construction of our *game* type is completed by proving

$$wf\ option\text{-}of. \qquad (31)$$

This is an immediate consequence of the well-foundedness of *is-option-of* and gives us an induction principle for *game*s.

7   The Partially Ordered Group Pg

In this section we formalize comparison, equality, addition and negation of games and show that they form a partially ordered group when considered modulo equality. We will not give any intuition behind these operations; ONAG provides plenty of intuition.

Easiest to define is the negation of games:

consts
  neg-game :: *game* ⇒ *game*
recdef *neg-game option-of*
  neg-game g = *Game* (*zimage neg-game* (*right-options g*))
            (*zimage neg-game* (*left-options g*))

The above statements define *neg-game* via well-founded recursion over *option-of*.

lemma *neg-game* (*neg-game g*) = *g*
  apply (*induct g rule*: *neg-game.induct*)
  ...

The short proof (8 lines) of the lemma above is by induction over *g* using the automatically generated and pre-proven induction rule *neg-game.induct*:

$$(\bigwedge g.\ (\forall x.\ zin\ x\ (left\text{-}options\ g) \longrightarrow P\ x)$$
$$\implies (\forall x.\ zin\ x\ (right\text{-}options\ g) \longrightarrow P\ x)$$
$$\implies P\ g) \implies P\ x \qquad (32)$$

Next comes comparison of games:

consts
  $ge\text{-}game :: (game \times game) \Rightarrow bool$
recdef $ge\text{-}game$ ($gprod\text{-}2\text{-}1$ $option\text{-}of$)
  $ge\text{-}game\ (G,\ H) =$
    ($\forall\,x.\ if\ zin\ x\ (right\text{-}options\ G)\ then\ ($
        $if\ zin\ x\ (left\text{-}options\ H)\ then\ \neg\ (ge\text{-}game\ (H,\ x) \vee (ge\text{-}game\ (x,\ G)))$
                    $else\ \neg\ (ge\text{-}game\ (H,\ x)))$
      $else\ (if\ zin\ x\ (left\text{-}options\ H)\ then\ \neg\ (ge\text{-}game\ (x,\ G))\ else\ True))$

The above definition uses the *if*-operator to give recdef the necessary hints for proving termination. A better definition can easily be derived:

$$ge\text{-}game\ (G,\ H) = (\forall\,x.\ (zin\ x\ (right\text{-}options\ G) \longrightarrow \neg\ ge\text{-}game\ (H,\ x))$$
$$\wedge\ (zin\ x\ (left\text{-}options\ H) \longrightarrow \neg\ ge\text{-}game\ (x,\ G))).$$

Because *ge-game* is essentially a function of two arguments which swaps the order of its arguments when calling itself recursively it is important to provide the right termination relation, *gprod-2-1 option-of*, where

$$gprod\text{-}2\text{-}1\ R \equiv \{((a,\ b),\ (c,\ d))\ |\ a = d \wedge (b,\ c) \in R \vee b = c \wedge (a,\ d) \in R.$$

It seems clear that $wf\ (gprod\text{-}2\text{-}1\ R)$ should follow from $wf\ R$; we need to prove this, otherwise recdef will reject above definition of *ge-game*. Actually, *gprod-2-1* is only a special case of a more general well-founded relation that crops up in most definitions and proofs dealing with games. Mamane calls the induction principle that this relation induces *permuting induction* [2, p. 41, p. 95]. He was not able to formalize the principle in CIC but only instances of it like *gprod-2-1*. We have a problem at this point, too; our general relation should not only deal with pairs of games, but with n-tuples of games for arbitrary n. So for $n = 2$ our relation should have type

$$((game \times game) \times (game \times game))\ set \tag{33}$$

but for $n = 3$ it must have type

$$((game \times game \times game) \times (game \times game \times game))\ set \tag{34}$$

and so on. We have no dependent types available in HOL, but there is a solution; we define our relation not on tuples, but inductively on lists.

consts
  $lprod :: ('\alpha \times '\alpha)\ set \Rightarrow ('\alpha\ list \times '\alpha\ list)\ set$
inductive $lprod\ R$
intros
  $(a,\ b) \in R \Longrightarrow ([a],\ [b]) \in lprod\ R$
  $(ah@at,\ bh@bt) \in lprod\ R \Longrightarrow (a,b) \in R \vee a = b$
    $\Longrightarrow (ah@a\#at,\ bh@b\#bt) \in lprod\ R$

Here $xs@ys$ denotes the concatenation of two lists xs and ys, $x\#xs$ denotes the consing of x to the list xs; $lprod\ R$ is really a generalized version of $gprod\text{-}2\text{-}1\ R$:

$$gprod\text{-}2\text{-}1\ R \subseteq inv\text{-}image\ (lprod\ R)\ (\lambda(a,\ b).\ [a,\ b]). \tag{35}$$

The inverse image *inv-image* $R\ f$ of a relation R under a map f is well-founded if R is. Therefore all we have to show is the well-foundedness of *lprod* R which then proves the well-foundedness of *gprod-2-1* R and similar relations. Using induction one shows

$$lprod\ R \subseteq inv\text{-}image\ (mult\ (R^+))\ multiset\text{-}of, \tag{36}$$

that is we reduce the well-foundedness of *lprod* R to the well-foundedness of the multiset order *mult* (R^+). The function *multiset-of* takes a list as its argument and returns the corresponding multiset. See [9, ch. 2.5] for more information on multisets and the multiset order. Luckily, multisets have already been formalized in Isabelle and the well-foundedness of *mult* (R^+) is available as a lemma. Therefore we show easily

$$wf\ R \implies wf\ (lprod\ R). \tag{37}$$

When showing that *ge-game* is a partial order, one has to show transitivity:

$$ge\text{-}game\ x\ y \implies ge\text{-}game\ y\ z \implies ge\text{-}game\ x\ z. \tag{38}$$

The proof of (38) that Conway gives in ONAG is particularly short and elegant. Mamane gives a much longer CIC proof [2, pp. 49-53]. We have a short proof (44 lines in Isar) that is in direct correspondence to the proof of Conway. The trick is to convert a statement of the form $P\ x\ y\ z$ where in this case we set

$$P\ x\ y\ z \equiv ge\text{-}game\ (x,\ y) \wedge ge\text{-}game\ (y,\ z) \longrightarrow ge\text{-}game\ (x,\ z), \tag{39}$$

into a statement of the form $\forall x\ y\ z.\ gs = [x,\ y,\ z] \longrightarrow P\ x\ y\ z$ and prove this by well-founded induction over gs with respect to *lprod option-of*. This ensures that when trying to prove $P\ x\ y\ z$ we can use the induction hypothesis $P\ a\ b\ c$ for all a, b and c that fulfill

$$([a,\ b,\ c],\ [x,\ y,\ z]) \in lprod\ option\text{-}of. \tag{40}$$

Currently one has to show manually that (40) holds for particular instances, typically involving proofs of two or three lines using the introduction rules for *lprod*. Of course this could be automated.

Equality (*eq-game*) is defined in terms of *ge-game*. Addition (*plus-game*) is defined recursively; there are no technical differences to the definition of *ge-game*. We also introduce the zero game (*zero-game*).

constdefs
  eq-game :: *game* $\Rightarrow$ *game* $\Rightarrow$ *bool*
  eq-game $G\ H \equiv ge\text{-}game\ (G,\ H) \wedge ge\text{-}game\ (H,\ G)$

  zero-game :: *game*
  zero-game $\equiv$ *Game zempty zempty*

consts
  $plus\text{-}game :: game \times game \Rightarrow game$
recdef $plus\text{-}game$ $gprod\text{-}2\text{-}2$ $option\text{-}of$
  $plus\text{-}game\ (G,\ H) = Game$
                $(zunion\ (zimage\ (\lambda\ g.\ plus\text{-}game\ (g,\ H))\ (left\text{-}options\ G))$
                        $(zimage\ (\lambda\ h.\ plus\text{-}game\ (G,\ h))\ (left\text{-}options\ H)))$
                $(zunion\ (zimage\ (\lambda\ g.\ plus\text{-}game\ (g,\ H))\ (right\text{-}options\ G))$
                        $(zimage\ (\lambda\ h.\ plus\text{-}game\ (G,\ h))\ (right\text{-}options\ H)))$

Most properties of addition and comparison are straightforward to prove; just copy the proofs that Conway gives and apply above reformulation technique. There is one proof though where this does not work because the proof that Conway gives is flawed. The proof is supposed to verify the theorem

$$ge\text{-}game\ (y,\ z) = ge\text{-}game\ (plus\text{-}game\ (x,\ y),\ plus\text{-}game\ (x,\ z)). \tag{41}$$

The error is on page 18 of ONAG in the proof of theorem 5. Conway claims that the truth of

$$x^R + y \le x + z \ \lor \ x + y^R \le x + z \ \lor \ x + y \le x^L + z \ \lor \ x + y \le x + z^L, \tag{42}$$

assuming furthermore $y \ge z$, implies the truth of

$$x^R + y \le x + y \ \lor \ x + y^R \le x + y \ \lor \ x + z \le x^L + z \ \lor \ x + z \le x + z^L, \tag{43}$$

obviously taking for granted

$$y \ge z \Longrightarrow x + z \le x + y. \tag{44}$$

But this is just what he is trying to prove!
  We can fix this error quickly; two of the assumptions in (42) lead immediately to a contradiction by applying the induction hypothesis:

$$x + y^R \le x + z \Rightarrow y^R \le z \le y, \quad x + y \le x + z^L \Rightarrow z \le y \le z^L. \tag{45}$$

The other two assumptions yield a contradiction by first unfolding the definition of $\le$ and then applying the induction hypothesis:

$$x^R + y \le x + z \Rightarrow \neg(x^R + z \le x^R + y) \Rightarrow z \not\le y, \tag{46}$$
$$x + y \le x^L + z \Rightarrow \neg(x^L + z \le x^L + y) \Rightarrow z \not\le y. \tag{47}$$

Note that we were able to apply the induction hypothesis in several different disguises because all of $[x, z, y^R]$, $[x, z^L, y]$, $[x^R, y, z]$ and $[x^L, y, z]$ are predecessors of $[x, y, z]$ with respect to $lprod$ $option\text{-}of$.
  Does the type $game$ form a group with respect to the defined operations? No, it does not! We only have the theorem

$$eq\text{-}game\ (plus\text{-}game\ (x,\ neg\text{-}game\ x))\ zero\text{-}game \tag{48}$$

not the stronger, but false statement

$$plus\text{-}game\ (x,\ neg\text{-}game\ x) = zero\text{-}game. \tag{49}$$

The equality relation *eq-game* is compatible with the other operations. Furthermore *eq-game* is an equivalence relation, that is transitive, reflexive and symmetric. Therefore we can define a new type *Pg* of Partizan Games that consists of the equivalence classes of *game* with respect to *eq-game*.

typedef $Pg = UNIV$ // { (p, q) . *eq-game* p q }

Using the techniques described in [12] we then lift the theorems we have shown about *game*s to theorems about *Pg*s. The icing on the cake is the Isabelle meta-theorem

instance Pg :: pordered-ab-group-add

that states that *Pg* is an instance of the axiomatic type class of partially ordered groups *pordered-ab-group-add*.

8   Conclusion

We have presented a formalization of Conway's Partizan Games. Our work can be split into two parts.

One part consists of the development of HOLZF in Isabelle and provides infrastructure for this logic. The main result in this context is to identify a notion of well-foundedness particularly suited to the ZF part of HOLZF and to connect this notion with the common notion of well-foundedness in HOL via (24). This allows us to use all of the HOL machinery when dealing with recursion. Furthermore we argue that HOLZF is not only theoretically stronger than both ZFC and HOL but that this difference is also of practical importance, as the example of Partizan Games shows. Interesting is that we have now available a new type of 'set' called zet which might be a valuable addition to the datatype package of Isabelle/HOL. For example, it might then be possible to define Partizan Games directly by

datatype *game* = *Game* (*game zet*) (*game zet*)

Also part of the developed infrastructure is the *lprod*-relation that allows defining of and reasoning about recursive functions of several arguments of the same type.

The second part of our work can be seen as an application of Isabelle/HOLZF. Knowing *wf is-Elem-of* it was easy to show that there is a unique fixpoint of Partizan Games. We have shown that Conway's proofs withstand uttermost scrutiny with the exception of the slip in the proof of (41).

Altogether we have written about 2200 lines of theory text[2]. About 60% is infrastructure development, about 40% specific to Partizan Games. This is not too much text; actually the total time of proving that Partizan Games form a partially ordered group was not more than a couple of days after the type *game* had been constructed and an induction principle for it had been established.

Acknowledgments. Stefan Berghofer told the author why (1) cannot work and caused him to look into the multiset order. Clemens Ballarin helped to prove the

---

[2] Which can be downloaded from [14].

properties of the *zunion* operator. Norbert Schirmer taught the author how to feed congruence rules to the recdef-package. Thanks to Bob Solovay for providing the initial idea and consistency proof of HOLZF, and to Tobias Nipkow for providing references to Mike Gordon's work. Special thanks to the anonymous referee who pointed out that *set-like* is the established name for property 2 of a ZF-well-founded relation.

References

1. John H. Conway. *On Numbers And Games*, 2nd ed., A K Peters Ltd., 2001.
2. Lionel E. Mamane. Surreal Numbers in Coq. *TYPES 2004*, LNCS 3839, Springer 2005, pp. 170-185.
3. Mike J.C. Gordon. Set Theory, Higher Order Logic or Both. *Theorem Proving in Higher Order Logics, 9th International Conference, TPHOLs'96*, LNCS 1125, Springer 1996, pp. 190-201.
4. Sten Agerholm. Formalising a Model of the λ-Calculus in HOL-ST. Technical Report 354, University of Cambridge Computer Laboratory, 1994.
5. Sten Agerholm, Mike J.C. Gordon. Experiments with ZF Set Theory in HOL and Isabelle. Technical Report RS-95-37, BRICS 1995.
6. Lawrence C. Paulson. Set theory for verification: I. From foundations to functions. *J. Automated Reasoning* 11 (1993), 353-389.
7. Lawrence C. Paulson. Set theory for verification: II. Induction and Recursion. *J. Automated Reasoning* 15 (1995), 167-215.
8. Tobias Nipkow, Lawrence C. Paulson, Markus Wenzel. *Isabelle/HOL: A Proof Assistant for Higher-Order Logic*, Springer 2002.
9. F. Baader, T. Nipkow. *Term Rewriting and All That*, Cambridge U.P. 1998.
10. Thomas Jech. *Set Theory*, 3rd rev. ed., Springer 2003.
11. Lawrence C. Paulson. Organizing Numerical Theories Using Axiomatic Type Classes. *Journal of Automated Reasoning*, 2004, Vol. 33, No. 1, pages 29-49.
12. Lawrence C. Paulson. Defining Functions on Equivalence Classes. *ACM Transactions on Computational Logic*, in press.
13. Steven Obua. Proving Bounds for Real Linear Programs in Isabelle/HOL. *TPHOLs 2005*, LNCS 3683, Springer 2005, pp. 227-244.
14. Steven Obua. *Partizan Games in Isabelle/HOLZF*. http://www4.in.tum.de/~obua/partizan.

Proof-Producing Program Analysis

Amine Chaieb

Institut für Informatik
Technische Universität München

Abstract. Proof-producing program analysis augments the invariants inferred by an abstract interpreter with their correctness proofs. If these invariants are precise enough to guarantee safety, this method is an automatic verification tool. We present proof-synthesis algorithms for a simple flow chart language and domains $\mathcal{V} \to \mathbb{V}$ mapping variables to abstract values and discuss some benefits for proof carrying code systems. Our work has been carried out in Isabelle/HOL and incorporated within a verified proof carrying code system.

1 Introduction

Formal verification of imperative programs using a theorem prover is not always an easy task since. Besides the formalization of syntax, semantics and a verification calculus, it especially involves finding appropriate invariants. If these are provided, the verification calculus reduces program correctness to proving a formula, the verification condition. This is in essence *reverifying* that the invariants really fit with the program semantics. In our proof carrying code (*pcc*) context, we automate safety proofs by letting an abstract interpreter infer the invariants. Since this analyzer already cares about the program semantics the reverification of its result, i.e. proving the verification condition, is double work.

This paper presents some techniques, that have been successfully implemented, to augment the inferred invariants with their correctness proofs, which results in an automatic proof method provided the invariants are strong enough to ensure program safety. Assume, for instance, the analyzer discovers the Hoare triple $\{P\}\ x := a\ \{Q\}$, then our method also proves that P implies $Q(x/a)$. We focus on domains $\mathbb{V}^{|\mathcal{V}|}$ (*which we denote by* $\mathcal{V} \to \mathbb{V}$) mapping each program variable $x \in \mathcal{V}$ to an abstract value $v_x \in \mathbb{V}$ that approximates the set of concrete values x may take during execution. For these domains we give algorithms in a generic functional programming notation and concrete examples for interval analysis. All the work we present has been successfully implemented for a subset of Jinja bytecode (Jinja [9] is a Java-like language, for which also a proof carrying code (*pcc*) infrastructure is verified in Isabelle/HOL, cf. [17]). All the proofs are synthesized in Isabelle/HOL [13].

Abstract interpretation [7,8] is a generic framework in which a program analysis is fully specified by an abstract domain, a complete lattice D, and a monotone abstract semantics to interpret programs over D. The correctness of the analysis is guaranteed by proving that (α, C, D, γ_D) is a a Galois connection and that the

K. Barkaoui, A. Cavalcanti, and A. Cerone (Eds.): ICTAC 2006, LNCS 4281, pp. 287–301, 2006.

abstract semantics safely approximates the concrete one. In this framework the invariants are the result of a fix-point computation, generally done iteratively. Termination of the analysis relies on the absence of infinite ascending chains (without loss of generality), which is ensured by restricting D or using widening [7]. Proving termination of iterative solvers, especially formally i.e. in a theorem prover, is hard work even if only lattices without infinite ascending chains are considered, cf. [5]. The verification of optimized solvers or the use of lattices of infinite height and widening is more complicated. The termination proof is, however, irrelevant to the correctness proof for the found invariants. Motivated by these arguments we develop a simple proof-producing analysis without formalizing abstract interpretation in a theorem prover. Alternatively we trust an abstract interpreter, external to the theorem prover, to terminate and then use its result to generate a correctness proof for every edge in the control flow graph (*cfg*). The proofs are compact, generic and make minimal assumptions on the underlying theorem prover machinery, which makes them portable and suitable for *pcc*-systems [12].

The rest of this paper is structured as follows. In § 2 we introduce notation and preliminary definitions. In § 3 we present the proof-synthesis for the found invariants. Benefits for theorem provers and *pcc* systems are subject of § 4.

Related Work. Proof carrying code has been introduced in [12]. Since then several extensions have been proposed to automate generation of proofs on the producer side. Abstraction carrying code (ACC) [1] proposes the use of the post-fix-point reached by the analyzer as a certificate. Note that this changes the *pcc* architecture: it assumes the consumer to have an implementation of the abstract domain used by the producer and that this implementation is *trusted* while proof-checking. Our method allows without loss of efficiency (w.r.t. ACC, i.e. we also need only one pass through the *cfg*) to produce a proof in terms of the safety logic and hence keeping the architecture as it is. This is important since the abstract interpreter may fail to find invariants that are precise enough to ensure safety. In such a case one still can carry out the proof by hand as before, which is not possible in the ACC approach.

An implementation of an abstract interpreter with some domains in Coq is presented in [11], where the goal was the generation of certified abstract interpreters. A different and more successful approach has been adopted in [5] and the authors also claim that termination of the analysis is the most tedious part, although they forbid lattices of infinite height (interval analysis would not be expressible there). After finishing this work we noticed that [15] presents a very similar approach, yet we developed this work independently. Our language is not structured and admits multiplication. Our method is more abstract and general. We implemented proof lifting (from $\mathbb{V}$ to $\mathcal{V} \to \mathbb{V}$) and we actually implemented the presented methods to synthesize correctness proof-skeletons for Jinja byte-code [9], integrated it with Isabelle/HOL[13] and a certified *pcc* architecture [17] and synthesize Isabelle/HOL theorems, and finally present an abstract description of its implementation. In [16] we presented an integration between our static analyzer (without proof-synthesis) and the *pcc*-framework.

2 Notation and Preliminaries

2.1 Logic

We make a difference between theorems (elements of an abstract type) and the formulae they prove (elements of a concrete datatype that allows pattern matching on the implementation level). To refer to a formula f proven by a theorem th we write th **as**‘f’. An inference rule with premises $A_1, \cdots, A_n$ and conclusion C is denoted by $[\![A_1; \cdots; A_n]\!] \implies C$. These rules allow manipulations on the logical connectives $\longrightarrow, \wedge, \vee, \neg$ and $=$, which stands for both equivalence and equality. Forward deduction is supported by a generalization of modus ponens $fwd : thm \to thm\ list \to thm$. If th is the theorem above and th_1 **as**‘B_1’, $\cdots, th_n$ **as**‘B_n’ are theorems, where every B_i is of the form $[\![H_i^1; \ldots; H_i^{m_i}]\!] \implies P_i$ and the P_i's match the premises $A_1, \cdots, A_n$ then the theorem $fwd\ th\ [th_1, \cdots, th_n]$ is th'**as**‘$[\![\Theta(H_1^1), \ldots, \Theta(H_1^{m_1}), \ldots, \Theta(H_n^{m_n})]\!] \implies \Theta(C)$’, where $\Theta = mgu\{A_1 = B_1, \cdots, A_n = B_n\}$. For simplicity we also assume that in the resulting theorem no premise occurs twice.

The theorems used along this paper are listed in appendix A. They are all almost trivial and included mainly for completeness and to illustrate the modularity of the method. Free variables in a theorem th could be instantiated from left to right by terms $t_1, \cdots, t_n$ by writing $th[t_1, \cdots, t_m]$, e.g. $thm_{\widetilde{\mathbb{T}}}[1, y, 3]$ is $[\![1 \le y \le 3]\!] \implies -3 \le y \le -1$. We also use a function *prove* to carry on simple proofs like $3 \le 5$ and $0 < 1$. If $(th$ **as**‘P’) is a theorem and x is a free variable in P then $gen\ x\ th$ returns a theorem th' **as**‘$\forall x.P(x)$’.

2.2 The Implementation Programming Language

We use a generic functional programming notation to present some algorithms. Lambda-abstraction uses a λ and permits pattern-matching. Because formulae (a concrete recursive type) and theorems (some abstract type) are quite distinct, we use pattern matching to refer to the formula proven by some theorem. If th is a theorem variable and f a formula pattern then we write th **as**‘f’, thus binding the formula variables in f. For example, matching the theorem $0 = 0 \wedge 1 = 1$ against the pattern th **as**‘$A \wedge B$’ binds th to the given theorem, A to the term $0 = 0$ and B to the term $1 = 1$. Patterns may be guarded by boolean conditions as in Haskell: $p \mid b$ is the pattern p that is guarded by the condition b. We denote by $x :: xs$ consing x to the list xs.

2.3 The Programming Language We Reason About

Syntax. We consider a flow-chart language [8] where a program is given by its *cfg* $G = (\mathcal{N}, \mathcal{E}, n_e, n_x, lab)$ and a set Val where each variable takes its values.

The set $\mathcal{N}$ of program nodes $\mathcal{N}$ contains at least the entry (n_e) and the exit (n_x) nodes. The set $\mathcal{E} \subseteq \mathcal{N} \times \mathcal{N}$ of edges contains an edge (n_1, n_2), if and only if control could pass from n_1 to n_2. The label $lab(n_1, n_2)$ describes the command that takes place. The language for labels is defined by:

$$Lab ::= v := exp|exp$$
$$exp ::= v \mid c \mid \mu e' \mid e_1 \beta e_2$$
$$\mu ::= \sim \mid \neg \quad ; \quad \beta ::= + \mid - \mid * \mid \leq \mid < \mid = \mid \wedge \mid \vee$$
$$v ::= x_1 \mid \ldots \mid x_{|\mathcal{V}|} \in \mathcal{V} \quad ; \quad c \in \mathsf{Val}$$

They represent assignments of expressions to a variable or a branching condition. In contrast to the operators of the logic, those used for the labeling language are set in bold face and are self explanatory, except $\sim$ which stands for unary minus. We consider only well formed control flow graphs, i.e. the expressions in the labels are well typed and if there exists $(n, m) \in \mathcal{E}$, where $b = lab(n, m)$ is a branching condition, then there exists a unique m', s.t. $(n, m') \in \mathcal{E}$ such that $\neg b = lab(n, m')$. We denote by $cmd(l)$ the command which has been translated to label l. We also assume that $(m, n_e) \notin \mathcal{E}$ and $(n_x, m) \notin \mathcal{E}$ for all $m \in \mathcal{N}$.

Deductive Semantics. Our concrete semantics is a predicate transformer semantics in backward style. It describes at each node an invariant which characterizes the set of states ascendant to an output state specified by an assertion $Q \in \mathbb{P}$. Assertions are predicates where the program variables occur freely. Those form a complete lattice $(\mathbb{P}, \longrightarrow, \mathit{False}, \mathit{True}, \vee, \wedge)$ partially ordered by the implication $\longrightarrow$. The predicate transformer wp, weakest precondition, is the transfer function and satisfies

$$wp\ (x := e)\ P = P(x/e)$$
$$\text{and } wp\ b\ P = b \longrightarrow P.$$

We emphasize that in the following wp is a function of the meta-language, i.e the programming language the theorem prover is written in. It is implicit in the implementation but fits with the definition above.

If $(D, \sqsubseteq_D, \bot_D, \top_D, \sqcup_D, \sqcap_D)$ is a complete lattice and $f^D : Lab \to (D \to D)$ a monotone transfer function and $i_D \in D$ an initial value, then the merge over all paths solution $d \in D^{|\mathcal{N}|}$ is the least solution to

$$\begin{cases} d_{n_e} = i_D \\ d_j = \bigsqcup_{(i,j) \in \mathcal{E}} f^D_{l_{ij}}(d_i), \text{ for } j \neq n_e, l_{ij} = lab(i, j). \end{cases}$$

The analyzer over-approximates the solution to these equations, i.e. find a postfix-point, using an iterative solver.

2.4   Abstract Interpretation

In abstract interpretation [7,8] a program analysis is fully specified by an abstract domain, a complete lattice D, and a monotone abstract semantics to interpret programs over D. Correctness of the analysis is guaranteed if one gives a Galois connection (α, C, D, γ_D) and if the abstract semantics safely approximates the concrete one. The Galois connection ensures safe abstraction ($\forall x \in C.x \sqsubseteq_C \gamma_D(\alpha(x))$) and safe concretization ($\forall d \in D.\alpha(\gamma_D(d)) \sqsubseteq_D d$). Moreover α and γ_D

are order-preserving, i.e. conserve information. A semantic f^D is said to safely approximate f^C iff. $\forall s \ s'. f^C(s) = s' \longrightarrow s' \sqsubseteq_C \gamma_D(f^D(\alpha(s)))$.

From a practical point of view, an abstract domain has to be implemented using efficient data structures. The abstract semantics is then a function manipulating elements of these data structures. Usually the correctness proof of an abstract interpretation is done on paper. The concretization γ_D is seldom implemented. In this paper we identify the abstract domain and its implementation, which reduces the correctness proof of the abstract interpretation to the correctness proof of the implementation. In order to make analysis results useful for the verification, the concretization γ_D has to be implemented. It transforms any $d \in D$ into $\gamma_D(d)$, an assertion pluggable into the verification environment. Predicates from $\gamma_D(D) \subseteq \mathbb{P}$ describe semantical aspects the analysis is interested in. Their syntactical shape is imposed by γ_D.

We use the lattice $D = \mathcal{V} \to \mathbb{V}$ to associate to each program variable $x \in \mathcal{V}$ an abstract value $v_x \in \mathbb{V}$, approximating the set of concrete values x may take. To each program node we associate $\bot_{\mathcal{V} \to \mathbb{V}}$, if it is dead, and $d \in \mathcal{V} \to \mathbb{V}$, where $\exists x_i \in \mathcal{V}. \ d(x_i) = v_i \neq \bot_{\mathbb{V}}$, otherwise. We define the concretization $\gamma_{\mathcal{V} \to \mathbb{V}}$ by

$$\begin{cases} \gamma_{\mathcal{V} \to \mathbb{V}}(\bot_{\mathcal{V} \to \mathbb{V}}) = \textit{False} \\ \gamma_{\mathcal{V} \to \mathbb{V}}(d) = \bigwedge \gamma_{\mathbb{V}}^{x_i}(d(x_i)), \text{for all } d(x_i) \neq \bot_{\mathbb{V}}. \end{cases}$$

The predicate $\gamma_{\mathbb{V}}^a(v_a)$ states that the values taken by the expression a during execution are among the concrete values represented by $v_a \in \mathbb{V}$. Consider the lattice $\mathbb{I}$ of intervals as an example for $\mathbb{V}$. An interval is either $\bot_{\mathbb{I}}$ or $[l, u]$, where $l \in \mathbb{Z} \cup \{-\infty\}, u \in \mathbb{Z} \cup \{+\infty\}$ and $l \leq u$. We then define $\gamma_{\mathbb{I}}^a$ by

$$\begin{cases} \gamma_{\mathbb{I}}^a(\bot_{\mathbb{I}}) = \textit{False}, \quad \gamma_{\mathbb{I}}^a([l, u]) = L^a(l) \wedge U^a(u) \\ L^a(-\infty) = \textit{True}, \ L^a(l \in \mathbb{Z}) = l \leq a \\ U^a(+\infty) = \textit{True}, \ U^a(u \in \mathbb{Z}) = a \leq u. \end{cases}$$

2.5 System Overview

Given a Jinja bytecode program p to be verified within the formalized *pcc*-framework [17], our work provides an interface (a tactic) that takes p, builds its *cfg* and runs our analyzer and annotates p, at junction nodes, with the inferred invariants. The analyzer also returns proofs that the inferred invariants fit with p's behavior. These proofs are generic, i.e. in an internal proof format. The tactic interprets these proofs in Isabelle/HOL to obtain Isabelle/HOL theorems, which are returned with the annotated program to the verification environment.

3 Proof Generation

Consider an edge $(n_1, n_2) \in \mathcal{E}$ labeled by l and let $c = cmd(l)$ and $d_1, d_2 \in D$ denote the inferred invariants at nodes n_1 and n_2. Our goal is to give a proof method for

$$\gamma_D(d_1) \longrightarrow (wp \ l \ \gamma_D(d_2)). \tag{$\star$}$$

The main observation is that at post-fix-point, cf. §2.3, we have :
$$f_l^D(d_1) \sqsubseteq_D d_2 \qquad \text{(post-fix-point result)}$$
hence $\qquad \gamma_D(f_l^D(d_1)) \longrightarrow \gamma_D(d_2) \qquad$ (γ_D is order preserving)
and finally $wp \ l \ (\gamma_D(f_l^D(d_1))) \longrightarrow wp \ l \ (\gamma_D(d_2))$ ($wp \ l$ is monotone).
We can therefore reduce our goal to providing proof methods for

- the monotonicity of wp, cf.§3.4,
- deriving $\gamma_D(d) \longrightarrow \gamma_D(d')$, for all $d \sqsubseteq_D d'$, cf.§3.4, and
- deriving $\gamma_D(d_1) \longrightarrow wp \ l \ \gamma_D(f_l^D(d_1))$, cf. §3.1-§3.3.

Note that by transitivity, they yield a proof method for $(\star)$. The first proof-method depends on the logic we use and the last two methods depend on the domain we consider, and express intuitively that we are able to prove the correctness of the implemented $\sqsubseteq_D$ and f_l^D operations, for all labels l. In the following we give a method for domains $D = \mathcal{V} \to \mathbb{V}$, where no dependency between program variables is present. Generally, a domain implementation gives a good guideline: just keep in mind that domain elements represent formulae.

3.1   Syntax Driven Proof Generation

In this section we present a generic mechanism to synthesize structural induction proofs. The main function *thm-of*, below, implements divide and conquer. It takes a problem decomposition function of type $\alpha \to \alpha \ list \times (\beta \ list \to \beta)$ and a problem t of type α, decomposes t into a list of subproblems ts and a recombination function *recomb*, solves the subproblems recursively, and combines their solution into an overall solution. This method is referred to as tactic style proving in [14] and represents a generic proof method by structural induction. Note that *decomp* determines the induction scheme.

> *thm-of decomp t =*
> **let** *(ts,recomb) = decomp t*
> **in** *recomb (map (thm-of decomp) ts)*

Example 1. Evaluating an expression e in an abstract state $d \in \mathcal{V} \to \mathbb{V}$, denoted by $[\![e]\!]^D d$ and defined below, approximates the set of values e may evaluate to. For an operator τ we denote by $\tau_\mathbb{V}$ its implementation for $\mathbb{V}$.

> $[\![e]\!]^{\mathcal{V} \to \mathbb{V}} d =$
> **case** e **of**
> $\quad c \Rightarrow \alpha(c)$
> $\quad x \in \mathcal{V} \Rightarrow d(x)$
> $\quad ue' \mid u \in \{\sim, \neg\} \Rightarrow u_\mathbb{V}[\![e']\!]^{\mathcal{V} \to \mathbb{V}} d$
> $\quad e_1 \beta e_2 \mid \beta \in \{+, -, *, \leq, <, =, \wedge, \vee\} \Rightarrow ([\![e_1]\!]^{\mathcal{V} \to \mathbb{V}} d) \beta_\mathbb{V} ([\![e_2]\!]^{\mathcal{V} \to \mathbb{V}} d)$

The correct evaluation of an arithmetical expression a in an abstract state d is stated by $\gamma_{\mathcal{V} \to \mathbb{V}}(d) \Longrightarrow \gamma_\mathbb{V}^a([\![a]\!]^{\mathcal{V} \to \mathbb{V}} d)$. The proof is by structural induction and is based on correctness of abstraction, i.e. $thm_\mathbb{V}^c : \gamma_\mathbb{V}^c(\alpha(c))$, for the unary operator, i.e. $thm_\mathbb{V}^{\sim} : \gamma_\mathbb{V}^a(v_a) \Longrightarrow \gamma_\mathbb{V}^{\sim a}(\sim_\mathbb{V} v_a)$, and for the binary operators $\beta \in \{+, -, *\}$, i.e. $thm_\mathbb{V}^\beta : [\gamma_\mathbb{V}^{a_1}(v_1); \gamma_\mathbb{V}^{a_2}(v_2)] \Longrightarrow \gamma_\mathbb{V}^{a_1 \beta a_2}(v_1 \beta_\mathbb{V} v_2))$. Note that for variables we just

$decomp\text{-}abounds_\mathbb{V}\ d\ a\ =$
case a **of**
$\quad c \Rightarrow ([], \lambda[].\ thm^c_\mathbb{V}[c])$
$\quad x \in \mathcal{V} \Rightarrow ([], \lambda[].\ trivial[\gamma^x_\mathbb{V}(d(x))])$
$\quad \sim a' \Rightarrow ([a'],\ fwd\ thm_{\widetilde{\mathbb{V}}})$
$\quad a_1\ \beta_r\ a_2 \mid \beta_r \in \{+,-,*\} \Rightarrow ([a_1, a_2],\ fwd\ thm^{\beta_r}_\mathbb{V})$

$prove\text{-}abounds_\mathbb{V}\ d\ a = thm\text{-}of\ (decomp\text{-}abounds_\mathbb{V}\ d)\ a$

Fig. 1. Proof synthesis for bounds on arithmetical expressions

assume the bounds in d. See Appendix A for the intervals versions. Fig. 1 shows a generic implementation for arithmetical expressions using *thm-of*.

Our Analyzer scrutinizes the expressions in order to deduce more precise approximations. This is also supported by the method we present for proof generation. For instance the following theorem may be used instead of $thm^*_\mathbb{I}$ when the operands are equal.

$$l \leq x \leq u \Longrightarrow (if\ 0 \leq l\ then\ l^2\ else\ if\ u \leq 0\ then\ u^2\ else\ 0) \leq x^2$$
$$\leq (if\ 0 \leq l\ then\ u^2\,else\ if\ u \leq 0\ then\ l^2\,else\ max\ l^2\ u^2)$$

Since domain elements represent semantic properties and the correctness of their manipulations is usually proved by structural induction, syntax driven proof-synthesis is a powerful tool for our purpose. We used this technique for a proof-producing quantifier elimination procedure for full Presburger arithmetic, which gives us the feeling that it will be also useful for domains more complex than $\mathcal{V} \to \mathbb{V}$.

3.2   Proofs for Approximate Bounds on Expressions

The transfer functions approximate the expressions in order to compute the next state. Hence proofs for the derived approximations on expressions are important steps for the correctness proofs for the transfer functions. The previous example dealt with arithmetical expressions. Now we investigate boolean expressions. The correct evaluation of a boolean expression b in an abstract state d is expressed by $\gamma_{\mathbb{V} \to \mathbb{V}}(d) \Longrightarrow b = b'$, where b' is a simplified version of b which may be different from $True$ or $False$. The last reflects the analyzers incapability of deciding b in the abstract state d. $prove\text{-}bbounds_\mathbb{V}\ d\ b$, cf. Fig. 2, returns a theorem for $[\![A_1; \ldots; A_n]\!] \Longrightarrow b = b'$, where A_i is $\gamma^{x_i}_\mathbb{V}(d(x_i))$ for some $x_i \in \mathcal{V}$ and hence a conjunct of $\gamma_{\mathbb{V} \to \mathbb{V}}(d)$. The call $prove^{\beta_r}_\mathbb{V}\ d\ a_1\ a_2$ derives a theorem for $[\![\gamma^{x_{j_1}}_\mathbb{V}(d(x_{j_1})); \ldots; \gamma^{x_{j_n}}_\mathbb{V}(d(x_{j_n}))]\!] \Longrightarrow a_1\beta_r a_2 = b'$, where $b' \in \{True, False, a'_1\beta_r a'_2\}$ and a'_1 and a'_2 are simplified versions of a_1 and a_2. This theorem expresses the correctness of the relation operators on the abstract values. Fig. 2 also gives an example for interval analysis. The call $prove\text{-}bbounds_\mathbb{I}\ \{x \mapsto [0,5], y \mapsto [-1,3]\}\ (x \leq y * y \land y \leq x^2 + 4)$ returns a theorem th as '$[\![0 \leq x \leq 5; -1 \leq y \leq 3]\!] \Longrightarrow (x \leq y^2 \land x \leq x^2 + 4) = (x \leq y^2 \land True)$'.

$decomp\text{-}bbounds_{\mathbb{V}}\ d\ b\ =$
case b **of**
   $\mathbf{tt} \Rightarrow ([], \lambda[].\mathit{refl}[True])$
   $\mathbf{ff} \Rightarrow ([], \lambda[].\mathit{refl}[False])$
   $b_1\beta_r b_2 \mid \beta_r \in \{\leq, <, =\} \Rightarrow ([], \lambda[].\mathit{prove}_{\mathbb{V}}^{\beta_r}\ d\ b_1\ b_2)$
   $\neg b' \Rightarrow ([b'],\ \mathit{fwd\ cong}_\neg)$
   $b_1\beta_l b_2 \mid \beta_l \in \{\wedge, \vee\} \Rightarrow ([b_1, b_2],\ \mathit{fwd\ cong}_{\beta_l})$

$prove\text{-}bbounds_{\mathbb{V}}\ d\ b = thm\text{-}of\ (decomp\text{-}bbounds_{\mathbb{V}}\ d)\ b$
$prove_{\mathbb{I}}^{\leq}\ d\ b_1\ b_2\ =$
let
   $th_1\mathbf{as}`[\ldots] \Longrightarrow l_1 \leq b_1 \leq u_1' = (prove\text{-}abounds_{\mathbb{I}}\ d\ b_1)$
   $th_2\mathbf{as}`[\ldots] \Longrightarrow l_2 \leq b_2 \leq u_2' = (prove\text{-}abounds_{\mathbb{I}}\ d\ b_2)$
in
if $u_1 \leq l_2$ **then** $\mathit{fwd\ cong}_{\leq \mathbf{tt}}[th_1, th_2, prove(u_1 \leq l_2)]$
else if $u_2 < l_1$ **then** $\mathit{fwd\ cong}_{\leq \mathbf{ff}}[th_1, th_2, prove(u_2 < l_1)]$ **else** $\mathit{refl}[b_1 \leq b_2]$

Fig. 2. Proof synthesis for approximations of boolean expressions

3.3   Proofs for the Abstract Transfer Functions

Assignment. For an assignment $x_k := a$ and an abstract state $d \in \mathcal{V} \to \mathbb{V}$ we have to provide a proof-method for $\gamma_{\mathcal{V} \to \mathbb{V}}(d) \longrightarrow \gamma_{\mathcal{V} \to \mathbb{V}}(f_{x_k:=a}^{\mathcal{V} \to \mathbb{V}}(d))(x_k/a)$, i.e.

$$\bigwedge_{i=1}^{|\mathcal{V}|} \gamma_{\mathbb{V}}^{x_i}(d(x_i)) \longrightarrow \bigwedge_{i=1}^{k-1} \gamma_{\mathbb{V}}^{x_i}(d(x_i)) \wedge \gamma_{\mathbb{V}}^{a}([\![a]\!]^{\mathcal{V} \to \mathbb{V}} d) \wedge \bigwedge_{i=k+1}^{|\mathcal{V}|} \gamma_{\mathbb{V}}^{x_i}(d(x_i)).$$

Since most of the conclusion occurs in the premise, the main challenge consists in proving $\bigwedge_{i=1}^{|\mathcal{V}|} \gamma_{\mathbb{V}}^{x_i}(d(x_i)) \longrightarrow \gamma_{\mathbb{V}}^{a}([\![a]\!]^{\mathcal{V} \to \mathbb{V}} d)$, which is almost the result of *prove-abounds*$_{\mathbb{V}}\ d\ a$. Assume we have a function *adjust*, which transforms a theorem for $[\gamma_{\mathbb{V}}^{x_{i_1}}(d(x_{i_1})); \ldots; \gamma_{\mathbb{V}}^{x_{i_m}}(d(x_{i_m}))] \Longrightarrow \gamma_{\mathbb{V}}^{a}([\![a]\!]^{\mathcal{V} \to \mathbb{V}} d)$ into a theorem for $\bigwedge_{i=1}^{|\mathcal{V}|} \gamma_{\mathbb{V}}^{x_i}(d(x_i)) \longrightarrow \gamma_{\mathbb{V}}^{a}([\![a]\!]^{\mathcal{V} \to \mathbb{V}} d)$, using the result $[th_1, \ldots, th_{|\mathcal{V}|}]$ of *destruct* d (note that th_j proves $\gamma_{\mathcal{V} \to \mathbb{V}}(d) \longrightarrow \gamma_{\mathbb{V}}^{x_j}(d(x_j))$, see Fig. 3). The implementation is simple and hence omitted: perform $\longrightarrow$ introductions then use the result of *destruct* d and *trans*$_\longrightarrow$. Fig. 4 gives the overall implementation. The result of *reconstruct* $[th_1\ \mathbf{as}`P \longrightarrow P_1', \cdots, th_n\ \mathbf{as}`P \longrightarrow P_n']$ is $th\ \mathbf{as}`P \longrightarrow \bigwedge_{i=1}^{n} P_i'$.

$destruct\ d \in \mathcal{V} \to \mathbb{V}\ =$
let
   $destructh\ n\ th\ =$
   if $n > 1$ **then** $(\mathit{fwd\ elim}_\wedge^1\ [th]) :: (destructh\ (n-1)\ (\mathit{fwd\ elim}_\wedge^2\ [th]))$
   else $[th]$
in $destructh\ |\mathcal{V}|\ triv[\gamma_{\mathcal{V} \to \mathbb{V}}(d)]$

Fig. 3. Proving $\bigwedge_{i=1}^{|\mathcal{V}|} \gamma_{\mathbb{V}}^{x_i}(d(x_i)) \longrightarrow \gamma_{\mathbb{V}}^{x_j}(d(x_j)), j = 1 \ldots |\mathcal{V}|$

$prove\text{-}aexp_\mathbb{V}\ d\ a = adjust\ (destruct\ d)\ (prove\text{-}abounds_\mathbb{V}\ d\ a)$
$prove\text{-}f^{\mathcal{V}\to\mathbb{V}}_{x_k:=a}\ d =$
let

$[th_1,\ldots,th_{|\mathcal{V}|}] = destruct\ d$
$th_a = adjust\ [th_1,\ldots,th_{|\mathcal{V}|}]\ (prove\text{-}abounds_\mathbb{V}\ d\ a)$
in $reconstruct\ [th_1,\cdots,th_{k-1},th_a,th_{k+1},\cdots,th_{|\mathcal{V}|}]$

Fig. 4. Proof synthesis for $f^{\mathcal{V}\to\mathbb{V}}_{x_k:=a}$

$prove\text{-}vcond_\mathbb{I}\ thms\ d\ (y \le a) =$
let

$th_a = prove\text{-}abounds_\mathbb{I}\ d\ a$
$th_y = trivial[\gamma^y_\mathbb{I}(d(y))]$
in $adjust\ thms\ (fwd\ bcond_{\le\mathbb{I}}[th_y,th_a])$
$prove\text{-}\ f^{\mathcal{V}\to\mathbb{V}}_{x_k\beta_r a}\ d =$
let

$[th_1,\ldots,th_{|\mathcal{V}|}] = map(\lambda th.(fwd\ weak_\to [th])[x_k\beta_r a])(destruct\ d)$
$th_b = prove\text{-}vcond_\mathbb{V}\ [th_1,\ldots,th_{|\mathcal{V}|}]\ d\ (x_k\beta_r a)$
in $reconstruct'\ [th_1,\ldots,th_{k-1},th_b,th_{k+1},\ldots,th_{|\mathcal{V}|}]$

Fig. 5. Proof synthesis for a case of $f^{\mathcal{V}\to\mathbb{I}}_{x_k r_\beta a}$

Example 2. We can now prove $0 \le x \le 5 \wedge -1 \le y \le 3 \longrightarrow 0 \le x + y^2 \le 14 \wedge -1 \le y \le 3$ by calling $prove\text{-}f^{\mathcal{V}\to\mathbb{I}}_{x:=x+y*y}\ \{x \mapsto [0,5], y \mapsto [-1,3]\}$.

Branching Conditions. For a branching condition b and an abstract state $d \in \mathcal{V} \to \mathbb{V}$ we have to prove $\gamma_{\mathcal{V}\to\mathbb{V}}(d) \longrightarrow b \longrightarrow \gamma_{\mathcal{V}\to\mathbb{V}}(d')$, where $d' = f^{\mathcal{V}\to\mathbb{V}}_b(d)$. This depends on $[\![b]\!]^{\mathcal{V}\to\mathbb{V}}d$. We distinguish three cases:

- $[\![b]\!]^{\mathcal{V}\to\mathbb{V}}d = \alpha(\mathbf{tt})$: then $d' = d$, since b does not restrict d. In this case our proof is simply $(fwd\ weak_\to[triv[\gamma_{\mathcal{V}\to\mathbb{V}}(d)]])[b]$.
- $[\![b]\!]^{\mathcal{V}\to\mathbb{V}}d = \alpha(\mathbf{ff})$: then $d' = \bot_{\mathcal{V}\to\mathbb{V}}$ and thus unreachable. Our proof is then synthesized by the following steps:
  - $adjust\ (destruct\ d)\ (prove\text{-}bbounds_\mathbb{V}\ d\ b)$ proves $\gamma_{\mathcal{V}\to\mathbb{V}}(d) \longrightarrow (b = b')$
  - prove $(b = b') \longrightarrow (b \longrightarrow False)$ by simplification
  - apply transitivity to get the goal.
- $[\![b]\!]^{\mathcal{V}\to\mathbb{V}}d \notin \{\alpha(\mathbf{ff}),\alpha(\mathbf{tt})\}$: in this case d' is d restricted by b. Let us consider the case where b is $x\beta_r a$, $x \in \mathcal{V}$, $\beta_r \in \{\le,=,<\}$ and let $v_a = [\![a]\!]^{\mathcal{V}\to\mathbb{V}}d$. The output state d' is $d[x \mapsto d(x) \sqcap_\mathbb{V} vcond(\beta_r,v_a)]$, where $vcond(\beta_r,v_a) \in \mathbb{V}$ approximates the set $\{y|y\beta_r a\}$, i.e. $\gamma^a_\mathbb{V}(v_a) \longrightarrow x\beta_r a \longrightarrow \gamma^x_\mathbb{V}(vcond(\beta_r,v_a))$. For intervals, we use for instance $vcond(\le,[l,u]) = [-\infty,u]$.

The proofs for $\mathcal{V} \to \mathbb{V}$ are again reconstructed from those for $\mathbb{V}$. Fig. 5 shows a representative case. $prove\text{-}vcond_\mathbb{V}\ d\ (x\beta_r a)$ deduces the restriction on x from the actual state, i.e. $\gamma_{\mathcal{V}\to\mathbb{V}}(d) \longrightarrow b \longrightarrow \gamma^x_\mathbb{V}(d(x) \sqcap_\mathbb{V} vcond(\beta_r,v_a))$. $reconstruct'$ synthesizes a theorem th **as**'$\bigwedge_{i=1}^{|\mathcal{V}|} P_i \longrightarrow b \longrightarrow \bigwedge_{i=1}^{|\mathcal{V}|} P'_i$ from the theorems th_1

$as'\bigwedge_{i=1}^{|\mathcal{V}|} P_i \longrightarrow b \longrightarrow P_1''$, ..., and $th_{|\mathcal{V}|}$ $as'\bigwedge_{i=1}^{|\mathcal{V}|} P_i \longrightarrow b \longrightarrow P_{|\mathcal{V}|}'$. It simply conjuncts the conclusions since the premises are the same.

Example 3. We can now prove $0 \leq x \leq 5 \wedge -1 \leq y \leq 3 \longrightarrow x \leq y^2 - 5 \longrightarrow 0 \leq x \leq 4 \wedge -1 \leq y \leq 3$ by calling *prove-$f_{x \leq y*y-3}^{\mathcal{V} \to \mathbb{I}}$* $\{x \mapsto [0,5], y \mapsto [-1,3]\}$.

3.4   Finishing the Proofs

Recall from the introduction to §3 that we have to provide three proof methods. The result of §3.3 is a proof method *prove-$f_l^{\mathcal{V} \to \mathbb{V}}$* to synthesize proofs for $\gamma_{\mathcal{V} \to \mathbb{V}}(d_1) \longrightarrow wp \; l \; \gamma_{\mathcal{V} \to \mathbb{V}}(f_l^{\mathcal{V} \to \mathbb{V}}(d_1))$. This section presents the simpler proof methods *prove-wp$_{\mathcal{V} \to \mathbb{V}}$* for the monotony of *wp* and *prove$_{\sqsubseteq \mathcal{V} \to \mathbb{V}}$* for proving $\sqsubseteq_{\mathcal{V} \to \mathbb{V}}$.

---

prove-wp-monoton$_D$ l (th $as'P \longrightarrow P''$) =
case l **of**
   $x := a \Rightarrow$ (*fwd spec* [*gen x th*])[a]
   $b \Rightarrow$ (*fwd weak$_\rightarrow$* [th])[b]

prove-wp$_D$ l d_1 d_2 =
let
   $th_1 = $ *prove-f_l^D* d_1
   $th_2 = $ *prove-wp-monoton* (*prove$_{\sqsubseteq_D}$* $f_l^D(d_1)$ d_2)
in *fwd trans$_\rightarrow$* [th_1, th_2]

Fig. 6. Overall proof

Proofs for $\sqsubseteq_D$. Proving $\gamma_D(d) \longrightarrow \gamma_D(d')$ for $d \sqsubseteq_D d'$ needs knowledge about D. This should be the result of *prove$_{\sqsubseteq_D}$* d d'. For $D = \mathcal{V} \to \mathbb{V}$ we have

$$prove_{\sqsubseteq_{\mathcal{V} \to \mathbb{V}}} \; d \; d' = reconstruct_\wedge \; (map \; (\lambda x.prove_{\sqsubseteq_{\mathbb{V}}} \; x \; d(x) \; d'(x)) \; [x_1, \ldots, x_{|\mathcal{V}|}]),$$

where the theorem *prove$_{\sqsubseteq_{\mathbb{V}}}$* x v_1 v_2 proves $\gamma_{\mathbb{V}}^x(v_1) \longrightarrow \gamma_{\mathbb{V}}^x(v_2)$, for $v_1 \sqsubseteq_{\mathbb{V}} v_2$. Moreover the call *reconstruct$_\wedge$* [$th_1 as'P_1 \longrightarrow P_1'', \ldots, th_n as'P_n \longrightarrow P_n''$] proves $\bigwedge_{i=1}^n P_i \longrightarrow \bigwedge_{i=1}^n P_i'$.

Example 4. For intervals we have

$$prove_{\sqsubseteq_{\mathbb{I}}} \; y \; [l, u] \; [l', u'] =$$
$$(fwd \; thm^{\sqsubseteq_{\mathbb{I}}} \; [prove \; l' \leq l, prove \; u \leq u'])[y],$$

where $thm^{\sqsubseteq_{\mathbb{I}}}$ is $[\![l' \leq l; u \leq u']\!] \Longrightarrow l \leq x \leq u \longrightarrow l' \leq x \leq u'$.

Monotonicity of *wp*. The final step is now to argue the monotonicity of *wp*. It is simple and given in Fig. 6. For an assignment $x := a$ we generalize the result of *prove$_{\sqsubseteq_D}$* d d' $as'P \longrightarrow P''$ to $\forall x.P(x) \longrightarrow P'(x)$ and then just specialize the theorem to the expression a. Recall that x occurs free before generalization. Monotonicity of *wp* for a branch condition is explicitly stated by *weak$_\rightarrow$*.

3.5   A Short Example for Relational Domains

The aim of this section is *not* to present proof-synthesis for a relational domain, but to give an example of the usefulness of the syntax-driven proof-synthesis for relational domains. The octagon domain [10] abstracts a state by a potential graph $g \in \mathcal{O}$. Unreachable states are represented by $\perp_\mathcal{O}$. Each variable $x \in \mathcal{V}$ is present in a graph $g = (\mathcal{V}^\pm, E, w)$ twice: positive as x^+ and negative as x^-. An edge $(u, v) \in E$ represents the constraint $u - v \le w(u, v)$. The concretization could therefore be given by

$$\begin{cases} \gamma_\mathcal{O}(\perp_\mathcal{O}) & = False \\ \gamma_\mathcal{O}((\mathcal{V}^\pm, E, w)) = \bigwedge_{(u,v) \in E} \gamma_{\mathcal{V}\pm}(u) - \gamma_{\mathcal{V}\pm}(v) \le w(u,v) \end{cases}$$

$$\text{and } \begin{cases} \gamma_{\mathcal{V}\pm}(x^+) = x \\ \gamma_{\mathcal{V}\pm}(x^-) = -x \end{cases}$$

For $(u, v) \in E$ we also write $u - v \le w(u, v)$ but mean $\gamma_{\mathcal{V}\pm}(u) - \gamma_{\mathcal{V}\pm}(v) \le w(u, v)$. All the proofs to be synthesized could be done by linear arithmetic, which is available in every state-of-the-art theorem prover, yet simulating the analyzers behavior would lead to shorter proofs.

If there is a path $[u_0, \dots, u_n]$ from u_0 to u_n of total weight $c =$, then the constraint $u_0 - u_n \le c$ holds (two consecutive edges represent $u_i - u_{i+1} \le c_i \wedge u_{i+1} - u_{i+2} \le c_{i+1}$, and hence $u_i - u_{i+2} \le c_i + c_{i+1}$ holds). Hence the most precise way to bound $u_0 - u_n$ is by c_{min} the total weight of the shortest path from u_0 to u_n. This operation of "tightening" the bounds is called strong closure and is based on the Floyd-Warshall algorithm for shortest paths, cf. [6] and represents a basic operation in the domain. Here we only show how to use *thm-of* to synthesize the main parts of the correctness proof for this transformation. Fig. 7 shows how to compile a non empty path $\pi = [u_0, \dots, u_n]$ into a theorem proving the new bound on $u_0 - u_n$ assuming the actual constraints.

Note that if the emptiness test by Bellman-Ford algorithm, cf. [6], returns cycle π of negative total weight, then the same algorithm derives the contradiction $x - x < 0$ represented by π, needed for an unreachability proof.

decomp-path $w\ \pi =$
case π **of**
    $[x_{n-1}, x_n] \Rightarrow ([], \lambda[].trivial[\gamma_{\mathcal{V}\pm}(x_{n-1}) - \gamma_{\mathcal{V}\pm}(x_n) \le w(x_{n-1}, x_n)])$
    $(x_i :: x_{i+1} :: xs) \Rightarrow ([x_{i+1} :: xs], \lambda[th].(fwd\ thm_\mathcal{O}^{\le +}\ [th])[\gamma_{\mathcal{V}\pm}(x_i), w(x_i, x_{i+1})])$
prove-path $w\ c = thm\text{-}of\ (decomp\text{-}path\ w)\ c$

Fig. 7. Deriving a new bound from a shortest path

3.6   Alternative Approaches for Proof-Synthesis

The most intuitive way to realize proof-producing program analysis is maybe to formalize the analyzer in a theorem prover as in [11,5]. This involves implementing the abstract domain and iterative solvers and finally proving *once and for all* the analyzer correct, i.e. its results are consistent with the semantics. Whereas this approach is completely in the formalized world (a theory of a proof assistant), one can say that the approach we presented is fully in the meta-language world, since it runs completely on the meta-level, the programming language the theorem prover is written in. Hence our method generates the correctness proofs for every instance of the problem.

One can think of a hybrid approach. The analyzer is extern to the theorem prover and returns as in our case the invariants and proofs skeletons. In the verification environment, programs are not only enriched by invariants (annotations), but also by their proofs, elements of a datatype P. The verification of a program consists not only in generating proof obligations, but rather checking the present proofs and generating obligations for the rest. The proof checker is naturally a function on the theory level. This notion of verification has to be proven once and for all in a theorem, say th_c. The invariants and proofs of the external analyzer are then *reified* and instantiated into th_c. Using reflection [2] the whole correctness proof reduces to reflexivity. This is of course balanced by the fact that the proof checker has to expand the definitions of the involved recursive functions to reach the normal form. Note that this principle is included in several prominent theorem provers like Coq [3]. Despite the loss of portability of the proofs to other theorem provers, this method has the great advantage, that the obtained proofs are small for theorem provers, e.g. Coq, where proofs are considered modulo normalization (the evaluation of the proof checker in our case).

4   Benefits for *pcc* and Theorem Proving

Special-Purpose Decision Procedures. When implementing proof-producing program analysis (using domain D) one implicitly implements a sound yet incomplete decision procedure for a subset of $\gamma_D(D) \subseteq \mathbb{P}$. Recall that $prove_{\sqsubseteq_D} d_1 d_2$, $prove\text{-}f^D_{x:=e} d$ and $prove\text{-}f^D_b d$ prove theorems corresponding to $\gamma_D(d_1) \longrightarrow \gamma_D(d_2)$ for $d_1 \sqsubseteq_D d_2$, $\gamma_D(d) \longrightarrow \gamma_D(f^D_{x:=a}(d))[x/a]$ and $\gamma_D(d) \longrightarrow b \longrightarrow \gamma_D(f^D_b(d))$, respectively. In our example the decision procedure is simple but useful for very simple non linear reasoning.

For $D = \mathcal{V} \to \mathbb{V}$ the most interesting part comes from the proof-producing safe approximation of expressions in abstract states, i.e *prove-abounds*$_\mathbb{V}$ and *prove-bbounds*$_\mathbb{V}$. These proof-producing procedures represent potential extensions for theorem provers, as tactics. The integration of these procedures is straightforward. This approach has also been used in [4], where sign analysis was used to simplify and maintain polynomials during (partial) quantifier elimination for real algebra. We integrated the interval arithmetic reasoning as a proof-producing decision procedure in Isabelle/HOL. The main challenge was, in fact, to reconstruct a good representation of the abstract state ($\in D$) from a given goal, allowing the user to state the interval constraints liberally. The tactics are still interesting even if the theorem prover already has decision procedures for a larger theory, since the "special purpose" tactics proofs are shorter.

Moreover the proofs are well structured and generic. A proof could be a skeleton, that may be interpreted on different theorem provers to synthesize the theorem we want. We naturally need the same *fwd* function and that the used theorems are proven on that platform. This may be useful for *pcc* systems as §4 suggests.

Proof Length. In order to give exact bounds on proof length, one has to define a syntax for proofs. We give here just approximate lengths in terms of the needed instantiations (i) and *fwd* operations (f). Let us consider an expression e with n nodes, n_l leaves, n_v among them are variable-occurrences. The function *prove-abounds d e* needs $n_l \cdot i + (n - n_l) \cdot f$ to obtain $[\![P_1; \ldots; P_{n_v}]\!] \implies \gamma_{\mathbb{V}}^e(v_e)$, where v_e stands for $[\![e]\!]^{\mathbb{V} \to \mathbb{V}} d$. The function *adjust (destruct d)* transforms it to $\gamma_{\mathbb{V} \to \mathbb{V}}(d) \longrightarrow \gamma_{\mathbb{V}}^{x_i}(d(x_i))$ after $(n_v - 1) \cdot f + 1 \cdot f + (n_v - 1) \cdot f$ steps. The summands thereby correspond to the three steps given in §3.3.

The function *destruct* generates the theorems $\gamma_{\mathbb{V} \to \mathbb{V}}(d) \longrightarrow \gamma_{\mathbb{V}}^{x_i}(d(x_i))$ in $i + 2f \cdot (|\mathcal{V}| - 1)$. The call to *reconstruct* takes $(|\mathcal{V}| - 1) \cdot f$. Hence finally the result of *prove-$f_{x_k := e}^{\mathbb{V} \to \mathbb{V}}$ d* is obtained after $(n_l + 1) \cdot i + (n - n_l + 2n_v + 3|\mathcal{V}| - 4) \cdot f$, which remains linear in expression length and the number of variables. Similar results could be obtained for the other functions presented in §3.

We should interpret these results as "the synthesized proofs for the found invariants are short", and not as "the synthesized program correctness proofs are short". This is due to the simple fact that the found invariants only approximate the program behavior and thus the synthesized proofs might gratuitously include arguments about infeasible execution paths. This problem is inherent to static analysis.

Benefits for *pcc* Systems. In *pcc* [12] the code consumer expects a proof for a verification condition that captures code safety and which is generated according to a predefined safety policy. If the invariants found by a static analyzer are precise enough to ensure safety then proof-producing program analysis represents a powerful tool for automatic certification. The extracted proofs could simply be transferred to the consumer. The generated proofs are small and hence suitable for complicated safety policies and larger programs. They are exclusively based on a small set of theorems required by abstract interpretation. This allows high sharing and hence compact representation of proofs.

5   Conclusion

We presented our approach to proof-producing program analysis, which resides in augmenting program analysis results by correctness proofs, a step towards automatic program verification in a proof assistant setting. We illustrated a generic proof synthesis method for domains of the form $\mathcal{V} \to \mathbb{V}$. The method we presented mimics the abstract interpretation framework: global proof synthesis is guaranteed, if it is locally possible. Since domain implementations usually argue their correctness by induction on the structure of their elements, we believe that the syntax-driven approach is the way to go. We emphasized this aspect in §3.5.

References

1. Elvira Albert, Germán Puebla, and Manuel Hermenegildo. Abstraction carrying code. In *11th International Conference on Logic for Programming Artificial Intelligence and Reasoning (LPAR)*. Springer, 2004.
2. Henk Barendregt and Erik Barendsen. Autarkic computations in formal proofs. *J. Autom. Reasoning*, 28(3):321–336, 2002.
3. Y. Bertot and P. Castéran. *Coq'Art: The Calculus of Inductive Constructions*, volume XXV of *Text in theor. comp. science: an EATCS series*. Springer, 2004.
4. Nikolaj Skallerud Bjorner. *Integrating decision procedures for temporal verification*. PhD thesis, Stanford University, 1998. Adviser-Zohar Manna.
5. David Cachera, Thomas Jensen, David Pichardie, and Vlad Rusu. Extracting a Data Flow Analyser in Constructive Logic. In *Proc. of 13th European Symposium on Programming (ESOP'04)*, number 2986 in Lecture Notes in Computer Science, pages 385–400. Springer-Verlag, 2004.
6. Cormen, Leiserson, and Rivest. *Introduction to Algorithms*. MIT Press, Cambridge Mass., 1990.
7. P. Cousot and R. Cousot. Abstract interpretation: a unified lattice model for static analysis of programs by construction or approximation of fixpoints. In *Conference Record of the Fourth Annual ACM SIGPLAN-SIGACT Symposium on Principles of Programming Languages*, pages 238–252, Los Angeles, California, 1977. ACM Press, New York, NY.
8. P. Cousot and R. Cousot. Systematic design of program analysis frameworks. In *Conference Record of the Sixth Annual ACM SIGPLAN-SIGACT Symposium on Principles of Programming Languages*, pages 269–282, San Antonio, Texas, 1979. ACM Press, New York, NY.
9. Gerwin Klein and Tobias Nipkow. A machine-checked model for a Java-like language, virtual machine and compiler. *ACM Transactions on Programming Languages and Systems*, 28(4):619–695, 2006.
10. A. Miné. Representation of two-variable difference or sum constraint set and application to automatic program analysis. Master's thesis, ENS-DI, Paris, 2000.
11. David Monniaux. Réalisation mécanisée d'interpréteurs abstraits. Rapport de DEA, Université Paris VII, 1998. French.
12. George C. Necula. Proof-carrying code. In *Proc. 24th ACM Symp. Principles of Programming Languages*, pages 106–119. ACM Press, 1997.
13. Tobias Nipkow, Lawrence C. Paulson, and Markus Wenzel. *Isabelle/HOL — A Proof Assistant for Higher-Order Logic*, volume 2283 of *LNCS*. Springer, 2002.
14. Lawrence C. Paulson. *Logic and Computation*. Cambridge University Press, 1987.
15. Sunae Seo, Hongseok Yang, and Kwangkeun Yi. Automatic construction of Hoare proofs from abstract interpretation results. In *The First Asian Symposium on Programming Languages and Systems, LNCS Vol. 2895*, pages 230–245, Beijing, 2003. Springer.
16. Martin Wildmoser, Amine Chaieb, and Tobias Nipkow. Bytecode analysis for proof carrying code. In *Proceedings of the 1st Workshop on Bytecode Semantics, Verification and Transformation*. Electronic Notes in Computer Science, 2005.
17. Martin Wildmoser and Tobias Nipkow. Certifying machine code safety: Shallow versus deep embedding. In Konrad Slind and Annette Bunker, editors, *Proc. 17th Int. Conf. on Theorem Proving in Higher Order Logics (TPHOLs'04)*, volume 3223 of *Lect. Notes in Comp. Sci.*, pages 305–320. Springer Verlag, September 2004.

A   Theorems

$thm_{\sqsubseteq}^{c}$ $x \leq x \leq x$

$thm_{\sqsubseteq}^{+}$ $[\![l_x \leq x \leq u_x; l_y \leq y \leq u_y]\!] \Longrightarrow l_x + l_y \leq x + y \leq u_x + u_y$

$thm_{\sqsubseteq}^{-}$ $[\![l_x \leq x \leq u_x; l_y \leq y \leq u_y]\!] \Longrightarrow l_x - u_y \leq x - y \leq u_x - l_y$

$thm_{\sqsubseteq}^{*}$ $[\![l_x \leq x \leq u_x; l_y \leq y \leq u_y]\!] \Longrightarrow \min\ F \leq x{\cdot}y \leq \max\ F$, where $F = \{l_x{\cdot}l_y, l_x{\cdot}u_y, u_x{\cdot}l_y, u_x{\cdot}u_y, \}$

$thm_{\sqsubseteq}^{\sim}$ $[\![l_x \leq x \leq u_x]\!] \Longrightarrow -u_x \leq -x \leq -l_x$

$thm_{\sqsubseteq}^{\sqsubseteq}$ $[\![l_x \leq x \leq u_x; l'_x \leq l_x; u_x \leq u'_x]\!] \Longrightarrow l'_x \leq x \leq u'_x$

$cong_{\leq tt}$ $[\![l_a \leq a \leq u_a; l_b \leq b \leq u_b; u_a \leq l_b]\!] \Longrightarrow a \leq b = True$

$cong_{\leq ff}$ $[\![l_a \leq a \leq u_a; l_b \leq b \leq u_b; u_b < l_a]\!] \Longrightarrow a \leq b = False$

$bcond_{\leq I}$ $[\![l_x \leq x \leq u_x; l_e \leq e \leq u_e]\!] \Longrightarrow x \leq e \longrightarrow l_x \leq x \leq \min\ u_x\ u_e$

$bcond_{\leq ff}$ $[\![l_x \not\leq u; l_x \leq x \leq u_x; x \leq u]\!] \Longrightarrow False$

$thm_{\ominus}^{\leq +}$ $[\![y - x \leq c; z - y \leq c']\!] \Longrightarrow z - x \leq c + c'$

$refl$ $P = P$

$cong_{\wedge}$ $[\![P = P'; Q = Q']\!] \Longrightarrow P \wedge Q = P' \wedge Q'$

$cong_{\vee}$ $[\![P = P'; Q = Q']\!] \Longrightarrow P \vee Q = P' \vee Q'$

$cong_{\neg}$ $[\![P = P']\!] \Longrightarrow \neg P = \neg P'$

$trans_{\rightarrow}$ $[\![P \longrightarrow Q; Q \longrightarrow R]\!] \Longrightarrow P \longrightarrow R$

$elim_{\wedge}^{1}$ $[\![P \longrightarrow Q \wedge R]\!] \Longrightarrow P \longrightarrow Q$

$elim_{\wedge}^{2}$ $[\![P \longrightarrow Q \wedge R]\!] \Longrightarrow P \longrightarrow R$

$trivial$ $[\![P]\!] \Longrightarrow P$

$triv$ $P \longrightarrow P$

$weak_{\rightarrow}$ $[\![P \longrightarrow Q]\!] \Longrightarrow P \longrightarrow R \longrightarrow Q$

$spec$ $[\![\forall x.P(x)]\!] \Longrightarrow P(a)$

$mp_{P\rightarrow}$ $[\![P \longrightarrow P'; P \longrightarrow P' \longrightarrow Q]\!] \Longrightarrow P \longrightarrow Q$

Reachability Analysis of Mobile Ambients in Fragments of AC Term Rewriting

Giorgio Delzanno and Roberto Montagna

Dipartimento di Informatica e Scienze dell'Informazione
Università di Genova
via Dodecaneso 35, 16143 Genova - Italy
{delzanno, montagna}@disi.unige.it

Abstract. In this paper we investigate the connection between fragments of associative-commutative Term Rewriting and fragments of Mobile Ambients, a powerful model for mobile and distributed computations. The connection can be used to transfer decidability and undecidability results for important computational properties like reachability from one formalism to the other. Furthermore, it can be viewed as a vehicle to apply tools based on rewriting for the simulation and validation of specifications given in Mobile Ambients.

1 Introduction

Models for mobile and distributed computation like the Mobile Ambients (MA) of Cardelli and Gordon [5] provide mechanisms for moving collections of processes across a network. The basic block of the MA model is the notion of ambient. Each ambient has a name, a collection of local agents, and a collection of sub-ambients. Local agents model the possible computations that can take place inside the ambient. Differently from standard process algebraic languages, MA agents have movement capabilities as well as primitives to dissolve the boundary of an ambient. Several variations of MA have been proposed in the literature. For instance, the Safe Ambients of [10] and the Boxed Ambients of [2] provide more sophisticated mechanisms for controlling the access to an ambient. In this paper we restrict our attention to *pure* and *public* versions of MA-like calculi. The pure public fragment of MA (ppMA) is obtained by forbidding the use of name restriction and of communication between local agents, two features inherited from the π-calculus. The ppMA fragment allows us to focus our attention on ambients and movement operations, the novel features with respect to the π-calculus. As shown in [11], ppMA is still Turing complete.

From an abstract point of view, the movement mechanisms of MA-like calculi can be viewed as update schemes for dynamically changing tree structures. Following this abstract view, in this paper we investigate the connection between fragments of MA and associative-commutative (AC) Term Rewriting, a natural operational model for manipulating unordered finite trees. To be as closest as possible to the MA syntax, we consider terms built via a constructor for representing parallel composition, a constructor for representing ambients (internal

K. Barkaoui, A. Cavalcanti, and A. Cerone (Eds.): ICTAC 2006, LNCS 4281, pp. 302–316, 2006.
© Springer-Verlag Berlin Heidelberg 2006

nodes), and a finite set of constants for representing local agents (leaves). We refer to this class of AC Term Rewriting as Tree Update Calculus (TUC).

The connection between the two computational models can be used to transfer properties from one formalism to the other. In this paper we focus our analysis on the *reachability problem* for fragments and variations of ppMA. For two processes P_0 and P_1, the reachability problem consists in checking whether there exists a reduction from P_0 to P_1. The same decision problem can be formulated for a set of rewrite rules and two fixed ground terms t_0 and t_1.

As a first analysis, we show how to express a reachability problem between ppMA-processes as a reachability problem between terms in TUC. Resorting to results on ppMA [1,11], we can exploit the encoding to show that the reachability problem is undecidable in TUC. This negative result motivates further investigations in search of fragments of TUC that can still model ambients and movement operations and in which computational problems like reachability

In this paper we focus our attention on *structure preserving* rewriting rules (TUC^{sp}). Intuitively, a structure preserving rule is such that its application never removes ambients (internal nodes) of a tree, while it can produce and consume leaves without any limit. Thus, structure preserving rewrite rules are monotonic with respect to the number of internal nodes of terms, but not with respect to their size. By exploiting this property, we show that TUC^{sp}-reachability is decidable via a reduction to a reachability problem for a Petri net. The latter problem is known to be decidable [12]. It is important to remark that the TUC^{sp} fragment is not directly related to other fragments of Term Rewriting for which reachability is known to be decidable [6,9,14,15].

By exploiting again the encoding from ppMA to TUC, we show that our decidability result for TUC^{sp} generalizes in an elegant way those proved in [1,3] for reachability in fragments of ppMA. Specifically, we show that the semantic restrictions for replication proposed in [1] (weak reduction) and the syntactic restrictions proposed in [3] (guarded replication) can be captured in a uniform way using the syntactic restrictions of TUC^{sp}. Furthermore, we apply our result to prove decidability of reachability for fragments of Safe and Boxed Ambients similar to those mentioned in [1,4]. It is important to remark that TUC^{sp} can express more general tree update schemes than those provided by the MA-fragments studied in [1,3,4]. Thus, TUC and TUC^{sp} can be viewed as operational models in which to reason on extensions of languages inspired by MA.

Plan. In Section 2 we introduce ppMA. In Section 3 we introduce TUC and study its relation with ppMA. In Section 4 we define TUC^{sp} and study its properties. In Section 5 we study the relation between TUC^{sp} and fragments of ppMA. In Section 6 we discuss related work. Finally, in Section 7 we address some conclusions.

2   ppMA: Pure Public Mobile Ambients

In this paper we consider the pure (without communication) public (without name restriction) fragment of MA (ppMA for short), studied in [1,3,11], in which processes comply with the following grammar:

$$open \; m.P \mid m[Q] \twoheadrightarrow P \mid Q$$

$$n[in \; m.P \mid Q] \mid m[R] \twoheadrightarrow m[n[P \mid Q] \mid R]$$

$$m[n[out \; m.P \mid Q] \mid R] \twoheadrightarrow n[P \mid Q] \mid m[R]$$

$$\frac{P \twoheadrightarrow Q}{P \mid R \twoheadrightarrow Q \mid R} \qquad \frac{P \twoheadrightarrow Q}{n[P] \twoheadrightarrow n[Q]} \qquad \frac{P' \equiv P \quad P \twoheadrightarrow Q \quad Q \equiv Q'}{P' \twoheadrightarrow Q'}$$

Fig. 1. Reduction semantics for ppMA

$$P \quad ::= \quad \mathbf{0} \mid n[P] \mid M.P \mid P|P \mid \;!P$$

$$M \quad ::= \quad in \; n \mid out \; n \mid open \; n$$

where n ranges over a denumerable set Amb of ambient names. The process $n[P]$ denotes an ambient with public name n. The process $M.P$ denotes sequential composition (action prefixing), while $P|Q$ denotes the parallel composition of P and Q. The replication $!P$ denotes an arbitrary number of parallel copies of P. Finally, $\mathbf{0}$ denotes the null process. Since ambients can be nested, the spatial structure of an MA process can be viewed as an unordered tree (with arbitrary width). Movement capabilities may change the ambient spatial structure of processes. The meaning of the operators becomes clearer by looking at the operational semantics defined in terms of a structural congruence $\equiv$ and of a reduction relation $\twoheadrightarrow$. The structural congruence $\equiv$ is the smallest one satisfying

$$P \mid Q \equiv Q \mid P \qquad P \mid (Q \mid R) \equiv (P \mid Q) \mid R \qquad P \mid \mathbf{0} \equiv P \qquad !P \equiv !P \mid P$$

The reduction relation $\twoheadrightarrow$ is defined in Fig. 1. We use $\overset{*}{\twoheadrightarrow}$ to denote the reflexive and transitive closure of the relation $\twoheadrightarrow$.

Definition 1. *Given two* ppMA *processes P and Q, the* reachability problem *consists in deciding whether $P \overset{*}{\twoheadrightarrow} Q$ holds or not.*

Example 1. Assume $P_0 = !P|pc[Q]$ and $P = trojan[in \; pc.virus[out \; trojan.P']]$. By using the congruence on $!P$ and the in capability, a copy of P can move inside the ambient pc yielding the process $P_1 = !P|pc[trojan[virus[out \; trojan.P']]|Q]$. By using the out capability, the $virus$ agent can now be released inside the ambient pc leading to $P_2 = !P|pc[trojan[\mathbf{0}]|virus[P']|Q]$. Thus, $P_0 \overset{*}{\twoheadrightarrow} P_2$ holds.

2.1 Safe and Boxed Ambients

In the Safe Ambients (SA) model [10] movement capabilities have co-capabilities used the regulate the access to an ambient. For instance, the SA reduction rule for the in capability is defined as:

$$n[in \; m.P \mid Q] \mid m[\overline{in} \; n.P' \mid R] \twoheadrightarrow m[n[P \mid Q] \mid P' \mid R]$$

i.e., ambient n enters m only if m grants the access to n using $\overline{in} \; n$.

In the Boxed Ambients (BA) model [2] the open capability is replaced by a parent-child communication mechanism. As an example, let $(x)^\uparrow P$ denote a process ready to receive a sequence of capabilities from a process in the parent ambient (x is a variable that may occur in P), and $\langle M \rangle.R$ denote a process ready to send M to a child ambient. Then, the following reduction rule models parent-child communication:

$$n[(x)^\uparrow P|Q] \mid \langle M \rangle.R \twoheadrightarrow n[P\{x := M\}|Q] \mid R$$

where $P\{x := M\}$ denotes the substitution of x with M in P.

3   TUC: A Fragment of AC Term Rewriting

In this section we define a fragment of AC rewriting, called Tree Update Calculus (TUC), that can be viewed as a generalization of the tree update schemes underlying ppMA.

Given two *finite* sets of constants $\mathcal{N}$ and $\mathcal{Q}$ with $\mathcal{N} \cap \mathcal{Q} = \emptyset$, we use a constructor $n\langle \ldots \rangle$ to represent an ambient (internal node) with label $n \in \mathcal{N}$, an AC constructor $\mid$ to build multisets of trees (the multiset of sons of an internal node), ϵ to represent the empty multiset, and the finite set of constants in $\mathcal{Q}$ to represent processes (leaves). For instance, given $\mathcal{N} = \{n, m\}$ and $\mathcal{Q} = \{a, b\}$ the term $n\langle a \mid a \mid n\langle \epsilon \rangle \mid m\langle a \mid b \rangle\rangle$ can be viewed as an abstract representation of an ambient n with two subprocesses of type a and two subambients. Since ambients can be dynamically populated, we keep terms like $n\langle \epsilon \rangle$ (the empty ambient) distinguished from leaves in $\mathcal{Q}$. Formally, given a denumerable set of variables ranging over multiset of terms (multiset-variables) $\mathcal{V} = \{X, Y, \ldots\}$ the sets TR (tree terms) and MS (multiset terms) are the least sets satisfying:

- the empty multiset ϵ is in MS, every multiset-variable $X \in \mathcal{V}$ is in MS;
- every constant in $\mathcal{Q}$ is in TR (leaf);
- If $m \in MS$ and $n \in \mathcal{N}$, then $n\langle m \rangle \in TR$ (internal node);
- If $t \in TR$, then $t \in MS$ (singleton multiset);
- If $m, m' \in MS$, then $m|m' \in MS$ (parallel composition).

A *ground* term is a term without variables. Notice that, with a little bit of overloading, we use the same notation for a term t and the singleton multiset containing t. The multiset constructor $\mid$ is associative and commutative, i.e., $m_1|(m_2|m_3) = (m_1|m_2)|m_3$, and $m_1|m_2 = m_2|m_1$ for $m_1, m_2, m_3 \in MS$. Furthermore, $m \mid \epsilon = m$ for any $m \in MS$.

From here on, we use the special symbol tuc to represent a forest $t_1|\ldots|t_n$ as a single tree term $tuc\langle t_1| \ldots |t_n\rangle$. We always assume that tuc never occurs in $t_1, \ldots, t_n$. Furthermore, we use the syntax $t[\;]$ to indicate a tree term with one occurrence of the constant $\circ$, and $t[s]$ to indicate the term obtained by replacing the constant $\circ$ in $t[\;]$ with s. We use $var(t)$ to denote the set of variables in t.

A TUC-rewrite rule $l \rightarrow r$ is such that $l, r \in MS$, $var(r) \subseteq var(l)$, the label tuc does not occur in l, r and every variable in l occurs within a tree term.[1] A TUC-theory $\mathcal{R}$ is a set of TUC rewrite rules.

The rules in the theory describe how the current tree configuration is updated during a computation in accord with the following operational semantics. For a fixed set of rules $\mathcal{R}$ and given two ground TR terms $t_1 = tuc\langle m_1 \rangle$ and $t_2 = tuc\langle m_2 \rangle$, $t_1 \Rightarrow t_2$ if and only if there exists a context $t[\ ]$, a rule $l \rightarrow r$ in $\mathcal{R}$, and a mapping σ from $var(l)$ to terms in MS (multiset of trees) such that $t_1 = t[\sigma(l)]$ and $t_2 = t[\sigma(r)]$. For a set of rules $\mathcal{R}$, we use $\overset{*}{\Rightarrow}$ to indicate the reflexive and transitive closure of $\Rightarrow$.

Definition 2. *For a set of TUC rules $\mathcal{R}$ and two ground terms $t_1 = tuc\langle m_1 \rangle$ and $t_2 = tuc\langle m_2 \rangle$, the reachability problem consists in deciding if $t_1 \overset{*}{\Rightarrow} t_2$ holds.[2]*

Example 2. Assume $\mathcal{N} = \{n\}$, $\mathcal{Q} = \{a, b\}$, and let $\mathcal{R}$ consist of the rules

$$a \rightarrow a \mid a$$
$$a \mid a \rightarrow a$$
$$n\langle X \rangle \rightarrow n\langle a \mid n\langle X \rangle \rangle$$

The first rule adds one occurrence of leaf a, while the second rule consumes one occurrence of a. The third rule inserts a new internal node n with leaf a on top of an existing n-rooted tree. The multiset-variable X represents the content of the node labelled by n. With these rules, the term $t = tuc\langle a \mid n\langle b \rangle \rangle$ can be rewritten into trees of arbitrary width and depth as shown by the following derivation:

$$t \overset{*}{\Rightarrow} tuc\langle a \mid a \mid n\langle a \mid n\langle b \rangle \rangle \rangle \overset{*}{\Rightarrow} tuc\langle a \mid n\langle a \mid a \mid n\langle a \mid n\langle b \rangle \rangle \rangle \rangle \overset{*}{\Rightarrow} \dots$$

As another example, we can use the rule $n\langle X \rangle \rightarrow X$ to remove an internal node by moving its sons one level up in the tree, while the rule $n\langle X \rangle \rightarrow a$ replaces an entire n-rooted subtree with the leaf a.

In the next section we will show that TUC is powerful enough to express reachability problems for ppMA.

3.1   From Reachability in **ppMA** to Reachability in **TUC**

In this section we show how to reduce the reachability problem for ppMA to reachability in TUC. Before going into the details of the reduction, we need however some preliminary considerations on the semantics of MA. Let us first notice that we can work with a congruence relation applied only to context different from $!P$ (as for the reduction semantics). Let us now reformulate the axioms $P \mid \mathbf{0} \equiv P$ and $!P \equiv P \mid !P$ as the following reduction rules

$$P \twoheadrightarrow P \mid \mathbf{0} \qquad P \mid \mathbf{0} \twoheadrightarrow P \qquad !P \twoheadrightarrow !P \mid P \qquad !P \mid P \twoheadrightarrow !P$$

---

[1] With this condition, we forbid rules like $X \rightarrow t$ where $X \in \mathcal{V}$.
[2] We assume that the label tuc does not occur in m_1 and m_2.

$$T(\mathbf{0}) = q_0 \quad T(!Q_1) = q_{!Q_1} \quad T(M.Q_1) = q_{M.Q_1}$$
$$T(n[Q_1]) = n\langle T(Q_1)\rangle \quad T(Q_1|Q_2) = T(Q_1)|T(Q_2)$$

Fig. 2. Encoding of processes into ground terms

In MA the empty ambient is represented by $n[\mathbf{0}]$. To maintain this property, we refine the reduction semantics of the *out* rule as follows

$$n[m[out\ n.P \mid R] \mid Q] \ \twoheadrightarrow \ m[P \mid R] \mid n[Q \mid \mathbf{0}]$$

Several computation steps of the modified semantics may correspond to one computation or congruence step in the original semantics. Reachability is preserved by the modified semantics: If Q is reachable from P_0 in the standard semantics, then there exists Q' reachable from P_0 in the modified semantics such that Q' is equivalent modulo the congruences for $\mathbf{0}$ to Q, and Q' is obtained by replacing every occurrences of a process $!R$ in Q with an equivalent process $!R'$ occurring in P_0. Given a process term P, let us now define the set of replicated or sequential processes $Der(P)$ that may become active during a computation (the *derivatives* of P).

$$
\begin{aligned}
Der(\mathbf{0}) &= \{\mathbf{0}\} \\
Der(!P) &= \{!P\} \cup Der(P) \\
Der(M.P) &= \{M.P\} \cup Der(P) \\
Der(n[P]) &= Der(P) \\
Der(P \mid Q) &= Der(P) \cup Der(Q)
\end{aligned}
$$

It is easy to check that $Der(P)$ is a finite set. Furthermore, if $P \overset{*}{\twoheadrightarrow} Q$ using the modified reduction semantics, then $Der(Q) \subseteq Der(P) \cup \{\mathbf{0}\}$.

Let us now consider the reachability problem $P_0 \overset{*}{\twoheadrightarrow} P_1$. To encode it into TUC, we use tree terms in which internal nodes have labels in $\mathcal{N} = Amb$, the set of ambient names, and leaves range over the finite set of constants

$$\mathcal{Q} = \{q_R \mid R \in Der(P_0)\} \cup \{q_0\}$$

Given a process Q derived from P_0, we define the ground term $T(Q)$ by induction on Q as shown in Fig. 2. The semantics of MA processes can be simulated by the TUC-theory $\mathcal{R}(P_0)$ of Fig. 3. Indeed, the following property holds.

Proposition 1. $P_0 \overset{*}{\twoheadrightarrow} P_1$ *if and only if* $tuc\langle T(P_0)\rangle \overset{*}{\Rightarrow} tuc\langle T(P_1)\rangle$ *in* $\mathcal{R}(P_0)$.

Proposition 1 allows us to transfer the undecidability result for reachability in ppMA proved in [1] to our fragment of AC Term Rewriting.

Theorem 1. *Reachability is undecidable in* TUC.

3.2   Expressiveness of TUC

In [11] it has been shown that ppMA is a Turing complete model. We can exploit this result and Prop. 1 to show that TUC is Turing complete as well. This

$$\begin{array}{ll}
(open) & q_{open\ n.Q} \mid n\langle Y\rangle \;\rightarrow\; T(Q) \mid Y \\
(in) & m\langle q_{in\ n.Q} \mid Y\rangle \mid n\langle Z\rangle \;\rightarrow\; n\langle m\langle T(Q) \mid Y\rangle \mid Z\rangle \\
(out) & n\langle m\langle q_{out\ n.Q} \mid Y\rangle \mid Z\rangle \;\rightarrow\; m\langle T(Q) \mid Y\rangle \mid n\langle q_0 | Z\rangle \\
(copyt) & q_{!Q} \rightarrow q_{!Q} \mid T(Q) \\
(absorbt) & q_{!Q} \mid T(Q) \rightarrow q_{!Q} \\
(zero) & q \rightarrow q \mid q_0 \qquad q \mid q_0 \rightarrow q \\
& n\langle X\rangle \rightarrow n\langle X\rangle \mid q_0 \qquad n\langle X\rangle \mid q_0 \rightarrow n\langle X\rangle
\end{array}$$

For any $n, m \in \mathcal{N}$, $q_{open\ n.Q}, q_{in\ n.Q}, q_{out\ n.Q}, q_{!Q} \in \mathcal{Q}$

Fig. 3. TUC theory for ppMA

property as well as the undecidability of reachability can be seen in a more direct way by defining an encoding of Two Counter Machines (2CMs) in TUC. Let us first define the instruction set of a 2CM with control states $s_1, \ldots, s_n$ and counters c_1 and c_2. When executed in state s_k, $INC_i(k, l)$ increments counter c_i and then moves to state s_k, while $DEC_i(k, l, m)$ decrements c_i and then moves to s_l if $c_i > 0$, and moves to state s_m if $c_i = 0$. A 2CM configuration consists of a control state and of the current values of the counters. Our TUC representation makes use of the constants $\mathcal{Q} = \{s_1, \ldots, s_n, zero_1, zero_2\}$ and of the labels $\mathcal{N} = \{c_1, c_2\}$. A 2CM configuration $C = (s_i, c_1 = n_1, c_2 = n_2)$, for $n_1, n_2 \geq 0$, is represented by the term $C^\bullet = tuc\langle s_i \mid c_1^{n_1}\langle zero_1\rangle \mid c_2^{n_2}\langle zero_2\rangle\rangle$, where $c_i^0\langle t\rangle = t$, and $c_i^{n+1}\langle t\rangle = c_i\langle c_i^n\langle t\rangle\rangle$ for $n \geq 0$. To encode $INC_i(k, l)$ and $DEC_i(k, l, m)$, we use the TUC rules

$$\begin{array}{ll}
(inc) \;\; s_k \mid c_i\langle X\rangle \rightarrow s_l \mid c_i^2\langle X\rangle & \qquad (incz) \;\; s_k \mid zero_i \rightarrow s_l \mid c_i\langle zero_i\rangle \\
(dec) \;\; s_k \mid c_i\langle X\rangle \rightarrow s_l \mid X & \qquad (test) \;\; s_k \mid zero_i \rightarrow s_m \mid zero_i
\end{array}$$

The latter encodes the zero-test on counter c_i. If the 2CM configuration C_1 evolves into C_2 via the instruction i, then the term $C_1^\bullet$ can be rewritten into $C_2^\bullet$ using the TUC rule encoding i. The following property then holds.

Theorem 2. *TUC is a Turing complete model.*

In the following section we introduce a non trivial subclass of TUC that can still be used to model movement operations of MA-calculi and for which reachability is decidable.

4   The Structure Preserving Fragment of TUC

The structure preserving fragment of TUC (TUC^{sp}) is obtained by restricting the syntax of rules so as to avoid that their application can remove internal nodes. This property does not imply that the resulting system is monotonic with respect to the size of terms. Indeed, although we forbid rules like $n\langle X\rangle \rightarrow X$ and $n\langle X\rangle \rightarrow a$ that delete internal nodes or subtrees, a rule that removes a leave like $a|a \rightarrow a$ is still definable in TUC^{sp}.

In order to define the syntax of TUC^{sp}-rules, we introduce two subclasses of tree terms, namely RT_L (restricted terms used in the left-hand side of rules) and RT_R (used in the right-hand side) with the following characteristics. Leaves in $\mathcal{Q}$ are the only ground terms we allow in RT_L. Every non ground tree term occurring in an RT_L term must be of the form $n\langle t_1 \mid \ldots \mid t_n \mid X\rangle$, where $n \in \mathcal{N}$, X is a variable and t_i is an RT_L term for $1 \le i \le n$ and $n \ge 0$. RT_R terms are slightly more general since they can have ground trees as subterms.

Formally, RT_L and RM_L are the least sets satisfying

- $\mathcal{Q} \subseteq RT_L$;
- if $t_1, \ldots, t_n \in RT_L$ and $X \in \mathcal{V}$, then $t_1|\ldots|t_n|X \in RM_L$ for $n \ge 0$;
- if $m \in RM_L$ and $n \in \mathcal{N}$, then $n\langle m\rangle \in RT_L$.

RT_R and RM_R are the least sets satisfying

- $\mathcal{Q} \subseteq RT_R$ and $\epsilon \in RM_R$;
- if $t_1, \ldots, t_n \in RT_R$, then $t_1|\ldots|t_n \in RM_R$ for $n \ge 1$;
- if $t_1, \ldots, t_n \in RT_R$ and $X \in \mathcal{V}$, then $t_1|\ldots|t_n|X \in RM_R$ for $n \ge 0$;
- if $m \in RM_R$ and $n \in \mathcal{N}$, then $n\langle m\rangle \in RT_R$.

In the rest of the paper we use $n\langle t_1, \ldots, t_n\rangle$ as an abbreviation for $n\langle t_1 \mid \ldots \mid t_n\rangle$ and $n\langle t_1, \ldots, t_n| X\rangle$ for $n\langle t_1 \mid \ldots \mid t_n \mid X\rangle$. Given a term t let $IntNds(t)$ denote the number of occurrences of labels in $\mathcal{N}$ (internal nodes) in t. $IntNds(t)$ is defined by induction on t as follows: $IntNds(\epsilon) = IntNds(X) = IntNds(q) = 0$ for $X \in \mathcal{V}$ and $q \in \mathcal{Q}$, $IntNds(t_1|\ldots|t_k) = IntNds(t_1|\ldots|t_k| X) = \Sigma_{i=1}^{k} IntNds(t_i)$, and $IntNds(n\langle m\rangle) = IntNds(m) + 1$. For instance, if $t = n\langle n\langle q|q'|X\rangle|n'\langle q\rangle\rangle$, $X \in \mathcal{V}$, $q, q' \in \mathcal{Q}$, then $IntNds(t) = 3$. We are ready now to define the class of structure preserving rules.

Definition 3. *A structure preserving rule $l \to r$ is such that*

1. *$l = t_1 \mid \ldots \mid t_n$, and $t_i \in RT_L$ for $i : 1, \ldots, n$;*
2. *$r = t'_1 \mid \ldots \mid t'_m$ and $t'_i \in RT_R$ for $i : 1, \ldots, m$;*
3. *l and r have the same set V of variables;*
4. *each variable in V occurs once in l and once in r;*
5. *$IntNds(l) \le IntNds(r)$.*

A TUC^{sp}-theory is a set of structure preserving rules.

By definition of RT_L and RT_R, with the first condition we associate one and only one variable to each node, whereas in the right-hand side we also admit internal nodes with ground subtrees. The last three conditions ensure that the tree structure of terms, involved in a rewriting step can only get larger: condition 3 and 4 ensure that subtrees can neither be eliminated nor duplicated, condition 5 ensures that internal nodes can never be eliminated. Since $IntNds(t)$ only counts the number of occurrence of labels of internal nodes, these conditions do not imply monotonicity with respect to the size of a term.

Some examples of TUC^{sp} rules are:

- $a \mid a \to a$ and $a \to a \mid a$ (resp. deletion and insertion of a leaf);
- $n\langle X\rangle \mid m\langle Y\rangle \to n\langle Y\rangle \mid m\langle X\rangle$ (swapping of subtrees);
- $n\langle q|X\rangle \mid m\langle q|Y\rangle \to n\langle r|n\langle X\rangle\rangle \mid m\langle r|m\langle Y\rangle\rangle \mid n\langle\epsilon\rangle$ (insertion of nodes).

As opposite, the following rules are not in the TUC^{sp} fragment:

- $n\langle X\rangle \to n\langle X\rangle \mid n\langle X\rangle$ (duplication of a subtree),
- $n\langle X\rangle \to X$ (removal of a node),
- $n\langle\epsilon\rangle \to n\langle\epsilon\rangle|q$ (ground term on the left-hand side),
- $n\langle X\rangle \to a$ (removal of a complete subtree).

Despite all restrictions of Def. 3, TUC^{sp} is still a powerful computational model. As a first example, it is easy to check that Petri nets can be encoded in TUC^{sp} by using terms with one nesting level only. For instance, if $Q = \{a, b, c\}$, then the ground term $tuc\langle a \mid a \mid b\rangle$ can be used to represent a marking in which places a, b and c have two, one, and zero tokens, respectively. The rule $a \mid a \to c$ represents a transition that removes two tokens from place a, and adds one token to place c. From this observation, it follows that TUC^{sp} reachability is at least as hard as Petri net reachability. Actually, in the next section we show that reachability between terms in a TUC^{sp}-theory can always be reduced to a reachability problem for a Petri net extracted from the terms and from the rules (Proposition 2). From this property and from the decidability of Petri net reachability [12], we obtain that TUC^{sp}-reachability is decidable (Theorem 3).

4.1   Decidability of Reachability in TUC^{sp}

Given a TUC^{sp}-theory $\mathcal{R}$, and two ground tree terms t_0 and t_f, let us consider the reachability problem $t_0 \stackrel{*}{\Rightarrow} t_f$. By definition, if there exist $t_1, \ldots, t_k$ such that $t_0 \Rightarrow t_1 \Rightarrow \ldots \Rightarrow t_k \Rightarrow t_f$, then $IntNds(t_i) \leq IntNds(t_f)$ for $i : 0, \ldots, k$. This property gives us an upper bound on the number of internal nodes, but not on the number of leaves, occurring in each intermediate tree t_i. As an example, consider the two TUC^{sp} rules $a \to a|a$ and $a|a \to a$ and the tree term $t = tuc\langle a\rangle$. In a derivation from t to t we find terms with any number of occurrences of a.

To keep track of the number of leaves we can resort however to a Petri net. The construction is based on the following key observations. Firstly, we can exploit the above mentioned upper bound on the number of internal nodes to isolate the finite set of possible *tree structures* (tree terms without leaves) that can occur in a derivation leading to t_f. The Petri net has a finite set of places (T-places) each one denoting one of these tree structures. Only one T-place can be marked in a reachable marking. Another finite set of places (L-places) is used to keep track of the current number of occurrences of leaves (constants in $\mathcal{Q}$) at every level of the tree structure denoted by the currently marked T-place. The association between an internal node of a T-place and the set of its leaves is maintained via a finite set of *position labels*. To make these ideas more formal, let us first introduce the set of terms we use to represent T-places, i.e., *tree structures* with position labels.

Let $\mathcal{P}$ be the set of position labels $\{\bullet_1, \bullet_2, \ldots, \}$. Then TS (tree structures) and MTS (multisets of TS terms) are the least set satisfying: if $t_1, \ldots, t_r \in$

TS and $\bullet_i \in \mathcal{P}$, then $t_1, \ldots, t_r | \bullet_i$ is in MTS for $r \geq 0$ and $i \geq 1$; if $m \in MTS$ and $n \in \mathcal{N}$, then $n\langle m \rangle$ is in TS. We still use $IntNds(t)$ to denote the number of occurrences of labels of internal nodes in t (we assume that $tuc \notin \mathcal{N}$). Furthermore, we use $Pos(t)$ to denote the multiset that keeps track of the number of occurrences in t of position labels in $\mathcal{P}$. As an example, let $\mathcal{N} = \{n, p, q\}$, then $t = tuc\langle n\langle \bullet_4 \rangle, p\langle p\langle \bullet_5 \rangle | \bullet_3 \rangle, \bullet_8 \rangle$ is a TS term with $IntNds(t) = 3$. Furthermore, we have that $Pos(t) = \{\bullet_3, \bullet_4, \bullet_5, \bullet_8\}$. Notice that a tree structure represents a skeleton for an infinite set of tree terms, all those obtained by populating internal nodes with multisets of leaves.

Given a natural number $N \geq 1$, $t \in TS$ is said to be N-well-formed if and only if $Pos(t) = \{\bullet_1, \ldots, \bullet_{k+1}\}$ for $k \leq N$, i.e., t has k internal nodes and $k+1$ position labels numbered $1, \ldots, k+1$ (the top level label in a multiset term is not associated to an internal node). We use WS_K to denote the set of MTS terms that are K-well-formed. As an example, WS_3 consists of MTS-terms like $n_1\langle \bullet_{i_1} \rangle | n_2 \langle \bullet_{i_2} \rangle | n_3 \langle \bullet_{i_3} \rangle | \bullet_{i_4}$, $n_1\langle n_2 \langle \bullet_{i_1} \rangle, n_3 \langle \bullet_{i_2} \rangle | \bullet_{i_3} \rangle | \bullet_{i_4}$, $\ldots$, where $n_i \in \mathcal{N}$ for $i : 1, \ldots, 3$, and (i_1, i_2, i_3, i_4) is a permutation of $(1, 2, 3, 4)$.

Let $\mathcal{R}$ be a TUC^{sp}-theory, t_0 and t_f be two ground tree terms and K be the number of internal nodes of t_f, i.e., $K = IntNds(t_f)$. The Petri net N associated to the reachability problem $t_0 \overset{*}{\Rightarrow} t_f$ has two kind of places. The set of T-places is defined as $\{tuc\langle w \rangle \mid w \in WS_K\}$ (the set of tree structures with at most K internal nodes with labels in $\mathcal{N}$). The set of L-places is defined as $\{\langle q, \bullet_i \rangle \mid q \in \mathcal{Q} \text{ and } i \in \{1, \ldots, K+1\}\}$. Transitions have in their preset and postset a single T-place together with a set of L-places.

To define the marking and transitions of the Petri net associated to t_0, t_f, and $\mathcal{R}$, we introduce two functions called *match* and *extract*. The intuition behind their definitions is as follows. Given a rule $l \rightarrow r$ and a T-place s, we first try to match the left-hand side l with a multiset term m occurring in s. The matching procedure works by a parallel inspection of the structure of l and m and returns a substitution θ for the variables in l. Every variable is associated to a multiset term labelled by a position. During the matching phase, we collect in a set S all the leaves occurring in l. Leaves are labelled with the position of the corresponding internal nodes. If the matching between l and m succeeds then we can build a transition t with $\{s\} \cup S$ as input places. To determine the output places, we first have to apply the substitution θ, computed during the matching phase, to the right-hand side r, and then extract the new tree structure m' and the corresponding leaves from $\theta(r)$. Since r can have ground subterms, during the visit of $\theta(r)$ we may need to introduce new position labels, distinct from those in s. New labels are collected in a set N. Finally, we have to replace m with m' in s to obtain the output T-place s' of the transition.

For instance, suppose that $s = n\langle m \rangle | \bullet_1$, $m = n'\langle n\langle \bullet_3 \rangle | \bullet_2 \rangle$, and that the rule $l \rightarrow r$ is such that $l = n'\langle q_1, q_2 | X \rangle$ and $r = n'\langle q_3 | X \rangle | n'\langle q_4 \rangle$. The mapping $\theta = [X \mapsto n\langle \bullet_3 \rangle | \bullet_2]$ can be used to unify m and l. The set $S = \{\langle q_1, \bullet_2 \rangle, \langle q_2, \bullet_2 \rangle\}$ contains the leaves in l partitioned according to the position labels in m. Furthermore, from $\theta(r) = n'\langle q_3, n\langle \bullet_3 \rangle | \bullet_2 \rangle | n'\langle q_4 \rangle$ we can extract the labelled term (without leaves) $m' = n'\langle n\langle \bullet_3 \rangle | \bullet_2 \rangle | n'\langle \bullet_4 \rangle$ after having associated the new position label

$\bullet_4$ to the ground tree $n'\langle q_4\rangle$. The set $S' = \{\langle q_3, \bullet_2\rangle, \langle q_4, \bullet_4\rangle\}$ contains the leaves of the new tree structure (again partitioned according to the position labels). Finally, let s' be the term obtained by replacing m with m' in s. Then, we can define a transition with input places $\{s\} \cup S$ and output places $\{s'\} \cup S'$.

Match. Since TUC has an AC constructor, we need to work with sets of matching substitutions. The function *match* takes in input a (multiset) term $s \in WS_{\mathcal{M}}$ and a term $t \in RM_L$ and returns a set of pairs $\langle \theta, S\rangle$, such that θ is a mapping from the variables in t to multisets of TS terms, and S is a multiset of L-places. Formally, $\langle \theta, S\rangle \in match(s, t)$ iff there exist $u, v, w \geq 0$ and $k \geq 1$ such that

- $s = n_1[s_1], \ldots, n_v[s_v], r_1, \ldots, r_u \mid \bullet_k$,
- $t = q_1, \ldots, q_w, n_1[t_1], \ldots, n_v[t_v] \mid X$ where $q_i \in \mathcal{Q}$ for $1 \leq i \leq w$
- $\langle \theta_i, S_i\rangle \in match(s_i, t_i)$ for $1 \leq i \leq v$,
- $\theta = \{X \mapsto (r_1, \ldots, r_u \mid \bullet_k)\} \cup \bigcup_{i=1}^{v} \theta_i$,
- $S = \{\langle q_1, \bullet_k\rangle, \ldots, \langle q_w, \bullet_k\rangle\} \oplus \bigoplus_{i=1}^{v} S_i$.

Here $\oplus$ denotes *multiset union*. Notice that if $v = u = 0$, then $\theta = \{X \mapsto \bullet_k\}$, and that if $v = u = w = 0$ then $S = \emptyset$. For instance, consider

$$s = a\langle b\langle a\langle \bullet_3\rangle \mid \bullet_2\rangle, c\langle \bullet_1\rangle, a\langle \bullet_4\rangle \mid \bullet_5\rangle \mid \bullet_6 \qquad t = a\langle b\langle q_1 \mid X\rangle, a\langle q_2 \mid Y\rangle \mid Z\rangle \mid W$$

Then, $match(s, t)$ returns

$$\theta = \{X \mapsto (a\langle \bullet_3\rangle \mid \bullet_2), \ Y \mapsto \bullet_4, \ Z \mapsto (c\langle \bullet_1\rangle \mid \bullet_5), \ W \mapsto \bullet_6\}$$
$$S = \{\langle q_1, \bullet_2\rangle, \langle q_2, \bullet_4\rangle\}$$

As another example, if $s = n\langle \bullet_1\rangle \mid n\langle \bullet_2\rangle \mid \bullet_3$ and $t = n\langle X\rangle \mid n\langle Y\rangle \mid Z$ then $\{X \mapsto \bullet_1, Y \mapsto \bullet_2, Z \mapsto \bullet_3\}$ and $\{X \mapsto \bullet_2, Y \mapsto \bullet_1, Z \mapsto \bullet_3\}$ are two possible substitutions returned by $match(s, t)$ (in both cases $S = \emptyset$).

Extract. Let θ be a substitution computed by $match(s, t_1)$. Suppose that t_2 is an RM_R term with the same variables as t_1. The term $\theta(t_2)$ obtained by applying θ to t_2 is such that all variables in t_2 are replaced by MTS terms (multiset of tree structures with position labels). The *extract* function extracts the tree structure of $\theta(t_2)$ and associates to each leaf in t_2 a position label accordingly to those injected by θ in t_2. The function *extract* returns a set of pairs $\langle s, S\rangle$, where s is an MTS term, and S is a multiset of L-places.

Formally, $\langle s, S\rangle \in extract(t)$ iff there exist $v, w \geq 0$, and $k \geq 1$ such that

- $t = p_1, \ldots, p_w, n_1\langle m_1\rangle, \ldots, n_v\langle m_v\rangle \mid \bullet_k$ or $t = p_1, \ldots, p_w, n_1\langle m_1\rangle, \ldots, n_v\langle m_v\rangle$
  with $p_j \in \mathcal{Q}$ for $0 \leq j \leq w$,
- $(s_i, S_i) \in extract(m_i)$ for $1 \leq i \leq v$,
- $s = n_1\langle s_1\rangle, \ldots, n_v\langle s_v\rangle \mid \bullet_k$, and
- $S = \{\langle p_1, \bullet_k\rangle, \ldots, \langle p_w, \bullet_k\rangle\} \oplus \bigoplus_{i=1}^{v} S_i$.

Notice that if a certain level of t there is no position label, then we choose one non-deterministically to label the corresponding level of s. As an example, given $t = a\langle q_1, b\langle q_2, a\langle \bullet_3\rangle \mid \bullet_2\rangle, a\langle \bullet_4\rangle\rangle$, $extract(t)$ contains the pair $s = a\langle b\langle a\langle \bullet_3\rangle \mid \bullet_2\rangle, a\langle \bullet_4\rangle \mid \bullet_5\rangle$, $S = \{\langle q_1, \bullet_5\rangle, \langle q_2, \bullet_2\rangle\}$, where $\bullet_5$ is a new label.

Let $\tau_\mathcal{R} = \emptyset$
For every rule $l \to r \in \mathcal{R}$
 For every T-place v and term $t = n\langle m \mid \bullet_k \rangle$ such that $v = v'[t]$
 Let $t' = n\langle l \mid Z \rangle$ for a variable $Z \notin var(l)$
  For every $\langle \theta, S \rangle \in match(m \mid \bullet_k, l \mid Z)$
   For every $\langle s \mid \bullet_{tmp}, S' \rangle \in extract(\theta(r))$ s.t. $w = v'[n\langle s \mid \theta(Z) \rangle]$ is K-well-formed
    Add a transition with preset $\{v\} \oplus S$ and postset $\{w\} \oplus S'$ to $\tau_\mathcal{R}$.

Fig. 4. Algorithm for computing Petri net transitions

Transitions. The set $\tau_\mathcal{R}$ of Petri net transitions associated to rules in $\mathcal{R}$ is computed via the algorithm of Fig. 4. Notice that, well-formedness ensures that all position labels introduced in w by *extract* must be distinct and new with respect to those in $Pos(t)$.

Markings. Given a ground tree term t, the set of Petri net markings $marking(t)$ associated to t is the set $marking(t) = \{M \mid \langle s, S \rangle \in extract(t), \ M = \{s\} \oplus S\}$. Intuitively, the marking associated to t has one token in the T-place s representing the tree structure of t, and k tokens in place $\langle q, \ell \rangle$ if q occurs k times at position ℓ in s. The following property then holds.

Proposition 2. *Let N be the Petri net associated to the reachability problem $t_0 \stackrel{*}{\Rightarrow} t_f$ and $\mathcal{R}$. Then, $t_0 \stackrel{*}{\Rightarrow} t_f$ holds iff there exist $M \in marking(t_0)$ and $M' \in marking(t_f)$ such that M' is reachable from M in N.*

Example 3. Given $t = a\langle q_1, b\langle q_2, q_2, q_3, a\langle q_2 \rangle\rangle, a\langle q_1, b\langle q_1 \rangle\rangle, a\langle q_1, q_2 \rangle\rangle$, $extract(t)$ returns $s = a\langle s' \rangle \mid \bullet_7$ where $s' = b\langle a\langle\bullet_1\rangle \mid \bullet_2\rangle, a\langle b\langle\bullet_3\rangle \mid \bullet_4\rangle, a\langle\bullet_5\rangle \mid \bullet_6$ and $S = \{\langle q_1, \bullet_6\rangle, \langle q_2, \bullet_2\rangle, \langle q_2, \bullet_2\rangle, \langle q_3, \bullet_2\rangle, \langle q_2, \bullet_1\rangle, \langle q_1, \bullet_4\rangle, \langle q_1, \bullet_3\rangle, \langle q_1, \bullet_5\rangle, \langle q_2, \bullet_5\rangle\}$. We obtain the marking M_t associated to $\langle s, S \rangle$ by putting 1 token in the T-place s, 1 token in the L-place $\langle q_1, \bullet_6\rangle$, 2 tokens in the L-place $\langle q_2, \bullet_2\rangle$, etc.

Now consider the rule $l \to r$ such that $l = a\langle q_2 \mid X \rangle \mid b\langle q_3 \mid Y \rangle$ and $r = a\langle q_1, b\langle q_1 \mid X \rangle \mid Y \rangle$. Then, we have that $t' = a\langle l \mid Z \rangle$ can be matched against s. Indeed $match(s', l \mid Z)$ returns among other possible solutions

$$\theta = \{X \mapsto \bullet_5, \ Y \mapsto (a\langle\bullet_1\rangle \mid \bullet_2), \ Z \mapsto (a\langle b\langle\bullet_3\rangle \mid \bullet_4\rangle \mid \bullet_6)\}$$
$$U = \{\langle q_2, \bullet_5\rangle, \langle q_3, \bullet_2\rangle\}$$

Another possibility is to swap the terms associated to Y and Z. Furthermore, $\theta(r) = a\langle q_1, b\langle q_1 \mid \bullet_5\rangle, a\langle\bullet_1\rangle \mid \bullet_2\rangle$ and $extract(\theta(r))$ contains the pair $\langle s', S' \rangle$, where $s' = a\langle b\langle\bullet_5\rangle, a\langle\bullet_1\rangle \mid \bullet_2\rangle \mid \bullet_{new}$ and $S' = \{\langle q_1, \bullet_2\rangle, \langle q_1, \bullet_5\rangle\}$. Thus, we build a transition τ with input places $\{s\} \cup U$ and output places $\{s'''\} \cup S'$ where

$$s''' = a\langle s', a\langle b\langle\bullet_3\rangle \mid \bullet_4\rangle \mid \bullet_6\rangle = a\langle a\langle b\langle\bullet_5\rangle, a\langle\bullet_1\rangle \mid \bullet_2\rangle, a\langle b\langle\bullet_3\rangle \mid \bullet_4\rangle \mid \bullet_6\rangle$$

Furthermore, since $U \subseteq S$ we have that τ is enabled at M_T. Its firing leads to the marking obtained by removing one token from the T-place s and from the L-places $\langle q_2, \bullet_5\rangle$ and $\langle q_3, \bullet_2\rangle$, and by adding one token to the T-place s''' and to the L-places $\langle q_1, \bullet_2\rangle$ and $\langle q_1, \bullet_5\rangle$. Namely, the newly marked L-places is

$$V = \{\langle q_1, \bullet_2\rangle, \langle q_1, \bullet_5\rangle, \langle q_1, \bullet_6\rangle, \langle q_2, \bullet_2\rangle, \langle q_2, \bullet_2\rangle, \langle q_2, \bullet_1\rangle, \langle q_1, \bullet_4\rangle, \langle q_1, \bullet_3\rangle, \langle q_1, \bullet_5\rangle\}$$

From the resulting marking we can reconstruct the term obtained by applying the rule. We just have to populate s''' with the corresponding leaves in V to obtain the term: $a\langle q_1, a\langle q_1, b\langle q_1\rangle, a\langle q_2, q_2\rangle\rangle, a\langle q_1, b\langle q_1\rangle\rangle\rangle$.

Proposition 2 allows us to reduce reachability in a TUC^{sp}-theory to a finite set of reachability problems for a Petri net. Since the latter problem is decidable [12], we obtain the following result.

Theorem 3. *Reachability is decidable in* TUC^{sp}.

5   Reachability Analysis of Fragments of **ppMA** in **TUC**^{sp}

As investigated in [1,3], the use of the *open* capability and of the congruence $!P \equiv !P|P$ represent two different sources for the undecidability of the reachability problem in ppMA. To overcome this problem, in [1] Boneva and Talbot proposed a weaker semantics for the open-free fragment of ppMA: the original semantics of $!P$ is replaced by the oriented reduction rule $!P \twoheadrightarrow P \mid !P$, thus dropping the *absorbtion* law $!P \mid P \twoheadrightarrow !P$ from the calculus. In [1], they prove that reachability is decidable in this "semantic" fragment of open-free ppMA. In [3] Busi and Zavattaro introduced instead a "syntactic" fragment of open-free ppMA for which reachability is decidable. In this fragment replication is allowed only when guarded by an action, i.e., in terms like $!in\ n.P$ and $!out\ n.P$. Differently from the Boneva-Talbot fragment, the semantics of replication is not modified with respect to the original MA model. In [4] Busi and Zavattaro proved also the decidability of reachability for the public BA with guarded replication and with parent-child communication defined only for finite sequences of capabilities.

Consistently with the above mentioned results, we first notice that, due to the presence of the rules *open* and *absorbt*, the TUC-theory that models a reachability problem in ppMA of Fig. 3 is not structure preserving. The semantic restriction of Boneva-Talbot can be mimicked here by dropping *open* and *absorbt* from the calculus. We now observe that the following TUC^{sp} rules naturally model the semantics of guarded replication:

$$q_{!M.P} \to q_{!M.P} \mid q_{M.P} \qquad q_{!M.P} \mid q_{M.P} \to q_{!M.P}$$

for any $!M.P$ occurring in the set $Der(P_0)$ associated to the initial process P_0. The syntactic restriction of Busi-Zavattaro can be mimicked by removing the rules *open*, *copyt*, and *absorbt* from the TUC theory in Fig. 3, and by adding the new rules for $q_{!M.P}$. Furthermore, under the same assumptions taken in [4], we can use a TUC^{sp}-theory to model parent-child communication. For instance, the rule

$$n\langle q_{(x)\uparrow P}|X\rangle \mid q_{\langle M\rangle.R} \to n\langle T(P\{x := M\})|X\rangle \mid T(R)$$

models the transmission of a finite sequence of capabilities M to a child ambient n. In all the above cases the resulting rewrite rules are structure preserving. Therefore, we can apply Theorem 2 to obtain a uniform and elegant way to prove the decidability of reachability in these fragments of MA and BA. A similar reasoning can be applied for other variations of the MA model. For instance, it is immediate to check that reachability in open-free pure public SA can be encoded as TUC^{sp} reachability. Indeed, safe movement operations like safe in can be modelled via the TUC^{sp} rules

$$m\langle q_{in\ n.Q}\mid Y\rangle \mid n\langle q_{\overline{in}\ n.R}\mid Z\rangle\ \rightarrow\ n\langle m\langle T(Q)\mid Y\rangle\mid T(R)\mid Z\rangle$$

which is structure preserving.

It is interesting to notice that in TUC^{sp} we can model tree update schemes that are not present as primitive operations in MA. For instance, the rule that swaps the sons of two ambients, i.e.,

$$n\langle X\rangle\mid m\langle Y\rangle\rightarrow n\langle Y\rangle\mid m\langle X\rangle$$

is structure preserving. Thus, when such a tree update scheme is added to ppMA, it does not break the good property of the above mentioned fragments.

6   Related Work

Reachability is known to be decidable for ground Term Rewriting Systems (TRSs) [7,13]. In our setting we consider however reachability problems with substitutions and rewrite rules with infinite sets of ground instances. Ground AC TRSs are equivalent to Process Rewrite Systems (PRS) a combination of prefix rewrite systems and Petri nets introduced in [14]. TUC^{sp} seems to be not directly related to PRS. Indeed, PRS does not allow synchronization rules of the form $n\langle X\rangle\mid m\langle Y\rangle\rightarrow n'\langle X\rangle\mid m'\langle Y\rangle$ which are expressible in TUC^{sp}. Using these kind of rules, it is easy to see that TUC^{sp}-rules can generate non-regular tree languages when viewing rewrite rules as grammar rules. Despite of the non regularity of the generated languages, the decidability of reachability gives us a way to decide the membership problem of a given term t in the set of terms reachable from a certain term via a set of TUC^{sp} rewrite rules. This property seems a distinguished feature from decidability results of TRSs based on tree automata like those obtained for right-linear and monadic TRSs [15], linear and semi-monadic TRSs [6], and decreasing TRSs [9]. To be more specific, the rule used to encode movement capabilities in Fig. 3 violate all the syntactic restrictions proposed in [15,9,6] since they contain a variables in a nested term in the right-hand side that also occurs in the left hand side. The completion algorithm for tree automata presented in [8] could be a useful heuristic for testing non-reachability of a given (set of) term(s). Concerning the reachability problem for fragments of ppMA, we are only aware of the work in [3,1,4]. As discussed in detail in Section 5, the decidability result for TUC^{sp} gives us a uniform and more general view of these results.

7   Conclusions

In this paper we have investigated the relation between fragments of Mobile Ambients and AC Term Rewriting. Our investigations show that a large class of tree update mechanisms that includes the movement capabilities of Mobile Ambients can be naturally expressed in simple fragments of Term Rewriting in which it is possible to decide important computational properties like reachability. On the practical side, we are currently investigating two main directions: the use of tools for manipulating AC Term Rewriting Systems for simulation and analysis of specifications given in Mobile Ambients, and of approximation techniques based on unfoldings for exploiting in an effective way the reduction of reachability in TUC^{sp} to Petri net reachability.

Acknowledgments. We thank Nadia Busi and Cristiano Calcagno for fruitful discussions and suggestions.

References

1. I. Boneva and J.-M. Talbot. When Ambients cannot be Opened! Theoretical Computer Science 333(1-2): 127-169, 2005.
2. M. Bugliesi, G. Castagna, S. Crafa. Boxed Ambients. In Proc. of TACS '01: 38-63, 2001.
3. N. Busi and G. Zavattaro. Deciding Reachability in Mobile Ambients. In Proc. of ESOP '05: 248-262, 2005.
4. N. Busi and G. Zavattaro. Deciding Reachability in Boxed Ambients. In Proc. of ICTCS '05: 143-159, 2005.
5. L. Cardelli and A. D. Gordon. Mobile Ambients. Theoretical Computer Science 240(1): 177-213, 2000.
6. J.-L. Coquidé, M. Dauchet, R. Gilleron, S. Vágvölgyi. Bottom-Up Tree Pushdown Automata and Rewrite Systems. In Proc. of RTA '91: 287-298, 1991.
7. M. Dauchet, S. Tison. The Theory of Ground Rewrite Systems is Decidable. In Proc. of LICS '90: 242-248, 1990.
8. G. Feuillade, T. Genet, V. Viet Triem Tong. Reachability Analysis over Term Rewriting Systems. Theoretical Computer Science 330(3): 501-551, 2005.
9. F. Jacquemard. Decidable Approximations of Term Rewriting Systems. In Proc. RTA '96: 362-376, 1996.
10. F. Levi and D. Sangiorgi. Mobile Safe Ambients. ACM Transactions on Programming Languages and Systems 25(1): 1-69, 2003.
11. S. Maffeis and I. Phillips. On the Computational Strength of Pure Ambient Calculi. Theoretical Computer Science, 330(3): 501-551, 2005.
12. E. W. Mayr. An Algorithm for the General Petri Net Reachability Problem. SIAM Journal of Computing, 1984.
13. R. Mayr and M. Rusinowitch. Reachability is Decidable for Ground AC Rewrite Systems. In Proc. of Infinity '98, 1998.
14. R. Mayr. Process Rewrite Systems. Information and Computation 156(1-2): 264-286, 2000.
15. K. Salomaa. Deterministic Tree Pushdown Automata and Monadic Tree Rewriting Systems. Journal of Computer Systems Science 37(3): 367-394, 1988.

Interesting Properties of the Real-Time Conformance Relation tioco

Moez Krichen[1] and Stavros Tripakis[2]

[1] Verimag Laboratory, Centre Equation 2, avenue de Vignate, 38610 Gières, France
[2] Verimag Laboratory and Cadence Berkeley Labs, 1995 University avenue, Berkeley, CA, USA
krichen@imag.fr, tripakis@cadence.com

Abstract. We are interested in black-box conformance testing of real-time systems. Our framework is based on the model of timed automata with inputs and outputs (TAIO). We use a timed conformance relation called tioco which is the extension of the untimed relation ioco. We show that considering only lazy-input TAIO is enough for describing all possible non-blocking specifications. We compare between tioco and the trace-inclusion relation. We prove that tioco is undecidable and that it does not distinguish specifications with the same set of observable traces. We prove tioco to be transitive and stable w.r.t both compositionality and action hiding for input-complete specifications. We compare between tioco and two other timed conformance relations, rtioco and $\sqsubseteq_{tioco}$.

1 Introduction

In this work, we are interested in so-called *black-box conformance testing*, where the aim is to check conformance of the *system under test (SUT)* to a given specification. The SUT is a "black box" in the sense that we do not have a model of it, thus, can only rely on its observable input/output behavior. The considered specification is a real-time system . Real-Time Systems are systems which operate in an environment with strict timing constraints.

Our framework is *expressive*: it can fully handle *partially-observable, non-deterministic* timed automata. More precisely, we model specifications as *timed automata with inputs and outputs – TAIO*. The semantics of TAIO are given as *timed labeled transition systems – TLTS*.

In a previous work [5], we introduced the *timed input-output conformance relation* tioco, an extension of the relation *ioco* [7]. In this work, we show some interesting properties of the conformance relation tioco.

The rest of this document is organized as follows. Section 2 introduces the TAIO Model. Section 3 shows how conformance is formally defined and compares between tioco and trace-inclusion relation. Section 3 also states some interesting properties of tioco, namely, undecidability, transitivity and stability w.r.t both compositionality and action hiding. Section 4 gives a comparison between tioco and two other timed conformance relations, rtioco [4] and $\sqsubseteq_{tioco}$ [3]. Section 5 presents conclusions.

K. Barkaoui, A. Cavalcanti, and A. Cerone (Eds.): ICTAC 2006, LNCS 4281, pp. 317–331, 2006.

2   Timed Automata with Inputs and Outputs

2.1   Real-Time Sequences

Let R be the set of non-negative reals. Given a finite set of *actions* Ac, the set $(\mathsf{Ac} \cup \mathsf{R})^*$ of all finite-length *real-time sequences* over Ac will be denoted $\mathsf{RT}(\mathsf{Ac})$. $\epsilon \in \mathsf{RT}(\mathsf{Ac})$ is the empty sequence. Given $\mathsf{Ac}' \subseteq \mathsf{Ac}$ and $\rho \in \mathsf{RT}(\mathsf{Ac})$, $P_{\mathsf{Ac}'}(\rho)$ denotes the *projection* of ρ to Ac', obtained by "erasing" from ρ all actions not in Ac'. For example, if $\mathsf{Ac} = \{a, b\}$, $\mathsf{Ac}' = \{a\}$ and $\rho = a\,1\,b\,2\,a\,3$, then $P_{\mathsf{Ac}'}(\rho) = a\,3\,a\,3$. The time spent in a sequence ρ, denoted $\mathsf{time}(\rho)$ is the sum of all delays in ρ, for example, $\mathsf{time}(\epsilon) = 0$ and $\mathsf{time}(a\,1\,b\,0.5) = 1.5$.

In the rest of the document, we assume given a set of actions Ac, partitioned in two disjoint sets: a set of *input actions* $\mathsf{Ac_{in}}$ and a set of *output actions* $\mathsf{Ac_{out}}$. Actions in $\mathsf{Ac_{in}} \cup \mathsf{Ac_{out}}$ are called *observable* actions. We also assume there is an *unobservable* action $\tau \notin \mathsf{Ac}$. Let $\mathsf{Ac_{\tau}} = \mathsf{Ac} \cup \{\tau\}$.

2.2   Timed Labeled Transition Systems

A *timed labeled transition system* (TLTS) over Ac is a tuple $(S, s_0, \mathsf{Ac}, T_d, T_t)$: S is a set of *states*; s_0 is the initial state; T_d is a set of *discrete transitions* of the form (s, a, s') where $s, s' \in S$ and $a \in \mathsf{Ac}$; T_t is a set of *timed transitions* of the form (s, t, s') where $s, s' \in S$ and $t \in \mathsf{R}$.

Timed transitions must be deterministic, that is, $(s, t, s') \in T_t$ and $(s, t, s'') \in T_t$ implies $s' = s''$. T_t must also satisfy the following conditions:

- $(s, t, s') \in T_t$ and $(s', t', s'') \in T_t$ implies $(s, t + t', s'') \in T_t$;
- $(s, t, s') \in T_t$ implies that for all $t' < t$, there is some $(s, t', s'') \in T_t$.

We use standard notation concerning TLTS. For $s, s_i \in S$, $\mu, \mu_i \in \mathsf{Ac_{\tau}} \cup \mathsf{R}$, $a, a_i \in \mathsf{Ac} \cup \mathsf{R}$, $\rho \in \mathsf{RT}(\mathsf{Ac_{\tau}})$ and $\sigma \in \mathsf{RT}(\mathsf{Ac})$, we have:

- $s \xrightarrow{\mu} \;=\; \exists s' \cdot s \xrightarrow{\mu} s'$;
- $s \xrightarrow{\mu_1 \cdots \mu_n} s' \;=\; \exists s_1, \cdots, s_n \cdot s = s_1 \xrightarrow{\mu_1} s_2 \xrightarrow{\mu_2} \cdots \xrightarrow{\mu_n} s_n = s'$;
- $s \xrightarrow{\rho} \;=\; \exists s' \cdot s \xrightarrow{\rho} s'$;
- $s \xRightarrow{\epsilon} s' \;=\; s = s'$ or $s \xrightarrow{\tau \cdots \tau} s'$;
- $s \xRightarrow{a} s' \;=\; \exists s_1, s_2 \cdot s \xRightarrow{\epsilon} s_1 \xrightarrow{a} s_2 \xRightarrow{\epsilon}$;
- $s \xRightarrow{a} \;=\; \exists s' \cdot s \xRightarrow{a} s'$;
- $s \xRightarrow{a_1 \cdots a_n} s' \;=\; \exists s_1, \cdots, s_n \cdot s = s_1 \xRightarrow{a_1} s_2 \xRightarrow{a_2} \cdots \xRightarrow{a_n} s_n = s'$;
- $s \xRightarrow{\sigma} \;=\; \exists s' \cdot s \xRightarrow{\sigma} s'$;

A sequence of the form $s_0 \xrightarrow{\mu_1} s \xrightarrow{\mu_2} \cdots \xrightarrow{\mu_n} s'$ is called a *run* and a sequence of the form $s_0 \xRightarrow{a_1} s \xRightarrow{a_2} \cdots \xRightarrow{a_n} s'$ an *observable run*.

2.3   Timed Automata

We use timed automata [1] with deadlines to model urgency [6,2]. A *timed automaton over* Ac is a tuple $A = (Q, q_0, X, \mathsf{Ac}, E)$ where: Q is a finite set of *locations*; $q_0 \in Q$ is the initial location; X is a finite set of *clocks*; E is a finite set of *edges*.

Each edge is a tuple (q, q', ψ, r, d, a), where: $q, q' \in Q$ are the source and destination locations; ψ is the *guard*, a conjunction of constraints of the form $x \# c$, where $x \in X$, c is an integer constant and $\# \in \{<, \leq, =, \geq, >\}$; $r \subseteq X$ is a set of clocks to *reset* to zero; $d \in \{\text{lazy}, \text{delayable}, \text{eager}\}$ is the *deadline*; $a \in \text{Ac}$ is the action.

We will not allow delayable edges with guards of the form $x < c$ and eager edges with guards of the form $x > c$.

A timed automaton A defines an infinite TLTS which is denoted L_A. Its states are pairs $s = (q, v)$, where $q \in Q$ and $v : X \to \mathbb{R}$ is a clock *valuation*. $\mathbf{0}$ is the valuation assigning 0 to every clock of A. S_A is the set of all states and $s_0^A = (q_0, \mathbf{0})$ is the initial state. Discrete transitions are of the form $(q, v) \xrightarrow{a} (q', v')$, where $a \in \text{Ac}$ and there is an edge (q, q', ψ, r, d, a), such that v satisfies ψ and v' is obtained by resetting to zero all clocks in r and leaving the others unchanged. Timed transitions are of the form $(q, v) \xrightarrow{t} (q, v + t)$, where $t \in \mathbb{R}, t > 0$ and there is no edge (q, q'', ψ, r, d, a), such that: either $d = \text{delayable}$ and there exist $0 \leq t_1 < t_2 \leq t$ such that $v + t_1 \models \psi$ and $v + t_2 \not\models \psi$; or $d = \text{eager}$ and $v \models \psi$. A state $s \in S_A$ is *reachable* if there exists $\rho \in \text{RT}(\text{Ac})$ such that $s_0^A \xrightarrow{\rho} s$. The set of reachable states of A is denoted $\text{Reach}(A)$.

2.4   Timed Automata with Inputs and Outputs

A *timed automaton with inputs and outputs* (TAIO) is a timed automaton over the partitionned set of actions $\text{Ac}_\tau = \text{Ac}_\text{in} \cup \text{Ac}_\text{out} \cup \{\tau\}$. For clarity, we will explicitly include inputs and outputs in the definition of a TAIO A and write $(Q, q_0, X, \text{Ac}_\text{in}, \text{Ac}_\text{out}, \text{E})$ instead of $(Q, q_0, X, \text{Ac}_\tau, \text{E})$.

A TAIO is called *observable* if none of its edges is labeled by τ.

Given a set of inputs $\text{Ac}' \subseteq \text{Ac}_\text{in}$, a TAIO A is called *input-complete* w.r.t Ac' if it can accept any input in Ac' at any state: $\forall s \in \text{Reach}(A) . \forall a \in \text{Ac}' . s \xrightarrow{a}$. It is simply said to be input-complete when $\text{Ac}' = \text{Ac}_\text{in}$. A is called lazy-*input* w.r.t Ac' if the deadlines on all the transitions labeled with input actions in Ac' are lazy. It is called lazy-input if it is lazy-input w.r.t Ac_in. Note that input-complete does not imply lazy-input in general.

A is called *deterministic* if

$$\forall s, s', s'' \in \text{Reach}(A) . \forall a \in \text{Ac}_\tau . s \xrightarrow{a} s' \wedge s \xrightarrow{a} s'' \Rightarrow s' = s''.$$

A is called *non-blocking* if

$$\forall s \in \text{Reach}(A) . \forall t \in \mathbb{R} . \exists \rho \in \text{RT}(\text{Ac}_\text{out} \cup \{\tau\}) . \text{time}(\rho) = t \wedge s \xrightarrow{\rho} . \tag{1}$$

This condition guarantees that A will not block time in any environment.

The set of *timed traces* of a TAIO A is defined to be

$$\text{TTr}(A) = \{\rho \mid \rho \in \text{RT}(\text{Ac}_\tau) \wedge s_0^A \xrightarrow{\rho}\}. \tag{2}$$

The set of *observable timed traces* of A is defined to be

$$\mathsf{OTT}(A) = \{P_{\mathsf{Ac}}(\rho) \mid \rho \in \mathsf{RT}(\mathsf{Ac}_\tau) \wedge s_0^A \xrightarrow{\rho}\}. \tag{3}$$

The TLTS defined by a given TAIO is called a *timed input-output LTS* (TIOLTS). From now on, unless otherwise stated, all the considered TAIO are defined w.r.t the same sets $\mathsf{Ac}_{\mathsf{in}}$ and $\mathsf{Ac}_{\mathsf{out}}$ and unobservable action τ. As for TAIO, a TIOLTS L is denoted $(S, s_0, \mathsf{Ac}_{\mathsf{in}}, \mathsf{Ac}_{\mathsf{out}}, T_d, T_t)$ instead of $(S, s_0, \mathsf{Ac}_\tau, T_d, T_t)$.

2.5   Parallel Composition of TAIO

Most of the time, it is easier to write models in a modular way. That is, to consider models which are the product of some interacting components. For that, we introduce the notion of parallel composition for the case of TAIO.

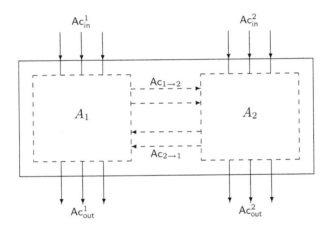

Fig. 1. The generic scheme of two interacting TAIO

We are given two TAIO $A_1 = (Q_1, q_0^1, X_1, \mathsf{Ac}_{\mathsf{in}}^1 \cup \mathsf{Ac}_{2\to1}, \mathsf{Ac}_{\mathsf{out}}^1 \cup \mathsf{Ac}_{1\to2}, \mathsf{E}_1)$ and $A_2 = (Q_2, q_0^2, X_2, , \mathsf{Ac}_{\mathsf{in}}^2 \cup \mathsf{Ac}_{1\to2}, \mathsf{Ac}_{\mathsf{out}}^2 \cup \mathsf{Ac}_{2\to1}, \mathsf{E}_2)$. The pair of TAIO (A_1, A_2) is said to be *compatible* w.r.t the pair of action sets $(\mathsf{Ac}_{1\to2}, \mathsf{Ac}_{2\to1})$ if $X_1 \cap X_2 = \emptyset$, the sets $\mathsf{Ac}_{\mathsf{in}}^1$, $\mathsf{Ac}_{\mathsf{out}}^1$, $\mathsf{Ac}_{\mathsf{in}}^2$, $\mathsf{Ac}_{\mathsf{out}}^2$, $\mathsf{Ac}_{1\to2}$ and $\mathsf{Ac}_{2\to1}$ are pairwise disjoint (as illustrated in Figure 1) and A_i is both input-complete and lazy-input w.r.t $\mathsf{Ac}_{(3-i)\to i}$, for $i = 1, 2$.

The two TAIO synchronise both on time and on their shared common actions $\mathsf{Ac}_{1\to2} \cup \mathsf{Ac}_{2\to1}$. When connected to each other, the interaction between the two TAIO is assumed to be unobservable from outside. We further assume that (A_1, A_2) is compatible w.r.t $(\mathsf{Ac}_{1\to2}, \mathsf{Ac}_{2\to1})$.

The parallel composition of A_1 and A_2 is denoted $A_1 \| A_2$. It is the TAIO $(Q_1 \times Q_2, (q_0^1, q_0^2), X_1 \cup X_2, \mathsf{Ac}_{\mathsf{in}}, \mathsf{Ac}_{\mathsf{out}}, \mathsf{E})$ such that

$$\mathsf{Ac}_{\mathsf{in}} = \bigcup_{i=1,2} \mathsf{Ac}_{\mathsf{in}}^i, \quad \mathsf{Ac}_{\mathsf{out}} = \bigcup_{i=1,2} \mathsf{Ac}_{\mathsf{out}}^i$$

and E is the smallest set such that:

- For $(q_1, q_2) \in Q_1 \times Q_2$ and $a \in \mathsf{Ac}_{in}^1 \cup \mathsf{Ac}_{out}^1 \cup \{\tau_1\}$:

$$(q_1, q_1', \psi_1, r_1, d_1, a) \in E_1 \Rightarrow ((q_1, q_2), (q_1', q_2), \psi_1, r_1, d_1, a) \in E; \quad (4)$$

- For $(q_1, q_2) \in Q_1 \times Q_2$ and $a \in \mathsf{Ac}_{in}^2 \cup \mathsf{Ac}_{out}^2 \cup \{\tau_2\}$:

$$(q_2, q_2', \psi_2, r_2, d_2, a) \in E_2 \Rightarrow ((q_1, q_2), (q_1, q_2'), \psi_2, r_2, d_2, a) \in E; \quad (5)$$

- For $a \in \mathsf{Ac}_{1 \to 2}$: $(q_1, q_1', \psi_1, r_1, d_1, a) \in E_1 \wedge (q_2, q_2', \psi_2, r_2, d_2, a) \in E_2$ [1]

$$\Rightarrow ((q_1, q_2), (q_1, q_2'), \psi_1 \wedge \psi_2, r_1 \cup r_2, d_1, \tau_a) \in E; \quad (6)$$

- For $a \in \mathsf{Ac}_{2 \to 1}$: $(q_1, q_1', \psi_1, r_1, d_1, a) \in E_1 \wedge (q_2, q_2', \psi_2, r_2, d_2, a) \in E_2$

$$\Rightarrow ((q_1, q_2), (q_1, q_2'), \psi_1 \wedge \psi_2, r_1 \cup r_2, d_2, \tau_a) \in E. \quad (7)$$

2.6   Parallel Composition of TIOLTS

Similarly, it is also useful to define parallel composition over TIOLTS. Given two TIOLTS L_1 and L_2, the corresponding parallel product is denoted $L_1 \| L_2$. $L_i = (S_i, s_0^i, \mathsf{Ac}_{in}^i \cup \mathsf{Ac}_{(3-i) \to i}, \mathsf{Ac}_{out}^i \cup \mathsf{Ac}_{i \to (3-i)}, T_d^i, T_t^i)$. The sets Ac_{in}^1, Ac_{out}^1, Ac_{in}^2, Ac_{out}^2, $\mathsf{Ac}_{1 \to 2}$ and $\mathsf{Ac}_{2 \to 1}$ are pairwise disjoint (as illustrated in Figure 1). The two TIOLTS synchronize on time delays and their common shared actions $\mathsf{Ac}_{1 \leftrightarrow 2} = \mathsf{Ac}_{1 \to 2} \cup \mathsf{Ac}_{\to 1}$. The parallel product of the two TIOLTS is $L_1 \| L_2 = (S, (s_0^1, s_0^2), \mathsf{Ac}_{in}, \mathsf{Ac}_{out}, T_d, T_t)$ such that

$$\mathsf{Ac}_{in} = \bigcup_{i=1,2} \mathsf{Ac}_{in}^i, \quad \mathsf{Ac}_{out} = \bigcup_{i=1,2} \mathsf{Ac}_{out}^i$$

and S, T_d and T_t are the smallest sets such that:

- $(s_0^1, s_0^2) \in S$;
- For $(s_1, s_2) \in S$ and $\delta \in \mathsf{R}$: $s_1 \xrightarrow{\delta} s_1' \in T_t^1 \wedge s_2 \xrightarrow{\delta} s_2' \in T_t^2$

$$\Rightarrow (s_1', s_2') \in S \wedge (s_1, s_2) \xrightarrow{\delta} (s_1', s_2') \in T_t; \quad (8)$$

- For $(s_1, s_2) \in S$ and $a \in \mathsf{Ac}_{in}^1 \cup \mathsf{Ac}_{out}^1 \cup \{\tau_1\}$:

$$s_1 \xrightarrow{a} s_1' \in T_d^1 \Rightarrow (s_1', s_2) \in S \wedge (s_1, s_2) \xrightarrow{a} (s_1', s_2) \in T_d; \quad (9)$$

- For $(s_1, s_2) \in S$ and $a \in \mathsf{Ac}_{in}^2 \cup \mathsf{Ac}_{out}^2 \cup \{\tau_2\}$:

$$s_2 \xrightarrow{a} s_2' \in T_d^2 \Rightarrow (s_1, s_2') \in S \wedge (s_1, s_2) \xrightarrow{a} (s_1, s_2') \in T_d; \quad (10)$$

- For $(s_1, s_2) \in S$ and $a \in \mathsf{Ac}_{1 \leftrightarrow 2}$: $s_1 \xrightarrow{a} s_1' \in T_d^1 \wedge s_2 \xrightarrow{a} s_2' \in T_d^2$

$$\Rightarrow (s_1', s_2') \in S \wedge (s_1, s_2) \xrightarrow{\tau_a} (s_1', s_2') \in T_d. \quad (11)$$

---

[1] We know that $d_2 = \mathsf{lazy}$ since a is an input w.r.t A_2.

It is not difficult to see that from each possible run λ of $L_1||L_2$ it is possible to extract two (unique) timed traces σ_1 and σ_2 of L_1 and L_2, respectively. For example for

$$\lambda = (s_0^1, s_0^2) \xrightarrow{1.5} (s,t) \xrightarrow{?a} (p,q) \xrightarrow{?b} (r,q) \xrightarrow{!c} (r,u)$$

we have $\sigma_1 = 1.5\,?a\,?b$ and $\sigma_2 = 1.5\,!a\,!c$, where $a \in \mathsf{Ac}_{2\to1}$, $b \in \mathsf{Ac}_{in}^1$ and $c \in \mathsf{Ac}_{out}^2$.

Conversely, two traces σ_1 and σ_2, respectively in $\mathsf{OTT}(L_1)$ and $\mathsf{OTT}(L_2)$, are said to be *synchronizable* in $L_1||L_2$ if there exists a run λ of $L_1||L_2$ from which the two traces can be extracted. In general, the run from which σ_1 and σ_2 can be extracted may not be unique, due to different possible interleavings . For instance, the two traces σ_1 and σ_2 given above can be also extracted from the run

$$\lambda' = (s_0^1, s_0^2) \xrightarrow{1.5} (s,t) \xrightarrow{?a} (p,q) \xrightarrow{!c} (p,u) \xrightarrow{?b} (r,u).$$

Let L_1' and L_2' be two new TIOLTS. For $i = 1, 2$, L_i' has the same sets of inputs and outputs as L_i. Moreover, L_1' and L_2' synchronize on the same set of actions $\mathsf{Ac}_{1\leftrightarrow2}$ as for L_1 and L_2. Let $\sigma_1 \in \mathsf{OTT}(L_1)\cap\mathsf{OTT}(L_1')$, $\sigma_2 \in \mathsf{OTT}(L_2)\cap\mathsf{OTT}(L_2')$, λ a run of $L_1||L_2$ and $\sigma \in \mathsf{OTT}(L_1||L_2)$ the observable timed trace corresponding to λ.

Lemma 1. *If σ_1 and σ_2 are the traces extracted from λ, then σ_1 and σ_2 are synchronizable in $L_1'||L_2'$ and $\sigma \in \mathsf{OTT}(L_1'||L_2')$.*

Let $A_1 = (Q_1, q_0^1, X_1, \mathsf{Ac}_{in}^1 \cup \mathsf{Ac}_{2\to1}, \mathsf{Ac}_{out}^1 \cup \mathsf{Ac}_{1\to2}, E_1)$ and $A_2 = (Q_2, q_0^2, X_2, , \mathsf{Ac}_{in}^2 \cup \mathsf{Ac}_{1\to2}, \mathsf{Ac}_{out}^2 \cup \mathsf{Ac}_{2\to1}, E_2)$ be two TAIO. Then we have the following.

Proposition 2. *If (A_1, A_2) is compatible w.r.t $(\mathsf{Ac}_{1\to2}, \mathsf{Ac}_{2\to1})$ then*

$$L_{A_1||A_2} = L_{A_1}||L_{A_2}.$$

3   Timed Input-Output Conformance: **tioco**

We assume that the specification of the SUT is given as a non-blocking TAIO A_S and that the SUT can be modeled as a non-blocking, input-complete TAIO A_I.[2]

3.1   Definition

Given a TAIO A and $\sigma \in \mathsf{RT}(\mathsf{Ac})$, A after σ is the set of all states of A that can be reached by some timed sequence ρ whose projection to observable actions is σ. Formally:

$$A \text{ after } \sigma = \{s \in S_A \mid \exists \rho \in \mathsf{RT}(\mathsf{Ac}_\tau) \,.\, s_0^A \xrightarrow{\rho} s \wedge P_{\mathsf{Ac}}(\rho) = \sigma\}. \tag{12}$$

Given state $s \in S_A$, $\mathsf{elapse}(s)$ is the set of all delays which can elapse from s without A making any observable action. Formally:

---

[2] We do not assume that A_I is known, simply that it exists.

$$\mathsf{elapse}(s) = \{t > 0 \mid \exists \rho \in \mathsf{RT}(\{\tau\}) \; . \; \mathsf{time}(\rho) = t \wedge s \xrightarrow{\rho}\}. \tag{13}$$

Given state $s \in S_A$, $\mathsf{out}(s)$ is the set of all observable "events" (outputs or the passage of time) that can occur when the system is at state s. The definition naturally extends to a set of states S. Formally:

$$\mathsf{out}(s) = \{a \in \mathsf{Ac_{out}} \mid s \xrightarrow{a}\} \cup \mathsf{elapse}(s), \quad \mathsf{out}(S) = \bigcup_{s \in S} \mathsf{out}(s). \tag{14}$$

The *timed input-output conformance relation*, tioco, is defined as

$$A_I \; \mathsf{tioco} \; A_S \equiv \forall \sigma \in \mathsf{OTT}(A_S) \; . \; \mathsf{out}(A_I \; \mathsf{after} \; \sigma) \subseteq \mathsf{out}(A_S \; \mathsf{after} \; \sigma). \tag{15}$$

We proceed in giving a number of properties of tioco. The first states that specifications that have the same set of observable timed traces are *equivalent* w.r.t tioco, in other words, they specify the same requirements.

Lemma 3. *Given two TAIO A_S and A'_S, if $\mathsf{OTT}(A_S) = \mathsf{OTT}(A'_S)$ then*

$$\forall A_I \cdot A_I \; \mathsf{tioco} \; A_S \Leftrightarrow A_I \; \mathsf{tioco} \; A'_S \; .$$

Proof. Let $\sigma \in \mathsf{OTT}(A_S) = \mathsf{OTT}(A'_S)$. We claim that $\mathsf{out}(A_S \; \mathsf{after} \; \sigma) = \mathsf{out}(A'_S \; \mathsf{after} \; \sigma)$. Indeed for any $a \in \mathsf{Ac_{out}} \cup \mathsf{R}$, $a \in \mathsf{out}(A_S \; \mathsf{after} \; \sigma) \backslash \mathsf{out}(A'_S \; \mathsf{after} \; \sigma)$ implies $\sigma a \in \mathsf{OTT}(A_S) \setminus \mathsf{OTT}(A'_S)$ which contradicts the hypothesis. Thus, for any implementation A_I, $\mathsf{out}(A_I \; \mathsf{after} \; \sigma) \subseteq \mathsf{out}(A_S \; \mathsf{after} \; \sigma)$ iff $\mathsf{out}(A_I \; \mathsf{after} \; \sigma) \subseteq \mathsf{out}(A'_S \; \mathsf{after} \; \sigma)$, and the result follows by definition of tioco. $\qquad\square$

The next lemma relates tioco to observable timed trace inclusion.

Lemma 4. *Consider two TAIO A and B.*

1. *$\mathsf{OTT}(A) \subseteq \mathsf{OTT}(B)$ implies $A \; \mathsf{tioco} \; B$.*
2. *If B is input-complete then $A \; \mathsf{tioco} \; B$ implies $\mathsf{OTT}(A) \subseteq \mathsf{OTT}(B)$.*

Proof. 1. Let $\sigma \in \mathsf{OTT}(B)$ and $a \in \mathsf{out}(A \; \mathsf{after} \; \sigma)$. $a \in \mathsf{out}(A \; \mathsf{after} \; \sigma)$ implies $\sigma a \in \mathsf{OTT}(A)$. Since $\mathsf{OTT}(A) \subseteq \mathsf{OTT}(B)$, $\sigma a \in \mathsf{OTT}(B)$. Thus, $a \in \mathsf{out}(B \; \mathsf{after} \; \sigma)$, or $\mathsf{out}(A \; \mathsf{after} \; \sigma) \subseteq \mathsf{out}(B \; \mathsf{after} \; \sigma)$. The result follows by definition of tioco.

2. Suppose there exists $\sigma \in \mathsf{OTT}(A) \setminus \mathsf{OTT}(B)$. Thus, there exist $\sigma_1, \sigma_2 \in \mathsf{RT}(\mathsf{Ac})$ and $a \in \mathsf{Ac} \cup \mathsf{R}$, such that $\sigma = \sigma_1 a \sigma_2$, $\sigma_1 \in \mathsf{OTT}(B)$ and $\sigma_1 a \notin \mathsf{OTT}(B)$. If $a \in \mathsf{Ac_{in}}$ then $\sigma_1 a \notin \mathsf{OTT}(B)$ is a contradiction since $\sigma_1 \in \mathsf{OTT}(B)$ and B is input-complete. If $a \in \mathsf{Ac_{out}} \cup \mathsf{R}$ then we have again a contradiction, since $\sigma_1 \in \mathsf{OTT}(B)$, $a \in \mathsf{out}(A \; \mathsf{after} \; \sigma_1)$ and $A \; \mathsf{tioco} \; B$. $\qquad\square$

3.2 Only lazy Inputs Are Needed in Specifications

In this section, we show that considering only *lazy-input* TAIO is enough for describing all possible (non-blocking) specifications. A lazy-input TAIO is one where every edge labeled with $a \in \mathsf{Ac_{in}}$ has deadline lazy. Given a TAIO A, let $\mathsf{Lazy}(A)$ be the TAIO obtained by setting the deadline of every edge of A labeled with input to lazy.

Lemma 5. *For any non-blocking TAIO A,* $\mathsf{OTT}(A) = \mathsf{OTT}(\mathsf{Lazy}(A))$.

Proof. It should be clear that $\mathsf{OTT}(A) \subseteq \mathsf{OTT}(\mathsf{Lazy}(A))$, since $\mathsf{Lazy}(A)$ is at least as "permissive" as A (i.e., every transition in the TLTS defined by A is also a transition of the TLTS defined by $\mathsf{Lazy}(A)$). It remains to prove that $\mathsf{OTT}(\mathsf{Lazy}(A)) \subseteq \mathsf{OTT}(A)$. Suppose there exists $\sigma \in \mathsf{OTT}(\mathsf{Lazy}(A)) \setminus \mathsf{OTT}(A)$. Let $s_0 \xrightarrow{\sigma_1} s_1 \cdots \xrightarrow{\sigma_N} s_N$ a possible run of $\mathsf{Lazy}(A)$ corresponding to the trace σ. Since $\sigma \notin \mathsf{OTT}(A)$, there must exist some $k \leq N$ such that $s_0 \xrightarrow{\sigma_1} s_1 \cdots \xrightarrow{\sigma_{k-1}} s_{k-1}$ is a possible run in A and $s_{k-1} \not\xrightarrow{\sigma_k}$ in A. Let q and v be the location and the clock valuation, respectively, such that $s_{k-1} = (q, v)$. Depending on the value of σ_k, two cases are possible:

- $\sigma_k \in \mathsf{Ac}_\tau$: By construction, location q has outgoing edges which are labeled with the same actions and have the same deadlines and clocks to reset, both in A and $\mathsf{Lazy}(A)$. Thus for the same valuation v, the discrete transition $s_{k-1} = (q, v) \xrightarrow{\sigma_k} s_k$, possible in $\mathsf{Lazy}(A)$, is also possible in A. Contradiction.
- $\sigma_k \in \mathsf{R}$: The fact that $s_{k-1} \not\xrightarrow{\sigma_k}$, in A, means that there is some delayable or eager outgoing edge e from q which prevents the delay σ_k from elapsing. e cannot be labeled with τ or an output action, since then it would block time in $\mathsf{Lazy}(A)$ as well. Thus, e is labeled with an input action. This implies that at state s_{k-1} time is blocked unless this input action is received, which contradicts the hypothesis that A is non-blocking. □

From Lemma 3 and Lemma 5, we obtain the following.

Proposition 6. *For any non-blocking TAIO A_S,*

$$\forall A_I \cdot A_I \text{ tioco } A_S \Leftrightarrow A_I \text{ tioco } \mathsf{Lazy}(A_S).$$

3.3   Making Specifications Input-Complete

A deterministic (and fully observable) specification can be made input-complete without changing its conformance semantics by adding edges covering the missing inputs and leading to a "don't care" location where all inputs and outputs are accepted. More precisely, this transformation is done as follows. Given a TAIO $A = (Q, q_0, X, \mathsf{Ac}, E)$, we build the corresponding input-complete TAIO $\tilde{A} = (\tilde{Q}, q_0, X, \mathsf{Ac}, \tilde{E})$. First, $\tilde{Q} = Q \cup \{q_{dc}\}$ where $q_{dc} \notin Q$ is the "don't care" location. Second,

$$\tilde{E} = E \cup \{(q_{dc}, q_{dc}, \mathsf{true}, \emptyset, \mathsf{lazy}, a) \mid a \in \mathsf{Ac}\} \cup$$
$$\{(q, q_{dc}, \neg\psi, \emptyset, \mathsf{lazy}, a) \mid q \in Q \wedge a \in \mathsf{Ac_{in}}\}$$

such that for each $q \in Q$ and each $a \in \mathsf{Ac_{in}}$, $\psi = \psi_1 \vee \psi_2 \vee \cdots \vee \psi_k$ where ψ_1, ψ_2, ... , ψ_k are the guards of the outgoing edges of q labeled with a. An example showing how this transformation works is given in Figure 2. We transform A to $\tilde{A}$. The TAIO A has only one input (a) and one output (b). The added edges are the dashed ones.

Let A_S be a deterministic and fully observable TAIO and let $\tilde{A}_S$ be the input-complete TAIO corresponding to A_S obtained by the transformation given above.

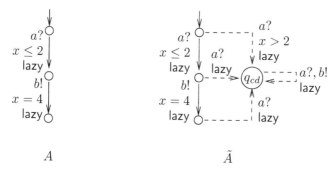

$$A \qquad\qquad \widetilde{A}$$

Fig. 2. How to transform a deterministic, fully-observable, but not input-complete specification to an equivalent input-complete specification

Proposition 7. *For any input-complete TAIO A_I, A_I tioco A_S if and only if A_I tioco $\widetilde{A}_S$.*

The proof of the above proposition is based on the following two lemmata.

Lemma 8. $\mathsf{OTT}(A_S) \subseteq \mathsf{OTT}(\widetilde{A}_S)$.

Lemma 9. *Let $\sigma \in \mathsf{OTT}(\widetilde{A}_S)$. If $\sigma \in \mathsf{OTT}(A_S)$ then $\mathsf{out}(A_S$ after $\sigma) = \mathsf{out}(\widetilde{A}_S$ after $\sigma)$. Otherwise, $\mathsf{out}(A_S$ after $\sigma) \subseteq \mathsf{out}(\widetilde{A}_S$ after $\sigma) = \mathsf{R} \cup \mathsf{Ac_{out}}$.*

Proof (of Proposition 7).

($\Rightarrow$) We assume that A_I tioco A_S and we prove that A_I tioco $\widetilde{A}_S$. So let $\sigma \in \mathsf{OTT}(\widetilde{A}_S)$. If $\sigma \in \mathsf{OTT}(A_S)$ then by Lemma 9 we have $\mathsf{out}(A_S$ after $\sigma) = \mathsf{out}(\widetilde{A}_S$ after $\sigma)$. Moreover since A_I tioco A_S we have $\mathsf{out}(A_I$ after $\sigma) \subseteq \mathsf{out}(A_S$ after $\sigma)$. So $\mathsf{out}(A_I$ after $\sigma) \subseteq \mathsf{out}(\widetilde{A}_S$ after $\sigma)$ and we are done. If $\sigma \notin \mathsf{OTT}(A_S)$, by Lemma 9 we have $\mathsf{out}(\widetilde{A}_S$ after $\sigma) = \mathsf{R} \cup \mathsf{Ac_{out}}$. Thus, we clearly have $\mathsf{out}(A_I$ after $\sigma) \subseteq \mathsf{out}(\widetilde{A}_S$ after $\sigma)$ and we are done once again.

($\Leftarrow$) We assume that A_I tioco $\widetilde{A}_S$ and we prove that A_I tioco A_S. Let $\sigma \in \mathsf{OTT}(A_S)$. By Lemma 8, we have $\sigma \in \mathsf{OTT}(\widetilde{A}_S)$. By Lemma 9, $\mathsf{out}(A_S$ after $\sigma) = \mathsf{out}(\widetilde{A}_S$ after $\sigma)$. Moreover, $\mathsf{out}(A_I$ after $\sigma) \subseteq \mathsf{out}(\widetilde{A}_S$ after $\sigma)$ since A_I tioco $\widetilde{A}_S$ and $\sigma \in \mathsf{OTT}(\widetilde{A}_S)$. Thus, $\mathsf{out}(A_I$ after $\sigma) \subseteq \mathsf{out}(A_S$ after $\sigma)$ and we are done.   □

Combined with Lemma 4, Proposition 7 implies that for deterministic and fully-observable specifications, tioco can be replaced by timed trace inclusion, modulo the above input-completing transformation. However, this transformation is not correct for non-deterministic or partially observable specifications. A counter-example is given in Figure 3. The specification A_S has one input (a) and two outputs (b and c). The implementation A_I is input-complete. [3] We have A_I tioco $\widetilde{A}_S$ but A_I ~~tioco~~ A_S.

---

[3] We omit self-loops labeled with a in order not to overload the figure.

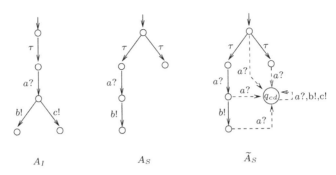

Fig. 3. An example showing that the transformation of Figure 2 is incorrect for non-deterministic or partially-observable specifications

Also note that the determinization of TAIO is undecidable in general [8]. Hence, reducing tioco to timed trace inclusion is not always possible and a specific framework for checking conformance w.r.t tioco needs to be established for non-deterministic or partially-observable specifications.

3.4 Transitivity

Next we show that tioco is a transitive relation, given the usual assumption that implementations are input-complete.

Proposition 10. *Let A, B and C be three TAIO such that A and B are input-complete, If A tioco B and B tioco C then A tioco C.*

Proof. Let $\sigma \in \mathsf{OTT}(C)$. Two cases are possible:

- $\sigma \in \mathsf{OTT}(B)$. From A tioco B and B tioco C, we obtain out$(A$ after $\sigma) \subseteq$ out$(B$ after $\sigma)$ and out$(B$ after $\sigma) \subseteq$ out$(C$ after $\sigma)$. Thus, out$(A$ after $\sigma) \subseteq$ out$(C$ after $\sigma)$.
- $\sigma \notin \mathsf{OTT}(B)$. By part 2 of Lemma 4, input-completeness of B and A tioco B, we get $\sigma \notin \mathsf{OTT}(A)$. Thus, out$(A$ after $\sigma) = \emptyset \subseteq$ out$(C$ after $\sigma)$.

The result follows by definition of tioco.   □

3.5 Undecidability

Proposition 11. *Checking* tioco *is undecidable.*

Proof. We reduce the timed trace inclusion problem for timed automata which is known to be undecidable [1] to the problem of checking tioco. Let A and B be two TA over the set of actions Ac. The timed trace inclusion problem consists in checking whether $\mathsf{OTT}(A) \subseteq \mathsf{OTT}(B)$. Let $\mathsf{Ac_{out}} = \mathsf{Ac}$, i.e., $\mathsf{Ac_{in}} = \emptyset$. Then, both A and B are input-complete. By part 2 of Lemma 4, $\mathsf{OTT}(A) \subseteq \mathsf{OTT}(B)$ iff A tioco B.   □

It is worth noting that the undecidability of tioco is not a problem for black-box testing: since the implementation A_I is unknown, we cannot check conformance directly, anyway.

3.6   Compositionality

Let A_1, A_1', A_2 and A_2' be four TAIO such that, for $i = 1, 2$, A_i and A_i' have the same sets of inputs and outputs, as shown in Figure 1. Suppose that all four automata are input-complete w.r.t their respective sets of inputs. Furthermore, suppose that A_1 and A_2 are compatible w.r.t $(\mathsf{Ac}_{1\to2}, \mathsf{Ac}_{2\to1})$, and so are A_1' and A_2'. Then, we have the following compositionality result.

Proposition 12. *If A_1' tioco A_1 and A_2' tioco A_2 then*

$$A_1' \| A_2' \text{ tioco } A_1 \| A_2.$$

Proof. Observe that both $A_1 \| A_2$ and $A_1' \| A_2'$ have the same set of inputs $\mathsf{Ac_{in}} = \mathsf{Ac_{in}^1} \cup \mathsf{Ac_{in}^2}$ and set of outputs $\mathsf{Ac_{out}} = \mathsf{Ac_{out}^1} \cup \mathsf{Ac_{out}^2}$.

– We first prove that $A_1 \| A_2$ is input-complete w.r.t $\mathsf{Ac_{in}^1} \cup \mathsf{Ac_{in}^2}$. A state s of $A_1 \| A_2$ is a pair (s_1, s_2) where s_i is a state of A_i for $i = 1, 2$. By assumption, each A_i is input-complete w.r.t $\mathsf{Ac_{in}^i}$. Thus for each $a \in \mathsf{Ac_{in}^i}$, $s_i \xrightarrow{a}$. By (4) and (5), for each $a \in \mathsf{Ac_{in}^1} \cup \mathsf{Ac_{in}^2}$, $s \xrightarrow{a}$.
– By the same reasoning, $A_1' \| A_2'$ is input-complete w.r.t $\mathsf{Ac_{in}^1} \cup \mathsf{Ac_{in}^2}$.
– Now, we show that $A_1' \| A_2'$ tioco $A_1 \| A_2$. By Lemma 4, it suffices to prove that $\mathsf{OTT}(A_1' \| A_2') \subseteq \mathsf{OTT}(A_1 \| A_2)$. Let $\mathsf{Ac} = \mathsf{Ac_{in}} \cup \mathsf{Ac_{out}}$, $\mathsf{Ac}_{1\to2} = \mathsf{Ac}_{1\to2} \cup \mathsf{Ac}_{2\to1}$ and $\sigma \in \mathsf{OTT}(A_1' \| A_2')$. Since $\mathsf{Ac}_{1\to2} \cup \{\tau\}$ are internal unobservable actions of $A_1' \| A_2'$, there exists $\gamma \in \mathsf{TTr}(A_1' \| A_2')$ such that $P_{\mathsf{R} \cup \mathsf{Ac}}(\gamma) = \sigma$. For $i = 1, 2$, let $\mathsf{Ac}_i = (\mathsf{Ac_{in}^i} \cup \mathsf{Ac_{out}^i} \cup \mathsf{Ac}_{1\to2})$ (i.e., the observable actions of A_i) and $\sigma_i = P_{\mathsf{R} \cup \mathsf{Ac}_i}(\gamma)$. Then $\sigma_i \in \mathsf{OTT}(A_i')$. By part 2 of Lemma 4, input-completeness of A_i and A_i' and the assumption A_i' tioco A_i, we get $\sigma_i \in \mathsf{OTT}(A_i)$. By Lemma 1, σ_1 and σ_2 are synchronizable in $A_1 \| A_2$ and $\sigma \in \mathsf{OTT}(A_1 \| A_2)$.   □

Note that the above result does not generally hold for the case of non input-complete TAIO. A counter-example is given in Figure 4. We consider four TAIO A_1, A_2, A_1' and A_2'. TAIO A_2 and A_2' are the same. The action a (dashed arrows in the figure) is shared between A_1 and A_2, as well as between A_1' and A_2'. That is, $\mathsf{Ac_{in}^1} = \{c\}$, $\mathsf{Ac_{out}^1} = \{d, e\}$, $\mathsf{Ac}_{2\to1} = \{a\}$ and $\mathsf{Ac_{in}^2} = \mathsf{Ac_{out}^2} = \mathsf{Ac}_{1\to2} = \emptyset$. The two TAIO A_1 and A_1' are input-complete w.r.t $\{a\}$. A_1 is not input-complete w.r.t $\{c\}$. The guards of the transitions of all the automata are equal to true with deadline lazy. We clearly have A_2' tioco A_2 since $A_2' = A_2$. It is also not difficult to see that A_1' tioco A_1. The figure also shows the two product automata $A_1 \| A_2$ and $A_1' \| A_2'$. After receiving input c, $A_1' \| A_2'$ may generate either output d or e while $A_1 \| A_2$ may generate only d. Thus, $A_1' \| A_2' \text{ } \overline{\text{tioco}} \text{ } A_1 \| A_2$.

3.7   Decreasing the Number of Observable Actions

Given a TAIO A and an observable action $a \in \mathsf{Ac}$, we denote by $A_{[\tau/a]}$ the TAIO obtained from A by replacing action a, anywhere it appears, by τ. We have the following result.

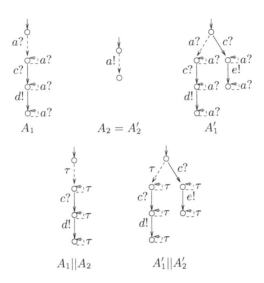

Fig. 4. A counter example showing that tioco is not compositional for the case of non-input-complete TAIO

Proposition 13. *Given two input-complete TAIO A and A′ and an observable action $a \in$ Ac, if A′ tioco A then $A'_{[\tau/a]}$ tioco $A_{[\tau/a]}$.*

The above result is not valid for non-input-complete TAIO, in general. We use the counter-example of Figure 4. We consider the two TAIO A_1 and A'_1. As already mentioned, A'_1 tioco A_1. It is easy to see that $A_{1[\tau/a]} = A_1 \| A_2$ and $A'_{1[\tau/a]} = A'_1 \| A'_2$. So, clearly $A'_{1[\tau/a]}$ ~~tioco~~ $A_{1[\tau/a]}$.

4   Comparison with Other Conformance Relations

4.1   The Relativized Timed Conformance Relation

In [4], the *relativized timed conformation relation*, rtioco, is defined. It is "relativized" in the sense that it compares the implementation $\mathcal{I}$ and the specification $\mathcal{S}$ w.r.t some given environment $\mathcal{E}$. Both $\mathcal{S}$, $\mathcal{I}$ and $\mathcal{E}$ are given as TIOLTS. $\mathcal{S}$ and $\mathcal{I}$ are assumed to be input-complete w.r.t $\mathsf{Ac_{in}}$; and $\mathcal{E}$ input-complete w.r.t $\mathsf{Ac_{out}}$. $\mathcal{S}$, $\mathcal{I}$ and $\mathcal{E}$ are also non-blocking. For comparing $\mathcal{S}$ and $\mathcal{I}$, the first step consists in making the parallel composition of each of them with $\mathcal{E}$. The used parallel composition is slightly distinct from the one we propose. To avoid confusion, we denote it $\|_r$. What is new with $\|_r$ is that it does not hide the actions on which the two TIOLTS synchronize (i.e., in (11) the action a remain observable after synchronization). Moreover, $\|_r$ is defined in a way such that $\mathsf{OTT}(\mathcal{S} \|_r \mathcal{E}) = \mathsf{OTT}(\mathcal{S}) \cap \mathsf{OTT}(\mathcal{E})$. The formal definition of rtioco w.r.t $\mathcal{E}$ is given by the following

$$\mathcal{I} \text{ rtioco}_{\mathcal{E}} \mathcal{S} \text{ iff } \forall \sigma \in \mathsf{OTT}(\mathcal{E}) \cdot \mathsf{out}((\mathcal{I} \|_r \mathcal{E}) \text{ after } \sigma) \subseteq \mathsf{out}((\mathcal{S} \|_r \mathcal{E}) \text{ after } \sigma).$$

Proposition 14. *Let $\mathcal{S}$ and $\mathcal{I}$ be two input-complete and non-blocking TLTS. Furthermore, let $\mathcal{E}$ be an environment of $\mathcal{S}$ given as an input-complete and non-blocking LTS. Then we have*

$$\mathcal{I} \text{ rtioco}_{\mathcal{E}} \mathcal{S} \;\Leftrightarrow\; (\mathcal{I} \,\|_r\, \mathcal{E}) \,\text{tioco}\, (\mathcal{S} \,\|_r\, \mathcal{E}).$$

Proof. $(\Rightarrow)$ Let $\sigma \in \text{OTT}(\mathcal{S} \,\|_r\, \mathcal{E})$. Since $\text{OTT}(\mathcal{S} \,\|_r\, \mathcal{E}) = \text{OTT}(\mathcal{S}) \cap \text{OTT}(\mathcal{E})$, $\sigma \in \text{OTT}(\mathcal{E})$. Since $\mathcal{I} \text{ rtioco}_{\mathcal{E}} \mathcal{S}$, $\text{out}((\mathcal{I} \,\|_r\, \mathcal{E}) \text{ after } \sigma) \subseteq \text{out}((\mathcal{I} \,\|_r\, \mathcal{E}) \text{ after } \sigma)$.
$(\Leftarrow)$ Let $\sigma \in \text{OTT}(\mathcal{E})$. Two cases are possible:

- $\sigma \in \text{OTT}(\mathcal{S})$. Since $\text{OTT}(\mathcal{S} \,\|_r\, \mathcal{E}) = \text{OTT}(\mathcal{S}) \cap \text{OTT}(\mathcal{E})$, $\sigma \in \text{OTT}(\mathcal{S} \,\|_r\, \mathcal{E})$ too. Thus, $\text{out}((\mathcal{I} \,\|_r\, \mathcal{E}) \text{ after } \sigma) \subseteq \text{out}((\mathcal{I} \,\|_r\, \mathcal{E}) \text{ after } \sigma)$ since $(\mathcal{I} \,\|_r\, \mathcal{E}) \text{ tioco } (\mathcal{S} \,\|_r\, \mathcal{E})$.

- $\sigma \notin \text{OTT}(\mathcal{S})$. Thus there exist $\sigma' \in \text{RT}(\text{Ac})$ and $b \in \text{R} \cup \text{Ac}$ such that: $\sigma'b$ is a prefix of σ, $\sigma' \in \text{OTT}(\mathcal{S})$ and $\sigma'b \notin \text{OTT}(\mathcal{S})$. Since $\mathcal{S}$ is input-complete we deduce that $b \in \text{R} \cup \text{Ac}_{\text{out}}$. Since $(\mathcal{I} \,\|_r\, \mathcal{E}) \text{ tioco } (\mathcal{S} \,\|_r\, \mathcal{E})$, $\sigma' \in \text{OTT}(\mathcal{E}) \cap \text{OTT}(\mathcal{S})$ and $b \notin \text{out}((\mathcal{S} \,\|_r\, \mathcal{E}) \text{ after } \sigma')$, we deduce that $b \notin \text{out}((\mathcal{I} \,\|_r\, \mathcal{E}) \text{ after } \sigma')$ either. The latter means that $\sigma'b \notin \text{OTT}(\mathcal{I})$ which, in turn, means that $\sigma \notin \text{OTT}(\mathcal{I})$ either. So, $\text{out}((\mathcal{I} \,\|_r\, \mathcal{E}) \text{ after } \sigma) = \text{out}((\mathcal{S} \,\|_r\, \mathcal{E}) \text{ after } \sigma) = \emptyset$ and we are done. $\qquad\square$

For the (universal) environment $\mathcal{E}_u$ such that $\text{OTT}(\mathcal{E}_u) = (\text{R} \cup \text{Ac})^*$, we clearly have $\mathcal{S} \,\|_r\, \mathcal{E}_u = \mathcal{S}$ and $\mathcal{I} \,\|_r\, \mathcal{E}_u = \mathcal{I}$. By Proposition 14, we have $\mathcal{I} \text{ rtioco}_{\mathcal{E}_u} \mathcal{S}$ iff $\mathcal{I} \text{ tioco } \mathcal{S}$. That is, tioco and $\text{rtioco}_{\mathcal{E}_u}$ are equivalent.

4.2 The Conformance Relation $\sqsubseteq_{tioco}$

An other conformance relation, $\sqsubseteq_{tioco}$, is introduced in [3]. The main goal of this work is to propose a testing framework which extends the notion of quiescence to the case of timed systems. $\sqsubseteq_{tioco}$ bears a lot of similarity with tioco. It is defined w.r.t TIOLTS. The considered TLTS are assumed to be non-blocking and input-complete. Given two TLTS $\mathcal{S}$ the specification and $\mathcal{I}$ the implementation, the first step for comparing $\mathcal{S}$ and $\mathcal{I}$ consists in identifying the *quiescent* states of both of them. A given state s of $\mathcal{S}$ is said to be quiescent if $\forall t \in \text{R} \cdot \text{out}(s \text{ after } t) = \text{R}$ (i.e., from s no discrete output can be generated if no input is received). For each detected quiescent state s, a self loop $s \xrightarrow{\delta} s$ is added to the TLTS. The obtained TLTS are denoted $\Delta(\mathcal{S})$ and $\Delta(\mathcal{I})$. $\sqsubseteq_{tioco}$ is defined w.r.t an arbitrary duration M. We let $\text{OTT}_M(\mathcal{S}) = \text{OTT}(\Delta(\mathcal{S})) \cap (\text{R} \cdot (\text{Ac} \cup \{M\delta\}))^*$. Given a state s and a set of states S, we let

$$\text{out}_M(s) = \{tb \in \text{R} \cdot \text{Ac}_{\text{in}} \mid s \xrightarrow{tb}\} \cup \{M\delta \mid s \xrightarrow{M\delta}\}; \quad \text{out}_M(S) = \bigcup_{s \in S} \text{out}_M(s).$$

The relation $\sqsubseteq_{tioco}$ w.r.t M, denoted $\sqsubseteq^M_{tioco}$, is defined as follows

$$\mathcal{I} \sqsubseteq^M_{tioco} \mathcal{S} \text{ iff } \forall \sigma \in \text{OTT}_M(\mathcal{S}) \cdot \text{out}_M(\Delta(\mathcal{I}) \text{after} \sigma) \subseteq \text{out}_M(\Delta(\mathcal{S}) \text{after} \sigma).$$

$\sqsubseteq_{tioco}$ and tioco are not identical. We consider the example given in Figure 5. For simplicity, both $\mathcal{S}$, $\mathcal{I}$, $\Delta(\mathcal{S})$ and $\Delta(\mathcal{I})$ are given as TAIO. It is easy to see

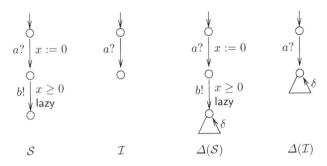

Fig. 5. A counter example showing that $\sqsubseteq_{tioco}$ and tioco are not identical

that $\mathcal{I}$ tioco $\mathcal{S}$. However for any M, we have $\mathcal{I} \not\sqsubseteq_{tioco}^M \mathcal{S}$, since $\Delta(\mathcal{I})$ produces δ after receiving a while $\Delta(\mathcal{S})$ does not.

Now, we check the other direction.

We first introduce the following intermediary result.

Lemma 15. *Let $\mathcal{S}$ be a non-blocking TLTS and S a set of states of $\mathcal{S}$.*

1. *For $b \in \mathsf{Ac_{out}}$: $b \in \mathsf{out}(S) \Leftrightarrow 0b \in \mathsf{out}_M(S)$.*
2. *For $t \in \mathsf{R}$: $t \in \mathsf{out}(S) \Leftrightarrow M\delta \in \mathsf{out}_M(S)$ or $\exists t'b \in \mathsf{out}_M(S) \cap \mathsf{R} \cdot \mathsf{Ac_{out}}$ such that $t \leq t'$.*

Proposition 16. *Given two non-blocking and input-complete TLTS $\mathcal{S}$ and $\mathcal{I}$ and a duration M. If $\mathcal{I} \sqsubseteq_{tioco}^M \mathcal{S}$ then $\mathcal{I}$ tioco $\mathcal{S}$.*

Proof. Let $\sigma \in \mathsf{OTT}(\mathcal{S})$. Since $\mathsf{OTT}(\mathcal{S}) \subseteq \mathsf{OTT}_M(\mathcal{S})$ then $\sigma \in \mathsf{OTT}_M(\mathcal{S})$ too. By the definition of $\Delta(\mathcal{S})$, it is not difficult to see that $\mathcal{S}$ after $\sigma = \Delta(\mathcal{S})$ after σ. Similarly, we have $\mathcal{I}$ after $\sigma = \Delta(\mathcal{I})$ after σ, as well. Let $b \in \mathsf{out}(\mathcal{I}$ after $\sigma)$. Two cases are possible then. Either $b \in \mathsf{Ac_{out}}$ or $b \in \mathsf{R}$.

- For $b \in \mathsf{Ac_{out}}$: By Lemma 15, we know that $0b \in \mathsf{out}_M(\Delta(\mathcal{I})$ after $\sigma)$. Moreover, since $\mathcal{I} \sqsubseteq_{tioco}^M \mathcal{S}$ then $0b \in \mathsf{out}_M(\Delta(\mathcal{S})$ after $\sigma)$, too . Then once again by Lemma 15, we have $b \in \mathsf{out}(\mathcal{S}$ after $\sigma)$ and we are done.
- For $b \in \mathsf{R}$: Quite similar to the previous case. $\square$

5   Summary

In this work, we gave a more detailed description of the class of timed systems we consider in our testing framework. We showed that considering only lazy-input TAIO is enough for describing all possible non-blocking specifications. We made a comparison between tioco and the trace-inclusion relation. We proved that tioco is undecidable and that it does not distinguish specifications with the same set of observable traces. We also proved that tioco is transitive and stable w.r.t compositionality and action hiding for input-complete sepcifications. We compared between tioco and the two relations rtioco [4] and $\sqsubseteq_{tioco}$ [3] as well.

References

1. R. Alur and D. Dill. A theory of timed automata. *Theoretical Computer Science*, 126:183–235, 1994.
2. S. Bornot, J. Sifakis, and S. Tripakis. Modeling urgency in timed systems. In *Compositionality*, volume 1536 of *LNCS*. Springer, 1998.
3. L. Briones and E. Brinksma. A test generation framework for quiescent real-time systems. In *FATES'04*, volume 3395 of *LNCS*. Springer, 2004.
4. A. Hessel, K. Larsen, B. Nielsen, P. Pettersson, and A. Skou. Time-optimal real-time test case generation using UPPAAL. In *FATES'03*, 2003.
5. M. Krichen and S. Tripakis. Black-box conformance testing for real-time systems. In *11th International SPIN Workshop on Model Checking of Software (SPIN'04)*, volume 2989 of *LNCS*. Springer, 2004.
6. J. Sifakis and S. Yovine. Compositional specification of timed systems. In *13th Annual Symposium on Theoretical Aspects of Computer Science, STACS'96*, volume 1046 of *LNCS*. Spinger-Verlag, 1996.
7. J. Tretmans. Testing concurrent systems: A formal approach. In *CONCUR'99*, volume 1664 of *LNCS*. Springer, 1999.
8. S. Tripakis. Folk theorems on the determinization and minimization of timed automata. In *Formal Modeling and Analysis of Timed Systems (FORMATS'03)*, volume 2791 of *LNCS*. Springer, 2004.

Model Checking Duration Calculus: A Practical Approach[*]

Roland Meyer[1], Johannes Faber[1], and Andrey Rybalchenko[2,3]

[1] Carl-von-Ossietzky-Universität Oldenburg
[2] Ecole Polytechnique Fédérale de Lausanne
[3] Max-Planck-Institut Informatik Saarbrücken

Abstract. Model checking of real-time systems with respect to Duration Calculus (DC) specifications requires the translation of DC formulae into automata-based semantics. This task is difficult to automate. The existing algorithms provide a limited DC coverage and do not support compositional verification. We propose a translation algorithm that advances the applicability of model checking tools to real world applications. Our algorithm significantly extends the subset of DC that can be handled. It decomposes DC specifications into sub-properties that can be verified independently. The decomposition bases on a novel distributive law for DC. We implemented the algorithm as part of our tool chain for the automated verification of systems comprising data, communication, and real-time aspects. Our translation facilitated a successful application of the tool chain on an industrial case study from the European Train Control System (ETCS).

1 Introduction

Verification of embedded hardware and software systems requires reasoning about data, communication, and real-time aspects. Duration Calculus (DC) represents these dimensions in one formalism. As a fundamental concept, it offers the use of data variables with possibly infinite data domains that are interpreted over dense real-time intervals.

To apply the automata theoretic approach of Vardi and Wolper [VW86] for model checking DC, we need to translate DC formulae into automata. This is a difficult task and it has been shown in [ZHS93] that it cannot be solved in general. Translation algorithms into automata-based semantics are known for restricted classes of DC only [Rav94, BLR95, Pan02, Frä04]. But they are not compositional and consider neither infinite data domains nor communication.

We identify a new class of DC formulae, called test formulae, that can be translated into automata, also referred to as test automata in this paper. Test

---

[*] This work was partly supported by the German Research Council (DFG) as part of the Transregional Collaborative Research Center "Automatic Verification and Analysis of Complex Systems" (SFB/TR 14 AVACS) and the Graduate School "TrustSoft" (GRK 1076/1). See http://www.avacs.org and http://www.trustsoft.org.

K. Barkaoui, A. Cavalcanti, and A. Cerone (Eds.): ICTAC 2006, LNCS 4281, pp. 332–346, 2006.

formulae (1) significantly extend the previously known classes and (2) take communication aspects and infinite data domains into account. Our expressiveness results suggest that the new class is among the richest for which satisfiability with respect to an automaton is decidable under a dense time interpretation.

Translations of DC suffer from an exponential blow up of the resulting automata in the number of operators. To overcome this problem, we provide an algorithm that decomposes a formula into sub-formulae that are translated independently. It allows for an efficient verification as it reduces the size of the automata. The decomposition is realised using a new operator for the DC that permits a distributive law of linear complexity.

We implemented our translation algorithm as part of a tool chain and provide evidence that it can handle industrial problems. We verify the emergency treatment of the European Train Control System (ETCS) [ERT02]. Our approach is the first that permits model checking of a comprehensive ETCS fragment considering communication, data, and real-time. Therefore, we bridge the gap between theoretical results and their practical applications. Due to our model's parameters and infinite data types, we apply the abstraction refinement model checker ARMC [Ryb06].

To summarise our contributions, we identify a novel class of DC formulae and give a translation algorithm into enhanced timed automata [AD94]. Since a direct translation leads to an exponential blow up of the automata, we give a normal form for our novel class to decompose given properties. The normal form is realised using a new distributive law of linear complexity based on a new operator for the DC. We implemented the algorithm and applied our tool chain to verify real-time properties of the ETCS case study.

The paper is organised as follows. After a short introduction to our case study, we recall the DC and the applied automaton model, phase event automata (PEA), in Sect. 2. The class of test formulae, the new operator, and the normal form are presented in Sect. 3. Based upon these results, Sect. 4 gives the test automata semantics and states its correctness. The case study and our model checking results are sketched in Sect. 5. Section 6, reviewing related work and suggesting future investigations, concludes the paper.

1.1 Motivating Example

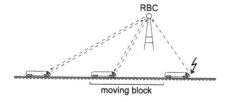

Fig. 1. Consecutive trains

The emerging European Train Control System (ETCS) is an international standard [ERT02] that shall replace national train control systems to ensure cross-border interoperability and to improve railway safety as well as track utilisation. In the final ETCS implementation level, the existing national trackside systems for detection of train speed, location, and integrity will not be used anymore. Instead, data values required for a moving train are ascertained in cooperation of the train's on-board ETCS unit with a radio block centre (RBC) that

controls the traffic in a well-defined area and grants movement authorities to
trains. RBCs and trains communicate over a GSM-R radio connection. To increase the possible traffic density, the ETCS employs the moving block principle,
by which the movement authorities are always given up to a position closely behind the preceding train (cf. Fig. 1). In our case study, we analyse the emergency
handling. In case of an accident, the train control system has to stop all trains
safely. The main desired property in our case study is that the trains will never
collide.

Verification approaches for safety requirements of industrial systems like the
ETCS have to consider the identified dimensions: data, communication, and real-
time. It is the first time, a fragment of the ETCS is verified considering all of
these aspects.

2 Preliminaries

Since we translate DC formulae into phase event automata (PEA), we review
the DC and PEA in this section.

2.1 Duration Calculus

Duration Calculus [ZH04] is an interval-based logic for the specification of real-
time systems. We use dense real-time, $\mathbb{T}ime := \mathbb{R}_{\geq 0}$. To represent a system state
at a point in time, DC uses state expressions. State expressions, denoted by φ,
are quantifier-free first-order formulae over time-dependent variables, so-called
observables $(X \in) SVar$. For every observable X there is a data domain $D(X)$.
The semantics of an observable X is given by an interpretation $\mathcal{I}$ assigning
a mapping $\mathcal{I}(X) : \mathbb{T}ime \to D(X)$ to the observable. Additionally, there are
predicates $p_{/n}$ of arity $n \in \mathbb{N}$ with interpretations $\hat{p} : D(X_1) \times \ldots \times D(X_n) \to \mathbb{B}$.

The semantics of a state expression φ depends on the semantics of the observables. Given an interpretation $\mathcal{I}$ of the observables in φ, the semantics of φ
is given by the mapping $\mathcal{I}[\![\varphi]\!] : \mathbb{T}ime \to \{0, 1\}$ as follows.

$$\mathcal{I}[\![p(X_1, \ldots, X_n)]\!](t) := 1 \text{ iff } \hat{p}(\mathcal{I}(X_1)(t), \ldots, \mathcal{I}(X_n)(t)) = tt \qquad (1)$$
$$\mathcal{I}[\![\neg\varphi_1]\!](t) := 1 - \mathcal{I}[\![\varphi_1]\!](t)$$
$$\mathcal{I}[\![\varphi_1 \wedge \varphi_2]\!](t) := 1 \text{ iff } \mathcal{I}[\![\varphi_1]\!](t) = 1 \text{ and } \mathcal{I}[\![\varphi_2]\!](t) = 1.$$

We require finite variability, i.e., for every predicate and every choice of observables the function in (1) has finitely many discontinuities on every finite interval.
Consider $\sim \in \{\leq, <, =, >, \geq\}$, $k \in \mathbb{R}_{\geq 0}$. The class of DC formulae $(F \in) \mathbb{F}orm$
is defined by

$$\mathbb{F}orm ::= \lceil\varphi\rceil \mid \ell \sim k \mid \neg\mathbb{F}orm \mid \mathbb{F}orm_1 \wedge \mathbb{F}orm_2 \mid \mathbb{F}orm_1 ; \mathbb{F}orm_2 \mid \exists X : \mathbb{F}orm.$$

Given an interpretation $\mathcal{I}$ of the observables in state expressions, the semantics
of a DC formula F is a mapping evaluating the formula on a given finite interval.

$$\mathcal{I}[\![\lceil\varphi\rceil]\!][b, e] := tt \text{ iff } \int_b^e \mathcal{I}[\![\varphi]\!](t) \, dt = e - b \text{ and } e > b$$
$$\mathcal{I}[\![\ell \sim k]\!][b, e] := tt \text{ iff } (e - b) \sim k$$
$$\mathcal{I}[\![\neg F]\!][b, e] := tt \text{ iff } \mathcal{I}[\![F]\!][b, e] = f\!f$$
$$\mathcal{I}[\![F_1 \wedge F_2]\!][b, e] := tt \text{ iff } \mathcal{I}[\![F_1]\!][b, e] = tt \text{ and } \mathcal{I}[\![F_2]\!][b, e] = tt$$
$$\mathcal{I}[\![F_1 \; ; F_2]\!][b, e] := tt \text{ iff there is } m \in [b, e] \text{ such that}$$
$$\mathcal{I}[\![F_1]\!][b, m] = tt \text{ and } \mathcal{I}[\![F_2]\!][m, e] = tt$$
$$\mathcal{I}[\![\exists X : F]\!][b, e] := tt \text{ iff there is } \mathcal{I}' =_{\backslash X} \mathcal{I} \text{ such that } \mathcal{I}'[\![F]\!][b, e] = tt.$$

Two interpretations are equal up to X, $\mathcal{I}' =_{\backslash X} \mathcal{I}$, if they coincide on all observables except X. The finite variability ensures that $\mathcal{I}[\![\varphi]\!]$ is integrable.

Two formulae F_1, F_2 are *satisfiability equivalent* iff for any interpretation $\mathcal{I}$ holds:

$$\exists t \in \mathbb{R}_{\geq 0} : \mathcal{I}, [0, t] \models F_1 \Leftrightarrow \exists t' \in \mathbb{R}_{\geq 0} : \mathcal{I}, [0, t'] \models F_2.$$

The definition of test formulae in Section 3 depends on the notion of events specifying changes in the values of Boolean observables (cf. transition formulae defined in [ZH04]). Let $\mathcal{E}$ be a Boolean observable. An *event* $\uparrow \mathcal{E}$ is valid at time t iff the value of $\mathcal{E}$ changes at t. A *forbidden event* $\not\uparrow \mathcal{E}$ holds at time t iff the value of $\mathcal{E}$ does not change at t. For an interval the *no event* formula $\boxminus \mathcal{E}$ holds iff the value of $\mathcal{E}$ is constant in the given interval.

2.2   Phase Event Automata

PEA [HM05] are a class of timed automata [AD94] that synchronise on both events and data variables. Let $\mathcal{L}(V)$ be the set of first-order formulae over variables in V.

Definition 1 (Phase Event Automaton). *A phase event automaton is a tuple* $\mathcal{A} = (P, V, A, C, E, s, I, P^0)$, *where*

- *P is a finite set of phases with initial phases $P^0 \subseteq P$,*
- *V, A, C are finite sets of real-valued state variables, events, and real-valued clocks, respectively,*
- *$E \subseteq P \times \mathcal{L}(V \cup V' \cup A \cup C) \times \mathbb{P}(C) \times P$ is a set of transitions,*
- *$s : P \to \mathcal{L}(V)$ associates with each phase a predicate that holds during the phase, and*
- *$I : P \to \mathcal{L}(C)$ associates with each phase a clock invariant.*

An edge (p_1, g, X, p_2) represents a transition from p_1 to p_2 with a guard g over (possibly primed) variables, clocks, and events, and a set X of clocks that are to be reset. Primed variables v' denote the post-state of v whereas v always refers to the pre-state. In addition, we postulate the presence of a stuttering edge $(p, \bigwedge_{e \in A} \neg e \wedge \bigwedge_{v \in V} v' = v, \varnothing, p)$ for every phase p.

The operational semantics of PEA is given by infinite sequences of configurations and events, called runs.

Definition 2 (Run of a PEA). *A* run *of a PEA $\mathcal{A}$ is a sequence*

$$\langle (p_0, \beta_0, \eta_0), t_0, Y_0, (p_1, \beta_1, \eta_1), t_1, Y_1, \ldots \rangle,$$

with phases $p_i \in P$, entry event sets $Y_i \subseteq A$, valuations of variables β_i and primed variables β'_i, where $\beta_i(v) = \beta'_i(v')$, clock valuations η_i, and points in time $t_i > 0$. Furthermore, we demand $p_0 \in P^0, \eta_0(c) = 0$ for all clocks $c \in C$, $\beta_i \models s(p_i)$, and $\eta_i + t_i \models I(p_i)$. For all transitions (p_i, g, X, p_{i+1}) we require $\beta_i, \beta'_{i+1}, \eta_i + t_i, Y_i \models g$ and $\eta_{i+1} = (\eta_i + t_i)[X := 0]$. We denote the set of all runs of $\mathcal{A}$ by $\mathbf{Run}(\mathcal{A})$.

PEA composed in parallel synchronise over common events and additionally over common variables. That is, a variable that occurs in both automata may only be changed if both automata agree.

Definition 3 (Parallel Composition). *The parallel composition of PEA $\mathcal{A}_1$ and $\mathcal{A}_2$ with $\mathcal{A}_i = (P_i, V_i, A_i, C_i, E_i, s_i, I_i, P_i^0)$ is given by*

$$\mathcal{A}_1 \parallel \mathcal{A}_2 := (P_1 \times P_2, V_1 \cup V_2, A_1 \cup A_2, C_1 \cup C_2, E, s_1 \wedge s_2, I_1 \wedge I_2, P_1^0 \times P_2^0),$$

where $((p_1, p_2), g_1 \wedge g_2, X_1 \cup X_2, (p'_1, p'_2)) \in E$ iff $(p_i, g_i, X_i, p'_i) \in E_i$ with $i = 1, 2$.

This parallel product allows for compositional verification, because once a safety property is proven for an arbitrary subset of parallel components, it is also true for the entire system.

3   Test Formulae

In this section, we introduce the DC subclass of test formulae, denoted by *Testform*. For test formulae we construct test automata in Sect. 4. Applying the automata theoretic approach [VW86, ABBL03], we can automatically decide whether a system satisfies a negated test formula. Thus, test formulae may be interpreted as undesired system behaviour.

We use so-called trace formulae to specify system executions. The class *Testform* is built up from trace formulae and admits a restricted use of negation.

Definition 4 (*Testform*). *The formula class Testform is defined inductively:*

$$Phase ::= \ell > 0 \wedge \ell \sim k \mid Phase \wedge \lceil \varphi \rceil \mid Phase \wedge \boxminus \mathcal{E}$$
$$Trace ::= Phase \mid \updownarrow \mathcal{E} \mid \nmid \mathcal{E} \mid Trace_1 ; Trace_2$$
$$Form ::= Trace \mid \neg Form \mid Form_1 \wedge Form_2$$
$$Testform ::= Form \mid Testform_1 ; Testform_2 \mid Testform_1 \wedge Testform_2 \mid$$
$$Testform_1 \vee Testform_2,$$

where $k \in \mathbb{R}_{>0}$, φ is a state expression, $\mathcal{E}$ is a Boolean observable, and $\sim \in \{\varnothing, \leq, <, >, \geq\}$. We use $\sim = \varnothing$ to indicate $\ell > 0$ is the only time bound. We impose the condition that the first element of a trace always is a phase.

In our running example, undesired behaviour is that the leading train sends an alert message, indicated by formula (2), but for longer than five time units neither the leading nor the following train applies the brakes, stated in formula (3), with $i = 1, 2$. Test formula (4) reflects the critical behaviour:

$$Warn := \lceil true \rceil \; ; \; \updownarrow Train_1\,ToRBC\_Alert \; ; \; \lceil true \rceil \; ;$$

$$\updownarrow RBCToTrain_1\_Warn_1 \; ; \; \lceil true \rceil \; ; \; \updownarrow RBCToTrain_2\_Warn_2 \qquad (2)$$

$$NoBrake_i := \boxminus ApplyEmergencyBrake_i \wedge \ell > 5 \qquad (3)$$

$$TF := Warn \; ; \; (NoBrake_1 \wedge NoBrake_2) \; ; \; \lceil true \rceil. \qquad (4)$$

A different approach would express the undesired behaviour directly in terms of test automata. The benefit of DC is its conciseness. A negated DC trace comprising n phases requires in the worst case a test automaton of size 4^n. Thus, even for simple behaviour the modelling of test automata by hand is error-prone, a disadvantage the automated compilation overcomes.

3.1 Sync Events

For arbitrary DC formulae F, G, H there is no distributive law between the chop operator and the conjunction, i.e., $F \; ; \; (G \wedge H) \not\Leftrightarrow (F \; ; \; G) \wedge (F \; ; \; H)$. To recover some form of distributive law, we introduce sync events $\underset{S}{\updownarrow}$, i.e., distinguished events occurring only once. They can be used to uniquely identify a chop point. For sync events the following distributivity holds:

$$F \underset{S}{\updownarrow} (G \wedge H) \Leftrightarrow \left(F \underset{S}{\updownarrow} G \right) \wedge \left(F \underset{S}{\updownarrow} H \right). \qquad (5)$$

Definition 5 (Sync Events). *Let F, G be DC formulae, S a Boolean observable not contained in F nor G. Let $\mathcal{I}$ be an interpretation, $b, e \in \mathbb{R}_{\geq 0}, b \leq e$. The* sync event $F \underset{S}{\updownarrow} G$ *is defined as follows:*

$$\mathcal{I}, [b, e] \models F \underset{S}{\updownarrow} G :\Leftrightarrow \exists t \in [b, e] : (\mathcal{I}, [b, t] \models F) \wedge (\mathcal{I}, [t, e] \models G) \wedge$$

$$(\mathcal{I}, [t, t] \models \updownarrow S) \wedge (\forall t' \in [0, t) \cup (t, \infty) : \mathcal{I}, [t', t'] \models \not\updownarrow S).$$

To introduce sync events to the class of test formulae, equivalence (6) in the following lemma allows the replacement of a chop operator with a fresh sync event not used in one of the formulae. Furthermore, an efficient distributivity between sync events and conjunctions is stated.

Lemma 1 (Sync Event Introduction and Linear Distributivity). *Let S be a Boolean observable not contained in $F, F_i, G, G_j, 1 \leq i \leq m, 1 \leq j \leq n, m, n \in \mathbb{N}$. The following equivalences hold:*

$$(F \wedge \ell > 0) \; ; \; G \Leftrightarrow \exists S : \left(F \underset{S}{\updownarrow} G \right) \qquad (6)$$

$$\left(\bigwedge_{i=1}^{m} F_i\right) \underset{\mathcal{S}}{\updownarrow} \left(\bigwedge_{j=1}^{n} G_j\right) \Leftrightarrow \bigwedge_{i=1}^{m} \left(F_i \underset{\mathcal{S}}{\updownarrow} true\right) \wedge \bigwedge_{j=1}^{n} \left(\lceil true\rceil \underset{\mathcal{S}}{\updownarrow} G_j\right). \qquad (7)$$

We know that the *true* phase before a sync event has a duration greater zero, i.e., $\lceil true\rceil$ holds, because events cannot happen at time zero. The distributivity in equivalence (7) results in $m + n + 1$ conjuncted formulae compared to the distributivity in (5) resulting in $m * n$ formulae:

$$\bigwedge_{i=1}^{m} \bigwedge_{j=1}^{n} \left(F_i \underset{\mathcal{S}}{\updownarrow} G_j\right) \Leftrightarrow \bigwedge_{i=1}^{m} \left(F_i \underset{\mathcal{S}}{\updownarrow} true\right) \wedge \bigwedge_{j=1}^{n} \left(\lceil true\rceil \underset{\mathcal{S}}{\updownarrow} G_j\right).$$

The introduction of sync events transforms a time-triggered real-time system specification using chopped formulae into an event-triggered specification with sync events replacing chops. Event-triggered system specifications allow for canonical operational semantics using labelled transitions whereas time-triggered specifications need some elaborate clock construction to represent the timing issues.

3.2 A Normal Form Theorem for Test Formulae

Our normal form is a disjunctive normal form (DNF) over traces.

Theorem 1 (Normal Form Theorem). *Every test formula is satisfiability equivalent with a formula of the form*

$$\exists \mathcal{S}_{ijk} : \bigvee_i \bigwedge_j T_{ij}, \qquad (8)$$

$$\text{with } T_{ij} ::= Tr_{ij} \underset{\mathcal{S}_{ij}}{\updownarrow} \lceil true\rceil \mid \lceil true\rceil \underset{\mathcal{S}_{ij1}}{\updownarrow} Tr_{ij} \underset{\mathcal{S}_{ij2}}{\updownarrow} \lceil true\rceil, \qquad (9)$$

where Tr_{ij} are (negated) traces, $k = 1, 2$, and $\mathcal{S}_{ijk}$ are fresh Boolean observables.

For the construction of the normal form, we assume the given test formula *TF* to end with a $\lceil true\rceil$ phase (cf. satisfiability equivalence, Sect. 2.1). We then replace every *Form* formula inside *TF* with its DNF. To obtain the outermost disjunctions in (8), we apply the known distributivities for disjunction and chop/conjunction to the resulting formula. We end with chop separated conjunctions of (negated) traces. For all these chops, we introduce sync events (6) and use distributivity (7).

The computation of the DNFs and the known distributivities may lead to an exponential blow up of *TF*. We tackle this problem by model checking all disjuncts separately. Distributivity (7) neither increases the number of (negated) traces nor the size of the product automata (cf. restriction, Sect. 4).

For example, we gain the normal form of formula (4) by introducing two sync events (6) and using the distributivity of sync events and conjunctions (7):

$$Warn \; ; (NoBrake_1 \wedge NoBrake_2) \; ; \lceil true\rceil$$
$$\Leftrightarrow \exists \mathcal{S}_0 : \exists \mathcal{S}_1 : Warn \underset{\mathcal{S}_0}{\updownarrow} \lceil true\rceil \wedge \bigwedge_{i=1,2} \lceil true\rceil \underset{\mathcal{S}_0}{\updownarrow} NoBrake_i \underset{\mathcal{S}_1}{\updownarrow} \lceil true\rceil.$$

4   Model Checking with Test Automata

To define whether a PEA model of a system satisfies a test formula, we need to clarify the meaning of satisfiability of a DC formula with respect to a PEA (cf. Definitions 1 and 2). Given Boolean observables $\mathcal{E}_1 \ldots, \mathcal{E}_n$ and observables $X_1, \ldots, X_m$, an interpretation $\mathcal{I}$ is said to *fit to a run* r iff

- the set of events A in the PEA can be identified with the set of interpreted Boolean observables, $A = \{\mathcal{E}_1 \ldots, \mathcal{E}_n\}$, the set of variables in the PEA is identical with the set of interpreted observables, $V = \{X_1 \ldots, X_m\}$,
- the observables used in the PEA are interpreted as imposed by the valuations in the run,
- a change in the interpretation of a Boolean observable $\mathcal{E}_i$ occurs at time t iff the PEA changes its state at time t and the variable is contained in the set of events, $\mathcal{E}_i \in Y$.

Every run of a PEA induces a fitting interpretation. Satisfiability of a formula by a PEA is defined over the interpretations fitting to the runs of the automaton.

Definition 6. *A PEA $\mathcal{A}$ satisfies a DC formula F, denoted by $\mathcal{A} \models_0 F$, iff all interpretations $\mathcal{I}$ fitting to a run r satisfy the formula from time zero:*

$$\mathcal{A} \models_0 F :\Leftrightarrow \forall \mathcal{I} : \forall\, r \in \mathbf{Run}(\mathcal{A}) : (\mathcal{I} \text{ fits to } r \Rightarrow \mathcal{I} \models_0 F).$$

4.1   Test Automata

Test automata (TA) are PEA with a distinguished state, called the *bad state*. The runs of a TA are the runs of the underlying PEA. A run is said to be a *test run* iff it reaches the bad state. Reaching the bad state in the parallel composition of the system with a TA means that the system can exhibit the undesired behaviour specified in the test formula the TA is constructed for.

We define the TA semantics for the normal form of test formulae. Therefore, we require three operations on TA: parallel composition to express the conjunction, sequential composition to represent the formula structure in (9), and restriction to model sync events.

The *parallel composition* of test automata, $TA_1 \parallel TA_2$, takes the parallel composition of the underlying PEA and defines the bad state of the composed automaton as the pair of the bad states of the original automata.

The *sequential composition* of two test automata, denoted by $TA_1 \bullet_{\mathcal{S},\gamma} TA_2$, means the second TA is started when the first one has accepted its formula. Since the acceptance of trace formulae depends on clock valuations, we cannot use bad states to check the acceptance in the TA for traces. Instead, we use a guard function γ yielding a first-order formula for every state. We define the sequential composition as follows. A transition between every state in the first automaton and every initial state in the second automaton is inserted. The new transitions demand an event $\mathcal{S}$ representing the sync events in (9). Furthermore, they require a guard that holds iff the test formula represented by the first TA is satisfied.

The guard is given by the function γ. All clocks in both automata are reset when the first TA is left.

As an example, consider the formula $tr \updownarrow_{\mathcal{S}} \lceil true \rceil$ for a trace tr. Figure 2 represents the structure of the TA for the sequential composition $\mathcal{P}(tr) \bullet_{\mathcal{S},\gamma_{tr}} \mathcal{P}(\lceil true \rceil)$ connecting the trace automaton $\mathcal{P}(tr)$ with the automaton $\mathcal{P}(\lceil true \rceil)$.

Given a test automaton TA, the *restriction of TA to the event* $\mathcal{S}$, denoted by $TA \setminus \{\mathcal{S}\}$, is defined by TA with the guards of the transitions changed: if the guard does not contain $\mathcal{S}$ in TA, the requirement $\neg\mathcal{S}$ is added in $TA \setminus \{\mathcal{S}\}$, otherwise, the transition remains unchanged. The restriction operator is used to make the occurrences of sync events unique.

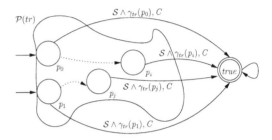

Fig. 2. Sequential composition (illustration)

4.2   A Test Automata Semantics for Test Formulae

We now define a test automata semantics for test formulae, i.e., a mapping that assigns to each test formula (in normal form, cf. Theorem 1) TF a test automaton $\mathcal{P}(TF)$. To begin with, we sketch the following non-compositional TA construction for traces. A trace tr consists of several subsequent phases. A state in the TA $\mathcal{P}(tr)$ represents a subset of these phases combined with a set of flags. For each phase p in this set all runs leading to the state accept the prefix of the trace up to p. The flags indicate the bound types $(\varnothing, \leq, <, >, \geq)$ that need to be used for every phase in this state. Given a state in the TA, a successor state is computed for every possible event set, clock and variable valuation. This results in a deterministic automaton, that may grow exponentially in the number of phases inside the trace. The phase p is accepted, if the given valuation and event set satisfy the guard function $\gamma_{tr,p}$ of this phase. The successor state contains the next phase in the trace. In Definition 7, the function γ_{tr} is the guard function of the last phase in the trace. Details of the construction and the guard function can be found in [Hoe06].

The disjunction in the normal form is not lifted to automata level but model checking is done stepwise for all disjuncts until a satisfied disjunct is found.

Definition 7 (Test Automata Semantics). *Let tr be a trace and $\mathcal{S}, \mathcal{S}_1, \mathcal{S}_2$ be Boolean observables. The test automata semantics for a test formula in normal form TF yields a PEA $\mathcal{P}(TF)$ defined as follows:*

$$\mathcal{P}(tr \updownarrow_{\mathcal{S}} \lceil true \rceil) := \left(\mathcal{P}(tr) \bullet_{\mathcal{S},\gamma_{tr}} \mathcal{P}(\lceil true \rceil) \right) \setminus \{\mathcal{S}\}$$

$$\mathcal{P}(\neg tr \updownarrow_{\mathcal{S}} \lceil true \rceil) := \left(\mathcal{P}(tr) \bullet_{\mathcal{S},\neg\gamma_{tr}} \mathcal{P}(\lceil true \rceil) \right) \setminus \{\mathcal{S}\}$$

$$\mathcal{P}(\lceil true \rceil \underset{\mathcal{S}_1}{\updownarrow} Tr \underset{\mathcal{S}_2}{\updownarrow} \lceil true \rceil) := \Big[\big(\mathcal{P}(\lceil true \rceil)\underset{\mathcal{S}_1,true}{\bullet} \mathcal{P}(Tr \underset{\mathcal{S}_2}{\updownarrow} \lceil true \rceil)\big) \setminus \{\mathcal{S}_2\}\Big] \setminus \{\mathcal{S}_1\}$$

$$\mathcal{P}(TF_1 \wedge TF_2) := \mathcal{P}(TF_1) \parallel \mathcal{P}(TF_2),$$

where Tr is a (negated) trace, TF_1 and TF_2 are in the form of (9). The function γ_{tr} guarantees that the trace tr is accepted.

Figure 3 shows the TA semantics for the formula $\lceil true \rceil \underset{\mathcal{S}_0}{\updownarrow} NoBrake_1 \underset{\mathcal{S}_1}{\updownarrow} \lceil true \rceil$, simplified by removing a transition with guard *false* from state 2 to state 4. State 2 and state 3 represent the states of the trace automaton $\mathcal{P}(NoBrake_1)$.

A test formula is satisfied by an interpretation on an interval iff the bad state in the TA is reachable in a run the interpretation fits to.

Lemma 2 (Characterisation of Satisfiability with Test Automata). *Consider the normal form $\bigvee_i \bigwedge_j \mathcal{T}_{ij}$ of a test formula. Given an interpretation $\mathcal{I}$ and $t \in \mathbb{R}_{\geq 0}$, the following equivalence holds for every disjunct:*

$$\mathcal{I}, [0, t] \models \bigwedge_j \mathcal{T}_{ij} \Leftrightarrow \exists \ test \ run \ r \in \mathbf{Run}(\mathcal{P}(\bigwedge_j \mathcal{T}_{ij})) :$$
$$\mathcal{I} \ fits \ to \ r \ and \ r \ reaches \ the \ bad \ state \ at \ time \ t.$$

With Lemma 2 we can reduce the problem whether a PEA satisfies a negated test formula to a reachability question. The correctness of our semantics with respect to model checking is stated in the following theorem.

Theorem 2 (Model Checking Theorem). *Let TF be a test formula with the normal form $\bigvee_i \bigwedge_j \mathcal{T}_{ij}$. The question whether the negated test formula is satisfied by a PEA $\mathcal{A}$ can be decided as follows:*

$$\neg(\mathcal{A} \models_0 \neg TF) \Leftrightarrow \exists i : \exists r \in \mathbf{Run}(\mathcal{A} \parallel \mathcal{P}(\bigwedge_j \mathcal{T}_{ij})) : r \ reaches \ a \ state \ (p, p_{Bad}),$$

where p is a state of $\mathcal{A}$ and p_{Bad} is the bad state of $\mathcal{P}(\bigwedge_j \mathcal{T}_{ij})$.

The decidability of the reachability problem depends on the constraints over the state variables of the PEA.

Model checking can be done separately for all disjuncts and terminates as soon as the bad state is reachable in one of the disjuncts. The parallel composition $\mathcal{A} \parallel \mathcal{P}(\bigwedge_j \mathcal{T}_{ij})$ only needs to be computed for the evaluated disjuncts.

A disjunct may consist of several conjuncted formulae. For model checking, a subset of these formulae may be chosen. If the bad state is reachable in the TA for the subset, further formulae may be added. Model checking is repeated for the new set of formulae gained by this iterative procedure. If the bad state is not reachable for the subset, we know that it is not reachable for the whole disjunct. This incremental approximation can significantly reduce the TA size.

5   Case Study: Real-Time Aspects of the ETCS

In this section we take up the case study of Sect. 1.1 for the experimental evaluation of our verification method.

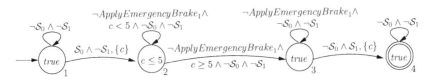

Fig. 3. Test automaton for $\lceil true \rceil \mathrel{\mathop{\Updownarrow}\limits_{\mathcal{S}_0}} NoBrake_1 \mathrel{\mathop{\Updownarrow}\limits_{\mathcal{S}_1}} \lceil true \rceil$

Complex systems like the ETCS consist of several components running in parallel, by the communications between these components, by internal data and state changes, and by real-time aspects. We use the declarative formal language CSP-OZ-DC [HO02] to model our case study. CSP-OZ-DC integrates the well-investigated languages CSP [Hoa85], Object-Z [Smi00], and DC [ZH04] into a unified formalism. CSP-OZ-DC is given an operational semantics [Hoe06] in terms of PEA.

Our case study incorporates five different components that can be modelled with CSP-OZ-DC in an object-oriented way using classes: *Train*, *RBC*, *Track*, *Driver*, and a communication layer *ComNetwork*, which is necessary to model the transfer times of messages between trains and RBC. Every CSP-OZ-DC class comprises an interface part (Fig. 4) defining channels that can be used for the inter-class communication.

The external and internal *communications* of parallel components are described with Communicating Sequential Processes (CSP) [Hoa85]. These processes communicate over channels (or events) that facilitate the transfer of data values, e.g., the main process of a train comprises the interleaving of three subprocesses. When the RBC

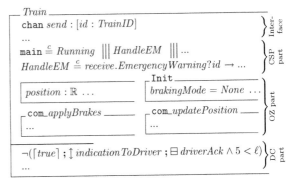

Fig. 4. Exemplary train class

sends an emergency warning, the train receives this message on the channel *receive* with the process *HandleEM* (Fig. 4).

Data aspects are specified with the object-oriented specification language Object-Z (OZ) [Smi00]. The OZ part consists of schemas describing data changes of a class. For instance, the OZ part of *Train* (Fig. 4) includes the state schema defining attributes of the class, e.g., *position*, the Init-schema defining that initially the train is not braking, and operation schemas, e.g., com_*applyBrakes* defining data changes that are performed at the same time when—in agreement with the CSP part of the class—the event *applyBrakes* occurs. In particular, our case study comprises, besides the real-time aspects, infinite data types, e.g., the positions, that are modelled as reals. Furthermore, the values of such infinite data types are also transferred via channels to other classes. Another important property of the data handling in CSP-OZ-DC is the use of parameters, i.e., we do not need to interpret all constants. Instead, it suffices to specify conditions that restrict the values adequately. In our case study, we have a parameter for the length of trains and the only condition we need is $length > 0$.

Real-time constraints are described using the logic DC [ZH04]. Since the full DC is too expressive for automatic verification, we only use counterexample-trace formulae, i.e., negated trace formulae according to Sect. 3.

The operational semantics of CSP-OZ-DC is given in terms of PEA, which can handle infinite data types and parameters. It is compositional in the sense that every part (CSP, OZ, and DC) of every component is translated into a single PEA, and the whole specification is translated into the parallel product of all these automata. For details we refer to [HM05, Hoe06].

The desired safety property in our case study is that the trains will never collide. For a setting with two trains, this can be expressed in the DC formula

$$\neg(\lceil true \rceil \, ; \, \lceil position_1 > position_0 - length_0 \rceil), \tag{10}$$

where $position_0$ is the position of the first train with length $length_0$. The variable $position_1$ represents the position of the subsequent train.

5.1 Tool Support

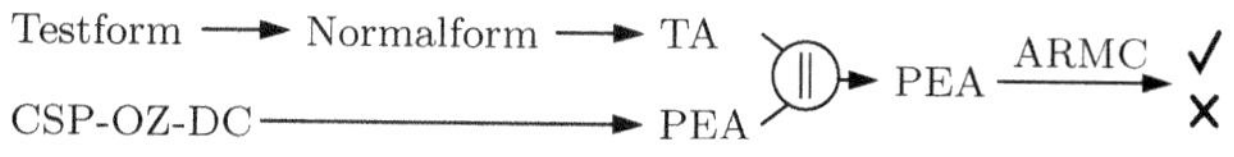

In order to verify whether a CSP-OZ-DC model satisfies a test formula, we execute the following steps (cf. Fig. 5).

Fig. 5. Flow of the verification process

We translate the model into PEA according to its semantics. The translation of the DC part is automated. To develop PEA for the CSP and the OZ part the graphical design tool Moby/PEA [HMF06] is available. The DC test formula is transformed into a set of test automata (TA), applying the algorithm introduced in Sect. 3 and 4. To this end, we implemented a compiler (available on [HMF06]) that automatically computes the normal form and the corresponding test automata semantics. In a next step, we compute the parallel composition of the test automata and the PEA of the model. Our tool generates outputs in the Uppaal [UUP05] and ARMC [Ryb06] supported formats. Finally, we apply a model checker on the product automaton. For our case study, Uppaal is of limited use, because it can neither cope with infinite data domains nor parameters.

We use the abstraction refinement model checker ARMC [Ryb06] for infinite state systems to prove the unreachability of bad states in PEA. We implemented a new abstraction refinement method in ARMC that allows us to handle large input PEA from the case study. ARMC automatically constructs a safe abstraction of the input PEA. The abstraction is defined by predicates over PEA variables,

Table 1. Experimental results (Athlon XP 2200+, 512 MB RAM)

Task	(1)	(2)	(3)	(4)	(5)	(6)	(7)	(8)
Running	178	6.1T	31	46	347	22	25s	26m
Running (decomp. 1)	8	150	20	11	11	8	2.5s	7.5s
Running (decomp. 2)	20	899	22	8	32	8	4.0s	21.5
Running (decomp. 3)	48	1.2T	27	13	93	10	5.9s	45s
Running (decomp. 4)	48	1.7T	27	11	70	7	6.3s	47.5s
Delivery	122	18T	20	41	2.2T	32	50s	86m
Delivery (decomp. 1)	14	366	14	9	29	8	2.7s	13.9s
Delivery (decomp. 2)	17	173	10	25	17	17	2.2s	1.9s
Delivery (decomp. 3)	12	71	9	12	9	9	1.9s	0.7s
Delivery (decomp. 4)	17	156	12	25	19	17	2.2s	2.6s
Delivery (decomp. 5)	7	28	4	3	5	3	1.6s	0.1s
Braking 1	44	240	17	45	44	3	3s	5.1s
Braking 2	172	1.6T	33	63	88	59	9s	35.3s

(1) program locations
(2) transitions
(3) variables
(4) predicates generated by ARMC
(5) abstract states
(6) refinements loops performed by ARMC
(7) runtime for generating test automata and parallel product
(8) runtime for model checking

T : thousand units
m : minutes   s : seconds

events, and clocks, and computed in the standard way [GS97]. The process of choosing the right abstraction is guided by spurious counterexamples that are found if the abstraction is not precise enough to verify the property [CGJ+00]. We apply the recent methodology for the extraction of new predicates from spurious counterexamples that is based on interpolation [HJMM04, McM03]. We designed and implemented an efficient algorithm for the computation of interpolants for linear arithmetic over rationals/reals based on linear programming, which are particularly needed for the verification of real-time systems.

5.2   Results

The model of the case study is too large to verify the global safety property (10) in a single step. Therefore, we decompose the model manually into smaller parts and verify local properties for the parallel components. The semantics of CSP-OZ-DC ensures that local properties hold for the entire system (cf. Sect. 2.2).

Table 1 shows our experimental results for a range of verification tasks. For instance, we consider the running behaviour of the train in isolation and verify (10) on the assumption that the first train does not apply the emergency brakes. To this end, we take only those PEA into account that influence the running behaviour, i.e., the automata for the subprocess *Running* (Fig. 4) together with the automata for the OZ and the DC part. The performance results of applying our model checking approach to this verification task are listed as "Running" in Tab. 1. The other entries (decomp. 1 – decomp. 4) contain our results for a further (manual) decomposition of "Running" into smaller tasks that allows for a more efficient verification. For the "Delivery" task (and also the decomposed variants) we verify that messages like an emergency message between train and RBC are not delivered too late. Bringing together the verification tasks and showing that they imply (10) for the entire model is subject of ongoing work.

The table illustrates that we can handle up to 18000 program transitions and up to 33 variables (with potentially infinite data types) in an order of 86 min. Hence, these results demonstrate that our new algorithm implemented in our tool chain can deal with problems in real world applications.

6   Related and Future Work

Our class of test formulae is a proper generalisation of previously known classes. It is based on the class of counterexample-trace formulae [Hoe06], that correspond to negated traces. Counterexample-traces cover the class of DC implementables [Rav94, Hoe06]. Non-negated traces with phases of exact length, i.e., $\ell = k$ bound, are covered by *Testform*. With this observation our class forms a proper superset of $\{\lceil \varphi \rceil, \ell < k, \ell = k, \ell > k\}$-formulae that have exactly one outermost negation [Frä04]. We conjecture that the classes of constraint diagrams used for model checking timed automata in [DL02] form proper subsets of *Testform*. We have not yet compared the expressiveness of our class with the results in [ABBL03].

For positive Duration Interval Logic formulae (DIL$^+$ formulae) a translation into Integration Automata (IA) is given in [BLR95]. DIL$^+$ formulae are covered by *Testform*, because they correspond to traces that contain phases of exact length. To give IA semantics to negated formulae, the authors of [BLR95] show that the negation of a strongly overlap free DIL$^+$ formula has a congruent DIL$^+$ formula. Since our translation for negated traces does not require overlap freeness, it covers a strictly larger class of negated formulae. Pandya proves the decidability of Interval Duration Logic with located constraints (LIDL−) by translation into event recording timed automata [Pan02]. Located constraints require disjoint phases, a condition our construction does not impose. In contrast, LIDL− is closed under negation even for phases with exact length.

The idea of sync events is closely related to the theory of nominals. In a DC extended with nominals [Han06], intervals can be identified uniquely using their names. Similarly, sync events identify chop points. In [KP05] phases in the QDDC are equipped with fresh observables to identify chop points. This yields decomposition results similar to ours. The benefit of our work is the integration of sync events with the operators of the full DC.

Related work on ETCS case studies like [ZH05, HJU05] focuses on the stochastic examination of the communication reliability and models components like the train and the RBC in an abstract way without considering data aspects.

We currently work on model checking DC liveness properties with the automata theoretic approach. In addition, enhancing our decomposition techniques is ongoing work. They allow for compositional verification of inherently parallel systems like the ETCS.

References

[ABBL03]   L. Aceto, P. Bouyer, A. Burgueño, and K. G. Larsen. The power of reachability testing for timed automata. *Theoretical Computer Science*, 300(1-3):411–475, 2003.

[AD94]   R. Alur and D. L. Dill. A theory of timed automata. *Theoretical Computer Science*, 126(2):183–235, 1994.

[BLR95]   A. Bouajjani, Y. Lakhnech, and R. Robbana. From duration calculus to linear hybrid automata. In *CAV*, volume 939 of *LNCS*, pages 196–210. Springer-Verlag, 1995.

[CGJ+00] E. M. Clarke, O. Grumberg, S. Jha, Y. Lu, and H. Veith. Counterexample-guided abstraction refinement. In *CAV*, volume 1855 of *LNCS*, pages 154–169. Springer-Verlag, 2000.

[DL02]   H. Dierks and M. Lettrari. Constructing test automata from graphical real-time requirements. In *FTRTFT*, volume 2469 of *LNCS*, pages 433–453. Springer-Verlag, 2002.

[ERT02]   ERTMS User Group, UNISIG. ERTMS/ETCS System requirements specification. http://www.aeif.org/ccm/default.asp, 2002. Version 2.2.2.

[Frä04]   M. Fränzle. Model-checking dense-time duration calculus. *Formal Aspects of Computing*, 16(2):121–139, 2004.

[GS97]   S. Graf and H. Saidi. Construction of abstract state graphs with PVS. In *CAV*, volume 1254, pages 72–83. Springer-Verlag, 1997.

[Han06]   M. Hansen. DC with nominals. Personal communication, March 2006.

[HJMM04] T. A. Henzinger, R. Jhala, R. Majumdar, and K. L. McMillan. Abstractions from proofs. In *POPL*, pages 232–244. ACM Press, 2004.

[HJU05]   H. Hermanns, D. N. Jansen, and Y. S. Usenko. From StoCharts to MoDeST: a comparative reliability analysis of train radio communications. In *WOSP*, pages 13–23. ACM Press, 2005.

[HM05]   J. Hoenicke and P. Maier. Model-checking of specifications integrating processes, data and time. In *FM 2005*, volume 3582 of *LNCS*, pages 465–480. Springer-Verlag, 2005.

[HMF06]   J. Hoenicke, R. Meyer, and J. Faber. PEA toolkit home page. http://csd.informatik.uni-oldenburg.de/projects/epea.html, 2006.

[HO02]   J. Hoenicke and E.-R. Olderog. CSP-OZ-DC: A combination of specification techniques for processes, data and time. *NJC*, 9, 2002.

[Hoa85]   C.A.R. Hoare. *Communicating Sequential Processes*. Prentice-Hall, 1985.

[Hoe06]   J. Hoenicke. *Combination of Processes, Data, and Time*. PhD thesis, University of Oldenburg, Germany, 2006. To appear.

[KP05]   S. N. Krishna and P. K. Pandya. Modal strength reduction in quantified discrete duration calculus. In *FSTTCS*, volume 3821 of *LNCS*, pages 444–456. Springer-Verlag, 2005.

[McM03]   K. L. McMillan. Interpolation and SAT-based model checking. In *CAV*, volume 2725 of *LNCS*, pages 1–13. Springer-Verlag, 2003.

[Pan02]   P. K. Pandya. Interval duration logic: Expressiveness and decidability. *ENTCS*, 65(6), 2002.

[Rav94]   A. P. Ravn. *Design of Embedded Real-Time Computing Systems*. PhD thesis, Technical University of Denmark, 1994.

[Ryb06]   A. Rybalchenko. ARMC. http://www.mpi-inf.mpg.de/~rybal/armc, 2006.

[Smi00]   G. Smith. *The Object-Z Specification Language*. Kluwer, 2000.

[UUP05]   Uppaal home page. University of Aalborg and University of Uppsala, http://www.uppaal.com, 1995-2005.

[VW86]   M. Y. Vardi and P. Wolper. An automata-theoretic approach to automatic program verification. In *LICS*, pages 332–344, 1986.

[ZH04]   C. Zhou and M. R. Hansen. *Duration Calculus*. Springer-Verlag, 2004.

[ZH05]   A. Zimmermann and G. Hommel. Towards modeling and evaluation of ETCS real-time communication and operation. *JSS*, 77(1):47–54, 2005.

[ZHS93]   C. Zhou, M. R. Hansen, and P. Sestoft. Decidability and undecidability results for duration calculus. In *STACS*, volume 665 of *LNCS*, pages 58–68. Springer-Verlag, 1993.

Spatio-temporal Model Checking for Mobile Real-Time Systems

Jan-David Quesel and Andreas Schäfer

Department of Computing Science, University of Oldenburg,
26111 Oldenburg, Germany
{jan-david.quesel, schaefer}@informatik.uni-oldenburg.de

Abstract. This paper presents an automatic verification method for combined temporal and spatial properties of mobile real-time systems. We provide a translation of the Shape Calculus (SC), a spatio-temporal extension of Duration Calculus, into weak second order logic of one successor (WS1S). A prototypical implementation facilitates successful verification of spatio-temporal properties by translating SC specifications into the syntax of the WS1S checker MONA. For demonstrating the formalism and tool usage, we apply it to the benchmark case study "generalised railroad crossing" (GRC) enriched by requirements inexpressible in non-spatial formalisms.

Keywords: model checking, real-time systems, mobile systems, spatial logic, temporal logic, Duration Calculus.

1 Introduction

Mobile real-time systems are omnipresent today, e.g. in airplane and railroad control systems. Failures in these systems may have severe consequences which can even endanger lives. Formal specification and automatic verification is a promising approach to increase the safety of such systems. As these systems often require the consideration of real-time *and* spatial aspects, real-time formalisms like Timed Automata [AD94] or Duration Calculus (DC) [ZHR91, HZ04] often fall short in these cases.

The main contribution of this paper is the development of a model checking approach for systems involving temporal and spatial aspects. We implemented our verification technique in a prototypical tool. Our approach is the first that enables the automatic verification of temporal and spatial properties. We successfully demonstrate our approach on the benchmark case study generalised railroad crossing [HL94]. Spatial aspects like movement and the distance of trains are modelled explicitly here, whereas they are usually abstracted in the analysis using real-time formalisms.

There are many well-understood formal techniques for the specification and verification of real-time systems, among them Timed Automata [AD94] and the interval temporal logic Duration Calculus (DC) [ZHR91, HZ04]. Tools like Uppaal [BDL04], Kronos [BDM+98], and DCValid [Pan00] for the automatic verification of systems specified in these formalisms contributed a lot to their

K. Barkaoui, A. Cavalcanti, and A. Cerone (Eds.): ICTAC 2006, LNCS 4281, pp. 347–361, 2006.

applicability. However, these formalisms are insufficient for problems with spatial requirements. A central point in the UNiFORM [KBPOB99] project in cooperation with the industrial partner Elpro was the development of a control for a single-tracked line segment (SLS) for tramways. The problem is to ensure the safety of trams if only one track is available and this track may be passed in both directions and occupied by up to two trams simultaneously as long as they head into the same direction. A controller has been derived, simulated and partially verified. However, the main safety requirement, i.e., mutual exclusion of trams with distinct directions on the critical section, is a spatio-temporal property and could not be expressed [Die99]. Similar problems arise in specifications for mobile robots [Sch05b] that may not leave certain working areas.

This led to the idea to extend a well-known formalism for real-time systems in order to be able to also describe spatial properties. The use of the formalism is similar to the use of pure temporal logics when no spatial reasoning is required. Thus, experienced users of temporal logics can easily adopt the new features.

To express spatio-temporal properties, we propose to use the Shape Calculus [Sch05a], a spatio-temporal extension of the interval logic Duration Calculus [ZHR91] introduced by Zhou, Hoare, and Ravn. The mutual exclusion property for the SLS can be expressed in Shape Calculus by the formula

$$\neg \Diamond_{e_x} \Diamond_{e_y} \Diamond_{e_t} \lceil \mathsf{tram}_1 \wedge \mathsf{tram}_2 \rceil$$

which reads as follows: It is not possible that somewhere ($\Diamond_{e_x} \Diamond_{e_y}$) sometimes ($\Diamond_{e_t}$) both tram_1 and tram_2 occupy the same place.

Although Shape Calculus is undecidable in general, decidability is obtained by restricting it to discrete *infinite time* and discrete *finite space*. Instead of developing a model checker from scratch, we present a modular approach translating Shape Calculus specifications into the WS1S input format of the well-known model checker MONA [KM01]. Thereby, we profit from the work done in this project concerning efficient internal representation and optimisations of the analysis. Subsequently, we introduce the formalism, the scenario of the case study, and demonstrate its applicability using the case study. In section 2, we describe the translation of Shape Calculus in monadic second order logic with one successor predicate (WS1S) before presenting the prototypical implementation of our model checking tool MoDiShCa in section 3. To allow for comparison with other real-time formalisms, we show the feasibility of the approach on the benchmark case study "generalised railroad crossing". To emphasise the strong points of Shape Calculus, we subsequently extend the setting of the case study and investigate the problem of two succeeding trains that cannot be tackled directly by standard real-time formalisms.

1.1   Generalised Railroad Crossing (GRC)

The generalised railroad crossing introduced by Heitmeyer and Lynch in [HL94] is a benchmark example for specification and verification formalisms for real-time systems. However, although the spatial behaviour is crucial in this system, these aspects are often neglected and abstracted in the analysis. The case study considers a railroad crossing and a controller that shall close the gates early enough when a train is approaching to ensure that the train cannot reach the gate while it is open. The controller uses a sensor to detect if the rails are empty, if there is a train approaching the gate or on the crossing. Figure 1 illustrates these different spatial zones before the railroad crossing. Using the safety requirement of the UNiFORM [KBPOB99] project, we

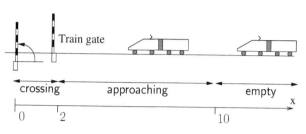

Fig. 1. The train gate zones

extend the classical case study by the following: For switching trains near railroad stations, railroad crossings may be passed successively by more than one trains moving in the same direction without intermediately opening the gates as illustrated in figure 1. In this case two trains shall not collide.

2 Shape Calculus

We introduce the Shape Calculus – proposed in [Sch05b] as an extention of Duration Calculus [ZHR91] – in a discrete spatio-temporal setting. System behaviour is modelled by observables which depend on the point in time *and* position in space. In [Sch05b] we have shown that Shape Calculus is not recursively enumerable for infinite discrete time and space domains, in contrast to Duration Calculus for which to corresponding subset is still decidable for infinite discrete time domains. Decidable subsets of Shape Calculus are discussed in [Sch05a] and it turns out that having only one dimension with infinite discrete domain and all other dimensions having only finite domains yields decidability and henceforth the feasibility of model-checking. With more than one infinite dimensions it is possible to encode the tiling problem for the Euclidean plane. We choose a discrete infinite time domain, here the set N, and a discrete *finite* space. The model-checking approach which we present here relies on the possibility to explicitly enumerate all spatial points. Since space is bounded in real-life applications, the restriction to a finite spatial domain is not severe in contrast to restricting to a finite temporal domain. Such a restriction would prevent us from verifying the absence of errors as the restricted observation interval could be chosen to small to exhibit the erroneous behaviour.

As we present a model checking technique by translation, we need to review syntax and semantics of Shape Calculus. A priory fixing a number n of spatial dimensions and an upper bound (its cardinality $card(i)$) for the space in each dimension, the semantics of an observable X is formally given by a trajectory $\mathcal{I}$ assigning each moment in time and point in space a boolean value. Instead of enumerating the dimensions by natural numbers, we will use mnemonic names like x, y to identify the spatial dimensions and t to identify the temporal dimension. The language of SC is built from state expressions and formulae. A state expression characterises a property of one point in time and space. They are denoted by π and built from boolean combinations of observables. The semantics is a function $\mathcal{I}[\![\pi]\!] : \mathbb{N} \times \prod_{i=1}^{n} \{0, \dots, card(i) - 1\} \to \{0, 1\}$ and is defined as a straightforward extension of trajectories of observables.

$$\mathcal{I}[\![\neg \pi]\!](z) \stackrel{df}{=} 1 - \mathcal{I}[\![\pi]\!](z) \qquad \mathcal{I}[\![\pi \wedge \pi']\!](z) \stackrel{df}{=} \mathcal{I}[\![\pi]\!](z) \cdot \mathcal{I}[\![\pi']\!](z)$$

Formulas are interpreted over n-dimensional intervals and — as usual for interval logics — they incorporate a special "chop" operator illustrated in figure 2 to partition the current interval into two parts. As we consider a higher dimensional logic, we allow chops along each axis. Formally, the set of *formulas* is defined by

$$F ::= \lceil \pi \rceil \mid \lceil \pi \rceil_{e_i} \mid \lceil \pi \rceil_{e_t} \mid F_1 \langle e_i \rangle F_2 \mid F_1 \langle e_t \rangle F_2 \mid$$
$$\ell_{e_i} \sim x \mid \ell_{e_t} \sim x \mid \neg F_1 \mid F_1 \wedge F_2$$

where e_i is the i-th unit vector and e_t denotes the unit vector in the temporal dimension. The terms ℓ_{e_i} and ℓ_{e_t} provide the diameter of the current spatial and temporal interval, respectively and can be compared with first order variables x over the natural numbers, i.e. $\sim \in \{=, \leq, \geq, <, >\}$. Comparison of interval lengths with constants is handled accordingly. Although the original definition in [Sch05b] does not distinguish temporal and spatial dimensions and intervals, the distinction is introduced here for clarification as all spatial dimensions are assumed to be finite whereas the temporal dimension is assumed to be discrete and infinite.

The boolean connectives and the quantifications over the natural numbers are defined as usual in first order logic, so we omit a description here and go into details only for the uncommon operators. In the following let D be an n-dimensional spatial, $[t_1, t_2]$ a one-dimensional temporal interval and $\mathcal{V}$ a valuation of the variables.

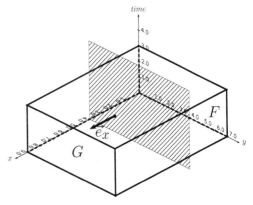

Fig. 2. The Chop Operation for $F \langle e_x \rangle G$

Notation. To give a concise definition of the semantics, we introduce the following notation. Let $D = [a_1, b_1] \times \dots \times [a_m, b_m]$ be a discrete m-dimensional interval. We denote the lower bound a_i of the i-th dimension by $\min_i D$ and the upper bound b_i by $\max_i D$ respectively. Furthermore, denote by $D \prec_i r \stackrel{df}{=} [a_1, b_1] \times \dots \times [a_i, r] \times \dots \times [a_m, b_m]$ the first subinterval obtained by chopping the original interval along the i-th axis at position r and the second part by $D \succ_i r \stackrel{df}{=} [a_1, b_1] \times \dots \times [r, b_i] \times [a_m, b_m]$. The "interior" D^- of D is defined by $D^- \stackrel{df}{=} [a_1, b_1) \times \dots \times [a_m, b_m)$. Using Z-notation, we define $x \oplus \{i \mapsto r\}$ to be the vector x having its i-th component replaced by r.

Almost Everywhere. The everywhere operator $\lceil \pi \rceil$ expresses that the state assertion π is true on all points in space and time. As not all system properties depend on all dimensions, Shape Calculus provides projections onto axes. The everywhere operator with projection on the ith axis $\lceil \pi \rceil_{e_i}$ performs a projection of all points fulfilling π onto the ith axis and then checks if every point on this axis is the target such a projection. This intuition is formally characterised by the following definitions.

$\mathcal{I}, \mathcal{V}, [t_1, t_2], D \models \lceil \pi \rceil$ iff $t_1 < t_2$ and for all $i, \min_i D < \max_i D$ and
$$\forall t \in [t_1, t_2) \, \forall \boldsymbol{x} \in D^- : \mathcal{I}[\![\pi]\!](t, \boldsymbol{x}) = 1$$
$\mathcal{I}, \mathcal{V}, [t_1, t_2], D \models \lceil \pi \rceil_{e_i}$ iff $\min_i D < \max_i D$ and
$$\forall r \in [\min_i D, \max_i D) \, \exists \boldsymbol{x} \in D^- \, \exists t \in [t_1, t_2) :$$
$$\mathcal{I}[\![\pi]\!](t, \boldsymbol{x} \oplus \{i \mapsto r\}) = 1$$
$\mathcal{I}, \mathcal{V}, [t_1, t_2], D \models \lceil \pi \rceil_{e_t}$ iff $t_1 < t_2$ and $\forall t \in [t_1, t_2) \, \exists \boldsymbol{x} \in D^- : \mathcal{I}[\![\pi]\!](t, \boldsymbol{x}) = 1$

Chop. A formula $F \langle e_i \rangle G$ is satisfied on an n-dimensional interval if there is a point $\boldsymbol{m}$ in the current observation interval such that the two n-dimensional subintervals induced by the hyperplane defined by the point $\boldsymbol{m}$ and the orthogonal vector e_i satisfy F and G respectively. As the n-dimensional observation interval is the n-fold Cartesian product of 1-dimensional intervals, the chopping operation in the i-th dimension can be formally defined by splitting the corresponding 1-dimensional interval.

$\mathcal{I}, \mathcal{V}, [t_1, t_2], D \models F \langle e_i \rangle G$ iff $\exists m \in [\min_i D, \max_i D] : \mathcal{I}, \mathcal{V}, [t_1, t_2], (D \prec_i m) \models F$
$$\text{and } \mathcal{I}, \mathcal{V}, [t_1, t_2], (D \succ_i m) \models G$$
$\mathcal{I}, \mathcal{V}, [t_1, t_2], D \models F \langle e_t \rangle G$ iff $\exists t \in [t_1, t_2] : \mathcal{I}, \mathcal{V}, [t_1, t], D \models F$
$$\text{and } \mathcal{I}, \mathcal{V}, [t, t_2], D \models G$$

Diameters. As ℓ_{e_i} refers to the diameter of the current spatial observation interval in direction e_i, and ℓ_{e_t} to the diameter of the current temporal observation interval, its semantics is defined as follows:

$$\mathcal{I}, \mathcal{V}, [t_1, t_2], D \models \ell_{e_i} \sim x \text{ iff } \max_i D - \min_i D \sim \mathcal{V}(x)$$
$$\mathcal{I}, \mathcal{V}, [t_1, t_2], D \models \ell_{e_t} \sim x \text{ iff } t_2 - t_1 \sim \mathcal{V}(x)$$

Abbreviations and Derived Modalities. Some abbreviations commonly used in Duration Calculus ease the handling. We will use d to denote spatial dimensions as well as temporal dimensions. The empty interval $\ell_{e_d} = 0$ is denoted by $\lceil \rceil_{e_d}$. The somewhere operator $\Diamond_{e_d} F$ is satisfied iff F is true on some subinterval:

$$\Diamond_{e_d} F \stackrel{df}{=} \text{true} \langle e_d \rangle F \langle e_d \rangle \text{true}$$

The dual globally operator $\Box_{e_d}$ expresses validity on all subintervals and is defined by

$$\Box_{e_d} F \stackrel{df}{=} \neg \Diamond_{e_d} \neg F.$$

2.1   The Railroad Crossing in SC

In this section we elaborate a formal model of the GRC case study in Shape Calculus. This model is used subsequently for the demonstration of the model checker MoDiShCa. In the first part, we model the standard GRC in Shape Calculus. In the second part, we elaborate a specification for two trains that pass the crossing successively.

The Standard Benchmark Version. We model the rails using one spatial dimension x and employ two observables: train and open. The observable train is true in a spatial point at a given time iff the train occupies this position at that point in time. The other observable models the gate status, it is true iff the gate is open. The train touches the bound of a spatial interval if this interval cannot be split such that there is no train on the first part. This is defined in SC as follows:

$$\text{trainPartWeak} \overset{df}{=} \neg(\lceil\neg\text{train}\rceil \langle e_x \rangle \, true).$$

While trainPartWeak is satisfied for the *empty* observation interval without enforcing the existence of a train, the existence is ensured by a stronger version additionally requiring the observation interval to be non-zero.

$$\text{trainPart} \overset{df}{=} \text{trainPartWeak} \wedge \ell_{e_x} > 0$$

Using this specification, the distance of the nearest train is captured by the following formula:

$$\text{dist}(\delta) \overset{df}{=} ((\lceil\neg\text{train}\rceil \vee \lceil\rceil_{e_x}) \wedge \ell_{e_x} = \delta) \langle e_x \rangle \, \text{trainPart}$$

Using the chop operator $\langle e_x \rangle$, we split the track into two parts such that the leftmost part has length δ and is not occupied by any train. As the rightmost part itself cannot be split again without the beginning being occupied, this expresses the maximality of the chopping position and therefore the maximum choice for the variable δ. Using this pattern, we can formally specify the three regions *empty*, *approaching* and *crossing*.

$$\text{empty} \overset{df}{=} \lceil\neg\text{train}\rceil \qquad \text{appr} \overset{df}{=} \text{dist}(\delta) \wedge 2 \leq \delta < 10 \qquad \text{cross} \overset{df}{=} \text{dist}(\delta) \wedge \delta < 2$$

Thus, the track is empty iff there is no train. The train is considered to be approaching (appr) if it is in the spatial interval $[2, 10)$, and it is crossing (cross) if it is in the interval $[0, 2)$. We model the train to proceed with velocity MAXSPEED spatial units per time unit and define the progress requirement by the following formula.

$$\text{runProgress} \overset{df}{=} \square_{e_t} \square_{e_x} \Big(((\ell_{e_x} = \text{MAXSPEED} \langle e_x \rangle \, \text{trainPart}) \wedge \ell_{e_t} = 1) \langle e_t \rangle \ell_{e_t} = 1 \Big)$$

$$\Rightarrow (\ell_{e_t} = 1 \langle e_t \rangle \, \text{trainPart})$$

The formula runProgress reads as follows. If for some spatio-temporal subinterval some part of the train has distance of MAXSPEED spatial units then one time-unit later it has distance zero. The operators $\Box_{e_t}$ and $\Box_{e_x}$ quantify over all spatio-temporal subintervals. A subinterval satisfies the antecedent of the implication if it can be chopped in time such that both subintervals have a temporal length of one. Furthermore, the first subinterval can be chopped in space such that the first part has length MAXSPEED and the second part satisfies trainPart. Henceforth, the antecedent is satisfied if the train is MAXSPEED spatial units away at the beginning. Similarly, the succedent is satisfied if the interval is chopped in the middle again and the train has arrived on the second part. Vice versa, we have to ensure that a train may only have distance zero now if it has been MAXSPEED spatial units away a second ago. Otherwise teleportation would be permitted by the specification.

$$\text{runMaxSpeed} \overset{df}{=} \Box_{e_t}\Box_{e_x}\left(\ell_{e_x} > \text{MAXSPEED} \wedge (\ell_{e_t} = 1 \langle e_t \rangle \text{ trainPart})\right)$$
$$\Rightarrow \left(\left((\ell_{e_x} = \text{MAXSPEED} \langle e_x \rangle \text{ trainPart}) \wedge \ell_{e_t} = 1\right) \langle e_t \rangle \ell_{e_t} = 1\right)$$

We need the following assumptions about the environment. Initially, the track is assumed to be empty and REACTTIME time units after some train is detected in the approaching or crossing region the gates are closed.

$$\text{initEmpty} \overset{df}{=} \ell_{e_t} > 0 \Rightarrow (\text{empty} \langle e_t \rangle \, true)$$

$$\text{reactBound} \overset{df}{=} \Box_{e_t}\left((\text{appr} \vee \text{cross}) \wedge \ell_{e_t} > \text{REACTTIME}\right)$$
$$\Rightarrow \left((\ell_{e_t} = \text{REACTTIME}) \langle e_t \rangle \lceil \neg\text{open} \rceil\right)$$

Using these assumptions, the main safety requirement can be automatically verified for predefined values of MAXSPEED and REACTTIME:

$$\text{runProgress} \wedge \text{runMaxSpeed} \wedge \text{initEmpty} \wedge \text{reactBound} \Rightarrow \neg\Diamond_{e_t}(\text{cross} \wedge \lceil\text{open}\rceil)$$

Extending the GRC. To allow for two trains to pass the crossing successively, we introduce two observables train_1 and train_2 and assume the constants MAXSPEED_1 and MAXSPEED_2 to describe the speed of first and the second train, respectively. The movement of both trains is modelled using the same patterns as in the previous section. The only new requirement that is needed is initial mutual exclusion, i.e,

$$\text{initExcl} \overset{df}{=} \neg\Diamond_{e_t}(\ell_{e_x} = 9) \langle e_x \rangle \lceil\text{train}_1 \wedge \text{train}_2\rceil$$

This formula reads as follows: It is never possible that on the last spatial position both train_1 and train_2 are true. Using this assumption and assuming that both trains have the same speed, i.e., $\text{MAXSPEED}_1 = \text{MAXSPEED}_2$, it is possible to verify a second safety requirement expressing that two trains never collide.

$$\text{safety}_2 \overset{df}{=} \neg\Diamond_{e_t}\Diamond_{e_x}\lceil\text{train}_1 \wedge \text{train}_2\rceil.$$

3   From SC to WS1S

Weak second order logic with one successor (WS1S) is a decidable subset of monadic second order logic. In addition to first order logic, second order logic introduces the possibility to use quantifiers over relations. *Monadic* second order logic permits only quantification over sets. In *weak* S1S the interpretation of the second order quantifiers $\exists X$ and $\forall X$ are changed into "there is a *finite* subset X of $\mathbb{N}$..." and "for all *finite* subsets X of $\mathbb{N}$...". However, this change of the interpretation does not affect the expressiveness of the logic [Tho97]. Weak S1S formulas can be constructed using the following EBNF grammar:

$$F ::= x \in X \mid \exists x : F \mid \exists X : F \mid F \wedge G \mid \neg F \mid S(x, y)$$

where X is a second order variable, x and y are first order variables, F and G are formulas and $S(x, y)$ is the successor predicate necessary for the temporal ordering; the expression $S(x, y)$ is true iff $y = x + 1$. The successor predicate can be used to define the ordering relations $<, \leq, =, > \geq$.

3.1   MONA

MONA [KM01] is a model checker for WS1S. Its development started 1994 at BRICS [HJJ+95]. MONA translates the formulas into finite automata and performs a reachability check representing the transition relation using BDDs. Among others, it is used as a backend by the model checker DCValid for Duration Calculus with discrete time [Pan00].

3.2   Model-Checking Shape Calculus

To use the model checker MONA for automatic verification with Shape Calculus, we translate the SC formulas into WS1S. Fixing the number of spatial dimensions to be n, we introduce for each observable X and each point x in the finite space one second order variable X_x – thus altogether $\prod_{i=0}^{n} card(i) \cdot |Obs|$ variables – such that X_x models the truth value of X at spatial position x on the time line. The intuition is that the observable X is true at spatial point x and point in time t iff $t \in X_x$. Assuming a temporal interval $[t_1, t_2]$ and a spatial interval D, we derive a WS1S formula that is satisfiable iff the SC formula is satisfiable on these intervals. The temporal interval is parametric, i.e,, t_1 and t_2 are first order variables, whereas D is known at translation time. The translation is accomplished by a translation function $SO([t_1, t_2], D)(F)$ taking the temporal interval $[t_1, t_2]$, the spatial interval D and the formula F as parameters. A Shape Calculus formula F is satisfiable iff there is a temporal interval $[t_1, t_2]$ and spatial interval D such that the translation to WS1S is satisfiable for these intervals. We present the definition of SO inductively on the structure of the Shape Calculus formula F. We use the same names for the axes as in the previous section.

State expressions are boolean combinations of observables and they translate straightforward into second order logic using set operations and boolean connectives. For simplicity in the following presentation, we only consider the simple state expression X involving no boolean operators, which is translated into $t_m \in X_{\boldsymbol{x}}$. Note that the state expression $\neg X$ is translated into $t_m \notin X_{\boldsymbol{x}}$ and $X \wedge Y$ is translated into $t_m \in X_{\boldsymbol{x}} \wedge t_m \in Y_{\boldsymbol{x}}$.

Translating $\lceil X \rceil$ *(everywhere-Operation).* As the formula is satisfied on a spatio-temporal interval, if X is true for all points in time and space, the second order translation involves quantification over all temporal and all spatial points. Due to the finiteness of all spatial dimensions, the universal quantification over spatial points can be expressed by a *finite* conjunction.

$$SO([t_1, t_2], D)(\lceil X \rceil) = t_1 < t_2 \wedge \bigwedge_{i=0}^{n} \min_i D < \max_i D \wedge$$

$$\forall t_m : t_1 \leq t_m < t_2 \Rightarrow \bigwedge_{\boldsymbol{x} \in D^-} t_m \in X_{\boldsymbol{x}}$$

Translating $\lceil X \rceil_{e_i}$ *and* $\lceil X \rceil_{e_t}$. The formula $\lceil X \rceil_{e_i}$ evaluates to true if for all possible values of $x_i \in [\min_i D, \max_i D)$ of the spatial observation interval, there is a point in time and space that a) satisfies X and b) projects on x_i. Clearly, this is a projection to the i-th spatial axis. The existential quantification over spatial points is expressed as finite disjunction over all possible points.

$$SO([t_1, t_2], D)(\lceil X \rceil_{e_i}) = t_1 < t_2 \wedge \min_i D < \max_i D \wedge$$

$$\bigwedge_{x_i = \min_i D}^{\max_i D - 1} \bigvee_{\boldsymbol{x} \in D^-} \exists t_m : t_1 \leq t_m < t_2 \wedge t_m \in X_{\boldsymbol{x} \oplus \{i \mapsto x_i\}}$$

The operator $\lceil X \rceil_{e_t}$ (all-the-time) expresses that for every point in time t there is a vector $\boldsymbol{x}$ such that X is true at the point $\boldsymbol{x}$ and time t. Obviously, this is a projection to the time line.

$$SO([t_1, t_2], D)(\lceil X \rceil_t) = t_1 < t_2 \wedge \forall t_m : t_1 \leq t_m < t_2 \Rightarrow \bigvee_{\boldsymbol{x} \in D^-} t_m \in X_{\boldsymbol{x}}$$

Translating chops. The temporal chop is defined as: there is a point t in the current temporal interval such that F is true in the interval $[t_1, t]$ and G is true in the interval $[t, t_2]$. Hence, we translate it using conjunction and changing the timestamp parameters.

$$SO([t_1, t_2], D)(F \langle e_t \rangle G) = \exists t_m : t_1 \leq t_m \leq t_2 \wedge$$

$$SO([t_1, t_m], D)(F) \wedge SO([t_m, t_2], D)(G)$$

The chop operator in e_i direction is defined as: there is a point x_m on the ith-axis such that F is true for the subinterval "below" x_m and G is true for the subinterval "above". To translate this operation, we use the same idea as for the translation of the temporal chop, but explicitly calculate all possible intervals $D \prec_i x_m$ and $D \succ_i x_m$ instead of changing the timestamps.

$$SO([t_1, t_2], D)(F \langle e_i \rangle G) = \bigvee_{x_m = \min_i D}^{\max_i D} \Big(SO([t_1, t_2], D \prec_i x_m)(F) \wedge$$
$$SO([t_1, t_2], D \succ_i x_m)(G) \Big)$$

Translating boolean connectives. The translation of conjunction and negation is straightforward. The requirement $t_1 \leq t_2$ is ensured by the overall construction, so we do not need to add it explicitly for the negation.

$$SO([t_1, t_2], D)(F \wedge G) = SO([t_1, t_2], D)(F) \wedge SO([t_1, t_2], D)(G)$$
$$SO([t_1, t_2], D)(\neg F) = \neg SO([t_1, t_2], D)(F)$$

Translating length expressions. Using $l_{e_t} \sim n$ with $\sim \in \{\leq, \geq, <, >, =\}$, we can determine the length of the temporal interval. In the temporal case, l_{e_t} is obtained as the difference of the two boundaries of the temporal interval, namely

$$SO([t_1, t_2], D)(l_t \sim n) = t_2 - t_1 \sim n.$$

As WS1S encompasses Presburger arithmetic with inequality this encoding is a valid WS1S formula. In contrast, expressions involving l_{e_i} — a length of the spatial observation interval — are to be calculated explicitly beforehand. Due to the finiteness of space, all spatial intervals are explicitly enumerated and therefore the length can always be calculated. Hence, the length of the spatial interval l_{e_i} is given by

$$SO([t_1, t_2], D)(l_{d_i} \sim n) = \begin{cases} true & \text{if } \max_i D - \min_i D \sim n. \\ false & \text{otherwise} \end{cases}$$

which can be evaluated during the translation process.

4   Automatic Verification of Shape Calculus Specifications

A prototype of the decision procedure presented beforehand is implemented in the tool MoDiShCa [Que05]. In the spirit of DCValid [Pan00] it translates a textual representation of the discrete SC into MONA syntax and uses MONA as a backend for satisfiability and validity checking. Additionally, MONA is able to generate satisfying examples and counterexamples. Beyond the operators defined in section 2 further operators are implemented in order to enhance the usability of the program. Additionally, MoDiShCa supports formula macros, constants and integer variables permitting structured specifications.

4.1   The Tool MoDiShCa

MoDiShCa supports an arbitrary number of spatial dimensions which have to be declared together with their cardinality as sketched in Figure 4. Observables can either be Boolean or bounded integers. Formula macros can be used to make the specifications more concise. The formula to examine is introduced by the keyword `verify:` in the last line in the file. As the translation of SC for satisfiability checking is different from the encoding for validity checking, the keyword `validity` is

Operation	SC	MoDiShCa
Everywhere	$\lceil \pi \rceil$	`[pi]`
Everywhere in direction x	$\lceil \pi \rceil_x$	`[pi]_x`
All the time	$\lceil \pi \rceil_t$	`[pi]_t`
Temporal chop	$\langle t \rangle$	`<t>`
Spatial chop	$\langle x \rangle$	`<x>`
Diameter of interval	ℓ_{e_t} or ℓ_{e_x}	`l_t or l_x`
Always	$\square_t$ or $\square_x$	`[]_t or []_x`
Eventually	$\Diamond_t$ or $\Diamond_x$	`<>_t or <>_x`
Boolean Connectives	$\wedge, \vee, \Rightarrow, \Leftrightarrow, \neg$	`&,|,->,<->,not`

Fig. 3. MoDiShCa syntax

used to switch MoDiShCa to validity checking mode, as shown in listing 1. An overview of the operator syntax is given in Figure 3.

4.2 Checking the Extended Generalised Railroad Crossing

The specification of the extended case study in MoDiShCa syntax is given abbreviatedly in listing 1. As the spatial points are explicitly enumerated, the spatial parameters have to be instantiated to concrete values. Henceforth, we assume MAXSPEED $= 1$ and REACTTIME $= 5$ in this specification and verified the

requirement increasing the cardinality of the spatial dimension. The results of the tests presented in Figure 5 were conducted on an AMD Sempron 2800+ with 1 GB RAM. For a spatial cardinality of 5 the safety requirement is not satisfied, as the train can proceed 5 spatial units during the reaction time. This behaviour is exhibited by the generated counterexample. Similarly to DCValid for Duration Calculus, MoDiShCa suffers from the nonelementary complexity

Declaration	Keyword	Example
Boolean observable	`bool`	`bool X`
Integer observable	`int`	`int a[5]`
Constant	`const`	`const ten = 10`
Spatial dimension	`dim`	`dim x = 3`
Formula macro		`$req = [X]<t>[Y]`

Fig. 4. MoDiShCa declaration part

Card.	MoDiShCa	file size	MONA
5	0.05 sec	192 K	0.3 sec
10	0.15 sec	1.7 M	2.7 sec
11	0.20 sec	2.3 M	4.2 sec
12	0.28 sec	3.2 M	7.8 sec
13	0.40 sec	4.4 M	13.7 sec
14	0.52 sec	5.9 M	26.2 sec
15	0.66 sec	7.8 M	Overflow of MONA BDD structure

Fig. 5. GRC: Results for checking safety

of the validity problem. The W1S1 formula grows polynomial in the size of the spatial dimension (its cardinality) and the degree of the polynomial is determined by the number of nested spatial chops. Hence, even small spatial dimensions

– here size of 15 – exceed the capacity of MONA, although the MONA developers devoted much attention to an efficient BDD based representation of the transition relation. The usage of projection in specifications permits more system behaviour and therefore increases the model checking complexity. Specifying the three zones *empty*, *approach*, and *crossing* using projection onto the x axis exceeds the capabilities of MONA even for a space of cardinality ten.

```
bool t1;               # declaration of observable t1 for the first train
bool t2;               # declaration of observable t2 for the second train
dim x = 6;             # declaration of dimension with cardinality 6
const speed1 = 1;      # declaration of the constant speed1 for
                       # the first train, the same for second train
const reactTime = 5;   # declaration of constant reactTime for
                       # the gate controller
validity; # checking for validity
## specification of the GRC in MoDiShCa Syntax
# The train−patterns
$trainPart1    = (( not ([not t1] <x> true)) & l_x > 0) ;
$trainPartWeak1 = (( not ([not t1] <x> true))) ;
# defining the three zones
$empty = ([not t1] & [not t2]);
$appr = ([(not t1) & (not t2)] & l_x < 5 & l_x >= 2)
  <x> not ([not (not t1) & (not t2)] <x> true);
$cross = ((([(not t1) & (not t2)] & l_x < 2 ) | l_x = 0)
  <x> ((not ([(not t1) & (not t2)] <x> true)) & l_x > 1);
# Defining the movement of both trains
$runProgress1 = ([]_t ([]_x
  ((((((l_x = speed1)<x> ($trainPart1))& l_t = 1) <t>(l_t=1))
    -> (l_t = 1 <t> (($trainPart1)))))));
$runMaxSpeed1 = ([]_t ([]_x
  ((l_x > speed1 & (l_t = 1 <t> ($trainPart1 & l_t = 1)))
    -> (((l_x = speed1) <x> ($trainPartWeak1))& l_t = 1)
          <t>(l_t=1))));
# ... the same for the second train ...
# specifying the reaction time of the gate controller
$reactAppr = ([]_t ((($appr | $cross) & l_t > reactTime)
      -> ((l_t = reactTime)<t>[not open])));
#assumptions on the Environment
$initEmpty = l_t > 0 -> ($empty <t> true);
$initExclusion = []_t (not (l_x = 5 <x> [t1 & t2] <x> true));
$assumptions = $reactAppr & $initEmpty & l_x = 6
  & $runMaxSpeed1 & $runMaxSpeed2 & $runProgress1
  & $runProgress2 & $initExclusion;
# the safety requirement
$safety = $assumptions ->
    ( (not <>_t <>_x [t1 & t2]) & not (<>_t ($cross & [open]))));
# formula to verify
verify: $safety
```

Listing 1. Extended Railroad crossing in MoDiShCa syntax

5   Discussion

We proposed a formal method extending the Duration Calculus that is able to express spatial aspects of system behaviour as well as temporal aspects, which is well suited for the specification and verification of mobile real-time systems. To the best of our knowledge, we presented the first implementation of a model checker for such a spatio-temporal formalism for mobile real-time systems. To benefit from research on efficient second order model checking, we decided to use the well proven second order model checker MONA as a backend rather than developing a new model checker from scratch. The applicability of the formalism and its model checking approach is demonstrated by elaborating on a well known benchmark case study, extended by explicit spatial modelling.

Related Work. There is a lot of work in the area of spatio-temporal logics, for example formalisms based on modal logic like in [BCWZ02, AvB01, RS85] or spatio-temporal logics [Gal95] based on the Region Connection Calculus by Randell, Cui and Cohn [RCC92] with applications in Artificial Intelligence. However, these approaches do not facilitate measuring time and space. The combination of different modal logics with Kripke semantics is extensively discussed by Gabbay et al in [GKWZ03]. As the logic presented in [WZ03] uses the very general class of metric spaces as semantic models, only one quantitative distance metric is available, losing the ability to distinguish directions.

Other approaches, like [Cai04] and [MWZ03] adopt the π-calculus' [Mil99] or ambient calculus' [CG98] notion of mobility, where mobility is interpreted as the change of links and ambients respectively. For the π-calculus and the logic [Cai04] tool support is available by the SPATIAL LOGICS MODEL CHECKER of Vieira and Caires [VC05].

Perspectives. As indicated by the results of the case study, further investigations of optimisation and reduction possibilities for the generated second order formula are important goals. However, since already for discrete Duration Calculus the validity problem is known to have non-elementary complexity, other approaches deserve further research. This comprises bounded model checking using a combination of SAT solvers and decision procedures as used in [BP06, DS04] or using a different target language as used in [Lam05] for checking real-time requirements. On the other hand, additional expressiveness can be gained by permitting first order variables over a finite domain in SC specifications enabling more concise specifications. Similar to Duration Calculus, a restricted Shape Calculus should be decidable for continuous temporal domains. Such a decision procedure is to implemented in the tool MoDiShCa.

Acknowledgements. The authors thank E.-R. Olderog, A. Platzer, R. Meyer and the other members of the "Correct System Design" group for draft-reading previous versions and fruitful discussions on this topic.

References

[AD94]   R. Alur and D. L. Dill. A theory of timed automata. *Theoretical Computer Science*, 126(2):183–235, 1994.

[AvB01]   M. Aiello and H. van Benthem. A Modal Walk Through Space. Technical report, Institute for Logic, Language and Computation, University of Amsterdam, 2001.

[BCWZ02]   B. Bennett, A.G. Cohn, F. Wolter, and M. Zakharyaschev. Multi-Dimensional Multi-Modal Logics as a Framework for Spatio-Temporal Reasoning. *Applied Intelligence*, 17(3):239–251, 2002.

[BDL04]   G. Behrmann, A. David, and K. G. Larsen. A tutorial on UPPAAL. In M. Bernardo and F. Corradini, editors, *Formal Methods for the Design of Real-Time Systems: 4th International School on Formal Methods for the Design of Computer, Communication, and Software Systems, SFM-RT 2004*, number 3185 in LNCS, pages 200–236. Springer–Verlag, September 2004.

[BDM+98]   M. Bozga, C. Daws, O. Maler, A. Olivero, S. Tripakis, and S. Yovine. Kronos: A model-checking tool for real-time systems. In A. J. Hu and M. Y. Vardi, editors, *Proc. 10th International Conference on Computer Aided Verification, Vancouver, Canada*, volume 1427, pages 546–550. Springer-Verlag, 1998.

[BP06]   G. M. Brown and L. Pike. Easy parameterized verification of biphase mark and 8n1 protocols. In H. Hermanns and J. Palsberg, editors, *TACAS*, volume 3920 of *Lecture Notes in Computer Science*, pages 58–72. Springer, 2006.

[Cai04]   L. Caires. Behavioral and spatial observations in a logic for the pi-calculus. In I. Walukiewicz, editor, *FoSSaCS*, volume 2987 of *Lecture Notes in Computer Science*, pages 72–89. Springer, 2004.

[CG98]   L. Cardelli and A. D. Gordon. Mobile ambients. In Maurice Nivat, editor, *FoSSaCS*, volume 1378 of *Lecture Notes in Computer Science*, pages 140–155. Springer, 1998.

[Die99]   H. Dierks. *Specification and Verification of Polling Real-Time Systems*. PhD thesis, University of Oldenburg, July 1999.

[DS04]   B. Dutertre and M. Sorea. Modeling and verification of a fault-tolerant real-time startup protocol using calendar automata. In Y. Lakhnech and S. Yovine, editors, *FORMATS/FTRTFT*, volume 3253 of *Lecture Notes in Computer Science*, pages 199–214. Springer, 2004.

[Gal95]   A. Galton. Towards a qualitative theory of movement. In *Spatial Information Theory*, pages 377–396, 1995.

[GKWZ03]   D. Gabbay, A. Kurucz, F. Wolter, and M. Zakharyaschev. *Many-Dimensional Modal Logics: Theory and Applications*. Elsevier, 2003.

[HJJ+95]   J.G. Henriksen, J. Jensen, M. Jørgensen, N. Klarlund, B. Paige, T. Rauhe, and A. Sandholm. Mona: Monadic second-order logic in practice. In *Tools and Algorithms for the Construction and Analysis of Systems, First International Workshop, TACAS '95, LNCS 1019*, 1995.

[HL94]   C. L. Heitmeyer and N. A. Lynch. The generalized railroad crossing: A case study in formal verification of real-time systems. In *IEEE Real-Time Systems Symposium*, pages 120–131. IEEE Computer Society, 1994.

[HZ04]   M. R. Hansen and Zhou Chaochen. *Duration Calculus: A Formal Approach to Real-Time Systems*. EATCS: Monographs in Theoretical Computer Science. Springer, 2004.

[KBPOB99]   B. Krieg-Brückner, J. Peleska, E.-R. Olderog, and A. Baer. The UniForM Workbench, a Universal Development Environment for Formal Methods. In J.M. Wing, J. Woodcock, and J. Davies, editors, *FM'99 – Formal Methods*, volume 1709 of *Lecture Notes in Computer Science*, pages 1186–1205. Springer, 1999.

[KM01]   N. Klarlund and A. Møller. MONA Version 1.4 User Manual. Technical report, Department of Computer Science, University of Aarhus, January 2001.

[Lam05]   L. Lamport. Real-time model checking is really simple. In D. Borrione and W. J. Paul, editors, *CHARME*, volume 3725 of *Lecture Notes in Computer Science*, pages 162–175. Springer, 2005.

[Mil99]   R. Milner. *Communicating and mobile systems: the π-calculus*. Cambridge University Press, 1999.

[MWZ03]   S. Merz, M. Wirsing, and J. Zappe. A Spatio-Temporal Logic for the Specification and Refinement of Mobile Systems. In M. Pezzè, editor, *FASE 2003, Warsaw, Poland*, volume 2621 of *LNCS*, pages 87–1014. Springer, 2003.

[Pan00]   P.K. Pandya. Specifying and deciding quantified discrete-time duration calculus formulae using dcvalid. Technical report, Tata Institute of Fundamental Research, 2000.

[Que05]   J.-D. Quesel. MoDiShCa: Model-Checking discrete Shape Calculus. Minor Thesis, University of Oldenburg, August 2005.

[RCC92]   D. A. Randell, Z. Cui, and A. Cohn. A Spatial Logic Based on Regions and Connection. In B. Nebel, C. Rich, and W. Swartout, editors, *KR'92.*, pages 165–176. Morgan Kaufmann, San Mateo, California, 1992.

[RS85]   J. H. Reif and A. P. Sistla. A multiprocess network logic with temporal and spatial modalities. *J. Comput. Syst. Sci.*, 30(1):41–53, 1985.

[Sch05a]   A. Schäfer. Axiomatisation and Decidability of Multi-Dimensional Duration Calculus. In J. Chomicki and D. Toman, editors, *Proceedings of the 12th International Symposium on Temporal Representation and Reasoning, TIME 2005*, pages 122–130. IEEE Computer Society, June 2005.

[Sch05b]   A. Schäfer. A Calculus for Shapes in Time and Space. In Z. Liu and K. Araki, editors, *Theoretical Aspects of Computing, ICTAC 2004*, volume 3407 of *LNCS*, pages 463–478. Springer, 2005.

[Tho97]   W. Thomas. Languages, automata, and logic. In Grzegorz Rozenberg and Arto Salomaa, editors, *Handbook of formal languages*, volume III, chapter 7, pages 389–455. Springer-Verlag New York, Inc., 1997.

[VC05]   H. Vieira and L. Caires. The spatial logic model checker user's manual. Technical report, Departamento de Informatica, FCT/UNL, 2005. TR-DI/FCT/UNL-03/2004.

[WZ03]   F. Wolter and M. Zakharyaschev. Reasoning about distances. In G. Gottlob and T. Walsh, editors, *IJCAI-03, Acapulco, Mexico, August 9-15, 2003*, pages 1275–1282. Morgan Kaufmann, 2003.

[ZHR91]   Zhou Chaochen, C.A.R. Hoare, and A.P. Ravn. A calculus of durations. *IPL*, 40(5):269–276, 1991.

Tutorial on Formal Methods for Distributed and Cooperative Systems

Christine Choppy[1], Serge Haddad[2], Hanna Klaudel[3], Fabrice Kordon[4],
Laure Petrucci[1], and Yann Thierry-Mieg[4]

[1] Université Paris 13, LIPN, CNRS UMR 7030
99 avenue Jean-Baptiste Clément, F-93430 Villetaneuse, France
{Christine.Choppy, Laure.Petrucci}@lipn.univ-paris13.fr
[2] Université Paris-Dauphine, LAMSADE, CNRS UMR 7024
place du Maréchal de Lattre de Tassigny, F-75775 Paris Cedex 16
haddad@lamsade.dauphine.fr
[3] Université d'Evry-Val-d'Essone, IBISC, CNRS FRE 2873
523, place des Terrasses de l'Agora, 91000 Evry - France
Hanna.Klaudel@ibisc.fr
[4] Université P. & M. Curie, LIP6/MoVe, CNRS UMR 7606
4, place Jussieu, F-75252 Paris Cedex 05, France
Fabrice.Kordon@lip6.fr, Yann.Thierry-Mieg@lip6.fr

Abstract.

1   Introduction

This tutorial is proposed by representatives of the MeFoSyLoMa[1] group. MeFo-SyLoMa is an informal group gathering several teams from various universities in the Paris area:

- Université Paris-Dauphine (LAMSADE laboratory),
- Université P. & M. Curie (LIP6 laboratory),
- Université Paris 13 (LIPN laboratory),
- ENST (LTCI laboratory),
- Conservatoire National des Arts et Métiers (CEDRIC laboratory).

These teams have extensive knowledge and experience in the design, analysis and implementation of distributed systems. The cooperation within the group aims at joining forces, sharing experiences and building joint projects to solve issues in the design of reliable distributed systems.

One of the major actions of this community is a collective book due to appear in the fall 2006, and entitled *"Formal Methods for Distributed Cooperative Systems"* (*Méthodes formelles pour les systèmes répartis et coopératifs* in french, published by Hermès). The purpose of this book is to gather a state of the art of

---

[1] MeFoSyLoMa stands for *Formal Methods for Software and Hardware Systems* (*Méthodes Formelles pour les Systèmes Logiciels et Matériels* in french).

K. Barkaoui, A. Cavalcanti, and A. Cerone (Eds.): ICTAC 2006, LNCS 4281, pp. 362–365, 2006.
© Springer-Verlag Berlin Heidelberg 2006

the most advanced techniques for modelling and formal analysis of distributed systems.

The book is divided into three parts, which constitute the basis for the tutorial we propose at ICTAC 2006. Following the design process, the first part deals with specification of distributed systems, the second one with analysis techniques and the third one presents actual experimentations of such modelling and verification techniques in real systems (i.e. industrial size case studies).

Each part of the book will correspond to a two hours tutorial presented by two of the authors of the corresponding part.

2   Part I: Dedicated Specification Languages and Models

This part is devoted to giving guidelines for designing a consistent system model. First, we present criteria to consider so as to build a specification satisfying the demands. Then, methodologies to write specifications are introduced.

Presenters: This part of the tutorial will be presented by:

- Laure PETRUCCI, Professor at University Paris 13, member of the CNRS laboratory LIPN,
- Christine CHOPPY, Professor at University Paris 13, member of the CNRS laboratory LIPN.

Outline: Many sorts of models can be used to specify a complex system. Hence, it might prove difficult, for a non-experienced designer, to choose among this large collection. Therefore, the first part of the presentation is dedicated to criteria that should be taken into account before choosing a modelling formalism: relevant concepts, abstraction level, specification goals, structuring, expected properties.

The *relevant concepts* are the different data types important in the system, timing issues, the structure of the system, i.e. its decomposition into subsystems, sequential or parallel execution mode, synchronous/asynchronous communication. When considering the *abstraction level*, one should keep in mind that the specification process may include incremental development and refinement. The *relevance* of the concepts and the abstraction level must be considered w.r.t. the goals for designing the specification, e.g. time is relevant when checking scheduling issues but may not be when verifying the correctness of a communication protocol. *Structuring the specification* into subsystems allows for both a better view of the different components and reusability. Finally, the *expected properties* must be written in a language consistent with the modelling technique.

Considering all these criteria should help the designer in choosing a specification paradigm, the appropriate level of abstraction and the relevant properties to be checked using the model.

The second part of the presentation is concerned with *guidelines* to start writing the detailed specification, considering data types structures, simple dynamic systems, and dynamic systems structured using subsystems. This approach can be combined with other approaches that guide the overall structuring of the specification using structuring concepts provided by *problem frames*, or *architectural styles*, and with a *component approach* to combine the specifications developed.

3   Part II: Dedicated Verification Techniques

This part is dedicated to efficient verification methods for distributed applications and systems.

Presenters: This part of the tutorial will be presented by:

- Serge HADDAD, Professor at University Paris-Dauphine, member of the CNRS laboratory Lamsade,
- Yann THIERRY-MIEG, Associate Professor at University P. & M. Curie, member of the CNRS laboratory LIP6.

Outline: The presentation comprises two parts.

The diversity of verification methods may puzzle the engineer facing the choice of the appropriate technique for analysing her/his system. So the first part of the presentation aims at clarifying the bases of such a choice by discussing three critical questions associated with the verification process:

- How to choose the formalism for verification?
- How to express the expected properties of the system modelled?
- Which verification methods apply on the model?

The second part of the presentation details one of the most successful verification methods in order to tackle the increasing complexity of the systems: the decision diagram based methods. It starts with a general introduction on data representation and manipulation using such structures. Then it shows how the reachability problem (the main verification problem) can efficiently be handled and how to generalise its application to the model-checking of temporal logic formulae. It concludes by detailing experiments in order to understand when and why the method is successful.

The whole presentation illustrates the different concepts with the help of (extended) Petri nets.

4   Part III: Application to Distributed Systems

This part is dedicated to the effective use of the techniques presented in the design and implementation of real systems.

Presenters: This part of the tutorial will be presented by:

- Fabrice KORDON, Professor at University P. & M. Curie and head of the MoVe (Modelling and Verification) team in the CNRS laboratory LIP6,
- Hanna KLAUDEL, Professor at University Evry-Val-d'Essonne and head of the LIS (Languages, Interaction, Simulation) team in the CNRS laboratory IBISC.

Outline: The presentation is divided into two parts. The first one is devoted to the PolyORB experience. PolyORB is a middleware dedicated to distributed real-time systems. It thus requires high reliability that is achieved by means of an original architecture on which formal verification of qualitative properties (such as absence of deadlock or livelock) is enforced thanks to Symmetric Petri Nets[2]. The presentation will explain how a strong interaction between the design of the software architecture, combined with new model-checking techniques, allows for coping with a high complexity of the formal specification.

The second part deals with the design of adaptive reactive systems, i.e. systems that dynamically adapt their architecture depending on the context of the execution. We use the formalism of timed automata for the design of the modules behaviour. Hence, it is possible to evaluate beforehand the properties of the system (regarding logical correctness and timelines), thanks to model-checking and simulation techniques. The approach is illustrated by a case study for which we show how to produce very quickly a running prototype satisfying the properties of the model, and how to evaluate *a priori* the pertinence of adaptive strategies.

5   Conclusion

This tutorial is thus intended for young researchers or engineers to have an overview of the specification process.

The first part is concerned with specification issues. Indeed, writing a specification from scratch is a difficult task for a non-experienced person. The criteria pointed out and the specification design methodology should help in choosing the appropriate formalism and starting the design of a system.

The second part is devoted to analysis issues. A complex model is intrinsically difficult to analyse. It is thus important to choose the appropriate technique to prove the expected properties of the system. Some advanced techniques are also shortly presented, which give a feeling on how to handle large systems.

Finally, the third part shows how these techniques have been succcesfully applied to real systems.

---

[2] Formerly called in the literature Well-formed Petri Nets.

Decision Procedures for the Formal Analysis of Software

David Déharbe[1,*], Pascal Fontaine[2],
Silvio Ranise[2,3], and Christophe Ringeissen[2]

[1] UFRN/DIMAp, Natal, Brazil
[2] LORIA, Nancy, France
[3] Univerisità di Milano, Italy
david@dimap.ufrn.br, fontaine@loria.fr, ranise@loria.fr,
ringeiss@loria.fr

1 Introduction

Catching bugs in programs is difficult and time-consuming. The effort of debugging and proving correct even small units of code can surpass the effort of programming. Bugs inserted while "programming in the small" can have dramatic consequences for the consistency of a whole software system as shown, e.g., by viruses which can spread by exploiting buffer overflows, a bug which typically arises while coding a small portion of code. To detect this kind of errors, many verification techniques have been put forward such as static analysis and model checking.

Recently, in the program verification community, there seems to be a growing demand for more declarative approaches in order to make the results of the analysis readily available to the end user.[1] To meet this requirement, a growing number of program verification tools integrate some form of theorem proving.

The goals of our research are two. First, we perform theoretical investigations of various combinations of propositional and first-order satisfiability checking so to automate the theorem proving activity required to solve a large class of program analysis problems which can be encoded as first-order formulae. Second, we experimentally investigate how our techniques behave on real problems so to make program analysis more precise and scalable. Building tools capable of providing a good balance between precision and scalability is one of the crucial challenge to transfer theorem proving technology to the industrial domains.

2 Designing Decision Procedures

Decision procedures, their combination, and their integration with other reasoning activities (such as Boolean solving or quantifier handling) have recently

---

* This author has been supported in part by CNPq grant 506469/04-2.
[1] See, for example, the challenge at http://research.microsoft.com/specncheck/
consel_challenge.htm

K. Barkaoui, A. Cavalcanti, and A. Cerone (Eds.): ICTAC 2006, LNCS 4281, pp. 366–370, 2006.

attracted a lot of attention because of their importance for many verification techniques (such as bounded model checking, software model checking, and deductive verification to name but a few). In this tutorial, we will describe some of the techniques which allow us to build, combine, and integrate decision procedures.

2.1 Building

A lot of papers in the literature address the problem of building decision procedure for theories of interest in program verification, such as [8]. The methods used in these papers are rather *ad hoc* and seem difficult to generalize.

We will present the so-called rewriting approach to decision procedures [2] for theories which can be axiomatized by a finite set of clauses (in first-order logic with equality) which are quite relevant for software verification: the theory of uninterpreted function symbols, theories of (possibly cyclic) lists, the theory of arrays (with or without extensionality), and their combinations. This approach allows us to synthesize such procedures in a uniform way by working in a well-understood framework for all the theories listed above. The proof that the decision procedures are correct is straightforward w.r.t. other correctness proofs given in the literature since it amounts to proving the termination of the exhaustive application of the rules of a calculus (see [2] for details). Furthermore, these theoretical results pave the way to synthesizing decision procedures from rewriting-based theorem provers (almost) taken off-the-shelf. We will present experimental results [1] which confirm the practical feasibility of this approach by showing that an automated theorem prover compares favorably with *ad hoc* decision procedures.

2.2 Combining

Verification problems frequently require more than just a single theory to model a given system and/or specify a property that we would like the system to satisfy. Hence, there is an obvious need to combine the decision procedures which are available for some component theories in a modular way so to obtain a decision procedure for unions of theories. This modular approach is particularly interesting to combine (fragments of) Presburger Arithmetics (for which the rewriting-based approach does not work) with rewriting-based decision procedures. There has been a long series of works devoted to the combination of decision procedures in the context of program verification. This line of research was started in the early 80's by two combination schemas independently presented by Nelson-Oppen [9] and Shostak [14] for unions of theories with disjoint signatures. Recently, a series of papers have clarified the connections between both combination schemas [13].

We will present a rational reconstruction of combination schemas [11] which will allow us to derive and prove correct Nelson-Oppen and Shostak combination schemas in a simple and uniform way. The reconstruction is based on a classification of the semantic properties that the theories being combined should satisfy (e.g., being stably-infinite). Then, we describe how some of the schemas might be generalized in order to find a better trade-off between the simplicity of Nelson-Oppen schema and the efficiency of Shostak's. We will discuss how to lift some of the requirements needed for the Nelson-Oppen combination schema to work; e.g., both theories need to be stably-infinite [12]. This is particularly relevant to software verification problems involving container data structures (such as lists, arrays, or sets) and the elements stored in such data structures whose theories may not satisfy the requirement of being stably-infinite (consider, for example, enumerated data-types). Finally, we will explain how rewriting-based procedures can be efficiently combined with arbitrary decision procedures in the Nelson-Oppen schema by showing that, under suitable assumptions, they derive all facts that need to be exchanged for the synchronization of the states of the procedures [7].

2.3 Integrating

When building decision procedures for certain theories or unions of theories, only the problem of checking the satisfiability of conjunctions of literals is considered. Now, verification problems often generate proof obligations consisting of complex Boolean combination of ground literals and may even contain quantifiers. So, to make the decision procedures really usable for software verification, it is crucial to integrate them with (i) Boolean solvers (such as SAT solvers or BDDs) and with (ii) mechanisms to handle quantifiers. Such system are called Satisfiability Modulo Theory solvers. The idea underlying (i) is to consider a propositional abstraction of the formula to be checked for satisfiability and then enumerating its propositional assignments. Such assignments are then refined back to conjunctions of ground literals which are checked for satisfiability by means of an available decision procedure. If all the (refined) propositional assignments are discarded as unsatisfiable with respect to the theory, we can conclude that the original formula is unsatisfiable. Otherwise, the formula is satisfiable. This is a very hot topic in automated deduction and verification as witnessed by many systems based on this type of integration.[2] The idea underlying (ii) is to pre-process the formula in order to abstract away the quantified sub-formulas by propositional letters and, at the same time, to enrich the background theory with enough information for a first-order theorem prover to refine the abstraction. In this way, we obtain a ground formula which must be checked for satisfiability modulo an extended theory. If the decision procedure can cope with the extended theory, it is possible to use (i) in order to solve the new satisfiability problem. We will discuss the encouraging experimental results obtained with an implementation of such techniques (see Section 3 for more details) on a set of benchmarks taken from the certification of auto-generated aerospace code [4].

---

[2] See the Satisfiability Modulo Theory Library at `http://combination.cs.uiowa.edu/smtlib` for pointers to the available systems.

2.4   Embedding

Formal system verification calls for expressive specification languages, but also requires highly automated tools. These two goals are not easy to reconcile, especially if one also aims at high assurances for correctness. Interactive proof assistants encode rich logics, which are at the basis of highly expressive (and user-extensible) modeling languages. Their verification environment is often built around a small kernel that ensures that theorems can only be produced from given axioms and proof rules; this approach helps to keep the trusted code base small and therefore gives high assurance of correctness. These tools however do not focus on automation, and much interaction is often required for even simple (but tedious) reasoning. At the other end of the spectrum one finds decision procedures, based on a restricted language, but that provide fully automatic (and efficient) deductive capabilities within that language.

There is a growing interest in making interactive proof assistants and automatic tools based on decision procedures cooperate in a safe way. This allows assistants to delegate proofs of formulas that fall within the scope of automatic tools. First, this involves translating formulas from the language of the assistant to the language of the automatic tool. Second, to comfort the confidence in the translation process and in the automatic tool, it is necessary to extract a proof from the automatic tool and certify it within the trusted kernel of the proof assistant. We will focus on proof extraction from decision procedures, but also mention state-of-the-art techniques for general first-order automatic theorem provers, and investigate proof certification for proof assistants. In particular, we will examine our recent [6] and ongoing work on combining the system **haRVey** (see Section 3) with the Isabelle [10] proof assistant.

3   Implementing Decision Procedures: haRVey

All the techniques discussed in Section 2 are implemented (or being implemented) in a system, called **haRVey**[3]. By now, the system has two incarnations. The former (called **haRVey-FOL**) integrates Boolean solvers with an automated theorem prover, to implement the rewriting-based decision procedures overviewed in Section 2.1 (see [3,4]). The latter (called **haRVey-SAT**) integrates Boolean solvers with a combination of decision procedures for the theory of uninterpreted function symbols and Linear Arithmetic based on the Nelson-Oppen schema and techniques to handle quantifiers and lambda-expressions (see [5]). Furthermore, **haRVey-SAT** can produce proofs which can then be independently checked by the proof assistant Isabelle (see [6]).

While **haRVey-FOL** offers a high degree of flexibility and automation for a variety of theories, **haRVey-SAT** is usually faster on problems with simpler background theories and ensures a high degree of certification by its proof checking capability. Along the lines hinted in [7], our current work aims at merging the two incarnations in one system which retains the flexibility and high-degree of

---

[3] http://harvey.loria.fr/

automation for expressive theories of **haRVey-FOL** and provides better performances on simpler problems as **haRVey-SAT**.

References

1. A. Armando, M. P. Bonacina, S. Ranise, and S. Schulz. On a rewriting approach to satisfiability procedures: extension, combination of theories and an experimental appraisal. In B. Gramlich, editor, *Frontiers of Combining Systems (FroCoS)*, volume 3717 of *Lecture Notes in Computer Science*, pages 65–80. Springer, 2005.
2. A. Armando, S. Ranise, and M. Rusinowitch. A Rewriting Approach to Satisfiability Procedures. *Information and Computation*, 183(2):140–164, June 2003.
3. D. Déharbe and S. Ranise. Light-Weight Theorem Proving for Debugging and Verifying Units of Code. In *Proc. of the Int. Conf. on Software Engineering and Formal Methods (SEFM03)*, pages 220–228. IEEE Computer Society, 2003.
4. D. Déharbe and S. Ranise. Satisfiability Solving for Software Verification. In *Proc. of IEEE/NASA Workshop on Leveraging Applications of Formal Methods, Verification, and Validation (ISoLA'05)*, 2005.
5. P. Fontaine. *Techniques for verification of concurrent systems with invariants*. PhD thesis, Institut Montefiore, Université de Liège, Belgium, Sept. 2004.
6. P. Fontaine, J.-Y. Marion, S. Merz, L. P. Nieto, and A. Tiu. Expressiveness + automation + soundness: Towards combining SMT solvers and interactive proof assistants. In *Tools and Algorithms for Construction and Analysis of Systems (TACAS)*, volume 3920 of *LNCS*, pages 167–181. Springer, 2006.
7. H. Kirchner, S. Ranise, C. Ringeissen, and D.-K. Tran. On Superposition-Based Satisfiability Procedures and their Combination. In *International Conference on Theoretical Aspects of Computing (ICTAC)*, volume 3722 of *Lecture Notes in Computer Science*, pages 594–608. Springer, 2005.
8. G. Nelson. Techniques for Program Verification. Technical Report CSL-81-10, Xerox Palo Alto Research Center, June 1981.
9. G. Nelson and D. C. Oppen. Simplification by cooperating decision procedures. *ACM Trans. on Programming Languages and Systems*, 1(2):245–257, Oct. 1979.
10. T. Nipkow, L. Paulson, and M. Wenzel. *Isabelle/HOL. A Proof Assistant for Higher-Order Logic*. Number 2283 in Lecture Notes in Computer Science. Springer-Verlag, 2002.
11. S. Ranise, C. Ringeissen, and D.-K. Tran. Nelson-Oppen, Shostak and the Extended Canonizer: A Family Picture with a Newborn. In Z. Liu and K. Araki, editors, *International Conference on Theoretical Aspects of Computing (ICTAC)*, volume 3407 of *Lecture Notes in Computer Science*, pages 372–386. Springer, 2005.
12. S. Ranise, C. Ringeissen, and C. G. Zarba. Combining data structures with nonstably infinite theories using many-sorted logic. In B. Gramlich, editor, *Frontiers of Combining Systems (FroCoS)*, volume 3717 of *Lecture Notes in Computer Science*, pages 48–64. Springer, 2005.
13. N. Shankar and H. Rueß. Combining Shostak theories. In S. Tison, editor, *Proc. of the 13th Int. Conf. on Rewriting Techniques and Applications*, volume 2378 of *Lecture Notes in Computer Science*, pages 1–18. Springer, 2002.
14. R. E. Shostak. Deciding combinations of theories. *J. of the ACM*, 31:1–12, 1984.

Author Index

Lecture Notes in Computer Science

For information about Vols. 1–4199

please contact your bookseller or Springer

Vol. 4246: M. Hermann, A. Voronkov (Eds.), Logic for Programming, Artificial Intelligence, and Reasoning. XIII, 588 pages. 2006. (Sublibrary LNAI).

Vol. 4245: A. Kuba, L.G. Nyúl, K. Palágyi (Eds.), Discrete Geometry for Computer Imagery. XIII, 688 pages. 2006.

Vol. 4244: S. Spaccapietra (Ed.), Journal on Data Semantics VII. XI, 267 pages. 2006.

Vol. 4243: T. Yakhno, E.J. Neuhold (Eds.), Advances in Information Systems. XIII, 420 pages. 2006.

Vol. 4241: R.R. Beichel, M. Sonka (Eds.), Computer Vision Approaches to Medical Image Analysis. XI, 262 pages. 2006.

Vol. 4239: H.Y. Youn, M. Kim, H. Morikawa (Eds.), Ubiquitous Computing Systems. XVI, 548 pages. 2006.

Vol. 4238: Y.-T. Kim, M. Takano (Eds.), Management of Convergence Networks and Services. XVIII, 605 pages. 2006.

Vol. 4237: H. Leitold, E. Markatos (Eds.), Communications and Multimedia Security. XII, 253 pages. 2006.

Vol. 4236: L. Breveglieri, I. Koren, D. Naccache, J.-P. Seifert (Eds.), Fault Diagnosis and Tolerance in Cryptography. XIII, 253 pages. 2006.

Vol. 4234: I. King, J. Wang, L. Chan, D. Wang (Eds.), Neural Information Processing, Part III. XXII, 1227 pages. 2006.

Vol. 4233: I. King, J. Wang, L. Chan, D. Wang (Eds.), Neural Information Processing, Part II. XXII, 1203 pages. 2006.

Vol. 4232: I. King, J. Wang, L. Chan, D. Wang (Eds.), Neural Information Processing, Part I. XLVI, 1153 pages. 2006.

Vol. 4231: J. F. Roddick, R. Benjamins, S. Si-Saïd Cherfi, R. Chiang, C. Claramunt, R. Elmasri, F. Grandi, H. Han, M. Hepp, M. Hepp, M. Lytras, V.B. Mišić, G. Poels, I.-Y. Song, J. Trujillo, C. Vangenot (Eds.), Advances in Conceptual Modeling - Theory and Practice. XXII, 456 pages. 2006.

Vol. 4229: E. Najm, J.F. Pradat-Peyre, V.V. Donzeau-Gouge (Eds.), Formal Techniques for Networked and Distributed Systems - FORTE 2006. X, 486 pages. 2006.

Vol. 4228: D.E. Lightfoot, C.A. Szyperski (Eds.), Modular Programming Languages. X, 415 pages. 2006.

Vol. 4227: W. Nejdl, K. Tochtermann (Eds.), Innovative Approaches for Learning and Knowledge Sharing. XVII, 721 pages. 2006.

Vol. 4226: R.T. Mittermeir (Ed.), Informatics Education – The Bridge between Using and Understanding Computers. XVII, 319 pages. 2006.

Vol. 4225: J.F. Martínez-Trinidad, J.A. Carrasco Ochoa, J. Kittler (Eds.), Progress in Pattern Recognition, Image Analysis and Applications. XIX, 995 pages. 2006.

Vol. 4224: E. Corchado, H. Yin, V. Botti, C. Fyfe (Eds.), Intelligent Data Engineering and Automated Learning – IDEAL 2006. XXVII, 1447 pages. 2006.

Vol. 4223: L. Wang, L. Jiao, G. Shi, X. Li, J. Liu (Eds.), Fuzzy Systems and Knowledge Discovery. XXVIII, 1335 pages. 2006. (Sublibrary LNAI).

Vol. 4222: L. Jiao, L. Wang, X. Gao, J. Liu, F. Wu (Eds.), Advances in Natural Computation, Part II. XLII, 998 pages. 2006.

Vol. 4221: L. Jiao, L. Wang, X. Gao, J. Liu, F. Wu (Eds.), Advances in Natural Computation, Part I. XLI, 992 pages. 2006.

Vol. 4219: D. Zamboni, C. Kruegel (Eds.), Recent Advances in Intrusion Detection. XII, 331 pages. 2006.

Vol. 4218: S. Graf, W. Zhang (Eds.), Automated Technology for Verification and Analysis. XIV, 540 pages. 2006.

Vol. 4217: P. Cuenca, L. Orozco-Barbosa (Eds.), Personal Wireless Communications. XV, 532 pages. 2006.

Vol. 4216: M.R. Berthold, R. Glen, I. Fischer (Eds.), Computational Life Sciences II. XIII, 269 pages. 2006. (Sublibrary LNBI).

Vol. 4215: D.W. Embley, A. Olivé, S. Ram (Eds.), Conceptual Modeling - ER 2006. XVI, 590 pages. 2006.

Vol. 4213: J. Fürnkranz, T. Scheffer, M. Spiliopoulou (Eds.), Knowledge Discovery in Databases: PKDD 2006. XXII, 660 pages. 2006. (Sublibrary LNAI).

Vol. 4212: J. Fürnkranz, T. Scheffer, M. Spiliopoulou (Eds.), Machine Learning: ECML 2006. XXIII, 851 pages. 2006. (Sublibrary LNAI).

Vol. 4211: P. Vogt, Y. Sugita, E. Tuci, C. Nehaniv (Eds.), Symbol Grounding and Beyond. VIII, 237 pages. 2006. (Sublibrary LNAI).

Vol. 4210: C. Priami (Ed.), Computational Methods in Systems Biology. X, 323 pages. 2006. (Sublibrary LNBI).

Vol. 4209: F. Crestani, P. Ferragina, M. Sanderson (Eds.), String Processing and Information Retrieval. XIV, 367 pages. 2006.

Vol. 4208: M. Gerndt, D. Kranzlmüller (Eds.), High Performance Computing and Communications. XXII, 938 pages. 2006.

Vol. 4207: Z. Ésik (Ed.), Computer Science Logic. XII, 627 pages. 2006.

Vol. 4206: P. Dourish, A. Friday (Eds.), UbiComp 2006: Ubiquitous Computing. XIX, 526 pages. 2006.

Vol. 4205: G. Bourque, N. El-Mabrouk (Eds.), Comparative Genomics. X, 231 pages. 2006. (Sublibrary LNBI).

Vol. 4204: F. Benhamou (Ed.), Principles and Practice of Constraint Programming - CP 2006. XVIII, 774 pages. 2006.

Vol. 4203: F. Esposito, Z.W. Raś, D. Malerba, G. Semeraro (Eds.), Foundations of Intelligent Systems. XVIII, 767 pages. 2006. (Sublibrary LNAI).

Vol. 4202: E. Asarin, P. Bouyer (Eds.), Formal Modeling and Analysis of Timed Systems. XI, 369 pages. 2006.

Vol. 4201: Y. Sakakibara, S. Kobayashi, K. Sato, T. Nishino, E. Tomita (Eds.), Grammatical Inference: Algorithms and Applications. XII, 359 pages. 2006. (Sublibrary LNAI).

Vol. 4200: I.F.C. Smith (Ed.), Intelligent Computing in Engineering and Architecture. XIII, 692 pages. 2006. (Sublibrary LNAI).